FULHAM OLD AND NEW

Being An

Exhaustive History of the Ancient Parish of Fulham

Volume II

by

Charles James Fèret

London
The Leadenhall Press, Ltd., 50, Leadenhall Street, E.C.

Simpkin, Marshall, Hamilton, Kent & Co., Ltd

New York: Charles Scribner's Sons, 153-157, Fifth Avenue
MDCCCC
(All Rights reserved)

[Above is a reproduction of the original 1900 title page].

The cover shows a Map of Fulham in 1813,
from Faulkner's `Fulham.'

Fulham Old and New (Vol. II),
first published in 1900,
is here republished by Michael Wood and FamLoc

FL

A FamLoc Book
Available in Print and eBook Format

Originally published 1900
This FamLoc Edition first published 2015
Copyright © 2015 Michael Wood
All rights reserved.

ISBN-13: 978-1519794154
ISBN-10: 1519794150

CONTENTS OF VOLUME II

List of Illustrations	Page v
Original 1900 Preface	Page xi
FamLoc Preface	Page xv
Chapter I: Fulham Church and Churchyard (Miscellaneous)	Page 1
Chapter II: Rectors and Vicars Of Fulham	Page 13
Chapter III: Tithes	Page 61
Chapter IV: New King's Road	Page 65
High Street to Burlington Road	Page 65
Burlington Road to Parson's Green	Page 97
Parson's Green to Waterford Road	Page 119
Waterford Road to Stanley Bridge	Page 132
Chapter V: Parson's Green	Page 138
General	Page 138
East Side	Page 144
Parson's Green Lane	Page 173
West Side	Page 188
South Side	Page 200
Chapter VI: Fulham Road	Page 256
High Street to Munster Road	Page 256
Munster Road to Percy Cross	Page 284
Percy Cross to Walham Green	Page 320
Walham Green to Stamford Bridge	Page 339

Chapter VII: Walham Green   Page 361

Chapter VIII: North End   Page 407

Chapter IX: North End Road   Page 417

    Walham Green to Lillie Road   Page 417
    Lillie Road to Gibbs Green   Page 429
    Gibbs Green to Hammersmith Road   Page 443

Chapter X: Hammersmith Road   Page 487

Notes to Text   Page 499

LIST OF ILLUSTRATIONS, VOL. II

Chapter IV: New King's Road:
Fulham Pottery, 1876
Statuettes of Lydia Dwight
    (now at the Victoria and Albert Museum)
Fulham Pottery, 1897
Pedigree Chart of Dwight Family
Token issued at the "King's Arms" in 1656
The old "King's Arms," 1878
Staircase at Chaldon House
A Room in Chaldon House
The New King's Road, 1896
Jasmine House, 1895
Hawkins's Alley (now Fulham Park Road), 1895
Elysium Row, 1868
Northumberland House, 1895
Draycott Lodge, 1895
Old Laurel Bank House
The Library, Osborne's Nursery
Dr. W. J. Burchell, 1854
Churchfield House, 1896
Ivy Cottage
Ivy Cottage, 1817
Eelbrook Common, looking towards Southfield Farm
Pomona Place, 1896
Plan of Pomona Place Estate
Wandsworth Bridge, 1895
The "Old Rose," 1895

Chapter V: Parson's Green:
Plan of Parson's Green in 1843
Parson's Green, looking towards Parson's Green Lane, 1896
East End House, circa 1851
The Grounds of East End House

The Grounds of East End House
Pedigree Chart of Child Family
Cedar Tree at East End House
Sir Francis Bacon
William Rumbold
Elm House, 1895
Belfield House, 1895
Albion House (back view), 1814
The Holt Yates Memorial Home and the Jubilee Home, 1896
Tea time at the Holt Yates Memorial Home
A bit of Parson's Green Lane, 1896
The old "Rose and Crown"
Rosamond's Bower, 1842
Audley Cottage just before its demolition in 1892
Facsimile of a Warrant for the payment of £30 to Sir Michael Wharton
Sketch plan from Mr. John Powell's lease, 1762
Old Rosamond's Bower and Park House, circa 1763
Park House (front view)
Park House (back view)
Rosamond's, 1896
Staircase at Rosamond's
Parson's Green Mission Hall
Rectory Place, 1896
Dr. Butts
Rectory House, After an Old Drawing
Broom Villa, 1895
Richardson's Villa, From an Old Drawing
Peterborough Lane
Old houses in Peterborough Place, 1893
Broom Farm, 1895
Peterborough Road, 1895
The Home Farm of Messrs. J. Veitch and Sons, 1895
John, Viscount Mordaunt
Charles, Earl of Peterborough
Peterborough House, south view, 1895
Fulham Volunteer, 1798
Silver Gilt Medal (ob.), presented to Nathaniel Chasemore
Silver Gilt Medal (rev.), presented to Nathaniel Chasemore

A Walk in the Grounds of Peterborough House, 1895
Peterborough Farm, 1895
A Walk in the Grounds of Peterborough House, 1895
An Alcove in the Grounds of Peterborough House, 1895
Old Stone Gateway at Peterborough House, 1895
The Ancient Ice Well, Peterborough Farm, 1895
Sir Thomas Bodley, kt.

Chapter VI: Fulham Road:
Fulham Road, looking towards High Street, 1867
Holcroft's
Holcroft's
Pedigree Chart of Withers Family
Holcroft's
Pedigree Chart of Cleybroke Family
Pedigree Chart of Frewen Family
Holcroft's Priory and Holcroft's Abbey
Ivy Lodge, 1895
Fulham Lodge, 1838
Eridge House, 1895
Fulham Park Gardens, 1895
Osborne (or Osborn) Lodge (or House)
Colehill Villa, front view, 1895
Colehill Villa, back view, 1895
Munster House, front view, 1895
Munster House, the Old Mulberry Tree
Munster House, back view, 1895
A Corner in the Grounds of Munster House
Pedigree Chart of Powell, Hinson and Williams Families
Pedigree Chart of Powell, Hinson and Williams Families (continued)
A supposed gun carriage in the Grounds of Munster House, 1895
Munster House: the Billiard Room in the Madhouse, 1895
Munster House, back view, about 1850
Munster House, principal entrance, 1895
King Charles's Bower, 1895
Doorway of King Charles's Bower, as seen from within
Munster Park Chapel, 1895
Vine Cottage, 1893

Percy Cross House
Fulham Public Library, 1893
Interior of the Reading Room
St. Peter's Lodge, 1896
Arundel House, 1896
Old Leaden Cistern at Arundel House
Arundel House (back view)
Wheatsheaf Alley, looking south, 1896
The "Wheatsheaf"
Ravensworth House
Fairlawn, back view, 1874
Peartree Cottage, 1894
The "Red Lion"
The old "King's Head," 1810
No. 404, Fulham Road, 1895
Oliver Stocken, founder of the "Swan" Brewery
Facsimile of frontispiece of an old price list of the "Swan" Brewery
Old "Swan" Brewery, back view
Pedigree Chart of Stocken Family
The old "White Hart"
Fulham Town Hall
Interior of the Large Hall, Fulham Town Hall, 1895
St. James's Church, 1895
St. James's Church, east end, 1895

Chapter VII: Walham Green:
Old houses on the site of Walham Green Broadway
Walham Green Broadway, 1895
St. John's Church, circa 1828
St. John's Church, 1828
St. John's Church interior, circa 1828
St. John's Church, east end (interior)
St. John's Church, after the restoration of 1893
St. John's Church, 1896
St. John's National Schools
Old houses which stood on the site of St. John's Terrace
The old "Cock," 1894
Jerdan Place, 1895

Pond Place, 1895
"The Maltsters," 1896
The Butchers' Almshouses (north side)
The Butchers' Almshouses (south side)
Farm Lane
Farm Lane, 1896
An old house in Farm Lane, 1896
The Manor House of Wendon, latterly incorporated in the premises of the old "Swan" Brewery
A room in the old Manor House of Wendon
Lane's Tenement: Deed of feoffment dated 24 April 9 Eliz. (1567)
John Norden

Chapter VIII: North End:
Normand House, south front, 1813
The old Entrance Gates, Normand House, 1896
The Mother Superior's Room, Normand House
The Grand Staircase, Normand House, 1896
The Ancient Staircase, Normand House, 1896
Normand House, south front, 1896

Chapter IX: North End Road:
The Conservative Club, 1896
Shorrold's
The Grange
Beaufort House
Beaufort House, 1896
Francesco Bartolozzi
The Hermitage, east front, about 1800
Samuel Foote
The Hermitage
The "Seven Stars" 1896
Old Tenements at Gibbs Green, 1895
An old House in Deadman's Lane, removed in 1880-1 in laying out St. Paul's School
Site of St. Paul's School
The Froebel Educational Institute
Baron's Court Estate, 1898
King's House, Baron's Court

North End House, 1897
Pedigree Chart of Earsby Family
Kensington Hall, 1896
Mornington Lodge, 1897
The Grange, circa 1800
Samuel Richardson, 1811
The Grange, 1896
Otto House, 1896
Pedigree Chart of Gresham Family

Chapter X: Hammersmith Road:
Monday morning at the Police Court, 1895
The Cedars, circa 1840
St. Mary's Church, 1896

ORIGINAL 1900 PREFACE

[FamLoc note: This preface repeats that of "Fulham Old and New" Volume I. It did not appear in the original Volume II, perhaps because all three volumes were sold together].

This work, the outcome of many years of patient research, will, it is hoped, be found to furnish the reader with full and accurate information regarding the interesting Parish with which it deals.

"A system built upon the discoveries of a great many minds," says Dr. Johnson, "is always of more strength than what is produced by the mere workings of one mind, which, of itself, can do little. There is not so poor a book in the world that would not be a prodigious effort were it wrought out entirely by a single mind, without the aid of prior investigators."

To no one is the truth of this statement more evident than to the student of topography. His work may be original, but his facts must be mainly gathered from the records of those who have preceded him. To reduce to order a vast mass of matter drawn from the most heterogeneous sources, to test each statement, and to separate the wheat from the chaff, is a task of immense magnitude. Those alone who have undertaken to write biography or history can realise the arduous labours necessary to secure absolute correctness. The Author has often had to say with Boswell, "I have sometimes been obliged to run half over London, in order to fix a date correctly: which, when I had accomplished, I well knew would obtain me no praise, though a failure would have been to my discredit."

In dealing with such an enormous and varied mass of matter as that involved in the compilation of "Fulham Old and New," some mistakes are almost inevitable, but throughout the work the utmost care has been exercised to ensure accuracy. With this purpose in view, the Author has, wherever possible, consulted manuscript documents as original sources of information, and therefore the least likely to err. Many of these records have happily been the means of throwing much, new light upon the history of our Parish, and of bringing into connection with it the names of very many distinguished personages famous in the annals of our country.

It would be impossible to enumerate here a tithe of the channels of information of which the Author has availed himself. The whole of the Court Rolls of the Manor of Fulham, commencing with the year 1382, have been carefully searched and have yielded a wonderful abundance of material of the deepest antiquarian interest. The accounts of the Churchwardens and Overseers of Fulham, dating from 1625, the Assessment and other Parish Books, preserved at the Fulham Town Hall, have all been explored. The Church Registers, beginning in 1675, have been fully examined. At the Probate Registry, the Public Record Office, the Bishop of London's Registry, the Ecclesiastical Commission, Lambeth Palace, Fulham Palace, the Guildhall, the Bodleian, the British Museum and numerous other places, very extensive searches have been made. Besides this, numberless original manuscripts, deeds, abstracts, letters, and other documents in private hands, have been consulted.

Nothing has been recorded upon mere surmise. In every instance in which historical facts have been given, the original authority for them has been sought out and examined, while the biographical notices of former residents have been culled from the most reliable sources. In many cases these notices have been supplemented by information furnished by the living representatives of the families concerned.

During the progress of this work the Author has been assisted to much information by old residents of Fulham, and by others who, in various ways, are connected with, or are interested in, the Parish. Among other kind contributors may be mentioned Lady Dilke, Lord Balcarres, His Excellency Sir Horace Rumbold, Bart., the Rev. W. C. Muriel, the Rev. J. S. Sinclair, Mr. A. Chasemore, Mr. G. Milner-Gibson-Cullum, the late Mr. C. E. Gildersome-Dickinson, Mr. John P. Hutchins, Mr. A. W. Stocken, Mr. Arthur Hussey, Miss Edith Harrison, Mrs. Lammin, Mrs. Roydhouse, Capt. George Merry, Mr. T. Aplin Marsh, Mr. F. W. Madden, Mr. F. G. Hilton Price, Mr. C. Mason, Mr. F. Manby, Col. Prideaux, Mr. John Rooth, Maj. General C. W. Robinson, Mr. T. E. Ravenshaw, Mr. R. F. Sketchley, Mr. D. Shopland, Mr. W. W.

Watts, Lt. Colonel G. Hunter-Weston, Mr. J. A. Wild, Mr. A. Ballhatchet, Mr. G. E. Lloyd-Baker, the Rev. M. H. Boden, Mr. F. Hitchin-Kemp, Mr. J. Ravenshaw, the late Mr. D. McMinn, Mr. William Thatcher and Dr. Woodhouse.

On many etymological points the Author has been favoured with the opinion of the Rev. Professor Skeat, M.A., the distinguished Anglo-Saxon scholar.

The Author has to express his especial thanks to Canon Fisher, M.A., the late Vicar of Fulham, to Mr. Charles Griffin, an old resident of this Parish, to Mr. W. J. Harvey, and to Mr. S. Martin, of the Hammersmith Public Library, for the generous assistance which, throughout the work, they have at all times so readily accorded him.

CHARLES JAMES FERET.
Fulham, 1900.

A bit of Parson's Green Lane.
From a photograph by Mr. T. S. Smith, 1896

Peterborough Road. From a photograph by Mr. T. S. Smith, 1895

PREFACE TO FAMLOC EDITION

For most of its history Fulham lay in the County of Middlesex, but, with the expansion of Greater London, it now forms part of the London Borough of Hammersmith and Fulham.

Fulham Old and New was first published in 1900. This Famloc Edition retains the three-volume format, and has been modified only slightly from Fèret's original:
A handful of typos have been corrected, and a small number of changes have been made to the punctuation, including indenting the quotations.
The original footnotes have been placed in an additional "Notes" chapter at the end of the book; the annotated text is underlined.
Some of the original chapters have been changed to sub-chapters.
The short number of entries in the original Errata page have been incorporated into the main text.

Always bear in mind the book was originally published in 1900, and all mention Fèret makes of relative dates, such as "two centuries ago", "thirty years ago," are with reference to that publication date. Also, Fèret often refers to Queen Elizabeth - obviously Queen Elizabeth I.

The photographs have been digitally adjusted, but please bear in mind the quality of photographs in 1900. We will make some of the photographs and family trees available on the FamLoc website.

Some now-unusual words and contractions, etc used in *Fulham Old and New*:

Vizt. was used for "namely", "that is to say", and "as follows".
&c. is an older form of "etc."
Esq. is a contraction of Esquire, much used until fairly recently as a polite title appended to a man's name in the absence of any other title. Originally a member of the English gentry ranking below a

knight.

Currency: The currency was Pounds, Shillings and Pence, abbreviated to £. s. d. There were twenty shillings to the pound, and 12 pence to the shilling. In old records, 3d. (for example) was written as iij^d with a "j" replacing the final i, and the "d" as a superscript. There is also the superscript ^{li} for "pounds" in some of the quotations.

Area of Land: As well as acres, there were the rod and pole, abbreviated to a, r and p.

Tombstones and memorials: Fèret uses the character "|" to differentiate separate lines on a memorial stone.

FAMLOC WEBSITE

Those wishing to find out more about Fulham local history and family history can visit FamLoc's website:

www.famloc.co.uk

- and navigate to the Fulham pages. Webpages can be added to continue the discussion of subjects in this book.

Finally, we would like to give our heartfelt thanks to Charles James Fèret, without whom much of the history of Fulham would have been lost.

Michael Wood, FamLoc, December 2015.

CHAPTER I:
FULHAM CHURCH AND CHURCHYARD
(MISCELLANEOUS)

The office of beadle is one of great antiquity. Among the officers of the ancient Manor, the "bedel," as the name was anciently spelled, received, on behalf of the Lord, surrenders made out of Court, reported at the Leet offences, etc., committed by the tenants, and generally kept order. In the Court Rolls the "bedel" is mentioned as early as the reign of Richard II.

With the advent of the parish constable and the headborough, the duties of the beadle became mainly confined to the church, though he still continued to assist in the maintenance of the peace, his offices including, as Shakespeare reminds us, the flogging of petty malefactors.

The beadle was a man of multifarious subordinate duties. When the Vestry was an adjunct of the church, he had to *bid* or cite parishioners to attend its meetings, and to be present at them himself; on the Sabbath he had to be at the church to keep order during Divine service, and generally to perform the duties now discharged by the verger.

The salary of the beadle in the time of Charles II was £4 per annum. The disbursements of the Overseers for 1669 include:

"paid Edw. Arnall (Arnold) Beadle a yeares wayges £4. 0. 0."

On 6 Nov. 1679, Thomas Wale was admitted "warder and beadle." The minutes for 1681 contain the following:

"Att a Vestry May ye 5th, 1681, Itt is ordered that a Capp, breeches and coate bee bought at the charge of the pish for Tho. Wayle, psent Beadle by Mr. Dodd Churchwarden."

Among the beadles of Fulham, none perhaps attained to a higher degree of importance than John Hodnott, or Hudnott. In the Parish Books are several entries relating to the rather expensive livery which this personage was allowed. Hodnott appears to have been a man who went in for the good things of this life, a jovial, jolly fellow, fond of his pipe and his beer. His portrait, painted in 1690, still hangs in the Tower of Fulham Church, in our account of which we have spoken of it. Old John himself survived till 1724, when he was interred in the Churchyard. The Church Registers contain the following quaint entry:

> 1724. John Hudnott Grave Digger als Old Forelock bu. 17 June.

The Words "als (i.e. alias) Old Forelock" have been scratched through, perhaps by some considerate Vicar, shocked at the ribald character of the sobriquet.

The cost of the beadle's livery, in the early years of the last century, may be gathered from the following extracts from the Parish Books:

1711:

> Paid Mr. Tibbals for the Beadles Hatt 15s. 6d.
> For making the Beadles cloths and necessaries £1. 7s. 0d.
> Paid Mr. Dauvis for Cloth for The Beadles Cloths £1. 15s. 0d.

1717:

> Paid for a sute of Cloaths and an hatt for the Beadle £4. 0s. 0d.

1730:

> Pd. for the Beadles Cloaths £5. 0s. 6d.
> Pd. for the gold lace £1. 11s. 6d.
> Pd. for a Hatt and Stockings 14s. 6d.

At a Vestry held on 6 July 1732, the salary of the beadle was increased to £10 per annum.

The following entry in the Parish Books concerning Joseph Bance, who was beadle for many years, is curious reading:

> "Paid Joseph Bance the beadle on a settlement of his affairs to get him discharged out of prison and for which he has given bond to repay it by

instalments out of his salary, etc. £27. 10s. 0d."

At a Vestry called for 20 May 1780, "to choose a Beadle and Bellman in the room of Mr. Fitch, deceased, Mr. John Woster was elected." The salary was now fixed at £20 per annum. Worster died in 1784, when another Joseph Bance was elected. Bance's death occurred in 1792, when Samuel Flooks was chosen beadle. In 1813 John Sadler was elected. He died in 1823, when William Pitts succeeded. Pitts resigned in 1826, when William Bryon was chosen. Two years later came an exciting contest for the beadleship, the candidates being John Morland and Samuel Bowstreed, each of whom was warmly backed by his friends. The following quaint handbill was issued on behalf of Morland:

"Trident against Crosier.
Morland versus Bowstreed for the beadleship. To the independent householders of the parish of Fulham. Ladies and Gentlemen, Our Reverend Vicar in his circular has told you by way of recommendation of Samuel Bowstreed that he has been regular in his attendance at church and that he, the Vicar, has known him in his own service and in the service of the Bishop of London for sixteen years 'Ego et Rex meus' - Cardinal Wolsey. John Morland, who offers himself as candidate for the vacant situation of beadle, I feel it but justice to state, has never been in the employ of any Bishop or priest but for many years in the arduous and honourable service of his king and country at sea; and I believe him to be a man of honest, sober and industrious habits, and his family long known in the parish as most respectable payers of parochial taxes and himself in every respect qualified for the office he solicits, and if successful will of course be 'regular in his attendance at church,' and the Evangelist says 'joy shall he in heaven over one sinner that repenteth more than over ninety and nine just persons which need no repentance.' No doubt, Ladies and Gentlemen, you will know how to discriminate and appreciate the services and merits of the two candidates and bestow your votes accordingly. An Old Parishioner.
John Morland anxiously solicits the early attendance of his friends at the Vestry Room on Thursday morning 12 instant, as the election commences at 11 o'clock and begs to state that it fortunate no exertion on his part shall ever be wanted to fulfil the important duties of his office.
Fulham, 10 June 1828."

Bowstreed, however, was the victor. He died in 1845, aged 58, and was buried at Fulham.

John Fletch became beadle in 1847. His successor was John Flood, called "Dukie" Flood, because his nose resembled in shape that of the Duke of Wellington. At Christmas time Flood, who had a weakness for ale and elderberry wine, would make himself extra agreeable to the villagers, and in the morning serenade the lasses:

Now, maidens, arise
Make your puddings and pies,
And don't forget the beadle.

The last beadle of Fulham was Mr. Charles Griffin. He, and his father before him, had carried on, from 1800 to 1850, the business of a baker at Walham Green. Mr. Griffin was elected in 1852, after a sharply-contested election. On assuming the office he discarded the red plush knee-breeches, and wore black trousers with a red cord, like our present postmen, and a black, instead of a red, waistcoat. The coat was of dark blue cloth, with heavy gold lace, to which was affixed a scarlet plush cape, also with two rows of gold lace. The cocked hat had previously given way to a top hat with gold band and edging.

The beadleship, in Mr. Griffin's day, involved attendance at the church on Sundays, the care of the gas, etc., and the charge of the boys in the aisle during divine service. During the week he had to be in attendance on the Vestry Clerk, and at Vestry and other parochial meetings, even at the school-room lectures, the Court Leet, Common entries for grazing, charity distributions, etc.

With the building of the new church his duties there were reduced to a minimum. There were no aisles full of boys to look after, no pulpit or vestry or chancel doors to open, in fact, no provision even for his old seat. From the east end of the south aisle he was relegated to a pew at the west end of the north aisle, near the Porch. Thus, in his declining years, he was able to take his place more as a worshipper than as an attendant. This was the more easy, for his quondam gay clothing had gradually given place to more ordinary garments. The cape was the first to go, then the coat, and at last only the gold band on the hat distinguished him from ordinary mortals. Archbishop Tait visited the old Church on

Sunday, 18 Jan. 1880, and thus records the fact in his "Diary" under that date:

> "Very few faces in Church which I recollect. Old Miss ___, and Griffin the beadle, despoiled by modern parochia economy of his splendid garments, and one or two others."
> - *Life of Archbishop Tait* (Davidson and Benham's) II., 524.

The last time Mr. Griffin occupied his old position of staff-bearer before the parish officers was on the occasion of the consecration of the Parish Church in 1881. He died 12 October 1884, having retained his beadleship to the last.

The first parish clerk of whom we have any knowledge was James Cluet, probably a relation of Dr. Cluet, the Vicar. In 1627 the Churchwarden

> "Paid James Clewett for writing ye accounts and ye assessments into ye Booke 4s. 0d."

In 1637 the parish clerk received the following payments:

> "Pd. the Clarke for washing the Church lynnen, broomes for ye church and oyle for ye bells £1. 0. 0d."

In 1642 the Churchwardens

> "Paid James Cluatt for 4 quarters for writing accts., etc. £4. 0. 0."

In the time of Adoniram Byfield the parish clerk and curate was Samuel Frazer or Frayser. In 1653 came Samuel Clarke, of whom we have spoken in our account of the School-house. On 5 Feb. 1653-54 Mr. John Gee was elected in Clarke's stead. He died in 1682. The following were the duties of the parish clerk as laid down at a Vestry held on 29 Jan. 1664-65:

> "It was agreed that, henceforth the Clerk of ye parrish for ye time being shall performe the seruices following, viz.: to cause the parrish lining to be washed, prouide oyle for ye bells, broomes and clensing ye Church and to ring ye 4 and 8 a Clock bell, keeping the Register and writeing ye transcript and entring ye Accounts and writing vpon all occasions in

the Vestry and alsoe take care of ye Clock and for his reward in doeing and performing ye aforesaid seruices he shall receiue six pounds by the yeare to be pd. vnto him by ye Churchwarden for ye time being."

John Gee's successor was Robert Clee. The Church Registers record:

1687. Robert Clee Clrke of ye pish bu. 18 Apill.

At a Vestry, held 11 May 1687, John Paul was chosen parish clerk. In consequence of ill-health, Paul resigned his office in 1731-32. Alexander Wells, who was next appointed clerk, held office for a lengthened period. William Law, who followed in the office, was, in 1778, succeeded by Edward Batsford, who held the post till his death in 1800, when Edward Batsford, junior, his son, was elected. In 1804, he was succeeded by John Besley. In 1808 Besley was dismissed for incapacity, when Edward Dalton was elected. Sergeant Roe notes in his "Diary," under date 10 Nov. 1808:

"A Vestry Clerk (Dalton) voted in this 10 Nov. A strong contest. Wilcox run hard."

Thomas Hackman was elected in 1818. On his death, in 1844, his son, Henry Hackman, was chosen. He died in 1865. The Vestry Clerkship was now separated from the Parish Clerkship, the last holders of the latter office being Knight and Nicholls. The separation of the civil duties from the office left the parish clerk exceedingly little to do. On the death of William Nicholls in 1879, no new appointment was made. His legal fees are now paid to the Churchwardens for the repair of the Parish Church.

List of Noticeable Incidents, Etc, in Connection with Fulham Church and Churchyard, Chronologically Arranged

1489. The first allusion to the "church of Fulham" in the Court Rolls of the Manor occurs in the minutes of a View of Frankpledge, held 11 May 1489.

1502. Marion or Maryon at Mere, by her will dated 17 Oct. 1502, proved 11 Dec. 1502 (P.C.C. 17 Blamyr) left to the "high awter" of Fulham church the sum of "xii^s." She and her husband, John at Mere, were buried in Fulham Churchyard.

1520. In the will of George Chauncey, receiver general to Bishop Fitzjames, dated 13 Dec. 1520, mention is made of "the image of the Crucifix in the parissh Churche of ffulh^m."

<u>1547-48</u>. In Roll 34 of 1 Edward VI Chantry Certificates (Augmentation Office) is the following return regarding Fulham Church:

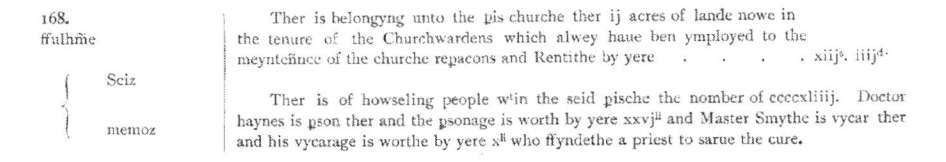

168. ffulhm̃e { Sciz memoz	Ther is belongyng unto the p̃is churche ther ij acres of lande nowe in the tenure of the Churchwardens which alwey haue ben ymployed to the meyntcñnce of the churche repacons and Rentithe by yere . . . . xiij^s. iiij^d. Ther is of howseling people w^{t}in the seid pische the nomber of ccccxliiij. Doctor haynes is p̃son ther and the p̃sonage is worth by yere xxvj^{li} and Master Smythe is vycar ther and his vycarage is worthe by yere x^{li} who ffyndethe a priest to sarue the cure.

"Howseling people" (from "housel," the Holy Eucharist) means, of course, those persons capable of receiving the mass.

1556. Fulham Church was often frequented by Bishop Bonner; but chiefly for the purpose of the public examination of heretics, not to preach. Thus, in April 1556, six Essex men (Lyster, Mace, Spencer, Joyne, Nichols and Hammond), who were afterwards burnt at Colchester, were examined here. In this year there were also examined here John Milles, Thomas Hinshaw and Robert Willis. On 9 May 1556 Hugh Laverock, a lame old man, and John Apprice, a blind man, were proceeded against and also sentenced in Fulham Church. On 15th of the same month they were burnt at Stratford-le-Bow. In a letter from Bonner, dated at Fulham "postridie Nativitatis 1556" to Cardinal Pole, it seems that he intended sentencing in Fulham Church twenty-two prisoners sent up from Colchester, but the Cardinal prevented it.

1588. Strype, in his "Life of Aylmer" (p. 97), gives the following curious particulars of a fracas which occurred in Fulham Church:

"In April 1588 the Bishop happened to have a ruffle with a mad blade named Maddocks, who had married a gentleman's daughter of Fulham. This man was a turbulent hot head and made great stirs in that town . . . He happened to have a contest with the Bishop about some private matters, as concerning the right of a pew in Fulham church; and with the townsmen about a passage to a ground of the Bishop's. Upon Easter day last [1588] he came in warlike manner with rapier and target to Fulham church, when the Bishop and all his men were at the Court, and there thrust in his mother and his sister into the Bishop's wife's seat, and troubled his daughters, being come to receive the communion."

The "mad blade" was probably John Maddocks, who married Frances, the daughter of Sir William Billesbie of Parson's Green. His son, William Maddocks, resided at Fulham and is several times mentioned in the Court Rolls.

1592. On 12 Nov. of this year John Sterne, S.T.B., was consecrated in Fulham Church Bishop Suffragan of Colchester. This was the last Bishop Suffragan consecrated under the Act of Henry VIII, until the office was revived in modern times.

1614. The following entry occurs in the "Domestic Chronicle" of Thomas Godfrey, M.P. for New Romney, the father of Sir Edmund Berry Godfrey:

> "Item, my wife had another mischance of a son at Hammersmith, at her father's house, 13th October 1614; the child was buried just against the little north doore of the Chancell in Fulham Churchyard, county of Middlesex."

Sir Edmund Berry Godfrey was the well-known magistrate who took the evidence of Titus Oates in connection with the bogus popish plot, concocted by that individual. Shortly afterwards, in Oct. 1678, the body of the magistrate was found murdered at Primrose Hill. The Godfreys owned a messuage called the Swan near Blind Lane (Blythe Lane,) Hammersmith.

1630. From the "Diary" of Bishop Laud:

> August 22. Sunday. I preached at Fulham.

1638. From the Churchwardens' Accounts:

> pd. for carrying Judeth Browne out of ye Church 1s. 0d.
> pd. for Communion wyne this yeare £4. 10s. 0d.
> pd. for Comm^n bread this yeare 6s. 8d.

1645:

> (Rec) more for 33lb. of Brass y^t came of (sic) the Graues 11s. 0d.
> [This entry clearly refers to the Wanton sale of brasses and brass ornaments affixed to the monuments in the Church]
>
> (Rec.) more for old lead taken of (sic) the Crosse 2s. 6d.

1658. At a Vestry, held on 7 June 1658, the following quaint resolution was passed regarding the attendance of pensioners at church:

> "Ordered that the Churchwarden and Overseers for the poore doe by ye 27 of June next cause to bee made fitt a convenient seate for sevrall penc^{rs} and receivers of bread from ye pish to sett in on Lords day and the(y) are desired to take care that they doe sevrally come to church twise a day and doe there continue dureing the time of performance of divine service and such as doe make default thereof their pension is to be taken from them vnless they cann show such sufficient cause for such absence as the said Churchwarden and overseers for ye poore for ye time being shall alow of."

1664. At a Vestry, held 14 Aug. 1664,

> "It is ordered y^t the psent Overseeres of the poore doe pay the seu'all pencons to the poore att no other place then the pish Church, vpon Sundaies, holydaies, Wedendayes and frydayes, and y^t the penconrs y^t is absent att the tymes and place aforesd shall forfeite one months pay (Except a Lawfull cause therefore showed)"

1689. On Sunday 13 Oct. 1689, a triple consecration took place at Fulham Church, Edward Stillingfleet being consecrated Bishop of Worcester, Simon Patrick, of Chichester, and Gilbert Ironside, of Bristol. The sermon preached in Fulham Church, on this occasion, by John Scott, D.D., was published in 1689 (4to, pp. 33). This sermon was reprinted in 1704 in Dr. Scott's "Sermons upon Several Occasions," pp. 331-385.

1689. At the consecration of Gilbert Burnett, Bishop of Salisbury, a sermon was preached in Fulham Church by the Rev. A. Horneck. It was published, sm. 4to, 1689.

1737. At a Vestry held on 26 Sept. 1737, it was agreed that Mr. William Gray, the Churchwarden, be empowered

> "to purchase a quantity of Linnen in order to make two surplices for the use of the minister and that the same be allowed in his accounts."

1758. In this year the Rev. William Cole, the antiquary, paid a visit to Fulham Church. He describes it as being very full of monuments, "some of which are very curious." He speaks of the Church as "an ordinary Building with a large stone Tower at the West End, having 8 Bells in it." The bulk of his narrative is devoted to the monuments. In 1764 the Rev. W. Cole, chancing to "pleasure on the Thames," paid a second visit to Fulham Church. The two manuscripts are dated 20 April 1758, and 18 June 1764, respectively.

[Cole Manuscripts (British Museum), vol. xxx., No. 5831.]

1777. From the Churchwardens' Accounts:

> "Pd. Mr. Postans Bill for Candles for use of the Church and for the Afternoon Preacher 9s. 4d."

1790. The following is a summary of the answers returned by the Rev. Graham Jepson to Bishop Porteus respecting the state of the parish in this year:

> "Divine service performed twice on Sundays: sermon in the morning by the Vicar; in the afternoon by the curate or lecturer: prayers on Wednesdays, Fridays and saints' days throughout the year. The Sacrament administered on the first Sunday in each month and on all the great festivals. Number of communicants varied from 20 to 70 or 80. Children were catechised during Lent, and some of them almost

every week in the year, in the Vestry after the service. Benefactions both of lands and money have been left to this parish which the Vicar believed had been properly applied. There was also a charity school for 18 boys and 18 girls supported chiefly by subscriptions and charity sermons. There were four Sunday Schools of about 20 each, two for boys and two for girls; an almshouse for 12 poor widows. There were very few papists in Fulham, but many in Hammersmith, which is a hamlet dependent on it. I have not heard of any late converts nor of any place of worship or priest resident. There is a popish school for girls at the North End of the parish but I know not whether any Protestant children go thither. There were some persons in the parish called Methodists and some Presbyterians. The church, chancel and vicarage house are in good repair. There are no glebe lands attached to the vicarage nor buildings."

1807. From the "Diary" of Mr. Joseph Roe:

5 July. Sunday. A Stranger Preached at Fulham whose Sermon was worth 1000 of Mr. Owens [i.e. the Rev. John Owen, M.A. curate and lecturer at Fulham]. It was stating the Duty of Sponsers to young children. An excellent sermon.

23 Aug. Sunday at Fulham Church. morning Owen Preached wherewith shall a young man etc. etc. a poor tool indeed.
[Throughout the "Diary" Mr. Roe seldom mentions Mr. Owen's name except with contumely.]

30 Aug. at Fulham Church in the morn^g I could not hear the preacher, in the evening I heard without being improved by it.

6 Sept. Sunday at Fulham Church. Owen both parts of the Day. very poor.

1808. Prom the "Diary" of Mr. Joseph Roe:

15 May. Sunday. Mr. Potchett [chaplain to the Bishop of London] gave us an excellent sermon. The Bp. was asleep. He sho^d have heard and understood that it pointed at his bad conduct and inattention.

1808. On Sunday, 25 Sept. 1808, the Rev. John Owen, M.A., preached a remarkable sermon, entitled "Youth Addressed," on the subject of three sad events which had then just taken place. The three events dealt with in this beautiful and impressive sermon were the death, in early girlhood, of Martha Plaw, daughter of Mr. Ezekiel Plaw, of Fulham, the suicide of a young man resident in the parish, whose name is withheld in the " Sermon," and the death, through a boating accident, of Mr. Richard Cooper, son of Mr. Cooper, of the "King's Arms," Fulham, and his sweetheart, Miss Hill, daughter and only child of Mr. Hill, boatbuilder, of Putney. This accident took place on the Thames, between Fulham and Putney, on the afternoon of Thursday, 15 Sept. 1808. This "Sermon" was published.

1810. In a return made in this year, preserved in the Diocese Book at Fulham Palace it is stated that the Parish Church was capable of containing about 1,000 persons.

1817. From the Churchwardens' Accounts:

> Paid Thomas Phelps for taking up a Corpse that was buried too shallow and reburying it 1s. 6d.

1818. From the Churchwardens' Accounts:

> Paid Mr. South for hanging the Pulpit for the Queen £1. 1s. 0d.
>
> Paid Mr. Rogers for black Cloth for the Pulpit etc. £20. 2s. 6d.
>
> Paid Mr. Faulkner for repairing Mr. Titley's Head, Foot and Coffin Stone, broken by the People at the Election of Parish Clerk and Sexton £6. 4s. 7d.

1820. From the Churchwardens' Accounts:

> Paid Mr. Rogers for cloth to hang the Pulpit and Communion on the death of King George the Third £40. 11s. 9d.

1855. On Sunday, 21 Oct. 1855, Bishop Blomfield notes in his "Diary" that he preached at Fulham Church. This was the last entry he ever made in it, for, on the night of the same day, he was seized with a paralytic attack from which he never recovered.

CHAPTER II: RECTORS AND VICARS OF FULHAM

From the earliest times the Parish Church was closely connected with the Manor, and, with the exception of one or two brief intervals, the Lord always exercised the right of patronage to the rectory.

Until the abolition of such benefices, by 3 and 4 Vic., c. 113, s. 48, the rectory of Fulham was a sinecure, that is, the incumbent had no spiritual function to perform. As the name Rectory or Parsonage House shows, the Rector or parson did, at one time, reside in the parish. It is probable, however, that at no time was the Rector bound to live in this house, and, as he usually held other preferment, which, perhaps, involved residence, he generally elected to live elsewhere. It was to his deputy or Vicar that the "cure of souls" was always committed.

In 1421 Richard Clifford, Bishop of London, appropriated the advowson of the church of Fulham, together with the vicarage, to the Priory of the Carthusians of Sheen (Richmond), founded by Henry V in 1414. For this appropriation the consent of the Dean and Chapter of St. Paul's was obtained, and it was confirmed by the King's Letters Patent. The following is a translation of the document (Patent Roll 9 Henry V, part i., mem. 1.):

> "The King to those etc. Greeting.
> Know ye that of our special grace we have granted and given license for us and our heirs so much as in us lies to the Venerable Father in Christ Richard Clifford Bishop of London and to the Dean and Chapter of the same place for the same Bishop with the consent of the same Dean and Chapter to give place and concede to our well beloved in Christ The Prior and Convent of the House of Jesu of Bethlehem of Shene in the County of Surrey of the Order of the Carthusians which are of our foundation One Acre of land in ffulham and the advowson of the Church of ffulham and the vicarage of the same Church to have and to hold to the same Prior and Convent and their Successors for ever.
> Dated at Dover 8 June in the 9th of our reign (1421)."

At a Court General, in 1422, the Prior was amerced. The entry in the minutes reads:

> "The Prior of the Carthusians of Schene, farmer of the Rectory of Fulham, for the destruction of the corn and pastures of the Lord at the time of August last, with pigs, is in mercy 40d."

Though the Prior evidently established himself at Fulham, it does not appear that the Convent ever presented to the benefice.

Presentation to the vicarage was vested in the Rector for the time being. On the abolition of the rectorship, the patronage of the vicarage was transferred to the Bishop of London.

The rectory and the vicarage continued to be separate benefices down to 1833. The Rev. William Wood, having in that year purchased the rectory, the livings may, from that date, be considered as one.

RECTORS

John Sylvester, 1242 to (?)

The first rector of Fulham, whose name has been preserved, was John Sylvester. He was presented to the living by Henry III, 30 Nov. 1242. He was still rector in 1259. The date of his resignation or death is unknown.
[Rot., Pat. 27 Hen. III, m. 4.]

John de Sancto Claro, 1289 (?) to (?)

The next known rector was John de Sancto Claro, otherwise de St. Clare (i.e. Sinclair). He was one of the executors named in the will of Richard de Gravesend, Bishop of London, dated 1289, in which he is described as Rector of Fulham. He was a canon of St. Paul's Cathedral, where he held the prebend of Wedland, or Wildland. He was also chaplain to Cardinal Gentili de St. Martin in Monte. He is mentioned as Rector of Fulham in Rot., Pat., 22 Edward I, m. 6 dorso. He was a witness to the confirmation of Ulhing Epis. and John de Silvester (perhaps identical with the preceding Rector of Fulham), anno 1298. In 1300 he was guilty of opposing Archbishop Winchelsey. He was still Rector of Fulham in the time of Bishop Baldock (1306 to 1313).
[Rot., Pat. 22 Ed. I, m. 6 dorso.]

William Vigorous, 1336 to 1360 (?)

This Rector is more fully described as William dictus Vygerous de London. In 1327 he was collated to the church of Thorley, Herts, which, in 1329, he exchanged with Stephen de Scaldeford for that of Finchley. The latter he resigned in 1332. He was presented to the archdeaconry of Essex, iv. Non. Dec. (2 Dec.) 1331, but resigned it about the following September. He was presented to the rectory of Fulham by the Bishop of London, 9 Nov. 1336.

From "Papal Petitions" (vol. I, p. 81) we gather that Hugh de Nevill, knight, the King's, envoy, petitioned on behalf of William Vigorous, Rector of Fulham, for a canonry of Wells, with expectation of a prebend. The petition was granted by Pope Clement I at Avignon, 3 Kal. Dec. (29 Nov.) 1344. Among the muniments of the Dean and Chapter of St. Paul's is a deed, dated 21 Ed. III (1347), in which Sir William Vigorous, Rector of Fulham, is described as one of the two executors of Stephen de Gravesend, Bishop of London. In a deed of 1360 William Vigorous is still mentioned as Rector of Fulham.
[Reg., Baudake, 99.]

John de Flamstead, 1361(F) to 1364

The precise date of the admission of John de Flamstead to the rectory of Fulham is unknown, but on 23 Sept. 1361 he presented Thomas Offring to the vicarage, showing that he must then have been in office. Flamstead was prebend of Tottenhall or Tottenham in St. Paul's. He died seized of both preferments in 1364.
[Reg. Sudbury, 4.]

Robert de Wyssyngeset, 1364 to 1365

Robert de Wyssyngeset, or Wyssingset, probably a native of Whissonsett in Norfolk, was presented to the rectory of Fulham, 16 Dec. 1364, on the death of John de Flamstead. He also held the vicarages of Old Ham, Essex, and Luton, Bedfordshire. He died in 1365.
[Reg. Sudbury, 35.]

William de Shirebourne, alias Ilberd, 1365 to 1413

William de Shirebourne, or Sherbourne, otherwise called

Ilberd the sub-deacon, was presented to the rectory of Fulham, 6 Dec. 1365.

> "An Englishman by birth, of a sharp wit and great judgment, very zealous in his private studies and of great applause in his publick exercises, excellently well vers'd, not only in philosophy but also in theology and in both kinds is said to have written with great commendation, and was famous in the year 1390"
> - (Pitt "de Illustr. Angl. Script." sub anno 1390).

"William Ilberd, parson of Fulham," is mentioned in a deed of conveyance, 4 Feb., 5 Ric. II (Public Record Office.) Among the Fulham Manor Rolls (portfolio 188, file 65) at the Record Office, is a bond, executed circa 1384, in which "William, rector of the church of Fulham," is mentioned. He died in 1413.
[Reg. Sudbury, 74.]

The rectory of Fulham, about 1421-42, was, as already observed, farmed by the Carthusians of Shene.

Nicholas Hirbury, B.D., (?) to 1428

Nicholas Hirbury, or Herbury, B.D., was presented to the prebend of Kentish Town, or Cantlers, in St. Paul's, 25 Sept. 1410, and, about the same time, to that of Holywell, alias Finsbury, in the same church. He was also archdeacon of Gloucester. His death, as Rector of Fulham, in 1428, is cited in Register Grey, fol. 17.
[Reg. Grey, 17.]

Richard Moresby, LL.B., 1428 to 1428-29

Richard Moresby, LL.B., was collated to the prebend of Hoxton in St. Paul's, 31 May 1427. On the death of Hirbury, he was presented to the rectory of Fulham, 13 May 1428, but, on 27 Feb. 1428-29, he exchanged it with Henry Mereston for the rectory of St. Magnus the Martyr, London. On 20 Jan. 1430-31, he was collated to the archdeaconry of London, which he resigned ante 23 Feb. 1442-43, on which date he was appointed rector of Brynghurst, Lincolnshire. He resigned the prebend of Hoxton circa Nov. 1443.
[Reg. Grey, 17, 26.]

Henry Mereston, 1428-29 to 1432-33

Henry Mereston, or Merston, was presented to the prebend of Oxgate in St. Paul's, 28 Nov. 1401. He was admitted to the rectory of St. Magnus, 6 May 1428. This living he exchanged for the rectory of Fulham, 27 Feb. 1428-9. He also held the prebends of Caddington Major in St. Paul's, of Southwell, of York, and of St. Stephen's, Westminster, and was rector of Doddington, in the diocese of Ely, and of Orpington, Kent. He died in 1432-33, and was buried "in the chapel of the King's free chapel of St. Stephen within the Palace of Westminster before the image of the crucifix."

His will, written in Latin, is dated 1 Jan. 1432-33. The exact date of probate is not recorded, but it must have passed the seal not later than 1433. (P.C.C. 18 Luffenam).
[Reg. Grey, 26.]

Nicholas Sturgeon, 1433(?) to 1452

Nicholas Sturgeon held the prebend of Hasilbury in Wells Cathedral, which he exchanged for the prebend of Reculverland in St. Paul's, 6 Nov. 1440. The exact date of his admission to the rectory of Fulham is uncertain, but he presented to the vicarage in 1439-40. He was appointed canon of Windsor, 23 Feb. 1441-42 (Pat. Roll, 20 Henry VI pt. 3, membrane 3). He became precentor of St. Paul's, 7 July 1442. On 23 May 1452, he was presented to the prebend of Kentish Town in St. Paul's, when he resigned that of Reculverland. He resigned the rectory of Fulham in 1452. He was also canon of Exeter. His death occurred in 1454.

He was buried "in the Chapell of our blessyd lady and Seynt Nicholas . . . atte the north dore of the Cathedral cherche of Seynt Pawle."

The will of Nicholas Sturgeon is dated 31 May, 1454. It was proved 8 June 1454 (P.C.C. 10 Rous).
[Reg. Kemp, 17.]

John Drewell, LL.D., 1452 to 1458

John Drewell, LL.D., was presented to the rectory on the resignation of Nicholas Sturgeon, 15 July 1452. On 27 May 1457, he was collated to the prebend of Oxgate in St. Paul's, and on 19 June 1458, he had the office of Treasurer of the Cathedral conferred upon him. He resigned the rectory of Fulham in

September 1458, and the other two appointments in 1467. He was also rector of Steeple Langford, Prebend of South Alton and four others in Sarum, and archdeacon of Exeter.

In 1454 he was presented for obstructing the way from Parson's Green to Broomhouse. Again, in 1457, he was presented for lopping the elms which grew before the Rectory House at Parson's Green. In 1461 "Master John Druell, doctor of either law," sat on a commission of oyer and terminer, held at Westminster on 14 Dec. of that year. (Pat. Roll, 1 Ed. IV) He died in 1469, and was buried in St. Botolph's, Cambridge.
[Reg. Kemp, 20.]

Robert Ballard, 1458 to 1465

Robert Ballard was admitted to the rectory of Shepperton in 1451, but resigned it in the following year. He was instituted to the rectory of Fulham on the resignation of John Drewell (after) 4 September 1458. He exchanged it with John Waynfleet for the prebend of Kentish Town in St. Paul's, 24 Nov. 1465. He also held the rectory of Hadham Magna. He was appointed Treasurer of St. Paul's, 9 July 1474.
[Reg. Kemp, 59.]

John Waynfleet, S.T.B., 1465 to 1476

John Waynfleet, Waynfleete or Waynflete, S.T.B., was, on the death of Nicholas Sturgeon in June 1454, presented to the prebend of Kentish Town in St. Paul's. This preferment he resigned circa Nov. 1465. On 24 Nov. 1465, he was instituted to the rectory of Fulham, which he resigned in 1476. He also held the prebend of South Alton in Sarum. His arms were once in the window of the chancel of Fulham Church. He is supposed to have been identical with John Patten, alias Waynfleet, who was archdeacon of Surrey in 1462. The latter was probably nephew of John Waynfleet, Dean of Chichester in 1425, whose brother, William Waynfleet, alias Patten (Bishop of Winchester, 1447-1487), founded Magdalen College, Oxford.
[Reg. Kemp, 98.]

Richard Alleyne, 1476 to 1488

Richard Alleyne, or Aleyn, was presented to the rectory of

Fulham by Thomas Kemp, Bishop of London, on the resignation of John Waynfleet, 5 May 1476. He held it till his death in 1488.
[Reg. Kemp, 155.]

Richard Hill, B.D., 1488 to 1489

Richard Hill, B.D., was dean of the King's Chapel, or, as it is fully termed, "Dean of the Chapel of the King's Household." Among the State Papers is a grant to him for life, dated 7 Mar. 1486-87, of the King's chapel, called the "Priory of the Hermytage, in Blackmore, co. Dorset." In the same year he received the prebend of Beaminster in Salisbury Cathedral, and was made archdeacon of Lewes. He was presented to the rectory of Fulham, 23 Nov. 1488, on the death of Richard Alleyne. His tenure was, however, brief, for, on 19 Aug. 1489, he was translated to the see of London. He was consecrated at Lambeth Palace by Archbishop Morton and others, 15 Nov. 1489. He died 20 Feb. 1495-96, and was buried in old St. Paul's, where a monument was erected to his memory. According to Dugdale this was among the monuments destroyed by the Puritans a century and a half afterwards. Bishop Hill's will, dated 26 April 1495, was proved in the P.C.C., 19 Mar. 1495-96.
[Reg. Kemp, 219.]

Henry Aynsworth, LL.D., 1489-90 to 1517-18

Henry Aynsworth, LL.D., who was born at Greenford, Middlesex, was rector of Greenford Magna, 1473 to 1489, rector of St. Martin, Ironmonger Lane, London, 1480 to 1481, and rector of St. Mildred's, Poultry, from 1483 till his death. On the promotion of Richard Hill to the see of London, Dr. Aynsworth was, on 4 Jan. 1489-90, presented to the rectory of Fulham by Henry VII by virtue of his royal prerogative. He resigned it in 1517-18. He also held the rectory of Olney, Bucks. He was a Fellow of New College, Oxford.
[Reg. Hill, 1.]

John Adams, S.T.P., 1517-18 to 1523-24

John Adams was educated at Merton College, Oxford, of which he was appointed Commissary in 1505. On 5 May 1509, he was collated to the vicarage of St. Sepulchre's, London. He became prebend of Holborn in St. Paul's, 11 Feb. 1510-11, holding this preferment till Jan. 1520-21. On 21 Jan. 1520-21, he became prebend of Mora *extra* London. On the resignation of Dr. Aynsworth he was presented to the rectory of Fulham, 30 Mar. 1517-18. He held this rectory jointly with the vicarage of St. Sepulchre's till his death, 25 Mar. 1523-24. He was buried in "the chancel of the Church of St. Sepulchre, before the usual stall" (ante stallum consuetum).

The will of John Adams, dated 12 March 1523-24, was proved 12 April 1524 (P.C.C. 17 Bodfelde). It is in Latin.
[Reg. Fitzjames, 72.]

Geoffrey Wharton, LL.D., D.D., 1523-24 to 1529

Geoffrey Wharton, LL.D., D.D., was, on 8 Oct. 1520, admitted an advocate. He held the appointment of Chancellor and Vicar-General to Bishop Tonstal. On 25 Nov. 1523, he became prebend of Isledon (Islington) in St. Paul's, and on 23 Mar. 1523-24, he was appointed Rector of Fulham. On 21 May 1525, he was presented to the vicarage of Tottenham, Middlesex, and on 29 Mar. 1526-27, he was collated to the archdeaconry of London. He was presented to the vicarage of Sawbridgeworth, Herts., 17 April 1526. He was highly skilled in the civil and canon law. He died circa Oct. 1529.
[Reg. Tonstal, 6.]

Robert Ridley, S.T.P., 1529 to 1536

Robert Ridley, Rydley or Rydeley, S.T.P., was the fourth son of Nicholas Ridley, of Willimoteswick, Northumberland, by Mary (Curwen) his wife, a family related to Bishop Tonstal. He studied at Paris and also at Cambridge, where he commenced S.T.P. in 1518. On 3 July 1523, he became rector of St. Botolph's, Bishopsgate, and on 21 Mar. 1523-24, he was admitted prebendary of Mora in St. Paul's. On 20 Feb. 1526-27, he was collated to the rectory of St. Edmund, Lombard Street, and on 3 April 1527, he received the prebend of Tottenhall in St. Paul's. Finally, on 30th of the same month, he was collated to the stall of Isledon in St. Paul's, and on 30 Oct. 1529, to the rectory of Fulham.

Robert Ridley was a man of great learning and a strenuous opponent of the Reformation. It was at his charge that his nephew,

Nicholas Ridley, ultimately Bishop of London, was maintained and educated at Cambridge, Paris and Louvaine. He died circa June 1536.
[Reg. Tonstal, 28.]

Simon Heynes, D.D., 1536 to 1552

Simon Heynes, Haynes, Haines or Heins, was the son of John Heynes, by Agnes, daughter of Thomas Rolfe of Reche, and grandson of Simon Heynes, of Mildenhall, Suffolk. He was born about 1498-1500, and received his education at Queen's College, Cambridge, where he graduated B.A. in 1515-16. In 1519 he proceeded M.A., and was elected a Fellow of his College. His first living was the rectory of Barrow, Suffolk, to which he was instituted 28 Nov. 1528. In this year he obtained the presidency of Queen's College.

Simon Heynes's entrance into political life dates from 1529-30, when he was appointed one of the delegates to make a determination as to the King's divorce from Katharine of Aragon. In 1531 he obtained the degree of D.D., and in 1532-33 became Vice-Chancellor of the University of Cambridge. On 23 May 1533, Dr. Heynes attested at Dunstable Archbishop Cranmer's instrument of divorce from the unhappy Queen. Bishop Stokesley, on 29 January 1534-5 appointed Dr. Heynes to the vicarage of Stepney, and in 1536 presented him to the rectory of Fulham, to which he was instituted, 27 July 1536. As a reward for his personal services, Henry VIII gave him a canonry at Windsor, in which he was installed, 24 Dec. 1535. In 1537 the King nominated Dr. Heynes to the deanery of Exeter. On his election, 16 July 1537, he resigned the vicarage of Stepney, as it involved residence, but retained the sinecure rectory of Fulham, which he held till his death. In his capacity as Dean of Exeter, he attended the baptism of Edward VI at Hampton Court. In 1538 he and Archdeacon (afterwards Bishop) Bonner were sent to Spain, where they joined in a commission with Sir Thomas Wyatt, the English Ambassador, to induce the Emperor Charles V not to attend the Pope's Council at Vicenza.

In 1540 Heynes was again concerned in the King's matrimonial affairs, for, on 9 July 1540 we find his signature to a decree invalidating the marriage of Henry with the Princess Anne of Cleves. As a further reward for his loyal services, he was made one of the first prebendaries in the cathedral church of Westminster. Trouble now overtook the prosperous doctor. He was an ardent opponent of the Act of the Six Articles. The canons of Exeter charged him with teaching against the mass, and the canons of Windsor with harbouring heretics. By an Act of Privy Council, 16 Mar. 1542-43, Dr. Heynes was committed to the Fleet for "lewd and seditious preaching." After being examined, he was warned and released on his own recognizances.

On 9 Dec. 1547, Dr. Heynes was appointed one of His Majesty's commissioners to the Chapter of Wells against ritual, and, in 1548, he served on a commission to examine and reform the offices of the church. On the passing of the Act repealing the Six Articles (1 Ed. VI) Dr. Heynes married Joan, daughter of Nicholas Wallron of Exeter.

The work by which Dr. Heynes is best remembered was the part he took as one of the compilers of the first English Liturgy in 1549. He died in Oct. 1552, leaving two sons, Joseph, who died in 1621, and Simon, who died in 1628. His will, dated 17 July 1552, was proved 11 Nov. following (P.C.C. 29 Powell).

The will of Joan Heynes, dated 7 Feb. 1585-86, was proved 31 Oct. 1587 (P.C.C. 28 .Spencer).
[Reg. Stokesley, 30.]

Edmund West, M.A., 1552 to 1554

Edmund West came of a Lincolnshire family. He was educated at Pembroke College, Cambridge, where he graduated B.A. in 1535 and M.A. in 1538. In 1540 he was elected to a Fellowship. He received the appointment of steward to Dr. Ridley, Bishop of London, who collated him to the prebend of Mora in St. Paul's, 24 Aug. 1551, and gave him the sinecure rectory of Fulham, vacant by the death of Dr. Heynes, 21 Oct. 1552. Subsequently West fell off from Protestantism, and endeavoured, though unsuccessfully, to persuade the Bishop to recant. This occasioned a memorable letter from Dr. Ridley to West, who resigned the rectory and died, it is said, of grief, 26 May 1554.
[Reg. Bonner, 315.]

Thomas Moreton, LL.B., 1554 to 1558

Thomas Moreton or Morton, LL.B., was presented to the rectory of Fulham, 29 April 1554. He was chaplain to Bishop Bonner. He was, in 1555, made prebend of Broomsbury or Brondesbury in St. Paul's. Ralph Allerton, who was burnt at Islington, 17 Sept. 1557, has left an account of his examination before Bonner and his chaplain, Thomas Moreton, at Fulham Palace, on 8 April 1557, "written by himself with his own blood." This is interesting as giving us Moreton's observations on the case. In 1558 he was sent down to Colchester and Harwich with Dr. Chedsey, on commission from Bonner and the Council, to try heretics in that part of the diocese. Bonner's commission for this inquisition is

> "datum in manerio nostro de Fulham, io die mensis Junii anno Domini 1557 et nostræ translationis anno decimo octavo."

Moreton died 1 Oct. 1558.
[Reg. Bonner, 451.]

Thomas Darbyshire, D.C.L., 1558 to 1559-60

Thomas Darbyshire or Darbishire, son of the sister of Bishop Bonner, was born in 1518. He was educated mainly at the expense of his uncle, who sent him to Bradgates Hall (now Pembroke College), Oxford, where he graduated B.A., 7 April 1544, B.C.L., 30 Oct. 1553, and D.C.L., 20 July 1556.

Through the influence of his uncle he was collated to the prebend of Tottenhall in St. Paul's, 23 July 1543. Bonner's own imprisonment, from 1549 to 1553, prevented him from doing much for his nephew during this period. On 26 May 1554, Bonner presented him to the rectory of Hackney. On 1 Oct. 1558, Darbyshire received the rectory of Fulham. On 28 Oct. of the same year he was collated to the archdeaconry of Essex, and on 27 Nov. following he was presented to the rectory of St. Magnus the Martyr, London. Bonner, in 1553, made his nephew Chancellor of the diocese of London. In this last named office he came into unfavourable prominence in assisting Bonner in the examination and condemnation of Protestants.

On the accession of Queen Elizabeth, in 1558, the bishops and

clergy, who refused to take the oaths of allegiance and supremacy, were deprived of all their preferments. Darbyshire strenuously defended the ancient faith and, in consequence, suffered deprivation, 1559-60. For two years he remained in England watching the course of events. In 1561, however, when the severe statutes against recusants came into force, he retired abroad. He attended the Council of Trent, then sitting, with a view to ascertaining whether the Fathers would assent to the "faithful" continuing to frequent Protestant churches, in order to avoid the penalties enforced against the recusants. He returned with the answer that attendance at the heretical worship would be a grave sin. While in England Dr. Darbyshire again got into trouble and was imprisoned in the Fleet. On his release he quitted England for ever. He visited various parts of France and Flanders, and at Rome, on 1 May 1563, entered the Society of Jesus, of which, in 1572, he became a professed Father. For some years he lectured in Latin at Paris to the members of the Sodality of the Blessed Virgin. In 1590, in consequence of failing health, he sought retirement in the country. After a short stay at Rheims, he went to reside at Pont a Mousson in Lorraine, where his eloquence drew around him, not only a peasant audience, but learned professors, eager to ascertain the secret of his phenomenal success. Here, at the age of 86, he expired, 6 April 1604, after an exile of over forty years.
[Reg. Bonner, 476.]

Edward Layfield, M.A., D.D., 1559-60 to 1583

Edward Layfield, Layfielde or Layfeilde, M.A., D.D., was presented to the rectory of Fulham on the deprivation of Dr. Darbyshire, 28 Feb. 1559-60. He was admitted to the prebendal stall of Holborn in St. Paul's, 21 Feb. 1574-75. He held the rectory of Fulham till his death, which occurred in 1583.
[Reg Grindal, 113.]

John Duport, M.A., D.D., 1583 to 1617

John Duport, Duporte, Dewport or Dewporte came of a Normandy family, which settled in Leicestershire, temp. Henry IV. He was the eldest son of Thomas Duport of Sheepshed, co. Leicester, by his wife, Cornelia Norton, of Kent. He was educated at Jesus College, Cambridge. By 1580 he had become M.A., a

Fellow of his College, and one of the proctors for the University. His first preferment was the rectory of Harleton, Cambs. Subsequently he was instituted to the rectory of Medbourne and Husbands-Bosworth, Leicestershire. On 24 Dec. 1583, he was presented to the rectory of Fulham. On 29 April 1585, he was instituted to the rectory of Bishops-Stortford, Herts., with the office of precentor of St. Paul's and the said rectory annexed. In 1590, being then D.D., he became Master of Jesus College. In 1593, 1594, 1601 and 1609 he filled the office of Vice-Chancellor of his University. In the last named year he succeeded to the 7th prebendal stall in the church of Ely. In 1611, he was chosen one of the translators of the Bible. He died in 1617, and was buried at Medbourne, 25 Dec. 1617. He married Rachel, daughter of Richard Cox, Bishop of Ely, by whom he had four sons, John, who died young, Richard, Thomas and James, and four daughters, Cornelia, Jane, Rachel and Lucy. His will, dated 21 Oct. 1617, was proved 19 Feb. 1617-18 (P.C.C. 14 Meade). He left £5 to the poor of Fulham.
[Reg. Grindal, pt. Aylmer, 212.]

Henry King, M.A., D.D., 1618 to 1641-42

Henry King was the eldest son of Dr. John King, Bishop of London, by his wife Joan (Freeman). He was born at Worminghall, Bucks, where he was baptized, 16 Jan. 1591-92. In 1608, he entered Christ Church, Oxford, and proceeded B.A., 19 June 1611, and M.A., 7 July 1614. On 24 Jan. 1615-16, he was collated prebend of St. Pancras in St. Paul's and appointed penitentiary or confessor in that cathedral, and rector of Chigwell, Essex. On 10 April 1617, he was made archdeacon of Colchester, and, on 18 Nov. 1618, he was presented by his father to the rectory of Fulham. About this time he was also appointed chaplain in ordinary to Charles I. On 3 March 1623-24, he became canon of Christchurch. On 19 May 1625, he was admitted to the degrees of B.D. and D.D. The deanery of Rochester was conferred upon him on 6 Feb. 1638-9, and on 6 Feb. 1641-42, he was raised to the see of Chichester, when his archdeaconry, prebendship and rectory became void. At the time of his elevation to the bench, he was also presented to the rectory of Petworth, Sussex. He was residing at the episcopal palace when Chichester surrendered to the

Parliamentarians in 1643. He was deprived of his bishopric and rectory, and his estates were sequestered. He retired to the house of his brother-in-law, Sir Richard Hobart, of Langley, Bucks, where he lived till 1651. On the Restoration, in 1660, Dr. King returned to Chichester, where he died, 30 Sept. 1669, and was buried in the cathedral. His will is dated 14 July 1653. King married Anne, eldest daughter of Robert Berkeley, of Ulcombe, Kent. There were five children, of whom only two, John and Henry, survived. Mrs. King died in 1624, aged 24, and was buried in St. Paul's Cathedral.

King's writings chiefly took the form of sermons and poems. In 1649 he published "An Elegy on Charles I," dated "From my sad Retirement," March 11 1648-9. His scattered poems were collected in 1657. His "Poems and Psalms" were, in 1843, edited by Archdeacon Hannah.

[Bishops' Institutions and First Fruits Composition Books at P.R.O.]

Thomas Howell, M.A., D.D., 1641-42 to 1644

Thomas Howell was the son of Thomas Howell, vicar of Llangam-March, co. Brecon, and of Abernant, co. Carmarthen. He was born in 1588 at Bryn, in the parish of Llangam- March. He entered Jesus College, Oxford, of which he eventually became a Fellow. Here he graduated B.A., 20 Feb. 1608-9, M.A., 9 July 1612, B.D. and D.D., 8 July 1630. He soon acquired notice as a preacher of great ability. Charles I appointed him one of his chaplains. In 1625 he was collated to the rectory of West Horsley, Surrey. On 13 April 1635, he became rector of St. Stephen's, Walbrook, but resigned in 1641. On 16 Nov. 1636, the King made him a canon of Windsor, and, on the translation of Dr. Henry King to the see of Chichester, his royal patron instituted him to the rectory of Fulham, 25 March 1641-42.

Though a Puritan, Dr. Howell was, at the outbreak of the Civil War, hotly attacked by the Parliamentary party. He was expelled from West Horsley in 1644, and in the same year his Fulham rectory was sequestered. In his extremity he sought refuge in the loyal city of Oxford. On the death of Thomas Westfield, Bishop of Bristol, Charles I appointed Dr. Howell to the see. He was consecrated by Archbishop Ussher in August 1644. His tenure of the bishopric, was, however, of short duration. On 10 Sept. 1645,

Prince Rupert surrendered Bristol to General Fairfax. The loyalist clergy were ejected. The Parliamentarian troops pillaged the bishop's palace, stripping the lead from the roof. Mrs. Howell, who was in childbed at the time, died from fright and exposure. Dr. Howell, who was very roughly treated, died in 1646. He was interred in Bristol Cathedral, where his grave bears the solitary word "Expergiscar" (i.e. "I shall awake"). The education of his young children was undertaken by the citizens of Bristol "in grateful memory of their most worthy father" (Barrett, "History of Bristol," p. 330). Fuller thus quaintly describes his preaching:

> "His sermons, like the waters of Siloah, softly gliding on with a smooth stream, his matter with a lawful and laudable felony, did steal secretly the hearts of the hearers."

Dr. Howell married Honor Bromfield, of Chalcroft, Hampshire, by whom he had six sons and two daughters.
[Reg. Laud, 109.]

Adoniram Byfield, 1646 to 1652

Adoniram Byfield, the noted Puritan divine, was the son of Nicholas Byfield, a Calvinist minister and voluminous writer. In 1615 the elder Byfield was appointed vicar of Isleworth, where he died in 1622. By his wife, Elizabeth, he had a family of eight children. Adoniram, the third child, was born about 1614. He was educated at Emmanuel College, Cambridge. He does not appear to have graduated, though Brook, in his "Lives of the Puritans," styles him "A.M." Zachary Grey calls him "a broken apothecary," but there is no evidence to show that Adoniram Byfield ever followed any profession other than a clerical one. For awhile he resided at Hackney. In 1642 we find him acting as chaplain to Sir Henry Cholmondeley's Regiment in the army of Robert, Earl of Essex, the generalissimo of the Parliamentarian forces. It was possibly about this period that he first became connected with Fulham, for Cromwell's forces were then quartered in the parish. At any rate, he must have been resident here as early as 1644, for his signature appears appended to the minutes of a Vestry held in that year.

On 3 July 1643, Adoniram Byfield, whom Wood describes as

"a most zealous covenanter," was appointed one of the two Scribes or secretaries to the Westminster Assembly of Divines, which sat, first in Henry VII's Chapel and afterwards in the Jerusalem Chamber, from Nov. 1644 till March 1649. The other Scribe was Henry Rowborough. The chief work of this Assembly was the compilation of a "Directory," giving full instructions as to the mode of conducting public worship without the aid of set forms of prayer. The Scribes themselves were not members of the Assembly, of which they kept the records, but, in common with the other divines, who were members, they were entitled to an allowance of four shillings a day. For their special trouble the Scribes received the copyright of the "Directory," which was published 13 March 1644-45. This little 85-paged pamphlet was sold at three pence a copy, and is said to have produced a profit of some £400, which was, presumably, equally divided between Byfield and Rowborough.

It was during the sitting of the Assembly that Adoniram Byfield obtained, first, the rectory and then the vicarage of Fulham. Colonel Edmund Harvey, as Lord of the Manor, presented him to both these preferments during the course of 1646. The Journal of the House of Lords, for 10 Nov. 1646, contains the entry of an application for "an order" for Dr. Aylett to institute and induct Adoniram Byfield to the rectory ("Reports," Hist. Manuscripts Com., vol. vi. House of Lords' Cal.) The Calendar for 29 Nov. 1647-48 also contains a draft order for the payment of £100 per annum to Adoniram Byfield,

> "One of the Scribes of the Assembly, and Vicar of Fulham, so long as he continues vicar there."
> - "Reports," Hist. Manuscripts Com., vol. vii., House of Lords' Calendar.

The name of Adoniram Byfield appears among the minutes of the Fulham Vestry from 8 May 1644, down to 19 April 1652. He resided, probably, at the Vicarage, and not, as has been thought, at the Rectory, for the latter was then in the occupation of the Nourses.

There is some confusion as to the date when Byfield resigned the rectory and vicarage of Fulham. Dr. Edmund Calamy observes that Isaac Knight "succeeded Adoniram Byfield both in the rectory and vicarage of Fulham, being presented to the former in 1645 by Edmund Harvy and to the latter in 1657 by Cromwell."

In this statement he has been followed by all subsequent writers. Byfield's signature to the minutes of the Fulham Vestry ceases on 19 April 1652, and soon after he must have resigned both preferments, for, on 18 Oct. 1652, we find that of "Isaac Knight, minister," a term answering to "vicar." On 9 June 1653, Knight appends to his signature the epithet "rector." We may take it, therefore, that Byfield's connection with Fulham ceased about 1652. About this time he obtained preferment to the valuable rectory of Collingbourne-Ducis, in Wiltshire, from which Dr. Christopher Prior had been ejected.

In 1652 Byfield was appointed one of the Assistant Commissioners for Wiltshire under the ordinance of 29 June for ejecting "scandalous, ignorant and insufficient ministers and schoolmasters." Walker, in his "Sufferings of the Clergy," 1714, gives a very full account of the active part which Byfield took in this work. Though he lived to see the downfall of his party, Byfield was not disturbed from the rectory of Collingbourne-Ducis. The exact date of his death is unknown, but it probably occurred in 1660.

The will of Adoniram Byfield, dated 29 October 1657, was proved 31st August 1660 (P.C.C. 164 Nabbs). In it he describes himself as "Adoniram Byfeild of Collingbourne-Ducis in the County of Wilts." To his son Adoniram and Katherine his wife he left "my two silver Tankards that have the Arms of the University of Oxford upon them." He left legacies to his children Nicholas and Martha, the former receiving "twenty of my books." To his grandchild Adoniram Shingle he left £20 payable when he was twenty-one. He directed that his son, Adoniram Byfield, and his "friend and brother," Mr. Thomas Bayly, should be joint executors. To the latter he gave "my best fringed gloves and Aynsworth upon the ffive Books of Moses." The will was proved "by the oath of Adoniram Bifeild," his son.

Katherine Byfield, on 12 Feb. 1660-1, took out letters of administration to the effects of an Adoniram Byfield, described as "of the Parish of St. Martin's-in-the-Fields in Middlesex lately deceased" (P.C.C. Admon. Act. Book for 1661 fo. 21). Dr.

Byfield, the notorious quack or sal-volatile doctor, as Granger terms him, was probably the eldest child of the Fulham Byfield.

A manuscript transcript of the Hackney registers, preserved at the Guildhall, shows that Adoniram Byfield had the following children baptized in that parish, vizt., John in 1635-6, Martha in 1637, Nicholas in 1639, and a second Martha in 1641.

In the Parliamentary Survey, made in 1649-50 "for Examinyng and finding out the number and yearly values of all parsonages and ecclesiasticall and spirittuall lyvings and benefices," etc. the Commissioners report:

> "That Mr. Adoniram Byfield is Viccar of ffulham and is an able honest and constant preacher of the Gospell of Jesus Christe and hath one Mr. Samuell Frayser A Man of honest lyfe and converson for his curate or officiate."

Butler, in "Hudibras" (pt. iii., canto ii.) portrays Byfield "as a type of those zealots for presbytery whose headstrong tactics opened the way for independency":

> Their dispensations had been stifled
> But for our Adoniram Byfield.

John Cleveland, the Leicestershire poet, alludes to him in his "Hue and Cry after Sir John Presbyter":

> If you meet any that do thus attire them,
> Stop them, they are the tribe of Adoniram.

Byfield's most important work consists of the notes of the debates of the Westminster Assembly. These are almost entirely in his own handwriting. Mitchell states that Byfield published a Catechism some years before the Assembly met. Byfield is also the supposed author of "A Brief View of Mr. Coleman, his new modell of Church Government," 1645. He also assisted Dr. Chambers in compiling his "Apology for the Ministers of the County of Wiltshire," 1654.

The Parish Books show that some of Byfield's descendants lived in Fulham for many years. In the Church Registers is the following:

1694. Dinah Byfield Wife of Iohn Byfield bu. 26 Mar.

This John Byfield was, probably, the son of Adoniram Byfield, baptized at Hackney in 1635-6.
[Institutions at the P.R.O.]

Isaac Knight, B.D., 1653 to 1660

Of Isaac Knight, Dr. Edmund Calamy, in his "Account of the Ministers, etc., Ejected," observes:

> "A Godly Man, and of a good Temper: But he wanted Academical Learning, and yet had the Honour of his Degree confer'd upon him for the Sake of the General."

This was the degree of B.D. granted to him by the University of Oxford, 8 March 1648-49. During the Civil War he held the appointment of Chaplain to General Fairfax, and became minister at the chapel of St. Paul's, Hammersmith. Though, as we have observed in our notice of Adoniram Byfield, Isaac Knight signed the minutes of the Fulham Vestry as "minister" as early as 18 Oct. 1652, and as "rector" as early as 9 June 1653, he had not then been legally admitted to the benefices. On the disappearance of Byfield in 1652, Knight, as minister at Hammersmith Chapel, had doubtless looked after the parent church, and probably received from Col. Harvey presentation to the livings which were in his gift. His formal admission to the rectory of Fulham is dated 24 Nov. 1654, and is in the following terms:

> "Know all men by these presents that the 24 day of November in the yeare 1654 there was exhibited to the Commissioners for Approbation of Publique Preachers a presentation of Isaac Knight clerke to the rectory of ffulham in the County of Middlesex made to him by Edmond Harvey Esquire patron thereof, as also an order of the late Committee for Plundered Ministers for his settlement thereupon together with a testimony in the behalfe of the said Isaac Knight of his holy and good conversation. Upon perusal and due consideration of the p^{r}misses and, finding him to be a person qualified as in and by the Ordinance for such approbation is required, the Commissioners above mentioned have adiudged and approved the said Isaac Knight to be a fit person to preach the Gospell and have graunted him admission and do admit the

said Isaac Knight to the rectory of ffulham aforesaid to be full and perfect possessor and incumbent thereof and do hereby signify to all persons concerned herein that he is hereby instituted to ye pfitts and perquisits and all rates and dues incident and belonging to the said rectory as fully and effectually as if hee had beene instituted and inducted according to ancient Lawes and Customes as have in this case formerly beene made, had and used in this Realme In witness whereof they have caused the Comon Seale to be hereunto affixed and the same to be attested by the hand of the Registrar by his Highness in that behalfe appointed. <u>Dated at Whitehall the 24th day of November 1654</u>."

The Commissioners on 21 Feb. 1655-56:

"Ordered that Mr. Isaac Knight incumbent of the Church of ffulham in the County of Middlesex do by himselfe or some other pson sufficiently authorised by him giue satisfaccon to those Trustees for the first fruites of the said Church, to which he is admitted, on the 28 of ffebruary instant at the place of their sitting in the old Pallace yard, Westminster, whereof he is in no wise to faile."

It was not till May 1657, the year quoted by Calamy, that Isaac Knight was formally admitted to the vicarage of Fulham, though he had actually been in the possession of it since 1652. In the Admissions at Lambeth is the following entry:

"Isaac Knight Cl. admitted the 4th day of May 1657 to ye Vicarage of ffulham in the County of Middlesex upon a presentation exhibited the same day from his Highnes the Lord Protector under the great seal of England."

Isaac Knight continued to hold the rectory and the vicarage down to the Restoration. His signature in the Parish Books occurs for the last time on 11 June 1660, shortly after which date he was deprived of both preferments.

He left one son, Thomas, who was educated at Magdalen College, Oxford, where, on 6 April 1652, he had the degree of B.A. conferred upon him by virtue of a letter of Oliver Cromwell as Chancellor. He is therein described as "A studious young man that is to leave the University and to apply himself to the study of the Lawe." He became a barrister of Gray's Inn.

[Admissions, Lambeth Palace Library, No. 585.]

George Stradling, M.A., D.D., 1660 to 1688

George Stradling, who was born in 1622, was the eighth and youngest son of Sir John Stradling, bart., of St. Donat's, Glamorganshire, by Elizabeth, his wife, daughter of Edward Gage, of Firle. He was educated at Jesus College, Oxford, where, on 6 Nov. 1640, he proceeded B.A. In 1643 he was elected a Fellow of All Souls, Oxford, and proceeded M.A., 26 Jan. 1646-47. On 6 Nov. 1661, he obtained his D.D. degree.

On the Restoration Dr. Stradling was <u>appointed chaplain to Bishop Sheldon, who, on 11 Jan. 1660-61, presented him to the rectory of Fulham</u>. His subsequent preferments were: rector of Hanwell cum Brentford, 25 Feb. 1661-62, vicar of Cliffe-at-Hoo, Kent, 13 Nov. 1663, and of Sutton-at-Hone, Kent, 1666, precentor of the church of Chichester, 22 July 1671, and vicar of St. Bride's, London, 23 April. 1672. He became a canon of St. Paul's, 19 Dec. 1660, and of Westminster in July 1663, and dean of Chichester in Dec. 1672. He is described as having been "an admirable lutinist."

Dr. Stradling married, on 3 Nov. 1666, Margaret, daughter of Sir William Salter, of Iver, Bucks, knt., carver-in-ordinary to Charles II. He died 19 April 1688, and was buried in Westminster Abbey on 24 April. He had two children, Margaret and George, both of whom were buried in the Abbey, the former on 1 July 1670, and the latter on 5 Dec. 1671. Mrs. Stradling was also buried there, 1 Oct. 1681. A volume of Dean Stradling's "Sermons" was published in 1692 with a preface by James Harrington.
[Reg. Henchman, 10.]

Thomas Turner, M.A., S.T.P., 1688 to 1714

Thomas Turner was the son of Thomas Turner, S.T.P., dean of Canterbury. He was born at Bristol about 1645-46 and was educated at Oxford. He became a scholar of Corpus Christi in 1663, and proceeded B.A. 15 Mar. 1665-66, and M.A. in 1669. In 1672 he was elected a Fellow of his College. In 1677 he took his B.D., and on 2 July 1683, his S.T.P. degree. On 13 Mar. 1687-88, he was elected President of Corpus Christi. He was incorporated at Cambridge in 1690.

In 1672 he received the vicarage of Milton next Sittingbourne,

Kent. He was appointed chaplain to Bishop Compton, who, on 4 Nov. 1680, collated him to the rectory of Thorley, Herts, and, on 20 Dec. following, to the archdeaconry of Essex. In 1682 he was made prebendary of Mapesbury in St. Paul's, and, four years later, was installed a prebendary of Ely.

On 7 May 1688, he was presented to the rectory of Fulham by his brother, Dr. Francis Turner, Bishop of Ely, Dr. Compton, Bishop of London, being at the time under suspension. In the following year he became precentor and prebendary of Brownswood in St. Paul's. He died 30 April 1714, and was buried in the chapel of Corpus Christi College, where there is a monument to his memory. His will, dated 24 Aug. 1706, is registered in the Probate Court of Oxford. It was proved 18 Oct. 1715. Dr. Turner left £100 to the parish of Fulham, which now produces £3 a year. This sum is still regularly paid, on application, by the Corporation of the Sons of the Clergy. It was formerly used for the purpose of putting out poor boys as apprentices.
[Reg. Compton, 104.]

John Wyvill, M.A., 1714

John Wyvill was educated at Trinity College, Cambridge, where he graduated B.A. in 1701 and M.A. in 1705. He was instituted to the rectory of Gilston, Herts, 15 June 1714. On 3 July 1714, he was presented to the rectory of Fulham, vacant by the death of Dr. Turner. On 29th of the same month he was collated to the prebend of Mora in St. Paul's. All these three appointments, which were in the gift of the Bishop of London, he resigned in November 1714, in order to be instituted to the rectory of Orsett, Essex, to which he had been presented by the Bishop of London. His institution and collation took place on 16 Oct. 1714. He held this benefice till his death, which occurred in 1717.
[Reg. Robinson, 11.]

George Bell, junior, M.A., 1714 to 1734

George Bell, junior, was born circa 1684, at Croft, Yorkshire, of which parish his father, George Bell, senior, was then incumbent. He was first sent to the grammar school at Richmond, Yorkshire. On 27 May 1701, he was admitted a pensioner of St. John's College, Cambridge. He obtained his B.A. degree in 1704

and his M.A. in 1708. He was presented to the prebend of Harleston in St. Paul's, 4 June 1714. He held this stall till August 1734. On 9 Nov. 1714, he was collated to the rectory of Fulham, which he held till his death in 1734.
[Reg. Robinson, 12.]

William Nicholas Blomberg, M.A., 1734 to 1750

William Nicholas Blomberg, who was born in 1702, was the son of Charles Blomberg, of St. Martin's-in-the-Fields, generally styled Baron Blomberg, a nobleman of Courland, Russia. He received his education at Merton College, Oxford. He proceeded B.A. 21 Feb. 1723-24, and M.A. 10 Mar. 1726-27, and was elected a Fellow of his College. He was admitted and instituted to the vicarage of Fulham by the Rev. George Bell, junior, the Rector, 15 June 1733, and was admitted and collated to the rectory of Fulham by Bishop Gibson, 24 Oct. 1734, the living having become vacant by the death of the Rev. George Bell in that year. On 7 Nov. 1739, he was collated to the rectory of Cliffe-at-Hoo, Kent. On 2 Nov. 1739, he obtained dispensation authorizing his holding both benefices together. He died 5 Oct. 1750. He had two children, William and Mary.

The will of the Rev. William Nicholas Blomberg, dated 8 June 1748, was proved 24 Oct. 1750 (P.C.C. 118 Greenly). From it we take the following extracts:

> "I William Nicholas Blomberg, vicar of ffulham in the county of Middlesex etc. If I die at ffulham to be buried within the Church there; if at Cliffe, to be buried in the Chancel there with a small stone to my memory over it. To my wife Ursula Blomberg all my household furniture (except Books and plate) in the Vicarage House in ffulham and in the Rectory House in Cliffe co. Kent, and all money due to me from the Rectory and Vicarage of ffulham or from the Rectory of Cliffe. To my son William Blomberg all my Books together with the Glass Book Case. I will that my manuscript sermons be Burnt within fourteen days after my decease."

The Rev. W. N. Blomberg published "An Account of the Life and Writings of Edmund Dickinson, M.D., Physician in Ordinary to King Charles and King James II: To which is added a treatise on the Grecian Games, printed from the Doctor's own manuscript."

London, 1739, 8vo. Dr. Dickinson was his maternal grandfather. [Reg. Gibson, 259, 266.]

Samuel Knight, M.A., 1750-51 to 1790

Samuel Knight was the son of Dr. Knight, archdeacon of Berkshire. He was educated at Trinity College, Cambridge, graduating B.A. in 1738 and M.A. in 1742. He also became a Fellow of his College. On 6 July 1745, he was incorporated at Oxford.

On 24 December 1750, the rectory being void, Bishop Sherlock admitted and collated the Rev. Samuel Knight to the vicarage of Fulham, and 15 Feb. 1750-51, he presented him with the rectory as well. Here, a year or two afterwards, Mrs. Samuel Knight died, a circumstance which "so deeply affected him," remarks the Rev. W. Cole in his manuscript *Account of Fulham Church*, "that he declared he could never reside there again." Bishop Sherlock accordingly allowed him to exchange the vicarage of Fulham for another living. "After a great many overtures," continues Cole,

> "with various people, and among the rest with my cousin Cock of Debden in Essex, who came to Fulham, but did not approve of the conditions, his Rectory being a very considerable one, he at last closed in with Mr. Cumberland, for the Bishop's Patience was almost tired out, as he began to think that Mr. Knight was of the same rambling Turn as his Father."

The Bishop had wished Mr. Knight to exchange both rectory and vicarage, but, as the former was a sinecure, and tenable with any other preferment, Mr. Knight was not to be persuaded to fall in with such a suggestion. The Rev. Denison Cumberland, who held the rectory of Stanwick, Northamptonshire, having agreed with the Rev. Samuel Knight for an exchange of livings, came to Fulham in the beginning of 1757, when he was formally admitted by Mr. Knight to the living, 29 Jan. 1757.

The Rev. S. Knight resided at Stanwick down to about 1770, when he moved to Milton, near Cambridge, the manor of which he had purchased.

The sinecure rectory of Milton, which was in the patronage of

King's College, Cambridge, becoming vacant in 1775, was conferred upon the Rev. Graham Jepson, a Fellow of the College. Mr. Knight, who was anxious, if possible, to acquire a second sinecure, induced Mr. Jepson, 13 March 1776, to exchange it for the vicarage of Fulham, which had again fallen vacant in .consequence of the death of the Rev. A. Hamilton, the successor of the Rev. D. Cumberland.

The Rev. Samuel Knight died at Milton, 6 Jan. 1790. By his wife Hannah, daughter of Talbot Pepys, of Impington, Cambridgeshire, he had one son, Samuel.
[Reg. Gibson, 340].

Michael Lort, M.A., D.D., 1790

Michael Lort, who was born in 1725, was the eldest son of Roger Lort, major of the Royal Welsh Fusiliers, by Anne, only child of the Rev. Edward Jenkins, vicar of Fareham, Hants. His father died 11 May 1745, from wounds he received in the battle of Fontenoy.

He entered, as a pensioner, at Trinity College, Cambridge, on 13 June 1743. In 1746 he took his B.A. degree, in 1750 his M.A., in 1761 his B.D., and in 1780 his D.D. He was incorporated at Oxford on 7 July 1759. His College offices were, Scholar, 20 April, 1744, Sub Fellow, 2 October 1749, Full Fellow, 4 July 1750, Senior Fellow, 1768, Sublector Primus, 1753, Latin Reader, 1754, Lector Primarius, 1755, and Greek Reader, 1756.

Terrick, Bishop of Peterborough, in 1761, appointed him his chaplain. About this date he received the vicarage of Bottisham, Cambridgeshire. From 1779 to 1784 he acted as chaplain to Archbishop Cornwallis, and, in 1785, became Librarian at Lambeth Palace. His subsequent appointments were: rector of St. Matthew, Friday Street, January 1771, prebend of Tottenhall in St. Paul's, 11 April 1780, and rector of St. Michael, Mile End, or Myland, adjoining Colchester, 1789. On 17 April 1790, Bishop Porteus instituted and collated him to the rectory of Fulham. He died at 6, Savile Row, London, 5 November 1790, from the effects of a carriage accident.

In May 1783, Dr. Lort married Susannah, daughter of Alderman Norfolk, of Cambridge. She died 5 February 1792. Dr. and Mrs. Lort were buried in the same vault in St. Matthew, Friday

Street, where a white marble tablet was erected to their memory. When, in 1881, this City church was demolished, the remains were removed to the City of London Cemetery at Ilford.

Dr. Lort was a man of great erudition. In 1755 he was elected a Fellow of the Society of Antiquaries, of which body he became Vice-President. In 1766 he became a Fellow of the Royal Society. In 1760 and 1770 he published a couple of sermons, and in 1790 "A Short Commentary on the Lord's Prayer."
[Bishop's Certificates, P.R.O.]

Graham Jepson, M.A., S.T.B., 1790 to 1811

Graham Jepson, who was born in 1734, was educated at King's College, Cambridge, where he graduated B.A. in 1758, M.A. in 1761, and S.T.B. in 1775. He was also elected a Fellow of his College. His first preferment was the rectory of Milton, Cambridgeshire, which, as already stated, he exchanged with the Rev. Samuel Knight for the vicarage of Fulham. To this vicarage he was admitted and instituted by Mr. Knight, 13 March 1776. On the death of Dr. Lort, Bishop Porteus presented him to the rectory of Fulham, his institution and collation taking place, 16 December 1790. Dr. Jepson died 24 May 1811, and was buried at Fulham.
[Regs. Osbaldeston, 65; Porteus, 303.]

William Wood, B.D., M.A., 1811 to 1841

William Wood was the son of William Wood, of Hatton, Salop, where he was born, 6 August 1769. He was educated at Christ Church, Oxford, proceeding B.A. in 1790, M.A. in 1793, and B.D. in 1801. He was proctor in 1800, and also acted as tutor at his University. He became domestic chaplain to Bishop Randolph. In 1810 he was made a prebendary of St. Paul's, and rector of Coulsden, Surrey. On 29 June 1811, Bishop Randolph, the rectory being vacant, instituted and collated the Rev. William Wood to the vicarage of Fulham, and, on 1 July following, to the rectory of this parish, void by the death of the Rev. Graham Jepson. In 1834 he was appointed a prebendary of Canterbury, when he resigned the vicarage of Fulham. He died at Coulsden, 11 April 1841, and was interred in the family vault at Fulham, 16 April.
[Reg. Howley, p. 2, f. 30.]

VICARS

Robert, 1320 (?) to (?)

THE first Vicar of Fulham of whom any record is preserved was one Robert. In "London and Middlesex Fines" is an entry showing that, in 1320, William de Northbrok and Egidia his wife purchased of Robert, Vicar of the church of Fulham, certain premises in the manor.
[Lond. and Midd. Fines, 14 Ed. II.]

Henry Martin, 1329 to 1361 (?)

Henry Martin de Colchester was presented to the vicarage, 19 November 1329. He was still here in 1333. The date of his resignation or death is unknown.
[Reg. Baudake, 72.]

Thomas Offring, 1361 to 1370-71

Thomas Offring, priest, was presented to the vicarage, 23 September 1361. On 5 February 1370-71, he exchanged with John Tette, chaplain.
[Reg. Sudbury, 4, 81.]

John Tette, 1370-71 to (?)

John Tette, chaplain, became Vicar of Fulham by exchange, 5 February 1370-71.
[Reg. Sudbury, 81.]

John de Stratford, (?) to 1392

John de Stratford was the next Vicar of whom any record has been preserved. His death, as Vicar of Fulham, is cited as having caused the vacancy to which his successor was presented, 16 October 1392.
[Reg. Braybroke, 100.]

John Godyng, 1392 to 1397 (?)

John Godynge, Godyng, or Goding, chaplain, was presented to the vicarage, 16 October 1392, on the death of John de Stratford. He is said to have been prebend of Layton Littlebury and Yeldham

Magna, Essex. He is mentioned in the minutes of a Court Baron, held 14 May 1397, as still Vicar of Fulham.
[Reg. Braybroke, 100.]

Gilbert Janyn, 1397-98 to 1410 (?)

Gilbert Janyn, chaplain, was presented to the vicarage, 8 February 1397-98.
[Reg. Braybroke, 157.]

Adam Jevecoke, 1410 to (?)

Adam Jevecoke was presented to the vicarage, 8 October 1410.
[Reg. Walden, pt. Clifford, 29.]

Walter Gerard, (?) to 1416

The date of the presentation of Walter Gerard to the vicarage is unknown. He exchanged it with John Stevenys, chaplain, vicar of Headcorn, Kent, 18 November 1416. He was also rector of Wishaw, Warwickshire.
[Cant. Reg. Chicheley, p. 1, f.79.]

John Stevenys, 1416 to (?)

John Stevenys, or Stevens, chaplain, vicar of Headcorn, exchanged his vicarage for that of Fulham, 18 November 1416. He was also rector of Bocking and Tey Parva, Essex.
[Cant. Reg. Chicheley, p. 1, f.79.]

From 1421-22, the Carthusians held the vicarage.

Richard Eaton, (?) to 1439-40

The date of the presentation of Richard Eaton, or Eton, is unknown. Richard Eaton, Vicar of Fulham, was, on 15 January 1439-40, recently deceased. He was, perhaps, identical with Richard Eaton, vicar of Arkesden, Essex, in 1407.
[Reg. Gilbert, 27.]

John Sudbury, alias Crall, 1439-40 to 1451

John Sudbury, *alias* Crall, became Vicar of Fulham, 15 Jan. 1439-40, and held the living till 1451, when he resigned. He also held the vicarages of South Weald, Springfield, Boswell and Wethersfield, all in Essex, of St. Magnus, London, and of St. Andrew Undershaft, and the prebends of Holborn, Brondesbury and York. He finally rose to be archdeacon of Essex and died about 1479-80. His will, dated 8 Dec. 1479, was proved 10 May 1480 (P.C.C. 13 Logge).

It was during the vicariate of John Sudbury that the Tower of Fulham Church was built. His arms, as we have mentioned, once existed in a window in the old Church.

Another John Sudbury, described as *capellanus*, lived at Fulham about this time, but was clearly distinct from John Sudbury, *alias* Crall, although the two names have hitherto been much confused. It is not improbable that the former was father of the latter. Both were most likely connected with the family of Simon of Sudbury, Bishop of London, 1362 to 1375. This John Sudbury was presented to the prebend of Broomsbury in St. Paul's, 20 Dec. 1418. At a View in 1428, it was presented:

"That John Suddebury, chaplain, has boughs and branches overhanging the way at Wenden (Walham) Green, wherefore he is amerced iiijd."

At a View, held in 1437, "John Suddebury, chaplain" was again presented for a like offence. The last allusion to him in the Rolls occurs in 1442. At a Court Baron, held in that year, "John Sudbury, Canon of the Church of St. Paul," surrendered certain lands at Fulham, including an acre in Bear Street, to the use of William Coxston. John Thorley of Fulham, whose will is dated 21 Dec. 1445, left to his wife all his lands in the parish "which I lately acquired of John Sudbury, clerk."

The registered copy of Sudbury's will (P.C.C. 29 Luffenam) is unfortunately now in very bad condition, and, in two places, several lines are almost obliterated. One of these includes the date, but a very careful examination of the document shows the words to be:

"In dei nomine Amen Undecimo die mensis Octobris Anno domini Millimo Quadringentisimo quadraginta quarto Regni vero Regis Henrici Sexti post conques anno Vicesimo tercio ego Johannes Sudbury," *etc.*

The date of the will is therefore 11 Oct. 1444. The grant attached is dated "6 Nov. anno suprascripto," i.e. 6 Nov. 1444, showing that Sudbury must have died between these dates. The following is an extract:

> "I give my soul to my Creator Omnipotent God to the Blessed Virgin Mary His Mother and to all the Saints and my body to be buried in the Churchyard called Pardon Churchawe near the Cathedral Church of St. Paul of London or in the Cloister about the same burying place according to the orders of my Executors. To Robert Normaville my servant as well for his good Services to me performed and to be performed and as also for his good diligence about the completion of this my will, my timber and all my wood at ffulham and a featherbed, 2 mattresses, pair of sheets, and 1 pair of coverlets, 1 brass pot, 1 brass porringer and other things, fixtures, hustlements and utensils at ffulham and all my apparati relating to heating and cooking there. The residue of my goods to be bestowed for the health of my soul and my parents' souls and ancestors' souls and my benefactors' souls and all faithful departed, for amending foul ways and bridges, to the delivery of prisoners, to poor honest maidens towards their marriage portions and all other works for the good of my soul."

[Reg. Gilbert, 27.]

Henry Smith, M.A., 1451 to 1452

Henry Smith, M.A., was presented to the vicarage, 17 Nov. 1451, but resigned it in the following year.
[Reg. Kemp, 13, 17.]

William Layton, M.A., 1452 to 1453-54

William Layton, M.A., was presented to the vicarage, 23 April 1452, but resigned it in the following year.
[Reg. Kemp, 17, 30.]

Henry Walfrey, 1453-54 to 1461-62

Henry Walfrey, priest, was presented to the vicarage, on the resignation of William Layton, 17 Feb. 1453-54. In 1461-62 he exchanged livings with William Redenese, vicar of Dagenham, Essex. At a View, in 1464, the following presentment was made:

> "Simon Walfrey unjustly and without leave has taken from John Oliver

a sword and a shield; in mercy xx^d."

This person was probably related to the Vicar. On 28 April 1455, Peter Hopkyn surrendered to the use of "Sr Henry Walfrey, vicar of the Church of Fulham," a garden in Bear Street. The minutes of a Court Baron, held 25 Nov. 1461, contain the following:

> "Henry Walfrey, vicar of the church of Fulham, on a day, *etc.,* made rescue of [*i.e.* resisted] John Tytmerssh, bailiff of the Liberty of the Lord, in attaching the said Henry by writ of our Lord the King to the same John directed unjustly and against the peace of the same Lord the King. Wherefore he is in mercy xij^d.
> And the same Henry unjustly and without authority to him committed at divers times in this year 30 lbs. of lead and 200 nails of iron of the value of [blank] of the goods and chattels of the church of Fulham took and carried away, wherefore he is in mercy viij^d.
> The said Henry Walfre has a ditch unscoured in Edwynns garden."

Edwin's garden was in Bear Street.
[Reg. Kemp, 30, 79.]

William Redenese, 1461-62 to 1463

William Redenese or Redenes, priest, exchanged with Henry Walfrey, 25 Feb. 1461-62, and resigned in 1463.
[Reg. Kemp, 79, 86.]

Richard Hendock, 1463 to 1465

Richard Hendock was presented to the vicarage, 9 May 1463, on the resignation of William Redenese. He resigned in 1465.
[Reg. Kemp, 86, 96.]

John Cooke, 1465 to 1466

John Cooke, priest, was presented to the vicarage, 28 Aug. 1465, on the resignation of Richard Hendock. He exchanged, 11 June 1466, with John Elton. Cooke was rector of St. Mildred's, Poultry, from 1479 to 1483.
[Reg. Kemp, 96, 101.]

John Elton, B.D., 1466 to 1467

John Elton, B.D., was presented to the vicarage, 11 June 1466, on the resignation of John Cooke. He was also rector of St. Bartholomew's, Exchange. He resigned the vicarage of Fulham in 1467.
[Reg. Kemp, 101, 105.]

John Chedworth, M.A., 1467

John Chedworth, Chadworth or Chadelworth, M.A., was collated to the prebend of Caistor in Lincoln Cathedral, 14 Dec. 1454, but resigned in 1457, when he was appointed archdeacon of Northampton, 19 Aug. 1457. He was collated prebend of Thame, 4 Sept. 1458. On 18 July 1464, he was presented to the prebend of Newington in St. Paul's. On 11 April 1465, he was installed prebend of Sutton *cum* Buckingham in Lincoln Cathedral. On 27 April 1464, he was collated to the archdeaconry of Lincoln. He became Vicar of Fulham, 17 April 1467, but resigned the living in the following August. He was rector of Stepney *circa* 1465 till his death, which occurred in August 1471.

His will, dated at his prebend of "Newnton" (Newington), 4 Aug. 1471, was proved at Lambeth, 9 Sept. 1471 (P.C.C. 3 Wattys), by William Chadworth, his father.
[Reg. Kemp, 105, 108.]

William Lax, 1467 to 1470

William Lax, priest, was presented the vicarage on the resignation of John Chedworth, 13 Aug. 1467. He resigned in 1470. He also held the vicarage of Nazeing, Essex.
[Reg. Kemp, 108, 124.]

William Harvey, M.A., 1470 to 1471

William Harvey or Hervey, M.A., was presented to the vicarage of Fulham, 10 Nov. 1470. He was also vicar of Ramsey, now a small island in Steeple parish, Essex. He died 5 Nov. 1471, and was buried in the chancel of Fulham Church (see vol. I).
[Reg. Kemp, 124, 131.]

John Peletot, M.A., 1471 to 1472

John Peletot, M.A., was presented to the vicarage, 18 Nov.

1471, vacant by the death of William Harvey. He resigned in the following year. He held the vicarage of Amwell, Middlesex, in 1479.
[Reg. Kemp, 131, 137.]

Walter Newton, 1472 to 1476

Walter Newton, priest, was presented to the vicarage on the resignation of John Peletot 20 Dec. 1472. He resigned in 1476.
[Reg. Kemp, 137, 159.]

Richard Seffrey, 1476 to 1476-77

Richard Seffrey or Seffery, priest, was presented to the vicarage on the resignation of Walter Newton, 8 Nov. 1476, but died before 15 March following.
[Reg. Kemp, 159, 160.]

Adam Sandaker, 1476-77 to 1479

Adam Sandaker or Sandakyr, priest, was presented to the vicarage, 15 Mar. 1476-77, on the death of Richard Seffrey. He died before 7 Sept. 1479.
[Reg. Kemp, 160, 174.]

John Cowper, 1479 to 1481

John Cowper or Couper, priest, was presented to the vicarage on the death of Adam Sandaker, 7 Sept. 1479. He resigned in 1481. He became vicar of St. Leonard's, Shoreditch. He also held preferments in Essex. He died about 1525, and was buried at St. Leonard's Church. His will, dated 16 Aug. 1521, was proved 10 July 1525 (P.C.C. 35 Bodfelde).
[Reg. Kemp, 174, 185.]

William Stokes, 1481 to 1499-1500

William Stokes, priest, was presented to the vicarage on the resignation of John Cowper, 30 July 1481. He resigned in Jan. 1499-1500.
[Regs. Kemp, 185; Hill, 36.]

William Payne, 1499-1500 to 1501(?)

William Payne, chaplain, was presented to the vicarage on the

resignation of William Stokes, 18 Jan. 1499-1500. He resigned *circa* 1501.
[Reg. Hill, 36.]

James Aynswokth, 1501(?) to 1502-03

James Aynsworth, chaplain, was the next Vicar. He resigned the living before 13 Feb 1502-03. He was also rector of Greenford Parva, otherwise Perivale, Middlesex, from 1494 to 1503, and vicar of Northall from 1502 to 1513. He died in 1513. He was probably related to Dr, Henry Aynsworth, Rector of Fulham, 1489-90 to 1517-18.
[Reg. Hill, 42, 43.]

John Woodhouse, B.C.L., 1502-3 to 1503

John Woodhouse, "in jure Civili Bac.," was presented to the vicarage, 13 Feb. 1502-3, on the resignation of James Aynsworth. He was also rector of Broomfield, Essex. He died in 1503.
[Reg. Hill, 42, 43.]

John Phipps, M.A., 1503 to (?)

John Phipps or Phippes, M.A., was presented to the vicarage, 15 Sept. 1503, on the death of John Woodhouse. The date of his resignation or death is unknown.
[Reg. Hill, 43.]

Simon Green, alias Foderby, D.D., (?) to 1506

Simon Green, Grene or Greene, *alias* Foderby, Fotherby or ffotherby, was educated at Lincoln College, Oxford. In 1494 he was admitted to the rectory of All Hallows, Honey Lane, London. He was for some time commissary of Oxford University, where he graduated D.D. in 1501. The precise date of his presentation to the vicarage of Fulham is unknown. In 1500 he witnessed the will of Thomas Wyndowt of Fulham. He resigned the living 13 May 1506. On 28 Mar. 1511-12 he was collated prebend of Empingham, and on 2 Dec. 1512, prebend of Biggleswade, both in Lincoln Cathedral. He was made precentor at the Cathedral, 28 May 1512, a position which he resigned in 1528. On 27 May 1528 he exchanged the stall of Biggleswade for that of Bedford Minor, also in Lincoln. He was rector of St. Peter's, Cornhill, till his death,

which occurred in 1536. He was buried in Lincoln Cathedral. His will, dated 26 Mar. 1536, was proved 12 April 1536 (P.C.C. 1 Crumwell).
[Reg. Hill, 55.]

Adam Forster, 1506 to 1511

Adam Forster, chaplain, was presented to the vicarage on the resignation of Simon Green, 13 May 1506. He died before 10 Oct. 1511. His will was proved in 1512.
[Regs. Hill, 55; Fitzjames, 31.]

James Aynsworth, 1511 to 1513

James Aynsworth, chaplain, was presented to the vicarage on the death of Adam Forster, 10 Oct. 1511. He died in 1513. He was probably identical with the James Aynsworth who resigned this vicarage, *circa* 13 Feb. 1502-3.
[Reg. Fitzjames, 31, 47.]

Robert Egremond, 1513 to 1529

Robert Egremond or Egremont, chaplain, was presented to the vicarage on the death of James Aynsworth, 18 Sept. 1513. He died in 1529. On 16 Dec. 1529 sequestration of the goods, *etc.,* of Sir Robert Egremond, Vicar of Fulham, deceased, who died intestate, was committed to Thomas Turner, apparitor general, and Robert Byrckhed, priest of St. Clement, Eastcheap.
[Vicar General's books, Reg. 1. fol. 190. Regs. Fitzjames, 47; Tonstal, 29.]

Robert Newton, 1529 to 1544-45

Robert Newton, priest, was presented to the vicarage on the death of Robert Egremond, 18 Dec. 1529. He also held the rectory of Wendon-Lowth or Wendon-Lofts, Essex. He was one of the witnesses to the will of Frances Ælmer of Fulham, proved 21 Mar. 1540-41. He died 1544-45. His will was proved in 1545.
[Regs. Tonstal, 29; Bonner, 151.]

John Smyth, S.T.B., 1545 to 1550

John Smyth, Smythe or Smith, S.T.B., was presented to the vicarage, 27 April 1545, vacant by the death of Robert Newton. In

1523, he held the rectory of St. Mildred's, Poultry, which, in 1527, he exchanged with Robert Harvey, vicar of Ardley, Essex. He died in 1550.
[Reg. Bonner, 151, 307.]

Nicholas Smyth, 1550 to 1569 (?)

Nicholas Smyth or Smythe was presented to the vicarage on the death of John Smyth, 19 April 1550. He compounded for the living 17 April 1550, his sureties being Richard Walaston, yeoman, and Peter Mewe, *alias* Maye, brickmaker, both of Fulham. On 7 July 1569, Nicholas Smyth was admitted to the vicarage of East Ham, when he probably resigned that of Fulham. He died about 1589, in which year letters of administration to his estate were taken out.
[Reg. Bonner, 307.]

William Hewett, 1569 (?) to 1591

William Hewett or Hewitt was apparently presented to the vicarage on the resignation of Nicholas Smyth. He resigned 3 April 1591.
[Reg. Grindal, 254.]

Christopher Goffe, M.A., 1591 to 1593

Christopher Goffe, M.A., was presented to the vicarage on the resignation of William Hewitt, 3 April 1591. On 30 Oct. 1593 he was admitted to the vicarage of Great Waltham, Essex, when he resigned that of Fulham.
[Reg. Grindal, 254, 278.]

Andrew Smyth, M.A., 1593 to 1598-99

Andrew Smyth or Smith, M.A., was presented to the vicarage on the resignation of Christopher Goffe, 14 Nov. 1593. He was deprived of the living in March 1598-99.
[Reg. Grindal, 278, 316].

Peter Lillye, M.A., D.D., 1598-99 to 1615

Peter Lillye, Lilly, Lilye or Lily is generally supposed to have been the son of Peter Lily, prebendary of Canterbury, and grandson of William Lily, the illustrious grammarian, the first high master of

St. Paul's School. The authority for this statement respecting the parentage of Peter Lillye, Vicar of Fulham, is Anthony à Wood, who, speaking of the grammarian, states that, at his death, he left behind him a son named George, *etc.,*

> "and Peter a dignitarie, as it seems, in the church of Canterbury, father of another Peter Lilye, D.D., sometime Fellow of Jesus College in Cambridge, afterwards a brother of the hospital called the Savoy."
> (I. col. 34).

Dugdale also calls him "grandson" of the grammarian. In the printed catalogue of the Bodleian, "Peter Lilly," the Vicar of Fulham, is called the son of "William Lilly," the grammarian, but, as the latter died in 1522, this relationship is very doubtful. George, the known son of the grammarian, was prebend of St. Paul's in 1557 and died in 1559. In the Cotton Manuscripts (Brit. Mus., Nero B. vi.) is a volume containing letters from this George Lily to one Starkey, *etc.* At fol. 152 George Lily speaks of himself as the only son left. The date of this letter, according to Gairdner ("Letters and Papers," vol. ix. No. 673), is "10 Kal. Nov. 1535." If George Lily be right in saying he was the only surviving son at the time of his father's death (1522), and if Agnes Lily, the grammarian's wife, predeceased her husband, having had only seventeen years of married life, it would be next to impossible for any son Peter to have died before 1522, leaving issue. Supposing he did and that a grandson Peter was born, say in 1521, he would have been 94 at his death in 1615, the known date of the death of Peter Lillye, Vicar of Fulham. It does not seem impossible that the Vicar was the son of George Lily, but there is no evidence whatever that such was the case.

Peter Lillye was educated at Jesus College, Cambridge, where he graduated B.A., M.A., and S.T.B. He was admitted and instituted to the vicarage of Fulham, 17 March 1598-99. He received the prebend of Caddington Major in St. Paul's, 16 April 1599. He was admitted to the rectory of Hornsey, 1 Nov. 1610. In Oct. 1613 he was made archdeacon of Taunton. He was nominated by James I among the first fellows of the Theological College established by the King at Chelsea. He was a brother of the Hospital of the Savoy, where he died, 15 May 1615. He was buried in the chancel of the Savoy Church, where were also interred his wife Dorothy, who died 1 June 1627, and his only daughter, who died 10 Oct. 1625. His will, dated 22 Feb. 1614-15, was proved 19 June 1615 (P.C.C. 64 Rudd.)

Peter Lillye published "Conciones Duæ," London, 1619.

[Reg. Grindal, 316.]

Thomas Walkington, D.D., 1615 to 1621

Thomas Walkington was educated at St. John's College, Cambridge, where he graduated B.A. in 1596-97 and M.A. in 1600. He became a Fellow of his College in 1602 and was incorporated as B.D., 14 July 1612 and D.D. in 1613.

He became vicar of Raunds, Northamptonshire, in 1608, and rector of Waddingham St. Mary, Lincolnshire, in 1610. He was admitted and instituted to the vicarage of Fulham, 25 May 1615, on the presentation of John Duport, the Rector. He was the author of "Rabboni, Mary Magdalen's Tears of Sorrow and Solace," preached at Paul's Cross on John xx. 16, Lond. 1620, and another single sermon on Ecclesiasticus xli. 10. He was a witness to the will of Dr. Thomas Edwardes of Fulham. (See vol. I). He died in 1621, in which year letters of administration to his estate were taken out.

[Reg. Bancroft, 191.]

Richard Cluet, M.A., D.D., 1621 to 1644

Richard Cluet, Cluett, Cleuett, Clewett, Cluit, Cluat, *etc.,* was educated at Oriel College, Oxford, where he proceeded B.A., 28 Jan. 1599-1600; M.A., 30 Oct. 1606 and B.D. and D.D., 25 June 1619.

He was instituted rector of St. Aldate's, Oxford, 1614. On 30 Nov. 1616, he was admitted to the prebend of Newington in St. Paul's. On 20 June 1617, he received the rectory of St. Anne and St. Agnes, London. On 16 June 1620, he was admitted to the archdeaconry of Middlesex. He was admitted and instituted to the vicarage of Fulham, 22 Nov. 1621, on the presentation of Henry King, Rector of Fulham. He was chaplain to Bishop John King, father of Henry King. He attended the Bishop at his death bed.

His signature "R. Cluet" or "R. Cluet, D.D." frequently occurs in the Parish Books, appended to the minutes of the Vestry.

Dr. Cluet was a staunch loyalist, and, after the outbreak of the Civil War, was speedily attacked by the Puritans. From the "Calendar of Proceedings of the Committee for the Advance of Money," we learn that "Dr. Clewett, vicar of Fulham," was assessed at £100, 24 Aug. 1643. On 5 Jan. 1643-44, however, he was discharged on his affidavit that he was not worth this sum. Soon afterwards all his preferments were sequestered, his vicarage at Fulham being filled by Adoniram Byfield. He died before the Restoration.

[Bishops' Institutions and First Fruits Composition Books.]

Adoniram Byfield, 1646 to 1652

Upon the sequestration of the preferments of the Rector and the Vicar, Col. Edmund Harvey, as Lord of the Manor of Fulham, presented Adoniram Byfield to both livings. This was the first occasion on which both rectory and vicarage were filled by the same person. [See "Byfield," *sub* "Rectors."]

Isaac Knight, B.D., 1652 to 1660

On the resignation of Adoniram Byfield in 1652, Col. Harvey presented the Rev. Isaac Knight to both rectory and vicarage. [See "Knight," *sub* "Rectors."]

Edmund Keene, M.A., 1660-61 to 1661

At the Restoration, the Rev. Isaac Knight was deprived of both rectory and vicarage, to make way for two Royalists, Dr. George Stradling being presented to the rectory (see "Stradling," *sub* "Rectors"), and the Rev. Edmund Keene, M. A., to the vicarage.

In the Calendar of State Papers (Domestic, Charles II vol. 23, p. 136) is a petition, dated 18 Dec. 1660, from "Edmund Keen" to the King, begging that he might be presented to the vicarage of Fulham. It is accompanied by a note from Bishop Sheldon, stating that the vicarage was in his own gift and that the petitioner, his chaplain, was eligible.

The Rev. Edmund Keene was presented to the vicarage, 11 Jan. 1660-61, being <u>admitted and instituted by the King</u>. The signature of "Edm. Keene, vicar" occurs for the first time in the Parish Books appended to the minutes of a Vestry held 11 Mar. 1660-61. It appears regularly down to 3 Nov. 1661, soon after

which he must have been suspended, for his name no further occurs.
[Reg. Henchman, 10.]

Thomas Greaves, D.D., 1662-63 to 1666 (?)

Judging from the Parish Books, it would seem that the vicarial duties were now undertaken by one Thomas Greaves, or Graves, D.D., whose signature to the minutes of the Fulham Vestry appears for the first time on 26 January 1662-63 and continues to 1665. The assessment for 1666 reads: "Dr. Greaue or his assignes 3s. 6d." Nothing is known about this person, who was certainly not regularly instituted to the vicarage. At a meeting of the Vestry, 13 Oct. 1662, the following resolution was passed:

> "It is ordered that Dr. Greaves the pnte [present] incumbent shall not bee assessed to any manner off assessment or taxe whatsoever relates *(sic)* to the church and pish of ffulham."
> - [Parish Books.]

Richard Stevenson, M.A., 1666 to 1691

Richard Stevenson, M.A., was presented to the vicarage, 11 April 1666, being admitted and instituted by the rector, Dr. George Stradling. He died 10 Sept. 1691, and was buried at Fulham. In the Church Registers is the following entry:

> 1691. Mr. Richard Stevenson, vic. mort. 10 buried 15 Sept.

The signature "Ric. Stevenson, vic." appears with remarkable regularity attached to the minutes of the Fulham Vestry, from 17 April 1666 to 14 April 1691.

Stevenson worked assiduously to alleviate the distress among the poor of Fulham in the time of the plague which was raging at the date of his presentation to the vicarage. At a meeting of the Vestry, on 14 April 1667, the following resolution was passed:

> "Ordered that Mr. Beauchampe, churchwarden, shall, in the next assessment for the parish, assesse ffive pounds to bee given to Mr. Stevenson, Vicar of Fulham, as a gratuity to him from the parish for his great pains in the tyme of the visitation."

The will of Richard Stevenson was proved in Oct. 1691. [Reg. Henchman, 117.]

Vincent Barry, M.A., 1691 to 1708

Vincent Barry, M.A., was the son of Vincent Barry, of Hampton Gay, Oxon, J.P. He was educated at Oriel College, Oxford. He proceeded B.A., 19 Feb. 1679-80 and M.A. in 1683. In 1682 he became a student at the Inner Temple. On 7 Aug. 1689, he was elected by the Vestry, "Lecturer" for the parish of Fulham. Upon the death of the Rev. Richard Stevenson, the parishioners strongly recommended him to the favourable notice of Bishop Compton and the Rector, Dr. Thomas Turner. He was admitted and instituted to the vicarage by the Rector, 23 Sept. 1691. At a Vestry held the next day the following quaint vote of thanks to the Bishop was passed:

> "Forasmuch as the Parishon[rs] and inhabitants within the pish of Fulham on Fulham side are very sensible of the many favours and kindnesses from tyme to tyme showne to them by the Right Rev. Father in God Henry Lord Bishop of London and more particularly of late in the kind recommendation of Mr. Vincent Barry for ye Vicaridge of this parish vpon the humble Peticon of most of the inhabitants vpon that account and conceaving themselves highly obliged in pointe of gratitude to returne their humble thanks to his Lordship for the same it is this present day by and with the unanimous consent of the said Vestry that their hearty and humble thankes be accordingly given to his Lordship and that S[r] Tho. Kency, Mr. Woodward, Mr. Dwaight, Mr. Antho. Nours, Mr. Rob. Limpany, Mr. Bliscow, Mr. Plukenett with the Churchwardens are desired to acquaint his Lordship with this order as also that his Lordship be humbly desired to recomend any fitt pson to supply ye place of Lecturer of the saide parish that place being now vacant which person the inhabitants here present doo declare that they will vse their utmost endeavor to elect him accordingly."

The Rev. Vincent Barry died at Fulham, 3 Dec. 1708, and was buried in the Churchyard. The Church Registers record:

1708. Mr. Vincent Barry Viccar. Died the 3 and Bu. 5 Dec.

By his wife Rebecca, he had five sons, Vincent, Francis, Robert, John and Philip, and two daughters, Jane and Elizabeth, all

baptized at Fulham.
[Reg. Compton, 119.]

Philip Dwight, D.D., 1708 to 1729

Philip Dwight was the fourth son of John Dwight, the founder of Fulham Pottery. He was born at Wigan, probably about the beginning of March 1670-71, as we find he was baptized there on the 6th of that month. Shortly afterwards his father moved with his family to Fulham. In 1685 Philip entered Westminster School, whence he proceeded to Christ Church, Oxford. In 1623 he obtained his B.A. degree and three years later his M.A. While a student at the University, he wrote one of the "Oxford Poems," celebrating the return of William III from Ireland in 1690.

On the death of the Rev. Vincent Barry, he was admitted and instituted by the Rector, Dr. Thomas Turner, to the vicarage of Fulham, 31 Dec. 1708. On 12 July 1712, his University conferred on him the degree of D.D. He married Jane, daughter of Captain Nathaniel Owen, of Mile End Old Town, an officer in the service of the East India Company. His wife at the time of her marriage was the widow of one Owen Wilson.

The Rev. Philip Dwight died 29 Dec. 1729, his wife Jane, predeceasing him only four days. Both were buried in a vault in Fulham Churchyard. The Church Registers record:

> 1729. The Reverend Phill Dwight and Jane his Wife inter'd in a valt together 2 Jan.

Dr. Dwight, by will dated 27 July 1727, proved 7 Jan. 1729-30 (P.C.C. 5 Dell), left

> "All furniture in my house at ffulham to my wife Jane. To her the life interest in my copyhold estate in the parish and manor of Westham *(i.e.* West Ham), co. Essex, with reversion to my only son, John Dwight and heirs for ever."

John Dwight, the Vicar's only son, in 1727, married Millicent Burbage of Fulham. The Burbages were a very ancient Fulham family. Richard Burbage, Shakespeare's friend and fellow actor, was related to them. It would appear, from a bookplate of "John

Dwight, Gentleman, 1728," that both his wife and mother were heiresses or eventually became so. The arms in 1 and 4 quarters are for Dwight. The escutcheon of pretence is clearly intended for Burbage and is identical with the coat of Richard Burbage, the actor, as recorded in the "Visitation of London," 1634. The blazon is as follows:

> "Argent, a chevron engrailed vert guttèe d'or between 3 boars' heads couped sable."

[Reg. Compton, 191.]

Thomas Wendey, M.A., 1729-30 to 1733

Thomas Wendey, or Wendy, was educated at King's College, Cambridge, where he graduated B.A. in 1709 and M.A. in 1713. On 29 July 1715, he was instituted to the vicarage of Wootton-Wawen, Warwickshire, a living which was in the gift of his College and which he held till he came to Fulham. He was admitted and instituted to the vicarage of Fulham by the Rector, the Rev. George Bell, junior, 22 Jan. 1729-30. He resigned in 1733.

[Reg. Gibson, 240.]

William Nicholas Blomberg, M.A., 1733 to 1750

William Nicholas Blomberg was admitted and instituted to the vicarage of Fulham by the Rector, the Rev. George Bell, junior, on 13 June 1733. [See "Blomberg, *sub* "Rectors."]

Samuel Knight, M.A., 1750 to 1757

Samuel Knight was admitted and instituted to the vicarage of Fulham by Bishop Sherlock 24 Dec. 1750. [See "Knight," *sub* "Rectors."]

Denison Cumberland, M.A., 1757 to 1763

Denison Cumberland was born about the year 1705. He was the second son of Dr. Richard Cumberland, archdeacon of Northampton and Bishop of Peterborough, author of "De Legibus Naturæ Disquisitio," a work written in opposition to Hobbes' philosophy. He was educated at Westminster School. He subsequently became a Fellow of Trinity College, Cambridge, which, by Royal Commission, conferred on him, in 1728, the degree of M.A. In the same year he married Joanna, the daughter of Dr. R. Bentley, the celebrated master of Trinity College, Cambridge. When only eleven years of age, she was celebrated by Dr. John Byrom as "Phoebe" in the ballad "My time, O ye Muses", which appeared in the *Spectator*. About 1727, Cumberland was presented to the rectory of Stanwick, Northamptonshire. In 1735 he was collated to a prebend at Lincoln Cathedral. About 1745 he gained great credit from the Government by enlisting, in his own neighbourhood, two full companies for the regiment raised by Lord Halifax; and, by strenuously supporting the Whigs in a contested election for Northampton in April 1748, he established a fresh claim which Lord Halifax recognized by appointing Cumberland's son, Richard, as his private secretary at the Board of Trade. Here, in his ample leisure time, Richard Cumberland, the future dramatist, amused himself in studying history and composing poems. In 1757, Denison Cumberland exchanged with the Rev. Samuel Knight, his rectory of Stanwick for the vicarage of Fulham, to which he was admitted and instituted by Mr. Knight, 29 Jan. 1757.

Richard Cumberland, in his "Memoirs," thus describes his advent to Fulham:

> "In the meantime the long and irksome residence in town, which my attendance upon Lord Halifax entailed upon me, and the painful separation from my family, became almost insupportable; and whilst I was meditating a retreat, my good father, who participated with me and the whole family in these sensations, projected and concluded an exchange for his living of Stanwick with the Rev. Mr. Samuel Knight, and with permission of the Bishop of London, took the vicarage of Fulham as an equivalent, and thereby opened to me the happy prospect of an easier access to those friends, so justly valued, and so truly dear.
> In point of income, the two livings were as nearly equal as could well be, therefore no pecuniary compensation passed between the contracting parties but the comforts of tranquillity in point of duty, or of convenience in respect of locality, were all in favour of Mr. Knight, and nothing could have prevailed with my father for leaving those whom he had so long loved and cherished as his flock, but the generous motive of giving me an asylum in the bosom of my family. With this kind and benevolent object in his view, he submitted to the pain of

tearing himself from his connections, and, amidst the lamentations of his neighbours and parishioners, came up to Fulham to take upon himself the charge of a great suburban parish, and quitted Stanwick, where he had resided for the space of thirty years in peace, beloved by all around him. He found a tolerably good parsonage house in Fulham, in which, with my mother and sister, he established himself with as much content as could be looked for."

In 1761 Denison Cumberland was collated to a prebendal stall at St. Paul's. In 1763 he vacated his prebendal stalls and the Fulham vicarage on his promotion to the bishopric of Clonfert in Ireland. From this he was, in 1772, translated, to Kilmore. He died in Dublin in November 1774, and was buried in the churchyard of his cathedral. Besides the son Richard, Denison Cumberland had two daughters.
[Reg. Gibson, 364.]

Anthony Hamilton, M.A., S.T.P., 1763 to 1776

Anthony Hamilton was educated at Corpus Christi College, Cambridge, where he graduated B.A. in 1760, M.A. in 1763 and S.T.P. in 1775. He was admitted, and instituted by the Rector, the Rev. Samuel Knight, to the vicarage of Fulham on 25 Sept. 1763. He held the living till 1776, when he received the rectory of Hadham. On 13 May 1780, he was appointed to the prebend of Cantlers in St. Paul's. He also held the vicarage of St. Martin's-in-the-Fields and the archdeaconry of Colchester. Dr. Hamilton married a daughter of Bishop Terrick.
[Reg. Osbaldeston, 8.]

Graham Jepson, M.A., S.T.B., 1776 to 1811

Graham Jepson was admitted and instituted to the vicarage of Fulham by the Rector, the Rev. Samuel Knight, 13 Mar. 1776. [See "Jepson," *sub* "Rectors."]

William Wood, B.D., M.A., 1811 to 1834

William Wood was admitted and instituted to the vicarage of Fulham by Bishop Randolph, 29 June 1811. [See "Wood," *sub* "Rectors."]

Robert George Baker, M.A., 1834 to 1871

Robert George Baker was a younger son of William Baker, of Bayfordbury, who sat as M.P. for Hertfordshire in five successive Parliaments, 31 to 47 George III. He was born 28 Oct. 1788. He was educated at Harrow, and afterwards at Trinity College, Cambridge, where he was a contemporary of Bishop Blomfield, his life-long friend and patron. He proceeded B.A. in 1810 and M.A. in 1813. In 1811 he was appointed to the curacy of Hertingfordbury, and in 1816, to that of Springfield, Essex. From Jan. to June 1819, he held the rectory of Hadley, near Barnet, the advowson of which his father had purchased. In 1822 he became rector of Springfield, in 1827 rector of Little Berkhampstead, and in 1833 rector of Stevenage. On 3 July 1834, the Rev. R. G. Baker was admitted and instituted to the vicarage of Fulham. In 1846 he was made a prebendary of St. Paul's, and in 1851 he was appointed rural dean of Fulham. In 1871, in consequence of advancing age, Mr. Baker resigned the vicarage of Fulham and retired to Ivy Cottage, Parson's Green, where he died, 21 Feb, 1878, in his 90th year.

Mr. Baker was twice married. His first wife, Emma, daughter of Mr. William Franks, died at Fulham Vicarage, 8 Jan. 1864. At the mature age of 77, Mr. Baker married, as his second wife, Mary, second daughter of the Rt. Hon. Laurence Sulivan, of Broom House, and niece of Lord Palmerston. This lady died 20 Oct. 1871.

The Rev. R. G. Baker was buried at All Saints. The funeral sermon, entitled "A Long Life," was preached by a former curate, the Rev. J. J. Coxhead, M.A.

Mr. Baker was very fond of antiquarian pursuits, and took a particular interest in the history of this parish. One of his lectures, entitled "The Olden Characters of Fulham," was printed in 1857. Mr. Baker also wrote "An Account of the Benefactions and Charitable Funds in the Parish of Fulham," published in 1846. He rebuilt the north-east end of Fulham Church. He also built the Schools in the High Street. He was the founder of the Fulham Friendly Society, in whose rooms there is a subscription portrait of him.

An account of the Rev. R. G. Baker appears in "Monken Hadley," by the Rev. F. C. Cass, M.A., rector. The late Prebendary Rogers, who became his curate in 1843, gives, in his

"Reminiscences," some interesting anecdotes concerning Mr. Baker.
[Reg. Blomfield, p. 1, vol.2, f.52.]

Frederic Horatio Fisher, M.A., 1871 to 1890

Frederic Horatio Fisher was educated at Rugby, whence he proceeded to Cambridge. He took his degree of B.A. in 1860 and proceeded M.A. in 1863. He did not at first take orders, being for seven years Assistant Master at Wellington College. He was ordained in 1867, and was for two years curate of Acton. On the retirement of the Rev. R. G. Baker, he was presented to the vicarage of Fulham, 29 June 1871, by Bishop Jackson, whose domestic chaplain he was and whose daughter, Agnes, he had married. He remained chaplain to Bishop Jackson till the latter's death in 1885. In 1890 he exchanged livings with the Rev. W. C. Muriel, vicar of Debden, Essex. The work by which Mr. Fisher will be best remembered in Fulham was the rebuilding of the Parish Church in 1880-81. In 1879 Mr. Fisher published "Ye Endowed Charities of ye Antiente Parishe of Fulham," printed from the original manuscript volume.

In 1899 the Rev. F. H. Fisher was made an honorary canon of St. Albans.
[Reg. Jackson, vol. 1, f. 34.]

William Carter Muriel, M.A., 1890 to -

William Carter Muriel, who, as above stated, exchanged livings with the Rev. F. H. Fisher in 1890, was born in Ely, 7 Nov. 1839. He was educated at St. Peter's College, Cambridge, where he graduated B.A. in 1862 and M.A. in 1868. He was curate of Sheen, Derbyshire, 1862-64, and chaplain of High Legh, Cheshire, 1864-67. He held the rectory of Debden, Essex, from 1867 to 1890, when he came to Fulham.

On his mother's side the Rev. W. C. Muriel is descended from the family of Archbishop Langham. His father's family can be traced back some seven centuries.

The old Chantry House, Ely, immediately opposite the Bishop's Palace, was long the home of the Muriels. His family have been connected with the town some 300 years, and many of the Cambridgeshire villages have had Muriels as rectors or vicars.

A son of a vicar of Soham was the first Muriel who settled in Ely, and the sisters of the Rev. W. C. Muriel still reside in the house which the family bought three centuries ago.

CHAPTER III: TITHES

In olden times two kinds of tithes existed in Fulham, known, generally, as Great Tithes and Little Tithes. The former, sometimes called Parsonage Tithes, belonged to the Rector, while the latter went to the Vicar.

Newcourt states that Richard de Belmeis, Bishop of London, in the reign of Henry I, granted to Henry, the master of the school belonging to the Cathedral Church of St. Paul, a meadow at Fulham, together with the tithes of Yling (Ealing) and Madeley, and that Richard Fitz-Neale, Bishop of London in the time of Richard I, gave to this school all the tithes arising "in his demesnes at Fulham and Horset." The name of the village of Horset (a corruption of Horse-heath) is now spelled Orsett. It is in Essex, a county which was long included in the diocese of London. The Rev. William Palin writes in "Stifford and Its Neighbourhood" (1871):

> "The Manor and Advowson were anciently held by the Bishops of London, one of whom, it appears, from a document in the time of Archbishop Langton, in the Lambeth Register, directed the rectors of his two livings of Orsett and Fulham to pay 9 marks each yearly to the Chancellor of St. Paul's, already well endowed by reason of the duties of his office, that of governing the schools of London. The rector of Orsett now pays £6 yearly to the Ecclesiastical Commissioners, as the Chancellor's representatives."

In 1327 the value of the rectory of Fulham was returned at 30 marks, or £20 per annum, exclusive of the sum of £6 per annum, then still paid to the Chancellor of St. Paul's. Subsequently the Fulham tithes due to the Chancellor were commuted by an annual payment of £4 15s. 0d. We have been unable to trace when the payment ceased to be made. In 1344 the annual value of the rectory is again given as £20. At a very early date the Great or rectorial Tithes became impropriate, *i.e.* they passed into lay hands. The holders of the sinecure rectory, not residing at Fulham, naturally turned the Rectory House and the Great Tithes to the most profitable account. For ages the rectorial tithes were leased for lives, the lessee paying a reserved rent, generally £40 per annum, to the Rector. According to a Parliamentary Survey, the glebe lands and tithes of the rectory, in 1610, were valued at £340 per annum. In 1641, Dr. Henry King, the Rector, granted a lease of the rectorial tithes to the Nourse, or Nurse, family.

When, in 1647, Col. Harvey purchased the Manor, he acquired from the Nourses their lease of the Great Tithes, as far as concerned the Manor House and the demesne lands belonging thereto. In the Survey of Church Livings, in 1656, when Mrs. Philippa Nourse held the Rectory House, we are told that the "tythes of corn and hay is worth Two hundred and nintye pounds per ann."

On the attainder, in 1660, of Col. Harvey, the Great Tithes became vested in the Crown. In the following year, Col. Arthur Eyre petitioned the King to grant him "a lease of lands in Fulham, part of the estate of Edmond Harvey, convicted of the death of the late king, excepted out of the grant of his estate made to the Duke of York." (Cal. of State Papers, Dom. Ent. Book 5, p. 190.) On 5 Feb. 1661-62, Col. Eyre's petition was forwarded to the Bishop of London, and, on 5 Mar. 1661-62, a grant was made to him

> "of a lease of the great tithes out of the Bishop of London's lands in Fulham during the lives of John Nurse, Jo. Nicholson and Thomas Hurst, which lease is forfeit to the Crown by attainder of Edm. Harvey."
> - (State Papers, Dom. Entry Book 5, p. 190.)

On 22 Jan. 1662-63, we find what is apparently a further grant to

> "Col. Ant. Eyre, of the tythes of Fulham vested in the Crown by the attainder of Edmund Harvey."
> - (Cal. of State Papers, Dom. Docquet, vol. lxvii.)

These grants were made to Col. Eyre in consideration of the services which he had rendered to the royal cause during the Great Rebellion. In 1666 the Great Tithes were held by Richard Child.

When next we hear of the rectorial tithes, they were the property of Sir John Elwes, of Grove House. On the death of Sir John they were enjoyed by his widow, Lady Elwes, from whom, in

1704, they were purchased by Sir Brook Bridges.

In 1730 Sir Brook Bridges demised the tithes to Joseph Benning, of St. Margaret's, Westminster (afterwards of Hammersmith). By his will, dated 21 Sept. 1732, he appointed his wife, Elizabeth, his sole executrix. Sir Brook Bridges died in 1733, his widow subsequently marrying the Hon. Charles Fielding. On the death of Joseph Benning, the Great Tithes came into the possession of Timothy Bullock (who had married Hannah, only daughter of Joseph Benning), Joseph Bullock (brother of Timothy Bullock and administrator of Anne, his late wife, who was the widow and executrix of Joseph Benning) and of John Willis, of St. James's, Westminster. On 25 Mar. 1738-39, on the surrender of the lease of 1730, the Hon. Charles Fielding and Elizabeth his wife granted to the two Bullocks a new lease of the Great Tithes of Fulham Rectory.

This lease is a document of much interest. It asserts that the parcels of land in Fulham which were then subject to rectorial tithes, comprised:

> "All that the scite of the Manor House of Fulham aforesaid, with one private Chappell, and all buildings, outhouses, etc., thereto belonging, and two footbridges and one great Bridge, and three Closes of pasture called the Warren, which premises are all incompassed with a Moate, about two poles over, and in most parts thereof floated and drained at pleasure, and do contain together with the moate 36½ acres by estimation."

It is further recited that the rectorial tithes were leviable on the following meads, *etc.*:

> Pale Mead, Rowberry Mead, Garlick Close, Gt. Hurlingham Field, Windmill Shot, Millbank, Stroud Mead, Church field, Wild Mead, Broom Field or Close, the Windmill and ground adjoining, Frogmill Bank, Crabtree Close, Dock Mead, Jackson's Mead, the Warren, near Broom House, the Coope and Pingle, parts of Fulham Fields, the ozier and reed ground adjacent to the Thames, and the royalty for fishing for salmon in the river.

On each occasion of the making of a new lease of the tithes, the Rector was entitled to receive a "fine." In the instance above cited, the Rector, the Rev. W. N. Blomberg, received £205 12s. 5d., a fourth part of which the lessee had to recoup to the lessor, while the former agreed to pay the latter "at the Church Porch at Fulham the yearly sum of 20 shillings at Michaelmas." In 1751 the rectorial tithes passed to the Hon. Edward Finch and Sir Cordell Firebrace, the devisees of Fielding. The lease eventually fell in to the Rector. In the time of the Rev. Samuel Knight, the Great Tithes were leased by the Rector to his son, Mr. Samuel Knight.

Bishop Porteus, on coming to Fulham in 1787, was called on by the holder of the rectorial tithes to pay those due on the Manor House and its demesne lands. In his "Brief Account of Three Residences," he tells us that, by the aid of the original deed of sale to Col. Harvey, he successfully resisted the claim, the conveyance to the regicide expressly stating that the lands were "Tythe free." It is impossible now to trace at what date, after the time of Harvey, the tithes were, by some irregular means, re-imposed, but it is not improbable that Bishop Sheldon, in his grant to Col. Eyre in 1661-62, overlooked the fact of their extinction. At any rate, as we have just seen, the Palace and its demesnes were included in the lease granted in 1738 by the Fieldings to the Bullocks.

The Rev. William Wood, the last Rector of Fulham, leased the Great Tithes to three members of his family. On his death the endowments were enjoyed by his widow and daughter in succession. The last life falling in in 1881, the Rectory House, lands and Great Tithes, in common with a large class of sinecure benefices of this character, became merged in the funds of the Ecclesiastical Commission, which had been formed in 1836 to take over all capitular and episcopal properties. The Great Tithes were commuted at £100 a year.

The Little or vicarial Tithes were, in the time of the Commonwealth, worth about £30 to £40 a year. In the Survey of 1656, the value of the Vicarage House, then in the occupation of Adoniram Byfield, is set down at £16 per annum, and "the small Tythes are worth thirty and six pounds *p. ann.*" Bowack tells us that, in his time (1705) the vicarial tithes were valued in the Queen's Books at £10 per annum, adding, "but it is thought worth about £150." <u>The vicarial tithes are commuted at £900 a year.</u>

CHAPTER IV: NEW KING'S ROAD

SECTION I: HIGH STREET TO BURLINGTON ROAD

We will now saunter along the New King's Road and its continuation, the King's Road, to Stanley Bridge.

Until 1894 the road, from the High Street to the south end of Burlington Road, was called Church Street; eastwards, to Harwood Road, it was termed the New King's Road; while, between Harwood Road and Waterford Road, we had Broxholme Road. In 1894 the whole thoroughfare was renamed the New King's Road.

In early times the New King's Road bore no distinctive name. In the Court Rolls for 1550 it is merely described as

> "a certain lane leading from Berestrete . . . towards hurlinghmfyld and towards psonesgrene,"

- that is, the lane which led towards Hurlingham, along what is now Hurlingham Road, and towards Parson's Green, along what is now the New King's Road. In the last century Church Street was generally described as "the lane to the 'Ship,'" or, "the lane from the 'King's Arms' to the 'Ship.'" Even as late as 1814 it is styled "the road to the 'Ship.'" Faulkner calls it Windsor Street, but that name never came into general vogue. Another occasional style for the way was Idle Lane.

NORTH SIDE

Fulham Charity Schools (later Fulham National Schools)

Commencing with the north side, the first point of interest will be the Fulham Charity Schools, with the first beginnings of which we have dealt in our account of the old Church. (See vol. I).

The endowment of the Fulham Charity Schools, now the <u>Fulham National Schools</u>, originated in a bequest made by one Edward Owen, who, about the year 1704, left the sum of £1,000 to "pious and charitable uses." He appointed his father, Captain

Nathaniel Owen, his executor. From the will of Nathaniel Owen, dated 27 Jan. 1707-8, and proved 3 Feb. 1707-8 (P.C.C. 137 Barrett), we learn that this £1,000 was still undealt with, for the testator left it to his daughter Jane, the wife of the Rev. Philip Dwight, Vicar of Fulham, whom he appointed residuary legatee and sole executor. On 27 Jan. 1710-11 the Court of Chancery made a formal order, in a suit instituted by the Vicar ("the Attorney General *v.* Dwight"), directing that £300, part of the £1,000, should be applied to the teaching of the poor children of the parish. This endowment is now represented by a sum of £337 10s. 1d. Consols. The total of the endowments is now rather over £3,000.

The history of the Fulham Charity Schools from the date of their removal from the Church Porch down to 1811, when a permanent school-house was erected in Church Street, is extremely vague. It is said that they were conducted in a cottage situated just opposite the site of the present building. In 1792 the Rev. Graham Jepson, the Vicar, issued the following statement:

> "Eighteen Boys and Eighteen Girls are clothed and educated in these Schools. They are instructed in the Principles of the Christian Religion: the Boys are taught to read, write, and cast accounts; the Girls to read, write, sew, knit, mark, etc., and both, when of proper ages, are bound Apprentice, or put to Service, etc."

In 1795 the income of the Schools was sufficient to clothe and educate 22 boys and the same number of girls. Faulkner writes in 1812:

> "There has been for many years in this parish a charity school, supported chiefly by voluntary contributions, and, the contributions exceeding the annual expense, it was determined by the trustees to extend the benefit to a greater number of poor children. Accordingly they erected in the year 1811, at the expense of £600, a new and spacious school, situated in the Town, capable of containing 200 boys, who are educated here according to the system first practised at Madras by the Rev. Dr. Bell. The school itself is a very neat building, and well adapted to the purpose. It is 36 feet in length and 26 in width, lighted from the top, the ends, and one of the sides; by which means also it is possible to keep it well aired. When there are sufficient funds for so important an object, it is intended to erect a school of the same dimensions for girls. At present there are about seventy girls educated

by voluntary contributions in two separate schools."

The essential feature of Dr. Andrew Bell's system, referred to in the above account, was that of using boys to teach boys, the origin of our monitor and pupil teacher system. Dr. Bell, in 1811, founded the National Society for the Education of the Poor in the Principles of the Established Church. It was, it will be noticed, in this very year, which witnessed the commencement of the movement for the extension of Church education, that the Trustees of the Fulham Charity Schools erected in Church Street, on a plot of ground belonging to Sir William Powell's Almshouses, the school-house which still exists. The school for the girls was added in 1813-14. The total cost of the premises for the master and mistress and of erecting the new school-house was about £700. The Schools were now renamed the United Charity Schools of the Parish of Fulham.

The site was let to the Trustees at a rent of £40 per annum, at which figure it remains to this day. The lease, which expired in 1835, has, we believe, never been renewed.

On the front wall of the school-room, now devoted to the infants, are two tablets inscribed:

FULHAM
CHARITY SCHOOL.
ERECTED ANNO DOM° 1811.

TRAIN UP A CHILD IN THE WAY
HE SHOULD GO;
AND WHEN HE IS OLD
HE WILL NOT DEPART FROM IT.

At a meeting of the Committee of Management, held on 6 Dec. 1811, a code of regulations for the government of the Schools was adopted.

In the early days of the Schools, each charity child was given two suits of clothes, one for week-day use and one for Sunday. The regulations of 1811 provided that twenty boys should be clothed at the cost of the Schools. In later times it became the custom to clothe

The 1st 20 boys entirely
The 2nd 20 boys everything except shirts
The 3rd 20 boys only shoes, stockings and caps.

The 1st 20 girls entirely
The 2nd 20 girls everything except flannel petticoats
The 3rd 20 girls only tippets and aprons.

<u>The boys wore jackets and waistcoats of brown frieze with cord trousers. The girls had blue serge dresses and white straw bonnets.</u>

In 1830 the infants' school was established. In 1831 there were 300 children in attendance.

The Fulham Charity Schools were, in the olden time, hardly models of good order. The late Rev. Prebendary Rogers, in his "Reminiscences," gives us the following account of them when he was a young curate at the Parish Church:

"It was at Fulham that I first tasted blood in the matter of education. The Bishop specially commended to me the National Schools, and I was prepared to go at them with a will. The boys' department, however, had not quite emerged from a state of rebellion, for one of the boys had thrown an inkbottle at the other curate's head and the School had been prematurely disbanded for the holidays. When I made my first appearance I heard a hiss, and I thought that the next thing might be an inkbottle. I told the boy who had hissed to stand up, which, after much reluctance, he did. I then ordered the Master to flog him on the spot; but, taking me aside, he said that he dare not, as the lad's father was the gardener at the Vicarage. I went at once to Mr. Baker, who seemed disposed to shield the boy, but I declared that, unless I was supported, I would quit the parish at once. The Vicar yielded, the lad was punished that afternoon and discipline was restored."

When the Workhouse boys were numbered among the scholars, very disgraceful scenes were sometimes witnessed. One day the master, William Popple, had occasion to flog a boy. "Shy the Bible at 'im," shouted the young urchin's brother, and away went the ponderous tome at the head of the unfortunate pedagogue. Mr. Popple, who was master from 1826 to 1840, though a good teacher, at times displayed great singularity of conduct. On one occasion he set all the boys to dig up and transplant a <u>tree in the school-yard</u>. His reason further failing, he had to relinquish his post. On his tomb at All Saints we read that "He was master of the Boys' National Schools in this parish during fourteen years and was obliged to relinquish that situation by the afflictive visitation of a wise but inscrutable Providence," a euphuism which we must surely attribute to Mr. Baker.

<u>The Schools from 1830 to 1862 comprised three buildings, one each for boys, girls and infants</u>. When, in 1862, the new branch for boys was opened in the High Street, the old boys' school in Church Street was appropriated to the girls, while the infants were transferred to the old girls' school, the girls using the former infants' school as a class-room. In 1871 the Rev. R. G. Baker added, at the rear of the infants' school, which faces the New King's Road, an additional class-room for the infants. On one of the walls in this room is a tablet inscribed:

"This class-room | was added to the Infants' School by the | Revd Robert George Baker, | a portion of the cost being contributed by some of his | parishioners, | as a mark of their esteem and respect, | on the occasion of his resigning | the Vicarage of Fulham; | July 1871."

The site, which was acquired in 1811-14, includes the flat-fronted brick house, No. 212, New King's Road, probably two centuries old. It was used as the residence of the master and two mistresses. Nothing is known as to its history.

Anciently the Charity Schools were quite free. In 1830 the authorities fixed a fee of a penny a week. This was successively raised, first to twopence and then to threepence. When, in 1892, the Free Education Act came into operation, the Schools were made into higher grade schools. The boys now pay 6d. and 9d., and the girls 4d., 6d. and 9d. per week. There are no fees in the infants' school.

In the copy of Faulkner's "Fulham" at the Hammersmith Public Library are preserved several leaflets relating to sermons to be preached at Fulham Church, and elsewhere, in aid of the Fulham Charity Schools. These are of great interest. After the sermon, when at All Saints, the Charity Children sang special hymns.

Lysons, in his "Environs," speaks of "A Sunday School and a School of Industry, a united establishment instituted in 1796." As late as 1814 an "Industry School" is mentioned in the assessments. In the Muniment Room at Fulham Palace is preserved "An Account of Money Earned and Work Done in the Parish School of Industry from 1 Jan. to 31 Dec. 1801." The boys, 76 in number, earned £349 16s. 6d.; the girls, of whom there were 56, £381 13s. 11d., making a total of £731 10s. 5d. for the year. The girls were chiefly employed in making underclothing, while the boys did stocking weaving, spinning, and house work.

Fulham Pottery

Between the Fulham Charity Schools and Burlington Road, stands Fulham Pottery, founded by John Dwight, between the years 1672 and 1673.

John Dwight came of an Oxfordshire family. Nothing is known of his parentage beyond the fact that his mother's name was Joan. In her will, dated 22 Oct. 1677, and proved 17 June 1680 (P.C.C. 77 Bath), this lady describes herself as "Joane Dwight of the Parish of St. Peter in the Bayley of the City of Oxford, widdow."

John Dwight was born about 1640. On 29 June 1661 he was appointed Registrar and Scribe of the diocese of Chester, a position which he held under the four successive episcopates of Dr. Bryan Walton, Dr. Henry Ferne, Dr. George Hall, and Dr. John Wilkins. He proceeded B.C.L. of Christ Church, Oxford, 17 Dec. 1661. In the Registers of St. Oswald's Church (part of Chester Cathedral) are the following entries:

1662. John sonne of John Dwaite Secretary to the Lord B[pp]. bapt. the 5th day of Nouembre.

This was John Dwight's first child.

1663. George sonne of Mr. John Dwaite bapt. the 18th ffebruary.
1665. Gertrude daughter of Mr. John Dwight bapt. the 18th Aprill.

Gertrude was a family name with Bishop Hall; both his mother and wife bearing it. We next trace John Dwight to Wigan. In the Registers of this parish are the three following entries:

> 1667. Lydia, daughter of Mr. John Dwight, Secretary to the Lord Bishop of Chester baptized 24 July.

> 1668. Samuel, son of Mr. John Dwight, Secretary to the Lord Bishop of Chester baptized 25 Dec.

> 1670-71. Phillip, son of Mr. John Dwight of Millgate, was baptized 6 March.

Dr. Hall, who was Bishop at the time of Lydia's baptism, held the rectory of Wigan *in commendam* and resided there a good deal. He died 23 August 1668, when he was succeeded by Dr. Wilkins, who was rector of Wigan at the time of Samuel's baptism. Millgate is a street in Wigan. It was probably here that Dwight was resident when, on 23 April 1671, he obtained his first patent for the protection of his invention.

Fulham Pottery. From a photograph by Mr. H. Ambridge, 1876

With Bishop Wilkins Dwight got into litigation. In Chancery Proceedings before 1714 ("the Bishop of Chester *v.* Dwight and Another," 462 Bridges), we find that, on 30 Nov. 1669, the complainant alleged that John Dwight, in his capacity as one of the executors of Bishop Hall, did confederate with Sir Amos Meredith, knt., another executor, on behalf of Mrs. Hall, and had got into his hands certain deeds, court rolls, muniments and other evidences of the see of Chester, whereby Bishop Wilkins was unable to establish his claim to certain rectories, *etc.*, the rents of which, he declared, had gone to Dwight and his friends. On 22 Jan. 1669-70, John Dwight, while admitting he had been Bishop's Hall's secretary, denied being his executor,

> "but did, on 7 May 1669, by permission of the said Sir Amos, look through the papers of the said Sir Amos left unto him by Mistresse Gertrude Hall, relict of the late Lord Bishop, and then and there found several counterparts of leases and one old Lieger book containing all ye rentalles and evidences for ye said Bishoprick which he [Defendant] delivered to ye Complainant on 10 May 1669, and denyeth all the other premisses and saith all the other muniments of the See were in the custody of the said Complainant at his Palace in Chester on 10 May aforesaid."

How the quarrel ended we have been unable to ascertain. It was not improbably due to this dispute that Dwight left Wigan for Fulham.

John Dwight was a man of considerable ability, and especially fond of scientific research. His secretarial work at Chester could hardly have been congenial to him, and doubtless his hours of relaxation from the Bishop's work were devoted to his favourite experiments with clays and other mineral substances. Having carried out these to his own satisfaction, he determined, like the shrewd business man he was, to patent his "discovery" before actually introducing his manufactures. The following is the text, *in extenso*, of a patent he obtained in 1671 (No. 164):

> "Know yee, that wee, being willing to cherish and encourage all laudable endeavours and designes of such of our subjectes as shall find out vsefull and proffitable artes, misteries, and invencons, by granting and appropriating vnto them for some terme of yeares the frvite and benefitte of their industry, whereby their labours and expenses in the attainm[t] thereof may be recompensed and rewarded vnto them, of our especiall grace, certaine knowledge, and meere mocon, have given and granted, and by theise presentes, for vs, oure heires, and successors, doe give and grant vnto the said John Dwight, his executors,

administrators, and assignes, speciall lycense and full and free libertye, priviledge, power, and authoritie, that he, the said John Dwight, his executors, administrators, and assigns, by him and themselves or by his or their deputies, servantes, workmen, or assignes, and none other, shall and may, from time to time, and at all and everie time and times hereafter, dureinge the tearme of fourteene yeares next ensueinge the date of these presentes, att his and their owne proper costes and charges, vse, exercise, practise, and enjoy the said mistery and invencon of makeing transparent earthenware, comonly knowne by the names of porcelaine or China, and Persian ware; and alsoe the mistery and invencon of makeing the stoneware, vulgarly called Cologne ware, within any convenient place, or places within our realme of England, dominion of Wales, or Towne of Berwick-vpon-Tweed, in such manner as to him or them in their discretions shall seeme meete; and shall and may have and enjoy the sole benefitte and advantage from, by, or under the said misteries, invencons, or manufactures of the said wares, or either of them, by him, the said John Dwight, found out and discovered, as aforesaid, ariseing or groweing from time to time during the tearme hereby granted, to have, hold, and enjoy the said lycenses, priviledges, powers, and authorities, benefitt, advantages, and other the premises in and by these presentes granted or menconed to be granted, and everie of them, vnto the said John Dwight, his executors, administrators, and assignes, from and dureing the terme of fourteene yeares from henceforth next ensueing and fully to be compleate and ended, yielding and paying therefore yearely and every yeare during the said tearme into the receipt of our Exchequer att Westminster, to the vse of vs, our heires, and successors, the yearly rent or sume of twentie shillings of lawfull money of England," *etc., etc.*

The patent then proceeds to

"require and streightly comand and charge all and everie person and persons, bodies pollitique and corporate, of whatsoever qualitie, degree, name, or condicon they may be, that neither they nor any of them, dureinge the tearme hereby granted, either directly or indirectly doe or shall vse or putt in practise the said misteries and invencons or manufacture of the said wares, or either of them, soe by the said John Dwight found out or discovered as aforesaid; nor doe or shall counterfeite, imitate, or resemble the same; and doe or shall make any addition, therevnto, or substraccon from the same, whereby to pretend themselves the inventors or devisors thereof, without the lycense, consent, and agreement of the said John Dwight, his executors, administrators, or assigns, in writing vnder his or theire handes and seales first had and obteyned in that behalfe, under pain and penalties."

The patent was ordered to be enrolled "before the clerke of the pipe within six months next after the date hereof."

Nothing is known as to the circumstances which led Dwight to settle at Fulham, <u>nor can the exact date of his advent be ascertained</u>. It is in 1674 that we find him, for the first time, assessed for a house in "Beare St.," so that it was probably about 1672 or 1673 that he came here.

At the Victoria and Albert Museum are two interesting pieces of pottery by Dwight. The first is a half length effigy of his little daughter Lydia, the registry of whose baptism in 1667 we have already mentioned. The child is represented with her head raised upon a pillow as she appeared after death. It is inscribed on the back "Lydia Dwight dyd March 3, 1673." Of this figure M. Solon observes in "The Art of the Old English Potter":

> "We fancy we can trace the loving care of a bereft father in the reproduction of the features and the minute perfection with which the accessories, such as flowers and lace are treated."

In "Marks and Monograms on Pottery and Porcelain," Chaffers writes:

> "But the most interesting relic of the Manufactory, executed in hard stoneware, is a beautiful half length figure of a lifeless female child lying upon a pillow with eyes closed, her hands on her breast clasping a bouquet of flowers and a broad lace band over her forehead, evidently modelled from the child after death."

Statuettes of Lydia Dwight,
now at the Victoria and Albert Museum

It was purchased at the Reynolds Sale for £158. The second piece, to which we have referred, is a full length figure of a female child, with hands clasped and wearing a shroud. At her feet lie flowers and a skull. From the similarity of the features to those of the child in the half length effigy, there can be little doubt that it also represents Lydia Dwight, though it bears no inscription. It was purchased at the same sale for £34 10s.

As the Fulham Registers do not commence till 1675, it is uncertain whether Lydia Dwight was buried here or not, but the absence of such entry from the Wigan Registers suggests that Dwight had already left the North when his child's death occurred.

In 1676, his youngest son, Edmond, was born at Fulham. The Church Registers record:

> 1676. Edmond son of Mr. John Dwight and Lydia His wife baptized 28 of August.

In 1682 John Dwight lost his eldest son, John, at the age of 20. The Church Registers record:

> 1682. John son of Mr. Jn° Dwite bu. 19 July.

In the following February we find the record of the interment of another son:

> 1682. ffell s. of Mr. John Dwight bu. 8 of ffebr.

On 12 June 1684, John Dwight obtained a second patent (No. 234) for a further period of fourteen years. The preamble to this sets forth that:

> "John Dwight gentl. has by his owne industry, and at his owne proper costes and charges . . . invented and sett vp at Fulham, in our County of Midd^x, several new manufactures, called by the names of White Gorges, Marbled Porcellane Vessells, Statues and Figures and Fine Stone Gorges and Vessells, never before made in England or elsewhere; and alsoe discovered the mistery of Transparent Porcellane, and Opacons, Redd and Dark coloured Porcellane or China and Persian Wares, and the mistery of the Cologne or Stone Wares and is endeavouring to settle manufactures of all the said wares within this our

Kingdom of England; and hee having humbly besought vs to grant vnto him our Letters Patents for the sole vse and exercise of the same for terme of fourteene years, according to the Statute in that case provided, We are gratiously pleased to condescend to that request."

This patent, it will be observed, mentions "Statues and Figures," showing that, during the preceding fourteen years, Dwight had aimed at producing work of an altogether higher order of artistic merit.

The value of Dwight's inventions was fully attested during the lifetime of the old potter. Even so early as 1677 Dr. Plot, keeper of the Ashmolean Museum, writes in his "History of Oxfordshire":

"The ingenious John Dwight, formerly M.A. of Christ Church College, Oxon., hath discovered the mistery of the stone or Cologne wares (such as d'Alva bottles, jugs, noggins) heretofore made only in Germany, and by the Dutch brought over into England in great quantities, and hath set up a manufacture of the same which (by methods and contrivances of his own, altogether unlike those used by the Germans) in three or four years' time, he has brought it to a greater perfection than it hath attained where it hath been used for many years, insomuch that the Company of Glass-sellers of London, who are dealers for that commodity, have contracted with the inventor to buy only of his English manufacture and to refuse the foreign. He hath discovered also the mystery of the Hessian wares, and vessels for reteining the penetrating salts and spirits of the chymists, more serviceable than were ever made in England or imported from Germany itself, and hath found ways to make an earth white and transparent as porcellane, and not distinguishable from it by the eye, or by experiments that have been purposely made to try wherein they disagree. To this earth he hath added the colours that are usual in the coloured china ware, and divers others not seen before. The skill that hath been wanting to set up a manufacture of this transparent earthenware in England, like that of China, is the glazing of the white earth, which hath much puzzled the projector, but now that difficulty is also in great measure overcome. He has also caused to be modelled statues or figures of the said transparent earth (a thing not done elsewhere, for China affords us only imperfect mouldings), which he hath diversified with great variety of colours, making them of the colour of iron, copper, brass, and party-coloured, as some Achat stones."

Another contemporary authority, John Houghton, in his

"Collection of Papers on Husbandry and Trade," 1694-5, thus alludes to Dwight's wares:

> "Of China ware I see but little imported in the year 1694, I presume by reason of the war and our bad luck on sea. This came only from Spain certain and from India certain twice. 'Tis a curious manufacture and deserves to be encouraged here, which without doubt money would do; and Mr. Dowoight at Fulham has done it; and can do it again for anything that is flat, but the difficulty is that if a hollow dish be made it must be burnt so much that the heat of the fire will make the sides fall. He tells me that our clay will very well do it; the main skill is in managing the fire. By my consent the man that would bring it to perfection should have for his encouragement one thousand pound from the publick though I help'd to pay a tax towards it."

Dr. Chamberlayne, in his "Present State of England" (20 ed., 1702, p. 50), mentions, among "other noble Inventions and Improvements," the "Earthen Ware of Fulham."

Dwight's claim to have made porcelain, as we now apply that term, has sometimes been disputed, but so high an authority as Prof. A. H. Church asserts that the applied ornaments on his grey stoneware jugs and flasks and even the substance of some of his statuettes were distinctly porcellanous.

In 1685 Dwight lost his eldest daughter, Gertrude. The Church Registers record:

> 1685. Gartrud da. of Mr. John Dwight and Lidiah his Wife bu. 18 of April.

The last few years of his life were further embittered by the death of two of his sons, George, his second, and Edmond, his youngest child. The Registers record:

> 1690. George, son of Mr. John Dwaight bu. 3 July.
> 1692. Edmond, son of Mr. John Dwaight bu. 1 Nov.

In consequence of certain persons having infringed his patent, John Dwight, was, in 1693, compelled to proceed against them. In Chancery Proceedings (B. and A. before 1714, 156 and 107 Bridges) are preserved the pleadings of John Dwight and the sworn evidence of the defendants, John Chandler, David Elers, John Elers, his brother, James Morley and Matthew Garner. Dwight urged that Chandler, who had been in his employ and had acquired knowledge and skill as to his inventions, had enabled the defendants to imitate his manufactures. The result of the action we have been unable to trace.

Dwight had a peculiar mania for hiding. According to tradition he buried within the precincts of the Pottery all his models, tools and moulds. This hidden horde has never been found and probably never will be. Mr. Cosmo Monkhouse thinks that Dwight's more artistic productions did not attract their due share of attention, and that, in consequence, he buried his models and tools in disgust. Marryat ascribes their burial to the circumstance that Dwight, "having failed to produce certain pieces of porcelain, grew so disheartened that he buried them so that he might not be induced to use them again." Prof. Jewitt is inclined to think that Dwight's object was "that his descendants or others should not be able to carry on that branch of the trade which he had been the first to invent."

More probably the burial of his tools and types was due to domestic reasons. Of his six sons, four had predeceased him. His eldest surviving son, Samuel, he disinherited on account of his "undutifulness," while the second, Philip, being destined for the Church, could not, of course, take an active part in the continuance of the business. It was therefore obvious to him that, though the manufacture of ordinary earthenware might be continued after his decease, the more artistic branch of the industry must cease, and that the implements connected therewith would be practically useless. In view of Dwight's will, from which we shall presently quote, it is quite possible that the tools, *etc.*, were disposed of by his widow.

In 1864-65 a curious discovery was made in a walled-up vaulted chamber at the Pottery. Some workmen, engaged in pulling down some decayed parts of the buildings and in digging foundations for a new erection, came upon the cellar in question. On being opened it was found to contain a number of stoneware greybeards or bellarmines, ale-pots, *etc.*, of Dwight's own manufacture. Many of the pieces found were more or less damaged, though some were in a fair degree of preservation. They were valued, and bought chiefly by Mr. Henry Willett, the collector. This gentleman lent some of the specimens for exhibition at the Alexandra Palace where they were unfortunately destroyed by fire. Mr. Thomas Baylis purchased other specimens.

In 1868 another interesting discovery was made at the Pottery. The late Lady Charlotte Schreiber, the well-known collector, found among a lot of old papers in one of the offices, two common looking note books, one bound in vellum and the other in parchment, with a silver clasp. They were both closely filled with the handwriting of John Dwight, the entries ranging in date from 1689 to 1698. They contained the results of sundry experiments, recipes and miscellaneous memoranda. The first six pages of the second book were torn out. On one of the remaining pages were the words:

>" Lydia Dwight
>   her Book.   8
>   12
>   4
> Fulham."

Chaffers states that these words were in the handwriting of a child, but this could hardly be the case. Lydia, the daughter of the potter, died in 1673, while Lydia, his granddaughter (the daughter of Dr. Samuel Dwight) was not born till 1716. The date in the entry certainly stands for 8 February 1704, and must have been made by Mrs. Lydia Dwight, the potter's wife, shortly after her husband's death. In the other book Dwight has written "all that is in this book was entered since 9^{ber} 15 1695." A few years ago these two books were sold by Messrs. Christie and Manson. Their present whereabouts cannot now be ascertained. When Prof. Jewitt wrote his "Ceramic Art in Great Britain," they were placed in his hands by Mr. C. I. C. Bailey, then the owner of the Pottery.

The tools and moulds were not the only things which Dwight stowed away. Prof. Jewitt quotes from the note books a number of most singular entries referring to various sums of money which the old potter had from time to time hidden away in sundry chinks and corners of the Pottery. Here are a few:

1693 9ber (November) In ye garret in a hole vnder ye fire place 240 G (Guineas) in a wooden box.

In ye old Labouratory at the old house, in two holes, vnder the file place, on both sides of ye ffurnace in 2 half pint Gor. (Gorges) couered 460 g.

Behind the door of the old Labouratory and within ye end of ye bench, in a pot couered 200.

In ye second presse in ye s(aid) Laboura(tory) vnder some papers at ye bottome in a bag some mill'd money.

Behind ye doore of the little parlor, old house, in a corner some mill'd money.

In ye same little parlour behind some boxes just going into ye kitchen some mill'd money.

In ye second side hole at the bottom of ye first ffurnace in ye kitchen on ye right hand going to ye chimney, pott of Gui.

Between a little furnace and great one that joynes to ye oven behind shouels and forks, a pott of Gui.

Close by those shouells wthin a hole into ye vent of ye same large furnace Gui.

In two holes of that great furnace running in almost to the Ouen, 2 boxes full of mill'd money. May be drawn out wth a long crooked Iron standing behind ye kitchen door.

1698 Vnder ye lower shelfe in ye kitchen near ye Ouen, 2 cans couer'd.

In severall holes of ye ffurnace in ye middle of the kitchen opening at ye top where the sande lyes is a purse of 100 gui: and seuerall Cans couer'd.

At ye further end of the bottome hole of my furnace in the little parlour a box of 200 G.

In some instances the pen had been drawn through the entries, indicating that the sums in question had been withdrawn.
John Dwight died in 1703. The Church Registers record:

1703. John Dwaight gentleman bu. 13 October.

His will, dated 13 Jan. 1702-3, was proved 23 Oct. 1703 (P.C.C. 165 Degg). The following is an extract:

"I John Dwight of ffulham co. Middx, gent. To be buried privately without charge or trouble to survivors. To the poor on the ffulham side of the parish of ffulham £10. To my sister Goweth £10 annually for life. To Mr. John Goweth of Oxford senior £10. To my godson John Dwight £200 to be invested in his behalfe. To my son Mr. Philip Dwight D.D. £100 yearly for next three years. To my undutifull son, Mr. Samuel Dwight, £5, desiring his mother, my executrix, according to her ability to confer on him what he may hereafter deserve when he shall return to his duty. To my wife, Mrs. Lydia Dwight, all my title in my now dwelling house and all my personall estate in full assurance she will employ it to the best advantage of her son or sons as one or both shall deserve which I myself would have done if my circumstances had permitted and if upon further Tryall it shall be thought fit to continue the manufacture by me invented and sett up at ffulham and the same in part or all shall be disposed of by my Executrix to the use and benefit of the said Mr. Philip Dwight and his son, then from such date the said yearly payment to him of £100 shall cease."

The will was proved by the widow, Lydia Dwight, but there are no records to show how the Pottery fared after the death of the founder. Mrs. Dwight survived her husband six years. The Church Registers record:

1709. Mrs. Lidia Dwight bu. 3 Nov.

It is most probable that the widow continued the Pottery and that, at her death, the son Samuel was admitted to the business.

We may, perhaps, pause here to say a few words about the career of Dwight's children. The eldest, John, died in 1682, as stated. The second, George, matriculated at Christ Church, Oxford, 2 July 1683, aged 20. He took his B.A. in 1687, and proceeded M.A. from Brazenose College, 5 Feb. 1689-90, but, as we have seen, soon afterwards died. Of Fell, the third son, nothing is known. Samuel, the fourth, was educated at Westminster School, which he entered in 1686. He matriculated as a gentleman commoner at Christ Church, Oxford, 12 July 1687, aged 18, proceeded B.A. on 23 May 1691, and M.A. on 14 Feb. 1693-94. Some verses of his occur among the academical rejoicings on the birth, in 1688, of James II's son, and others are in the collection celebrating the return of William III from Ireland in 1690. The following entry of his marriage appears in the Vicar-General's Allegation Books at Lambeth Palace:

"1716. Sept. 26 Appeared personally Margarett Price of the parish of ffulham, co. Middlesex, spinster, aged 30, and alleged that she intended to marry with Sam^ll Dwight of the same parish, bachelor, aged 40 . . . at the church of St. Mary Aldermary, London."

As Samuel Dwight was born in 1668, his age is understated by eight years, but Margaret was probably ignorant of this fact. Lydia, their only child, was baptized at Fulham Church, 2 Mar. 1716-17.

Samuel Dwight was admitted a licentiate of the College of Physicians, 25 June 1731. On the title pages of two of his books he is described as a doctor of medicine, but his degree was not recognized by the College. He was the author of three curious medical works, (1) "De Vomitare, ejusque excessu curando; nec non de emeticis medicamentis," *etc.,* 8vo. London, 1722; (2) "De Hydropibus; deque Medicamentis ed eos utilibus expellandos," *etc.,* 8vo. London, 1725; and (3) "De Febribus symptomaticis . . . deque earum curatione," 8vo. L o n d o n, 1731. The last named treatise is dedicated to Sir Hans Sloane, bt., whom Dr. Samuel Dwight was in the habit of consulting in difficult cases. He was in practice at Fulham from about 1720 down to the time of his death, which occurred on 10 Nov. 1737. A curious confusion has arisen between John Dwight, the founder of Fulham Pottery, and his son Samuel. Thus, in the obituary notice in the *Gentleman's Magazine* for 1737, we read:

"Dr. Dwight, author of several curious treatises in Physick, died at Fulham 10 Nov. 1737. The first that found out the Secret to colour earthenware like china."

The Church Registers record:

1737. Saml. Dwight bu. 17 Nov.

Of the fifth son, the Rev. Philip Dwight, we have already spoken (see Chapter II of this volume).

The youngest child, Edmond, entered Westminster School in 1687. He matriculated at Christ Church, Oxford, 2 July 1692, aged 16, but died soon afterwards.

John Dwight, the son of the Rev. P. Dwight, and grandson of John Dwight the potter, settled at Wandsworth, where he died in 1746. He was buried at Fulham. The Church Registers record:

1746. John Dwight bu. 13 Dec.

The following is an extract from his will, dated 3 Oct. 1745, and proved 6 Dec. 1746 (P.C.C. 348 Edmunds):

> "In consideration of the many great favours I have for some years past received from ffrances Want widow who now lives with me and in all respects more like a Mother than a common ffriend I therefore devise to her all my freehold estate I lately purchased of Mr. Richard West of the parish of Wandsworth and in which I now dwell, for her life. And after her death to my son, Philip Dwight, and his heirs for ever. To my son George Henry Dwight £100 to be paid him when he has served an apprenticeship and £15 to augment the £5 he received from Christ's Hospital. To my son Philip Dwight £50 when he shall have served his apprenticeship with Mr. David Ashley. To my daughter Jane Dwight £200 at 21. To ffrances Want widow 30 guineas and to her daughter ffrances Want spinster 10 guineas to buy her a piece of plate in my memory. All my furniture to ffrances Want for life, and afterwards to my son Philip Dwight. Executors to be Thomas Warland of ffulham gent, (to whom I give 5 guineas for a ring) and ffrances Want widow."

John Dwight the younger, by his wife Millicent, had four children, Philip, who was married to Sarah How, of Wandsworth, 8 Oct. 1752, Jane, who was born 19 Aug. 1728, and baptized at Fulham, 5 Sept. 1728, George Henry, and Millicent, who was buried at Fulham, 3 May 1732. The children of Philip were Millicent, Jane, and John. Frances Want, the faithful housekeeper of John Dwight, was buried at Wandsworth, 19 Nov. 1749.

Fulham Pottery. From a photograph by Mr. T. S. Smith, 1897

On the death of Dr. Samuel Dwight in 1737, the Pottery was carried on for awhile by his widow, Margaret Dwight. In the assessments for 1739, the name of "Margarett Dwight" is crossed through and that of "Tho. Warland" inserted. This Thomas Warland had married Lydia (the third of that name), daughter of Samuel and Margaret Dwight. The following is the entry of the marriage license issued by the Consistory Court of the Bishop of London:

"1737 Nov. 24: Appeared personally, Thomas Warland of the Parish of ffulham co. Middlesex, bachelor, aged upwards of 22 years alledged that he intended to marry with Lydia Dwight of the same parish, spinster, aged upwards of 20 years, with consent of Margaret Dwight, widow, her natural and lawful mother, at St. Bennet, Paul's Wharf. William Skelton and Margaret Dwight of the Parish of Fulham alledge to the truth thereof."

It was doubtless *de jure uxoris* that Thomas Warland became a partner with Margaret Dwight in the Pottery business. Affairs do not seem to have prospered, for we learn from the *Gentleman's Magazine* for Jan. 1746, that "Margaret Dwight and Thomas Warland of Fulham, potters," were adjudged bankrupts. In the Registers of the Bankruptcy Court occurs the following entry of the bankruptcy:

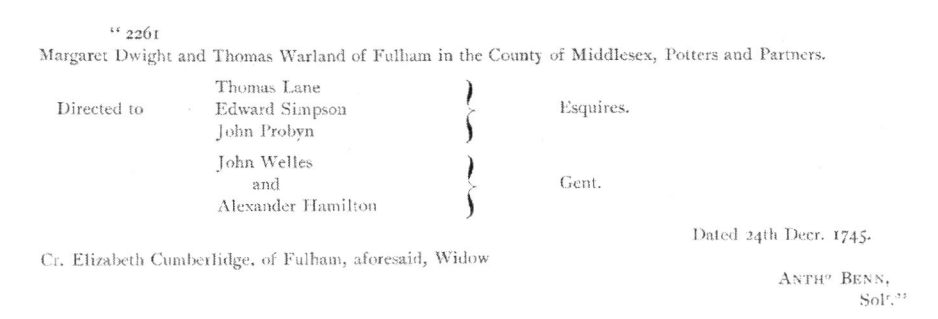

"2261

Margaret Dwight and Thomas Warland of Fulham in the County of Middlesex, Potters and Partners.

Directed to	Thomas Lane Edward Simpson John Probyn	Esquires.
	John Welles and Alexander Hamilton	Gent.

Dated 24th Decr. 1745.

Cr. Elizabeth Cumberlidge, of Fulham, aforesaid, Widow

ANTH? BENN,
Sol?."

Thomas Warland died three years later and was buried at Fulham, 12 Jan. 1748-49. Mrs. Margaret Dwight died in 1750. The Church Registers record:

1750. Margarett Dwight bu. 3 Apl.

Lydia Warland subsequently married a William White, or Wight, as the name is occasionally spelt, This William White appears to have done his best to restore to the Pottery some of its former reputation. In the "Annual Register" for 1761 (p. 95) is the following:

"The Society for the Encouragement of Arts, Manufactures and Commerce gave a premium to Mr. William White, master of the Stone Pot House at Fulham for his inventing the art of making crucibles of British materials which not only equal but excel those imported from abroad."

In 1762 this "Mr. William White of Fulham in the County of Middlesex, potter," took out a patent for 14 years for "a new manufacture of crucibles (set up at Fulham) for melting metals, salts, etc., called white crucibles or melting pots," for which, as we have seen, the Society for the Encouragement of Arts, etc., had awarded him a premium. The business remained in the hands of this family for a great number of years. Lysons, in 1796, speaks of the Pottery as being then "carried on at Fulham by Mr. White, a descendant in the female line of the first proprietor."

On the death, in 1829, of William White, son of the above

named, the Pottery was continued by Charles E. White, son of the younger William. Mr. C. E. White, who married a sister of Sir Richard Mayne, the well-known chief of the police, committed suicide in 1859 in the counting house at the Pottery. The executors managed the concern down to 1863. In 1864 the style was altered to Mackintosh and Clements or Clements and Co. In this year Mr. C. I. C Bailey purchased the freehold of the Pottery, which he very greatly enlarged and improved.

In February 1889, the property was brought under the auctioneer's hammer. It was put up in four lots. The first, consisting of the Pottery works, with frontages in Church Street and Burlington Road, and covering an area of about 30,200 superficial feet, was not sold. Lot two, consisting of the goodwill of the Pottery business, together with Mr. Bailey's extensive stock, was withdrawn. The remaining lots, comprising the freehold shops and dwelling houses, Nos. 57a and 57b, High Street, sold for £760 and £1,100 respectively. The works have since been acquired by the Fulham Pottery and Cheavin Filter Company, Limited.

Mr. Baylis of Pryor's Bank, who brought together an unrivalled collection of Fulham ware, published in the *Art Journal* for 1862 an interesting account of the Pottery and its manufactures. He writes:

> "The manufactory was in the reign of Charles II much employed in matters relating to the Court of this monarch and that of James II. Since that time its productions have been confined principally to stoneware, such as jugs, bottles and similar utensils in general use. These are of the kind usually termed 'stoneware,' but, it is believed, marked by a superior excellence in glazing and getting up and in the embossed subjects often in high relief on the surface. There is one curious specimen of a gallon jug with a grey beard spout, with a lid of the same ware, and, what is more remarkable, with *hinges* also of the same material. This was evidently meant to be a curiosity in its way and reminds one of those dungeons at Baden Baden and elsewhere where the door jambs and hinges are said to be hewn out of the solid rock. The date of 1800 is on this jug and the initials W. W. (William Wight)."

Mr. Baylis thus describes one of the more important pieces of the ware then in his collection:

"The first is a dish, said - and with more than mere probability - to be one of a dinner set manufactured for the especial service of Charles II. It is of a round form and large, being 64½ inches in circumference. The groundwork is a rich blue, approaching to ultramarine; it is surrounded by a broad rim nearly four inches wide, formed by a graceful border of foliage and birds in white and shaded with pale blue. The whole of the centre is occupied by the Royal Arms surmounted by its kingly helmet, crown and lion crest. The arms themselves are encircled with the garter on which is inscribed the well-known motto: *Honi soit qui maly pense.* The arms and supporters rest upon a groundwork of foliage, in the middle of which is the motto: *Dieu et mon Droit.* The workmanship of this piece of crockery is of a very superior character, and a dinner set of similar ware would make many a modern one look poor. The solitary specimen left of this once magnificent royal dinner service is believed to be by far the finest extant of this early English manufacture."

Some examples of the ware are to be seen at the Geological Museum, and in various private collections. Among the latter Professor Jewitt mentions the historically interesting flip-can belonging to "Robinson Crusoe," and carefully preserved by his family. It bears the incised inscription:

"Alexander Selkirke. This is my one (own). When you take me on bord of ship, Pray fill me full with punch or flipp, Fulham."

Howell, the author of the Introduction to the "Life and Adventures of Alexander Selkirk," 1829, discovered his grandnephew, a teacher at Canonmills, near Edinburgh, in whose possession he found this curious relic. It is said that Selkirk obtained this flip-can from Fulham about the middle of 1703, while waiting for the equipment and sailing of the Cinque Ports galley, to which he had been appointed sailing master. It doubtless accompanied him on his voyage to Juan Fernandez.

Most of the specimens belonging to Mr. Baylis were purchased by Mr. C. W. Reynolds. In 1871 the Reynolds' Collection was sold by auction, many of the pieces going to the British and Victoria and Albert Museums. In 1886 the authorities of the former institution acquired twelve additional pieces, thus forming the most complete series of Fulham ware ever brought together. The following is a list of the principal pieces:

		Lot
Large bust of Prince Rupert, miscalled James II.	Reynolds	271
White female bust, said to be Mrs. Pepys.		
Brown figure of Mars.	Reynolds	288
,, ,, ,, Meleager.	,,	289
White figure of Flora.	,,	276
,, ,, ,, Sportsman.	,,	279
,, ,, ,, Girl and Lamb.	,,	275
,, ,, ,, Meleager.	,,	280
,, ,, ,, Minerva.	,,	269
Hand of a child.		
Marbled jug with figures in relief and C.	Reynolds	282
White mug.		
Brown mug, partly engraved.		
Cylindrical white mug, silver mounted.		
Ordinary stoneware jug.		
Nineteen brass stamps, said to have been used to make the ornaments.		

Besides these there is an equestrian figure of the Duke of Cumberland, marked "W. D.," presumably for Warland and Dwight, but this is doubtful.

Before we quit the Pottery, we may, perhaps, mention an interesting tradition - for we fear it is nothing better - which ascribes its establishment to a younger brother of John and Cornelius De Witt, the famous Dutch statesmen, who were barbarously murdered by the populace. This "younger" brother is said to have escaped the massacre, and to have fled with his mother to England. The story is thus told by Lysons:

> "An erroneous tradition has prevailed that this Manufacture was set up by a younger brother of the unfortunate Dutch minister, Dewit, who escaped the massacre of his family and fled to England, *anno* 1672, with his mother. The tradition describes circumstantially the character of the old lady who is said to have maintained a kind of sullen dignity in her misfortunes, and to have been inaccessible except to the King, who sometimes visited her at Fulham, and to persons of the highest rank. The fallacy of the whole story, however, is evident, not only by a letter of Mrs. White, granddaughter of John Dwight (wherein she mentions that he was the son of a gentleman in Oxfordshire, who gave him a liberal education at the University, and that he afterwards became chaplain to three bishops of Chester), but also by a commonplace book (which, as well as the letter, is now in the possession of Mr. White,

who obligingly favoured me with the use of them), drawn up by Mr. Dwight, wherein he has inserted precedents of all forms of business which came before the Bishop's court in his own time and that of his predecessors."

There can be no doubt that the name is one of Dutch origin, though we have no means of determining how or when the family settled in England.

Charles James Fèret

PEDIGREE OF THE DWIGHT FAMILY

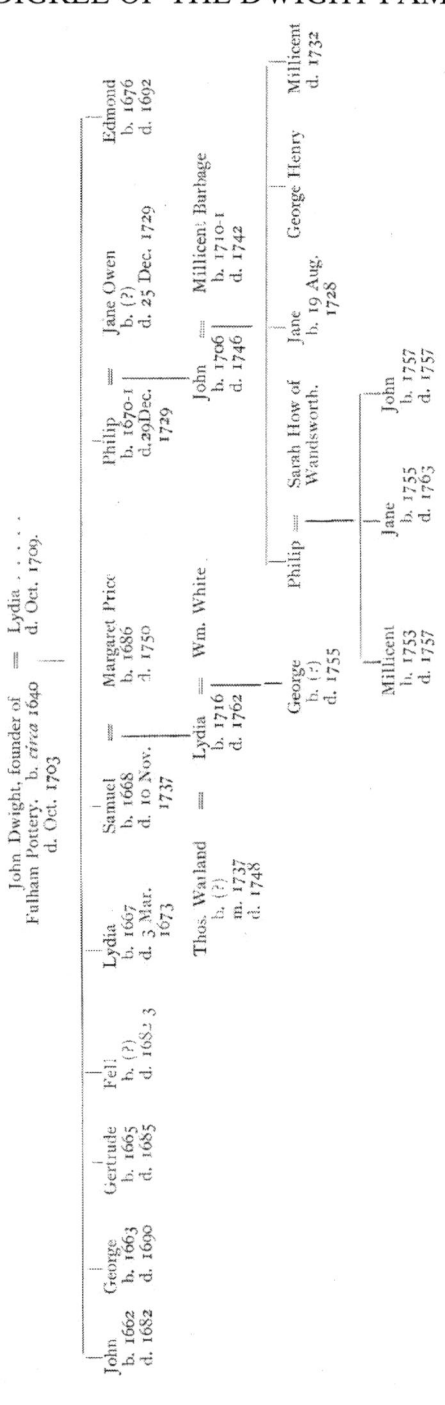

John Dwight, founder of Fulham Pottery. b. *circa* 1640 d. Oct. 1703 = Lydia ...... d. Oct. 1709.

- John b. 1662 d. 1682
- George b. 1663 d. 1690
- Gertrude b. 1665 d. 1685
- Fell b. (?) d. 1682-3
- Lydia b. 1667 d. 3 Mar. 1673
  - = Thos. Warland b. (?) m. 1737 d. 1748
- Samuel b. 1668 d. 10 Nov. 1737 = Margaret Price b. 1686 d. 1750
  - Lydia b. 1716 d. 1762 = Wm. White
    - George b. (?) d. 1755 = Sarah How of Wandsworth.
      - Philip
        - Millicent b. 1753 d. 1757
        - Jane b. 1755 d. 1763
        - John b. 1757 d. 1757
- Philip b. 1670-1 d. 29 Dec. 1729 = Jane Owen b. (?) d. 25 Dec. 1729
  - John b. 1706 d. 1746 = Millicent Barbage b. 1710-1 d. 1742
    - Jane b. 19 Aug. 1728
    - George Henry
- Edmond b. 1676 d. 1692
- Millicent d. 1732

SOUTH SIDE OF NEW KING'S ROAD

King's Arms Public House

On the right of the New King's Road, as we enter it from the High Street, is the "King's Arms," one of the oldest inns in Fulham.

In the reign of Henry VIII an alehouse on this site was kept by a Roger Hawkyns, who, in 1526, was fined for failing to make smooth his alepole.

For many years the house was owned by the Limpany family. In 1575, "Robert Lympenye of Fulham Street" was amerced 3s. 4d. because he kept a tavern "contrary to the order of the last Court."

Taylor, the water poet, in his "Catalogue of Tavernes in Ten Shires about London," 1636, mentions the "King's Arms" at Fulham. For more than a quarter of a century, the house was in the occupation of Francis Stutsbury. In 1656 this person issued a copper token from which the annexed illustration is taken. The initials on the reverse stand for "FranciS Stutsbury." In 1668, John Dickens mortgaged the "King's Arms," still in the occupation of Stutsbury, to Henry Shephard, citizen and haberdasher of London. In 1672 the house became the property of Mrs. Susanna Hamerton.

Token issued at the "King's Arms," in 1656, now in the possession of Mr. A. Chasemore. From a drawing by the owner.

In 1677 the inn passed to Neve Hamerton, who, in 1686, surrendered the whole to the use of Robert Limpany. From the abstract of Limpany's will, given in our account of Church Row (see Volume I), it will be seen that the testator charged the "King's Arms" with the annual payment of £4 10s. to be laid out in loaves for the poor, and in "wiggs" (buns) and ale for the Charity

Children, *etc.* When, in 1880, the house became the property of the late Metropolitan Board of Works, the rent charge of £4 10s. was commuted by them for £150 6s. Consols.

Anciently the "King's Arms" was the resort of smugglers on their way from Portsmouth, Eastbourne, *etc., via* Wimbledon Common to London. When the old house was pulled down, a rusty old rapier was found behind some of the wainscotting. Who knows but what some venturesome highwayman, resting here, may have hidden the weapon where it was discovered and left it behind him?

The "King's Arms" was essentially a coaching inn. Travellers from London drove in under a gateway which led to the yard and so through to the back of the house. The old four-horse coaches, such as the "Royal Mail," the "Rocket," the "Red Rover," and the "Times," running from London to Southampton, Petworth, Littlehampton, *etc.,* used to make their first change of horses here.

Down to some sixty years ago, it was the custom to hold every year in the "Long Room" at this old hostelry a dinner on 1st September to commemorate the Great Fire of London. Faulkner observes:

> "It is said to have taken its rise from a number of Londoners who had been burnt out, and, having no employment, strolled out to Fulham, and in their way collected a quantity of nuts from the hedges round Fulham Fields and resorted to this house with them. A capital picture used to be exhibited on this day of that great conflagration."

The origin of the dinner may have been as Faulkner states, but certainly, in later times, it merely served as an excuse for a convivial gathering of the old parishioners, some of whom would grow so merry over their wine as to resort to practical jokes of various kinds. Sometimes - possibly in dim memory of the Great Fire - they would shovel a lot of pence among the embers in the grate in order that, when the coins were red hot, they might throw them out of the windows and relish the fun of seeing the small boys burning their fingers' ends in a pell-mell scramble.

At times the amusement would be varied by cold coins being showered out mixed with "hot 'uns."

The disbursements of the Overseers for 1787 include:

"Paid at the King's Arms for Election Dinner when chosen and for dinner for the ringers £12. 8s. 0d."

The old "King's Arms."
From a photograph by Mr. H. Ambridge, 1878

In 1888 the old inn was taken down and the present handsome house erected.

There is still preserved, in the Muniment Room at Fulham Palace, a summons which was served on Bishop Sherlock citing him to appear at the "King's Arms" on 15 Dec. 1751, for neglecting to pay his poor rate.

Chaldon House

On the south side of Church Street, facing Back Lane, was Chaldon House, a fine old residence which stood behind a high wall. A small house, which previously existed on this site, was once in the occupation of a family named Woodward. Bowack, in 1705, writing of the Town of Fulham, says:

"At the entrance to this Town by the Queen's Gate is the convenient house of Captain Woodward one of Her Majesties Justices of the Peace for Middlesex, 'tis but small but very well contriv'd, his gardens also are very handsome."

Staircase at Chaldon House.
From an oil painting by Miss Jane Humphreys

The Woodwards were an old Fulham family. In the Rate books the name of Richard Woodward first appears under the year 1672. In 1690 Richard Woodward and Mary his wife surrendered their messuage to their eldest son Richard and Rebecca his wife. Richard Woodward, junior, is described as of the Middle Temple.

In 1750, William Skelton, of Church Row, obtained the Lord's license to demolish the old house and to apply the building materials to his own use. For this license he paid a fine of 10s. 6d. Shortly afterwards Chaldon House must have been built. In 1754 John Barlow of St. George's, Hanover Square,

> "surrendered to the Lord all that new built brick messuage or tenement with the stable, garden and appurtenances to the same belonging, enclosed by a brick wall," *etc.*,

to John Duer, late of Kensington, in whose occupation the house then was. The Rev. W. Cole, in his manuscript account of Fulham Church, dated 20 April 1758, informs us that he was then "on a visit to John Duer Esq., of this Place and one of his Majesties Justices of the Peace for Middlesex." John Duer died at Chaldon House, 1 Dec. 1764. The Churchwardens' Accounts for that year include:

"Expences at receiving a fine for John Dure, Esq., being buried in Linen 1s. 0d"

The Church Registers record:

1764. John Duer Esq bu. 8 Dec.

A room in Chaldon House.
From a painting by Miss Jane Humphreys

In the same vault lie other members of the family, including his wife, Frances Duer, who died 3 July 1787.

In 1779 Mrs. Phoebe McPhædris, widow of Colonel McPhædris, succeeded Mrs. Duer. She continued to reside here till 1821. In 1822 the house was taken by Mr. Thomas Chinnall Porter, J.P., the well-known picture collector, who lived here with his daughters. His wife, Mrs. Martha Porter, was a niece of Mrs. McPhædris.

The Porters were generous benefactors to the parish. Miss Martha Porter, who died in December 1836, by a codicil to her will dated 18 Aug. 1823, charged the sum of £1,403. 7s. 0d. 3 per cent

Consols with the payment of £10 annually for the benefit of the Fulham National Schools. The balance of the interest derived from this sum is shared between two parishes in Worcestershire. By a deed, dated 28 July 1838, the Misses Phoebe and Anne Porter gave £400 3 per cent Consols, the dividends accruing from which were to be applied by the Vicar in the purchase of clothing and bedding for poor inhabitants of Fulham not in the receipt of parochial relief. By her will, dated 11 Mar. 1859, Miss Phoebe Porter gave £100 for distribution among the poor of Fulham. This sum was invested in 3 per cent Consols, the dividends on which were applied to the Parochial Clothing Club. Miss Anne Porter, who died in 1871, left £100 for the poor inhabitants of Fulham, This sum was invested in Metropolitan 3½ per cent Stocks (£96. 12s. 3d.), and the income applied to the Clothing Club. The three last named benefactions are now merged in the United Charities.

After the death, in 1871, of Miss Anne Porter, Chaldon House for awhile stood tenantless. In 1874 it was taken by the late Mr. Charles Augustus Howell, D.C.L., the well- known dealer in works of art. Mr. Howell previously resided at North End Grove, North End, the removal of his elegant furniture from here to Chaldon House costing no less than £278. The transfer was effected by means of a procession of twelve cabs wending to and fro for over a week. When Mr. Howell took the house he found it practically a wreck. Every room became, in the hands of this celebrated connoisseur, a picture. The fire-hearths were paved with the costliest of tiles, Portuguese and Japanese. One window was designed by Burne-Jones and another by Rossetti. The house was speedily turned into a home of aestheticism. The rooms of this "Paradise of Beauty," as it was termed, were "arrangements" in blue and gold, in green and gold, and other colours. In 1879 the Metropolitan District Railway Company required the site of the house for the extension of their line to Putney. Mr. Howell, who used the house for the purposes of his business, preferred a claim for interest in the lease, compensation for money laid out in artistic decorations and expense for removing his valuable furniture, *etc.* The jury awarded him £3,650.

Chaldon House was reputed to be ghost haunted, the favourite *locale* of the spectre - said to be that of Miss Anne Porter - being the housekeeper's room.

At the junction of the New King's Road and the Hurlingham Road, where the District Railway now crosses, was an inn known as the "Ship." In the Parish Books the earliest mention of the house is in 1753. It had pleasant tea gardens at the rear, running along Hurlingham Lane. It was at the "Ship" that the Fulham Philanthropic Society was established.

SECTION II:
BURLINGTON ROAD TO PARSON'S GREEN

Before proceeding with this section of the New King's Road, we may perhaps conveniently speak of a piece of meadow or wareland, a portion of the demesne of the Manor, which lay on either side of the road, from about the end of Church Street as far as Parson's Green. Anciently this land was known as Bearcroft or Bearfield, a name identical in origin with that of Bear Street.

It is first mentioned in the Court Rolls for 1422, when John Webbe surrendered it to his daughter, Elizabeth, the wife of William Conyngton. William Coxston was, at a View in 1446, presented because he had ploughed up one furrow of land belonging to the church (subaravit unum sulcum terre ecclesiastice) in a field called "Berefeld." At a Court Baron in 1454 it was presented that

> "Henry Wakefield holds one acre in Berecroft parcel of ffolase tenement for which he ought to render annually xij^d but he pays only ix^d."

The following entry occurs in the minutes of a View in 1489:

> "At this Court Nicholas Sturgeon took of the Lord to farm by master Walter Ondeby, custodian of the temporalities of the bishopric during the vacancy of the See, six acres of the demesne lands in "Berecroft alias Berefield in Fulham, between the lands of John Edwyn on the south, the King's highway extending from the Church of Fulham to Grove House on the north, and the land formerly of Master John Suddebury on the east, which the same Nicholas heretofore held of Robert Lovell, farmer there, at the annual rent of 5s."

After about the end of the 15th century the name Bearcroft or

Bearfield ceases, that of Churchfield coming into use to designate practically the same district.

Churchfield, or Longclose, was some thirteen acres in extent. Its southern boundary was the old way to Broomhouse, now Hurlingham Road. Northwards it extended towards the London Road. It seems to have obtained its name from some ancient connection with the church. As we have just seen, in our account of Bearcroft, William Coxston went beyond the boundary of his own land there, ploughing up some which was the property of the church. This entry clearly shows that Fulham Church once possessed some land in Bearcroft or Churchfield, though no records now exist showing how much it was, or how it passed into other hands. It may possibly have been the acre granted, together with the rectory of Fulham, in 1420, to the Carthusian Priory at Sheen.

Churchfield was let out by the Lord of the Manor to his tenants. It was usually leased in two portions, the western part consisting of six acres, and the eastern part of seven acres. The former lay "next the Town of Fulham," and extended as far as the alley at the west end of Elysium Row; the latter adjoined it at this point.

The New King's Road.
From a photograph by Mr. T. S. Smith, 1896

As we have seen in our account of Church Street, the King's Road in ancient times bore no distinctive name. In Rocque's Map, 1741-5, the section of the road between Fulham Town and Parson's Green is called Fulham Lane.

The way was originally a farm track, giving access to the adjacent fields, used mainly by those tenants of the Manor whose lands abutted thereon.

It was during the Stuart dynasty that the King's Road emerged from this primitive condition. The State Papers throw an interesting light on the origin of "the King's Private Road," as the way came to be termed. The most direct way from St. James's and Whitehall to the royal palace at Hampton Court lay along this road, which the King would traverse, crossing the river at Fulham Ferry over to Putney. The frequent ringing of the bells in the old Church at Fulham, when the King "passed through the Town," was doubtless due to the journeyings of royalty along this road. In 1626 an order was issued to one Thomas Hebbs, surveyor of the King's Highways, "to take special care for the repair of the way leading from Chelsea to Fulham," This looks as if Charles I was at that time in the habit of using it. It was not, however, till the days of Charles II that the way was widened and turned into a "private road" for the convenience of the King when he travelled from London to Hampton Court.

In May 1704, we find "Michael Studholm, Esquire," keeper of Her Majesty's Private Roads, petitioning the Lord High Treasurer to be reimbursed certain moneys which he had laid out in respect to the repair of this road. During the three preceding reigns, the Surveyor points out, there was continued on the establishment of the royal household an allowance of £270 per annum for the repairs of the private roads to Fulham, and he therefore prays payment of £135 for the half-year ending Midsummer 1702, he having expended that amount. But Queen Anne, though she found the road very convenient for her use, did not see the force of continuing the payment which had been annually made by her predecessors. Studholm could hardly have relished the reply he received, for the petition is minuted in the following peremptory terms:

"Read 10 May 1704. If there be anything due on this allowance in ye late King's time, it will be paid when there is money for arrears of that kind, but the Queen never intended to establish any allowance for these roads."

In May 1711, Studholm again memorialized the Lords of the Treasury, this time for an order to put padlocks on the gates of "Her Majesty's private road to Fulham," whilst under repair. The memorial is minuted:

"8 May 1711 Order'd that he lock up the gates and make two gates in the places agreed upon by Mr. Surveyor Gen[ll] and himselfe."

But Studholm, with all his ingenuity, failed to discover any satisfactory plan by which he could preserve the road for the sole use of his royal mistress. The market gardeners of Fulham, the farmers, the brewers and the brickmakers insisted on taking their wares along it. In July 1711, we find Studholm again writing to the Lord High Treasurer, reminding him of the good old times when Charles II, James II and William III allowed £270 a year for the repair of the road, but he goes on to confess that he cannot find that the farmers' carts can be kept off, "their habitations [he probably means the farmers', not the carts'!] being all along in most parts of the road." The produce, he tells the Lord High Treasurer, had always been carried in heavy carts, through some parts, in least, of the road to the London market. As for the brewers' drays and the brick carts, which had always done the greatest damage, there was no preventing, sighs the poor Surveyor, "unless Her Majesty buys the several houses that join to each gate or makes an allowance annually to the persons that live in them." Perhaps, he suggested, for £5 a-piece the gate keepers would be "encouraged to keep out those heavy drays." The result of this application we do not know.

On 9 July 1712, the "Officers of Works" reported to the Lord High Treasurer on Studholm's estimate for the repair of the "Queen's" Private Road, which he proposed to mend with gravel and bavins. The document is minuted:

"17 July 1712. My Lord does not approve the filling up with bavins. To propose a more substantial way; then the estimate to be considered."

On or about 6 Sept. 1721, Joseph Carpenter memorialized the Lords of the Treasury for an advance of money for repairing the King's Private Road. This document is minuted:

"6 September 1721. 600^{li} to be issued to the paym^r upon accot. of these works now in hand."

In 1731 His Majesty's Surveyor issued to certain persons entitled to use the road small metal tickets, bearing, on the obverse, "The King's Private Road," and, on the reverse, the Crown and the letters " G.R." For the next hundred years the King continued to exercise a semblance of right over the road. It was not until 1830 that the King's Road was thrown open to the unrestricted use of the people. In the "British Almanac and Companion" for 1831, we read:

"The King's Private Road from London to Fulham has been given up to the public, and will be kept in repair by the parishes through which it passes."

Down to this date no less than six bars spanned the road, two of which were in Fulham parish and four in Chelsea. The first of the two in Fulham, known as the King's Gate, immediately faced Elysium Cottage. The second gate crossed the King's Road at Sand's End, where the "Lord Palmerston" now stands.

Among the Treasury Papers is a petition, dated 1722-23, from the six gatekeepers of His Majesty's Private Road, asking for payment for three years' work. William Watkins, the King's Surveyor, notes against the petition:

"22 Feb. 1722-3. The allow^{ce} of £5 p. ann. each to be established in the Office of Works, and to be p^d from the time they were employed in this service."

In an accompanying document, the Surveyor observes:

"The Gatekeepers have worked on this road thro' 3 years past, wch is ever since the houses were built, in hopes and upon my promise that I would use my endeavours to obtain some small allowance for them."

NORTH SIDE

We will now take the road from Burlington Road to Parson's Green, visiting the north side first.

Next but one to Burlington Road was the "Old Original Fulham Dairy, established 1790." In 1897 the Dairy and the other houses between Burlington Road and Vine Cottage were rebuilt. Passing Jasmine House (No. 200), and Burlington House (No. 198), we come to Buer Road, built on the demolition of Fulham Prison. Elysium Cottage (No. 182), was formerly the tollkeeper's residence, built circa 1720.

Fulham Park Road, which here enters the New King's Road, approximately marks the position of an ancient alley which crossed to the London (now Fulham) Road. This was known, from the tenant of an adjacent holding, as Hawkins's Alley. In 1832 Dr. Robert Roy, of Burlington House, paid £200 for permission to close the alley, the money being given to the New Almshouses.

Jasmine House. From a photograph by Mr. T. S. Smith, 1895

We now come upon a line of old houses, built, according to a tablet near the centre of the block, in 1738, and rejoicing in the classical appellation of Elysium Row, a name which, to the present day, the less educated residents of the Town persist in calling "Leeshum Row." The ancients were, we know, very uncertain as to the geographical position of that blissful region known by the name of the Elysian Fields. Some supposed them to be the Fortunate Islands on the coast of Africa, Virgil placed them in Italy, while Lucian thought they were in the Moon. The speculative builder, in the Fulham of long ago, may have fancied that he recognized the Elysian Fields in the lovely expanse of nursery grounds which, till recent times, faced the houses of which we are about to speak. When Elysium Row was built, it enjoyed an uninterrupted view right across the river to the rising ground at Wimbledon.

Some tenements apparently stood on the site before Elysium Row was built. Faulkner, in a manuscript note left in his own copy of his book, observes, speaking of the headstone in Fulham Churchyard to the memory of Mrs. Maria Cotton (p. 108):

"This was my grandmother who resided in Elysium Row where she died in 1727 and was buried in the south west corner of the churchyard. The inscription was written by my grandfather, C. Cotton Esq. The original lines are still in the possession of the family. T. F."

Hawkins's Alley, now Fulham Park Road.
From a photograph by Mr. T. S. Smith, 1895

For many years in the first half of this century Mr. Joseph Murr lived at No. 2, Elysium Row. Murr, who was a schoolmaster and an eccentric character, is perhaps best remembered as the author of one of the quaintest epitaphs which Fulham Churchyard boasts.

During 1866, Mrs. Tait, the wife of Archbishop (then Bishop) Tait, took this house and its neighbour, No. 3, which she turned into an orphanage for girls who had been deprived of their parents through the cholera visitation of that year. This was the origin of the St. Peter's Orphanage at Broadstairs. The Archbishop, in "Catharine and Craufurd Tait," p. 48, gives the following account of the Orphanage:

> "This visitation of the cholera led to the crowning labour of her life . . . My wife hired a house at Fulham for the girls, and . . . soon established St. Peter's Orphanage. . . . The Fulham Orphanage contained thirty girls. It was distant from the Palace about five minutes' walk. When we were at home there was constant communication between her and the inmates. She visited them almost every day. On Sundays the children would come and have a Scripture lesson; and she would read to them the 'Pilgrim's Progress,' or some such book in the great hall, or on the lawn. From time to time they attended the services of the Palace Chapel, and no sound could be more pleasant than that of the hymns and carols with which, standing in the frosty garden, they would waken us on Christmas morning. The Orphanage remained at Fulham for about five years. But as soon as we ourselves were called away by my translation, she resolved that it should be moved and made available for my new as well as my old diocese. . . . About this time I was enabled by the bequest of a relation to purchase a private and more permanent home for my family in the Isle of Thanet. Here she arranged with me in 1869 to secure in perpetuity two-acres of ground on one of the most healthy sites in England; and in course of time she caused a handsome building to be erected capable of receiving 80 children," etc.

At No. 3 lived the Rev. Arthur Simon Latter, M.A., curate at Fulham Church from 1835 to 1864. In 1890 he became vicar of Outwell, Wisbeach, and died 2 Feb. 1894. No. 5 (formerly known as Ilex House) and No. 6 (Carboldisham House) are mainly associated with the memories of the Osbornes of nursery fame. At No. 7 (Oak House) resided the Bassanos, of whom we have spoken in our account of Fulham Church.

At No. 8 (Claybrooke House) lived the Rev. Christopher Lipscomb, another curate of Fulham. The house is, however, mainly of interest as the residence of the Watsons. Mr. William Henry Watson, barrister-at-law, came of an old Northumbrian family. In 1812, at the age of 16, he was gazetted to the Royal

Dragoons, with whom he served in Spain, receiving the Peninsular medal. On the breaking out of the war, in 1815, he was appointed to the Inniskilling Dragoons, and was sent over to Belgium with reinforcements which reached Ostend just after the battle of Waterloo had been fought. At the close of the war he was placed on half pay, and, to avoid being idle, came up to London and studied law. He was called to the Bar in 1831, when he went the Northern Circuit, and continued to do so till 1856, when he was appointed Baron of the Exchequer and knighted. He served intermittently in Parliament as a Whig. In 1859 his health broke down, but he persisted in continuing his judicial duties. On 13 March 1860, while charging the Grand Jury at Welshpool, he fell back in his chair, and in a few minutes expired. Mr. Watson went to reside at No. 8, Elysium Row on his marriage, in 1826, with the sister of Lord Armstrong. Baron Wiercinski lived at No. 8 in 1861-63.

Elysium Row. From a photograph by Mr. H. Ambridge, 1868

No. 9 (Northumberland House) was, from 1875 to 1882, the residence of the Sullivans. Mr. Frederick Sullivan, the actor, famous as the Judge in "Trial by Jury," brother of Sir Arthur Sullivan, the composer, died here in 1877. Their mother, Mrs.

Charlotte Sullivan, died at Northumberland House in 1882. Sir Arthur, who often visited the house during his family's connection with it, composed here "The Lost Chord" while attending his brother in his last illness. Northumberland House is often spoken of as being haunted. Former residents have averred that the ghost of a dog has been seen to run about the house and to disappear up the large hall chimney.

Northumberland House.
From a photograph by Mr. T, S. Smith, 1895

No. 11 was, from 1814 to 1836, the residence of the Rev. George Wagner, who lies buried at Fulham. The Rev. Thomas Raleigh Birch, who moved here from Church Row, was at one time chaplain at the Fulham Union. Mr. Birch is best remembered as a profound Greek and Hebrew scholar. His death occurred 24 Mar. 1884.

No. 12 (Elysium Villa, now named Villa Romano) is associated with several noteworthy names. Mr. Peter Brames, of the Fulham Nursery, died here in 1834. Miss Santley, the actress, resided here for awhile, and, on occasion, Serjeant William Ballantine, the well-known criminal lawyer. In the basement of this house is a fine ice well. In the garden there survives an old mulberry tree, one of the few now left in Fulham.

Elysium Row has somewhat outlived its day, and is no longer

the attractive residential quarter it was once.

The twelve houses of which the Row consists are now numbered with those of the main thoroughfare, Nos. 1 to 12 being represented by Nos. 180 to 158 (even numbers) of the New King's Road.

Draycott Lodge. From a photograph by Mr. T, S. Smith, 1895

Just eastwards of Elysium Row stands an old-fashioned residence now known as Draycott Lodge. This was originally a small cottage, built about 1813, House. by Colonel, afterwards General McLeod, who resided here down to 1837. In 1838 the house was taken by Mr. Thomas Miller, and in 1841 by Mr. Peter Truefit, in whose time it obtained the name of Andover House. In 1850 the house was the residence and property of Mr. Henry J. Dixon. In 1852 it was let to Miss C. F. Gieslor, who lived here till 1859. Captain Arthur Palliser purchased Andover House in 1865, and renamed it Draycott Villa. From 1870 to 1879 it was the residence of Mr. Robert Vetch Grahame. For a short while it was the home of Madame Patti. In the last-named year Captain Palliser sold the house to Mr. William Holman Hunt, the distinguished painter and one of the founders of the Pre-Raphaelite movement. Mrs. Alice Meynell, describing Holman Hunt's Fulham home in the "Art Annual" for 1893, writes:

> "The house itself is not remarkable for its architecture - it is a house of its period, and has at least the look of privacy which its period prized. And it is a house that has more or less moulded itself upon the ways of its inhabitants, and has been shaped by their quiet pleasures and their leisurely necessities. A bow the more, a lengthened window, are amongst the signs of long occupation, interest and attention. The ivy has had time not only to grow, but to be pruned and clipped, and to grow again, until it fits window and porch like a glove."

The chief rooms of Draycott Lodge are low and long. The drawing-room and the dining-room were turned by the great artist into veritable museums of Eastern art. Attached to the house is a pleasant grassy lawn, overhung with trees, and cooled in summer time by a plashing fountain. Mr. Hunt's studio is at the back of the house.

Next to Draycott Lodge stands Laurel Bank House, a residence, enclosed by a high wall, standing in pleasant grounds which measure 1a. 1r. 20p. The original freehold of this estate was purchased of Francis Gotobed by Alexander Catcott in the year 1720. The piece of ground is thus described in a schedule of the Catcott property in the possession of John Rooth, Esq., of Laurel Bank House:

> "Half an acre of garden ground, and one Cottage (formerly two) lying in the p^{ish} of fulham, abutting for almost the whole length on the east and west sides on garden ground, now or lately belonging to Ric^d Lant of Kingston, Gent., and shooting tow^d the North on a p^{ce} of land called Bumbey, [*i,e*, Bombay's, *q. v.*] and abutting on the south, on the road leading from parson's green to fulham, called also the King's road from London to fulham bridge."

This cottage became a tavern, at first called the "Duke of Cumberland's Head," a name subsequently shortened to the "Duke's Head." The alehouse stood on the south-east corner of the property which we are about to describe, facing the New King's Road. The date of its erection is not known. It is not unlikely that it was originally styled in honour of the Duke of Cumberland, the victor of Culloden in 1746.

The date of the erection of the original Laurel Bank House is not known. From a plan of the "Duke's Head Alehouse," circa 1768, it appears that, behind the "Duke's Head," lay a yard and garden, while, on the site where the present Laurel Bank House stands, was "An handsome House," let to a Mr. Kimes. From this person, old Laurel Bank House passed into the possession of Lady Lonsdale. In a later plan of the Catcott estate, the house is described as

> "A Handsome house formerly in the possession of Mr. Kimes, since in the possession of Lady Lonsdale, but lately much improved and is now in the possession of Mr. Justice Hyde of famous Memory."

This was Mr. William Hyde, the magistrate. Among the items of disbursements in the accounts of the Churchwardens for 1794 is the following:

> "Paid at the Duke's Head expences of the Jury who sate on the body of Mr. Hodgson's carter 8s. 0d."

In its later days the "Duke's Head" was occupied by a "French immegrant." Justice Hyde, in 1802, pulled down the alehouse and built on the site "a new white house." Curiously enough, another "Duke's Head" arose in the King's Road, near the corner of Peterborough Place. Justice Hyde was succeeded by Colonel, subsequently General, Bradshaw of the Guards.

Though Laurel Bank House remained in the possession of the Catcotts, it does not appear to have been occupied by them. Charles Mathews, the comedian, occupied the house from 1811 to 1814. He was the father of the younger Mathews, who, in later years, also lived in the King's Road and at Holcroft's in the Fulham Road. The elder Mathews was the son of a bookseller, who, when the stage proved more attractive to his son than the shop, gave him twenty guineas and his indentures, with permission to follow his inclinations, and twenty guineas more if he would abandon histrionics and "turn to an honest calling." For sixteen years previous to his death this talented comedian was accustomed to entertain audiences by his single efforts in a species of entertainment entitled "Mathews at Home." He died at Liverpool,

28 June 1835. In 1838 the "Memoirs of Charles Mathews" was published by his widow. Speaking of his pecuniary embarrassments, Mrs. C. Mathews remarks:

> "These difficulties were occasioned by the inconsiderate purchase of a cottage, which, in his overweening love for a country residence, he had prematurely bought of General Bradshaw in the King's Road, Fulham, although he could not conceal from himself that the first outlay and expence of starting it must inevitably prevent him from enjoying it except by snatches."

Mathews sold the lease of his Fulham cottage to a Mr. James Thompson. About 1841-47 Laurel Bank House was the home of Charles Joseph Hullmandel, of whom we shall speak in connection with Dungannon House.

Old Laurel Bank House.
From an original sketch plan in the possession of John Rooth, Esq.

In 1872 the house was rebuilt by Mr. John Rooth, the father of John Rooth, Esq., the present owner and occupier, a descendant of the Catcotts. Alexander Catcott, who bought the property in 1720, had a granddaughter, Augusta Catcott, who married Mr. Richard

Smith, a surgeon of Bristol, the home of the Catcotts. Her brother, Mr. Thomas Catcott, at his death, left the property to his nephew, another Richard Smith, a surgeon of Bristol. The last named devised the property to two sisters, co-heiresses, the Misses Smith, one of whom married Mr. John Rooth, and the other, Mr. Goodwin Rooth, respectively the father and uncle of the present owner. The leases of the property fell in in 1865, and since then they have been held in fee simple, trustees being appointed to manage the estate.

Laurel Bank House is a handsome residence. Its spacious hall is a noteworthy feature. The drawing-room and the dining-room are pleasant apartments overlooking the well-kept grounds, in which, to the present day, may be seen the stump (now covered with ivy) of the old tree which is such a prominent feature in the back view of Justice Hyde's house.

On the west side of Munster Road, at its junction with the New King's Road, stood Vine Cottage, known in its later days as Belle Vue Lodge, taken in 1833 by Mrs. Hannah Walford. Mr. John S. Clarke, the popular actor, was here in 1872. The house was pulled down a few years ago. Its grounds were 1a. 2r. 31p.

Along the New King's Road, on the east side of Munster Road, lay a piece of nursery ground (extending back to Rectory Road), the property of the Osbornes and afterwards of the Veitches. Here was a large glass house, in which the flowers and plants were exhibited. Adjacent to it was a seed warehouse.

A few yards further east, just before Parson's Green is reached, was a house known as "The Shrubbery," which stood back from the road in a large garden. Here lived Oliver Frederick Stocken. It was taken in 1869 by Mr. William Watling, of pork pie fame. The grounds were 1a. 0r. 26½p.

SOUTH SIDE

One of the most celebrated nurseries in Fulham, and one of the last to survive, was the establishment known as Osborne's in the New King's Road. It extended from near the western end of this thoroughfare as far as the grounds of Ivy Cottage, its southern limits being Back Lane, now Hurlingham Road.

The history of Fulham Nursery, as it was formerly called, dates back to the Grays, market gardeners in the time of George I and George II. From them it went to William Burchell and his nephew, Matthew Burchell. About 1813 it passed into the hands of Messrs. Whitley and Co., otherwise Messrs. Whitley, Brames and Milne. In 1845 the Rate books give the style of the firm as Messrs. Whitley and Osborne, but, in the following year, it appears as Messrs. Osborne.

The Osbornes, who held the lease of Fulham Nursery from the Burchell trustees, were one of the most respected families in Fulham. Mr. William Osborne, the first of the family associated with the firm, died in 1824. For years the business was conducted under the style of Messrs. Robert Osborne and Sons. On the death, in 1868, of Mr. Robert Osborne, the nursery was continued by his sons, William and Thomas. Lastly, Mr. Robert Osborne, junior, a son of Mr. Thomas Osborne, succeeded to the nursery. The business was broken up in 1882, when the Burchells sold the property for building purposes.

Faulkner, who calls it the Fulham Nursery and Botanic Garden, tells us that amongst the botanists and travellers who enriched it by their contributions, were Mark Catesby, Peter Collinson and Philip Miller. A part of Bishop Compton's collection at Fulham Palace is said to have been sold to the nursery in the time of Bishop Robinson. When Faulkner wrote, Fulham Nursery still contained many rare trees, such as the *quercus suber*, or cork tree, the *ailanthus glandulosa*, or tree of heaven, the *quercus rubra*, or red oak, the *pishamin Virginianum*, or Virginian date plum, the *Celtis Occidentalis*, or nettle-tree, etc.

A private path between high ornamental hedges led from the New King's Road to Back Lane. About the centre of this stood a pretty Tudor Gothic lodge, called Ivy Villa, the residence of some of the members of the Osborne family. Near this house was a very remarkable tree called the Fulham Oak. The nursery covered 19a. 3r. 6p.

Almost facing Draycott Lodge stood Churchfield House, long the home of the Burchell family, by whom it was built over a century ago. The name, of course, recalls the ancient Churchfield, on a portion of the site of which it stood.

The Burchells were a family of well-to-do gardeners, who came to Fulham early in the reign of George III. The first we hear of them is in 1770 when William Burchell obtained from the

Bishop of London a lease of part of Great Hurlingham Field which, in 1760, had been granted to Christopher Gray, gardener. In 1773 he obtained 7 acres in Churchfield. Other leases followed, the Burchell estate extending, as we have just seen, along the King's Road as far as Ivy Cottage, which it eventually included.

The Library, Osborne's Nursery.
From a photograph by Mr. H Ambridge

William Burchell, who took his nephew, Matthew, into partnership, died 25 February 1800, and was buried in Fulham Churchyard, where his wife Jane had been interred three years previously. Matthew Burchell died 12 July 1828, being buried in the family vault. His widow, Jane, died 18 January 1841. Mrs. Burchell is rated for Churchfield House down to 1831. In 1832, and thence regularly down to 1863, the assessments are in the name of William John Burchell, D.C.L., its most noteworthy occupant.

This famous African traveller, the eldest son of Matthew Burchell, was the first explorer who demonstrated that the "Dark Continent" could be opened up via the Zambesi. His first appointment was that of schoolmaster and acting botanist at the Island of St. Helena. On 15 February 1808, he was elected a

Fellow of the Linnæan Society of London. At St. Helena he .made the acquaintance of John Janssens, the last Dutch Governor of the Cape, and Dr. Martin Lichtenstein, the naturalist. Burchell, in 1811, left St. Helena for the Cape, for the purpose of exploring the interior of the country. His travels lasted about four years, during which period he brought together some 63,000 natural objects, besides which he amassed huge collections of astronomical, meteorological and other observations and notes.

In 1822-24 he published his "Travels in Southern Africa," long regarded as a standard work and a model of literary style. In 1825 Dr. Burchell explored Brazil, returning home in 1829. In 1834 the University of Oxford conferred on him the degree of D.C.L.

The doctor was a curious old gentleman, about whom some strange stories are told. Mr. E. Lacey Robinson, in a letter which is preserved at the Fulham Free Library, remarks:

> "The oldest inhabitant may remember Dr. Burchell and the tame ocelot or small panther which wandered about his house and grounds, much to the alarm o£ any nervous lady or gentleman who might happen to call on him."

Dr. W. J. Burchell. From a drawing by T. H. Maguire, 1854

On 23 March 1863, Dr. Burchell shot himself under the large cedar tree in front of Churchfield House. The wound not proving fatal, he terminated his existence by hanging himself in a small outhouse at the back. The doctor, who was in his eightieth year, was buried in the family vault at Fulham. The Church Registers record:

1863. Wm. John Burchell, Fulham bu. 28 Mar.

His botanical collections were presented to Kew Gardens after his decease; his manuscripts are now in the Library there. Besides being an indefatigable naturalist, Dr. Burchell was a good artist and musician.

Miss Anna Burchell, his sister, died at Churchfield House, 2 October 1863, and was also buried in Fulham Churchyard. This lady, by her will, dated 8 April 1865, left £200 3 per cent Consols for the maintenance of the family tombs and the relief of the poor. The fund is now included in the United Charities.

In 1867 Churchfield House was taken by Mr. John Thomas Dicks, the owner of *Bow Bells*. He refronted the house and greatly improved the property. Mr. Jonas Turner, the well-known bootmaker, took Churchfield House in 1871. From 1880-82 the house was occupied by Mr. John George Waite. Its last resident was Mr. A. Moseley, the District Surveyor.

During Mr. Moseley's residence Churchfield House was further improved. Its heavy red-tiled, pitched roof was removed and another floor added. The old house had a door in the centre, fronting the road. To the right of this entrance, which was approached by a drive, was the library, subsequently a dining-room, an interesting apartment, panelled to the ceiling. To the left was the drawing-room. Between these was the staircase, evidently the original one. When Cristowe Road was formed, on the east side, the front entrance was done away with, and a door made at the side. From this led a corridor crossing what was once the drawingroom. At the rear was a large billiard-room.

In Maclure's "Survey" the grounds are given as 1a. 2r. 20p. Lewes House (No. 347, New King's Road), the residence of Mr. Sydney Knight, Ranelagh Mansions, built in 1896, and Churchfield Mansions, built in 1898, mark the frontage of the grounds to the main road. Churchfield House was demolished in the last named year.

On the east side of Ashington Road stand the Church of the Holy Cross and the Roman Catholic Schools. The latter were built by Canon Keens in 1884. In 1886 the church, a temporary edifice, was opened. It seats 300 persons.

Churchfield House.
From a photograph by Mr. T. S. Smith, 1896

Continuing our way westwards along the south side of the New King's Road, we arrive at the site of Ivy Cottage, which stood at the north-west corner of Broom Lane, now Broomhouse Road. This curious old cottage was situated in the midst of an equally quaint garden, 3a. 0r. 28p. in extent. Faulkner states that, in his day, a tradition existed to the effect that, on the site of Ivy Cottage, there was once a house which had been the residence of Oliver Cromwell, called the Old Red Ivy House, and that part of the walls of this building formed the west side of Ivy Cottage. There are few parishes around London which do not enjoy some supposed association with the memory of the Protector, and to this class Fulham forms no exception. A careful examination of all available records has failed to afford us the least evidence that Oliver Cromwell ever sojourned in Fulham. On this point we have already touched in our account of Passor's. In Rocque's "Map" (1741-45), a house is shown as standing on the site of the cottage which we are about to describe, but no memorials exist regarding it.

Ivy Cottage, a long, low, picturesque tenement, was constructed by Mr. Walsh Porter about the year 1802. It was built in a style which may be described as a debased Gothic. Faulkner, speaking of this "unique villa," writes:

> "The whole, comprising about five acres, is enclosed in a ring-fence, and has the appearance, from its situation, of a complete wood. The grounds, garden, and pasture-land are beautifully laid out. The farm is the exact model of one near Leyden in Holland."

Mr. Walsh Porter resided here till 1805, when he moved to Pryor's Bank. Sir Robert Barclay, 8th baronet, to whom he sold Ivy Cottage, came of an ancient Ayrshire family. For some years Sir Robert was employed by the Government on confidential missions to the Continent. In 1798 he fell into the hands of the French, who imprisoned him in the Temple. He was twice tried by a Military Commission, but was on each occasion acquitted. In Nov. 1799 he was released and sent to England by the special orders of Napoleon Bonaparte. Sir Robert lived at Ivy Cottage till 1817.

Ivy Cottage. From a photograph by Mr. H. Ambridge.

Faulkner, who visited Ivy Cottage in Sir Robert Barclay's time, gives a detailed description of its apartments. In later years the exterior was very considerably altered, especially the entrances to the house and stables.

The following cutting from a newspaper, published in 1818, is preserved in Faulkner's copy of his "History."

"Ivey Cottage, near Parson's Green, Fulham, little more than 3 miles from Hyde Park Corner — To be sold for an unexpired term of 15 years these desirable premises with the furniture complete fit for the immediate reception of a family of distinction. The house consists of good spacious dining and drawing rooms with a beautiful library, 3 best bedrooms and good attics, kitchen, servants' hall, housekeeper's room, larder and cellaring; detached is a small cottage fitted up at a great expense and containing a capital laundry with various bed and other rooms, a large double coach-house, 6 stalled stable, excellent poultry yard, pigeon house, garden and tool houses, etc., and other requisites; a greenhouse stocked with plants; a small hot-house, pleasure grounds, most tastefully laid out and extensively planted, a large garden stocked in the best manner and a paddock adjoining. The whole containing about 4 acres in the most perfect condition.

For further particulars, apply to Messrs. White & Fownes, Lincoln's Inn, where tickets for viewing the premises may be had."

Ivy Cottage. From an engraving by I. Matthews, after a drawing by I. H. A. Hassell, in the "Antiquarian Itinerary," 18 April 1817

The property was purchased by the Burchells, who let it to various tenants. Here, on 15 March 1827, died Mr. James Thompson, who lies buried in Fulham Churchyard.

In 1842 it became the residence of Mr., afterwards Sir, John

Dean Paul, bart., partner in the banking firm of Strachan, Paul and Bates. In 1854 the firm was rather a respectable credit, having a small, but very good, private connection. In 1855 the awkward discovery was made that the partners had been using their customers' money for their own pleasures or necessities. They were prosecuted, convicted and sentenced to fourteen years' transportation. On his liberation, Sir J. D. Paul changed his name and went to Australia. Returning to England, he died at St. Albans in 1868. An interesting account of the famous failure and trial will be found in "Facts, Failures and Frauds."

In 1850 Ivy Cottage was taken by Dr. Travers Cox. In 1858 it became the residence of Mr. E. T. Smith, of "Bloomer" costume fame, one of the world's born showmen, and owner of Drury Lane Theatre. During his tenancy he called the cottage Drury Lodge. Its next noteworthy occupant was the Rev. Robert George Baker, M.A., Vicar of Fulham from 1834 to 1871. He retired hither on his resignation of the vicarage. Here he died, 21 Feb. 1878, at the advanced age of 90. By his will, dated 30 Mar. 1872, he left a personal estate worth £40,000.

To perpetuate the old tradition in reference to the Protector, the house was, for awhile, renamed Cromwell Lodge. It was, in 1884, taken down and the site built over.

SECTION III:
PARSON'S GREEN TO WATERFORD ROAD

The next section of our journey comprises the remainder of the New King's Road, namely, from Parson's Green to Waterford Road.

NORTH SIDE

Resuming our route along the north side, we cross the south side of Parson's Green. Passing the end of East End Road, we reach the Poole Park estate, a Estate. collection of modern streets of no particular interest. One of these, Crondace Road, runs parallel with the New King's Road, from which it is separated by a narrow strip of land, now regarded as a portion of Eelbrook Common. Parallel with Crondace Road are Delvino, Ackmar,

Basuto and Campana Roads, while at right angles to Crondace Road are Molesford, Irene, Elthiron, Parthenia and Favart Roads. In Ackmar Road is the Ackmar Road Board School, opened 13 April 1885. It was enlarged (400 places) in 1892. It accommodates 480 boys, 480 girls, and 630 infants; total, 1590.

The Poole Park estate, which glories in the possession of such classically named thoroughfares, marks a portion of the site of Aston's or Austin's Field.

This was one of the oldest place-names in Fulham. In the Court Rolls it appears as early as 1386. The district to which the name was applied was a very extensive tract, bordering on what is now the New King's Road. It lay between Parson's Green on the west, and Eelbrook on the east.

Aston's, or Austin's, is a corrupt form of Augustine's. The name is spelled in a variety of ways: Austeyne's, Austyne's, Austine's, Austen's, Awsten's, Aston's, etc.

Aston's, or Austin's, Field, was let by the Lord of the Manor to his tenants in acre and half-acre strips, in accordance with the custom of feudal times. The Court Rolls contain a vast multitude of entries relating to admissions to, and surrenders of, these strips. One or two specimens will serve to show their general character. In 1517 Sir Sampson Norton, of Parson's Green, surrendered eight acres in "Astonfeld" to the use of John Norton. Ralph Parker, of King's Langley, in 1552, surrendered to Henry Parker, his son, "one acre in Astonfeld," to which he had been admitted on the death of his father, John Parker. The following order was enforced at a Court General held in 1577:

> "All tenants of lands in Austens fyld abutting upon the Common of Hellbrooke to make their ditches."

Sir Thomas Smith, of Brightwell's, died seized of "one parcel in a certain field called Austene feild." The last mention of Austin's Field, which we have observed in the Court Rolls, occurs under the year 1740.

Thomas Bonde, who died in 1600, left 2¼ acres of freeland in this field for the benefit of the poor of Fulham. This gift is fully described in the ancient "Register Book." We have already spoken of it in our account of the Bonde monument (See vol. I, Chapter

XIII: Fulham Church: Its Monuments and Epitaphs). The site, known as Bondfield, was certainly identifiable down to the beginning of this century, though it cannot now be ascertained.

Leaving the Poole Park estate, we arrive at the open space known as Eelbrook Common. In ancient times this was a portion of the Waste of the Manor, a boggy swamp, extremely dangerous to wayfarers.

The Common, as we now know it, lies, roughly speaking, between the District Railway on the north, the New King's Road on the south, Favart Road on the west, and Musgrave Crescent on the east. A narrow piece of the Eelbrook, as we have said, extends westwards, between Crondace Road and the New King's Road. This strip used to be known as Fulham Common. The present extent of Eelbrook is about 13½ acres, but in olden times it was much larger.

The origin of the name "Eelbrook," has given rise to a good deal of guesswork, and the fact that eels have been caught in the old brook here has been deemed sufficient evidence to account for the present appellation of the Common. The spelling, "Eelbrook," is, however, quite modern and a mere accommodation. As far as we have been able to trace, it does not occur before the present century.

In the Court Rolls for 1410, the Common is termed the "Hillebrook." In 1442 we have "Hellebrook." Later on we find the spellings "Helbrook" and "Hilbrook." Then, the aspirate falling away, we have Elbrook, or Ellbrook, and finally Eelbrook. In the absence of a 13th century spelling, two conjectures are possible. The 15th century spelling is always dubious as to the final "e." Hence the "Hellebrook," which occurs in 1442, may have been, in the 13th century, either Helbrook or Hellebrook. Helbrook may mean "hill-brook," which is by far the most rational explanation of the name. In the Anglo-Saxon word "hyll," meaning an elevation of the ground of considerable size, the "y" was sounded like the German "ü" in "glück." This split, dialectically, into (a) "hill" in the north and midland districts, "hull" in the southern, and "hell" in Kent. But the form "hell," though strictly Kentish, was known in some places outside the dialect. The meaning "hill-brook" is not only etymologically possible, but also geographically probable. "A hill" in the vicinity of Eelbrook is several times referred to in the older Court Rolls. Thus, at a View in 1442, Thomas Hasele was presented because he had six perches of his ditch "at the hill against hellebrook" unscoured. The sense "hell-brook" is, however, just possible, the Middle English word for "hell" being "hellé," a dissyllabic form which often occurs in compounds such as "helle-put," the pit of hell. It would, however, be difficult to account for such a name as "hell-brook," for our ancestors could hardly have likened the shallow little stream, which trickled down to the Thames, to a bottomless depth.

We will now take in review some of the references to the Common found in the old records of the parish. The first mention is in the minutes of a View held in 1410, when John Norbury was presented for an unscoured ditch at "Hillebrook." In 1442 Thomas Hasele was amerced "vj^d" because he had

> "accroached to himself from the common of hellebrook . . . in his lands next a certain parcell containing in length xx perches and in breadth x feet where he has cut a ditch to the great prejudice of the Lord and of his Lordship of ffulham and to the common nuisance of the tenants."

This Thomas Hasele was the owner of Rosamond's, which, in the neighbourhood of Parson's Green Lane, must have bordered upon "Hellebrook." John Shireborne, in 1448, was presented for an unscoured ditch at "Hellebrook."

Elbrook Common, looking towards Southfield Farm.
From a watercolour drawing by Miss Jane Humphreys

Until modern times Eelbrook was partially hedged round by ditches, while others crossed the surface of the Common. The Rev. John Kirkeby, a tenant of Sandford Manor, was, in 1454, presented for blocking "a ditch called Hellebrookdyk." In 1473 Dame de Wavers was, like the previous owner of Rosamonds, presented for encroaching on "the Common called Helbrook." Three years later she was required at a View to scour "the ditch called Helbrook-ditch."

In the same year (1476) Thomas Coxston was presented because he had "a ditch not scoured in Helbrook called Helbrookdich." In 1493 three tenants of the Manor were presented on account of the state of their ditches "in Elbroke." John Powell, for keeping three cows upon "the Common of Helbroke," was, in 1577, fined 10s. At a Court, in 1603, certain regulations were adopted regarding the depasturing of cattle on "Helbroke." In 1615 further forfeitures were laid down in the case of

> "all those persons or person that shall presume to put any cattle into any of our Commons before the accustomed times, that is to say, into Wormwold Wood and Helbrook, from Candlemas next until May eve, nor into our Common Fields or Meadows until all our corn and hay be cut down and carried away out of the fields or meadows."

In 1656 Col. Edmund Harvey, Lord of the Manor of Fulham, agreed to pay 50s. yearly to the poor "for taking in the Common called Helbrook." Harvey's attainder, following soon afterwards, probably frustrated this iniquitous "agreement." The following entry in the minutes of a Court General, in 1658, is of interest:

> "Thomas Betham did stopp upp the passage and way into a certaine place of Comon called Helbrooke and would not let one Stephen Read, a tennant unto Mr. Thomas Wyld, coppyholder of this Mannor of whome hee holdeth Coppyhold land of the same Thomas and so hath right of Comon there to put his two horses into the same unles hee would pay him v[s] the w[ch] for that purpose he received the same v[s] therefore he is amerced v[s]."

The first we hear of a keeper for the Common is in the minutes of a Court Baron in 1682, when William Rochford was appointed "woodkeeper for Hellbrooke." In the time of William and Mary,

Eelbrook Common fell into a deplorable condition,

> "The said Comon being overflowne and become of litle use or benefitt to ye Comon^{rs} for want of scowring and cleansing ye Ditches thereof and draining the same by reason that certaine Whelmes and Floodgates erected for the drayning thereof are much out of repaire and in great decay, And the water continuing upon the said Comon makes the same noysome."

To cover the cost of draining and placing the Common in order the Homage ordered that each tenant should pay 40s. for every head of cattle put in. In 1694 Mr. Robert Limpany was chosen "Treasurer for ye Comon of Helbroke." A fine of 20s. was, at this Court, inflicted upon William Tucker for "breaking up the lock of the floodgate belonging to Hellbrooke." The Homage in 1696 presented:

> "We order that noe person or persons whatsoever shall put any cattle into the Comon of Helbrooke. before publick notice shall be given in the Church for that purpose by the Treasurer for the time being upon payne of forfeiting to the Lord of this Manor xx^s a head."

The Homage, in 1701, laid down the following regulations:

> "Wee p'sent and order That every person that shall turne into the Comon of Helbrook haueing any right of Comon shall pay for every head hee soe turns in for the ensueing yeare one shilling and for every head soe turned in and not paid for the same to bee pounded till six shillings eight pense bee paid to the use of the Lord of this Mannor And that all cattle that shall bee turned in by persons haueing noe right of comon to bee pounded till they pay six shillings and eight pence to the Lord of this Mannor."

Abuses in regard to commoning grew to such an extent that we find the following presentment laid before the Court Baron in 1727:

> "We also present the Printed Orders here annex'd as part of our presentment tho' it was presented at this Court as it appears in the first of King James the First tho' but little minded as We Observ'd since, Therefore We the now Jury Impannell'd (or some of us) being sensible

of the growing Abuses more and more every year think fitt to present additional orders for a more speedy method to preserve our comoning.

We present any person that shall hereafter buy any horse or cow for one shilling or the like small sum purely to impose upon the Tenants of their herbage that season and then to exchange the horse or cow for the said shilling such persons both buyer and seller shall forfeit the sum of Forty Shillings one third to the Lord one third to the informer and one third to the Treasurer then in being for the repairs of the Fences and Roads to the said Comon.

We present that upon oath if it shall appear that the Wood Keeper at anytime shall connive or keep secret any person guilty of the above fraud and not to discover the same to the then Overseers shall forfeit the like sum of Forty Shillings and it is to be distributed as above.

...

We present Hellbrook as a Wett peice of Comon and if the Overseer does not understand the proper times of scouring and cleansing the ditches and the proper materials that is to be laid upon the Boggy slows in the Comon to preserve the cattle that then the Overseer is to let three or four of the Homage to Joyn with him in this Transaction that the Tenants may have the more Benefit of the herbage for now the said Comon is in a very Ruinous condition.

...

We also present any person that will turn any Cow or Horse into Hellbrook in any other way than Walham Green shall forfeit Twenty Shillings per head to ye Lord of the Manor."

The following entry occurs in the disbursements of the Overseers for 1770:

"Paid 20 Jurymen (groats) as satt on the inquisition touching the death of Mary Collins who was drowned in the Hell Brook 6s. 8d."

In 1773 John Powell Powell paid £100 "for apiece of land taken from the Common called Elbrook," the interest arising therefrom to be divided equally between Fulham and Hammersmith and distributed in bread and meat to the poor. In 1785 further orders were made regarding "Elbroke otherwise Helbroke Common."

Faulkner describes Eelbrook as consisting of eleven acres of land "which might with little expense be converted into excellent garden ground." In his day it served merely for the grazing of a few head of cattle. The Church Registers record:

1828. A male child found murdered on Eelbrook 9th Mar 1828 supposed about six weeks bu. 12 Mar.

In 1878 the Ecclesiastical Commissioners enclosed the portion of Eelbrook formerly known as Fulham Common with a view to its sale. On 13 March of that year a monster protest meeting was held at Beaufort House. Subsequently some of the less law-abiding inhabitants adjourned to the disputed site and made a bonfire of the fences. Nothing further in the matter was ever done by the Commissioners.

Until comparatively recent times a twelve-foot ditch ran round the Common. There was also another across the centre. The ditches were well stocked with fish, including carp, tench, roach, eels, etc. Some seventy years ago an otter was caught in Eelbrook ditch.

In 1832 horse and pony races were held on Eelbrook in commemoration of the passing of the great Reform Bill. The old pound, on its removal from Walham Green, was re-erected at the north end of Eelbrook. Mr. S. J. Walden and Mr. B. T. Wright were the last treasurers of Eelbrook.

Eelbrook Common is now under the control of the London County Council. It has been bordered all round by young trees and large numbers of shrubs have been planted upon it. A drinking fountain was added in 1894.

The subsoil of Eelbrook consists of rich black mould, capable of growing almost anything. Market gardeners, on several occasions, have made unsuccessful attempts to purchase it.

Leaving Eelbrook we arrive at Harwood Road. At its south-west corner is the Harwood Road Board School, opened 27 Oct. 1873, and enlarged (421 places) in 1878. It accommodates 392 boys, 355 girls and 441 infants; total, 1,188. It was the first Board School built in Fulham.

Before the formation of Broxholme Road there existed, between Eelbrook or Hillbrook Terrace and Sands End Lane, a peculiar bend in the New King's Road. In this angle stood Water Slade Court, the residence of Colonel W. Harwood. The name Harwood Terrace is now applied to what was, before the formation of Broxholme Road, the bend in the New King's Road. We will now return to Parson's Green, taking the South Side.

SOUTH SIDE

That portion of the south side between Broomhouse Road and Peterborough House we shall deal with under Parson's Green.

On 11 Jan. 1810, at Garraway's famous Coffee House in 'Change Alley, Cornhill, Mr. White bought under the hammer a piece of land, on which a few houses had already been erected, thus described in the auctioneer's catalogue:

> "Particulars of a valuable freehold estate consisting of about 26 acres of excellent garden ground with house and buildings thereon, a meadow or paddock with a cottage and iron gates bordered by a young plantation and a grove of fine young thriving timber trees, the whole having a frontage extending from Sands End to Peterborough House, a most eligible situation for the erection of villas or houses, being on the south side of the King's Road near Parson's Green, Fulham, Middlesex, only three miles from Hyde Park Corner and in one of the most select roads round the Metropolis."

Pomona Place. From a photograph by Mr. T. S. Smith, 1896

The site was disposed of in eight lots as shown in the subjoined sketch. Lot 1, including a house and building thereon, was in the occupation of Richard Wilcox, gardener; Lot 2, in the occupation of William Wilcox, gardener, was sold subject to an old "Mount," situated in it, being reserved out of the lease, with a right of way to it from the King's Road. Lots 4 and 5 comprised the grove of fine thriving young timber trees next to the King's Road and extending back to the wall of Lot 1. Lots 6, 7 and 8 consisted of the meadow or paddock anciently known as Pesecroft, Peasecroft or Pearscroft. The whole estate sold for £7,645.

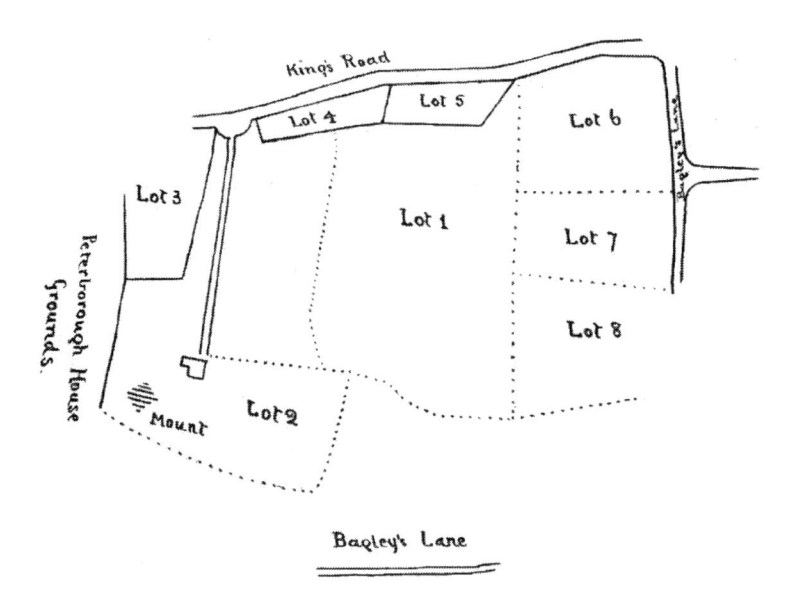

Plan of Pomona Place Estate

The "grove of fine thriving young timber trees" soon gave place to a line of houses, called Pomona Place, in allusion, possibly, to the neighbouring orchards of Peterborough House. Pomona Place was completed about 1823.

The "Peterborough Hotel," No. 65, New King's Road, was built in 1892. The original "Peterborough Arms" was erected about 1773, at a spot nearly adjoining Peterborough House, whence, of course, its name. The first house on the present site was built in 1831-32 by John Knight, of Walham Green. The "Peterborough Arms" is almost too modern to possess a history of any importance. It was in the parlour of this house that, on 12 June 1833, the first benevolent society was founded in Fulham, and to it it gave its name. It was here, down to 1850, when a move was made to the "Red Lion" at Walham Green, that the weekly meetings of the Peterborough Benevolent Society were held.

Just beyond the "Peterborough Hotel" is Wandsworth Bridge

Road, which runs southwards to Wandsworth Bridge. The late Fulham District Board of Works was involved in a tiresome litigation with the Wandsworth Bridge Company regarding this road. Eventually it was decided that the Board should make the thoroughfare, the Company previously depositing a sum of £1,750 in payment of the estimated cost. The Wandsworth Bridge Road is now a fine broad thoroughfare, lined with neat red-brick houses, the colour of which is relieved by the pleasant green trees planted along each side.

Starting from the south end of Wandsworth Bridge Road and taking the east side, the first point of interest is St. Matthew's Church, at the south-west corner of Rosebury Road. The St. Matthew's Mission was founded in 1884. A substantial brick and slate Mission Room was erected, the foundation stone of which was laid by Miss Sulivan, 19 May 1884. The building, which is capable of holding 250 persons, was opened by the Bishop of London on 1 August of the same year. In 1893 the permanent church was commenced on a site presented by Miss Sulivan. On 23 Oct. of that year the Duchess of Albany laid the foundation stone. On 27 April 1895 the church was consecrated by the Bishop of London. St. Matthew's seats 847 persons. The architects were Sir Arthur Blomfield and Sons, and the builders, Messrs. S. E. Parmenter and Sons.

A district taken entirely out of the parish of St. James was assigned to the new church in August 1895, and formed into a separate parish. The patronage of the church is in the hands of trustees, who, with their friends, contributed £2,000 towards its erection. The cost of the church, including fittings, was £7,925.

On the north side of Broughton Road, at its junction with the Wandsworth Bridge Road, is a Primitive Methodist Chapel, built in 1892. Along the front are numerous memorial stones, the central one being inscribed:

"This stone was laid by Mrs. H. Lowenfeld Sept. 1st, 1892. Rev. G. Spooner, minister, W. Wray, architect, Atkin & Green, builders."

On the west side, in Hugon Road, is the Hugon Road Board School, opened 29 Oct. 1894. It accommodates 360 boys, 360 girls and 466 infants; total, 1,186.

The South Branch of the Fulham Public Library (No. 132) stands on a site given by Miss Sulivan. A tablet on a wall at the entrance records that the building was designed by Messrs. Arthur Billing, Son and Rowle, and that it was opened by Mr. W. H. Fisher, M.P., 20 Jan. 1896. The builder was Mr. J. F. Collinson.

At the south end of the road is Wandsworth Bridge, which connects Fulham with Wandsworth. This structure was designed by Mr. J. H. Tolmé, and constructed by Messrs. C. de Bergue and Co.

The Bridge was promoted by a company which, by the Wandsworth Bridge Act, 1864, was empowered to raise a capital of £80,000.

On 27 September 1873, the Bridge, which had been about two years in course of construction, was formally opened by the late Colonel (subsequently Sir) J. McGarel Hogg, then Chairman of the Metropolitan Board of Works.

Wandsworth Bridge. From a photograph by Mr. T. S. Smith, 1895

The total cost was about £40,000. It is divided into five spans. Those at either end are 113 ft. 6 in. each, and the three in the stream are 133 ft. 4 in. each. The headway of the end spans is 14 feet clear, rising, in the centre span, to 20 feet clear. The structure is supported by eight wrought iron cylinders ranged in pairs. The cylinders, which are 7 feet in diameter, are filled with concrete. They are sunk in the bed of the river to a depth of 14 ft. and rest on a substantial bed of concrete. They are ornamented with polished capitals and are braced together at the top, under the planking of the Bridge, by longitudinal ties. The road is carried by lattice girders, made continuous throughout. The main girders are connected by cross girders. Upon the latter are laid diagonally the sleepers, and upon these is placed a layer of planking longitudinally, the whole being covered with macadam and wood pavement to form a roadway. The width is 30 feet.

Wandsworth Bridge was declared free of toll by the Prince and Princess of Wales, 26 June 1880, the Metropolitan Board of Works having acquired the property for £52,761, with £500 additional for land.

Resuming our walk along the New King's Road we come to Eelbrook Terrace, perversely altered, in 1879, to Hillbrook Terrace. The continuation of this thoroughfare is known as Bagley's Lane, from Charles Bagley, a market gardener. To the left is the land of the Gas Light and Coke Company, laid out in plots and cultivated by the employees. From the northern end of Bagley's Lane, two or three genteel streets lead towards the newly built Wandsworth Bridge Road estate, but, passing these, we come across a region of poverty and squalor, commencing with Sandilands Road, a name which perpetuates the memory of the Rev. R. S. B. Sandilands. At the corner of Victoria Road is the "Queen Elizabeth." In Langford Road is the Langford Road Board School, opened 16 June 1890. It was enlarged (600 places) in 1892. It accommodates 480 boys, 480 girls and 635 infants; total, 1,595. At the corner of Stephendale Road is Grove House, of which we shall speak in connection with its famous namesake. Southwards, Bagley's Lane led to the now vanishing Town Meads.

At about the centre of Harwood Terrace is the Imperial Road, which runs parallel with Bagley's Lane. This thoroughfare was formed as the outcome of negotiations between the Fulham District Board of Works and the Imperial Gas Company, now the Gas Light and Coke Company, the latter body agreeing to pay £1,000, and to construct the road in consideration of the permission accorded them to partially close Sands End Lane. It was completed in 1879.

The land on the south side of the New King's Road, west of Eelbrook Terrace and Bagley's Lane, was anciently known as Peasecroft or Pearscroft. As early as 1425 the Court Rolls make mention of "Pesecroft." In 1576 if was ordered: "All the tenants of lands in Peasecroft abutting upon the Common of Helbroke to make their ditches sufficient." On a portion of the site of Peasecroft, Peterborough Villas were built.

Certain freelands in Peasecroft bore the name of Coffers, Cofferes, Coferes or Cofferers. Generally speaking, the "Manor" of Coffers was held by the owners of the freelands or "Manors" known as Rosamond's at Parson's Green and Lane's at Walham Green. In 1476 "the tenants of the lands called Coferes" were required to scour their ditches "in Pesecroft abutting upon Helbrook."

SECTION IV:
WATERFORD ROAD TO STANLEY BRIDGE

This section, which takes us to the parish boundary at Stanley Bridge, covers what is now known as the King's Road in contradistinction to the New King's Road which we have just traversed.

The eastern, like the western, end of this thoroughfare, was, in olden times, known by no special name. As late as 1686 it is described in the Court Rolls as "the highway leading from Sandyend to helbroke." In Rocque's "Map" of 1741-45, the thoroughfare from Waterford Road to Stanley Bridge is marked as "The King's Road."

NORTH SIDE

At the corner of Waterford Road is the "Lord Palmerston" (No. 648), a modern house dating from about 1862. Here, as we have mentioned, was a bar across the King's Road.

An amusing incident, in connection with this bar, occurred early in the century. A couple of men, who had engaged in a prize-fight on the Common facing Pomona Place, having settled their differences, started for London. When they neared the bar, the old woman in charge of it, having been apprised of events, sallied forth from the gatehouse, and, holding up a rusty old sword, in the King's name defied the evil-doers to pass. The two men promptly caught hold of her and, having locked her securely in her toll house, pursued their way in peace.

Where Cornwall Street now joins the King's Road was the

commencement of an old lane which swept round in a north-westerly direction, joining the Fulham Road near the northern end of Britannia Road. The next turning was Bull Alley, which ran northwards to the Fulham Road, on the site now marked by Stamford Street. Of Bull Alley we shall speak in our account of Fulham Road.

In the King's Road, at the south-west corner of Bull Alley, was a tavern known as the "Bull," mentioned in the Parish Books as early as 1713. One of Sir Richard Steele's letters to his wife, dated 9 Aug. 1710, is thus directed:

"To Mrs. Steele,
At Mrs. Bradshaw's house, at Sandy-end,
Over-against the Bull Alehouse, in Fulham-road."

By "Fulham Road" was doubtless intended the "King's Road." In the letter he tells Lady Steele to "come home by this morning's coach, if you are impatient, but if you are not here before noon, I will come down to you in the evening." In front of the "Bull," which was pulled down many years ago, were some seats for the use of customers, shaded by pleasant trees.

Just before reaching Stanley Bridge was another turning between the Fulham and King's Roads, known as Bull Lane. This, in later times, became Harriet Street, a name which, in 1888, was changed to Wandon Road. Here is Chelsea Station, built in 1866. When the railway was formed, Harriet Street was considerably raised. The old tenements on the west side still show the original level.

SOUTH SIDE

This ancient lane, which led from the eastern end of the "bend" in the King's Road to the Town Meadows, is now almost obliterated, the small portion, which still exists, bearing the designation of Waterford Road.

Sands End Lane, in olden times, was by far the most important thoroughfare in the neighbourhood of Sands End. In the Parish Books the earliest mention of the name is in 1646. At a Vestry, held on 19 May of that year,

"Information was brought in from Thomas Walter of Richard Coales in sand end lane keeping of 3 familyes being inmates in his house, lately out of Barnes and haue noe other profession but Begging."

The Vestry agreed that Thomas Walter should prosecute Coales "according to the statute in that case made and prouided." The greater portion of Sands End Lane is now incorporated in the site of the works of the Gas Light and Coke Company. (See vol. I, Chapter XVII: High Street East Side).

On the east side of Sands End Lane was a noted inn called the "Rose," a house which still exists under the name of the "Old Rose," while another "Rose," a more modern house, now faces it. The earliest notice of the "Rose" occurs in the minutes of a Court General in 1708, when

"Francis Whettman surrendered one cottage at Sandy End called by the name of the sign of the 'Rose' to the use of Richard Sanders of Fulham, innkeeper, and heirs."

In the Highway Rate books the house is mentioned under the year 1753:

"Paid two labourers to scavenge ye footpath from Mr. Bowacks to the Rose 3s. 0d."

The "Old Rose." From a photograph by Mr. T. S. Smith, 1895

The sporting fraternity were great patrons of the "Rose." Shooting competitions were not infrequent events at this house. Here is one for 1839:

> "The 'Rose.' To be shot for at the 'Rose,' Sandsend, Fulham, on Monday the 8th April 1839, a very handsome chased silver snuffbox by twelve members at nine sparrows each. Entrance 6/6. To be handicapped, 16 and 19 yards rise; 40 yards bounds. To commence at two o'clock. The box at the bar for inspection."

Ben Gaunt, the pugilist, was a patron of the "Rose" in its palmy days.

It was in a cottage at Sands End Lane that John Bowack lived from 1730 down to 1756. He seems to have moved here from Church Street, Chelsea, where, in 1705-6, he commenced to publish "The Antiquities of Middlesex." In 1731 he paid a fine of £5 5s. "for being excused serving the office of overseer." In his younger days Bowack, who wrote a beautiful hand, held the post of writing master at Westminster School. A fine specimen of his skill in penmanship is to be seen in Harleian Manuscript 1809, a thin vellum book containing two neat drawings in Indian ink, and various accounts of English books, etc., sent to Lord Oxford in December 1712. In July 1732 he received the appointment of Clerk to the Commissioners of the Turnpike Roads, and in 1737 he was made Assistant Secretary to the Westminster Bridge Commissioners. The Church Registers record:

> 1739. Dorothy W. of John Bowack bu. 13 Apl.

An old path ran from Sands End Lane to Bagley's Lane. In 1835 Mr. Robert Gunter paid £100 for permission to close it.

The "Hand and Flower," (No. 617, King's Road), was formerly a well-known inn, with pleasant tea-gardens and a bowling-ground. In the Parish Books it is not mentioned by name till 1845.

Passing Edith Row, formerly Barr's Alley, we come to Sotheron Road, formerly Grove Road, to Cambria Street, formerly Stanley Park Road, and to Little Stamford Street. At the back of these is Stanley Road, which runs from Waterford Road to

Cambria Street. South of this road are the Imperial Gas Works, of which we speak under Sands End.

No. 541, King's Road is the "Nell Gwynne," a comparatively modern house, which preserves the name of an older one which stood not far off. It was so named from the supposed association of Nell Gwynne with Sandford House.

Along this side of the King's Road was, in the latter part of the last century, a noted nursery, kept by Mr. Henry Parry ("Parry and Co."). It was sold by Mr. Raine at the "Rainbow Coffee House" in Cornhill, 22 April 1803. In the auctioneer's sale bill it is described as:

> "A very valuable freehold estate consisting of a plot of ground of 4 acres bounded on one side by Chelsea Creek and on another by the King's Private Road; in front of which it extends 162 feet, consisting of a small but neat brick dwelling house in front of the said King's Road with a piece of garden ground nearly encircled by a brick wall, held by Mr. Henry Parry, florist, at the low rent of 12 guineas per annum."

A good deal of confusion has hitherto existed between the old forms of the names of the bridges across the creek between Fulham and Chelsea.

The ancient name of the bridge over the creek, where it crossed the Fulham Road, was Samford or Sandford Bridge, *i.e.* the bridge at the sand ford. This we shall more fully touch on when we reach Stamford Bridge. The bridge which, in early days, continued the King's Road from Chelsea into Fulham was the "Stanbregge," or Stonebridge. No "ford" is ever added to the name, for the simple reason that, while at the more northern point on the Fulham Road, the creek was fordable, at the King's Road it was not.

The stone bridge on the King's road was, like the other bridges within the Manor, repairable by the Lord. The Court Rolls contain numerous references to its state of disrepair. The first is in 1409, when "Stonbregge" required amendment. The next mention of the bridge is in 1422, when the name is written "Stanbregge." In 1448 the Lord was called upon to amend "Stanbregge leading towards Fulham mead." Again, in 1450, the Lord was asked to amend "Stanebregge." In 1455 the bridge is specifically termed

"Stanbregge atte Sonde," *i.e.* the stone bridge at Sands End. In 1522 there is a presentment that "the Lord ought to repair the bridge called Stenebrege."

In the last century the name Stonebridge or Stanbridge fell out of use. The proximity of the old "Bull" alehouse led to the bridge being called Bull Bridge, and the creek, Bull Bridge Creek. In the early part of this century the bridge was generally known as the King's Road Bridge. Stanley Bridge, which now marks the site of the ancient "Stanbregge," is a modern structure. Its name is due to the Stanleys of Chelsea, whose house stood just on the other side of the bridge, on the north side of the King's Road.

Other Noteworthy Residents of the King's Road

According to Pulteney's "Anecdotes of Botany," Mark Catesby, the eminent naturalist, once lived at Fulham, his home being in or near the King's Road.

Catesby, who was born about 1679, started, in 1710, on a voyage to America,
returning to England in 1719 with a magnificent botanical collection. In 1722 he visited Carolina, returning in 1726. In 1733 he published his "Natural History of Carolina, Florida, and the Bahama Islands." He was made a Fellow of the Royal Society. He died 23 Dec. 1749.

In a house on the King's Road lived, about 1686-93, John Dunton, said to have been the well-known bookseller. In the minutes of a View in 1686 is the following:

> "We present John Dunton for not scowering up his ditch belonging to ye meadow late in the tenure of Capt. Colingwood next the highway leading from Sandyend to helbroke."

An altar tomb in Fulham Churchyard formerly bore the words:

> "John Dunton ob: 27 January 1693 æt. 40."

As the eccentric bookseller survived till 1733, it is clear that this John Dunton must have been a different person.

CHAPTER V: PARSON'S GREEN

SECTION I: GENERAL

Between the New King's Road and the Fulham Road lies Parson's Green, in bygone times by far the most aristocratic quarter of Fulham. Bowack states that, in his day, it was inhabited "mostly by Gentry and Persons of Quality," who resided in "several very handsome Houses all standing very airy upon a dry, clean Green." The Green itself forms an irregular triangle, the King's Road constituting its base and the southern end of Parson's Green Lane its apex.

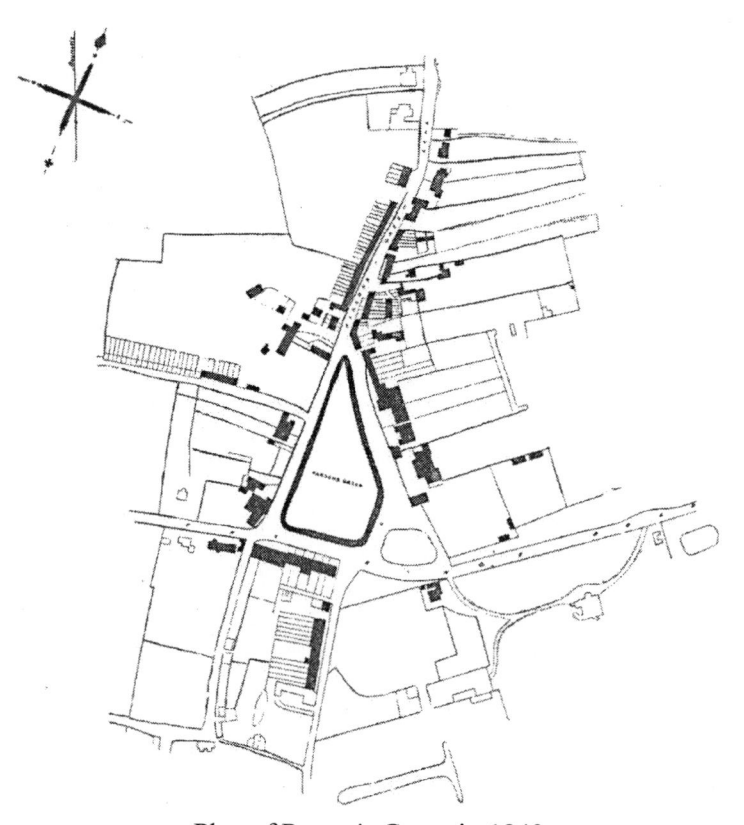

Plan of Parson's Green in 1843

Parson's Green, looking towards Parson's Green Lane.
From a photograph by Mr. T. S. Smith, 1896

The earliest allusion to Parson's Green occurs in the Court Rolls for 1391, when the name is written "P'sonsgrene." In ancient documents the Green is spoken of as a portion of the Waste of the Manor.

Parson's Green owes its name to the Parsonage or Rectory House, which stood about midway on the western side of the Green. Bowack remarks:

> "Before the said House is a large Common which, within the Memory of several Ancient Inhabitants now Living, was us'd for a Bowling green, belonging to the said Rector, and served for his own and his domesticks' Diversion, from whence 'tis most likely the place was literally call'd Parson's Green."

The Green was occasionally called the Parsonage Green. As late as 1708 this form occurs in the Church Registers:

> Robert the son of Richard Readman, Parsonidg Green bu. 4 ffeb.

As was the case with other commons in the Manor, it was an offence to fell
timber here without the permission of the Lord. At a Court General in 1456 it was presented that:

"Agnes Hasele has cut down 2 Elms of timber of the Lord growing upon Psonage grene without license of the Lord."

At a Court General in 1476 Alice Parker was presented because she possessed a pig which was not ringed, "so that it goeth on to the lands and upon the Common of the Lord called psenagegrene, to the common nuisance."

In 1625 there were sixteen rated inhabitants at Parson's Green representing a population of, say, 80. In 1641 the number was only 23, equivalent to a population of about 115. In 1649 there were 37 persons rated, or, say, 165 inhabitants. In 1658 the Churchwardens:

"Paid for lookinge to a poore woman that fell in Travill vpon Parson's Greene, 5 daies and for passinge her away to London 9s. 6d."

Lysons, quoting from *Perfect Occurrences*, 31 March 1648, says:

"It was reported in the House of Commons in the month of March 1648, that a Doctor, one of his Majesty's Chaplains, had several times preached about Parson's Green, once in the great brick house, another time in the high white house when there was a great resort of people and many of them disaffected to the Parliament. The Doctor was sent for and, after examination, committed to custody."

The assessments for 1666 show 49 persons rated under Parson's Green, or a population of about 245; in 1674 there were 72 ratepayers or, say, 360 inhabitants.

In 1664 posts were erected "att and too" Parson's Green. On this occasion there was

"paid to Carpenters and Labor[rs] for pininge the Posts and setting them 17s. 6d."

The following presentments were made at a Court Baron in 1688:

"We p[r]sent William Ranger for lopping an Elme tree growing upon the Lords Waste in Parsons Greene w[th]out leave of ye Lord of the Manor and doe amerce the said William Rainger three shillings and foure pence.
We p[r]sent John Haines victualler for setting vp posts before his house at Parsons Greene without leave of the Lord of the Manor and doe

amerce the said John Haines six shillings and eight pence and order yt he remove them by the first of Aprill next under the paine of twenty shillings."

The Highway Rate books for 1722 record:

"For Stocking Ruts and mending ye Bank at Pars Green 6s. 0d."

The population of Parson's Green in 1739 was about 225. In 1834 a cricket match was played on Parson's Green: "Married versus Single Women." The married women won. Shortly before his death in 1878, the Rev. R. G. Baker erected the handsome polished granite drinking fountain on the Green facing the New King's Road.

Down to within living memory Parson's Green was little better than a dreary grass plot, surrounded by posts and chains. A narrow muddy pathway crossed from Rectory Place to Elm House, while another trended towards the Duke's Head. It still boasted several fine old trees, including a row of large elms on the east side and a row of plane trees facing Pitt Place.

Towards the south-east corner of the Green was the pond, a rather large sheet of water, one end of which was very deep. The East End Road now crosses the eastern portion of the pond; the other terminated about opposite Peterborough Road. According to tradition the neighbouring Baptists occasionally used it for the purposes of the immersion of their members. It was doubtless at one time a clear pool, but those of us who remember it in its later and dirtier days have not the most agreeable recollections concerning it. Even within living memory some of the village boys were wont to take a dip in the pond. Dogs and ducks patronized it, and market gardeners led their horses into it to bathe. The first known reference to it occurs in the Court Rolls for 1559, when the following presentment was made:

"William Maynarde mercer has fished in the pond (*stagnis*) at psongrē contrary to the orders of the Homage."

In the minutes of Courts held in 1606 and 1626, references are made to the "pond on Parson's Green called Colepitt." The only reference to the pond in the Parish Books occurs under date 1727:

"To money paid for scouring Parson's Green Ditch 4s."

The pond was fed by a natural spring. When, some years ago, the main drainage of the King's road was laid, the spring was destroyed and the pond was filled up.

Parson's Green formerly had its fair, an annual institution which is said to have been first established in the reign of William III. Addison, in No. 452 of the *Spectator* for 19 Aug. 1712 (8th Aug. O. S.), amusingly alludes to the deadly dullness of the western suburbs of the London of his day. "They advise from Fulham," he writes, "that things remained there in the same state they were." Then, in the same vein of satire, the great essayist continues:

"They had intelligence just as the Letters came away, of a Tub of excellent Ale just set abroach at Parson's Green but this wanted confirmation."

This ale-tapping was, of course, an incident in the annual revels of the village folk. The fair generally lasted three days (6th, 7th and 8th Aug. O. S., or 17th, 18th and 19th Aug. N. S.) Mr. C. Griffin, writing of "Parson's Green in the olden times," in the Parish Magazine for Aug. 1884, observes:

"At such times, besides the rows of booths arranged under the trees on the east side of the Green - of which, alas, so few remain - might be seen the usual concomitants of an ancient country fair, such as greasy pole climbing, treacle bobbing, ale-broaching, and competitive hot tea drinking."

"Honest" John Phelps, who well remembered the fair, thus described it:

"I've been to the Fair many a time. It was held on the 17th, 18th and 19th August each year, and if one day happened to be a Sunday, it was continued to the 20th. My mother sold oysters there. I can tell you a story about one of the Hudnotts - William, a sailor - and Parson's Green Fair. He came home from sea and Parson's Green Fair being on at the time, he went there. The canvas booths were all ranged about under the trees, where they sold gingerbread and such like commodities. Well, William was so active as a sailor that he climbed on one of the booths which broke away, and he went through on to all the things below, while the people were asleep inside, and he had to pay the damage. It was a wonderful nice fair, but I remember one thing that wasn't nice. Poor live cocks used to be tied up by their legs and people threw sticks at them."

Parson's Green Fair was essentially a pleasure fair. Along the King's Road side, it was the general custom to arrange the puppet shows and acting booths. On the west side were the refreshment stalls. At the top of the Green, near the "White Horse," were the fish stalls, oysters and whelks always being in large demand.

In the early years of this century, "Billy" Button, a noted clown, used to ride a horse at the fair. After going through its antics, the intelligent animal would throw its rider off and "bolt" for the stables of the "White Horse" inn. The "Diary" of Sergeant Roe contains a few allusions to Parson's Green Fair; thus:

"1807. 17 Aug. My Boy here to-day and at the fare Parsons Green. I think he is better."

"1808. 17 Aug. being the fair at P. Green to which all the children went and Mrs. R. and self in the Evening."

The following "Public Notice" was issued about 1810:

"Fairs: At Parson's Green and Blue Green, alias Brook Green, Hammersmith. Whereas a report has lately been circulated with great industry through the parish of Fulham and elsewhere that the late fair at Parson's Green was held under the authority and with the approbation of the Bishop of London, as Lord of the Manor, and that all the profits of it were appropriated to his use and also the profits of the fair at Blue Green alias Brook Green, Hammersmith, now, we, the underwritten Rector, Curate and Churchwarden of the Parish of Fulham are authorized by his Lordship to contradict the said scandalous report in which there is not one word of truth."

This quaint notice is signed by Graham Jepson, Rector of Fulham, John Owen, curate, and George Matyear, churchwarden.

Norris Brewer, in "London and Middlesex" (1816), observes:

> "Some fastidious persons attempted a few years back, to suppress this annual festival, but, after a long altercation between hired constables and the inhabitants, the harmless amusements were suffered to proceed."

In April 1823, Parson's Green Fair was suppressed by the Magistrates.

SECTION II: EAST SIDE

We will now notice some of the old houses which once bordered the Green. We will first take the east side.

At the south-east corner there survived, until 1884, one of the most notable residences in Fulham, known in ancient times as Hollybush House, but, in later days, as East End House. It was built about the end of the reign of Queen Elizabeth. Its first known occupant was Sir William Billesbie, knight, of whom we have spoken in our account of Fulham Church (See vol. I). Sir William, who died 25 March 1607-8, sold the estate, in 1606, to Sir Thomas Smith of Brightwell's. The surrender is thus recorded in the minutes of a Court General in 1606:

> "On 11 May 1606, William Billesbie kt. and Dame Anne his wife surrendered a certain tenement of new erection called Holybushe House on a parcel of the Waste of Parsons Greene which the said William had taken of the Lord and also a parcel of land in Austens field and other lands late in the tenure of Hugh Parlor, gent., deceased, abutting upon the pond in Parsons Green called Colepitt . . . to the use of Thomas Smith and his heirs which said Thomas was on 11 May 1606 admitted."

Sir Thomas, on his death in 1609, left his estate at Parson's Green to his son, Robert Smith, but his widow, Lady Frances Smith, was to "receive the profits during her life." In 1615 this lady became the wife of Thomas Cecil, first Earl of Exeter. Robert Smith predeceased his mother, dying in 1626, when his sister, Margaret, who had married Thomas Carey, became heiress to the estate. At a Court General, in this year, she was duly admitted. The minute recording the admission describes the site as a place "where elms and hollybushes grow," a description which accounts for the name of this vanished mansion and its still existing neighbour, Elm House. At the next Court Baron, in 1626-7, Thomas and Margaret Carey surrendered Hollybush House to Robert Dickson of St. Martin's-in-the-Fields.

East End House. From a drawing by Miss Daniel, *circa* 1851.

Robert Dickson died in 1644, leaving a son Robert, who, in 1657, mortgaged the estate for £600 to one James Short. From the minutes of a Court, in 1658, we gather that a part of this sum had by that date been repaid by Robert Dickson, but, his death having occurred, Short was admitted to hold under his successor till payment of the residue.

Robert Dickson's heir was a third Robert Dickson, his nephew, son of his brother, Thomas Dickson. In some unexplained way Hollybush House very shortly afterwards passed into the possession of William Mason of Lambeth.

Its next owner was Robert Blanchard, a distinguished London goldsmith, partner with Sir Francis Child in the Fleet Street bank still known as Child and Co. He came to live at Fulham in 1666. At a View in 1675, the Lord, "of his special grace and upon the petition of Robert Blanchard of Parson's Green," granted him a parcel of the Waste on which to erect "unam sheddam quæ convertatur et inserviat pro uno domo," that is, a structure which he might turn into and use for the purpose of a coachhouse.

Blanchard appears to have done much to raise the status of his Bank, which was known by the sign of "Ye Marygold." This Bank was originally established by a family named Wheeler. The first of the family of whom we possess any record was John Wheeler, a London goldsmith, who carried on business in the Cheap. He died in 1575. The business was continued by his son, a second John Wheeler, who moved into Fleet Street. He died in 1609. On his death the concern came into the hands of William Wheeler, son of the younger John Wheeler. William moved his shop to "Ye Marygold" which had, until then, been an inn, next to Temple Bar. He died in 1663. William Wheeler's son, a second William, who was admitted a member of the Goldsmiths' Company by patrimony, 27 April 1666, continued the Bank. The date of his death is unknown. The business now fell to Robert Blanchard, who had married Martha, the widow of William Wheeler senior. On 2 Oct. 1671, Francis Child, of whom we shall presently speak, married Elizabeth, daughter of William Wheeler senior. Blanchard appears shortly afterwards to have taken Child into partnership with him. In "The Little London Directory" of 1677, the firm of Blanchard and Child of "Ye Marygold" is given in a list of "all the Goldsmiths that keep Running Cashes."

Robert Blanchard died 6 June 1681, apparently at his premises at Temple Bar. In his ledger, which is still preserved, are notes by him of sundry payments to his doctors and "chirurgeons" made during his fatal illness. The last is on 6 June 1681, when he writes:

"Spent on the Doctor at the 'Devil Tavern' 7s. 6d."

In accordance with his will his remains were interred at Fulham. The Church Registers record:

1681. Mr. Robert Blanchard   bu. ye 10 of June.

At the next Court General, in 1682, Mrs. Martha Blanchard was admitted to Hollybush House.

The following is an extract from the will of Robert Blanchard. It is dated 17 Aug. 1680, and a codicil, 27 May 1681. It was proved 15 June 1681 (P.C.C. 87 North):

"I, Robert Blanchard, cittizen and goldsmith of London. My lands in Hayes co. Middlesex to my friends Mr. Christopher Cratford, Mr. Francis Child and Mr. John East in Trust for £80 per annum to my sister Mrs. Alice Veel for life and after her death to Richard Blanchard of Westminster, eldest son of Thomas Blanchard of Ringwood co. Hants who was son of Arthur Blanchard brother to my late father Thomas Blanchard deceased, and whereas my wife is seized of two houses near the Savoy, she to give same to her grandson Robert Child. My copyhold in Fulham to my wife for life and afterwards to Elizabeth Child daughter of my said wife and heirs for ever.
To my wife my houses in Fleet St. and Blackfryers and at her death to her grandson John Child. I give five pounds to the Poore of Fullham on Fullham syde to be given and distributed by the Vestry to such as are old and have been sober, honest, laborious and Frequenters of the Church."

Mrs. Blanchard died at Hollybush House in 1685-86. The Church Registers record:

1685. Mrs. Mary Blanchard w^d of Mr. Rob. Blanchard bu. 23 of Jan.

In accordance with the will of her husband, Hollybush House descended to her daughter, Elizabeth, the wife of Francis Child.

Sir Francis Child was born at Heddington in Wiltshire in 1642. His father was Robert Child, a clothier. Coming to London at an early age, Child was, in March 1655-6, apprenticed for eight years to William Hall, a London goldsmith. An entry, which is still preserved among the records of the Bank, made by Francis Child himself, reads:

"Memorandum that I ffrancis Childe sonn of Robert Childe of Headdington in the County of Wiltts clothyer doe putt myself aprintize unto William Hall, cittizen and goldsmith of London for the tearme of eight yeares from the feast of St. Mary the Blessed Virgin next ensuing. FRANCIS CHILD."

Child, having served his articles, was, on 24 Mar. 1663-64, admitted to the freedom of the Goldsmiths' Company, and on 17 April following he was enrolled a freeman of the City of London. On the death of Robert Blanchard, he succeeded to his fortune. In

July 1681, the firm of Blanchard and Child became Francis Child and John Rogers, the latter being Sir Francis's cousin. Pennant justly calls Child "the father of the profession." He was certainly the first banker who dropped the goldsmiths' trade.

On 6 Jan. 1681-82, Child was chosen for St. Dunstan's precinct of the Ward of Farringdon Without in the Court of Common Council and in October 1689 he was elected Alderman of the Ward. On 29 Oct. 1689 he was knighted by William III at the Guildhall on the occasion of the mayoralty banquet. Finally, on 29 September 1698, Sir Francis was elected Lord Mayor of London. According to Luttrell, Child's mayoralty left him £4,000 out of pocket. In Feb. 1689-90, he was admitted a member of the Honourable Artillery Company and in March 1693-94 he was elected one of the six colonels of the City Trained Bands. In 1702 he sat as a Whig as one of the four representatives for the City in the first Parliament of Queen Anne.

Sir Francis Child was a munificent supporter of Christ's Hospital, a portion of which, in 1705, he rebuilt. Osterley Park, the seat of his son, Robert Child, was purchased by Sir Francis about 1711.

Very little is known about Child's life at Fulham. In 1690 he was admitted to the adjacent messuage known as Parlor's tenement. At a Court Baron, in 1693, he was elected the Lord's reeve for Hollybush House.

Sir Francis died at Hollybush House, 4 Oct. 1713, and was buried in a vault in the Churchyard (see vol. I, "Fulham Churchyard" chapter). The Church Registers record:

1713. Sir Francis Child knight bu. 9 Oct.

Sir Francis had fifteen children, of whom twelve were sons, namely Robert, Francis, James, Christopher, William, Leonard, George, John, Thomas, Stephen, Samuel, and one other, and three daughters, namely Martha, Elizabeth and Jane. Sir Robert and his brother, known as Sir Francis the younger, followed their father's business. Christopher and William were twins, baptized at St. Dunstan's. George is believed to have taken holy orders. John died in childhood. Thomas appears to have been a merchant. Stephen was a goldsmith in partnership with a Mr. Tudman at the "Crown" in Lombard Street. Samuel, the youngest son, was also a goldsmith. Martha became the wife of Anthony Collins of Parson's Green. Elizabeth married <u>Tyrringham Backwell, son of Alderman Edward Backwell</u>, and Jane married a Mr. Guydott. Only Robert, Francis, Samuel, Elizabeth and Jane survived their father.

The following is an extract from the will of Sir Francis Child, dated 2 Feb. 1710-11 and proved 2 Dec. 1713 (P.C.C. 269 Leeds):

> "I Sir Francis Child of London knight. To my wife all my copyholds in the parish of ffulham and all my Freehold messuages, lands, *etc.*, in the said parish for life Remainder to my eldest son Sir Robert Child for life Remainder to Mr. John Tidcomb of London merchant and Mr. Stephen Child, citizen and goldsmith of London in Trust for heirs in tale male of my said son Robert and in default to my next son Francis Child for life and heirs male of body and in default to my son Samuel Child and heirs male of body and in default to my own right heirs for ever. My personal estate to be divided into three parts, one part thereof to my wife, another part to my children Robert, Francis and Samuel Child equally, my daughter Martha having been fully preferred by me in marriage and after died, and my daughter Elizabeth being likewise fully preferred by me in marriage, and my daughter Jane being likewise fully preferred by me in marriage. Of the remaining third part, £500 to my wife on condition she release her right of Dower in my freehold estate in Hemlock Court co. Middlesex. To each of my said three sons £1,000. To my son-in-law Collins £50. To my son-in-law Backwell and his wife £50 apiece. To my son-in-law Guydott and his wife £50 apiece. Unto the Child my Daughter Backwell is now enseint with £100. Unto the poor of Headington where I was born, St. Dunstan West, London, and Fulham £10 to be distributed by the Churchwardens."

Lady Elizabeth Child died at Hollybush House, 23 February 1719-20. She was buried in the family vault at Fulham. The Church Registers record:

> 1719. Lady Eliz. Child bu. 27 Feb.

Her will, dated 20 May 1714, was proved in 1720.
On his mother's death, Sir Robert Child came into possession of Hollybush House. He resided at Osterley Park, where he died, 6 Oct. 1721. He was also buried at Fulham. The Church Registers

record:

1721. Sr Robert Child bu. 11 Oct.

In 1720, Hollybush House was let by Sir Robert Child to Admiral Sir Charles Wager, knt., who spent here nearly the last twenty-two years of his life.

This famous English Admiral was born in 1666, and achieved his great success in the war of the Spanish Succession. The operations of Commodore Sir Charles Wager, who was knighted by Queen Anne in recognition of his bravery, afford us a vivid picture of what a cruising fight was in the days when Spanish galleons from El Dorado were coveted prizes in the eyes of English seamen. In the spring of 1708, the Commodore received intelligence that Spanish treasure ships had sailed from Carthagena for Portobello. In the month of May, Wager, with only four English men-of-war, attacked seventeen Spanish galleons as they were creeping along the South American shore. At sunset the battle began. About midnight the Spanish Admiral's ship, the *San Jose,* blew up. Six hundred men and seven millions in gold and silver went down. Vastly more wealth was destroyed than taken, yet the gallant Commodore managed to secure prize-money amounting to about £100,000. On his return home he received the honour of knighthood, 8 Dec. 1709.

Sir Charles Wager, who, in 1733, was made First Lord of the Admiralty, is said to have died at Stanley House, Chelsea, 24 May 1743. Lysons notes:

"Mr. Collinson, in his manuscript Diary, remarks that in the year 1756, a tulip tree, which had been given to Sir Charles Wager, having been raised from seed thirty years before, flowered for the first time in his garden opposite Peterborough House."

The grounds of East End House

The grounds of East End House.
From a drawing preserved in the Vicarage "Faulkner."

Charles James Fèret

PEDIGREE OF CHILD FAMILY

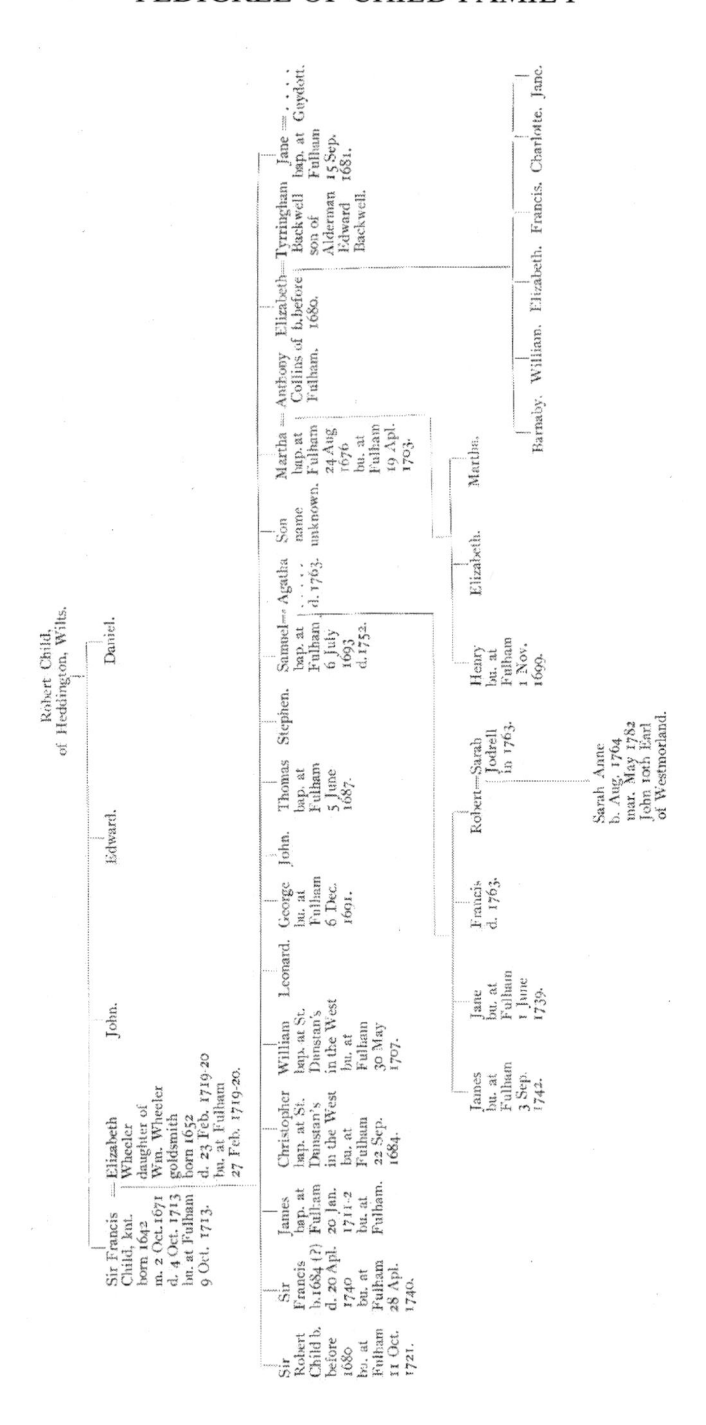

Robert Child, of Heddington, Wilts.

- Sir Francis Child, knt. born 1642, m. 2 Oct. 1671, d. 4 Oct. 1713, bu. at Fulham 9 Oct. 1713. = Elizabeth Wheeler, daughter of Wm. Wheeler goldsmith, born 1652, d. 23 Feb. 1719-20, bu. at Fulham 27 Feb. 1719-20.
- John.
- Edward.
- Daniel.

Children of Sir Francis Child and Elizabeth Wheeler:

- Sir Robert Child b. before 1680, bu. at Fulham 11 Oct. 1721.
- Sir Francis Child b. 1684 (?), d. 20 Apl. 1740, bu. at Fulham 28 Apl. 1740.
- James bap. at Fulham 20 Jan. 1711-2, bu. at Fulham.
- Christopher bap. at St. Dunstan's in the West, bu. at Fulham 22 Sep. 1684.
- William bap. at St. Dunstan's in the West, bu. at Fulham 30 May 1707.
- Leonard.
- George bu. at Fulham 6 Dec. 1691.
- John.
- Thomas bap. at Fulham 5 June 1687.
- Stephen.
- Samuel bap. at Fulham 6 July 1693, d. 1752. = Agatha ......, d. 1763.
- Son name unknown.
- Martha bap. at Fulham 24 Aug 1676, bu. at Fulham 19 Apl. 1703. = Anthony Collins of Fulham.
- Elizabeth b. before 1680.
- Tyrringham Backwell son of Alderman Edward Backwell. = Jane bap. at Fulham 15 Sep. 1681. = Guydott.

Children of Samuel and Agatha:

- Francis d. 1763.
- Jane bu. at Fulham 1 June 1739.
- Robert = Sarah Jotrell in 1763.
- Henry bu. at Fulham 1 Nov. 1699.
- Elizabeth.
- Martha.

- James bu. at Fulham 3 Sep. 1742.
- Sarah Anne b. Aug. 1764, mar. May 1782 John 10th Earl of Westmorland.

Barnaby. William. Elizabeth. Francis. Charlotte. Jane.

152

Sir Francis Child the younger, who came into possession of Hollybush House in 1721, died 20 April 1740, and was buried at Fulham. The Church Registers record:

1740. Honble Sr Francis Child bu. 28 Apl.

On his death, his brother, Samuel Child, was admitted. He continued to let the property as his brothers had done. At his death, in 1752, it was sold to the Powells.

From about 1751 to 1762 Francis Gashry, Paymaster at the Ordnance Office, resided at the house. He was buried in Fulham Churchyard. The Church Registers record:

1762. Francis Gashry Esq. bu. 29 May.

His widow, Mrs. Martha Gashry, was rated for the property down to 1777; in 1778 Mr. John Powell was rated, and in 1788 his heir, Mr. A. A. Powell, of whom we shall speak in connection with High Elms House, Percy Cross. By Mr. John Powell, Hollybush House was much modernized and re-named East End House.

Dr. Jeffery Ekins, Dean of Carlisle, according to Faulkner, resided here. Before he took orders, Ekins, according to the "Memoirs" of Richard Cumberland, "composed a drama of an allegorical cast, which he entitled *Florio; or The Pursuit of Happiness*." He successively held the rectories of Quainton, Sedgefield and Morpeth. In 1771 he published "A Translation of the Loves of Medea and Jason," by Apollonius of Rhodes. Dr. Ekins died 20 Nov. 1791, and was buried at Fulham (see vol. I, "Fulham Church: Its Monuments" chapter).

In 1793 the house was rented by Sir John Hales, bart., who died here in 1802. The Church Registers record:

1802. Sir John Hailes bu. 3 Mar.

In 1808 East End House was taken by the famous Mrs. Fitzherbert, who was visited here by her royal admirer, the Prince of Wales, afterwards George IV. This remarkable woman was Maria Anna Smythe, daughter of Walter Smythe, of Brombridge, Hants. She was born 26 July 1756. Her first husband was a Mr.

Weld, of Lulworth, a wealthy Roman Catholic gentleman. Her second marriage was with Mr. Fitzherbert, of Swinnerton, Staffs. Though denied by Fox and other Ministers, there is no doubt that the Prince of Wales was secretly married to her in 1785. Mrs. Fitzherbert, who left Parson's Green in 1810, died at Brighton, 27 Mar. 1837.

After a short tenancy by Mr. John Bayford, East End House was, in 1814, bought by Mr. John Daniel, a wealthy West India merchant, who spent large sums of money in structural improvements. In his day, there was no man better known, or more highly respected, in Fulham than "Squire" Daniel, as he is yet familiarly remembered. He died at East End House in 1853 and was interred at All Saints (see vol. I, "Fulham Church: Its Monuments" chapter).

A family of the name of Stainsby succeeded the Daniels. From 1856 to 1859 East End House was the residence of Dr. Baillie. Next came Maria Piccolomini, the clever operatic singer. In 1864 the house was sold by the devisees of Squire Daniel to Mr. Grant Heatly Tod-Heatly, who, in 1870, let it to Major Arthur James Ewens. Mr. Tod-Heatly was its last occupant. Here, on one occasion, he entertained the Prince of Wales. In 1884 the old mansion was razed to the ground. Nos. 17 to 41 Parson's Green now mark the site.

East End House, in the days of its greatness, was a perfect specimen of what is known as the Queen Anne style of architecture. It was of red brick. The front door was of solid mahogany. The inner doors, panelling, floors, staircases and shutters were of oak, some of which was quite dark with age. Bowack, describing the house in 1705, speaks of it as "well-built with brick after the modern manner and looks very stately, the gardens also are very good."

The grounds (covering a land area of 16a. 3r. 30p.), which were laid out with great taste, included an orangery, a rose garden and a fruit garden. They were planted with a number of very fine trees, among which was a veteran cedar. On the demolition of the house, this tree, which the old Duke of Portland was wont to worship, was blown up with gunpowder. In the copy of Faulkner's "Fulham" at the Vicarage is a pencil sketch of the great tree with its huge branches, taken in Sept. 1854.

Cedar Tree at East End House.
From a drawing preserved in the Vicarage "Faulkner."

On the back of the drawing are the following details:

"Measurement of the Cedar Tree at Parson's Green in 1853. The six branches are taken at 6 feet 6 inches branches 100 feet. Age about 150 years. 1853."

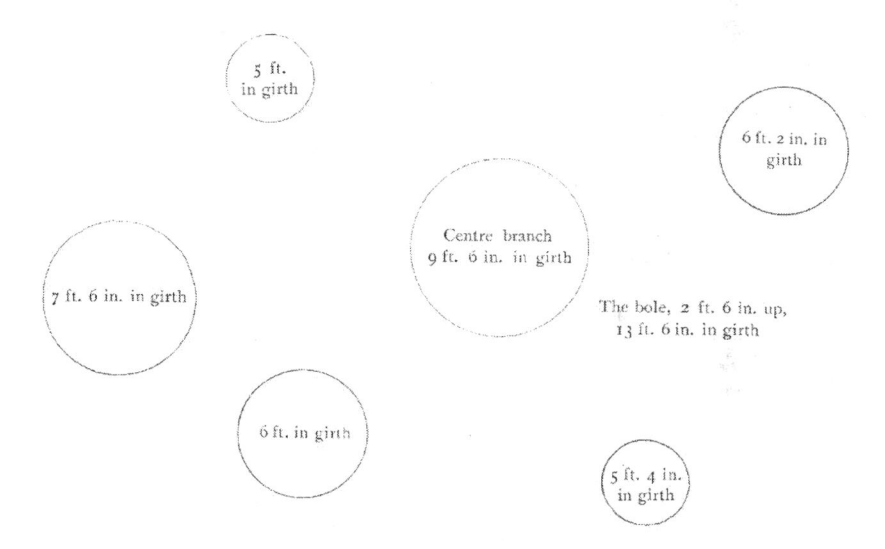

- 5 ft. in girth
- 6 ft. 2 in. in girth
- 7 ft. 6 in. in girth
- Centre branch 9 ft. 6 in. in girth
- The bole, 2 ft. 6 in. up, 13 ft. 6 in. in girth
- 6 ft. in girth
- 5 ft. 4 in. in girth

Where Belfield House and Elm House stand was anciently an extensive messuage which extended back as far as Austin's Field. As the early history of Belfield House is much interwoven with that of Elm House, it will, perhaps, be best to deal with the two tenements together.

The most ancient designation of the messuage was that of Hore's, a name which doubtless recalls that of the family which first occupied it. In a list of the tenants of the Manor, in 1401, we find one Richard Hore, about the last representative of the name in Fulham. In the minutes of a Court General in 1392 it is presented that "John Parker holds ½ acre parcell of Hore's."

During the reign of Richard II Hore's was in the occupation of the Rev. Robert Hunt, son of William Hunt, of Fulham. In 1395 Robert Hunt surrendered to Elizabeth, the wife of Gerard Hokelem, the five acres of which Hore's then consisted. Gerard Hokelem died in 1422 possessed of this estate which then passed to Agnes, his daughter, wife of William Conyngton, who, in the same year, sold Hore's to John Adam senior and John Adam junior.

Hore's tenement was held by the Adam family during the greater part of the fifteenth century. In 1491 William Adam sold the estate to Owen Meredith. In 1512 Meredith sold Hore's tenement to Sir Sampson Norton, knight, Master of the Ordnance, of whom we have spoken in our account of his monument at Fulham (see vol. I, "Fulham Church: Its Monuments and Epitaphs" chapter). Sir Sampson's estate at Parson's Green consisted of eight acres of land in Austin's Field and the tenement called Hore's. "In his last sickness," in 1517, he surrendered this estate to his cousin, John Norton, who paid a fine of "xj^s iiij^d" on admission.

On the death of this John Norton, in 1571, his youngest son, a second John Norton, was admitted, but, in 1577, the latter sold the property to John Wytte, Whitte or White, yeoman, a cousin of John Tamworth, of Brightwell's. Among the minutes of a Court General, in 1579 is the following curious presentment:

> "John Whitte, because he has not exonerated the parish of ffulham of a certain infant called a sawyer's child risen and born within the.cottage of the said John, contrary to the mandate of the last Court is amerced xxx^s."

In 1582 he surrendered Hore's to Joan, wife of Maurice Pyckering. Joan Pyckering died in 1596, when her son, Hugh Parlor, succeeded to Hore's, which now became known as Parlor's tenement.

Margaret, daughter of Sir William Billesbie of Hollybush House, married Hugh or Hugo Parlor, described as of Plumstead, but doubtless identical with the Hugh Parlor of Parson's Green. Sir William Billesbie left his wife Anne "two crofts called Ore's crofts," most likely a portion of Hore's messuage. Francis, son of Hugh Parlor, was, in 1606, admitted to Hore's tenement.

In 1616 this Francis Parlor, described as "of Plumsted," sold the whole of his estate at Parson's Green to Thomas Gresham of North End. It consisted of the messuage called Hore's, then comprising nine acres, and three small tenements.

Sir Francis Bacon.
From an engraving after an original portrait by Van Somer.

At the time of this sale, Hore's tenement was in the occupation of Sir John Vaughan, kt., who resided here several years. It was to the house of this noblemanat Parson's Green that Lord Chancellor Bacon, when he fell into disgrace, repaired for six weeks. A part of the sentence passed upon Bacon was that he should never again come "within the verge of the Court." In order, however, to settle certain personal affairs, James I granted him license to repair to "our City of London," and "to abide there for the space of one month or six weeks." Accordingly he obtained a warrant, dated 13 Sept. 1621, under the King's signature, enabling him "to be and remain at Sir John Vaughan's house at Parson's Green, the said clause of confinement notwithstanding." Sir John Vaughan was Comptroller of the Prince's Household. Though styled "Sir John" in the warrant of 13 Sept. 1621, he had, on the previous 29 July, been created Lord Vaughan of Mullingar in the county of Westmeath. In the Fulham Rate books he is styled "the Lord Vaughan." Subsequently he became Earl of Carberry.

In 1617 Thomas Gresham sold Hore's tenement to Thomas Iles, junior, "of Christ's Church in Oxford, clerk."

We now, for the first time, hear of a cottage which was evidently situated between Hore's tenement (identical with Elm House) and Hollybush House (East End House of later times). This cottage, to which was attached 1½ acre of ground, practically occupied the site of Belfield House. It was probably one of the three tenements mentioned in the surrender of 1616.

Dr. Thomas Iles, who became the owner of Hore's in 1617, was, in 1619, admitted to the adjacent cottage, in which he resided for some years. Dr. Iles's house is several times mentioned in the Court Rolls. Thus, in 1627, it was reported that:

> "William Gooderich one of the Customarie Tenants hath taken upp or caused to bee taken upp certayne stakes in Parson's Greene upon the Wast there ouer against Doctor Iles his house and other of the Tennants of this Manno[r] w[ch] said stakes weare put in there at the app[t]ment of the jurie of this Manno[r] after the Lo[d] and Tenants both ffreehold and copiehold had granted to the said Doct[r] Iles the Wast ground ouer against the sayd House where the said stakes weare driven and therefore hath forfeited to the Lord 1s."

At a Court held in the following year it was ordered that

> "William Gooderidge shall driue or cause to be driuen in certayne stakes w[h] he formely tooke up in Parson's Greene ouer against Doctor Iles his house in the places where thother weare beefore Midsomer Day next or ells shall forfeite to the Lo[d] of this Manno[r] the some of viij[s]."

Dr. Thomas Iles was a noteworthy character. He matriculated at Christ Church, Oxford, on 23 May 1604. He proceeded B.A. on 9 June 1608 and M.A. on 18 April 1611. He obtained his B.D. and D.D. on 23 June 1619. His first preferment was the rectory of

Lasborough, co. Gloucester, in 1609. In 1618 he was appointed rector of Toddenham, co. Gloucester. He was principal of Hartford Hall, Oxford, from 1621 to 1633. He was appointed canon of Gloucester in 1622. In the same year he became canon of Oxford. Finally, in 1635, he received the rectory of Little Mongeham, Kent. In 1648 he was ejected from his preferments and robbed of his private property. He died at Oxford, 20 June 1649. On 6 July following administration of his estate was granted to Thomas Iles, his eldest son.

Dr. Iles married, as his first wife, Elizabeth, daughter of Dr. John Weston, prebendary of Christ Church, Oxford. This lady was sister to the Rev. John Weston, M.A., of Fulham, rector of All Hallows, Lombard Street. Dr. Iles is best remembered as the founder of the. Almshouses at Brook Green. On the front of these buildings is the following inscription:

"Quod Pauperibus datur
In Christum Conferitur
1629."

The houses, which were rebuilt in 1840, were actually erected by Mr. Thomas Iles, the father of Dr. Iles, who owned a considerable estate at Hammersmith.

Hore's tenement, on its vacation by Lord Vaughan, became the property and residence of Charles Holloway, sergeant-at-law, who, for many years, held the post of steward to the Bishop of London.

Next we find both Hore's tenement and Dr. Iles's house in the possession of John Hicks, who, in 1651, had purchased the former from Charles Holloway, of the Inner Temple, son of the above Charles Holloway.

The Hickses were a notable family. John Hicks' father was a tallow chandler of London. He himself was a member of the Vintners' Company. In the Bishop of London's Registry is an entry of the marriage of John Hicks, gent., of Fulham, aged 58, and Anne Needier of the same, aged about 58, "at Fulham or SS. Anne and Agnes, London, 27 April, 1640." Mrs. Anne Needler, the widow of Henry Needler, who was buried at Fulham m 1638, had for some years resided at Dr. Iles's house at Parson's Green, whither John Hicks, who had previously been assessed for a house in "ffulham streete," now came to live. Subsequently, about 1647, he moved to Church Row. <u>Robert Hicks or Hickes, the son of John Hicks, a woollen draper, lies buried in Fulham Church</u>. (see vol. I, "Fulham Church: Its Monuments" chapter).

In 1658 Robert Hicks sold Dr. Iles's cottage to Edward Peirce, or Pearce, the grandson of John Pearce, of Glynde, co. Sussex, and son of Edward Pearce, of London, by Mary, daughter of Thomas Bishop, of London. He married Mary, second daughter of Sir Dudley Carleton by his second wife, Lucy Crofts, of Croft Castle, co. Hereford. They had two sons, Edward and Dudley, and three daughters, Mary, Lucy and Bridget.

In 1665-66 Hore's tenement and Dr. Iles's cottage became the property of <u>William Rumbold</u>. In the minutes of a Court Baron, held 14 Feb. 1665-66, are the following admissions:

> "Presented that on 9 June, 17 Car. II. (1665) Edward Pearce and Mary his wife surrendered one cottage and 1½ acre in Austen Field and one parcel of the Waste at Parson's Green in which Thomas Iles D.D. deceased did formerly inhabit to the use of William Rumbold of London, Esq., and Mary his wife."

> "Edward Pearce and Mary his wife surrendered a messuage and nine acres near Parson's Green and half an acre of arrable land in Austen's Field formerly in the occupation of Charles Holloway, Esq., to the use of William Rumbold and Mary his wife. Now at this Court the said William Rumbold in his proper person and said Mary his wife by her attorney, Stephen Kibblewhite, were admitted."

With the career of William Rumbold, Comptroller of the Great Wardrobe in the reign of Charles II, we have dealt at length in our account of Fulham Church (see vol. I, "Fulham Church: Its Monuments" chapter).

At a View, in 1668, the death of William Rumbold was presented. It is difficult to say exactly what happened on his demise. Mrs. Rumbold, who survived her husband only three months, appointed Lord Mordaunt and others the guardians of her young children, who, she desired, might be brought up by her mother, Mrs. Barclay. All of them were of tender age, Edward, the only surviving son, being but two years old.

At some date, which cannot now be ascertained, the greater portion of the Rumbold estate at Parson's Green, "the messuage and nine acres," passed into the possession of Sir Walter Plunkett, kt., who may, perhaps, have held it in the capacity of a guardian. As soon as Edward Rumbold attained his majority, he set to work to recover his patrimony. At a Court Baron, held in 1687, Sir Walter Plunkett renounced his claim to the property in favour of Edward Rumbold.

William Rumbold. From an oil painting in the possession of C. J. A. Rumbold, Esq., of Brighton

At a Court Baron, in 1687-88, Edward Rumbold formally presented himself, and, on paying fines and heriots, amounting to 15s., was duly admitted to the copyholds of his father. He immediately mortgaged the whole to Roger Jackson, of St. Clement Danes, for upwards of £1,000. This done, Edward Rumbold, who was then living in a house in St. James's, let his mortgaged property to one John Starkey and his wife, for one year from 1 Nov. 1689, with option of renewal for a further period, at £30 per annum. Financial difficulties preventing Edward Rumbold from paying off his mortgage, Jackson claimed possession, and, in

1691, was actually admitted by the Homage of the Manor. Immediately upon his admission, this person sold the estate to Sir Francis Child, of Hollybush House, who, in turn, was admitted.

John Starkey, who was desirous of renewing his lease of the premises for eleven years, and who had spent a considerable sum on their repair, took proceedings against Edward Rumbold. <u>In an information, sworn 23 Oct. 1690,</u> Starkey asserts that he took the house for one year only, as he "did not then knowe whether the aire there would agree with him and his wife," but, finding that it did, and

> "having repaired the said premises to the extent of £5 and much more out of his pockett in beautifing the same and in soileing planting and improveing the gardens and walls and in new Gravelling the walkes and in making the same convenient for him and resolving to take a further lease therein, disposed of another house which he thought no(t) so convenient and signified to said Rumbold."

Starkey, who failed to get the desired renewal, goes on:

> "But so please it, the said Rumbold having entered into a confederacy with Sr Francis Child knt. who hath one or more houses adjoining the said house he the said Rumbold doth deny that he made said agreement of renewal of lease at pleasure of Y^r Orator and further said Rumbold doth pretend that his estate is only of the Nature of a copyhold holden of the Manor of Fulham and that he hath no power to make such lease of said premisses and Y^r Orator also saith he hath spent at least £50 on said premisses and said Sr Francis Child was the person that first advised Y^r Orator to take lease of sd premisses and further when Y^r Orator had prepared a release he showed it to said Child who seemed well pleased therewith and with your Orators neighbourhood and wished your Orator joy and comfort therein or to that very effect and said Rumbold now pretends he hath mortgaged said premisses to said Sr Francis Child before the contract made with your Orator and y^r Orator telling Sr Francis Child of Rumbold's unkindness, said Sr Francis Child then but never till then did inform your Orator that he had a mortgage in said premisses and intended to be admitted tenant thereto."

Edward Rumbold, in his defence, pleaded that he never professed power to lease the premises, being copyhold, for a longer term than one year, and that, about 16 Mar. 1687-88, in consideration of £800, he surrendered the premises to Sir Francis Child for repayment of £848 on 16 Mar. following, which sum, not being paid, the premises had become forfeited. To show his fairness, he expressed his willingness to make the complainant some allowance "for what he may have laid out if he hath laid out anything."

Judgment must have gone against John Starkey, for Child remained in undisturbed possession of the estate. Edward Rumbold seems to have made a further agreement with Sir Francis Child for the repurchase of the property, but, at a Court Baron, in 1691, it is recorded that he had failed to carry out his undertaking. From this date we hear no more of Edward Rumbold in connection with Fulham.

Here we may perhaps be allowed a slight digression. It is curious to note that, though the Comptroller's family disappears from our local records, the descendants of his brother Henry, who was buried at Fulham, 28 Mar. 1690-91, returned to the parish, though not to the old home at Parson's Green. The Comptroller's brother Henry had two sons, Henry and William. The latter, who was buried at Fulham, 5 Sept. 1728, had a son, William, who is rated for a house somewhere in the neighbourhood of Percy Cross, from 1727 to 1735. Its precise site is somewhat doubtful. This William Rumbold, who married Dorothy Maur, *nee* Cheney, daughter of Richard Cheney, of Hackney, and widow of Captain John Maur, of the East India Company's service, was a remarkable character. He is recorded to have had a considerable fortune, which he dissipated in gambling. The house, said to have been a large white one, was apparently given up by William Rumbold about the time of the birth of his son, Sir Thomas Rumbold, who became Governor of Madras, and was created a baronet after the capture of Pondicherry.

In 1691 the Hon. Francis Villiers was admitted to Dr. Iles's cottage, which, on his death in 1694, descended to his two sons, the Hon. Charles and William Villiers. The heirs, however, immediately sold it to Charles Chambrelain, an alderman of London.

In the meantime Hore's (or Parlor's) tenement had been let by Sir Francis Child to Ralph Grange, or "Councellor Grange," as he is usually styled, on whose death it was purchased by Charles

Chambrelain, who died 29 Jan. 1704-5. In his will, dated 18 Oct. 1703, he devised all his lands to his "daughter Rebow." This was Abigail, who had married Lemyng Rebow.

In 1711 Lemyng Rebow was one of the Surveyors of the highways of the Manor. The date of his death is unknown, but in 1721-23 Mrs. Rebow was rated for the property. In 1724, Lemyng and Abigail Rebow being both dead, their youngest son, Isaac Lemyng Rebow, was admitted. Being a minor, his custody was given to his grandfather, Sir Isaac Rebow, knight. In 1729 Dr. Iles's cottage (Belfield House) came into the possession of Charles Chambrelain Rebow, who, in 1752, surrendered the property to William Tresilian, of St. Paul's, Covent Garden, who resided here till 1760. In the account of this surrender, we learn that the messuage or cottage, with a piece of waste attached to it, was held of the Lord at a rent of 2s. per annum. Before the house was another piece of ground, 98 feet in length, 44 feet broad at the end next to East End House, "and at the end next the occupation of Ralph Grange (Elm House) two inches with fruit trees growing thereon."

In his will Charles Chambrelain further provided that the other portion of Parlor's tenement, after the death of his daughter Abigail, should go to his granddaughter Rachel. This Rachel, who married John Gerard de Hopman, d'Hoppman, or d'Hopman, was, in 1724, admitted to the property (Elm House). In 1728 the d'Hopmans obtained license to let the estate. In *The Country Journal,* No. 157, for 5 July 1729, it is thus advertised for letting:

> "On Parson's-Green, near Fulham, Middlesex, To be Lett a large convenient House, with an Orchard, well-planted Gardens, Stables, Coach-Houses, and Out-Houses, a Row of large Elms before the Gates, pleasantly situated on a very healthy Ground. The House is fit for either Courtier, Merchant, or large Boarding-School. Enquire at the House near the White House on Parson's-Green, on Mondays, Wednesdays, and Fridays."

In 1731 Elm House was leased to Henry Meriton, of St. George's, Hanover Square. For some years its occupants were persons of no note. In 1803 it was taken by the Rev. William Pearson, who conducted here, down to 1811, a school for young gentlemen. In 1809 Mr. Pearson published "Short Speeches, selected for the use of Young Gentlemen of the Seminary at Parsons Green, Fulham." This little volume which is in octavo, is now extremely scarce. For the next three years Elm House was conducted as a Roman Catholic School by Francis Quequet. The school was continued by Henry Daniel. In 1822 it passed into the hands of Mr. Owen Morrice, on whose death, in 1826, it was carried on by his son, the Rev. William Richard Morrice. The school was broken up about 1832.

Elm House. From a photograph by Mr. T. S. Smith, 1895

In 1848 Elm House, which had been purchased in 1820 by Squire Daniel, was leased by his daughter, Miss Ann Daniel, to Captain, afterwards Lt.-Colonel, James Nicholas Abdy, of the East India Company's service. He resided there till 1854, when the house was taken by Colonel Jebb, afterwards Major-General Sir Joshua Jebb, K.C.B., Director General of Convict Prisons. Elm House, which long stood empty, was, in 1890, converted into a School of Discipline for Girls, a Roman Catholic institution.

The history of Dr. Iles's cottage, or Belfield House, may be briefly concluded. In 1776 it became the home of Captain Kirke, who was followed, in 1785, by Lady Ann Simpson.

For a short time it was the residence of the famous "Mrs.

Jordan," with whom the Duke of Clarence, afterwards William IV, contracted a secret alliance. This lady, whose real name was Dorothy Bland, was born about 1762. When only 15, she made her debut on the Dublin boards. In 1782 she came to England. Three years later, at Drury Lane Theatre, she took the part of "Peggy," in "The Country Girl." She soon became a great favourite in London society. It was about this time that the Duke fell in love with her. He continued to live with her till 1811, when the connection was suddenly broken off. After again taking to the stage, she went to France, dying at St. Cloud, 3 July 1816. By the Prince she had ten children, eight of whom survived their father, who left them £2,000 apiece, with equal shares in a life policy for £40,000!

During the earlier part of the century the house was successively in the occupation of Thomas Lancaster, Mrs. Frances Kirke, Mrs. Mary Banks, and Miss Emma Banks. The name of the last-mentioned lady appears in the Rate books down to 1820, when the house was bought by Squire Daniel. From 1825 to 1849 it was the residence of his nephew, Mr. Thomas Daniel Belfield. In 1850 Belfield House, as it was now called, was taken by Major Edmund Sheppard, R.A., who moved here from Arundel House. In 1855 he was succeeded by Mr. Henry Brinsley Sheridan, barrister-at-law, who resided here till 1863. The devisees of John Daniel, in 1864, sold Belfield House to Mr. Grant Heatly Tod-Heatly. The house, which remained empty for many years, was, in 1890, purchased by Mr. Theodore Roussel, the distinguished painter.

Belfield House is a flat-fronted brick residence, with two extensive wings. The central portion, which is the most ancient, is doubtless upwards of 250 years old.

During the long period of non-occupation which preceded the advent of Mr. Theodore Roussel, Belfield House fell into a state of dilapidation. With the true instincts of the artist, Mr. Roussel set to work to restore the house. To escape the window tax, a previous tenant had blocked up as many of the windows as could possibly be spared. These Mr. Roussel had re-opened. The fine oak staircase was relieved of its successive coats of paint and restored to its former beauty.

The plan of Belfield House is somewhat novel. The hall, which is spirit-painted in white, is handsome and commodious. A door leads from it into the dining-room, which overlooks an extensive garden at the back. In the north wing, on this floor, are the blue and yellow rooms. In the south wing is a pretty morning room, and, at the back of the old house, the studio, formerly used as a billiard room. Ascending the stairs we arrive, on the first floor, in a lobby which is very similar in form to the hall. Its chief feature is its fireplace with some curious carving, bearing the monogram W. and J. for "William" and "Jordan." On a door on this landing, leading to the servants' staircase, is a lock, on which is wrought the royal crown, a piece of very elegant workmanship. The floors, doors and much of the general woodwork are of oak.

Belfield House. From a photograph by Mr. T. S. Smith, 1895

No. 9, Parson's Green marks the site of three successive houses of much interest. The most ancient one was known as Stowte's or Stoute's Tenement, doubtless, like others, from the original owner. The first we hear of it is in the minutes of a Court General in 1391, when

> "Richard Langton surrendered ½ acre parcel of Stoughtes tenement abutting upon a garden of Richd Charteshous in Astons feld near P'sons grene to the use of Richard Mooreden."

In 1422 Gerard Hokelem died, seized of five acres of wareland at "P'sons Green," together with "one garden parcel of Stoutes," when his daughter Agnes, wife of William Conyngton, was admitted.

Next we find Stowtes in the possession of Johanna Parker of Brightwell's, who also held the five acres of wareland above mentioned. She died in 1437, when her son, Thomas Parker, was admitted. In 1542 Ralph Parker, gent., was elected the Lord's bailiff for "Stowtts." Among the presentments at a Court General, in 1543, is the following:

> "Ralph P'kr (Parker) has obstructed a certain gateway at Parsonsgrene."

At a Court, in 1551, Ralph Parker surrendered Stowte's to Henry Parker, his son. It was probably to this family that John Parker, the husband of Susanna Svanders, mentioned on the Svanders' brass in Fulham Church, belonged.

The Parkers were succeeded by the Dodds. In 1561, Thomas Dodd was elected bailiff for Stowte's. In the minutes of a Court, in 1569, we read:

> "The Lord of his special grace granted out of his hands to Thomas Dodde one parcel of wast ground adjacent to his house and lying at Parsons Green within this Manor in length 84 feet and in breadth 9 feet to hold the same to the said Thomas and heirs by the rod."

Thomas Dodd, who died in 1571, surrendered Stowte's to his eldest son, James Dodd, who, in 1602, mortgaged it to Richard Ward, or Warde, rector of Chelsea, and Katherine his wife.

This worthy rector had been vicar of Epping, of which living he was deprived in 1556, Queen Elizabeth made him her cofferer. His wife, Katherine, was buried at Chelsea, 16 Dec. 1605. On 2 Jan. 1606-7, he married, in the old Church at Chelsea, Elizabeth Fisher. In 1612 "Rich Ward, clerk" sought license of the Bishop of London to demise Stowte's and one acre at Parson's Green to Thomas Lovell, maltster, of Chelsea. The Rev. Richard Ward was buried in the grave of his first wife at Chelsea Church, 2 Sept. 1615. His widow, Elizabeth Ward, who succeeded to Stowte's, married, as her second husband, John Hambden, S.T.P., who, in 1630, sold the property to James Taylor, of Fulham, baker. In 1645 he surrendered Stowte's to John Grant, a brewer. In 1673 Henry Carter sought admittance to Stowte's "to his own use for life, heretofore surrendered by George Kelsey, deceased, to Ann, late wife of said Henry Carter." Henry Carter died in 1679 possessed of Stowte's, when Ann, his youngest daughter, then wife of John Bowater, was admitted.

The ancient tenement was taken down about the time of William III. In 1702, Bowater sold to Robert Child, the eldest son of Sir Francis, "one acre upon which formerly stood a tenement called Stouts tenement." On the site of Stowte's tenement was built Albion House, or the "White House," a mansion at one time of some consequence. There is, however, little to record as to its history. From 1714 to 1725 it was the residence of Lady Temple.

Albion House (back view). From an original oil painting by E. Dorrell, 1814, now in the possession of the London Female Preventive and Reformatory Institution, 200, Euston Road, N.W.

In the above illustration, the white house is Albion House, the original school of Mr. William Maxwell. The dark one to the right is the additional house acquired by Mr. Maxwell in 1813. Further to the right are No. 6 (now incorporated with No. 7, the Jubilee Home), and Nos. 5, 4 and 3, now the Holt Yates Memorial Home. To the extreme left is Elm House.

Towards the close of the last century this house was in the occupation of the Rev. Mr. Waring, who, in 1797, was succeeded by Mr. William Maxwell. This gentleman, who, in 1813, acquired a second house on the north side, kept a boarding school for boys. <u>Albion House School was continued down to about 1828</u>. Shortly afterwards the property was purchased by Mr. John Daniel, who pulled down Albion House and built upon a portion of the site the residence now known as Park House.

This mansion was erected by Messrs. Cubitt about 1841. It is said that Squire Daniel designed it so that it might last a thousand years. Some of the floors are of solid oak. The front gates, with their wrought iron figures and roses, are very handsome. It has had only two tenants. The first was Mr. Charles Robinson, who resided here from 1844 to 1847. In 1848 the house was taken by Mr. Park Nelson, solicitor to the Fulham Vestry, and a member of the firm of Park Nelson and Co., of Essex Street, Strand. He died at Parson's Green, 19 Dec. 1876. The house has recently been taken by the Fulham Guardians for boarding pauper children.

The property now occupied by the London Female Preventive and Reformatory Institution was originally known as Nos. 3, 4, 5, 6 and 7, Parson's Green. These houses possessed no interest of an antiquarian nature. Mr. William Maxwell, of whom we have spoken in connection with Albion House, took No. 7 for the purpose of enlarging his school. Here, between 1863-65, lived Prince Peter Dolgouroukow.

Eventually the houses came into the possession of Dr. Holt Yates and his wife, who was a daughter of Mr. William Maxwell. Dr. Yates, the author of Yates' "Egypt," and founder of the Suediah Mission near Antioch, was a well-known philanthropist. In 1860 he attended one of the earliest midnight meetings organized by the London Female Preventive and Reformatory Institution for the purpose of rescuing outcast women. He was so impressed by what he saw that he offered the Institution the use of Nos. 3, 4 and 5, Parson's Green, rent free, if the Committee would adapt them for another Home for the fallen.

This offer was gladly accepted. Subsequently Dr. and Mrs. Holt Yates allowed the Institution, for a nominal rent, the use of No. 7, Parson's Green, which was fitted up for preventive work among respectable friendless young women and girls.

Dr. Holt Yates died on 26 July 1874. The houses at Parson's Green being trust property, over which Dr. and Mrs. Holt Yates had not absolute control, a special effort was made by the Institution to

raise money for their purchase. These were the three houses, Nos. 3, 4 and 5, which were pulled down when the present Rescue Home,
No. 5 Parson's Green, was erected in memory of its founder. It is known as the Holt Yates Memorial Home. In 1886 a further effort was made to commemorate the Queen's Jubilee by extending the preventive work carried on at No. 7. This was done by incorporating No. 6 with No. 7, the two houses being turned into one, affording accommodation for fifty young girls who are here trained for domestic service. It is now numbered 7, and known as the Jubilee Training Home. In front of the house is a tablet inscribed:

> "This Memorial Stone was laid by Mrs. Frank Bevan, June 19, 1886, to commemorate the extension of the Training Home in this place for Young Girls. Completed in the Jubilee Year of the Reign of Queen Victoria 1886, Aug. 17."

The Holt Yates Memorial Home and the Jubilee Home. From a photograph by Mr. T. S. Smith, 1896

In the grounds attached to the Home (No. 7), there still stands a venerable mulberry tree. Here, under the shade of the old tree, on a warm summer evening, Dr. Holt Yates would often gather the inmates of the Home and conduct a short religious service. The whole of the property is in trust. The Homes are not endowed, being entirely supported by voluntary gifts.

Tea time at the Holt Yates Memorial Home.
From a photograph by Mr. T. S. Smith

The "White Horse," now rebuilt, stands at the junction of Ackmar Road with Parson's Green. The "White Horse" enjoys, by virtue of ancient tenure, a square foot of ground on which stands its sign at the northern end of the Green. It was formerly supported in a curious piece of iron scrollwork.

There is little of interest to be noted in connection with the "White Horse." In the Parish Books it is first mentioned in 1777. Its most noted host was John Wright, of whom a well-known incident is related. A boy named Fennell, nicknamed "The Giant," had, on one occasion, the misfortune to incur the displeasure of the host of the "White Horse," and was so severely chastised by him that he died. Thenceforward Wright was known as "Jack, the Giant Killer."

It was at the "White Horse," Parson's Green, that the old Fulham Albion Cricket Club used to meet. This was the pioneer cricket club in Fulham.

SECTION III: PARSON'S GREEN LANE

Before we cross to the west side of the Green, we will take a stroll along Parson's Green Lane, as far as Percy Cross.

The name "Parson's Green Lane," as applied to this thoroughfare, is modern, coming in, perhaps, with the present century. Old Parson's Green Lane, as elsewhere observed, was the road which bounded, on its west side, the Peterborough estate. This lane, in course of time, became known as Peterborough Lane, its former designation being transferred to the lane of which we are about to speak.

In ancient documents, the present Parson's Green Lane is always spoken of as the "lane from Parson's Green to Purser's Cross," or by some similar phrase.

EAST SIDE

Along this side there is little to detain us. Elysium Cottage (No. 61), lying a little way back, is a curious place. Along the high pavement, as far as Crown Street, were some very old houses pulled down in 1898-99. "The Alma" (No. 51), established in 1799, was rebuilt in 1899. No. 49, adjoining Crown Street, was, from 1843 to 1847, used as a meeting house by the Roman Catholics before the building of St. Thomas's. On the demolition of this portion of Parsons Green Lane, in 1898-9, the ground was levelled.

Crown Street, long a disreputable way, was, in 1896, renamed Novello Street, when its houses were remodelled.

From the end of Novello Street a narrow path led through to Eelbrook. The ground has recently been cleared, and the entrance to the Common greatly improved.

Returning to Parson's Green Lane, we arrive at the "Rose and Crown" (No. 47). The old house, which stood on high pavement, boasted some antiquity. It was pulled down about seventeen years ago, when the present house was built. In the time of Mr. J. T. Liley, a collection of curios, once owned by Mr. Robert Roskell, of

Park House, adorned the bar. The present landlord, Mr. E. Willby, the son-in-law of Mr. Liley, still possesses Mr. Roskell's well-known "swish."

A bit of Parson's Green Lane.
From a photograph by Mr. T. S. Smith, 1896

Near where the railway line crosses Parson's Green Lane, stood a very old red-brick house. It lay back from the road and had some fine trees in front. Blenheim House (No. 43), which stood next to it, still survives. The name, which recalls Marlborough's victory over Marshal Tallard, probably indicates the period of its erection. Very little can be gathered about its early history. It was here that Felice Orsini resided.

This notorious Italian was a prominent mover in the revolution of 1848, from which period he continued to conspire against the French Government. He was confined for a time in prison at Mantua. Escaping, in 1856, he came to England, settling for awhile at Blenheim House. For his attempt on the French Emperor he was executed in March 1858. The house was last occupied by Baron

May, but is now empty, he having left in 1900. Next door, attached to Blenheim House, is Chilton Lodge, a similar house of about the same age. Nothing of interest is connected with its history.

The old "Rose and Crown"

Just northwards of Chilton Lodge stood Audley Cottage, formerly called Brunswick Cottage. To perpetuate the legend concerning the supposed connection of Fair Rosamond with Parson's Green, Mr. T. Crofton Croker, when he took the house in 1837, bestowed upon it the fantastic designation of Rosamond's Bower. Finally, Mr. Thomas James Bell, who, in 1847, succeeded Mr. Croker, altered the name to Audley Cottage.

The original building (the portion nearest to Chilton Lodge) was composed mainly of rubble. Mr. Croker writes in his "Walk":

"The foundation of the present 'Rosamond's Bower,' judging from the brickwork on the south side, and the thickness of the walls, is probably as old as the time of Elizabeth. I mean the original building which consisted of two rooms, one above the other, 12 ft., square, and 7 ft. in height. On the north side of this primitive dwelling was a deep draw-well. Subsequently two similar rooms were attached, one of which (the present hall) was built over the well, and two attics were raised upon this very simple structure, thus increasing the number of rooms from two to six. Then a kitchen was built (the present dining-room), and another room over it (the present drawing- room), at the back of the original building, which thus from a labourer's hut had assumed the air of an eight-roomed cottage. It was then discovered that the rooms were of very small dimensions, and it was considered necessary to enlarge four of them by the additional space to be gained from bay windows in the dining-room, drawing-room, blue bedchamber, and dressing-room. But the spirit of improvement seldom rests content, and when it was found that the kitchen, which looked upon the garden, was a more agreeable sitting-room, both as to aspect and quiet, than the more ancient and smaller room which looked upon the road, it was determined to create another attachment on the north side by building a kitchen of still larger dimensions, with a scullery and storeroom behind, to replace the old scullery and out-offices by a spacious staircase, and over this new kitchen to place a room of corresponding size, or equal to that of the two bedrooms upon the same line of building. Thus in 1826 did 'Rosamond's Bower' become a cottage of ten rooms; and as it was soon afterwards presumed from the march of luxury that no one could live in a decade cottage without requiring a coach-house and stable, an excellent one was built not far from the north side, making the third, though not the last, addition in that direction."

Rosamond's Bower, from an engraving, 1842

Audley Cottage stood back from the road. At its rear was a large garden. Here was a weeping ash, the circumference of which measured 56 feet. Under its branches, on 22 June 1842, Gunter laid a breakfast for Croker and a party of thirty-eight friends. The house, when Croker took it, became a rendezvous for the literati of his day.

Mr. Crofton Croker, who left Rosamond's Bower in 1846, was the only son of Major Thomas Croker of the 38th Regiment of Foot, of a family of good standing in Ireland. From boyhood he evinced a love for antiquities, and this was cherished during several excursions which he made in the South of Ireland between 1812-15. At that early period Croker commenced his collections of legends and songs of the peasantry of Ireland which he interweaved in many of his subsequent writings. In 1819 he received an appointment in the Admiralty through its secretary, Mr. Wilson Croker. It is somewhat singular that Crofton Croker went to the same Government department as his namesake, Wilson Croker, and that both the Crokers made Fulham their home, though they were in no way related.

Audley Cottage, just before its demolition in 1892

Among Crofton Croker's more important works are his "Researches in the South of Ireland" (1824), "Fairy Legends of Ireland" and "Legends of the Lakes; or Sayings and Doings at Killarney" (1829). To most of us residing in this part of the Metropolis, Croker is best remembered for his interesting "Walk from London to Fulham," a work to which we have to express our own indebtedness. The "Walk," which originally appeared in the pages of *Fraser's Magazine,* was revised and considerably extended by his son, Mr. T. F. Dillon Croker, who published it in book form in 1860. Mr. Croker also wrote "A Description of Rosamond's Bower, Fulham," 5 parts, 1842-43. This was privately printed, only fifteen copies being issued.

After the tenancy by Mr. Thomas J. Bell, Audley Cottage was taken by Mr. William Douglas, the well-known South Kensington builder.

In consequence of its dilapidated condition, it was, in 1892, thought advisable to pull down Audley Cottage. It was long rumoured that secret passages existed beneath the old building. Its demolition, however, revealed nothing beyond thick walls of ancient construction. The quaint oak staircase of the cottage was traditionally said to have belonged to what Croker terms the "veritable Rosamond's Bower," by which, we presume, he means the old house which once existed on the opposite side of the lane, the ancient manor house of Rosamond's.

Blenheim House, Chilton Lodge and Audley Cottage were purchased by the Metropolitan District Railway Company in 1883 in connection with the Fulham Extension Line to Putney.

WEST SIDE

Roughly speaking, the west side of Parson's Green Lane, from Percy Cross to Rectory Road, westwards towards the Fulham Road, indicates the site of the ancient freelands or "Manor" of Rosamond's.

There has long lingered in the neighbourhood a tradition to the effect that "the fair Rosamond," whom Henry II loved not wisely but too well, once inhabited a "palace" or "bower" at Parson's Green. Lysons notes the tradition, and old people still living will relate the stories handed down to them by their fathers, regarding a subterranean passage alleged to be yet existent. According to some, this underground way leads from the old tenements, still known as Rosamond's, under the Lane to the site of Audley Cottage. Others will have it that it runs from Rosamond's, under the Green, in the direction of Arragon House. The stories are all more or less vague in details. There is not, however, a shred of evidence to show that the fair daughter of Walter, Lord Clifford, ever had the remotest connection with Fulham.

In the course of this work we have shown that nearly all the more noted residences or "tenements" in the Manor were called after the surnames of their original owners. Thus, at Parson's Green, we have Hore's, Parlor's, Stowte's, etc. The case with regard to the freelands or "Manor" of Rosamond's is precisely similar. The family of Rosemont, Rosemond or Rosamond, appears to have long dwelt at Parson's Green, and to this circumstance, there can be no reasonable doubt, the name of "Rosamond's" is due. In the minutes of a Court General, held in 1414, occurs the name of "Robert Rosemount, clerk." At a Court Baron, in 1418, it was presented that:

> "Robert Rosemond held and occupied one acre of customary wareland called Mathewes bithewode (i.e. Mathew's by the Wood) and for long time held without license of the Court to the prejudice of the Lord, wherefore the said tenement is seized into the hands of the Lord."

In 1431 we read in the minutes of a Court:

> "Robert Rosomond has trees overhanging Bridgecroft lane and the same Robert has made a gate between Parsonsgrene and Lordesfeld."

This Robert Rosamond, who was a bachelor in laws, was public notary and procurator of the Court of Canterbury. He died 29 June 1431. John Style, a vintner of London and a kinsman of the Rosamonds, by his will; dated 28 June 1440, left a tenement in Gracechurch Street to the rectors, churchwardens and parishioners of All Hallows,

> "so that they might maintain an honest chaplain to serve in a perpetual chantry to be called Rosamondeschauntrie in the aforesaid church for the soul of Master Robert Rosamond," etc.
> (Sharpe's "Wills.")

Robert Rosamond was the last of the family connected with Fulham. After the Rosamonds the estate passed through several hands. In or about 1440 Nicholas Philpot and William Huntley devised the Manor, together with other property, to Sir Thomas Hasele or Haseley, who held very extensive estates in the parish.

At a View in 1442 Thomas Hasele was amerced "ij^d" because he suffered the branches of his trees to overhang the king's highway "between Berestret and Wendenesgrene," in length eight perches. The king's highway thus indicated was, of course, the London or Fulham Road, so that we may infer that the Manor of Rosamond's extended north-westwards to it. Eastwards it probably reached as far as Eelbrook, for we find him several times presented for endeavouring to encroach upon the Common. Thus, at a Court Baron in 1443:

> "Thomas Hasele has encroached on the Common at Hellebrook."

Sir Thomas died about 1448. At a View in 1450 it was presented that "The wife of the late Thomas Hasele has made encroachments upon the Common at Hellebrook." Dame Agnes Hasele, the widow, was, in 1454, indicted for over-commoning.

The piece of wareland, which had been occupied by Mathew by the Wood, consisted of a field anciently known as Prefette's or Presette's Field. It lay adjacent to Rosamond's and was apparently regarded by the owners of that Manor as a piece of freeland which they had the right to occupy. The Bishop, on two or three occasions, claimed the field and ordered its seizure by his bailiff. Thus, it is recorded in the minutes of a Court Baron held in 1448:

> "Ordered to seize into the hands of the Lord one customary tenement with appurtenances and two acres in P'fettes feld which Thomas Hasele kt claimed to hold as freeland."

Dame Agnes Hasele, who married, as her second husband, Gilbert Debenham, about 1459 alienated Rosamond's to Sir Henry, or Harry, Waver, kt., citizen and draper of London, a kinsman, who died possessed of the estate in 1469-70. His nuncupative will, dated 4 Feb. 1469-70, was proved 11 Aug. 1470 (P.C.C. 31 Godyn). By it he devised all his lands in Fulham and elsewhere to his wife Christian. At a Court General in 1473 it was presented that "Dame de Wavers has encroached on the common called Helbrook." Dame Christian Waver died in 1479, seized of this estate. The entry in the "Cal. Inq. Post Mortem," 19 Ed. IV, reads: "Christiana Waver Rosamondes maner' in Fulham." The Manor of Rosamond's was then valued at 10 marks per annum.

The next heir to the estate appears to have been another Christian, daughter of Henry, the son of the first named Henry Waver, but it does not appear that this lady ever had possession.

The next tenant of Rosamond's of whom we have any knowledge was one Thomas Broun, or Browne, who held other tenements in the parish, such as Dowbeler's, Lane's, etc. In 1492-93 Thomas Browne was in default for "Rosamond's." From 1508 to 1514 William Browne owned the estate, etc.

In 1527 Humphrey Dymock was the tenant of Rosamond's and Lane's. In 1539 they passed into the hands of Humphrey Dymock the younger, who, in 1550, sold the two free tenements to Nicholas Holmes and Thomas Thorneton. Nicholas Holmes died in 1575.

For many years the history of Rosamond's is a blank. In 1632 we find Sir Michael Wharton, or Warton, knight, in possession.

Sir Michael, who was high sheriff of Yorkshire in 1616, was knighted at Ripon, 16 April 1640. He married Elizabeth, third daughter and co-heiress of Ralph Hansby of St. Giles's, Beverley.

About 1637 Sir Michael let Rosamond's to Andrew Arnold, who died in 1646. In the old Register Book it is recorded that "Mr. Andrewe Arnold gent." by his will gave the poor of Fulham the sum of 40s.

In 1647 Sir Michael Wharton was elected one of the Lord's reeves. He was evidently a worshipper at Fulham Church, for, in 1649, there was received "for puage"

"Sr Michaell Wharton 10s."

In the same year the Churchwarden paid:

"To a Joyner for Boards and workmanship in altering and making a Pew for Sir Mic. Wharton £3 0s 0d."

Sir Michael is rated for Rosamond's down to the time of his death. He died 8 Oct. 1655, in his 82nd year, and was buried at Beverley Minster. His son, Michael, who married Catherine, daughter and co-heiress of Christopher Maltby of Maltby, Yorkshire, was killed by a cannon ball at Scarborough Castle. He left a son, a third Michael, who died in London, 9 Aug. 1688, and was interred in Beverley Minster, 23 Aug. 1688. By his wife, Susannah, third daughter of John, first Lord Poulett, he left a son, a fourth Michael. As to how Rosamond's fared during the ownership of the three last named Whartons we know extremely little.

In the time of the fourth Michael we obtain a glimpse of Rosamond's. This Sir Michael, who was born about 1652, was elected M.P. for Hull in 1681. In the reign of William and Mary we find him espousing a scheme promoted by "the King and Queen's Corporation" for fostering the manufacture of linen in England. For this purpose he let to the Company "a house" at Parson's Green for their use. Judging from the high rental charged (£30 a year), it seems probable that it was the manor house of Rosamond's which the "Corporation" took.

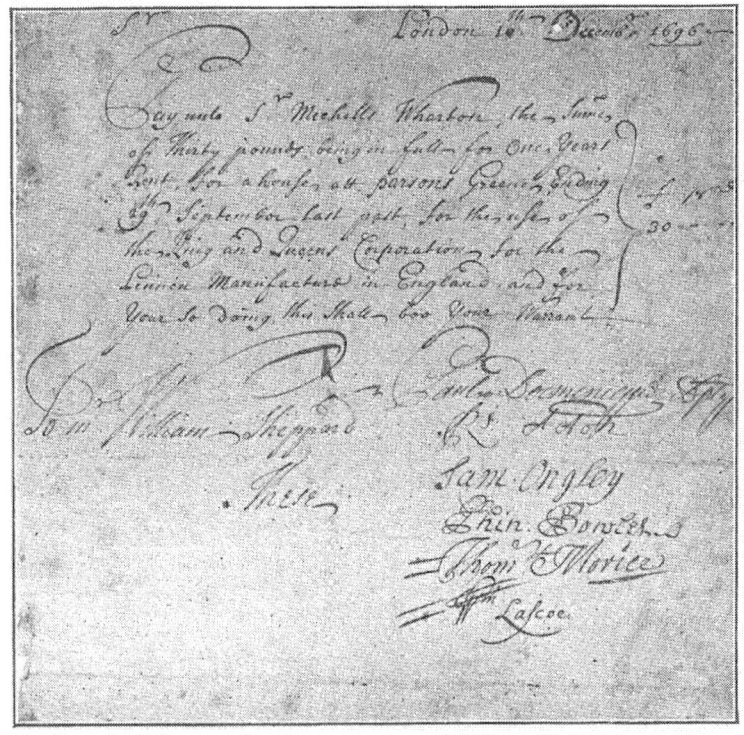

Facsimile of a Warrant for the payment of £30 to Sir Michael Wharton.
From the original in the possession of the Author

Sir Michael died 25 March 1725, aged 73. According to Lysons, Rosamond's was, on his death, divided between the co-heirs, "of whom, or their representatives, it was purchased by the late John Powell, Esq." The Court Rolls show that, on the death of the fourth Sir Michael, in 1725, his youngest sister, Lady Mary Pennyman, wife of Sir James Pennyman, bart., was admitted to "the heriotable messuage called Rosamond's." This lady probably sold the estate.

The history of Rosamond's during the years immediately following the death of Sir Michael, is involved in much obscurity. Croker, in his "Walk," tells us that the mansion was known as Quibus Hall,

> "a name, as is conjectured, bestowed upon it in consequence of some dispute respecting possession between the co-heirs of Sir Michael Wharton."

Where Croker obtained this story we do not know. The name, Quibus Hall, nowhere occurs.

It may be mentioned that the site on which Park House came to be eventually built, was a half acre strip of copyhold land, on which some three or four tenements had stood, belonging to the Bishopric of London, bounded north and south by the "free-lands" of Rosamond's. In 1749 this piece of land was leased to James Sayers. On 15 May 1762, Mr. John Powell, of the Pay Office, Whitehall, obtained a similar lease of the property, described as "all that half acre of land formerly arable and afterwards an orchard and a brick messuage and three other tenements," etc.

The old brick messuage and the three small tenements Mr. Powell pulled down, erecting, in their stead, "one large capital messuage." <u>This was High Elms House, familiar to a later generation as Park House</u>.

In 1763 we find Mr. John Powell first assessed for his new "mansion house." The house was designed by Mr. Henry Holland.

In explanation of the name High Elms House, we may, perhaps, be allowed a slight digression. There is no doubt that, in ancient times, some great elms grew at the junction of the Fulham Road with Parson's Green Lane, precisely as we know a clump of elms once marked the site of the cross roads where the Queen's Elm now stands. As early as 1571, we hear of a "headland called High Elmes," presumably identical with this point of land at Percy

Cross. In 1603 reference again occurs in the Court Rolls to the "High Elmes" at this spot. At a Court General in 1609 it was presented that:

> "Certain of the tenants shall carry away their dung lying in the kinges highway neer the great elme in ffulham streete."

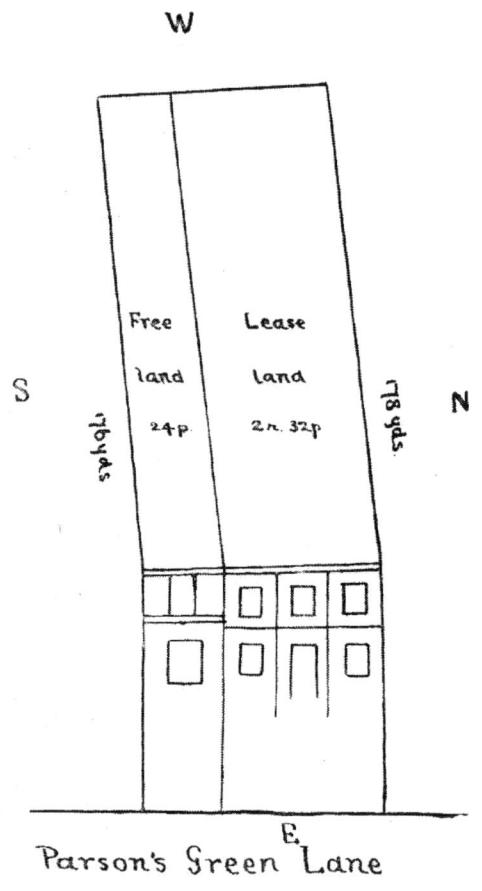

Sketch plan from Mr. John Powell's lease, 15 May 1762.

On the death of Mr. John Powell, in 1784, his executors obtained a renewal of the lease. In this indenture High Elms, or Fulham Park House as it came to be called, is described as in the occupation of the Rev. Thomas Bowen, M.A., chaplain of Bridewell Hospital and minister of Bridewell Precinct. Here, in the year just named, Mr. Bowen established a boys' school, which he conducted with much success.

In 1791 the Bishop granted to Mr. Arthur Annesley Powell, the nephew and heir of John Powell, a new lease of the estate.

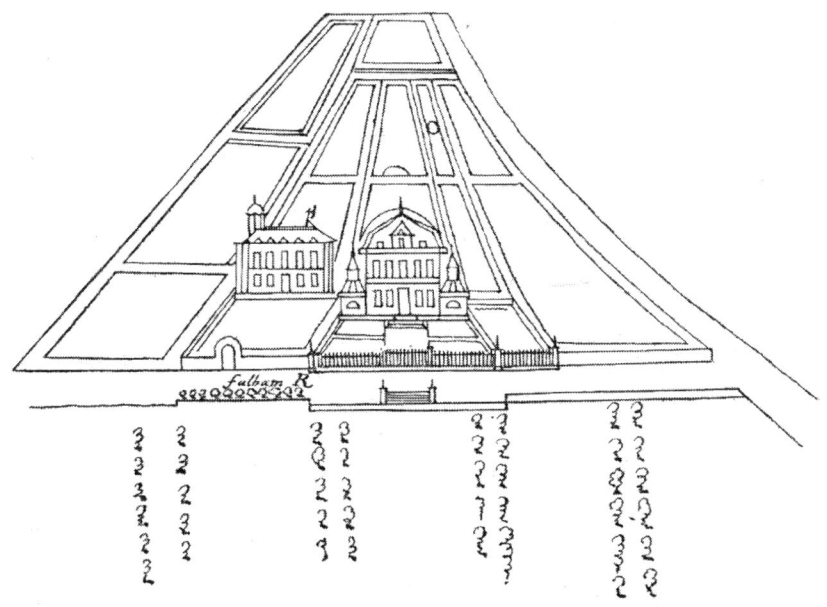

Old Rosamond's Bower and Park House, circa 1763. From a sketch by Doharty, formerly in the possession of J. P. Powell, Esq. ['fulham R' in the road in front of the house is properly Parson's Green Lane.]

Park House (front view)

Park House (back view).

The Rev. Thomas Bowen died in 1800. With the assistance of the Rev. Joshua Ruddock, M.A., the widow continued Fulham Park House School down to 1818. One of the most distinguished pupils at this school was Lord Lytton, the eminent novelist.

On the death of Mr. A. A. Powell, a new lease was, in 1823, granted to Mr. John Powell Powell, of Quex Park, Thanet, who made the house his occasional residence. In 1825-26 Mr. J. P. Powell pulled down the ancient building, known as Rosamond's Bower, believed to have been of about the time of Elizabeth. Subsequently, the stables of Park House were built on the site. Mr. J. P. Powell died in 1849.

Captain Henry Perry Cotton, of Quex Park, son-in-law of Mr. J. P. Powell, resided at Park House till 1860. He died at Quex Park, 20 Nov. 1881.

From 1862 till his death in 1888, Park House was the residence of Mr. Robert Roskell, of the firm of Hunt and Roskell, jewellers, of Bond Street. Mr. Roskell, who lies buried in St. Thomas's Churchyard, was a very benevolent man, greatly beloved by the poor of Parson's Green. He died at Park House, 22 July 1888, aged 83.

Park House was very picturesquely situated. Its grounds (13a. 2r. 25p.) were finely timbered and included a large meadow together with a canal and watercourse. It was pulled down in 1889, to make way for the Park House estate, which now covers the site.

Park House was familiar to wayfarers on account of a small stone tablet let into the right pier of the gateway inscribed:

> Purser's Cross
> 7th August
> 1738.

The date recorded the death of a highwayman who fled before his pursuers across Fulham Fields. The desperado was, however, run to earth, and, to escape capture, blew out his brains after throwing his ill-gotten gains to the labourers who witnessed his suicide. In the *London Magazine* for August 1738 (p. 411), the monthly chronologer thus records the incident under date Monday, 7 Aug.:

> "An Highwayman, having committed several Robberies on *Finchley-Common* was pursued to *London* when he thought himself safe, but was in a little Time discovered at a Publick House in *Burlington Gardens*, refreshing himself and his Horse; however he bad Time to remount, and rode thro' *Hyde Park*, at which Place there were several Gentlemen's Servants airing their Horses, who taking the Alarm, pursued him closely as far as *Fulham-Field,* where finding no probability of escaping, he threw Money among some Country People, who were at Work in the Field, and told them they would soon see the End of an unfortunate Man; he had no sooner spoke these Words but he pull'd out a pistol, clap'd it to his Ear, and shot himself directly, before his Pursuers could prevent him. The Coroner's Inquest brought in their Verdict, *Self-Murder*, and he was buried in a Cross Road with a Stake drove thro' him: But 'twas not known who he was."

The sequel to this grim story is thus told in the Church Registers:

> 1738. A strong built man, 5 feet 7 or 8 inches high, aged about 26, robb'd a Gent, on Finchley Common Aug[t] 7 and was pursued to ffulham ffield near the Windmill, where he shot himself thro' the Head, and was buried in the Common Highway, Pursor's Cross 8 August.

The tablet has been refixed against the wall of the house which now stands at the comer of the cross roads.

Next to the Park House estate, going towards Parson's Green, is Park Lodge (No. 24 Parson's Green Lane), once the residence of Mr. John A. Waring. Brunswick Place was built about 1825 by a Mr. Akers on a site which had belonged to the Plaws. At No. 1 resided, for some years, the late Mr. Samuel Bridges, who, by his marriage with the widow of Mr. Akers, became the owner of this property. Passing Brunswick Place we come to Purser's Cross Road, which preserves, in contradistinction to Percy Cross, the older spelling of the name of this spot. Parson's Green Station, where the Metropolitan District Line crosses the Lane, was opened for traffic 1 Mar. 1880.

SECTION IV: WEST SIDE

We will now return to the Green, making our way down its western side. At its north-west corner and a little way back from the road, lying behind the "Ray of Hope" coffee house, the visitor will come upon what is by far the oldest house now standing in the neighbourhood. "Rosamond's," as this building is called, was most probably built about the time of Elizabeth, but no records exist as to its early history. About the commencement of this century it is said to have been known as Rosamond's Dairy. The house is now divided into three tenements. In the centre house is an ancient square staircase, now much broken and decayed. Once it must have been the principal staircase of the house.

Rosamond's. From a photograph by Mr. T. S. Smith, 1896

From Mr. Thomas Flaw, Rosamond's passed to his son-in-law, Mr. Henry Solomon, from whom it was purchased by Miss Sulivan, of Broom House.

A curious story attaches to Rosamond's. On the death of Mr. James Stockdale, in 1815, his widow, Mrs. Frances Stockdale, the only daughter of Oliver Stocken, the founder of the "Swan" Brewery, took this house, where she carried on a boys' school. In the course of some work, which Mrs. Stockdale was having carried out about 1816, the men, on removing some panelling, discovered a space between this woodwork and the original wall, on the latter of which still hung some valuable oil paintings. It is said that they were claimed by, and passed into the possession of, the Lord of the Manor.

Staircase at Rosamond's.
From a photograph by Messrs. C. G. and A. C. Wright

At No. 10, Parson's Green, formerly known as Rosamond Place, lived William Wainwright, brother of Henry Wainwright who was hanged for the murder of Harriet Lane at Whitechapel. The notoriety which the house thus attained led the owner to change its name to Ash House Cottage.

At the north-east corner of Rectory Road stands Parson's Green Mission Hall, built in 1876 by Miss Sulivan, of Broom House. It was designed by Mr. Arthur Billing. Here, before the erection of St. Dionis, services were held.

Rectory Road, which marked the boundary between the freelands of Rosamond's and the glebe lands of the Parsonage, rejoiced, in the last century, in the characteristic name of Muddy Lane. In a "Book for the Surveiour," for 1752, we read:

"Paid a Man to spread the stuff in Muddy Lane 1s. 0d."

Parson's Green Mission Hall.
From a photograph by Mr. H. Ambridge.

Down to the early years of this century, the only habitation in the lane was a small wooden hut about half way down. The old cottages, on the north side of the road, were built by John Faulkner. A stone tablet against them still recalls their original name, "Rectory Place."

Rectory Place. From a photograph by Mr. T. S. Smith, 1896

The ancient Rectory or Parsonage House, built in 1707, stood on the west side of Parson's Green, a portion of its site now being occupied by St. Dionis Church and the new Vicarage house. It was a square, not unpicturesque looking, brick building with a red gabled roof and rows of small dormer windows set in heavy frames. In front of the house was a neat garden. The grounds, at the back, were latterly about an acre in extent, though once much larger. The rooms of the Rectory were mostly dark and small, hardly suggestive of affording any large amount of comfort.

From time immemorial the Rectory or Parsonage House stood on this spot. The earliest allusion to it occurs in the minutes of a Court held in 1401. During the latter part of the reign of Henry V, the Parsonage lands at Fulham were farmed by the Carthusian monks of Shene, of whom we have spoken in our account of the Parish Church and the Rectory. Dr. Drewell, Rector of Fulham, was, at a Court Baron in 1457, found guilty of lopping some elms growing in front of the Rectory House. The entry in the minutes reads:

> "Ordered to distrain John Drewell Rector of the Church of Fulham that he may be at the next Court to answer because he has cut off the heads (*capitavit*) of certain elms growing upon the waste at psonesgrene opposite the Rectory there and the underwood thus forthcoming carried away without license of the Lord."

That the lands of the Rectory adjoined, on the north, those of Rosamond's, is clear from the following minutes of a Court General in 1477:

> "One Nicholas has ploughed up one mere between the lands of the Lady Waffer (Waver) and the lands of the Rectory of Fulham, 10 perches, from which cause they are not able to determine the boundaries of the said lands."

During the rectorship of Dr. Simon Heynes the Rectory House was leased to Sir William Butts, chief physician to Henry VIII, who, as we have previously remarked, probably died here in 1545. From the annexed extracts from the will of Lady Butts, his widow, who died in 1547, it will be observed that she disposed, in her lifetime, of her interest in the Parsonage House to a Mr. William ffitzwilliam, who had, apparently, also purchased the farm stock belonging to it. The will, which is dated 3 Oct. 1547, was proved 15 Nov. 1547 (P.C.C. 48 Alen):

> "I Dame Margaret Buttes of Milton in ye pishe of Egham in the countie of Surr[y] wydowe, late the wife of S[r] Willm Buttes knight now deceased. My body to be buryed in the pishe Churche of fulham besides the s[d] S[r] William. To the chest in the saide Church of ffulham aforesaid in redy money xij[d] whiche I will shalbe distributed to the powre people by the discretion of the Church Wardens their. I will that there be bestowed at the daye of my buryall in the said pishe of ffulham £5. To S[r] Nicholas Smyth my Chapleyn Clerk a feather bed, a bolster, and a couyng to the same lying at ffulham and xl[s] in redy money. All my plate and juelles (one Rynge of Gold excepted which I will and bequeth to the good wyfe Warrand of fulham) to be solde.
> Whereas Mr William ffitzwilliam of Fulham aforesaid gent hath bought of me my cartes horses mylne brewhouse wood cole haye and myn interest title and right in the psonage of myn of fulham aforesaid for which I the said Dame Margaret have receyved of him xlviij[li] xvj[s] and whereas the said Mr ffitzwilliam hath bought of me all my wheate Rye barley otes pease and tares paying after the rate of the most highe prise that shall be had upon sales made in Newgate m'ket w[th]in Newgate in London and the same Mr Willm ffitzwilliam must stande to the charges of the thresshers therof whiche thresshers shalbe at the appointment and denomination of me the said Dame Margaret and shall haue in consideracon of the same charges the strawe thereof issuying.
> Residue of goods to John Hebbern and Margaret his wife and same John and Mr Doctor Haynes of ffulham my Execut[rs]."

Dr. Butts. After the original picture by Hans Holbein

We may here pause to mention a quaint custom which, from remote times, existed in connection with the Parsonage House of Fulham. This was the obligation, on the part of the Rector, as the owner of the Great Tithes, or of the farmer of these tithes, to keep a common bull and a common boar for the general use of the kine and sows of the inhabitants of the parish, for the increase of calves and pigs. In many parishes it was once usual to keep what was known as the "town bull," which could be hired by persons who kept cows. How long in Fulham this primitive system for calving existed we cannot say, but it certainly existed down to about 200 years ago. At a Court General, in 1550, the following presentment was made:

"The Rector of Fulham or his firmar shall keep and find one bull and one boar for the inhabitants and the same rector or his firmar shall keep and haue common upon the common of the Lord for his team (*carut' suam*) and not more cattle."

The custom is alluded to by Shakespeare in Henry IV (Act 2, Sc. 2), and in the last chapter of Sterne's " Tristram Shandy."

About 1580, that is, during the rectorship of the Rev. Edward Layfield, one Thomas Heath was residing at the Parsonage House. A letter among the State Papers, believed to have been written in the year named, was sent by Thomas Heath, junior, to his father, Thomas Heath, "dwelling in the Parsonage at Fulham." In it the writer desires to be placed with another tutor. Thomas Heath, senior, died in 1583. The following is an extract from his will, dated May 1583, and proved 22 October 1583 (P.C.C. 6 Butts):

"I Thomas Heath of the parrishe of ffulham in the Countie of Middlesex ffermer of the personage of ffulham. To be buried in the Chauncell of the parrishe Churche of ffulham yf yt please God to call me to his mercie in the same parrishe. Whereas Thomas Heathe my Sonne at this present remayneth beyonde the Seas I will and my mynde and intente is that if he shall at annye time wthin three yeares at the moste nexte after my deceasse returne home into this Realme or otherwise shall wthin the same three yeares obtayne a sufficient Licence from her Maiestie to tarye longer at his Studye beyonde the Seas then I devise to him all my lands etc. in Perivall, litle Grinford, and Elinge which I purchased of Mr Roger Townesend and to the heirs male of his body and for default to my Son Jerome and his heirs male and in default to my daughter Mary and her heirs male."

In 1598 the Rectory was the residence of Lady Ursula Walsingham, the widow of Sir Francis Walsingham, Elizabeth's faithful ambassador and "lieger" in France. It was after the death of Sir Francis, which occurred on 6 April 1590, that Lady Walsingham came to the Parsonage House, probably as a rural retirement. She did not, however, long enjoy it, for she fell into financial difficulties. To Secretary Windebank she presented a piteous memorial, dated 2 June 1602, pointing out how, the previous year, she had purchased land of the Queen at a cost of £2,700, "which else had been purchased over her head by some other." The money, the appeal sets forth, she took upon interest, and for repayment she had been constrained to sell, not only Walsingham House, her town residence, but Fulham Parsonage to boot. [State Papers, Dom., Eliz., vol. 284, No. 24.]

James I, in 1612, in answer to an appeal by Sir Francis Walsingham's daughter Frances and her husband, the Earl of Clanricard, gave a sum of £3,000 in discharge of the dead queen's liabilities to her Secretary of State.

In 1641, Dr. Henry King, Rector of Fulham, granted a lease of the Rectory to the Nourse or Nurse family, of Wood-Eaton, Oxfordshire.

The following information about the Rectory House is given in the "Survey of Church Livings," furnished to the Commonwealth in 1656:

"Presentment of the Jurie hereunder named:
Fulham.
Wee p^{r}sent that there is one parsonage there, the p^{r}sent Incumbant is the aforesaid (see 'Rectors' vol. ii. pp. 18-20) Mr. Adoniram Byfield, is worth fforty pounds p. ann., and is Impropriate, the p^{r}sentacon is in Edmond Harvie Esq. ass Wee are informed beeing Lo: of the said Man^r. The Tennant in possession is Mrs. Phillippa Nurse Widdow or her Assigns and holdeth the same by Lease for Three lives it being as wee are informed the Parsonage with twentie acres of Glebes Land Barnes and Stables thereunto belonging is worth ffifty pounds p. ann. The Tythes of Corn and hay is worth Two hundred and Nintye pounds p. ann."

Col. Arthur Eyre, who, in 1662, obtained from Charles II a lease of the rectorial lands and tithes, forfeited to the Crown on the attainder of Col. Harvey, was probably the next resident at the Rectory. In the assessments his name recurs till 1674.

In the latter part of the reign of Charles II Edward Limpany, brother of Robert Limpany, rented the Rectory House. The quaint custom of bull and boar, to which we have already referred, was, we find, still in existence, for, at a Court General in 1680, Limpany was fined for its breach. The entry runs:

> "Wee do present Mr. Edward Lympany (renting the parsonage within this parish) for not keepinge a bull and a Boare at the Parsonage yard for the Comon use of the Tenants and Inhabitants within this parish according to ancient custome and do order him to provide and keepe a sufficient Bull and boare for the use aforesaid by Michas next otherwise wee do ffine and amerce him ffive pounds."

Sir John Elwes, of Grove House, who died in 1701, was the next owner of the rectorial property.

Bowack writes of the Rectory House in 1705:

> "This house in which the Rectors of Fulham used to reside, is now very Old, and much decayed, but by the care that has been lately taken of it, is in good Tennantable Condition. There is, adjoyning to it, an Old Stone Building, which seems to be of about three hundred or four hundred years' standing, and Design'd for Religious Use; in all probability a chappel for the rectors and their Domesticks, which might be many in number, this Living being worth some Ages since £800 per annum, which building is now let in tenements."

This old stone building was taken down about 1740. It is not unlikely that, in pre-Reformation days, it served as a kind of oratory. In Bowack's time the Rectory House was tenanted by Mr. Thomas Carter.

Lady Elwes, the widow of Sir John, in 1704, sold the Rectory House to Sir Brook Bridges, who, in July 1707, obtained from Bishop Compton leave to take down such parts of the "Parsonage House and buildings" as he should judge needful, upon condition that he should erect upon the ground two or more substantial brick houses "of equal value goodness or dimensions as those expressed in the models shown to the Commissioners." Two houses were, we find, accordingly erected by Sir Brook Bridges, and constituted the old Rectory House which survived down to our own time.

Rectory House. After an old drawing

In 1733 the Rev. George Bell, junior, then Rector of Fulham, granted the Rectory House and lands to Dame Elizabeth Bridges, relict of Sir Brook Bridges, "late of Goodnestone, Kent," who continued to let the property, as her husband had done. The Rectory House was, in 1739, leased by the Rev. William Nicholas Blomberg, then Rector, to the Hon. Charles Fielding, of Goodnestone, and Elizabeth his wife, relict of Sir Brook Bridges.

In 1749 the Hon. Lady Jane Boyle took one of the Rectory houses, where she resided for thirty years. A Mrs. Batchellor, later on, occupied the other house. She was the widow of Mr. John Batchellor, who died 8 Aug. 1766, and was buried at Fulham (see vol. I, "Fulham Church: Its Monuments" chapter).

In 1751 the Rev. Samuel Knight, then Rector of Fulham, granted a lease of the Rectory House to the Hon. Edward Finch, of St. James's, and Sir Cordell Firebrace, of Long Melford, Suffolk, bart., the devisees of the Hon. Charles Fielding. The Rectory property next passed into the hands of Samuel Knight, of the

Middle Temple, son of the Rev. Samuel Knight. In 1822 the Rev. William Wood, then Rector, leased to James Wood

> "all the rectory or parsonage of Fulham and all glebe lands, meadows, pastures, and edifices and also all those two brick messuages or tenements erected and built in the stead of the old parsonage house and on the ground belonging thereto and all the houses, out-houses, buildings, gardens, orchards, rent - tithes, fruits, oblations, obventions and all manner of profits to the said Rectory or Parsonage pertaining or in any wise belonging (except all trees and woods growing on the premises and every of them and also the breaking of the ground in the chancel of the church of Fulham aforesaid for burial and the gift of the vicarage which are hereby excepted and to the parson and his successors always reserved), to have and to hold the said Rectory or Parsonage, etc., unto James Wood his heirs and assigns."

Subsequently the Rectory House reverted to the Rev. William Wood, on whose death it passed to his widow. Mrs. Wood, though she became a Roman Catholic, continued to enjoy the emoluments of the rectory and was popularly known as the "Roman Catholic rectoress." On her death her daughter, Miss Wood, became the owner. The last life in the lease, that of the Rev. W. Wood, vicar of Christ Church, Lancaster Gate, fell in in 1881, when the Rectory property reverted to the Ecclesiastical Commissioners.

For the last fifty years of its existence, the old Rectory House was used as a school. The Rectory House School was established about 1832 by Mr. Charles Roach, who died here, 28 March 1838. His son, Mr. John Roach, continued the school down to 1867. From 1848 to 1853 Dr. George Lambert, his brother-in-law, was in partnership with him. In 1868 Dr. Henry Laumann opened at the Rectory House his well-known Military Academy, a school for young gentlemen preparing for the Army. The inception of a Military School is said to have been due to Dr. Laumann's second wife, who had been governess to the Princess Mary, Duchess of Teck, sister of the Duke of Cambridge. The school seems to have gained a high reputation; indeed, it was a current belief that a term or two at Dr. Laumann's would be sure to qualify the dullest boy for "a pass." Dr. Laumann was assisted in the school by Mr. William Alexander Elderton. Upon the doctor's retirement, in 1876, Mr. Elderton continued the school.

In 1882 the Rectory House was demolished, a portion of the site being granted by the Ecclesiastical Commissioners for the erection of the new church of St. Dionis. On another portion a vicarage house was built in 1898.

The farm lands belonging to the Parsonage House must in ancient times have been very large, extending back from the Green probably as far as Munster Road. We have seen that, when Adoniram Byfield was rector, the glebe lands consisted of 20 acres. At a more remote period there existed, either included in or contiguous to the parsonage lands, a wood known as "Parsonage" or "Parson's Grove," first mentioned in the minutes of a Court General in 1424. At a Court General in 1488 it was presented that

> "The Rector of the Church of Fulham has not lopped the branches of his trees overhanging the highway on the north part of the wood called Parsones Grove."

The foundation stone of this church was laid by Miss Daniel on 28 July 1884, the consecration by Dr. Temple, Bishop of London, taking place on 19 June 1885.

St. Dionis Church is a remarkable instance of the adaptation of old institutions to the needs of modern times, since it usefully replaces an ancient City church which had long outlived its day. In 1876 an Order in Council was obtained for the demolition of the old City Church of St. Dionis Backchurch, and for the erection of a new church at Parson's Green, with an ecclesiastical district carved out of that of the Parish Church. The funds for the building of the new edifice were mainly derived from the proceeds of the sale (£47,000) of the old church, the Ecclesiastical Commissioners granting £7,000 for the building of the church and £3,000 for its endowment.

St. Dionis is built in the style of the West Country churches of the fifteenth century, with a wagon, three-gabled, roof. It consists of a nave and two low side aisles. It was designed by the late Mr. Ewan Christian, and built by Messrs. W. H. Brass and Son. It affords seating accommodation for rather over 800 persons.

The church contains several features of great interest. The fine oak pulpit (designed by Grinling Gibbons, if not carved by him) came from Sir Christopher Wren's church. The octagonal font, composed of black and white marble, and the altar table were also brought from old St. Dionis. The organ, built by Messrs. W. Hill and Sons, was opened on 19 Dec. 1885. The brass lectern was designed by Messrs. Singer, of Frame. The handsome east window, in five panels, was executed by Mr. Henry A. Hymers. The centre light was the gift of Dr. Hugh Webb. The colours are rich and harmonious, and the figures clear, well-drawn and full of dignity. The three inner lights contain a representation of the Nativity, while above is a choir of angels, rejoicing and singing the praises of the Holy Family. The two outer lights show a single figure of an angel in each. In the Vestry are some interesting souvenirs of the old City church. The ancient plate is very valuable. A very large paten, of solid hammered silver, is inscribed

> "The gift of Mr. Peter Hoet the elder of the Parish of St. Dionys Backchurch, London, the 6th day of June 1674."

There are three fine flagons. One is inscribed

> "The gift of Mr. Peter Hoet ye elder of the Parish of St. Dionys Backchurch, London, the 6th day of June 1674."

The others bear the inscriptions:

> "The guift of ye Reverend father in god John Warner Bishop of Rochester late parson of this parish of St. Dionis Backchurch 1642."

> "The guift of Edward Cooke Apothecarie to St. Dionis Backchurch An° Dom. 1632."

There are four chalices. The two smaller ones, the gift of a lady, bear the following inscription:

> "The gift of Mrs. Frances Say of the Parish of St. Dionis Back Church, daughter of Myles Wisken late Parish Clerk to this Parish."

One of the two larger ones records that it was

> "The gift of Mr. Peter Hoet ye elder of the Parish of St. Dionys Backchurch, London, the 6th day of June 1674."

The other is inscribed:

> "This chalice, with the patten and spoone, is dedicated to be vsed for the service of the Lord's Supper in St. Dionis Back Church, 1671."

The Order in Council for the formation of the consolidated chapelry of St. Dionis, Parson's Green, is dated 12 Dec. 1885.

The tower of St. Dionis, which, through want of funds, was left incomplete when the church was erected, was finished in 1896. The dedication of the tower was performed by the Bishop of Marlborough, 23 May 1896.

The Rev. John Stewart Sinclair, M.A. Oxford, was vicar of the church down to June 1898, when he was succeeded by the Rev. W. S. Carter, D.D.

Continuing our walk southwards along the west side of the Green, there is little more to note. The makings of Messrs. Swannell and Sons, formerly at the south corner, established early in this century by Mr. Joseph Swannell, were removed many years ago.

SECTION V: SOUTH SIDE

We have now to take the south side of Parson's Green, from Gosford Lodge to Peterborough House. This section of our journey is really a portion of the New King's Road.

At the south-west corner of the Green is Broomhouse Road, which runs southwards to the east end of Hurlingham Road. Here it turns an angle, the remaining portion of the road trending away southwards to the river. In this chapter we take the first section only, the latter being dealt with under the head "Broom-house."

Down to quite recent times Broom Lane, as it was always called, possessed very few houses. At the top, on the west side, was Ivy Cottage, described under the "New King's Road" chapter. On the east side, by Bell's Alley, were two semi-detached houses, built probably over two hundred years ago. Of these two houses, Fern Bank and Broom Villa, only the latter now survives.

Practically nothing can be gathered regarding Broom Villa before the present century. About 1818 it was purchased by Mr.

William Bell, the brewer. The oldest portion of the Villa is evidently the northern end, though the whole of the front boasts a respectable antiquity. About 1840 Mr. Bell made an extensive addition at the rear of the house.

Broom Villa. From a photograph by Mr. J. Dugdale, 1895

The grounds (1a. 1r. 1½p.) are exceedingly pretty. They extend back to Peterborough Road. A fine mulberry tree is probably as old as the house. On the south side of the house is the passage known as Bell's Alley, leading from Hurlingham Road to Peterborough Road.

Mr. William Bell, who died here 31 Jan. 1858, left two sons, William and Joseph Friend Bell. Mr. William Bell junior resided at Broom Villa till his death, when Mr. J. F. Bell, who had previously lived in the adjoining house, moved into it.

Old Fern Bank was pulled down by Mr. J. F. Bell in 1878, when the present Fern Bank was erected, on a site a little to the north of it.

Assheton Villa, subsequently the Lonsdale Club, was formerly the residence of Admiral Hawkins.

Spring Cottage, on the same side but a little further north, was pulled down some years ago. It was built about 1805 and was the residence of Mr. Stephens, the builder of Gosford Lodge and

Arragon House.

We will now return to Parson's Green. Facing the Green, on the site now occupied by Arragon House and its neighbour, Gosford Lodge, was an ancient tenement known, in its later years, as Richardson's Villa.

According to tradition the villa was once the dower house of Queen Katharine of Arragon. There is no doubt that the young widow of Prince Arthur occasionally stayed at Fulham, though it is impossible to assert that this old house was really the place which she frequented. Among the State Papers is preserved a letter, dated 28 Oct. 1506, written by. Henry VII to the princess, his daughter-in-law. He tells her that he has received her letter of 27 Oct., dated from Eltham, and is pleased to hear that his last letter was so agreeable to her. "The house at Fulham," he informs her, had been kept for the ambassadors of the King of Castile (Philip), who were expected, but, as she wishes to go to it and thinks it will improve her health to be so near him, it is certainly at her disposal and the ambassadors must lodge elsewhere. The letter is dated from Windsor and is addressed "To the Most lllustrious Princess Katharine Princess of Wales, my most beloved daughter."

Richardson's Villa. From an old drawing

In the time of Charles II, Richardson's Villa was the property of Sir Paul Whichcote, baronet. In 1678-79 it was purchased of Sir Paul by "Edmund Saunders, Esquire," afterwards Sir Edmund Saunders, the eminent jurist, who, in 1682, rose to be a chief justice of the Court of King's Bench. The statement as to this purchase we make on the authority of an entry in "London and Middlesex Fines." Lysons states that, in 1792, he was shown the actual deeds, then in the possession of Thomas Northmore, the proprietor. Sir Edmund died on 19 June 1683 at, it is said, his house at Parson's Green.

The house is celebrated as having been the villa residence of Samuel Richardson, the novelist, of whom we shall speak in connection with The Grange, North End. Richardson, who came to Parson's Green in Oct. 1754, writes in a letter, dated 26 Nov. 1754, ("Richardson Corr.," iii. 99):

> "The Speaker was so good as to call upon me at Parson's Green. He liked the house and situation."

In another letter, dated 30 Dec. 1754, Richardson says:

> "My wife . . . bids me . . . tell you that she, as you foretold, likes her removal to Parson's Green, every day more and more."

Thomas Edwards, the well-known critic, died while on a visit to Richardson at Parson's Green, 2 Jan. 1757. He was the author of the "Canons of Criticism," 1747.

It is not improbable that Richardson moved from North End to Parson's Green in order to be nearer Fulham Church. At any rate he was, down to the last, a regular worshipper here. His pew was "No. 7 North Gallery." His death occurred at his villa at Parson's Green, 4 July 1761. He was twice married, first to Miss Allington Wilde, his master's daughter, who died in 1731, and secondly to a Miss Leake of Bath. By the first marriage he had five children, all of whom died in infancy. By his second wife, who survived him, he had four daughters.

In Dodsley's "Collection of Poems in Six Volumes by Several Hands," 1782 (p. 316), are the following verses by Mrs. Bennet, sister of Edward Brigden, a son-in-law of Richardson:

Upon an Alcove
Now at Parson's Green
By Mrs. Bennet.

O Favourite Muse of Shenstone, hear !
And leave awhile his blissful groves;
Aid me this sweet alcove to sing,
The Author's seat whom Shenstone loves.

Here the soul-harrowing genius form'd
His Pamela's enchanting story !
And here divine Clarissa died
A martyr to our sex's glory !

'Twas here the noble-minded Howe
With every gen'rous passion glow'd
And here the gentle Belford's eyes
With manly sorrows overflow'd.

Here Clementina, hapless maid !
With wild distress each bosom tears:
And here the lonely Harriet own'd
A virgin's hopes, a virgin's fears.

Here Emily, sweet artless girl,
Fills every breast with strange delight !
And when we fear her early fall
Secures her conquest by her flight.

Here sprightly Charlotte's hum'rous wit
Dispenses mirth to all around;
But ah ! we tremble, whilst we smile,
Lest its fine edge herself should wound.

Here Grandison, to crown the whole,
A bright exemplar stands confest !
Who stole those virtues we admire
From the great Author's glowing breast.

> O sacred seat! be thou rever'd
> By such as own thy master's power;
> And, like his works, for ages last,
> Till fame and language are no more.

Mrs. Richardson continued to live at Parson's Green, where she died in Nov. 1773.

Little is known about the subsequent history of Richardson's house. Lysons, in 1796, states that it was then in the occupation of a Mr. Dawson. Lambert, who wrote in 1805, speaks of it as still standing. It was probably pulled down in this year. In Lysons' "Supplement," published in 1811, occurs the following passage:

> "The old house in which Richardson lived at the corner of Parson's Green has been taken down, and a house, now occupied by Dr. Taylor as a school, built on the site."

Gosford Lodge (No 249, New King's Road), which occupies a corner of the grounds of Richardson's Villa, was erected by Stephens about 1805-6. It was named by an early tenant, Captain Acherson, a distant relation of the Gosford family. In 1854, it became the residence of the late Mr. Charles Baylis Child.

The history of Arragon House (No. 247, New King's Road), which was built by Stephens about 1805-6, dates from 1808, when it was taken by Dr. James Taylor, who, for ten years, conducted a boys' school here. About 1846 it was turned into a girls' school, kept by Miss Sarah Brown, who continued it down to 1873. In 1875 the house became the property of Mr. James Wray.

Arragon House, named of course to perpetuate the tradition regarding Queen Katharine's connection therewith, is a flat fronted residence possessing no claim to beauty. The windows of the basement appear to be much older than those in the other parts of the house. It is possible they may have belonged to Richardson's Villa.

Strictly speaking, the name Pitt or Pitt's Place, now numbered with the houses in the New King's Road, was applied to the terrace of old-fashioned houses, six in number, standing between Arragon House and Peterborough Road, namely Belgrave House (No. 6),

Sefton House (No. 5), Cradley House (No. 4), Albyn House (No. 3), its nameless neighbour (No. 2), and the corner house, now the Duke's Head (No. 1). Sometimes, however, Arragon House and Gosford Lodge were regarded as included under the designation.

The six houses comprising Pitt Place are somewhat older than Arragon House, having been built about 1795. No. 1, Pitt Place, at the north-west corner of Peterborough Road, is now the "Duke's Head," rebuilt in 1893. The original house did not face the Green, but stood a little way down Peterborough Lane, at the rear of the present house. The original house, which, for convenience sake, we will speak of here, was an old inn, known as the "Pond Head Ale House," from the fact that it faced the pond on Parson's Green. The first we hear of it is in 1714, when Hicks Burroughs sold to Sir Robert Child certain property at Parson's Green, including "one cottage known by the sign of the 'Pond-head Alehouse,'" then in the occupation of John Paine. On the death of Sir Robert the "Pondhead Alehouse" went to his brother, Samuel. The sign was changed to the "Duke's Head," probably about 1802, when the "Duke's Head," near the Laurel Bank House was pulled down. It was a riotous house, frequented chiefly by the gardeners from Rench's and Fitch's nursery. Early in this century a terrible fight occurred at this house, resulting in the deaths of four men.

The transfer of the "Duke's Head" from its old premises to its present position took place on the death of Dr. James Humphrey Keats, which occurred at No. 1, Pitt Place in 1861. Dr. Keats resided at Parson's Green nearly all his life, the first appearance of his name in the Rate books being in 1819. Keats was a remarkable character. He used to visit his patients habited in a long, shabby, dark green frock coat with prominent brass buttons. There used to be a saying in Fulham, in reference to thread-bare clothes, that a person wore Dr. Keats's livery. Despite his apparent poverty, he used to keep a pack of harriers, which might often have been seen on Parson's Green, Eelbrook, Wimbledon Common, etc. In his time Keats said, or is reported to have said, many smart things. Perhaps one of his quaintest dicta concerned the Vicar and his beadle: "There's Griffin the baker of Walham Green and Baker the griffin of Fulham!"

The houses in Pitt Place, Nos. 1 to 6, are now renumbered 235 to 245 (alternate numbers), New King's Road.

Old Peterborough Lane or Place dates from the time of Charles I. Among the House of Lords' Manuscripts is preserved a curious petition, dated 19 Nov. 1660, presented to the House by Dame Margaret Herbert, late wife of Sir Edward Herbert, which throws some light on the early history of the old Lane. In the year 1633, the owner of the mansion, since known as Peterborough House, was Thomas Carey, who had married Margaret, daughter of Sir Thomas Smith, the preceding owner of the estate. After Carey's death, his widow married, as her second husband, Sir Edward Herbert, mentioned in the petition.

Peterborough Lane.
From a water-colour drawing by Miss Jane Humphreys

It appears that, about the year named, there lay near Carey's grounds some three acres of wet marsh common ground belonging to the freeholders and commoners of the Manor. Carey, for the accommodation of his own and his neighbours' dwellings, agreed to change a like quantity of good ground for this marsh ground, and to leave a way from Parson's Green to Southfield at the west end of the marsh ground, and thereupon, at a great charge, he subdivided, enclosed, drained and planted the marsh ground, leaving the way as agreed. The path which Carey thus formed in 1633 was the Peterborough Lane of later days.

The arrangement which Carey made remained undisturbed

until shortly after the death of Sir Edward Herbert, which occurred in 1657. In this interval great events had taken place. Charles I had gone to the scaffold, the Bishop of London had been ejected from Fulham Palace, and in his place ruled Col. Harvey. The Republican soldier, "the usurped Lord of the Manor," as Dame Margaret Herbert calls him, combining with one Francis Thorne, a tailor, locked up the gate at the end of the way leading into Southfield, and then quietly claimed a right of way through the grounds of the widow of that staunch loyalist, Sir Edward Herbert. Accordingly, Dame Margaret, as soon as the happier days of the Restoration returned, petitioned the House to give her redress, and to confirm by Act of Parliament the enclosure and way from Parson's Green to Southfield.

Old houses in Peterborough Place.
From a photograph by Mr. T. S. Smith, 1893

Annexed to this petition is an Order of the Committee, to whom the matter was referred, effecting a compromise between the parties, 24 Nov. 1660. In 1661 an Act was passed confirming the enclosure as prayed by Dame Margaret.

The appellation Peterborough Place or Lane dates, of course, only from the time when the Peterborough family became connected with Parson's Green. Its earliest designation was, as we have noted, Parson's Green Lane. As early as 1650 the name Parson's Green Lane occurs in the accounts of the Churchwardens. Among those who this year shared in the distribution of "beef and bred," the "gift of D'cor King deceased," we find "Old Harding in Parson's Greene Lane" and "Old Bainbrigg in the same place."

Later on, when the Renches held Southfield Farm in Parson's Green Lane, the way was often termed Rench's Lane. Peterborough Road retains, even to the present day, several quaint old houses, some in a dilapidated condition.

WEST SIDE

On the west side, just as we turn into it from Parson's Green, are four or five flat fronted tenements which must date from the early part of the last century. A little beyond these is a row of white fronted houses. Against one of these (No. 33) is an inscription reading:

Peterborough Place.
1792.

This line of houses terminates in what was formerly the "Crown" Brewery, founded about the beginning of this century by a Mr. Whittingsall. In 1824 it was purchased by Messrs. Chase and Bell. Shortly after this event Mr. Chase met with a fatal accident. Thenceforward the "Crown" Brewery was conducted by Mr. William Bell alone. On his death, in 1858, the business was carried on by his sons, William and Joseph Friend Bell, and, on the death of the former, by Mr. J. F. Bell alone. The "Crown" Brewery was chiefly noted for its ales. In 1890 Mr. Bell gave up his maltings, when the premises were for a time converted into the Grape Brandy Distillery.

Southwards to the Town Mead Road, Peterborough Road degenerates to the dimensions of a rural pathway.

EAST SIDE

The east side of Peterborough Road, starting from Parson's Green, is, for a considerable distance, now covered with prim red-brick villas.

Just before we reach Bryan's Lane is Broom Farm. Here is an ancient homestead associated with the memories of a well-known family of gardeners. The Renches, to whom we refer, were connected with Parson's Green for something like two centuries. The first we hear of the name is in the year 1641 when the Churchwarden

"rec^d for a knell Wrench 6d."

Broom Farm. From a photograph by Mr. J. Dugdale, 1895

For many years the Renches remained a very obscure family. The first of note was Thomas Rench, who was born about 1630. He seems to have lived near Parson's Green Lane, if not actually in it, for in 1674 we find him assessed for property at "Broom Feilde." In 1688 "Thomas Ranch" was elected a Surveyor of the highways.

The Renches were a prolific family. The Church Registers literally teem with entries relating to them, commencing with the year 1676.

The connection of the Renches with the property owned by them in Parson's Green Lane in later times dates, apparently from 1711, when George Wood surrendered a cottage in this lane to "Thomas Ranch, of Fulham, gardiner." Thomas Rench died 31 Mar. 1727-28, aged 98. The Church Registers record:

1728. Thomas Rench sen^r bu. 4 Apl.

He left four sons, Benjamin, Nathaniel, George and Daniel, and several daughters. The will of Thomas Rench, dated 27 Jan. 1727-28, was proved 10 April 1728 (P.C.C. 121 Brooke). The following is an extract:

> "I Thomas Rench of the parish of ffulham, Gardener, To my wife Susannah Rench my two messuages at Wandons Green in said county which I lately purchased of Robert Richardson for the term of her widowhood, and after her decease to be sold and proceeds equally divided amongst my children as well those of my former wife as this I now have and whereas my Daughter Sarah Brassett is lately dead I do hereby give her share by such sale to her little daughter Anne Brassett.
> To my two sons Benjamin Rench and Nathaniel Rench all my crops upon my grounds and my lease together with the carts and horses, wheelbarrows and all other materials whatsoeuer belonging to the gardening and it is my will that they shall elect and choose four honest and indifferent men to part and distribute equally the crops or grounds planted between them."

Southfield Farm appears to have been carried on for some years by the brothers Benjamin and Nathaniel Rench. Benjamin Rench died in 1732. The Church Registers record:

1732. Benjamin Rench bu. 18 June.

Nathaniel Rench, on the death of his brother, carried on the business alone. He seems to have been a horticulturist of no mean ability. According to Faulkner, Thomas Rench, the father of Nathaniel Rench, produced at Southfield Farm "the first pine strawberry and Chinese strawberry and also the first auricula ever blown in this country," while the son, Nathaniel, reared "the large arbutus trees some of which attained 50 feet in height. . . . The moss rose tree was first introduced here by this celebrated gardener."

Peterborough Road. From a photograph by Mr. T. S. Smith, 1895

Nathaniel Rench died 18 Jan. 1783, aged, according to his gravestone in Fulham Churchyard, 101 years. In the Sussex Advertiser for 3 Mar. 1783, occurs the following:

"A few days ago, died at Fulham aged 101, Mr. Wrencher (sic), gardener. It is remarkable that he died in the same house in which he was born, and had by two wives thirty two children."

The *Mirror* for 1833 records:

"Mr. Rench, of Fulham, who planted the elms in Birdcage Walk from saplings reared in his own nursery, died in 1783, aged 101, in the same room in which he was born."

The Church Registers, however, show that he was by no means a centenarian, assuming his baptism to have occurred in infancy. They read:

1701. Nathaniel, son of Thomas and Susan Ranch, borne __ , gardener bap. 3 Aug.

1783. Nathaniel Rench bu. 26 Jan.

Unfortunately the blank after the word "borne" prevents the matter from being absolutely determined.

The *Gentleman's Magazine* and the *Sussex Advertiser*, which record his death, appear to be the authorities originally responsible for the story about the birth and death of Nathaniel Rench having occurred in the same house. As the premises in Parson's Green Lane did not come into the possession of his father, Thomas Rench, till 1711, it is not easy to see how it can be true. His will, dated 25 Sept. 1781, was proved 31 Jan. 1783 (P.C.C. 43 Cornwallis).

Mr. Rench seems to have had a peculiar affection for the name "Nathaniel," many of his sons, who mostly died in infancy, being so called.

Thomas Rench, by his two wives, had 33 children, while his son, Nathaniel, by his two wives, had no less than 35. The *Gentleman's Magazine* ascribes 32 children to him.

The marriage of Elizabeth, daughter of Nathaniel Rench, with Daniel Fitch, of Kilburn, brought Southfield Farm into the hands of the Fitches, who also acquired property on the other side of Bryan's Lane, now the Home Farm of Messrs. James Veitch and Sons, of Chelsea. Daniel Fitch died in 1818. His widow, Elizabeth, conducted the business for many years. She died in 1834.

The Home Farm of Messrs. J. Veitch and Sons.
From a photograph by Mr. T. S. Smith, 1895.

On 20 June 1825, some of the property was leased to Nathaniel Rench Fitch, the son of Daniel and Elizabeth Fitch, but he died in the same year. For some years Southfield Farm was in the hands of three brothers, Henry, Daniel and William Fitch. On Henry's death, Daniel and William, two enormous men who turned the scale at twenty-one stone each, conducted the business. Daniel Fitch, the last survivor, died at Southfield Farm, 16 Feb. 1858. The business was for some years later continued by Miss Fitch.

The Fitches resided in the house which is now in the occupation of Messrs. James Veitch and Sons, whose connection with this property dates from 1870.

Continuing our journey eastwards along the south side of Parson's Green we arrive at Peterborough House, one of the most historically interesting sites in the parish.

In ancient times the estate about here was known as Brightwell's, a very large messuage which eventually extended from Peterborough Lane to Bagley's Lane and southwards almost as far as Bryan's Alley.

As with other tenements, there is little doubt that Brightwell was the name of some early owner, though a wild guess has been made that the name arose from the bright or clear waters of certain wells here.

The history of Brightwell's tenement we have fortunately been able to trace back over a period of five centuries. In the minutes of a Court Baron in 1386, "John Parke(r) and Joan his wife were admitted to a free tenement in Fulham called Bryghtwelles tenement."

A cottage which stood on the freelands of Brightwell's was known as Chartres or Charteshous, doubtless after Richard Charteshous who resided here in the time of Richard II. In 1393 William Swap sold to Richard Meadon (or Mooreden) "one cottage with curtilage in P'sones grene called Chartres parcell of Brightewelles."

On the death of John Parker, Brightwell's continued in the occupation of his widow, Joan. At a Court Baron, in 1437, it was presented that

"Johanna Parker who held of the Lord one free tenement called Bryghtwell is dead and William is her son and next heir."

William is probably an error for Thomas, who, as the son and heir of Joan or Johanna Parker, was, at the same Court, admitted to his mother's other tenement called Stowte's. From the minutes of a View, in 1456, we learn that Thomas Parker was still in the possession of a croft called "Brightwellsfield." In 1489 Brightwell's was in the occupation of a John Parker. His right to the tenement seems to have been disputed, for the Homage, in 1491, issued "precept to distrain the tenant of Brightwell at psonegrene to come to next court and show his title." John Parker apparently established his claim, for, as late as 1510, he was the tenant of Brightwell's. Though the family continued for many years longer in the possession of Stowte's tenement, we cannot connect them with Brightwell's after 1510. For some years following this date the history of the latter tenement is uncertain. Not improbably it passed into the hands of the Essex family of whom we elsewhere speak.

The next known owner of Brightwell's was John Tamworth, a descendant of Sir Nicholas de Tamworth, treasurer and keeper of the Town of Calais in the time of Edward III. John Tamworth was Clerk of the Crown in the reign of Elizabeth, besides which he was one of Her Majesty's grooms and a member of her Privy Council. The date of his admission to the free tenement of Brightwell's is uncertain, but it was probably about 1562. In 1565 he was fined sixpence because he failed to pay suit of Court. <u>He died at Parson's Green, 19 April 1569.</u>

By his wife Christian, daughter of William Walsingham, he had one daughter who died young. He was buried at St. Botolph's, Aldersgate, 26 April 1569.

The will of John Tamworth, dated 22 Mar. 1568-69, was proved 2 Mar. 1569-70 (P.C.C. 8 Lyon). From this will, a very long one, the testator appearing to have held land in various counties, we extract the following:

"I John Tamworth of London, Esq., one of the Groomes to the queenes Matie of her highenes moste honorable privey Chamber.
To be buried in the parrishe Church of St. Buttolphes w^{t}oute Aldrichegate of London in the same Chappell where now my pue is.
I will and bequeath that <u>my cousin Wythe</u> and her husband shall have the house that they Dwell in at London and at Fulham for their lives.
I will to Thomas Knowlls the reversion of my Manor of Honeylandes and Pentriches in Middlesex and Herts and my lands in Fulham which I have hereunto conveyed to him."

Brightwell's, as we see from the foregoing will, was bequeathed by John Tamworth to Sir Thomas Knowlls, Knowles, Knowlles or Knolles, kt. A Court Baron in 1569 directed "the heirs of John Tamworth Esq. to lay pales upon the road."

Sir Thomas Knowles, in 1603, sold his estate at Parson's Green, partly to Sir William Billesbie and partly to Sir Thomas Smith. The latter purchased the estate known as Brightwell's, together with 24 acres of adjacent land, enclosed in a pale, for the sum of £530. Sir Thomas Smith resided here till 1609.

This distinguished man was born at Abingdon about the year 1556. According to Anthony à Wood, he was "born of sufficient parents in a town called Abingdon in Berkshire."

In Harleian Manuscript 1551, 69[b], it is stated that he was the son of Thomas Smyth, of Abingdon, by Jone his wife, daughter of Thomas Jenings. The marriage license of the sister of Sir Thomas Smith describes her as:

"Marye Smithe of the Savoy London, spinster, daughter of   Smithe of Abingdon co. Berks, gent."

Thomas Smith received his early education at the Free Grammar School at Abingdon, In 1573 he was entered as a student of Christ Church, Oxford, where he graduated B.A., 17 Dec. 1574 and M.A., 17 June 1578. Between 1582-94 he was the public orator of the University, and in 1584 he was appointed proctor.

About the close of his stay at the University he became secretary to Robert Devereux, the hapless Earl of Essex. His abilities soon brought him to the front. He was, in 1587, appointed one of the Clerks of the Privy Council. He sat as M.P. for Cricklade in 1588-89 and for Tamworth in 1593. In 1597 he became Clerk to the Parliament. James I knighted him at Greenwich, 20 May 1603, and in the same year made him his "Secretary of the Latin Tongue," with a salary of forty marks a year, and Secretary to the Council of the North. Finally, in 1608, he was made Master of the Court of Requests, a court of equity, inferior to the Court of Chancery, instituted in the reign of Henry VII for the relief of such persons as addressed the King by petition.

In 1606 Sir Thomas purchased of Sir William Billesbie his estate at Parson's Green. He died at Brightwell's, 28 Nov. 1609, and was buried in the chancel of Fulham Church on 7 Dec. The "Inq. Post Mortem," touching his estate is dated 3 July 1610 (see vol. I, "Fulham Church: Its Monuments and Epitaphs" chapter).

Sir Thomas married Frances, daughter of Sir William Brydges, fourth Lord Chandos. By her he had issue two children, Robert and Margaret. Robert Smith was educated at Christ Church, Oxford, where he matriculated in 1620. He died *s. p.* in 1626 (Harleian Manuscripts 1551). As already stated, Margaret married, first, the Hon. Thomas Carey, second son of Robert, first earl of Monmouth, and, secondly, Sir Edward Herbert, Attorney General and Keeper of the Great Seal to Charles II during his exile. Of this lady and her husbands we shall again have occasion to speak.

The following is an extract from the will of Sir Thomas Smith, dated 12 Sep. 1609, and proved 21 Dec. 1609 (P. C. C. 113 Dorset):

> "My body to be buried after a X'ian manner decently and christianly but without any needles and superfluous solemnitie or expence.
> Next concerning my worldlie estate thoughe very meane in respecte of the long tyme and travaile by me for the getting thereof yet far beyond my deserte (yf it were much lesse than it is) the same beyng Gods benefitt wherof throughe my synnes I am alltogeather unworthie. Whereas yt doth consiste partly of a little Land partlie of some fewe Leases partlie of some money plate and other moueables.
> My dwelling house at Parson greene in the parish of Fulham with the land purchased with yt and to yt I do give to my sonne Robert Smithe but my wife Frances to receive the profits during her life. My house and land called Hertley or Hartley Court in the parish of Shinfield near Reading being at present lett by me on lease to my brother Richard Smithe or £100 per an. I do likewise devise to my said son. The land which I lately bought of my friend Hughe Middleton in the manor of Barwicke uppon Tease co. Yorke to said son and to his heirs for ever and in default to my daughter Margaret Smythe that is to say my estate at Parsons Green to my said daughter and her heirs for ever with reserval of the profitts to my wife during her life as abovesaid and all my said other lands to said daughter for life Remainder to my brother Richard Smithe and the heirs male of his body and for Default said lands to return to the heirs of my said daughter for ever.
> To Sir Thomas Bodley for the Librarie in Oxforde twentie markes to be bestowed on some bookes at his Discretion. To the poore of the towne and parishe of ffulham where my nowe dwelling is I give and bequeath £20. My wife sole executrix but my son executor of his part and my

good friends Sr John Benett, kt., Sr Owen Oglethorpe, Mr. John Buckeridge, D.D., my brother Richard Smithe and Mr. Hugh Middleton to be overseers."

Both Sir John Bennet and Sir Owen Oglethorpe lived at Fulham.

After the death of Sir Thomas Smith, his widow continued to reside at Parson's Green. In 1615 Lady Smith re-married, her second husband being Thomas Cecil, first Earl of Exeter, warden of Rockingham Forest. The Earl died 7 Feb. 1621-22. By his will, without date, he left to his wife all his "household stuffe which I used att psons Greene house att the tyme I lay there." It was proved by Lord Burleigh, sole executor, 11 Mar. 1621-22 (P. C. C. 23 Swann). The Countess of Exeter resided at Parson's Green for some years longer. The earliest existing Assessment book (1625) shows "the Lady Exeter or tenant" rated to the poor at "vj^s." By the second marriage there was no issue.

In the Parish Books the name of the Countess of Exeter ceases with the year 1632, when she apparently surrendered Brightwell's, or Parson's Green House, as it now came to be termed, to the use of her daughter and son-in-law. The Countess, who was 38 years junior to her second husband, survived till 1663, when she was buried under a flat stone in Winchester Cathedral, and not, as is often asserted, in Westminster Abbey, where there is a stately monument to the memory of the Earl of Exeter and his two wives. Dean Stanley, in his "Memorials of Westminster Abbey," writes:

> "The first Earl of Exeter, after a life full of years and honours, lies in the chapel of St. John the Baptist. His tomb was built for himself and his 'two most dear wives.' "

The tomb, which is composed of black and white marble, occupies the centre of the chapel Upon it are the recumbent effigies of the Earl and his first wife, and there is an unoccupied space for that of his second consort, the lady of whom we have been speaking. It is said that she directed by her will that her effigy should not be placed upon the tomb, her reason being that she objected to being placed on the left of her husband.

The early death, in 1626, of Robert, the only son of Sir

Thomas Smith, made Margaret sole heiress to the estate at Parson's Green.

Thomas Carey, or Cary, the first husband of Margaret, was Groom of the Bedchamber to Charles I. He was born at Berwick-on-Tweed, where he was baptized, 16 Sept. 1597. His father, Sir Robert Carey, knt., was the tenth son of the first Lord Hunsdon, Deputy Warden of the Western Marches towards Scotland, and afterwards Chief Warden of the Marches and one of the Gentlemen of the Bedchamber to James I, who, on 5 Feb. 1625-26, made him Earl of Monmouth. His mother was Elizabeth, daughter of Sir Hugo Trevanion of Carhayes, co. Cornwall, knt., by Sybilla, daughter of Sir Thomas Morgan (who was buried at Fulham in 1595) and sister of Anne, Lady Hunsdon (see vol. I, "Fulham Church: Its Monuments and Epitaphs" chapter).

The date of Thomas Carey's marriage with Margaret Smith is unknown, but he was evidently residing at the house of his mother-in-law at Parson's Green as early as 1628, for the assessment this year reads:

"The Countesse of Exeter and Thomas Carey, Esquire xxx^s"

In 1633 it is in the name of the

"Hon. Mr. Thomas Carey xx^s"

During the residence of the Hon. Thomas Carey at Parson's Green, the house was usually known as Villa Carey, or Carey House.

Lysons regards it as probable that the Hon. Thomas Carey rebuilt the house. However this may be, he certainly employed Francis Cleyne, or Klein, the historical painter of Rostock, to embellish its walls and ceilings. A statement to this effect appears in Saunderson's "Graphice" (1658).

Among the State Papers (Domestic, vol. 260, No. 49), is a certificate, dated 10 Feb. 1633-34, as to the value of a messuage and lands at Parson's Green, Fulham,

"whereof Thomas Carey stands seized in right of Margaret his wife, sister and next heir of Robert Smith, deceased, son of Sir Thomas

Smith, worth £6 per annum, 8 James I. ; now £66. 13. 4."

Thomas Carey died at Whitehall, 9 April 1634, and was buried in the family vault in Westminster Abbey. It is erroneously said by some writers that Carey died of grief at the death of his royal master, Charles I. This error is apparently due to Anthony à Wood ("Fasti," i. 352) whose account has been quoted, *in extenso*, by the Rev. J. W. Ebsworth in the Appendix Notes (p. 238) of his edition of "Carew." The will of Thomas Carey (undated) was proved 18 July 1634 (P.C.C. 66 Seager).

By his wife Margaret, Thomas Carey had issue three daughters, his co-heirs, vizt.: Philadelphia, Lady of the Bedchamber, married, as first wife, to Sir Henry Lyttelton, dying *s. p.* 2 Aug. 1663, aged 32; Frances, aged three years at the death of her father, died unmarried: buried in "Lord Hvnsdons Valte" in Westminster Abbey, 24 Nov. 1653; and Elizabeth, aged 18 months, in 1634. This lady, of whom we shall have more to say, eventually became sole heiress and married John Mordaunt.

Thomas Carey's widow was painted by Vandyck in 1636, the picture being engraved by Faithorne and Van Gunst. According to this portrait, which is now at Halswell House, Goathurst, Somersetshire, the seat of Halswell M. Kemeys-Tynte, Esq., the Hon. Mrs. Carey had but few pretensions to good looks.

Parson's Green House, in 1640, passed into the possession of Sir Edward Herbert, who, in that year had married the widow of the Hon. Thomas Carey.

Edward Herbert, who was the son of Charles Herbert, of Aston, Montgomeryshire, by Jane, daughter of Hugh ap Owen, was born about 1591. In 1609 he was admitted to the Inner Temple, and nine years later was called to the Bar. In 1620 he was elected Member of Parliament for the borough of Montgomery. Between 1625 and 1629 he sat for Downton, Wilts. On 1 July 1630 he was made Steward of the Marshalsea. He was appointed Attorney General, 20 Jan. 1634-35, and Solicitor General, 25 Jan. 1639-40. On 28 Jan. 1640-41 he was knighted by Charles I at Whitehall. On 3 Jan. 1641-42 the King instructed Sir Edward to exhibit articles of impeachment against Lord Kimbolton and the five members of the Commons who had been instrumental in the passing of the "Grand Remonstrance." On the same day the

Solicitor General charged them before the House of Lords with traitorously conspiring to subvert the fundamental laws of the realm and with other offences tantamount to high treason. A strong protest, however, by Parliament caused the King not to proceed with the impeachment. The tables were now turned on the Solicitor General, who was impeached by the Commons of high crimes and misdemeanours for the part he had played. Sir Edward pleaded that the articles of impeachment against the implicated members of the Commons had been furnished to him by the King, and Charles was magnanimous enough to avow the fact. The impeachment of Sir Edward Herbert was allowed to proceed. A verdict of guilty was returned, but the House refused to inflict punishment. On the outbreak of the Civil War, Sir Edward joined the King's party. In July 1646 he was placed by Parliament on the list of delinquents incapable of pardon, and his estates were sequestered.

In the Fulham assessments for 1647 the poor rate in respect to Parson's Green House appears in the name of

"S^r Ed. Harbert or his tenn^t 3s. 4d."

Doubtless the great crisis in the history of the nation had already compelled him to leave Parson's Green. On the execution of King Charles, Sir Edward Herbert retired to the Hague, throwing in his lot with that of the King's son. He accompanied Prince Charles in his exile, and was made by him Lord Keeper of the Great Seal and his Attorney General. In 1653 his name is found described as of Parson's Green among those loyalists whose estates were ordered to be sold. He certainly never returned to his old home, though at a Court General, held at Fulham as late as 19 Oct. 1657, he was formally fined 4d. for failing to pay suit of Court. In the December following he died in Paris from gangrene.

Sir Edward Herbert left three sons, Arthur, Edward and Charles, all of whom became men of eminence. Arthur Herbert was created Earl of Torrington and raised to the rank of Admiral. He died in 1716. The second son, Sir Edward Herbert, followed his father's profession. In 1685 he was chosen by James II to succeed Jeffreys as Chief Justice. At the Revolution in 1688 he followed the King into exile, and died in Paris in 1698. The third son, Charles Herbert, became Colonel of the 23rd Regiment. He fought under General Ginckel in the battle of Aghrim, 12 July 1691, but, being taken prisoner, he was murdered by his captors.

The history of Parson's Green House during the time of the Commonwealth is somewhat obscure. Possibly the mansion underwent a temporary sequestration, for the name of the Herberts ceases in the Rate books. A Mr. Robert Wallopp is assessed for the property in 1649-50.

Dame Margaret Herbert survived her. husband many years. At the Restoration she obtained a grant of the King's New Year's Presents, less £1,000, for three years in consideration of her late husband's services, losses and sufferings in the royal cause. From the petition which she presented to the House of Lords in 1661, regarding the way from Parson's Green to Southfield, it is clear that Dame Margaret retained some interest in connection with her old home. The probability is that she resided with her daughter, the Lady Elizabeth Carey, who had now become the wife of John, Lord Mordaunt. She died apparently in 1677-78. The Church Registers record:

1677. The Lady Elizabeth Herbert sepult 27 ffeb.

There can be little doubt that this entry is intended to record the burial of Dame Margaret Herbert, the use of the name "Elizabeth" for "Margaret" being due to the confusion of the Christian name of the daughter, Elizabeth Carey, with that of the mother. This supposition is further strengthened by the fact that Lady Mordaunt (nee Elizabeth Carey) enters in her "Diary," under date "Jan. ye 28 1677," "A Prayr for my Mother," which points, of course, to her illness at that time.

In 1660, the year of the Restoration, we find John Mordaunt, Baron Mordaunt of Reigate, in Surrey, and Viscount Mordaunt of Avalon, in Somersetshire, in possession of the estate at Parson's Green by virtue of his marriage, in 1657, with Elizabeth Carey.

The Mordaunts came of ancient lineage. They were in the train of William, Duke of Normandy, when that ambitious prince accomplished the conquest of England. John Mordaunt, who was the second son of John, the first, and brother of Henry, the second Earl of Peterborough, was born on 11 June 1627. He was entered as a student of Brasenose College. While the Civil War was waging between King and Parliament, he was receiving his education in France and Italy. Returning to this country, he married the Lady Elizabeth Carey, whom Clarendon describes as "A young, beautiful lady, of a very loyal spirit and notable vivacity of wit and humour, who concurred with him in all honourable dedication of himself."

John, Lord Mordaunt. After an original engraving

No sooner had Lord Mordaunt reached the age of manhood than he determined to use his best energies to restore the exiled King. He accordingly communicated his intentions to the Marquis of Ormonde, who was then with Prince Charles abroad. When the Marquis returned to England, Cromwell, who had received information of what was astir, sent for "Mr." Mordaunt, and closely questioned him as to whether he had seen Lord Ormonde. Though he managed, by evasive answers, to get out of the

Protector's clutches, he was speedily "sent for" again and committed to the Tower, 1 May 1658.

All the ringleaders in the Royalist plot, Mordaunt included, were brought to trial, John Lisle, one of the regicides, being the President of the Court. When Mordaunt's examination came on, 1st June 1658, Lady Mordaunt, by some unexplained means, succeeded in keeping out of the way one of the principal witnesses against her husband. During the hearing of the case Col. Pride was seized with illness and had to retire. The remainder were equally divided in their opinion as to his guilt, and Mordaunt was acquitted only through the casting vote of the President.

The acquittal of Lord Mordaunt elicited the following outpourings from the heart of Lady Mordaunt. We again quote from her "Diary":

> "1658 June ye 2nd. In the yere of our Lorde 1658, on the first of June, my Deare Husband was tryed for his Life by a Corte, calede the Highe Corte of Justis, and on the second day of June was cleerd by one uoys only, 19 condemning of him and 20 sauing of him, and. thos twenty had not preualed, but by God's emedeate Hand, by striking one of the Corte with an illness, which forsed him to goe out, in whous absens, the uots wer geuen, and recorded, so that his returne no way preiudis'd Mr. Mordaunt tho' in his thoughts he resolued it (Prid was the person). Many outher meracolus blesings wer shod in his presentation for which Blesed Be God. He was the first exampule that pleded not gilty, that was cleerd before thes Cortes."

Lady Mordaunt, according to her fashion in this "Diary," then bursts forth into a song of praise, ending with a long prayer.

No sooner was Mordaunt at liberty than he again set to work to accomplish the restoration of the monarchy. The death of Cromwell, in September 1658, raised the hopes of the King's friends. Mordaunt and his associates worked with redoubled vigour. When General Monk had matured his plans for the restoration of the King, he despatched Sir John Grenville to Breda. Mordaunt accompanied Sir John and returned with him, bearing the famous "Declaration of Breda" and other documents from the exiled prince.

On 25 May 1660 Charles and his two brothers, the Dukes of York and Gloucester, landed at Dover, where they were met by

Monk, Mordaunt and other Royalists. His Majesty, in recognition of the faithful services which Mordaunt had rendered him, created him Baron Mordaunt of Reigate in the county of Surrey and Viscount Mordaunt of Avalon, Aviland or Aveland in the county of Somerset. The letters patent bear date 10 July 1659. Lord Mordaunt was soon afterwards made K.G. and constituted Lord Lieutenant of Surrey, Constable of Windsor Castle and Ranger of Windsor Forest, offices which he held till his death.

The last fifteen years of his life seem to have been chiefly spent on his estate at Parson's Green. <u>Gardening was one of his favourite recreations</u>. Among his visitors here was John Evelyn, who remarks in his "Diary," under date 29 Nov. 1661:

> "I dined at the Countess of Peterborow's, and went that evening to Parson's Greene's house with my Lord Mordaunt with whom I staid that night."

In 1661 Lord Mordaunt gave the poor "on this side the pish of Fulham" a sum of £7: at the same time Lady Mordaunt gave £10. Lord Mordaunt, in 1662, had a serious illness. Lady Mordaunt enters in her "Diary":

> "A prayr of thanksgeuing For my deare Hosband's recouery from His greate and dangerus illnes July ye 16th 1662."

In the following year he was thrown out of his coach near Weybridge. Again his wife notes:

> "July ye 29th 1663 A thanksgeuing for my deare Hosband's deleuranc [deliverance] from any dangerus ill, when he was ouerturned in ye Coche near Wabridg."

In 1664 Lord Mordaunt accompanied the King's brother, James, Duke of York, in a sea fight with the Dutch, but speedily returned to Parson's Green. Lady Mordaunt notes in her "Diary":

> "A Prayr of thanks Geuing for my Deare Hosbands safe returne Home, when he went out with the Duck of Yorck to see Wensday Decern. ye 7th 1664."

Lord Mordaunt had a love for versifying, but, if we may believe Pepys, his compositions were not of a very brilliant nature. The old chronicler writes in his "Diary," under date 22 Dec. 1664:

> "Met with a copy of verses, mightily commended by some gentlemen there, of my Lord Mordaunt's in excuse of his going to sea this late expedition with the Duke of York. But, Lord ! they are sorry things, only a Lord made them !"

Lady Mordaunt also was a versifier. A specimen (one of many) of Lady Mordaunt's power of rhyming occurs in her "Diary" under date 1666, taking, as usual, the form of a thanksgiving on "Wednesday, May ye 2nd 1666, the day I fell of my Horse."

Lord Mordaunt does not appear to have frequently attended the meetings of the Fulham Vestry. His bold, firm signature to the minutes occurs, for the first time, on 18 June 1665.

The cessation of the Plague and the extinction of the Great Fire of London elicited Lady Mordaunt's thanksgiving in verse. The entries are dated respectively:

> "Monday ye 1st July 1666 A thanks geuing for the preservation of my Deare hosband, myselfe, childerne and famely from the plage of pestilenc, and for our saffe retorne home, and for the sesing of that plage of pestilenc in this nation."

> "Sep. ye 6th 1666 Thursday A thanks geuing for the stoping of the Fire in London."

In 1666 Lord Mordaunt added 44 acres of copyhold land to his estate at Parson's Green. The additions comprised Stroud Mead (4 ac.), Bushy Close (25 ac.) and Legatt Shot and New Close (15 ac.). These closes lay to the south of the estate and extended to the lands of Grove House on the east, to Southfield on the west, to the Coope and Pingle, the Warren and Broomfield on the south and to the Peasecroft on the north. This land had once been in the possession of John Nurse or Nourse, Bachelor of Law, and, at the time of the lease to Mordaunt, was in the possession of Samuel Harvey, son of Col. Edmund Harvey. The whole of Lord Mordaunt's estate at Parson's Green must now have measured close upon 60 acres.

Lord Mordaunt's later life was unfortunately marked by a disgraceful incident in connection with the daughter of one William Taylor, Surveyor of Windsor Castle. Pepys many times refers to it in his "Diary." It is, perhaps, undesirable to give the details here.

A fire at Parson's Green House is thus recorded in Lady Mordaunt's "Diary":

> "June ye 12 1670. A thanks geuing for our deleueranc from the fire at Persons Greene ye 12 of June to be sayed, this or sume outher, euery Sonday."

And the recovery of her "dear childerne" from the small pox, in Jan. 1674-75, brought forth yet another prayer.

Lord Mordaunt died from fever, 5 June 1675, aged 48. His remains were interred, with great ceremony, in a vault in Fulham Church. The Church Registers record:

> 1675 The Rt. Hono^ble John Lord Viscount Mordaunt departed this mortall life ye 5day of June and was Interred in a new vault in ye south Ile ye 14 of ye same month of June.

Lady Mordaunt, in her "Diary," inserts a very long prayer on the occasion of her husband's death. The entry is headed:

> "After the death of my deare Hosband who dyed June ye 5 1675 Satorday in the afternoune (wreton July ye 30)."

Lord Mordaunt's will, dated 4 March 1673-74, was proved 11 June 1675 (P.C.C. 67 Dycer) by Lady Elizabeth Mordaunt. He left £20 to the poor of Fulham and £30 for the binding out of apprentices. He bequeathed all his lands to his son Charles. To his wife he left his interest in the Coale Farm and the Manors of Shepton Mallet and Currey Mallet, co. Somerset.

Lady Mordaunt continued to reside at Parson's Green House. John Evelyn, who calls her "the most virtuous lady in the world," notes in his "Diary" under 2 December 1675:

> "I visited Lady Mordaunt at Parson's Green, her son being sick. This

pious woman delivered to me £100 to bestow as I thought fit for the release of poor prisoners for charitable uses."

On 1 April 1676 Lady Mordaunt enters in her "Diary":

"A thanks geuing for delueranc from fire in my chamber begun."

One of the last entries in her "Diary," is of the date

Wensday Feb. y^e 14 167$\frac{7}{6}$.

It reads:

"When I was asalted thrise in my chare, and preserued from all ill, by the great mercy of my God."

Lord Mordaunt left issue seven sons and four daughters. His eldest son, Charles, named by Mordaunt after his royal master, was born about the year 1658. He became the third Earl of Peterborough. Of this distinguished man we shall presently speak at length. John, the second son, was born 22 April 1659. The third son, Harry, born 29 Mar. 1663-64, is the first mentioned by Lady Mordaunt in her "Diary." She writes:

"A thanks geuing to my God for ye berthe of my sone Hary, and my Hapy and safe deleuery of him after so greate a fitt of scicknes and weknes, he was borne upon a Sonday ye 29th of March 1663."

Harry Mordaunt became a Lieut.-General in the Army, and Treasurer of the Ordnance in 1699. Louis, the fourth son, was born 22 Dec. 1665. His mother notes:

"A thanks geuing for the berthe of my sone Louis, born in Oxford, Decem, the 22nd 1665."

Louis became a Brigadier General in the Army. Osbert, the fifth son, was born in April 1668. The "Diary" contains:

"A thanks geuing for my safe deleuery of my son Osbert, born at Mumpiler [i.e, Montpelier) ye   of April 1668."

Lady Mordaunt, who had been staying at Montpelier for her health, returned to Parson's Green in April of the following year. The "Diary" contains:

> "A prayr of thanks geuing to my God, for the Recouery of my helthe, and my safe retourne home, to my hosband and childerne, after my long Jorny to Montpiler in that week condetion, to be sayd euery Saturday, that or sum outher, for I came safe to Persens Green apon Saterday ye 2 of Aprell in the yere of our Lord 1669."

The sixth son, Osmund, was born in Oct. 1669. The "Diary" sets forth:

> "A thanks geuing for the berthe of my son Osmond (borne Octo. ye 1669) and for my restoration to helthe."

Osmund Mordaunt, who also entered the Army, was killed at the battle of the Boyne, 1 July 1690. George, the seventh son, was born after his father's death, in Nov. or Dec. 1675 The Church Registers record:

> 1675. Georg s. of Lady Mordaunt bap. 6 Dec.

Further on in this list is a second entry of the baptism. In her "Diary," under date "Jan. i67" (qc insert image of date, p 143, 3/4 down) Lady Mordaunt enters another prayer "After the berthe of my son Gorg." This son, who took holy orders, married Elizabeth, daughter of Sir John D'Oyly of Oxon., bart. This lady was buried at Fulham (see vol. I, "Fulham Church: Its Monuments" chapter), the Church Registers recording:

> 1718. Elizabeth the Wife of the Hon[ble] Geo. Mordaunt bu. 24 Mar.

The Rev. George Mordaunt died in 1728. The eldest daughter of Lord and Lady Mordaunt was Elizabeth, the date of whose birth is unknown. The second daughter, Carey, was born 29 July 1661. In the "Diary" we read:

> "Agust ye 31st 1661.
> A Prayr of thanks geuing for my safe delueranc from ye payn of Child

berthe of my daughter Cory borne July 1661 ye 29th day."

This lady died in 1714. The Church Registers record:

1714. The Lady Carrey Mordaunt from London bu. 3 Jan.

The third daughter, Sophia, was born in July 1664. The "Diary" reads:

"1664 July ye 15th.
A thanksgeuing for ye Bearthe of my daughter Sophia."

The fourth daughter, Anne, was born 5 Mar. 1665-66. Lady Mordaunt notes:

"March ye 5th 1666.
A thanks geuing for my safe deleuery of my Daughter Anne."

This daughter married James Hamilton of Tollymore Park, co. Down. Their daughter, Cary Eleanor, lies buried at Fulham (see vol. I, "Fulham Church: Its Monuments" chapter). Lady Mordaunt survived her husband four years, dying in April 1679. The Church Registers record:

1679. Elizabeth Viscountess Mordaunt sepult primo Maij.

Prefixed to the "Diary" published by Lord Roden is a portrait of Lady Mordaunt copied from an original picture, painted in 1665, by Louise, Princess Palatine, daughter of the Queen of Bohemia. The original picture is in the possession of Lord Roden. The excellent engraving of Lord Mordaunt, by Faithorne, from the picture by Vandyck, is prefixed to an account of his trial, published in 1661 (folio).

Lady Mordaunt's "Diary" shows her to have been a devout Churchwoman, a loving wife and a generous friend to the poor around her.

We now come to one of the most remarkable characters to be found in English history, Charles, Lord Mordaunt, subsequently the third Earl of Peterborough, eldest son of John, Lord Mordaunt, and his successor to the estate at Parson's Green.

Charles Mordaunt is generally believed to have received his early education at Eton, whence he proceeded to Oxford. He matriculated at Christ Church, 11 April 1674. He did not stay long at the University, for, in Nov. 1674, he entered as a volunteer on board the Cambridge under his mother's step-brother, Arthur Herbert, afterwards Earl of Torrington, Admiral of the Fleet, and went out to the Mediterranean in the squadron under Admiral Sir John Narbrough.

By the death of his father, in 1675, he became Viscount Mordaunt and, through his mother, owner of the estate at Parson's Green. In 1680 he embarked for Africa with the Earl of Plymouth. He greatly distinguished himself at Tangier, then besieged by the Moors. In a few months he returned to England and ultimately settled down at Parson's Green.

On the accession of James II, Charles Mordaunt proved a sturdy opponent to the tyrannical measures of that monarch, and from his seat in the House of Lords hotly opposed the repeal of the Test Act. Disliking the proceedings of the Court, he obtained leave to go to Holland, where he was one of the first of the refugees to offer his services to William, Prince of Orange, in his intended expedition to England. In the Revolution of 1688 he played a conspicuous part. He accompanied the Prince of Orange to England, was sworn in a Privy Councillor and made a Lord of the Bedchamber. In order to attend the coronation of the Prince and Princess of Orange as an Earl, he was, on 9 Apl. 1689, created Earl of Monmouth. In 1692 he made the campaign in Flanders under William III. In 1697, on the death of his uncle, Henry, 2nd Earl of Peterborough, he succeeded to that earldom. During the War of the Spanish Succession the Earl of Peterborough was declared General and Commander-in-Chief of the British Forces in the Iberian peninsula. In the early summer of 1705, he landed in Spain with a force of only 5,000 men. Here he took on board the Archduke Charles of Austria, who claimed the Spanish Crown, and at once proceeded to Valencia. His first intention was to make a dash on Madrid, with the idea of finishing the war at a blow, but the Archduke and the Prince of Hesse overruled. Peterborough then laid siege to Barcelona, which was defended on one side by the sea and on the other by the fortifications of Monjuich, of which, by a brilliant *coup de main*, he made himself master. Barcelona fell, and soon all Valencia lay at his feet. But for the obstinacy of the Archduke Charles and political dissensions at home, there is little reason to doubt that Peterborough could have placed the Austrian Prince on the throne of Spain. His plans being rejected by the Archduke, the Earl, in ill humour, left the command and retired to Italy.

In 1707 he once more returned to Valencia, but his wise counsels were not followed and he was soon afterwards recalled. The tide of fortune now went strong against the Austrians, but we need not follow the matter further. The brilliant career of Charles, Earl of Peterborough, as a military and as a naval commander, was over.

Charles, Earl of Peterborough.
From an engraving by W. T. Fry, published 1 May 1829,
after an original painting by Dahl

Historians regard him as one of the greatest soldiers which this country has ever produced. His achievements in Spain were enveloped in a haze of romance and his deeds of daring read more like fiction than actual history.

Peterborough's great vices were his vaingloriousness, his craving for novelty and popularity, and his childish love of mischief. When he returned home, though a Whig, he made common cause with the Tories in order to spite his great rival, the Duke of Marlborough. The story runs that, on one occasion, the populace mistook him for the Duke, who was at that moment in somewhat bad odour. "Gentlemen," exclaimed Peterborough, "I shall convince you by two good and sufficient reasons that I am not the Duke of Marlborough. First, I have only five guineas in my pocket, and secondly, here they are at your service," flinging the coins among the crowd, a pretty satire on the wealth and greed, the besetting sins of the victor of Blenheim.

In his estate at Parson's Green, Peterborough took great delight. Bowack, who was the Earl's contemporary, gives the following account of the grounds as they existed in his day:

> "This seat is a very large, square, regular pile of brick, and has a gallery all round it upon the roof. 'Twas built by a branch of the honourable family of the Monmouths and came to the present Earl in right of his mother, the Lady Elizabeth Carey, Viscountess De Aviland. It has abundance of extraordinary good rooms with fine paintings, etc., but is mostly remarkable for its spacious gardens, there being above twenty acres of ground inclos'd: the contrivance of the grounds is fine, tho' their beauty is in great measure decay'd. And the large cypress shades, and pleasant Wildernesses, with fountains, statues, etc., have been very entertaining."

The 44 acres of copyhold land, which came into the possession of Harry, the second Earl of Peterborough, were, in 1702, leased to Thomas Gibson. In 1722 they were leased to Charles, Earl of Peterborough. At the same time the Earl was granted by the Bishop of London:

> "All that cottage and one acre of land enclosed with quicksett being the northward part of a close called ffour acres, and the northward part of a close called Damaris close and lying and being next unto the garden,

orchard and ground of the said Charles Earl of Peterborough, enclosed with a brick wall, which said acre doth extend in length from the greengate coming out of the ground of the said Earl of Peterborough on the west part unto the end or corner of the aforesaid wall on the east part."

The one acre field, in which this "cottage" stood, lay at the north-east corner of Peterborough Lane and is now traversed by Coniger Road. Southward of this, and also adjacent to Peterborough Lane, was the close called "ffour acres," through which Coniger Road also extends. About 150 yards down the Lane was the "greengate," the entrance to old Peterborough House. This gate was destroyed in 1874. Portions of the ancient wall bounding "ffour acres" are still standing. Damaris close, which adjoined "ffour acres," recalls the name of a former owner, one Edward Damarie, who lived at Parson's Green in the time of Charles I.

At Peterborough House, as the mansion now came to be called, the Earl entertained most of the literati and wits of the day, including Addison, Swift, Prior, Pope, Locke and Bolingbroke. Several of Swift's letters mention the Earl's hospitality, and some verses by this writer, beginning:

"Mordanto fills the trump of fame,
The Christian world his deeds proclaim,
And prints are crowded with his name,"

convey a lively image of his figure and a description in playful caricature of his manners and mental qualities. "His activity of body and mind," says Swift, "was incessantly hurrying him into suspicious designs and perils of a thousand kinds." Peterborough loved to fly round Europe; in fact, he is said to have seen more kings, princes and postillions than any other living man. He used to travel at such a tremendous speed that the ministers were wont to say that they wrote at rather than to him. He would dictate to his secretaries six or seven letters simultaneously. Mackay, in his amusing "Memoirs," says of Peterborough:

"He affects popularity and loves to preach in coffee houses and public places, is an open enemy to revealed religion; brave in person; hath a good estate; does not seem expensive, yet always in debt, and very poor; a well-shaped, thin man, with a very brisk look, near fifty years old."

He was said to have been a man absolutely without fear, but when he was asked whether this was so, he replied, "No, I am not, but I never saw the occasion to fear."

In 1727 Voltaire, an atheist like Peterborough, visited the Earl at Parson's Green, where he stayed three weeks. Addison, who chanced also to be present, was seized with one of those fits of taciturnity which formed the most lamentable trait in his character. The Earl was the author of a "Song by a Person of Quality."

His favourite dining-room at Parson's Green was on an eminence in his gardens. It was a handsome building, and was in a good state of preservation down to the beginning of the present century. Norris Brewer, who was told the anecdote by Faulkner, writes:

> "When his Lordship gave a large dinner it was his practice to assume the apron and to supervise, in person, the preparation and arrangement of the various dishes. When the banquet was ready, he threw aside his culinary appendages, and entered the drawing room with the grace of a refined courtier, but more proud of having exercised the talent of a skilful cook, which he acquired during his arduous campaigns in Spain."

A writer in the *Westminster Magazine* for January 1778 tells a similar story:

> "While he (Peterborough) was upon his journeys he was frequently in danger of perishing from want of food, and when he could get it, was so often constrained to dress it himself that he became a good cook; and such was the force of habit that, till disabled by age, his dinner was constantly of his own dressing. Those who have dined with him at Parson's Green say that he had a dress for the purpose, like that of a tavern cook, and that he used to retire from the company an hour before dinner time, and, having dispatched his culinary affairs, would return properly dressed and take his place amongst them."

At these dinner parties at Peterborough House, the Earl was wont to entertain his company by reciting his adventures abroad, especially those relating to his Spanish campaign.

When quite a youth, Peterborough, then Charles Mordaunt, married Carry, daughter of Sir Alexander Fraser, of Durris, Kincardineshire. By this lady, who died 13 Mar. 1708-9, he had four sons, Thomas, John, Harry and George, and one daughter, Henrietta. Harry was baptized at Fulham. The Church Registers record:

> 1683. harry son of Charles Lord Viscount Mordaunt and Sarah his Lady bap. 28 of April.

"Sarah" is apparently an error for "Carry." Thomas died in 1684 and was buried at Fulham. The Registers record:

> 1684. Tho. son of the Ld. Viscount Mordaunt a child bu. 1st of Nov.

> 1685. George son of John the Ld. Viscount Mordaunt and Sarah his Lady bap. 17 of Sept.

Here the Christian names of both father and mother are incorrect.

> 1685. Geo. son of the Ld. Viscount Mordaunt a child bu. 19 of Sept.

The sons John and Harry died of smallpox in 1710. The daughter Henrietta married Alexander, Duke of Gordon.

In his old age the Earl of Peterborough fell in love with Miss Anastasia Robinson, the celebrated opera singer, whose beauty and talents were surpassed only by her modesty and worth. She was the daughter of a Mr. Robinson, an artist, who resided in the neighbourhood of Golden Square. Returning from his studies in Italy, Mr. Robinson instructed his young daughter in Italian. Her vocal and musical talent obtained for her a place at the Opera where she attracted the attention of the Earl of Peterborough. About 1723 she retired from the stage in consequence of her marriage with the Earl. The affair was, however, kept secret, and it was not till after the lapse of some years that Peterborough could be persuaded openly to admit that which all the world knew. It is stated that he took a house at or near Parson's Green, where Anastasia and her mother resided. A writer in the *Westminster Magazine* observes:

"During the residence of Mrs. Robinson at Parson's Green, she had a kind of musical academy there, in which Bononcini, Martini, Tosi, Greene and others were frequent performers."

During the last few years of his life, Peterborough resided chiefly at an estate near Southampton, known as Bevois Mount, near the present village of Bevois. He suffered from stone and was advised, as his only chance of recovery, to undergo an operation. Before so doing he convened a family party at the rooms of his nephew, the Right Hon. Stephen Poyntz, in St. James's Palace, where, according to Dr. Burney ("Hist. of Music" iv. 247-49), he formally introduced his wife as the Countess of Peterborough. Shortly afterwards he was publicly married to her. His wife, who nursed him with great tenderness, accompanied him on a voyage to Lisbon, for the benefit of his health. He reached the port, but died six days after his arrival, 25 Oct. 1735. His widow brought the body back to England, where it was buried in the family vault in Turvey church, Turvey, Bedfordshire.

Lady Peterborough, during her widowhood, resided chiefly at Bevois Mount, where she died in 1750.

The will of Charles, Earl of Peterborough and Monmouth, dated 9 Sept. 1735, was proved 26 Nov. 1735.

It recites that, by indentures of lease and release, dated 3 and 4 Sept. respectively, between himself of 1st, John Mordaunt, one of his grandsons of 2nd, Lady Mary Countess Dowager of Pembroke of 3rd, and Lord Lymerick, Stephen Poyntz, Esq., P.C., Colonel John Mordaunt and Colonel Charles Mordaunt, two of his brother's sons, of 4th part he conveyed "the Mansion House and freehold lands at Parson's Green in Fulham," to be held in trust and the same to be charged with an annuity of £25 per ann. to "Mrs. Anna Maria Mordaunt when she is admitted a Maid of Honour."

The executors let Peterborough House to various tenants. Lady Howe resided here from 1737 to 1744. From 1745 to 1749 the Hon. John Mordaunt is rated for the property. The Hon. John Cleveland was here in 1760-61.

Colonel Charles Mordaunt died in 1762 and was buried at Fulham. The Churchwardens' Accounts record:

"For the burial of Charles Mordaunt Esquire in ye Church £4 0s. 0d."

The Church Registers record:

1762. Charles Mordaunt Eq. bu. 3 May.

His brother, Colonel John Mordaunt, died in 1767 and was buried at Fulham. The Registers record:

1767. The Hon[ble] Colonel John Mordaunt (from London) bu. 5 July.

In 1761 Peterborough House became the residence of Charles, 4th Earl of Peterborough, who died here in August 1779. He was buried at Fulham. The Church Registers record:

1779. The Right Hon[ble] Charles Earl of Peterborough and Monmouth bu. 7 Aug.

His Countess had predeceased him in 1755, the Church Registers recording:

1755. Mary Countess of Peterborow bu. 24 Nov.

In the Churchwardens' Accounts for 1755 is the following:

"Rec[d] for the Countess of Peterborough being buried in Linnen £2 10s. 0d."

Before we pass from the Peterborough family, it may be mentioned that, though the only memorials to it in Fulham Church are the monument recording the career of John Mordaunt, the devoted adherent of Charles II, and a stone to his daughter-in-law, the Hon. Elizabeth Mordaunt, many members of it have been interred here. Some of these we have already mentioned. One or two of the Lawsons, connections of the Peterboroughs by marriage, were also buried here. James II, in 1685, created one Wilfrid Lawson, a baronet. His descendant, a third Sir Wilfrid Lawson, M.P. for Cockermouth and one of the Grooms of George I, was married at Fulham. The Church Registers record:

1723. Sʳ Wilfrid Lawson Bart, and Mrs. Eliz. Lucy Mordaunt by License mar. 14 March.

Elizabeth Lucy Mordaunt was the daughter of the Hon. Henry Mordaunt, brother of the second Earl of Peterborough. The third Sir Wilfrid died in 1737. The eldest son of Sir Wilfrid and Lady Lucy Lawson was another Sir Wilfrid. This fourth baronet died in infancy at Kensington, 2 May 1739 "of a mortification of the bowels." The Fulham Church Registers record:

1739. Sʳ Wilfred Lawson Bart bu. 4 May (died 2 May)

On the death of this child, his titles and estates passed to his only brother, Sir Mordaunt Lawson, who also died in his minority, 8 Aug. 1743, and was buried at Fulham. The entry in the Registers reads:

1743. Sʳ Mordaunt Lawson Bart. bu. 13 Aug.

Lady Elizabeth Lucy Lawson, above referred to, was also buried at Fulham. The Registers record:

1765. Lady Elizabeth Lucy Lawson (in the Church) bu. 29 Nov.

The Registers also record:

1725. The Lady Mohun bu. 21 May.

This lady was the widow of Lord Mohun, who was killed in a duel with the Duke of Hamilton. She subsequently married the Hon. Charles Mordaunt. The minutes of a meeting of the Fulham Vestry, held 30 May 1725, set out that

> "It was agreed by a majority that the sum of 25 guineas should be paid for the vault erected in the south Isle in which the Corps of the late Lady Mohun was lately interr'd before any faculty be granted for the appropriating of the same."

Other members of the Mordaunt family buried at Fulham include

Thomas Mordaunt, bu. 12 Oct. 1721; Henry Mordaunt, bu. 6 May 1724; Margaret Mordaunt, bu. 29 Dec. 1788, and Lt.-Genl. Thomas Osbert Mordaunt, bu. 18 Feb. 1809.

We will now resume the history of Peterborough House. By lease and release, dated respectively 11 and 12 April 1782 (release made between Robiniana, Countess Dowager of Peterborough and Monmouth and Charles Henry, 5th Earl of Peterborough and Monmouth), Peterborough House was conveyed to Mr. Richard Heaviside, a timber merchant, who lived here till 1795.

Peterborough House south view.
From a photograph by Mr. J. Dugdale, 1895

By lease and release (both dated 12 Sept. 1797), between Mr. R. Heaviside and Mr. John Meyrick, Peterborough House was conveyed to the latter. Mr. Meyrick was, at the time he purchased the Peterborough estate, living at Westfield House, now the Fulham Public Library. As old Peterborough House was not to his tastes, he decided to pull it down and to erect another house. The historic mansion, which he demolished in 1798, faced the south-east corner of Parson's Green, and stood near an ancient maze. The new Peterborough House, which Mr. Meyrick made his home, stands about the same distance back from the New King's Road, but considerably more to the east.

Mr. Meyrick, who was Churchwarden in 1800, will chiefly be

remembered in connection with the active part he took in forming the Fulham Volunteer Corps, of which he became the first Colonel Commandant.

The first Company of Volunteers was formed in Fulham in 1798. Rowlandson, who illustrated the whole of the platoon exercises by one of the London corps in every motion, has represented the "Fulham Volunteer" in the second motion, as shown below. The fears of a French invasion gave an immense impetus to the Volunteer movement, and an Act was passed for strengthening the National Defences. Napoleon, in his ambition to become dictator of Europe, contemplated the invasion of England. The air was very full of rumours of war, and preparations were on all sides being made to meet the threatened crisis. In Feb. 1798 the parishioners of Fulham were called together for the purpose of appointing a local Committee to receive contributions in aid of the subscription list which had been opened at the Bank of England for the "Defence of the Kingdom." The Vicar, the Rev. Graham Jepson, was appointed treasurer. Mr. Meyrick, however, determined to do something even more practical, than mere money-collecting, and, with this object, he raised a small body of artillery.

Fulham Volunteer. From a coloured print by Rowlandson, published by Ackermann, 18 July 1798

The Declaration, Rules and Regulations of the Fulham Volunteer Corps of Light Infantry contain the following declaratory preface:

> "We whose names are hereunto subscribed, Inhabitants of the Parish of Fulham, on the Fulham Side, do agree to form a Volunteer Corps of Light Infantry, to enable His Majesty more efficiently to provide for the

Defence and Security of the Realm during the present War, agreeable to the Provisions of an Act of Parliament passed in that behalf. And We do further agree and bind ourselves by this our Declaration, to be trained and exercised, and to March to any Part of Great Britain, for the Defence of the same, in case of Actual Invasion, or the Appearance of an enemy in Force upon the Coast; and for the Suppression of any Rebellion or Insurrection arising or existing during any such Invasion, whenever we shall be summoned by the Lieutenant of the County or in Consequence of any general Signal of Alarm. And for the more solemnly attesting our Agreement, to this our Declaration, We have taken and subscribed the following Oath:

'I _____ do sincerely Promise and Swear that I will be faithful and bear true Allegiance to His Majesty King George the Third, and that I will faithfully serve His Majesty in Great Britain, for the Defence of the same against all his Enemies and Opposers whatsoever,
So Help me God.' "

The Corps consisted of eight companies. Mr. Edward Batsford acted as secretary. The colours were presented to the Corps by Mrs. Meyrick.

The illustrations above represent a handsome silver gilt medal, obverse on the left, and reverse on the right, from the original, now in the possession of his grandson, Archibald Chasemore, Esq. The medal was presented by Captain Meyrick to Mr. Nathaniel Chasemore in the year 1800. Mr. Chasemore was a sergeant in the old Fulham Volunteers, and the medal, presented by their Colonel Commandant, was won by him in a shooting match with the old brown Bess, which took place in the grounds of Peterborough

House.

Upon Col. Meyrick's resignation, Lord Ranelagh was appointed to the command. The Corps subsequently fell off and, in 1816, was disbanded.

In Faulkner's own copy of his history of Fulham are inserted the following verses, dedicated by G. Hussey to the "Captain, Ensign, and the other officers and gentlemen of the Corps" of Fulham Volunteers:

"Ye Sons of Loyalty attend
And hear the Poet's lays
With me, the heart's effusion send
Pour'd out in songs of praise.

To an expanded diner's mind,
Whom all the Corps reveres:
The Toast's - The Captain, brave and kind
Of Fulham Volunteers.

What ardour fills the soldier's breast,
By lib'ral acts inspir'd;
The noble hero stands confest
With martial honour fir'd.

When men like him the standard raise
Here old and young appears
And proudly join the song of praise
With Fulham Volunteers.

This day your blazon'd Colours fly,
Received from Beauty's hand,
Let plaudits echo to the sky
The Heroines of our land.

Who smile the soldier to reward,
When martiall'd he appears,
And vows the British Maids to guard
Like Fulham Volunteers.

Ye envy'd Corps ! By far and near,
Around your banners stand;
By freedom's chart you're sure to steer
While Meyrick takes command;

Your leading men are England's boast;
And all the ladies give this toast -
The Fulham Volunteers.

Let this your Ensign's natal day
With manly mirth be crown'd;
Let ev'ry heart be blithe and gay,
With martial music sound.

In mem'ry see this day record
Wishing him health and years;
He's brave, and worthy the regard
Of Freedom's Volunteers.

Now when the olive wreath is won
And smiling Peace is seen;
When ev'ry hostile act is done,
And soldiers dance the green;

When wives around the conquerors cling,
And children lose their fears,
We'll teach the lisping babes to sing
Of Fulham Volunteers."

With the collapse of Napoleon and the cessation of danger of invasion, volunteering fell off and the movement slumbered till the great awakening of 1857.

Mr. Meyrick was an ardent lover of antiquities, of which he had a great collection at Peterborough House. He was a Fellow of the Society of Antiquaries. He died at Peterborough House on 27 Nov. 1805 and was buried at Fulham. The Registers record:

1805. John Meyrick Eq. bu. 6 Dec.

He was one of the last persons to be buried in linen.

By his wife Hannah, daughter and co-heiress of Samuel Rush, of Ford House, Herts, and Chislehurst, Kent, he was the father of Sir Samuel Rush Meyrick, author of "A Critical Inquiry into Ancient Armour." By his early marriage he greatly offended his father, who determined that his property should devolve upon his son's children instead of upon his son. The early death of Samuel

Meyrick's only son destroyed the effect of this disposition.

A Walk in the grounds of Peterborough House.
From a photograph by Mr. J. Dugdale, 1895

Mrs. Meyrick, who died in 1832, remained for a short while at Peterborough House, but, in 1807, the estate was offered in lots for sale by public auction. By lease and release, dated respectively 9 and 10 Dec. 1807, the trustees of the will of Mr. John Meyrick conveyed Peterborough House and the greater portion of the grounds to Major John Scott Waring, who resided here till 1813. The remainder of the estate was, in 1808, leased to Mr. Peter Denys, who let it to Messrs. R. and W. Wilcox. This portion lay to the south of Pomona Place and comprised 18a. 0r. 38p. It was used as a market and fruit garden by the Wilcoxes and subsequently by the Fitches.

Mr. Anthony Sampayo, in 1813, removed from Munster House to Peterborough House, where he resided till his death, 30 June 1832. On 14 May 1815, his wife, Mrs. Frances Sampayo, died at Peterborough House, and was buried at Fulham, 20 May 1815. His daughter, Frances Sampayo, died here, 27 July 1829, and was buried in her mother's grave, 1 Aug. 1829. Mr. Sampayo's son, Mr. Osborn H. Sampayo, to whom, in 1829, Peterborough House had been conveyed in fee simple, resided here till 1839. The house was now let to various tenants. Lady Sophia Margaret Kent and her son, Sir C. E. Kent, both died at Peterborough House in 1834, and were buried in Fulham Church (see vol. I, "Fulham Church: Its Monuments" chapter). In 1840-41 Peterborough House was the home of William Beckford, author of "Vathek," a romance written in elegant French. Of this work, Lord Byron observes, "As an eastern tale, even Rasselas must bow before it; his Happy Valley will not bear a comparison with the Hall of Eblis." Beckford died in 1844.

Peterborough Farm.
From a photograph by Mr. T. S. Smith, 1895

In the following year we find Peterborough House in the occupation of the Countess Dowager of Listowel. In this year (1845) the mansion once more came under the auctioneer's hammer. The details of the sale were thus announced:

> "Particulars and Conditions of Sale of an important Freehold Estate situate at Parson's Green, in the Parish of Fulham, comprising The Noble Residence called Peterborough House, a mansion in every way calculated for a Family of Distinction, seated in a Beautiful Park. Also of most valuable fruit market garden grounds in the occupation of Messrs. Fitch, thus combining an Elegant Residence and Solid Investment, in the whole comprising about 41a. 3r. 1p. Which will be Sold by auction by Messrs. Hedger, at the Auction Mart, opposite the Bank of England, on Tuesday June 17th, 1845 (unless previously

disposed of by private contract), at Twelve o'Clock, in one or in four lots "

A walk in the grounds of Peterborough House.
From a photograph by Mr. J. Dugdale, 1895

Peterborough House, which was included in Lot 1, is described as:

"A mansion of most costly erection, and as a specimen of architecture and solid construction certainly not surpassed. It is very commandingly placed, a pleasant remove from the King's Road, from which it is screened by a Noble Wall and Terrace, with Iron Fencing and approached by two very Handsome Entrances, with Lodges and Carriage Drives to the House."

The purchaser of this estate was Captain William Terry, a typical military man, blunt and bluff to a degree. In 1862 the estate, on Captain Terry's death, passed to his son, William Terry, a wealthy man with a mania for collecting, no matter what. He possessed perhaps the finest collection of violoncellos in this country. Mr. William Terry died at Peterborough House, 8 July 1884. Mrs. Terry continued to reside here for a short while. In 1885 the collections accumulated by the deceased were sold by Mr. J. C. Stevens, of King Street, St. James's.

An alcove in the grounds of Peterborough House.
From a photograph by Mr. J. Dugdale, 1895

In 1885 Peterborough House, which is now the property of Major William Terry, was taken by Mrs. Gardiner Hill, who removed here from Earl's Court House, where for many years she conducted an asylum for insane ladies.

Peterborough House is a somewhat handsome building. Its walls, which are of considerable thickness, are composed entirely of Suffolk bricks. It is approached by a fine semicircular double flight of steps. A pair of enormous Corinthian columns rise almost to the roof. The spacious vestibule, at the end of which is a noble circular stone staircase, is, perhaps, the finest feature of the mansion. It measures 30 ft. by 22 ft., and is 13 ft. high. The house is built in the French style prevailing at the period of its erection, nearly the whole of the rooms having their corners rounded.

Old Stone Gateway at Peterborough House.
From a photograph by Mr. J. Dugdale, 1895

On the left of the hall is the drawing-room (45 ft. by 20 ft.), an apartment extending from the front to the back of the house. It formerly had a painted ceiling and its walls were covered with *moiré* silk. To the right of the hall is the dining-room, formerly the library (18½ ft. by 16 ft.). It has a wood skirting of polished teak. The original dining-room was the apartment behind the present one. Passing through the hall to the back of the house, we reach a pretty circular boudoir, still preserved in its original state, with its blue walls and painted ceiling. A pair of French windows open on to the sloping lawn at the rear of the house.

On the west side of the house is a wing, comprising billiard and smoking rooms, etc., added by Captain William Terry. Beyond this is a further block of 24 rooms added for the accommodation of patients. The original kitchen is a dark and dingy room. The larder and dairy have black and white marble floors.

The Ancient Ice Well, Peterborough Farm.
From a photograph by Mr. T. S. Smith, 1895

The grounds of Peterborough House are now 12a. 2r. 27p. in extent. They are finely timbered. Some of the elms are 200 years of age. One of these is 150 ft. high. Beech, oak, chestnut, sycamore, ash - in fact, almost every English type of tree is represented in these grounds. A stone alcove in the grounds dates back, probably, to the days of the "great Earl." On the west side is a handsome stone gateway which originally formed an approach to the old house. The stable-yard and walls here are in almost the same state as they were a century and a half ago.

In the grounds there were formerly three ponds. The Church Registers record:

> 1709. Elizabeth the Dau. of ffrancis Draper was drounded in the Earl of Peterborough's pond. bu. 13 May.

A noticeable feature in the grounds of Peterborough House was an ice-well which survived till the recent building operations of Mr. J. Nichols. It was situated in what became the market and fruit garden of Messrs. Wilcox. In the pleasure grounds of the house was a building called the Armoury, in which was a marble bath.

The line of frontage of the Peterborough estate at its western end originally ran in a much more south-westerly direction. Between it and the New King's Road, just facing Parson's Green Pond, was a piece of waste. Under a grant by the Lord of the Manor, this piece of ground, subsequently known as the Shrubbery, was attached to the Peterborough estate. It is now covered by the houses between Peterborough and Coniger Roads.

In 1897 parts of the Peterborough estate were let for building purposes. Peterborough House will itself shortly come down to make way for further building operations.

OTHER NOTEWORTHY RESIDENTS OF PARSON'S GREEN

Sir Henry Barker, resided at Parson's Green from 1609 to 1631. By his will, dated 1631, he left £20 for the poor of Fulham. Sir Henry, who belonged to a Berkshire family, was knighted in July 1603.

Another distinguished resident of Parson's Green was Sir Thomas Bodley, who lived here from 1605 till his death in 1612. Thomas Bodley was the eldest son of John Bodley, of Exeter, by Joan, daughter and heiress of Robert Hume, of Ottery St. Mary. He was born 6 March 1544. During the reign of Queen Mary, John Bodley, on account of his religion, went into exile, settling at Geneva. On the accession of Elizabeth, the family returned to England, young Bodley being sent to Magdalen College, Oxford. In 1563 he proceeded B.A., and in the same year was chosen probationer of Merton College. He obtained the degree of M.A. in 1566, and three years later was elected a proctor of the University. The Queen, in 1583, made him one of her gentlemen ushers. In 1585 he married Anne, daughter of Mr. Carew of Bristol, a widow lady of large fortune. Elizabeth employed him on several embassies to Germany, Denmark, and Holland. In 1597 Bodley obtained his final recall, and in the same year set to work to restore the public library at Oxford, which was completed in 1599. To this library he presented a collection of books worth £10,000. Shortly after the accession of James I he was knighted. It was probably at Parson's Green that he wrote his life, which he completed down to 1609.

Other collections of books being sent to the Bodleian, the restored library no longer afforded sufficient accommodation.

Bodley now proposed to enlarge the building, and, on 19 July 1610, laid the first stone of the new foundation. He did not, however, live to see it completed, dying 28 Jan. 1611-2.

Sir Thomas Bodley, kt.
From an engraving after the original portrait at Oxford

In the "Annals of the Bodleian Library," by W. D. Macray, Oxford, 1890 (pp. 402-12), is the will of Sir Thomas Bodley, dated 2 Jan. 1611-12. The following is an extract:

> "I Thomas Bodley Knight being now of the age of threescore and seven complete and more. To be buried at Merton College, Oxford. To Mr. Richard Litler for small remembrance of my loue I geue my newest yron chest and my greate stone pot trimed wth Siluer dubble guylt, together wth ye case belonging to it, and to his vertuous wife my little Damske Cabbinett in my vpper studie at ffulham, yf it be not displaced, intreating him earnestly to afforde my Executo^{rs} his counsaile and aide wherein soe^{r} they shall neede it for ye gathering of my debts or otherwise. To the poore of the p^{r}ish of little St. Bartholomewes ten pounds and as much to ye poore of the p^{r}ish of ffulham to be distributed in both places as my Executo^{rs} shall thinke meete."

In a codicil he gives a legacy of "two little spoone boles double guylt, together wth my siluer fruicte basket," to the Bishop of London.

In the manuscript collection of Sir A. A. Hood, bart., is a folio paper, 17th century, containing a copy of a letter from Sir Thomas Bodley to Sir Francis Bacon, dated "From Fulham Feb. 19 1607." In another Bacon writes to Bodley: "I pray you send me some good news of Sir Thomas Smith, and commend me very kindly to him." In the "Cabala" are other letters from Bodley to Bacon. He was buried in the chapel of Merton College, Oxford.

In 1649 Sir Roger Burgoyne came to live at Parson's Green. Sir Roger was the eldest son of Sir John Burgoyne, of Sutton, co. Bedford, bart. He was knighted at Whitehall, 18 July 1641. He lived at Parson's Green, probably till the death of his father, circa 1654, when he succeeded to the title.

The Claytons were an old Parson's Green family. As early as 1638 the Churchwardens' Accounts record:

"rec. for knell Clayton   1s. 0d."

A Mr. Jasper Clayton is rated for a house at Parson's Green down to 1650. In 1664 a Lady Clayton comes into the rating, and in 1670 Sir John Clayton, knt. The following entries respecting the Clayton family occur in the Parish Registers:

1675. Jasper, son of Sir John Clayton and Dame Alice eius Dom[a] Baptizat 22 Oct.

1678 Sharlotte sonne of S[r] John Clayton and Allice his lady Bap. 23 Aprill.

1686. Mrs. Eliz. Clayton da. of S[r] Jno Clayton bu 6 of May.

In 1673 Sir John Clayton, kt, described as of "Parson's Green," and George Blake, of London, merchant, held letters patent for erecting lighthouses. Capt. Blake was, in 1674, a neighbour of Sir John's at Parson's Green.

Anthony Collins, the well-known deistical writer, was born in 1676, his father being Henry Collins, a man of good position. Anthony was educated at Eton and at King's College, Cambridge, and was a student at the Temple. In 1698 he married Martha, daughter of Sir Francis Child, the elder, of Hollybush House. Soon afterwards he became the intimate friend of John Locke, to whom he wrote many affectionate letters. Mrs. Martha Collins died in 1703, and was buried at Fulham. The Registers record:

1703. Martha, wife of Anthony Collins, Gent. bu. 19 Apl.

Locke observes of Collins that he had "an estate in the country, a library in town and friends everywhere." In 1715 he retired to Essex. By his wife Martha he had two sons and two daughters. In 1724 he married Elizabeth, daughter of Sir Walter Wrottesley, by whom there was no issue. He died 13 Dec. 1729, and was buried in Oxford Chapel, where a monument was erected by his widow.

Sir Thomas Fisher, knt. and bart., of Parson's Green and of Islington, was the son of Thomas Fisher by Susan, daughter of Thomas Tindall and sister of Sir John Tindall. He married Sara, daughter of Sir Thomas Fowler, of Islington, knt. Sir Thomas Fisher died 22 March 1635-36.

In 1630 the "Rt. Hon. the Lo: Morton" comes into the rating under Parson's Green.

William, seventh Earl of Morton, K.G., was born in 1582, succeeding to the earldom in 1605. He held the positions of Privy Councillor, Gentleman of the Bedchamber to James I and Charles I, High Treasurer of Scotland, and Captain of the Yeomen of the Guard. Douglas describes him as "one of the richest and greatest men in the kingdom." Like so many other residents of Parson's Green, he was a staunch supporter of the King, and made great sacrifices for the Royalist cause, selling for it the great estate of Dalkeith. He died in Orkney, 1648.

Daniel Finch, third Earl of Nottingham, died at Parson's Green, probably at the Rectory House, 2 Aug. 1769, aged 81 years. The Earl was twice married, first to Frances Fielding (d. 27 Sep. 1734), daughter of the fourth Earl of Denbigh, and secondly to Mary, fourth daughter of Sir Thomas Palmer. She died 8 Aug. 1757. By his first wife the Earl had one child, Charlotte, born 7 July 1731. By his second wife he had eight daughters, of whom four survived him. His second wife, Mary Palmer, was sister of Ann Palmer, who married Charles Fielding, who held the Fulham rectorial tithes.

Simon Willimot resided in Fulham, first in Bear Street and

then at Parson's Green, throughout the reign of Charles I, dying in 1648. On 13 Oct. 1639 he gave

> "for ever to the Poore Parishioners and auncient dwellers of Fulham on Fulham side 20^{li} to the care and truste of the Vicar and Churchwarden of Fulham on Fulham side from tyme to tyme being."

He directed that this money should be lent to young men dwelling in the parish at the rate of 6 p. c. per annum, the interest to be given in bread to the poor. But the donor added:

> "And if at any time there shall be in stocke for the poore on Fulham syde a fitting sume to buy some landes to the use of ye sayd Poore then it is the Doners will that the sayd 20^{li} be joyned with other moneyes to make a Purchase, Provided that out of the yeerelye Proffits of the sayd Landes 24^s be yeerly bestowed as is before expressed, as the gift of the sayd Simon Willimot for ever. And considering the casualtyes of moneyes once let out, if it shall happen that the sayd 20^{li} should miscarry or be ost [sic, lost?], it is not the Donors will, that the Vicar and Church-warden (hoping that they will discharge the trust that is comitted unto them carefully,) shall any way be tyed to make it good or be any way molested for the same."

The money has long since been entirely lost. In the ancient "Register Book" is a detailed entry of the benefaction signed by "Symon Willimott."

At a Court General, held in 1648-49, the following presentment was made:

> "Simon Wilmott, free tenant, died since last Court and John and James Wilmott are his sons and next heirs."

CHAPTER VI: FULHAM ROAD

SECTION I: HIGH STREET TO MUNSTER ROAD

Returning to the top of the High Street, we will now bend our course along old the Fulham Road.

Fulham Road, looking towards High Street, in 1867.
From a photograph by Mr. H. Ambridge.

The present name is of quite modern introduction. In the Court Rolls the first allusion to the road occurs under date 1442, when it is described as "the King's highway between Berestret and Wedenesgrene," i.e. that part between the High Street and Walham Green. In 1496 it is called the "highway leading from Fulham towards Wendon grene." In 1516 it is spoken of as "the King's highway" leading to London. In 1553 occurs the expression "from Fulhamstrete to Wandongrene." In 1568 the eastern end is described as "the Queen's highway between Standford Bridge and Wendon Grene," i.e. the part between Stamford Bridge and Walham Green. Sometimes we find it spoken of as Fulham Street.

Once (in 1507) the expression London Lane occurs in the Court Rolls.

In course of time, as the thoroughfare gradually superseded the river as the more speedy means of reaching town, it began to be called the London Road. It was not until about 1870 that the designation Fulham Road completely supplanted the older name. Faulkner, who wrote in 1812, speaks of the thoroughfare as the "Fulham Road."

Perhaps, in olden times, no artery leading out of London was encompassed by greater dangers to travellers than the Fulham Road. An open ditch on each side, complete darkness at night, countless ruts, and, in wet weather, seas of mud, were some of the difficulties which had to be coped with, to say nothing of the footpads who made it a favoured haunt.

Cases of robbery and outrage on the Fulham Road are frequently reported in the old magazines. On 16 April 1765, Mr. James House Knight, of Walham Green, while returning along it, was waylaid, robbed and murdered. He was buried at Kensington, the Registers recording that he was "shot in Fulham Road near Brompton." The Overseers' disbursements for 1743 include:

"19 June (Pd.) ffor taking a Highwayman 17s. 4d."

The Fulham Road became a favourite coaching road for Portsmouth, Guildford, Southampton, Isle of Wight, Chichester, Havant, etc. Among some of the better known coaches which used to traverse it were the "Rocket," the "Red Rover," and the "Earl of March."

NORTH SIDE

Our first section of the Fulham Road will be from the High Street to Munster Road. We will take the north side.

The Holcroft's estate, at the junction of the Fulham Road with the Fulham Palace Road, marks the site of a noteworthy house, known as Holcroft's or Holcroft's House or Hall, a somewhat heavy-looking residence which stood in grounds measuring 5a. 0r. 24p.

The name "Holcroft's" is of doubtful origin. It is possible that the original house - for the Holcroft's, which many of us remember, had a predecessor - was so called after the maternal ancestors of Lady Margaret Legh, whose grandmother was a Margaret Holcroft. Lady Margaret Legh was buried at Fulham in 1603, while forty three years later the name Holcroft's is recorded in the Court Rolls. In 1646 John Richards, guardian of Richard Richards, let "a messuage in ffulham called Holcrofts" to Edmund Snowe. In 1658 William Richards, merchant taylor of London, was chosen reeve for Holcroft's. On 19 January 1662-63 this William Richards surrendered

> "All that messuage called Holcrofts and all his field called Great Colehill containing 5½ acres in the occupation of Thomas Willett to the use of Paul Docminique of Hackney, Middlesex, merchant, and his heirs."

It will be observed that the above acreage is almost identical with the figure we have already given, taken from Maclure's "Survey" of 1853. Of Colehill we shall more particularly speak when we reach the Fulham Palace Road. Paul Docminique, the elder, held Holcroft's until 1675, when he surrendered it to his only son, Paul.

Paul Docminique, junior, who was a London merchant, in 1694, sold the messuage to William Sherington of the Middle Temple. About the year 1700 Robert Limpany purchased the estate and built upon it the house which survived until our time. In 1708 he sold the property to Sir William Withers, his cousin.

William Withers, who was born in 1650, was a member of the Fishmongers' Company. In 1698 he was elected Alderman of the Ward of Farringdon Without, and, on 20 October 1699 he received, at Kensington Palace, the honour of knighthood. At the Parliament, elected in 1701, Sir William was returned as a Whig for the City of London. In the same year he was chosen Sheriff and, in 1707, became Lord Mayor of London. During his term of office, Sir William Withers, at a bye-election occasioned by the death of Sir R. Clayton, was returned as a Tory! At each of the succeeding Parliaments, elected in 1708, 1710 and 1713, he headed the poll for the City.

Sir William was President of Bridewell and Bethlehem

Hospitals. His election to this position took place at a Court of these Hospitals, held 15 December 1708, his predecessor being Sir Thomas Rawlinson, kt., another Fulham worthy. At a Court, held 13 August 1713, Sir William Withers was thanked for the gift of some ornamental pavement and a pair of iron gates, then erected in front of the chapel of Bridewell. At the next Court, 20 August 1713, it was ordered that the following inscription in gold letters should be put over the chapel door:

"These Iron Gates and Marble Pavement were the gift of the Right Worshipfull Sir William Withers, Knt. and Alderman, President of this Hospital. Anno Dni. 1713."

Holcroft's. From a photograph by Mr. H. Ambridge

These old gates, which bear his arms, are still preserved at the offices of the Bridewell Royal Hospital in New Bridge Street, Blackfriars. In one of the old Court Books of the Hospital is the following quaint entry:

"Court, 5th Decr 1718.
A motion being made that the R^t Worshipfal Sir William Withers Knt. and Alderman and President of these Hospitals be desired to sit for his picture, to be put up in the great Hall of this Hospital, where there are the pictures of three former Presidents, and that the same may be drawn

at ye Hospital charge, as some acknowledgment to remain to posterity of the high esteem the Governors have for his person, and their gratefull sense of his eminent care and paines for the service of these Hospitals during the time he has done them the honour to be their President, besides his generous donation of the Marble Pavement and Iron Gates of the Chappell his Worship desired that the question might not be putt But it being unanimously insisted upon, he was pleased to say since the Governors thought fitt to give his picture a place in the Hospital, It should be done without any expense to the house."

And again:

"Court, 6th August 1719.
The thanks of this Court were unanimously given to the R^t Worshipfal Sir Wm Withers Knt. and Alderman of this City and President of these Hospitals for his picture on horseback (set up in the Dining room of this Hospital) in the manner he had the honour to attend her late Majesty Queen Ann in her procession to St Paul's the nineteenth day of August 1708 to return Thanks to Almighty God for ye victory over the French near Oudenard, which picture his Worship was pleased to give to the Hospital at his own charge when this Court desired him to sitt for it at the Charge of the Hospital."

This portrait was preserved at Bridewell Hospital until 1862, when it was offered to the authorities at Guildhall and accepted by them in 1864. On being received, it was found to be too large for any of the public rooms. After being kept rolled up, it was, in February 1886, returned by the City Lands Committee to Bridewell. To make it a more "sizeable" picture, the head and shoulders were cut out and framed. It still hangs at Bridewell and Bethlehem Hospitals.

Sir William Withers married Margaret, daughter of Thomas Hayes, of Chertsey Abbey, by whom he had nine children.

Lady Margaret Withers died at Holcroft's, 6 Aug. 1711. Sir William expired here, 31 January 1720-21. The Church Registers record:

1711. The Lady Margaret Withers Wife of Sr William Withers knight bu. 12 Aug.

1720. Sr William Withers knight bu. 7 Feb.

The will of Sir William Withers, dated 19 Feb. 1718-19, was proved 16 February 1720-21 (P.C.C. 39 Buckingham). The following is an extract:

> "I Sʳ William Withers knt. and alderman of London. To be buried privately in ffulham churchyard without any pomp or ostentation. To my daughter Sarah £5275 19s. and to her the Wrought Bed with the Beding, Boulster, etc., and the White India Satin quilt, etc. To my cozen, Robert Limpany and his wife £10 each."

Testator left a legacy of £200 to Bridewell and Bethlehem; to the poor of St. Mary-le-Bow £5; to the poor of Fulham £10, to be distributed "to such as are or have been housekeepers of the communion of the Church of England."

The death of Sir William Withers was immortalized in verse by Elkanah Settle, the opponent of the poet Dryden. The only known existing copy of this poem is now in the possession of Thomas E. Ravenshaw, Esq., a descendant of Sir William. The title page reads:

> "Augusta Lacrimans | A | Funeral Poem | To the | Memory | Of the Honourable | Sir William Withers, knt. | Mors Sola fateter | Quantula sunt Hominum corpuscula | By E. Settle, City-Poet | London | Printed for the Author, 1721."

The cover bears the following arms:

Dexter: A chevron between three crescents (Withers); *Sinister*: A chevron between three wolves' heads erased (Hayes).

The closing lines in this fulsome panegyric run thus:

> "Now Honoured Fulham, thou, who by thy Side,
> Seest the proud neigh'bring Thames's Current glide
> Thy Towers the watry mirror overlook,
> And plume their beauties in the Silver Brook.
> Here a fair Rural Dome of Honour blest
> With that bright Head, thy Honourable Guest,
> Here in the Short Recesses he could spare,
> (His Dear Augusta still his nearest care !)
> He his retiring Hours of Life bestowed,

Betwixt his Friends, his Closet, and his God.
Hither his sleeping Worthy to convey
To his enstalment on his Throne of Clay,
Behold his Cavalcade of Sorrow move,
The last just Debt of Piety and Love.
We to thy Temple bell his Dust resign
The Withers narrower Mausoleum thine
But what, tho' thus to his long Requiem led ?
He lives in those young Eyes that mourn him dead;
Copies that shall the Original renew
And made the Stock immortal whence they grew."

Holcroft's. From a photograph by Messrs. W. Field and Co.

Little is known about William Withers, the son and heir of Sir William. He appears to have been a Colonel in the Army. He married Elizabeth Turner, and survived his father only two years. In Mawson's "Obits" is the following:

"Nov. 18 1722. Died at his House in Fulham in the County of Midd[x] Col. Withers Son to the late S[r] W[m] Withers, kn't and Alderman, and was buryed in the Church Yard there, in the Tomb of the Alderman his Father."

On "9^{br} (i.e. November) 11th 1723" the parish officers disbursed 8s. "To a warrant and expencs in Receiving Col. Withers' money being buried in Linnen," while on the contra side of the account is an entry of the receipt of £5 "for Wm. Withers Esq. his being buried in Linen."

In his will, dated 4 Oct. 1722, proved 2 Mar. 1722-23, and extract entered in the old "Register Book," 7 Jan. 1724, William Withers bequeathed the whole of his property to his wife, Elizabeth, subject to a rent charge of £5 per annum to the Governors of the Hospitals of Bridewell and Bethlehem, to pay it to the Minister and Churchwarden of Fulham, to be applied by them for the repair, etc., of

> "the Vault and Tomb or Monument by me lately Erected to the Memory of my late Honoured Father, Sr William Withers kt., deceased, in the Church Yard belonging to the Parish Church of Fulham, the money, when not wanted, to be given to the poor."

From other parts of this will, it is clear that Col. Withers intended the tomb for his own sepulture, though the monument contains no reference to him. The Church Registers, however, contain the following entries of the burial of Col. Withers and his wife, the latter of whom died at the age of 29:

> 1722. Will Withers Esq. bu. 26 Nov.
> 1727. Elizabeth Withers bu. 19 May.

A grandson of Sir William Withers, a third William, described as of Dummer, co. Hants, was born 23 August 1717. He died 29 Oct. 1768, and was also buried in the Fulham vault. The Church Registers record:

> 1768. William Withers, Esq. bu. 5 Nov.

His widow, Rebecca, died at Chelsea, and was buried at Fulham, 11 November 1779. This William Withers was also buried in linen. The disbursements of the Churchwardens for 1769 include:

> "Expenses going to London to the undertaker to receive the fine for Sir

(sic) William Wythers's being buried in linnen 2s. 6d. "

His will, dated 27 Nov. 1767, was proved 12 November 1768. He resided chiefly in Hampshire. The descent of Holcroft's is for awhile somewhat doubtful. On Colonel Withers' death his widow let the property.

PEDIGREE OF WITHERS FAMILY

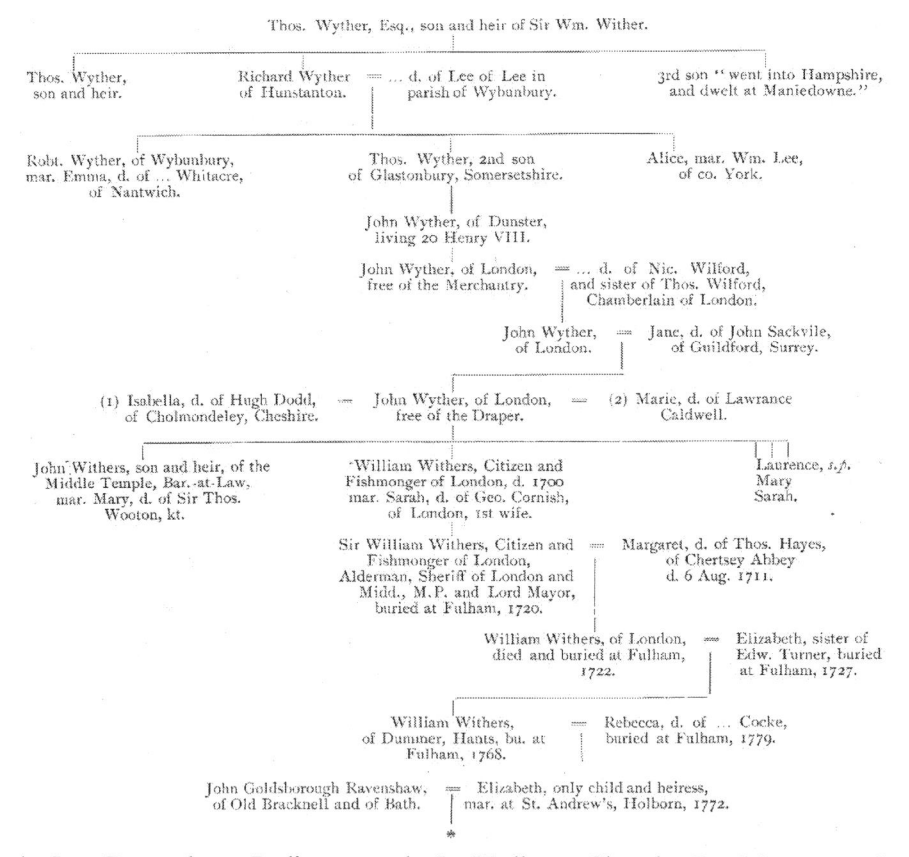

Thos. Wyther, Esq., son and heir of Sir Wm. Wither.

- Thos. Wyther, son and heir.
- Richard Wyther of Hunstanton. = ... d. of Lee of Lee in parish of Wybunbury.
- 3rd son "went into Hampshire, and dwelt at Maniedowne."

Children of Richard Wyther:
- Robt. Wyther, of Wybunbury, mar. Emma, d. of ... Whitacre, of Nantwich.
- Thos. Wyther, 2nd son of Glastonbury, Somersetshire.
- Alice, mar. Wm. Lee, of co. York.

John Wyther, of Dunster, living 20 Henry VIII.

John Wyther, of London, free of the Merchantry. = ... d. of Nic. Wilford, and sister of Thos. Wilford, Chamberlain of London.

John Wyther, of London. = Jane, d. of John Sackvile, of Guildford, Surrey.

(1) Isabella, d. of Hugh Dodd, of Cholmondeley, Cheshire. = John Wyther, of London, free of the Draper. = (2) Marie, d. of Lawrance Caldwell.

- John Withers, son and heir, of the Middle Temple, Bar.-at-Law, mar. Mary, d. of Sir Thos. Wooton, kt.
- William Withers, Citizen and Fishmonger of London, d. 1700 mar. Sarah, d. of Geo. Cornish, of London, 1st wife.
- Laurence, s.p. Mary Sarah.

Sir William Withers, Citizen and Fishmonger of London, Alderman, Sheriff of London and Midd., M.P. and Lord Mayor, buried at Fulham, 1720. = Margaret, d. of Thos. Hayes, of Chertsey Abbey d. 6 Aug. 1711.

William Withers, of London, died and buried at Fulham, 1722. = Elizabeth, sister of Edw. Turner, buried at Fulham, 1727.

William Withers, of Dummer, Hants, bu. at Fulham, 1768. = Rebecca, d. of ... Cocke, buried at Fulham, 1779.

John Goldsborough Ravenshaw, of Old Bracknell and of Bath. = Elizabeth, only child and heiress, mar. at St. Andrew's, Holborn, 1772.

* See Ravenshaw Pedigree, vol. I, "Fulham Church: Its Monuments" chapter).

Charles, ninth Earl of Suffolk, resided at Holcroft's between the years 1730-33. He died in the latter year.

The next distinguished owner of Holcroft's was Sir Martin Wright, grandson of William Wright, an Alderman of the City of

Oxford and one of its representatives in Parliament, 1678-81. The father of Sir Martin, another William Wright, was a barrister of the Inner Temple. In 1688 he became Recorder of Rochester, and a Welsh judge in 1714. He died in 1721, leaving issue, by his wife, Dorothy Finch, two sons, Martin and Thomas.

Martin Wright was born 24 March 1691-92 and entered Exeter College, Oxford, March 1708-9. He was called to the bar of the Inner Temple, 1718-19, and became a bencher of that inn and serjeant-at-law in 1733. In 1739 he was made a Baron of the Exchequer, and in November 1740 a Justice of the King's Bench. In the Fulham assessments for 1742, the name of "Mr. Justice Wright" appears for the first time. He retired from his Justiceship in February 1755. He died at Holcroft's, 26 September 1767.

The Churchwardens' Accounts contain several entries referring to the "pewing of Sr Martin Wright." In 1753 the Surveyor paid a man 3s. for "scaveing ye Town from Judg. Wright's to ye 'King's Arms.'"

By his wife, Elizabeth, daughter of Hugh Willoughby, M.D., of Barton-Stacey, Hants, Sir Martin left two sons and two daughters. The elder son, Martin Wright, of Epsom, died from injuries received through a fall from his horse while hunting, 6 October 1783. The younger son, Thomas Wright, was born about 1727 and educated at St. John's College, Cambridge. He was a barrister of Lincoln's Inn.

None of the four children of Sir Martin Wright married. Elizabeth, the last surviving daughter, appears to have lived on at Holcroft's, her name figuring in the Rate books as Mrs. Wright. She died at her house at Fulham in September 1794.

The Fulham property descended to the issue of Sir Martin's younger brother, Thomas Wright, of Lawrence Lane, who had married Elizabeth, eldest daughter and co-heiress of William Woodford, M.D., of Epsom. The issue of this marriage was an only daughter, Elizabeth, who, on 28 June 1770, married John Guise of Highnam Court, co. Gloucester. He was created a bart. in 1783 and died in May 1794.

In the assessments for 1795 the name of Lady Guise appears. She resided at Holcroft's till her death in 1808. Sir William Berkeley Guise, bart., the eldest son of Sir John and Lady Guise, succeeded to the property.

In 1811 Sir William let Holcroft's to Lawrence Parsons, second Earl of Rosse, the last joint Postmaster-General for Ireland.

A curious suit occurred about this time. Thomas Wright, the brother of Sir Martin, died 14 March 1814, aged 87, possessed of a large property. By his will he disposed of it in a most remarkable manner, several of his legatees being persons who were wholly unknown to him. Lady Frances, the wife of Sir Henry Wilson, of Chelsea Park, daughter of Thomas, Earl of Ailesbury, he made his residuary legatee, leaving her his estates in Hampshire, deer parks and fisheries, worth about £3,000 per annum. Lady Frances was wholly unacquainted with the testator, but, on going to his lodgings to see him in his coffin, she recognized him as a person who was accustomed to annoy her at the opera by staring at her. Sir Berkeley Guise, his first cousin once removed and heir-at-law, contested the will.

For some time Holcroft's appears to have stood tenantless. Mr. Alexander Campbell was here in 1809-10. From 1827 to 1833 Mr. Francis Alven resided here. In the latter year it became the residence of Mr. Kenrick Collett, Registrar of the Court of Chancery, an extraordinary buck, reputed, in his day, to be the handsomest man in Fulham. He died in 1841. In 1843 Mr. John Laurie, who had previously resided at Westfield House, Percy Cross, and had married Mr. Collett's daughter, succeeded to Holcroft's. Mr. Laurie was a nephew of Sir Peter Laurie and a partner in the well-known firm of Laurie and Marner, coachbuilders.

In 1845 he let the house to Major-General Sir John Fox Burgoyne, Wellington's engineer- in-chief during the Peninsular War. He was the natural son of General the Rt. Hon. John Burgoyne, M.P. for Preston. He was created a baronet in 1856, and was made Constable of the Tower of London in 1865. Sir John, who died in 1871, used to give at Holcroft's some clever dramatic entertainments. In 1854 the house was taken by Mr. Charles James Mathews, the comedian, and his illustrious wife, known as Madame Vestris.

Mr. C. J. Mathews was the son of Charles Mathews, the popular comedian, of whom we have spoken in connection with the New King's Road. He was born in 1803, and was first trained, under Pugin and Nash, for the profession of an architect. In 1835 he became joint manager of the Adelphi, and in the same year first appeared in public at the Olympic in the "Humpbacked Lover," written by himself. His success was secured. In 1838 he married Madame Vestris, became the manager of Covent Garden Theatre, and, after three seasons, found himself encumbered with debt. He continued, however, to play in almost all parts of the world.

Holcroft's. From a photograph by Messrs. W. Field and Co.

Madame Vestris was Lucia Elizabeth Bartolozzi. She was the elder daughter of Gaetano Bartolozzi, son of Francisco Bartolozzi, the engraver, of Cambridge Lodge, North End. She was born in 1797, and, at the age of sixteen married M. Armand Vestris, ballet master at the King's Theatre, Haymarket. Her reputation dates from her successful performance of the part of the hero in a burlesque of "Don Giovanni," from which time she remained unrivalled in light comedy. Left a widow in 1825, she became lessee of the Olympic in 1829, and made it the most popular theatre in London.

Mr. and Mrs. Mathews resided for some time at Gore Lodge, Brompton Park. On moving to Holcroft's, they re-named the house, Gore Lodge. Madame Vestris, who now gave up the stage, died at Gore Lodge, 8 August 1856. Subsequently Mr. Mathews married Miss Davenport. He resided at Gore Lodge till 1864. John Phelps, the old waterman, used to tell the following true story:

"One day Mr. Charles Mathews hired me to take him and his lady in my boat across the river. When they got out at the Duke's Head, at Putney, he wanted some change and so he says to me, 'My man, have you got a sixpence?' 'I am never without one, Sir,' I replied. 'Then you're a lucky fellow,' rejoined Mathews in grim allusion to his own financial troubles."
- *Fulham Chronicle.*

In 1865 Mr. Henry Anderson, better known as the "Wizard of the North," took Holcroft's. Mr. H. Streatfield Baker, who, in 1867, moved from Percy Villa to Holcroft's, was the son of Mr. James Baker, an officer in the Marines. He was educated at Christ's Hospital. For some years he resided in Portugal, and afterwards became a partner in the firm of Messrs. Robert MacAndrew and Co., of Bond Court, Walbrook. Mr. Baker died in 1872. His widow continued to reside here till 1880. The last occupant was Mr. W. H. Lammin, who moved here from Shorrold's at Walham Green. Mr. Lammin for twenty three years represented Fulham at the late Metropolitan Board of Works. In 1886 he went to Eridge House. In the following year Holcroft's House was pulled down, the whole estate having been sold by the Lauries for building purposes. The following are the particulars of sale of five lots comprising the Laurie property in Fulham:

Lot 1, comprising Holcroft's, Ivy Bank, High Bank, St. Mary's Villa and Holcroft's Lodge, about 8 acres £16,000.

Lot 2, comprising Colehill Cottage with nearly two acres of land was purchased by the tenant, Mr. J. Addison, for £3,140.

Lot 3, comprising Holcroft's Abbey and Holcroft's Priory £920.

Lot 4, comprising a vacant piece of land at the corner of Burlington Road and High Street £405.

Lot 5, consisting of ground rent on Nos. 1 and 3 High Street, sold for £215.

Total, £20,680.

Continuing our walk eastwards, there is little to detain us till we reach Munster Road. Robert Bagley, one of the "kings of Fulham," long owned along this side of the Fulham Road nursery grounds, which stretched almost as far as the "Durell Arms." This house, at the corner of Munster Road, was built about 1868.

SOUTH SIDE

We will now take the south side. This was an extensive messuage, situated on the south side of the London Road, at its junction with Back Lane, which formed its western boundary. It extended southwards as far as Northampton Place. In legal documents the site is still styled Clay Brook's, Cley Brook's, or Brook's.

The first glimpse which we catch of the estate takes us back to the days of Edward III, when it was in the possession of a family of the name of Broder, or Brother. From the Brothers the property passed, in 1452, to John Lok, an alderman of London and a wealthy mercer. His will, dated 19 July 1459, was proved 19 July 1463 (P.C.C. 1 Godyn). In it he directs that he shall be buried in the Chapel of St. Thomas the Martyr in the Church of St. Mary le Bow. Twelve torches, two of which were to be placed in Fulham Church, were to be burned at his funeral. He left 40s. for the repair of Fulham Church.

In 1478 his widow, then Elizabeth York, surrendered the messuage to John Sutton, who died soon afterwards. His will, dated 9 September 1479, was proved 27 October 1479 (P.C.C. 37 Wattys). In it are a few allusions to Fulham. He bequeathed for distribution among the poor of the parish £5, and, to the support of the Church, a similar sum. His lands in Fulham he left to his wife Beatrice.

In the time of Henry VII the property was possessed by a family named Tylney, or Tilney, who held lands in various parts of the Manor, including the "pisshes of ffulhm and Mustow." On the death of Ralph Tilney, a member of the Grocers' Company and Sheriff of London in 1488, the estates descended to his widow Joan, who died in 1509. The following local references occur in her will, dated 12 July 1509, and proved 4 December 1509 (P. C. C. 23 Bennett):

"I bequeth to eu'y poore pisshen householders dwelling in the pisshes of o^r Lady of Aldermanbury, Seynt Martyn in Iremongerlane, o^r Lady of Colchurch and ffulhm the tyme of my decease to thentent that they haue the soules of my said late husbond and of me recomended in their devout prayers xij^d as feire as the some of vj^{li} xiij^s iiij^d sterl woll stretche and amount amonges theym to be distributed aft' the same rate. All my londes w^{t}all and singuler their app^{r}tennces beyng freehold lying in the pisshes of ffulhm and Mustow which I had of the gift of Rauf Tilney late my husbond in his last will in this wise folowing ffirst I will that John Tilney my son shalhaue for eu'more all my londes oonly except the said ten^t and gardeyn w^t thapp^{r}tennces of the Chief lorde of the fee by such [rent] therof due and accustomed And the which ten^t and gardeyn w^t thapp^{r}tennces lye in Bere Strete in ffulhm being freehold as is aforesaid I geve unto Elizabeth Aunsham my doughter and her heirs."

In 1507 John Tilney, the son, was fined 6s. 8d. because he had "insulted and made an affray upon John Johnson, the deputy beadle in the execution of his office." In 1515 he was presented because he had a cesspool "to the grievous nuisance of those going in the high street," of Fulham. In 1518 Tilney sold his estate at Fulham to Giles Cleybroke.

The Cleybrokes were a Kentish family settled in the Isle of Thanet. Giles Cleybroke's first wife, according to the Visitations of Kent, 1574 and 1619, was Margery "daughter of . . . Norton." On 6 September 1523

"one Giles Cleybroke, sojourning in the Hospital of St. Thomas Aeons, had license from the Bishop of London to marry with one Christian Barton, of the parish of St. Thomas the Apostle, London, at St. Thomas Apostle aforesaid."

This was probably his second wife. The hospital of St. Thomas of Aeon was in the Cheap. In 1525 Giles Cleybroke was ordered to lop the branches of his trees overhanging "a lane called Mustewlane (see 'Munster Lane' in this volume), leading from ffulhm field towards Shortcroft." The date of his death is not known, but it must have occurred before 1547.

Cleybroke's, the messuage we are describing, together with other lands in the Manor, descended to James and Stephen, the sons of Giles. Stephen resided chiefly at Hammersmith. At the Record Office is preserved a pardon, granted to "Stephen Cleybroke of Hamersmyth in the parish of Fulham, Middlesex," for killing one John Strakeford, at Hammersmith on 30 April, 28 Henry VIII (1536), for which offence he had been indicted before John Stokkeriekell, one of the coroners for Middlesex, and before the Justice of the Peace for the County. The pardon was granted by the King at Windsor Castle, 2 October 1537, and delivered at Westminster 7th of that month. [P.S. Pat. p. 1 m.21].

In 1565 precept for escheat was issued against Stephen Cleybroke in these words:

> "Precept is given to the Bailiff to seize into the hands of the Lord the customary lands of Stephen Cleybroke forfeited for divers causes, contempts, offences and acts perpetrated by the said Stephen against the customs of the Manor."

In spite, however, of his misdeeds, Stephen Cleybroke continued a tenant of the Manor. In 1570 he was elected bailiff or collector of the rents of the Lord "for his tenement called Brokes." In 1575 he surrendered "an orchard in Fulham Street" to the use of his eldest son William Cleybroke.

Stephen Cleybroke, who died circa 1575, married, first, Jane, formerly wife of Thomas Burton of Sandes (Sands End) and secondly Margaret, daughter of Thomas Wolfe. He left three sons, William the elder, Thomas and William the younger. His will, dated 13 March 1574-75, was proved 30 March 1575-76 (P.C.C. 12 Pyckering).

The eldest son, "William Clebroke of Fulham," was, in November 1557, admitted a student of the Inner Temple. He possessed property both in Fulham and Hammersmith, but he seems to have resided chiefly at Thanet in Kent. He was buried in the church of St. John's, East Margate. By his wife, Ann, daughter of Paul Johnson, he left two sons, Stephen and Paul.

Thomas, the second son of Stephen Cleybroke, married Mary, daughter of Thomas Burton of Sands End, whose widow Jane, as we have seen above, became the wife of Stephen, father of Thomas Cleybroke. The first we hear of Thomas Cleybroke is in 1568, when his wife was admitted to a garden near Fulham Churchyard and other lands vacant by the death of her brother, Edmund, son of Thomas Burton of Sands End.

Thomas Cleybroke died in September 1587, and was buried in Fulham Church. His will, dated 2 September 1587, was proved 13 October 1587 (P.C.C. 51 Spencer). The following is an extract:

> "I Thomas Cleabroke of fulham, gent, to be buried in the parish church of Fulham. [Testator devised his copyhold lands in Fulham to his brother 'William Cleybroke of St. John's in the Isle of Tennett in Kent, gent.' to hold the same in trust for ten years to uses of will and at the end of that period 'to my son William Cleybroke and his heirs for ever.'] To eldest daughter Elizabeth Cleybroke £50 payable March 1588, to daughter Christian Cleybroke £100 payable March 1590, and to daughter Mary Cleybroke £100 payable March 1592, to daughter Winifred Cleybroke £100 payable March 1594, to daughter Sara Cleybroke £100 payable March 1596, and to son William Cleybroke £50 payable Michaelmas 1597. All my household furniture to Elizabeth my eldest daughter (except all my wainscottes and glasse in and aboute my houses). William Cleybroke my eldest brother sole executor. My well-beloved brother, William Cleybroke the younger and Henry Thornton and Thomas Bonde gent, to be overseers."

The name of "Thomas Claybroke, gentleman," the son of Stephen Claybroke, occurs among the

> "Midd. Liberi Tenentes cujuslibet hundr' in com. Midd. Anni xvij° and xviij° Dne Elizabeth Regina: Hundred de Ossulston in com. pred. ffulham apd. Londn."

Thomas, second son of the above Thomas Cleybroke, held the messuage down to about 1626. After this date we hear nothing more of the family in Fulham.

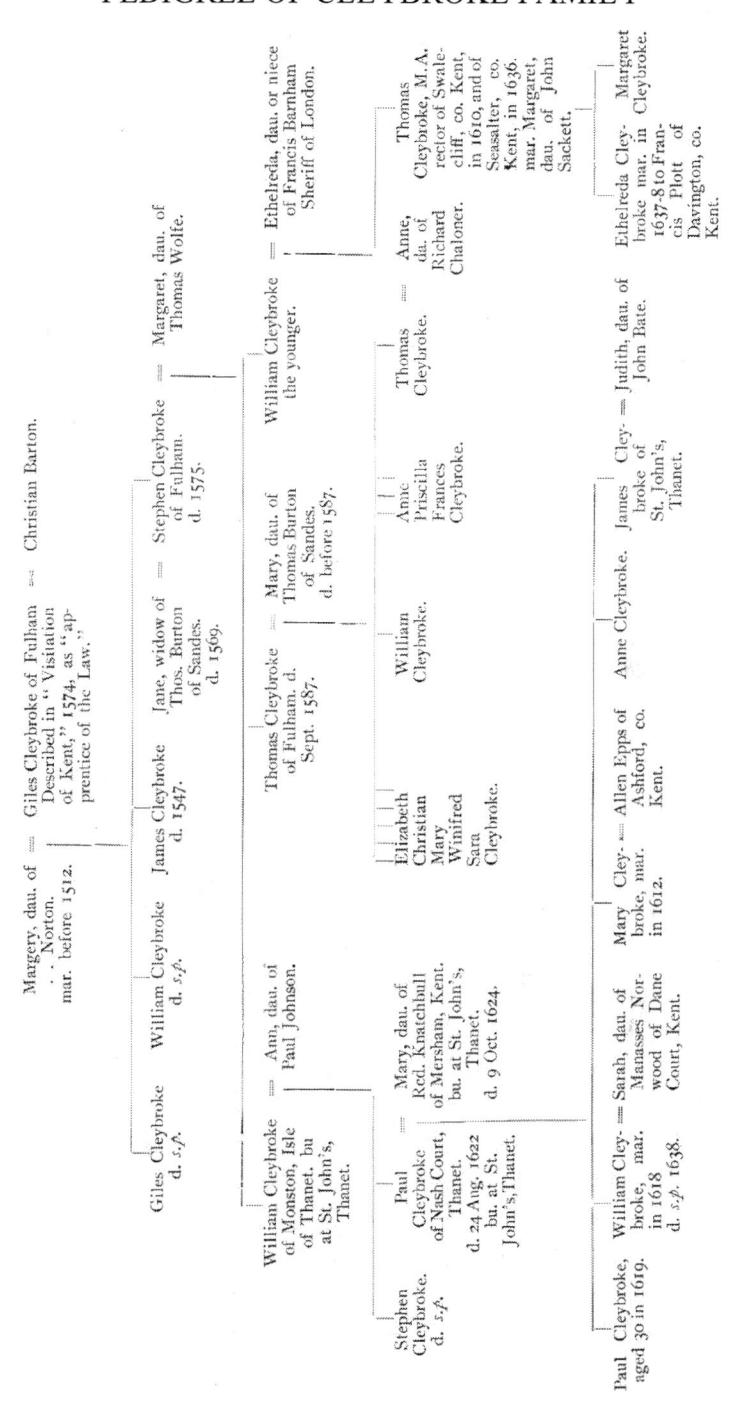

PEDIGREE OF CLEYBROKE FAMILY

Margery, dau. of ... Norton. mar. before 1512. = Giles Cleybroke of Fulham Described in "Visitation of Kent," 1574, as "apprentice of the Law." = Christian Barton.

Giles Cleybroke d. s.p.

William Cleybroke d. s.p.

James Cleybroke d. 1547.

Thomas Cleybroke of Fulham. d. Sept. 1587. = Jane, widow of Thos. Burton of Sandes. d. 1569. / Mary, dau. of Thomas Burton of Sandes. d. before 1587.

Stephen Cleybroke of Fulham. d. 1575. = Margaret, dau. of Thomas Wolfe.

William Cleybroke the younger. = Ethelreda, dau. or niece of Francis Barnham Sheriff of London.

William Cleybroke of Monston, Isle of Thanet. bu at St. John's, Thanet. = Ann, dau. of Paul Johnson.

Paul Cleybroke of Nash Court, Thanet. d. 24 Aug. 1622 bu. at St. John's, Thanet. = Mary, dau. of Rcd. Knatchbull of Mersham, Kent. bu. at St. John's, Thanet. d. 9 Oct. 1624.

Elizabeth Christian Mary Winifred Sara Cleybroke.

William Cleybroke.

Anne Priscilla Frances Cleybroke.

Thomas Cleybroke. = Anne, dau. of Richard Chaloner.

Thomas Cleybroke, M.A. rector of Swalecliff, co. Kent, in 1610, and of Seasalter, co. Kent, in 1636. mar. Margaret, dau. of John Sackett.

Stephen Cleybroke. d. s.p.

William Cleybroke, mar. in 1618 d. s.p. 1638. = Sarah, dau. of Manasses Norwood of Dane Court, Kent.

Mary Cleybroke, mar. in 1612. = Allen Epps of Ashford, co. Kent.

Anne Cleybroke.

James Cleybroke of St. John's, Thanet. = Judith, dau. of John Bate.

Ethelreda Cleybroke mar. 1637-8 to Francis Plott of Davington, co. Kent.

Margaret Cleybroke.

Paul Cleybroke, aged 30 in 1619.

273

The next owner of Cleybroke's was John Wolverstone, the third son of Humphrey Wolferstone or Wolferstan, baptized at Newbold-Verdon in 1606. In 1634 he was elected to the office of overseer for Fulham. In the Parish Books for 1655 he is described as "Alderman Wolverston." His signature, attached to the minutes in the Parish Books, ceases in 1657. He died probably about the period of the Restoration.

Judith, the daughter and sole heiress of John Wolverstone, married Thomas Frewen, who, on the death of his father-in-law, succeeded to the Cleybroke estate. They were formally admitted, 3 December 1660.

The Frewens were a notable family. John Frewen, who was born in 1560, was rector of Northiam, Sussex, a typical Puritan divine. He died, leaving issue several sons, the most distinguished of whom was Dr. Accepted Frewen, who eventually obtained the archiepiscopal see of York. He died in 1664.

Stephen, a younger brother of Accepted Frewen, was a London merchant and Master of the Skinners' Company. He supplied ermine to the judges. His brother, Accepted, left him 27,000 guineas, which he straightway brought from the funeral at York in his coach to London and deposited with Sir Richard Vyner, the King's goldsmith. This fortune he lost on the shutting up of the Exchange. He died in 1679.

His eldest son, Thomas Frewen of Fulham, was born in 1630. He was trained for the legal profession, and was called to the bar of the Inner Temple. He married thrice. His first wife was, as we have stated, Judith, daughter of John Wolverstone "of Claybrooke House, Fulham." She died in child-birth, 29 September 1666, aged 27. There were five children of the marriage. She was buried in the Lady Chapel at York Minster, where there is a marble slab to her memory.

Thomas Frewen's second wife was Bridget, daughter of Sir Thomas Layton, of Layton, co. York. She died at Brickwall, and was buried at Northiam, 11 September 1679. She left six children. The third wife was Jane, relict of Sir Dawes Wymondsold of Putney and daughter of Sir R. Cooke of Gloucestershire. Her grandfather, Sir William Cooke, was first cousin to Lord Bacon and first cousin once removed to Lady Jane Grey. She died in 1718.

Thomas Frewen was M.P. for Rye from 1679 to 1689, and again from 1694 to 1698. He died in 1702 and lies buried with his third wife in the Wymondsold vault in Putney Church. The Fulham Church Registers record:

1680. Thomas son of Thomas Frewen Esq bu. 7 Dec.

This was the eldest son of Thomas Frewen of Cleybroke's.

On the death of Thomas Frewen, in 1702, Cleybroke's passed to his second, and eldest surviving, son Edward. This Edward Frewen, who was born in 1662, became a major of the 1st Regiment of the Cinque Ports. He acted as a canopy-bearer at the coronation of James II, who, for his loyal services, knighted him in the royal bedchamber, 4 March 1684-85. He married Selina, daughter of John Godschall, merchant, of East Sheen. There were five children, but Sir Edward's issue became extinct in the second generation. Lady Frewen died suddenly at Hawkhurst, 25 November 1714, aged 54 years. In 1714 Sir Edward Frewen was elected reeve for Cleybroke's. He died 8 October 1723. The Church Registers record:

1699. Edward son of Sr Edward ffrewen knight bu. 1 Aug.

This was the third son of Sir Edward.

1704. William Ives gent, and Jane ffrewin mar. p. Lyc. 23 July.

This was the eldest daughter of Sir Edward.

Sir Edward Frewen does not seem to have resided much at Fulham. In 1720 he surrendered Cleybroke's to his only son, Thomas Frewen, of Lincoln's Inn, who, in 1732, sold it to Robert Limpany.

Charles James Fèret

PEDIGREE OF FREWEN FAMILY

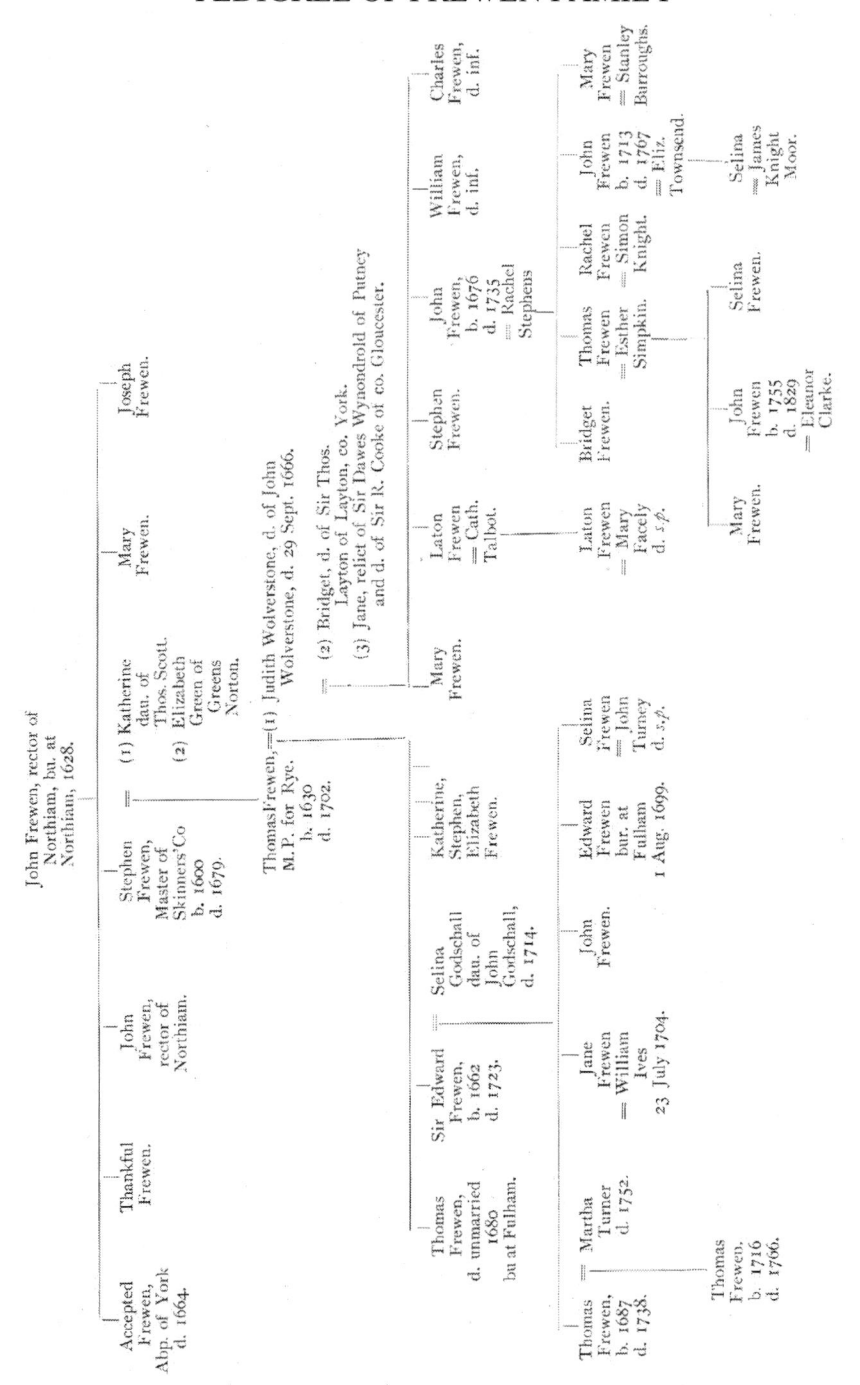

John Frewen, rector of Northiam, bu. at Northiam, 1628.

Children:
- Accepted Frewen, Abp. of York, d. 1664.
- Thankful Frewen.
- John Frewen, rector of Northiam.
- Stephen Frewen, Master of Skinners' Co, b. 1600, d. 1679. = (1) Katherine dau. of Thos. Scott. (2) Elizabeth Green of Greens Norton.
- Mary Frewen.
- Joseph Frewen.

Thomas Frewen, M.P. for Rye, b. 1630, d. 1702. =
(1) Judith Wolverstone, d. of John Wolverstone, d. 29 Sept. 1666.
(2) Bridget, d. of Sir Thos. Layton of Layton, co. York.
(3) Jane, relict of Sir Dawes Wynondrold of Putney and d. of Sir R. Cooke of co. Gloucester.

Children of Thomas Frewen:
- Thomas Frewen, d. unmarried 1680, bu at Fulham.
- Sir Edward Frewen, b. 1662, d. 1723. = Selina Godschall dau. of John Godschall, d. 1714.
- Jane Frewen = William Ives 23 July 1704.
- John Frewen.
- Katherine, Stephen, Elizabeth Frewen.
- Edward Frewen bur. at Fulham 1 Aug. 1699.
- Selina Frewen = John Turney d. s.p.
- Mary Frewen.
- Laton Frewen = Cath. Talbot.
- Stephen Frewen.
- John Frewen, b. 1676, d. 1735 = Rachel Stephens.
- William Frewen, d. inf.
- Charles Frewen, d. inf.
- Mary Frewen = Stanley Burroughs.

- Thomas Frewen, b. 1687, d. 1738. = Martha Turner d. 1752.
- Laton Frewen = Mary Facely d. s.p.
- Bridget Frewen.
- Thomas Frewen = Esther Simpkin.
- Rachel Frewen = Simon Knight.
- John Frewen b. 1713 d. 1767 = Eliz. Townsend.
- Selina James Knight Moor.

- Thomas Frewen, b. 1716, d. 1766.
- John Frewen b. 1755 d. 1829 = Eleanor Clarke.
- Selina Frewen.
- Mary Frewen.

276

Limpany, who died in 1735, left his copyhold and freehold estate "at the upper end of the Town of Fulham," including "the mansion house of Sir Edward Frewen," to Elizabeth Cotton, youngest daughter of Thomas Cotton. This lady, on attaining age in 1746, sold the Cleybroke estate to Joseph Hustwich.

The subsequent history of Cleybroke House is of little interest. Its last occupants were the Mayers, who resided here nearly half a century. About 1780 the house was taken by Messrs. Mayers and Chant. On the decease of Mr. Frederick Mayers, about 1795, his widow, Mrs. Cornelia Theodosia Mayers, carried on Cleybroke House as a boarding school for young ladies. Mrs. Mayers gave up the school about 1824. The old house, after standing empty for some years, was taken down in 1843.

Holcroft's Priory and Holcroft's Abbey: these two tiny Gothic houses were built on a portion of the site of Cleybroke House. They were erected by Mr. Ben Johnson, about 1844, for Mr. John Laurie of Holcroft's, whence, of course, their name. The Abbey, which was pulled down in 1895, contained, upstairs, two small bedrooms, and, on the ground floor, an entrance lobby and modest sitting-room. The Priory, a similarly-sized building, demolished in 1897, was adjacent to Holy Cross House, with which it was incorporated a few years since.

Holcroft's Priory and Holcroft's Abbey.
From a photograph by Mr. H. Ambridge

Facing Oxberry Avenue stood Wimberley House, pulled down in 1898. It owed its name to one Bartholomew Wimberley, who resided in the parish for a great many years. We first meet with his name in 1718. The Church Registers record:

1755. Bartholomew Wimberley Esqr. bu. 7 June.

From 1755 to 1758, Mrs. Wimberley is assessed for the house (see vol. I, "Fulham Church: Its Monuments" chapter).

In the early part of this century Wimberley House was a school for boys. For upwards of forty years it was conducted by Mr. Thomas Hackman, who died in 1844 (see vol. I, "Fulham Churchyard" chapter).

The school was, for some years, carried on by Mr. Thomas Cooper, who died in 1861, and by his son, Mr. Thomas Mason Cooper, who died in 1878.

In 1881 the house was taken by the Wantage Sisterhood, who kept it as a home for incurable children and female patients. They re-named the place Holy Cross House, and fitted it for the purpose of a miniature hospital. About 1889 a little chapel was erected in the grounds for the use of the patients. This was connected with Holy Cross House by means of a cloister. So many appeals reaching the Sister Superior, it was finally decided to dispose of the property, and to transfer the patients to more commodious premises at Worthing.

Holy Cross House presented few features of interest. Most of the rooms had been divided up, and were very small. The front drawing-room and the dining-room were spacious apartments. The oak staircase had been completely spoilt by the addition of successive coats of paint. Shops have recently been built on the site.

A little way further along the road, on the same side, stood Ivy Lodge, demolished in 1896. This unpretentious, flat-fronted house was probably about two centuries old. From 1728 to 1732 it was the residence of Sir Thomas Samwell, bart. Subsequently the property came into the occupation of Thomas Moore of the Middle Temple, whose executors, in 1746, surrendered it to Catherine Baldwin of Tonbridge.

Ivy Lodge. From a photograph by Mr. T. S. Smith, 1895

Ivy Lodge was chiefly noteworthy on account of the residence here, from 1826 to 1831, of Rudolph Ackermann, the fine art publisher. This ingenious and enterprising tradesman was born at Stolberg, in Saxony, in 1764. Shortly before the outbreak of the French Revolution, he came to England, where he first found employment as a carriage draughtsman. This led to his forming the acquaintance of artists, and, ultimately, to his opening his printseller's shop in the Strand. It was while residing at Ivy Lodge, in the spring of 1830, that Ackermann was struck with paralysis. For the benefit of his health he removed, in 1831, to Finchley, but he died there three years later.

Ivy Lodge was, for 32 years (1843-75) occupied by Mr. Charles Smith, the founder of the well-known firm of Messrs. C. Smith and Son, the gold and silver lacemen of Piccadilly, now of New Burlington Street. In 1878 it was taken by Mr. Gordon Donaldson Peters. Its grounds were 1a. 3r. 22p.

The site of Ivy Lodge is now covered by a terrace of red-brick flats, known as The Drive, Fulham Park Gardens.

South of Fulham Road and west of Munster Road, lay Fulham Park, a picturesque estate, the early history of which merges in that of ancient Churchfield. In its grounds, which measured about thirteen acres, stood Fulham Lodge, at a point where Fulham Park Road now crosses through to the New King's Road.

Here it was that Hughes Minet, the son of the Rev. John Minet, M.A., rector of Eythorne, Kent, resided from 1788 to 1803. Hughes Minet, who came of an old Huguenot family, was born in 1731. He was adopted by his uncle, William Minet, of Fenchurch Street, and became a partner in his business. In 1761 he married Mary, daughter of Anthony Loubier. He died, 23 December 1813, at Westerham, Kent.

In an advertisement of the sale of the house in The Times of 21 March 1804, it is described as

"A compact and convenient detached villa, with new-built coach house, stables and billiard room, walled gardens, pleasure ground, lawn, shrubbery, hothouse and two meadows containing together ten acres."

In this secluded little villa lived Mrs. Eliza Carey, an actress, who came here in 1808. " This cottage, for it was no more," writes Croker, "was a favourite retirement of the late Duke of York." This was Frederick, the second son of George III. The lady, in whom the Duke took such an exceptional interest, is described by old residents of Fulham as a tall and handsome woman. Theodore Hook's manuscript "Diary" contains several references to dinners, etc., in which he took part at Fulham Lodge in Mrs. Carey's time. Mrs. Carey's name disappears from the Rate books after 1827.

Major John Gibbes resided here for a short period in 1827-28. From 1829 to 1831 we find Mr. William John Lenthall rated for Fulham Lodge. He is said to have been a lineal descendant of William Lenthall, the celebrated Speaker of the House of Commons in 1640. Mr. Richard Roy, brother of Dr. Robert Roy of Burlington House School, lived at Fulham Lodge from 1832 to 1838.

On 7 June 1838 the property was sold at the Mart by Mr. George Robins. In the catalogue of the sale the total extent of the grounds in given as 12ac. 2r. 24p. The auctioneer's description of the property reads:

"Fulham Lodge; Particulars and conditions of sale of a delightful villa, secluded front the public gaze by its luxuriant, full grown plantations, and within three miles and a half of Hyde Park Corner. It has long been distinguished from its numerous rivals in this admired vicinity as Fulham Lodge. The gardens, pleasure grounds and rich paddocks, all in the highest order and cultivation, including nearly 13 acres, disposed in the best taste and the land of the richest quality; ten acres are copyhold of inheritance equal to freehold, being held of the Manor of Fulham at the quit rent of 9s. 6d. and a fine certain of the same amount and a heriot of 3s. 4d. The remainder, containing about two acres three roods, is freehold."

Fulham Lodge.
From a view on Plan attached to Conditions of Sale, 1838

Mr. Robins thus describes the Lodge itself:

"On the ground floor is a Doric portico leading into the entrance hall with a conservatory; and in communication with the pleasure grounds are a dining-room, drawing-room, breakfast parlour and library. A verandah encloses two sides of the dwelling and terminates in the conservatory."

Besides a laundry and a farm, the auctioneer tells us that

"in the extensive grounds will be found a snug little cottage for a bachelor and in a private place a hermitage fitted up in excellent taste."

It was next tenanted by Mr. Park Nelson, who resided here till 1847, when he moved to Parson's Green. Soon afterwards the old cottage was taken down by Mr. William Potter, who bought the estate for building operations.

For Mr. John Glenny, of the firm of Thresher and Glenny,

India outfitters of the Strand, Mr. Potter built, on a portion of the site of old Fulham Lodge, a new residence called Fulham Lodge, near the corner of Fulham Park Road and the Fulham Road. Mr. John Glenny was a brother of Mr. George Glenny of Dungannon Nursery, on the opposite side of the Fulham Road. In 1867 the house was taken by Mr. Frederick Wright, who re-named it Eridge House. Mr. and Mrs. Wright died here on the same day, 20 May 1881. They are buried in Fulham Cemetery. Mr. John Robert Wright, barrister-at-law, of the Inner and Middle Temples, only surviving son of Mr. F. Wright, was thrown from his horse and killed whilst riding down Clayton Hill, Sussex, 5 April 1882. He is buried in the same grave.

Eridge House. From a photograph by Mr. T. S. Smith, 1895

After a brief tenancy by Colonel Cooke, Eridge House was bought by the late Mr. W. H. Lammin, who moved here from Holcroft's. He died here on 21 January 1890. The house is still in the occupation of the family.

The Fulham Park estate was developed by Messrs. Gibbs and Flew between 1877 and 1885.

At No. 10, Fulham Park Gardens, resides the well-known painter, Mr. Rinaldo Werner. His father was the distinguished aquarellist, the late Professor Carl Werner. After studying at the Royal Academy of Art at Vienna, Mr. Werner returned to Rome -

his birth-place - where he remained till 1888, enjoying the patronage of most of the eminent families who visited the Eternal City. Many of his works are in the possession of the Imperial family and the aristocracy of Russia. For some years he worked for the late King William and Queen Olga of Wurtemburg.

Fulham Park Gardens. From a photograph by Mr. J. Dugdale, 1895

Osborne (or Osborn) Lodge (or House).
From a photograph by Mr. H. Ambridge

Munster Place and Munster Terrace, now incorporated in the Fulham Road, were built by Mr. William Potter, for Mr. Robert Roy, about the year 1840.

No. 1, at the eastern end of the Terrace, was the residence of Colonel John, and Lady Walpole, who were succeeded by Mr. Thomas Osborne, of the firm of Robert Osborne and Sons, the King's Road nurserymen. After him the house was called Osborne Lodge. Mr. Mortimer Menpes, the well-known impressionist artist and etcher, greatly beautified the house, converting its rooms into delicious "harmonies." He resided here some eleven years. Since the tenancy of Mr. Menpes, Osborne Lodge has been re-christened Osborn House. At No. 5 lived Mr. Barnard Oswald Colnaghi, the well-known picture connoisseur. Munster Lodge and Leinster Lodge were long the homes respectively of Mr. H. M. Suft and Mr. Thomas Rousby.

SECTION II: MUNSTER ROAD TO PERCY CROSS

Before we resume our tour along the Fulham Road, it will be convenient if we first take a glance at Munster Road, as the original form of the name of this thoroughfare fortunately sets at rest the disputed question as to how Munster House came to be so called.

On Rocque's "Map," Munster Lane, as it was formerly styled, is shown as trending away from Fulham Fields, past Munster House, to a point about midway between Fulham Road and King's Road, where it joined Muddy Lane, now Rectory Road, and so brought the wayfarer to Parson's Green.

This thoroughfare, under the name "Mustewlane," is first mentioned in the minutes of a Court General in 1486. All those who had branches overhanging "Mustowlane," in 1553, were ordered to lop them. In the Court Rolls for 1579, the name is spelled "Mustowe Lane." In 1604, 1608, 1627 and 1658 are other references to it where it is also called "Mustowe Lane." The following order was made at a Court in 1611:

> "Mr. Kender of ffulham shall plowe backe againe two furrowes of lande wch is taken and plowed from Mr. Thomas Clebrokes (i.e.

Cleybroke's) lande neere to Mustowe lane end in Fulham fielde."

In 1666 William Richards of Holcroft's surrendered a cottage and three acres "near Sand Lane (i.e. Colehill Lane) on the north and abutting upon Mustow Lane on the east," to one Robert Sidenham. This shows that Sand Lane, or Colehill Lane, as we now know it, then, as at present, ran into Munster Road. In 1667 the name is written "Mustoe Lane." The next century sufficed to convert "Mustow" into "Muster." Thus, in 1755, we find in the Highway Rate book the entries:

"Eleven men filling Gravel Cart and spreading the same in Muster Lane 16s. 6d.

Two men a Day in Muster Lane 3s. 6d."

And, in 1759,

"For plowing and levelling Muster Lane 6s. 0d."

And, in 1771,

"Pd. 3 men Stocking Muster Lane 5s. 0d."

It was during the next fifty years that the intrusive "n" gained a permanent foothold in the word. We thus see that the stages of the name have been Mustew, Mustow, Muster and Munster.

In early times, when the village of Fulham extended no farther than the top of the High Street, Mustow was a name assigned to a somewhat undefined region, north of the Fulham Road. In fact, we hear of Mustow, and even of Mustow "parish," long before we hear of Mustow Lane.

The earliest use of the name occurs in the minutes of a Court Baron, held in 1397, where it is recorded that John Glover had died seized of certain lands, including "one acre in Mustow." In the fifteenth century the district is often spoken of as Great Mustow and Little Mustow.

There is not much to be said about the history of Munster Lane. Until very recent days it was a rural way with very few houses along it.

Its northern end joins the Crown Road at what is now styled "Fulham Cross." Opposite Bedford Place is the eastern entrance to Fulham Cemetery, to the right of which is the Parish Mortuary, erected on a site offered to the Fulham Vestry by the Burial Board. It was built by Mr. R. Cox in 1888-89. South of the Cemetery is Messrs. Batey's Fulham Brewery, which covers between two and three acres of ground. At the north-east corner of Colehill Lane, at its junction with Munster Road, stood, until 1895, Colehill Villa, for many years a nursery. The back portion, which was of wood, was very old. In Sherbrooke Road, on the east side of Munster Road, is the Sherbrooke Road Board School, opened 5 Jan. 1885 and enlarged (398 places) in 1887. It accommodates 480 boys, 480 girls and 631 infants; total 1,591.

Colehill Villa, front view.
From a photograph by Mr. J. Dugdale, 1895

Facing Colehill Villa, on the east side, was Munster Farm, long in the occupation of the Bagleys. On its site Messrs. Gibbs and Flew built their workshops. On the triangular site, between Bishop's Road and Filmer Road, stands Munster Road Board School, opened 26 June, 1893. It was enlarged (389 places) in 1895. It accommodates 474 boys, 474 girls and 643 infants; total

1,591.

The Munster Park estate, which lies about here, was developed by Messrs. Gibbs and Flew between 1877 and 1883.

Colehill Villa, back view.
From a photograph by Mr. J. Dugdale, 1895

It was not till 1832 that Munster Lane was continued southwards from the western end of Rectory Place into the New King's Road. In that year a proposal was made to form a new road through the nursery grounds, continuing Munster Lane southwards, as a substitute for Hawkins's Alley, then on the point of being closed.

On the west side of Munster Road, near the Fulham Road, are the twin houses, Fulham Lodge and Kenmure Lodge, York Lodge and Wire Elm House. Next we come to The Hollies, or Holly Lodge, built by Mr. William Potter. For many years it was the residence of the late Sir John Waller Clifton, J.P. Next again is Cobham Lodge, the home of Mr. J. H. Neave.

On the same side, where the Railway crosses, are the Parish Stables, the foundation stone of which was laid by Mr. C. A. Walter, 1 Jan. 1889. The stables are designed to accommodate 44 horses in a building arranged in three wings, two of them being 49 feet long and the main block 70 feet long. They were erected by Messrs. A. R. Flew and Co. at a cost, including drainage, of £5,631 6s. 2d.

NORTH SIDE

Resuming our tour along the Fulham Road, we will again commence with the north side.

The Munster House estate, adjoining Munster and Fulham Roads, marks the site of what was, at the time of its demolition, one of the oldest houses in Fulham.

Munster House, front view.
From a photograph by Mr. T. S. Smith, 1895

Munster House, which faced the Fulham Road, stood behind high castellated walls, a veritable landmark to travellers along the road. Unfortunately no records exist which afford the slightest clue to the date of the erection of the house or its earliest occupants. From a careful examination which we made, it seems most probable that the oldest portions of the house were of about the latter part of the reign of Elizabeth. Its pseudo-Gothic embellishments, added in quite modern times, gave the house an appearance of age which, taken as a whole, it did not really possess. The earliest account of Munster House is that of Bowack, who wrote in 1705:

"In the road towards Walham Green, somewhat north-east of the Town, is a handsome, ancient house, belonging to Sir Joseph Williams or his son, Joseph Williams, esquire. Mr. March, chirurgeon, lives here at present."

Next we come to Lysons, who observes in his "Environs" (1796):

> "Mustow (commonly called Munster) House, on the north side of the road to London, between Fulham and Purse's Cross, was, during the greater part of the last century, the property of the Powells from whom it came to Sir John Williams of Pengethly, Monmouthshire, Bart. It is now the property of Arthur Annesley Powell, Esq., and is occupied by Mrs. Davies."

Faulkner, in 1812, gives a somewhat similar account, and adds:

> "It is said by tradition to have been a hunting seat of King Charles II. The garden-grounds round it were formerly a park, and part of the ancient walls are yet standing."

Norris Brewer, who visited the house in 1814, observes:

> "Some remains of ancient wall denote much former consequence; but the mansion has experienced so many alterations that few traces of its original character can now be discovered."

Crofton Croker, in criticizing Faulkner's statements, ingeniously suggests that Munster House owed its name to Melesina Schulenberg, "created by George II in 1716 Duchess of Munster," and he caps his guesswork by adding, "according to Faulkner it was also called Mustow House - this was not improbably the duchess's pronunciation." The suggestion is, however, entirely erroneous. The evidence which we have produced from the Court Rolls, respecting the origin of the name Munster Road, of course applies with equal force in respect to Munster House, which, naturally enough, was simply named from the way which formed its western boundary. As early as 1666 we find in the Parish Books the following assessment:

> "Mr. Deane mustow house ground 5s. 0d."

In Blome's "London and Middlesex Gentry," 1673, the name again appears as "Mustow House." It is so printed in Ogilby's "Map of Middlesex," 1677.

This is incontestible evidence that, as far back as the reign of

Charles II, Munster House was called "Mustow House," precisely as the adjacent way was styled "Mustow Lane."

Then "Mustow House" changed to "Muster House," an alteration which was doubtless due to a careless pronunciation of the name. Thus, in "A Booke for the Surveior only on Fulham side Beginning in the year 1716," we find under date 1719:

> "For Labour and Expences takeing away ye Earth by Muster House £1. 2s. 0d."

Again, in Rocque's "Map of London," 1741-45, the name is spelled "Muster House." Lastly, towards the end of the eighteenth century, the all-confusing "n" stole in.

It may be as well to state here that Ehrengarde Mélusine von Schulenberg, Duchess of Munster, Marchioness and Countess of Dungannon, Baroness of Dundalk and Duchess of Kendal, was never rated for any property at Fulham. She lived pretty well between St. James's and Herrenhausen. When George I died, she retired to Isleworth, where at "Kendal House," the "Maypole," as people irreverently styled her, the gaunt duchess died, 10 May 1743.

The Powells, the earliest known owners of Munster House, were a Welsh family whose connection with Fulham dates back to the days of the "Virgin" Queen. The ancestral estate was situated at Pengethly, in Sellack parish, five miles north-west of Ross in Herefordshire.

Richard Powell, described as of Harewood, a parish in Ross district, left, besides other children, two sons, John and Edmund Powell. The elder brother, John, married Annes, daughter of Richard Dod of Salop. The younger, Edmund, married by license dated 26 January 1578-79, Catherine, daughter and heiress of Richard Young. According to some authorities, John Powell purchased the Pengethly estate in 1583, but the old deed, conveying Pengethly to John and Edmund Powell, states that it was purchased from Edmund Brown of Harewood for 1,000 marks, this sum being due from Edmund Brown to John Powell.

Both brothers appear to have settled at Fulham. The first we hear of the elder is contained in the following minute of a Court General in 1572:

"John Powell gent, prays license to intake 8 ft. of land in breadth and 100 ft. in length from the wast of the Lord and erect pales against his house provided the same be not to the hurt of the Lord.
To whom the Lord of his special grace granted license, rendering annually to the Lord and his successors 12d. at Lady Day and St. Michael by equal portions as a quit rent."

In 1575 he was ordered to make a fence "between Gill Hale and the premises of John Burton at Sands Ende." In 1577 he bought of the Bishop of London land "in the meadow called the Wylde Meade." At a Court Baron in 1578 it was reported that

"John Powell keeps three cows upon the common of Helbroke contrary to order of former Courts wherefore he forfeits iij^s iiij^d per cow, in all, x^s."

Munster House: the Old Mulberry Tree.
From a photograph by Mr. J. Dugdale, 1895

He owned a house known as "Grenes *alias* Byrdes" at Walham Green, of which we shall speak later on. He also held land in other parts of Fulham, including four acres in Longland Shot, two acres under Eylands (Aylands), 1 acre 1 rod in Town Mead, 5½ acres in Fulham Fields, and half an acre in Charlow Mead, to all of which he was admitted between 1572 and 1590.

In the "Custos Rotulorum and Justices of the Peace of the County of Essex Manuscripts," there is a letter signed "John Lond." (Bishop Aylmer), dated from Fulham, 24 July 1589, in which mention is made of John Powell. It is directed to the Justices of the Peace for the County of Essex and deals with the action of one Thomas Pegrim, who, it appears, had been imposing himself on certain of the Essex folk as an officer of the Bishop of London with authority to meddle in the affairs of his Lordship's manor of Stockforde. The writer remarks:

> "Theis are to signify vnto you and the rest of the Bench that I knowe no such officer by the name of Thomas Pegrim as you writt of to haue to doe in any lordships of myne to be warented as a Clerke of the Markett, but contrariwise I knowe for certenty that one Mr. Powell, Her Majesties servant, my honest neighbour at Fulham, since my late coming hether, did with the Mannor of Stockforde deale by vertue of the . . . Marketts office supplying vnder Her Majesties grant to him all things that belong to that office whatsoever."

On the death of John Powell, in 1606, the whole of his estate in Middlesex went to his only child, Elizabeth, who had married Sir William Stonehouse, bart.

The will, a very long one, is dated 27 May 1606 and a codicil, 26 July 1606. After a legal dispute, it was proved, 2 Dec. 1606 (P.C.C. 22 Stafford). The following is a brief extract:

> "I John Powell of the Parish of ffulham in the County of Middlesex Esquire. To the Viccars of the parishes of ffulham and Sellecke 6s. 8d. apeece. To the poor of the parishes of ffulham, St. Margaret's Westminster, St. Martin's in the fields, Chelsey and Kensington one Annuity or yerely rent of Twentie Shillings payable for ever unto the poor of said parishes out of one messuage in Kinges street, Westminster. To John Powell son of Edmonde Powell my brother my lease of an house in London which I hold of the Bishop of London towards his mayntenance at schoole.
> To Annes, my wife divers articles of furniture with such other necessarie lumber for house according to the same proportion . . . out of my now dwellinge house in the parish of ffulham. To Elizabeth Stonehouse my daughter my best salt, etc. To John Stonehouse my grandchild and godsonne 6 silver spoones, etc.
> And forasmuch as it hath nott been the good pleasure of God to blesse me with any heire male but onely with one daughter the nowe wife of

William Stonehouse before mentioned to which daughter I do leave all my lands, etc. in co. Mid^x.

All my lands in co. Hereford to Edward Powell son and heire apparent of my brother Edmond and heirs of Body Remainder to John Powell 2nd son of said Edmond and heirs of Body Remainder to Richard Powell son of my brother David Powell and heirs of body.

With proviso that if said brother Edmonde Powell and Katherine his nowe wief do after the death of Annes my now wife convey said lands to said Wm Stonehouse etc. with all the state and interest of said Edmonde and Katherine of all that messuage where I nowe dwell in Wandons Grene in the parish of ffulham.

To my worshipfull good friende Sr Thomas Smith Knight Secretary of the Kinges Ma^{ty} in the Latin Tounge 20s. in gould to make him a ringe in remembraunce of my love towardes him, and 20s. to his Ladie for like purpose.

To my brother Dauid Powell my best violet cullored cloake beinge faced with velvet and my best hat wch are as Pengethlye."

The following entry occurs in the old "Register Book":

"John Powell, Esq. of the Parishe of Fulham deceased gaue by his last will and testam^t a Legacie of Twentie shillings p. annum for ever to the Poore of the foresayd Parishe, and it is to be payd yearlie by Wm Stonehouse Esquier or his assignes, unto the Churchwardens for the tyme being, out of an house in the Kings-streete, within the Citye of West-minster wherein now dwelleth one Elizabeth Dod, widdowe."

This Elizabeth Dod was doubtless a relation on his wife's side. The house in King Street bore the curious name of the Butter Churn. The erection of Westminster Bridge, in 1746-50, necessitated the demolition of the house, when the Trustees sold their interest in it for £30.

Of Mr. Edmund Powell, the younger brother, not much is known. The old "Register Book" records a gift of £5 by him to the poor of Fulham.

Edmund Powell is the first of the Powells unquestionably connected with the estate at Mustow. James Knowles, of Walham Green, in his will dated 23 January 1613-14, left 40s. "to my lovinge friend Mr. Edmond Powell of Mustoe in fulham." In the assessments for 1625 we find under "North End"

"Edmond Powell gent vj^s iiij^d."

From 1630, however, his name appears under "Fulham Street." He died in 1638. The Churchwardens' Accounts for this year include:

"rec^d for buryall Powell 9s. 0d."

Edmund Powell left three sons, Edward, who was knighted and of whom we shall presently speak, Richard of St. James's, Clerkenwell, and Maurice, all of whom held lands in Fulham.

Richard Powell, the second son of Edmund, is sometimes styled in the Parish Books "Captain Richard Powell." He is rated under "Fulham Street" from 1633 to 1640.

Edmund Powell's death was followed by a dispute between the sons Richard and Edward, the latter having come into possession of everything. In the State Papers is preserved a curious petition from Richard Powell, dated 1 November 1639, addressed to the King. The petition recites that

> "Divers suits are like to arise between petitioner and his brother, Sir Edward Powell, touching the will and estate of their deceased father, which, besides being very unnatural, may, in respect of the charge tend to the utter ruin of the petitioner and his family, his brother Sir Edward having possession of the whole estate, both real and personal."

In 1640 Fulham was visited by the plague, when, among the houses attacked, was that of Richard Powell. The Churchwardens' Accounts contain the following quaint entries:

"Itm. for the reliefe of Powell's house from the first of November to the 7th of Decemb. £3. 12s. 0d.

Itm. pd. to James ffranckes Smyth for a barr of Iron wt.9^{li}½ at 3d. p. pound to close vp Powells house doore 2s. 4½d.

Itm. for brodds and his manns labour to sett on the barr 6d.

Itm. to goodman Burr for one weeks pay for warding 5s. 0d.

Itm. to goodman Osborne for wardinge £3. 0s. 8d.

Itm. for one bushell of Coles for ye visit hou^s 1s. 3d."

One of the family probably fell a victim to the scourge, for the Churchwardens' Accounts for 1640 include:

"rec^d for knell Powell   6d."

Richard Powell, by his first wife, Sarah, daughter of Sir Richard Warburton, of Arley, Cheshire, left two sons, Richard Powell, of St. James's, Clerkenwell, who married <u>Barbara, daughter of Henry Cary, of Clovelly</u>, co. Devon, and Benjamin Powell.

Munster House, back view.
From a photograph by Mr. J. Dugdale, 1895

Of Maurice little is known. In 1625 we find him admitted, along with his brothers, Richard and Sir Edward Powell, and his uncle, John Powell, to the trusteeship of the "Poores Land" at Parr Bridge. In 1627 he is returned as a defaulting tenant of the Manor.

Sir Edward Powell, the eldest son of Edmund Powell, certainly resided at Munster House. In the minutes of a Court General, in 1617, reference is made to the landholders "between Purser's Cross and Mr. Powell's house." This entry leaves little room for doubt that Munster House is referred to. The name of Sir Edward Powell thus appears at the head of the oldest poor rate assessment (1625) under "Fulham Street":

"Sir Edward Powell, kt. Barronet xx^s."

Edward Powell, who was created a baronet 18 Jan. 1621-22, was one of the Masters of the Court of Requests. He married Mary, fourth daughter of Sir Peter and Lady Jacoba Vanlore (Van Loor or Van Loer), of Tilehurst, co. Berks. He seems to have spent most of his time on his Pengethly estate, bequeathed to him by his uncle, John Powell. From 1628 to 1633 he appears to have surrendered Munster House to the use of "the Lady Vanloare," his wife's mother, who, in 1627, had been left a widow. In 1636 the assessment entry reads:

"The executors of the Ladie Vanlore or tenante £1. 1s. 0d."

Lady Vanlore died in April 1636, at the residence of her daughter, Lady Mary Powell, the wife of Sir Edward, in Church Street, Chelsea. The Chelsea Registers record:

1636. The ritte worshipful Lady Wanlore was buried the last day of April.

She left, by her will, dated 6 September 1633, £10 to the poor of Fulham and Hammersmith.

Sir Edward Powell's marriage did not prove a happy one. In 1638 Lady Mary Powell addressed the King by petition, pointing out numerous grievances against her husband, and praying His Majesty to interfere on her behalf and to "give some final order for the petitioner's redress." Shortly afterwards we find Lady Powell again petitioning the King in regard to her grievances and praying that reference of the differences between her and her husband might be made by some persons of honour to be appointed by His Majesty, "who may hear and report the true state of matters and assign such allowance to petitioner for her maintenance in the meantime as they shall think fit." This petition is underwritten,

"His Majesty is pleased to refer the examination of the differences between Sir Edward and his wife to the Archbishop of Canterbury, the Lord Keeper, the Earl of Dorset and Secretary Windebank. 26 Mar. 1639."

Through some hasty expressions which Sir Edward Powell used against Archbishop Laud, one of the arbitrators in the dispute, he was brought before the Court of the Star Chamber. Lady Powell finally left her husband and retired to the house at Chelsea. Here it was she died 6 Oct. 1651. There was no issue of the marriage.

A corner in the grounds of Munster House.
From a photograph by Mr. J. Dugdale, 1895.

During the troublous days of Charles I, Sir Edward Powell played a not altogether consistent part. In 1640, under a writ of Privy Seal, he lent His Majesty a sum of £3,000, which was to have been repaid three years later out of the revenue of the Court of Wards, but he never got it back from his impecunious sovereign. When the Civil War broke out, we find Sir Edward living in a house in Dean's Yard, Westminster, a district which was known as the "Parliament's quarters." Whether the old baronet actually countenanced the cause of the Roundheads, we cannot say, but at any rate his residence in the disaffected quarter served as a pretext for a seizure of his Pengethly property by the King's forces, and he was, we find, obliged to compound with Sir Henry Lingen for his estate.

How Munster House fared is not quite clear. From 1639 to 1642 we find Sir Edward duly rated for the house. The assessments from 1642 are somewhat incomplete, but his name does not recur in those that still exist. In the minutes of a View in 1646 is the following presentment:

"Wee order and payne Sr Edward Powell kt. and bart. for inclosinge a Church way leading from Wandon's Greene to Pursers Crosse wthin the field held by the widowe ffishe."

Sir Edward Powell died in 1653, when the title became extinct. According to the editor of the "Remembrancia" (p. 498), his death occurred "at his manor of Munster House, Middlesex." On what authority this statement is made, we do not know. His place of burial is uncertain. There is no entry of the death of Sir Edward in the Sellack Registers.

The will of Sir Edward Powell, dated 6 Feb. 1651-52, was proved 27 May 1653 by William Powell, alias Hinson, the sole executor, "and by virtue of a Sentence of Court." (P. C. C. 299 Brent.) This phrase indicates that the validity of the will had been disputed. The following is an extract:

"I Sr Edward Powell of Chelsey in the County of Middlesex, knight and baronet. To be buried at discretion of executor. To Elizabeth Manwaring of ffulham my loving sister £100. To my sister Suzan Cranmer widow of Rotterdam in Holland beyond ye seas in respect she hath been long absent from mee and I have not had opportunity or convenience to do for her as I have for my other sisters £200. To my brother Richard Powell Esq. although he hath been and continued most unaturally my enemy and hath neglected to show himself with w^t duty and respect he owed unto my deceased father ye summe of 20s. To all his younger children, I having otherwise plentifully provided for his eldest son, £50 each to be paid them wthin one moneth after my said executor shall receive a debt of £3000 or thereabout to mee due from ye late King Charles and directed to be paid out of ye late Court of Wards. To my brother Maurice Powell £20, to buy him blackes for mourning. To my kinsman D'cor. Zouch and his now wife £20 each, as my respects to them to buy them blackes. To William Powell alias Hinson of ye Middle Temple, Esq., my nephew, and to his heirs for ever, in respect I have ever found him dutifull, faithfull and diligent unto me in all my business, all my manors, messuages, lands and tenements, together with all my chattels and he sole executor."

Edmund Powell, the father of Sir Edward, had four daughters. Katherine, the eldest, became the wife of John Hart of Fulham and died 23 Oct. 1605; Elizabeth, married Thomas Manwaring, of Fulham; Susan, who married one Cranmer, possibly a Rotterdam merchant, and Anne, who married Thomas Hinson, of Dublin, afterwards of Fulham.

This Thomas Hinson settled at Fulham about 1640, probably on his marriage. He died in 1669. The Overseers thus explain why they collected only is. 6d. out of an assessment of 3s. levied upon him:

"Mr. Henson dyed att the half yeares end 1s. 6d."

He left two sons, Thomas and William. The elder, Thomas Hinson, graduated B.C.L. and held the post of Registrar General for the province of Munster, Ireland. In the Fulham Parish Books his name first appears in 1661. On 22 June 1666 he married Mary Filmer (Philmer), widow. He died in 1685. The Church Registers record:

1685. Mr. Tho. Hinson bu. 29 of Nov.

The second son, William Hinson, was that ever "dutifull, faithfull and diligent" nephew whose conduct Sir Edward rewarded by making him heir to his estates, the only condition which he attached being that he and his issue male should assume the surname of Powell.

In the Assessment books the name, "William Hynson," first appears in 1643. In 1649 he is styled "William Powell, alias Hinson." Thence onwards he is either William Powell, alias Hinson, or simply William Powell. As Sir Edward Powell did not die till 1653, it is obvious that the condition as to the heirship must have been arranged long before the execution of the will. He is described as of the Middle Temple.

William Powell, alias Hinson, married, as his first wife, Katherine, daughter of Richard Zouch, LL.D., Judge of the Admiralty. In the Sellack Registers the first wife is erroneously called Alice. Thus, the baptism of his eldest daughter is entered:

1643. Margaret daughter of William Powell and Alice his wife was baptized the 18th day of May.

Another child by his first wife died in infancy and was buried at Fulham in 1650. Katherine Powell, alias Hinson, died 6 October 1651, and was buried in Fulham Church. William Powell, alias Hinson, married, as his second wife, on 31 December 1655, Dame Mary, relict of Sir John Bridges, of Wilton, co. Hereford, bart., and daughter and heiress of John Pearl, of Acornbury, co. Hereford. By his second wife he had two daughters, Katherine, baptized 1660, and Mary, baptized 1662. He was created a baronet by Charles II, 23 January 1660-61, by the name of Sir William Powell, alias Hinson, of Pengethly, in the county of Hereford. He was, however, allowed to retain his paternal coat of arms, vizt.: az., a chevron between three suns or and a bordure ermine, which bordure had been granted to Thomas Hinson, his father, in 1644, by the Ulster King of Arms in Ireland for services rendered in that kingdom.

In 1660 Sir William Powell was elected to represent Hereford in Parliament. In 1664 his estate was sequestered. A copy of the Royal Mandate is printed in Webb's "Memorials of the Civil War."

According to tradition Munster House was frequented by the Merry Monarch when he felt inclined for the chase. The temporary sequestration of Sir William's estate in 1664 seems to offer a simple explanation as to how it might have been possible for Munster House to have been used by the King in some of his hunting exploits.

It is impossible to say how long Sir William Powell was ousted from his estates. He was apparently again in possession of Munster House in 1673, for in "London and Middlesex Gentry," by Blome, published in that year, we find, "Sir William Powell of Mustow House, Fulham, knt." Sir William died at Pengethly, 2 December 1680. The Sellack Registers record:

1680. Sir Wm. Powell (alias Hinson) Bart, died Dec[r] 2nd and was buried on 16th of the same month.

His will, dated 2 December 1680, the day of his death, was proved 5 January 1680-81 (P.C.C. 8 North). On 2 April 1706 it received further proof by William Williams, Esq., grandson and next of kin of the testator. The following is an extract:

> "I Sr William Powell [alias] Hinson of ffulham Barronett. To be buried in the Church of ffulham in the south Isle neare unto my late loueing wife Katherine daughter of Richard Zouch Doctour of Lawes and Judge of the High Court o^f Admiralty late deceased as conveniently may be if I dye nearer to the said Church of ffulham then to the Parish Church of Sellake in the County of Hereford otherwise att the west end of the said Church of Sellake.
>
> To my wife Dame Mary Powell, formerly wife of Sr John Bridges Baronet deceased, for life all the rents of my manor of Pengethley in the parishes of Sellake hentland and Pitstowe, etc. To my brother Thomas Hinson of ffulham Bachelor of Lawes for life my ffarm in ffulham ffeild now in the possession of widdow Holderness whereof part is freehold and part copyhold and another copyhold in ffulham now in the possession of Mrs. Aurelia Hicks widow and another copyhold messuage at ffulham in the possession of Richard Kirby glasier and also another copyhold messuage at ffulham now in the possession of Edward Lympany, chandler, and another messuage in ffulham in possession of Thomas Pyner carpenter and that capitall Inn called the Naggs head in ffulham aforesaid now in the possession of Humphrey Painter innkeeper. The house now in the possession of my said brother Thomas Hinson at Fulham to the said Thomas and Mary his wife or longes liver. To Thomas Bishop and Dorothy his wife for lives or longer liver the Inn known by the signe of the George in Wandsons greene wherein they now dwell. At the termination of all such life estates, reversion to my onely daughter Dame Mary Williams wife of Sr John Williams of Eltham co. Kent, knight, by Dame Mary my wife.
>
> And in regard (to) the greatest part of the lands by me in this my will disposed of were freely given and settled upon me by my said late uncle Sr Edward Powell deceased upon his desire and to the intent that I should take upon me the sirname of Powell which I have punctually observed, I do hereby desire and make it my earnest request that every such person of the male sex shall take the name of Powell."

As Sir William Powell left no male heirs, the baronetcy, on his death, for the second time became extinct.

On the death of Sir William Powell, Munster House and the Pengethly estates passed into the possession of his son-in-law, Sir John Williams, knight, and his wife, Lady Mary Williams, his only surviving child. In 1687 Sir John was elected one of the Surveyors of the highways for Fulham. The Fulham Church Registers record:

> 1678. Ludd son of S^r St. Johns Guillim, knt. sepult. 2 Junij.
>
> 1678. Dorothea da. of S^r St. Johns Guillim sepult 12 Juni.
>
> 1679. Mary daughter of Sr John Williams kn^t et Mary his Lady bapt. 17 Maij.
>
> 1682. Charlott da. of Sr Jno Gwiliams bu. 22 of June.

The Sellack Registers record:

> 1691. Dorothy dau. of Sir J. Williams and Dame Mary of Pengethly his wife was buried Augst 9th.

Sir John had two other daughters, Susanna, who married Henry Cornewall of Moccas and Penelope, who married Thomas Symonds, son of Robert Symonds, of Lincoln's Inn. Pengethly is still in the possession of the Symonds family.

In 1705 William Williams, the son of Sir John Williams, was admitted to Sir William Powell's estate at Fulham.

PEDIGREE OF POWELL, HINSON AND WILLIAMS FAMILIES
(continued on next page)

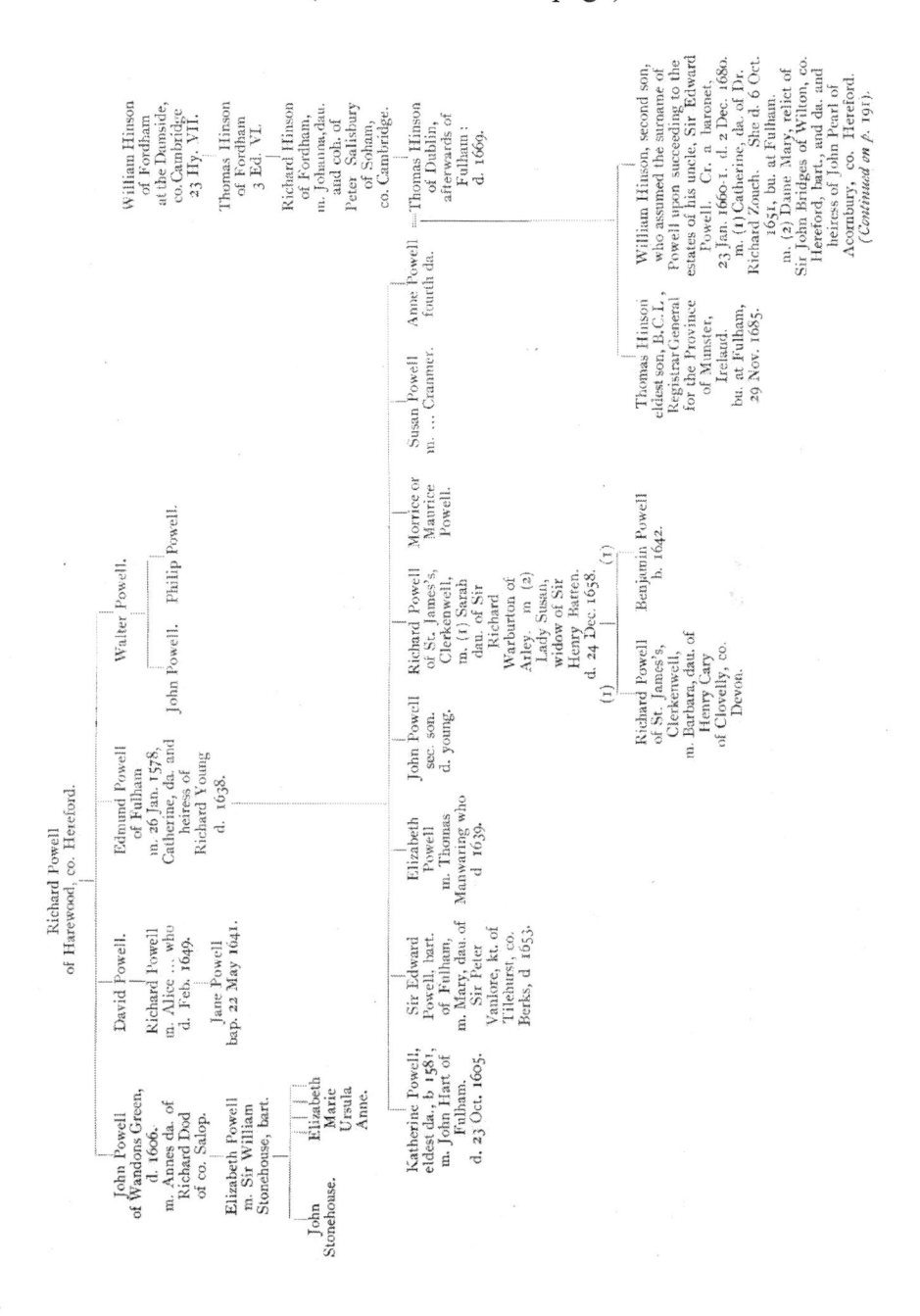

Richard Powell of Harewood, co. Hereford.

David Powell.

Richard Powell m. Alice ... who d. Feb. 1649.
- Jane Powell bap. 22 May 1641.

Edmund Powell of Fulham m. 26 Jan. 1578, Catherine, da. and heiress of Richard Young d. 1638.
- John Powell.
- Philip Powell.

Walter Powell.

Children of Edmund Powell:

John Powell of Wandons Green, d. 1666. m. Annes da. of Richard Dod of co. Salop.
- Elizabeth Powell m. Sir William Stonehouse, bart.
  - John Stonehouse.
  - Elizabeth
  - Marie
  - Ursula
  - Anne.

Katherine Powell, eldest da., b 1581, m. Thomas Hart of Fulham. d. 23 Oct. 1605.

Sir Edward Powell, bart. of Fulham, m. Mary, dau. of Sir Peter Vanlore, kt. of Tilehurst, co. Berks, d 1653.

Elizabeth Powell m. Thomas Manwaring who d 1639.

John Powell sec. son. d. young.

Richard Powell of St. James's, Clerkenwell, m. (1) Sarah dau. of Sir Richard Warburton of Arley. m (2) Lady Susan, widow of Sir Henry Batten. d. 24 Dec. 1658.
- (1) **Richard Powell** of St. James's, Clerkenwell, m. Barbara, dau. of Henry Cary of Clovelly, co. Devon.
- (1) **Benjamin Powell** b. 1642.

Morrice or Maurice Powell.

Susan Powell m. ... Cranmer.

Anne Powell fourth da. = **Thomas Hinson** of Dublin, afterwards of Fulham: d. 1669.

- **Thomas Hinson** eldest son, B.C.L., Registrar General for the Province of Munster, Ireland. bu. at Fulham, 29 Nov. 1685.
- **William Hinson**, second son, who assumed the surname of Powell upon succeeding to the estates of his uncle, Sir Edward Powell. Cr. a baronet. 23 Jan. 1660-1. d. 2 Dec. 1680. m. (1) Catherine, da. of Dr. Richard Zouch. She d. 6 Oct. 1654, bu. at Fulham. m. (2) Dame Mary, relict of Sir John Bridges of Wilton, co. Hereford, bart., and dau. and heiress of John Pearl of Acornbury, co. Hereford. (*Continued on p. 191*).

William Hinson of Fordham at the Damside, co. Cambridge 23 Hy. VII.

Thomas Hinson of Fordham 3 Ed. VI.

Richard Hinson of Fordham, m. Johanna, dau. and coh. of Peter Salisbury of Soham, co. Cambridge.

303

Charles James Fèret

POWELL, HINSON AND WILLIAMS FAMILIES
(continued from previous page)

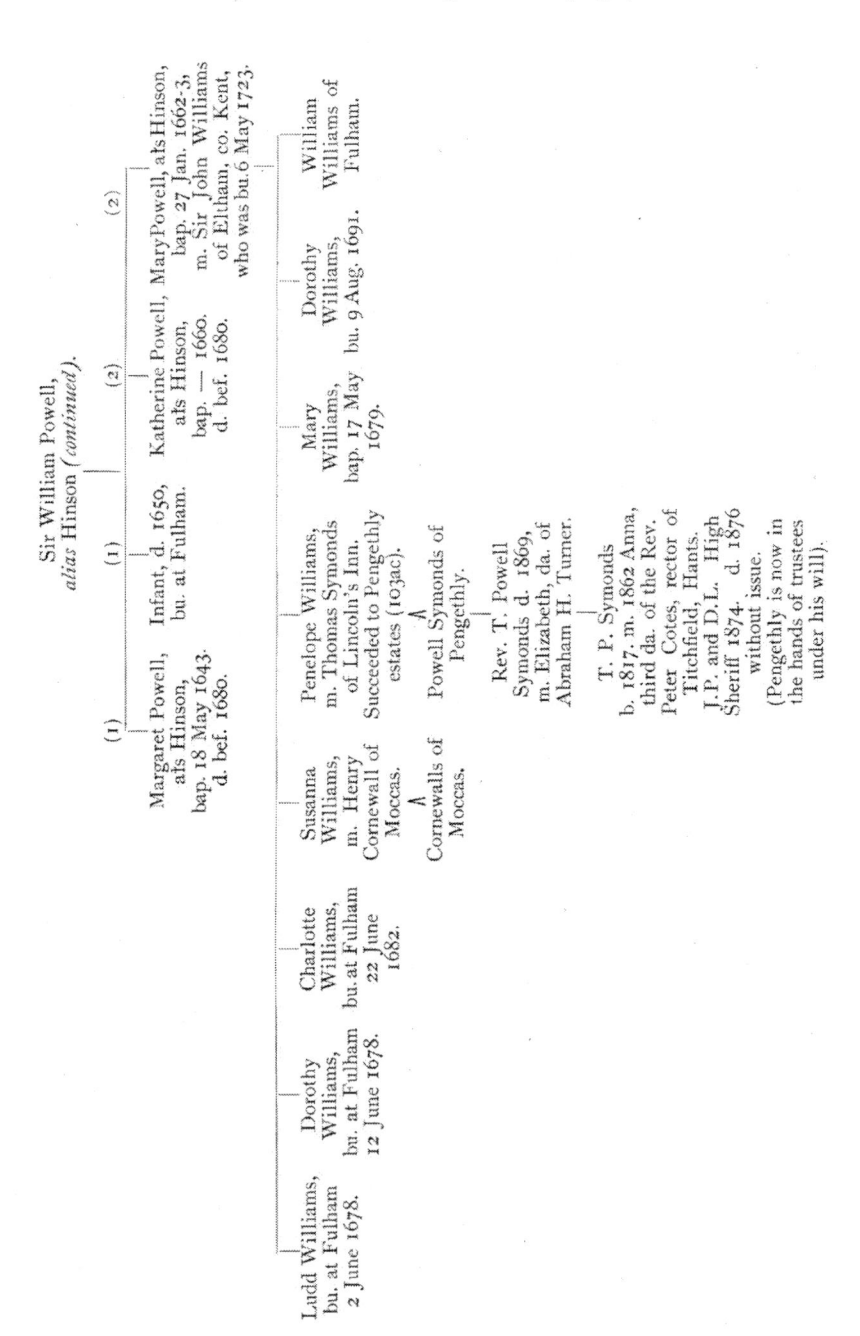

Sir William Powell, alias Hinson (*continued*).

(1) Margaret Powell, als Hinson, bap. 18 May 1643. d. bef. 1680.

(1) Infant, d. 1650, bu. at Fulham.

(2) Katherine Powell, als Hinson, bap. — 1660. d. bef. 1680.

(2) Mary Powell, als Hinson, bap. 27 Jan. 1662-3, m. Sir John Williams of Eltham, co. Kent, who was bu. 6 May 1723.

Children of Mary Powell and Sir John Williams:

- Ludd Williams, bu. at Fulham 2 June 1678.
- Dorothy Williams, bu. at Fulham 12 June 1678.
- Charlotte Williams, bu. at Fulham 22 June 1682.
- Susanna Williams, m. Henry Cornewall of Moccas.
  - Cornewalls of Moccas.
- Penelope Williams, m. Thomas Symonds of Lincoln's Inn. Succeeded to Pengethly estates (103c).
  - Powell Symonds of Pengethly.
    - Rev. T. Powell Symonds d. 1869, m. Elizabeth, da. of Abraham H. Turner.
      - T. P. Symonds b. 1817. m. 1862 Anna, third da. of the Rev. Peter Cotes, rector of Titchfield, Hants. J.P. and D.L. High Sheriff 1874. d. 1876 without issue. (Pengethly is now in the hands of trustees under his will).
- Mary Williams, bap. 17 May 1679.
- Dorothy Williams, bu. 9 Aug. 1691.
- William Williams of Fulham.

304

Sir John Williams and his son William appear to have let Munster House, whose subsequent occupants, for some years, were persons of little note. The following entry occurs in the Highway Rate books:

> "1723. For a team of Horses and a Cart to Fetch Gravel and Labourers to mend Sir John Williams Walk 13s."

Sir John Williams died in 1723, and was buried at Sellack, 6 May. In the Sellack Registers he is described as "of Pengethly," no mention being made of Fulham. There is a quaint eulogy of him in the Registers, where he is spoken of as "gloria hujus agri."

The will of Sir John Williams, dated 7 April 1723, was proved 24 July following by Thomas Symonds, his son-in-law. The proof was confirmed by sentence, 26 July 1723 (P.C.C. 179 Richmond). The following is an extract:

> "I Sr John Williams of the parish of Sellake in the County of Hereford Knight and Baronet being in good health (a cold only excepted). To be buried in Sellake Churchyard near or under the West Window of the addition made to the Church by my wife's ffather Sr William Powell Baronett with a decent plain mable Stone over my Grave raised about two Foot above the Ground with this inscription upon it: Here lyeth the body of Sr John Williams Knight and Baronett husband to the Virtuous and Excellent Mary Sole daughter and Heire to Sr William Powell mentioned on a monument in the said addition by me erected."
> [Testator gives a number of curious directions about the manner of his funeral, and others about a charity at Eltham, co. Kent, founded by him, for teaching six poor boys].

About 1751 Munster House was turned to the purposes of an asylum. In the *Public Advertiser* for 13 December of that year occurs the following announcement:

> "At Purser's Cross, near Fulham, in a healthful Situation, and open Air, there is lately fitted up, in a decent and genteel Manner, a commodious House, for the Reception of Gentlemen, Ladies, and others, who are afflicted with Nervous, or Melancholy Disorders.
> The House is convenient, and the Gardens are pleasant, and well laid out for the Amusement of Persons under such unhappy Circumstances. The Public may be assured of the most careful Attendance, with all

imaginable Tenderness and Humanity, as the Person solely engaged in this important Undertaking is one who, for some time past, hath made it his peculiar Study to learn the proper Method of managing such unhappy Patients."

Munster House continued in the possession of the Powells. From John Powell it passed to his nephew, Arthur Annesley Roberts.

At the death of his uncle, in 1783, Mr. A. A. Roberts assumed the surname of Powell. He appears to have let Munster House. In 1796 a Mrs. Davies carried on a girls' school here. In 1809 the house was taken by Mr. Anthony Sampayo, a wealthy Portuguese merchant, who, in 1813, removed to Peterborough House, when Munster House became the home of the Rt. Hon. John Wilson Croker, M.P., Secretary to the Admiralty.

This distinguished man was the son of Mr. John Croker, of a Cornish family settled in Ireland. He was born in county Galway, 20 December 1780. Having acquired the first rudiments of learning at an Irish day school, he entered Trinity College, Dublin. He graduated in 1800. Shortly afterwards he entered himself as a law student of Lincoln's Inn and was called to the Irish Bar. His success does not seem to have been great, and his leisure hours were spent chiefly in literary work. On 22 May 1806 he married Rosamond Pennell, eldest daughter of William Pennell, H.M.'s Consul-General in Brazil, by whom he had an only son, who died in early childhood. So afflicted were Mr. and Mrs. Croker at the loss of their child, that they determined to adopt Rosamond Hester Pennell, the youngest daughter of William Pennell. In 1808 Croker entered Parliament for Downpatrick. In 1809 he was appointed Secretary to the Admiralty, a position which he held for twenty-two years. At Munster House, which he purchased for £1,200, he resided down to 1826. In 1832 Croker settled Munster House on his adopted daughter, who, in that year, had married Sir George Barrow, second baronet, a quiet, silent man, with chronic ill-health. Sir George, who was for some years Chief Clerk at the Colonial Office, died in 1876. The Barrows did not live at Munster House, which, for some years, stood tenantless and ghost-haunted.

Sir Charles Lennox Peel, the nephew of the great Sir Robert, was born at Munster House in 1823. In 1841 it was taken by the

Rev. Stephen Reed Cattley, curate at Fulham Church, but better known for his scholarly editorship of an issue of Foxe's "Book of Martyrs."

A supposed gun carriage in the grounds of Munster House.
From a photograph by Mr. J. Dugdale, 1895

In 1849 Munster House was acquired by Mr. Cyrus Alexander Elliott for the purposes of an asylum for insane gentlemen. He had in partnership with him his brother, Dr. William Elliott - known as the "mad doctor," who, singularly enough, himself became insane and was actually confined here.

Munster House: the billiard-room in the madhouse [sic].
From a photograph by Mr. J. Dugdale, 1895

There is preserved in the copy of "Faulkner" at Fulham Vicarage a very interesting card, which was issued by Mr. Elliott as an advertisement for his asylum. On one side is a view of Munster House, and, beneath, the words "A Home for gentlemen nervously and mentally afflicted. Proprietor, Mr. Cyrus A. Elliott." On the back is the following:

"Munster House, near Fulham, London, Three Miles from Hyde Park Corner, For the Care and Recovery of Nervous, Epileptic and Insane Gentlemen. Proprietor, Mr. C. A. Elliott.
Munster House, once the Hunting Seat of his Majesty King Charles 2nd, contains twenty-nine Rooms. It is situated on the road from London to Fulham, in the highest part of the Parish, and upon a gravelly soil. The Pleasure grounds are eight acres, walled in, studded with noble Trees, and comprise Lawns, a Meadow, Orchard, Bowling Green, Green House, Bowling Alley, Billiard and Reading Rooms, and detached Buildings for recreation and amusements.
An additional House has been built, containing a Hall, large and lofty Dining, Sitting and Bed Rooms, seventeen Separate Rooms, Washing and Bathing Rooms, a padded Room, and a Refractory Ward, doing away with Mechanical restraint and rendering classification complete.
Those patients whose cases permit will be allowed (accompanied) to walk and ride into the Country, and attend Divine Worship, and if change of air is considered requisite, will by the request of their friends be sent to the Sea Coast, where the Proprietor has a cottage always in readiness."

Mr. Elliott conducted Munster House down to 1870, when it was taken by Dr. Samuel Cartwright Reed, who had married the daughter of one of the patients. In 1873 the asylum passed into the hands of Dr. G. Fielding Blandford, the eminent lunacy specialist, who conducted it in partnership with Mr. John Lamond Hemming and Mr. Charles Frederick Williams. In 1878 Mr. William Kaylet Curtis took the place of Mr. Hemming. In 1894 Dr. Blandford broke up the asylum and sold the property. During the spring of 1895 Munster House was pulled down and the site turned to the purposes of a builders' estate.

In the days of Mr. Elliott it was no uncommon occurrence for inmates to escape. Sometimes they would hide in Dancer's Nursery opposite, but at others they would get further afield before their recapture could be effected. On the night of 28 September

1874, a lunatic, in a state of nudity, got out from Munster House, and ran down the Fulham Road and through the High Street till he reached the old Toll House at the foot of the Bridge. It was just 3.30 a.m. The toll keeper, the late Richard Green, seeing his strange visitor, rang the alarm bell for assistance. Meanwhile he managed to persuade the madman to lie down on the sofa while he made up the fire and covered him. "Oh, I am so good," exclaimed the poor fellow, "I left such a pretty blue-eyed girl .behind me. I kept on calling her, but she would not come, and so I had to come alone." Jack Kelley, the waterman, and two or three policemen arrived on the scene, quickly followed by three or four keepers from Munster House. They wrapped up their charge in a blanket and conveyed him back. The unfortunate man died within a month of this occurrence.

Munster House, back view, about 1850. From the original drawing engraved by T. H. Ellis, now in the possession of his son, T. H. Ellis, Esq.

Externally, Munster House was a curious looking building. Inside there was little that was of any special interest. There is a tradition that the front gates and lamps came from the Admiralty, brought here by Croker when he was Secretary to that department. Sir Arthur Blomfield, in his lecture on "The Olden Times of Fulham," delivered 27 June 1856, remarked:

"Not many years ago there stood on the gateposts of Munster House two composition lions of such ferocious aspect and of such strange forms, that the common idea was, I believe, at that time, that the real name of the place was 'Monster House.' "

Mr. Elliott, though not responsible for the leonine adornments, certainly put up the imitation Gothic front and battlements and other doubtful embellishments. The plaster figures at the entrance were principally added by Croker. One was the effigy of the Venerable Bede. A relief against the wall was suggestive of a Jewish sacrifice.

Munster House, principal entrance.
From a photograph by Mr. J. Dugdale, 1895

The prettiest view of the house was from the back. Here a long narrow room, with an old fashioned bay window, commanded a very agreeable view of the fine grounds. About twenty five years ago a large addition was made to the east side of the
house for the accommodation of the patients. A curious fact about Munster House was that none but the outside walls were built of brick, the others being lath and plaster. Among these hollow partitions droves of rats and mice could at night be heard careering

around.

We will now take a glance at the interior of the old house, commencing at the top. The highly pitched red-tiled roof was a noteworthy feature. On the two highest floors were numerous bedrooms. The oak panelling of some of the deeply recessed cupboards was very old. The dining-room and the first reception-room were fine apartments. At the back of the house was the long narrow drawing-room to which we have referred. This room led to the new part of the house where the patients lived. This was an extensive range of buildings, the accommodation being first, second and third class. Here was a large billiard-room, 60 ft. by 40 ft. The curiosities of this part of the house included a padded-room and an extra strong bedroom with double door.

In the grounds were some detached buildings, including a laundry, which stood against the Munster Road wall, and a picturesque octagonal building at the north end of the grounds. It had doubtless once been used as a summer house, and was traditionally known as King Charles's Bower. It was, in more prosaic times, used as a dead house for the temporary reception of the bodies of patients who died at the asylum.

King Charles's Bower.
From a photograph by Mr. T. S. Smith, 1895

Doorway of King Charles's Bower, as seen from within.
From a photograph by Mr J. Dugdale

The grounds were finely timbered. Among the more noticeable trees were a grand old mulberry supported by chains, a deciduous cedar, about the tallest in England, and two splendid acacias. Bordering one of the paths was an old stone, which looked suspiciously like the bed of a piece of ordnance, and may have come from the Admiralty.

At the junction of Chesilton Road with Fulham Road is Munster Park Chapel, a neat edifice in the Gothic style, erected by Messrs. Gibbs and Flew from the designs of Mr. J. Weir. The foundation stone was laid 28 June 1881. The chapel accommodates one thousand persons.

Eastwards along this portion of the Fulham Road, there is little to call for notice till we reach Vine Cottage at the south-west corner of Winchendon Road. It is, perhaps, the most picturesque bit of old Fulham now remaining on this road of new houses. Little can be traced of its early history. It is said once to have been the home of Anastasia Robinson, the wife of the celebrated Earl of Peterborough. William Robert Bertolacci, the artist, resided here in 1868-69.

Munster Park Chapel. From a photograph by Mr. T. S. Smith, 1895

Vine Cottage. From a photograph by Mr. T. S. Smith, 1893

Vine Cottage was the house which Wilkie Collins evidently had in his mind when, in 1870, he wrote "Man and Wife." In the 53rd chapter of this novel he gives a minute description of it. He makes it the home of one of his characters, Reuben Limbrick, formerly a dealer in salt, who, coming to Fulham, purchased a piece of freehold land on which he built a cottage which he called Salt Patch. The novelist tells us that one of Limbrick's eccentricities was to live in perpetual dread of thieves, and he describes how he sheathed his window shutters with iron and attached alarm bells to them. Vine Cottage, at the present day, exactly answers the description which Wilkie Collins gives of Salt Patch; even the bell turret on the roof is mentioned. The house, which is now the residence of Mrs. Roydhouse, the mineral water manufacturer, enjoys the distinction of having been the first in the parish to be electrically lighted.

Percy Cross House.
From a photograph in the possession of the Rev. F. H. Fisher, M.A.

Where Clonmel Road now enters the Fulham Road, stood Percy Cross House, a fine mansion whose grounds, 6a. 1r. 28p., extended back to Bishop's Road. It was erected about 1830. From 1832 to 1839 it was the residence of Mr. John Borley. In 1840-41 Mr. Thomas Paley resided here. From 1842 to 1853 it was the home of a celebrated lawyer, the late Serjeant Digby Caley Wrangham. Mr. John da Silva was here from 1854 to 1859. Mr. Henry Jubber, the proprietor of Long's Hotel, Bond Street, lived at Percy Cross House from 1860 to 1870. In 1872 it was purchased by Mr. Joseph Napier Higgins, Q.C. In 1895 the house was pulled down and the site built over.

Westfield House and the neighbouring Terrace take their name from an ancient close known as the "West Field." Little is recorded about the early history of the house. From 1764 to 1775 we find Abraham Dupuis assessed for a "mansion house" called "West Field." In 1787 it became the residence of Mr. John Meyrick, of whom we have spoken in connection with Peterborough House. (See "Parson's Green, South Side").

Mr. John Druce, J.P., took Westfield House in 1797, and resided here down to his death in 1818. Pie lies buried at Fulham. For the next twenty years it was the residence of Mr. John Pensam.

On the death of the Rev. George Dupuis, its owner, Westfield House was sold at Garraway's Coffee House, 'Change Alley, for £1,200, its purchaser and occupant being Mr. John Laurie, who subsequently lived at Holcroft's. In 1845 Mr. Laurie let Westfield House to Mr. Thomas Sawer, who lived here down to 1864. From 1868 to 1875 it was the residence of Mr. Joseph Wright Turnley, who earned distinction as the foreman of the jury in the notorious Tichborne case. On his death, in 1875, it was taken by Mr. John Goldsmith.

In 1887 Westfield House was turned into a Public Library. The Library Commissioners carried out several structural alterations, and spent a considerable sum of money in adapting the old premises to their new uses. In 1888 the new reading-room, at the rear of the house, was built by Mr. Charles Wall, from the designs of Mr. John C. Hall. The decorations were executed by Signor Mirolda and Signor Cananova. Its cost was £2,480.

At the end of this handsome room, which measures 31 feet by 71 feet, in a central niche, is a large painted design which bears the following inscription:

"Fulham Free Public Library. This reading room was opened Oct. 20 1888."

Then follows the names of the Commissioners, etc.

Fulham Public Library.
From a photograph by Mr. T. S. Smith, 1893.

Interior of the Reading Room

The Marist Convent and St. Peter's Collegiate school for girls consisted, until 1896, of two separate houses, built by Mr. John Laurie, of Holcroft's, about 1841.

The south wing of the present block was known as Percy Villa. From 1845 to 1850 it was the residence of Mr. Joseph Holmes. In 1853 it was taken by Mr. George Henderson, and in 1860 by Mr. H. Streatfield Baker, who resided here down to 1867. In 1868, Mr. E. T. Smith, of Drury Lane Theatre, took Percy Villa, but soon quitted it. In the following year it was leased to Mr. Joseph A. Yglesias. From 1877 to 1884 Madame Cornelia d'Anka, the actress, lived at Percy Villa with her husband, Mr. John Ingham.

The northern portion of the block was St. Peter's Lodge, originally St. Peter's Villa. Madame Garcia was its first occupant. From 1845 to 1847 it was tenanted by Mr. William Schan Lindsay. In 1857-58 the Rev. A. S. Latter resided here. After a short tenancy by Mr. John Pybus, in 1860-61, the house was taken by Mr. Robert Henderson Rust, who changed its name to St. Peter's Lodge. In 1882 it was leased to Mr. John Hales.

In 1895 Percy Villa and St. Peter's Lodge were purchased by the Marist Sisters, when the two houses were united by the erection of a central block. In the wall at the back of this new part is a stone inscribed:

> "Laid by the Right Reverend Monsignor Fenton On Ascension Day MDCCCXCV. Nisi Dominus ædificaverit domum in vanum laboraverunt qui ædificant eam."

At the top of this new building is a chapel. The convent and school were originally established in Bishop's Road. At the present time there are, in the Marist Convent (the Percy Villa portion), some fifteen Sisters. The other part (the St. Peter's Lodge portion) comprises the St. Peter's Collegiate School. There is accommodation for about 120 scholars, of whom a few are boarders. The grounds measure 1a. 0r. 24p.

At 40, Darlan Road, just at the rear of the Marist Convent and St. Peter's Collegiate School, is a Roman Catholic club for men and boys, established by Monsignor Fenton in 1896 at a cost of about £2,000.

St. Peter's Lodge. From a photograph by Mr. T. S. Smith, 1896

SOUTH SIDE

Opposite Munster House was Dancer's Nursery, an establishment which occupied an extensive frontage to the Fulham Road, stretching from Munster Road to the grounds of Park House and extending back towards Rectory Lane and Parson's Green Lane. It covered about 47 acres.

The Dancers were one of the oldest families connected with the parish. In 1625 we find Nathaniel Dancer rated for his homestead at North End, where he died in 1657. His will, dated 6 September 1656, was proved 2 September 1657 (P.C.C. 338 Ruthven). The following is an extract:

"I Nathaniel Dauncer of ffulham in the County of Middlesex yeoman. To be buried in the parish Church of ffulham neare unto my Wife Dorithie and neare unto my wonted pewe. My parcell of copyhold land in occupation of Thomas Day and situate at Wandons Greene and all my tenements in a Lane comonly called Dawes Lane neare Wandons Greene to the use of myselfe and my now wife Jane for joint lives and longer liver. My two acres at High Elmes which I lately bought of Obadiah Burton and Katherine his wife to my wife Jane Dancer. I giue to the poore of the parish of ffulham on ffulham side the yearly summe of Thirtie Shillings for ever Twentie Shillings thereof to be giuen to fortie poore Inhabitants of the said parish in bread and Tenn Shillings in monie att the Parish Church of ffulham and att or upon everie ffirst day of Januarie by the Church Wardens for the tyme being. I doe giue and bequeath unto the Minister of ffulham for the time being the Summe of Tenn Shillings for his paines in preaching of a Sermon att or upon each and everie first Day of January for ever The whiche said forty Shillings I doe will shall be paid out the proffitts of the two Acres of Land lying near the High Elmes."

In the old "Register Book" is a detailed account of the gift. This rent charge of 40s., payable on certain lands which can be identified, is still regularly paid. Under the last Scheme of the Charity Commissioners, the gift was included among the "pensions" of the "United Charities." Before the new Scheme, Dancer's gift was devoted to the bread and beef distribution, which was made by tickets for 1s. 6d. worth of beef and 6d. worth of bread at Christmas.

Nathaniel Dancer, son of the above Nathaniel Dancer, in 1689, married Elizabeth Cranke, who died in 1711. Nathaniel Dancer, junior, died in 1741-42. Thomas Dancer, brother of Nathaniel Dancer, senior, also lived at North End. His name appears in the Court Rolls down to 1662. His widow, Joan, died in 1670, when his son, William, was admitted to the property at North End. He died in 1705. The farm of William Dancer at North End lay adjacent to the old Creek. The two acres of land lying "neare the High Elmes," referred to in the will of Nathaniel Dancer, senior, were on the Fulham Road, and doubtless formed the nucleus of the great nursery.

The early history of the nursery is difficult to trace. Its site had originally formed a portion of the ancient Manor of Rosamond's (see "Parson's Green: Parson's Green lane" chapter). In the last century it was in the occupation of the Grinsteeds. Mr. Thomas Grinsteed, gardener, died 16 December 1788. On his death the nursery appears to have been taken by Mr. William Dancer, who is assessed for it from 1790 to 1826, when he was succeeded by his son, Mr. Alexander W. Dancer. The latter's son, another Alexander, conducted it down to about 1884, when the nursery was broken up and the site covered with a builders' estate. Dancer

Road recalls the name of the nurserymen.

On a portion of the site of Dancer's Nursery has been built the Stukeley Park Estate, a name which recalls the memory of Dr. William Stukeley (1687-1765), the learned antiquary and author of the "Itinerarium Curiosum." It should, however, be stated that Dr. Stukeley had no connection with Fulham, the naming of the estate being due to the circumstance that he happened to be an ancestor of one of the promoters of the undertaking, Messrs. Fleming and Co.

SECTION III: PERCY CROSS TO WALHAM GREEN

The neighbourhood of the Fulham Road, at its junction with Parson's Green Lane, is known as Purser's Cross or Percy Cross.

Faulkner could find no satisfactory explanation of the name. In the "Beauties of England and Wales" it is stated that Purser's Cross is said to have been corrupted from Parson's Cross, and the vicinity of Parson's Green is mentioned in support of the conjecture. The name is, however, easily explained. Purser's Cross is merely a corrupt form of Purser's Croft or Field. In the Court Rolls the first occurrence of the name is in 1552, where it is spelled "Purserscrosse." At a View in 1569 it was ordered that:

> "Everyone having trees overhanging the highway from Wendon Green to Pursere Croft shall lop the same before St. John or forfeit 12d. per perch."

Again, in 1605:

> "Willm Rippyn and Mr. Danson shall lay out the foote pathe by the lane yt leadeth to Pursers Crosse as it hath byn heretofore used wth sufficient styles to the same."

The following entry occurs in the minutes of a Court General held in 1617:

> "Edward Cole shall scour his ditch from Pursers ground to Robert Norris grounde."

Nothing can be gathered as to the person whose little homestall bestowed an abiding name upon this part of the Fulham Road. The Parish Books record:

> 1625. "It. pd to a woman of Kingston for keeping Richard Purser's childe from ye 25th of Aprill 1625 to ye 20 of March 1s. p. weeke £2. 7s. 0d."

> 1627. "Paid the woman of Kingston for keeping pursers Daughter two monethes ending the 19th of Maye 8s. 0d."

> 1627. "Paid John Rowe with pursers daughter when put apprentice for five yeares £3. 0s. 0d."

It is possible that this Purser belonged to the family of the Pursers whose Croft adjoined this road. The change from Croft to Cross seems to have taken place in the reign of Elizabeth. In the Court Rolls for 1572 we read:

> "George Burton has not cut the boughs from Poursers Cross to Berestrete according to precept wherefore he is fined 2s. 4d."

In 1575 Thomas Holmes was presented "for his ditch" from "Pourcers Crose to Bowmbye Stile." Bombay's Stile was on the London Road, near what is now Fulham Park Gardens (see "New King's Road: Burlington Road to Parson's Green" chapter) The disbursements of the Churchwardens for 1641 include:

> "Itm for graue and expences in buryall of the man that dyed att pursers Crosse 1s. 0½d."

The transition from Purser's to Percy Cross, which has been in course of progress during the past fifty years, is doubtless due to the tendency to represent a word, the meaning of which has, perhaps, passed out of mind, by one tolerably similar in sound but wholly distinct in sense.

In the Rate-books for 1746 occurs, for the first time, the name of Mrs. Turberville, rated for a house at Purser's Cross. In the *Annual Register* for 1781 is the following notice of her and her sister:

"Died 30th December 1780 at Purser's Cross, Fulham, Mrs. Elizabeth and Mrs. Frances Turberville, in the seventy seventh year of their ages, of an ancient and respectable west country family; they were twin sisters, and both died unmarried. What adds to the singularity of this circumstance, they were both born the same day, never were known to live separate, died within a few days of each other, and were interred on the same day."

In the *London Chronicle* for 2-4 January 1781 (vol. 49, p. 11), is a similar paragraph. They were interred at Petersham in Surrey. The Church Registers record:

1733. Mary a foundling Infant dropt near Pursors Cross, for that reason surnam'd Pursor. bap. 13 Feb.

1734. Mary Pursor Inf^t bu. 4 Sep.

1761. Samuel Royld, Mr. Souchs man kill'd by a fall of a House at Pursers bu. 12 Nov.

NORTH SIDE

This section of the Fulham Road takes us from Percy Cross to Walham Green. Taking the north side, we come first to the Arundel Gardens estate, the site of Arundel House, a flat, brick-fronted mansion which, till 1898, stood between the Marist Convent and Wheatsheaf Alley. Croker writes:

"It is a house of considerable antiquity, judging from the stone mullions brought to light by some repairs, - probably as old as the time of Henry VIII. ; although the brick front . . . appears to be the work of the latter part of the seventeenth century."

During some alterations at the house in 1890, other mullions of wood, forming what had once been an entire window, were discovered, built into the wall behind a panelled recess in the library, telling evidently of an older Tudor mansion. Unfortunately there are no records now discoverable which throw any light on the early history of the house.

A tradition still lingers to the effect that the house was once occupied by one of the mistresses of Charles II, and it is even said that an old mulberry tree in the garden was planted by the Merry Monarch.

Arundel House. From a photograph by Mr. T. S. Smith, 1896

The date of the erection of Arundel House is not certainly known, but some of the older fire-places, etc., pointed to the time of Queen Anne. The Rate books for the earlier years of the last century are missing, but there are good reasons for believing that the house was, for some years, the residence of the Earl of Annandale. Against the east wall of the house there existed a very curious leaden cistern, now preserved at the Public Library, bearing on its front an earl's coronet, a monogram, and the date 1703, probably the year of the reconstruction of the house. This cistern was formerly in the scullery. The monogram is difficult to decipher and has been read in several ways, but it seems to us to show the combination of the two letters "J" and "D." These, apparently, were arranged for "Johnstone" and "Douglas." The widow of James Johnstone, second Earl of Annandale, was the fourth daughter of William, first Marquis of Douglas. Her son was created Marquis of Annandale, 4 June 1701. The Rate books from 1728 to 1735 show a Marchioness of Annandale assessed for a house at Purser's Cross, and, judging from the amount of the assessment, her home, there can be little doubt, was the house of which we are now speaking. The only person at this period entitled to be styled Marchioness of Annandale was Charlotte Vanlore, only child and heiress of John Vanden Bempde of Pall Mall, relict of William, first Marquis and third Earl of Annandale, K.T. She married, as her second husband, Colonel John Johnstone, who was killed at Carthagena in 1741. This lady, who brought a large fortune to the Johnstones, ultimately died at Bath, 23 November 1762.

Old Leaden Cistern at Arundel House.
From a photograph by Mr. J. Dugdale

In no ancient records which we have searched does the name Arundel House appear. Croker, who confesses himself unable to state to whom the monogram belonged, adds, "For the name of Arundel I am equally unable to account." To us the explanation appears to be this: in the assessments of the Marchioness of Annandale, the name is variously spelled Annandale, Anandale, Anundale, Anundell, etc. An alteration of the first "n" into "r" would give us Arundell or Arundale, which, curiously enough, is the oldest form of the name so far as our research has gone. When or under what circumstances Annandale House first assumed the guise of Arundale or Arundell House we cannot say, but there can be no reasonable doubt that such a change occurred.

With other property at Purser's Cross, Walham Green and Knightsbridge, the house was bought by Miss Prudentia Trevor, daughter of the first Viscount Dungannon (created Lord Trevor), whose family, until 1896, owned the estate. The vendor was a Joseph Burch, described as the son and heir of Samuel Burch, of St

Margaret's, Westminster.

For a short while, in 1819, Henry Hallam, the historian and essayist, resided at Arundel House. During his sojourn here he was visited by numerous literary friends, prominent among whom was young Alfred Tennyson, who formed an ardent friendship with the historian's eldest son, Arthur Henry Hallam, whose sudden death at Vienna, in 1833, closed a career of great promise. It was this event which produced Tennyson's "In Memoriam."

Mr. George Forsyth Maule was living at "Arundell House" in 1820. For some years the house stood empty. In 1846-47 it was occupied by Mr. William Kinder, who was succeeded by Major Edmund Sheppard. In 1851 Arundel House was taken by Mr. William Good, who, for the remarkable period of fifty years, was clerk at Somerset House. Mr. Good is remembered as a kind-hearted and benevolent man. In 1870 he died quite suddenly, in his favourite spot in the old garden. The next occupant of Arundel House was Baron May, who lived here from 1871 to 1886. The Rev. John S. Sinclair, M.A., the late vicar of St. Dionis, resided at Arundel House from 1888 to 1898.

The rooms of Arundel House, though not large, were exceedingly comfortable, and they had about them an air of quiet seclusion which almost made the visitor fancy he was in some country mansion, instead of in a house situated on the verge of one of the busiest highways in Fulham. The square staircase which faced the visitor as he entered was of pine painted white. The library was to the left; to the right, overlooking the delightful grounds, was the dining-room. Immediately above the latter was the principal drawing-room, before which was a quaint-looking verandah of wood by which access to the garden was gained. Above were several bedrooms and a curious little apartment known as the "powdery room," reminding one of the time when perfumed starch and chalk were in greater vogue with the fair sex than they are to-day. The foundation walls of the house were of remarkable thickness.

The back of Arundel House was much more picturesque than the front, and displayed the Dutch characteristics of architecture which found so much favour in England in the time of William III. and Queen Anne. A quaint turret and an old-fashioned garden porch of wood were noteworthy features.

Arundel House (back view).
From a photograph in the possession of the Rev. J. S. Sinclair, M. A.

The grounds, which were rather over an acre in extent, were finely laid out. Originally they were planned in the formal Dutch style with box edgings in stiff geometrical lines. Considering their situation, they were singularly pretty and possessed some fine trees. At the far end was an old arbour formed by yew trees which had long since gone to decay. It was here that Hallam used to write. A few yards away stood a pump, bearing date 1758. On the west side of the grounds was the venerable mulberry tree already mentioned.

Passing a narrow passage known as Wheatsheaf Alley (closed in 1900), leading to Bishop's Road, we reach the new "Wheatsheaf." Its predecessor, which stood a few yards eastwards of the present house, was a small, old-fashioned roadside inn, pulled down in 1889.

In former days, when the Fulham Road was a little frequented highway, the old "Wheatsheaf" was a resort favoured by footpads and other congenial spirits. In 1757 the inn was leased by the Bishop of London to James Sayers, from whom it passed, in 1762, to John Powell, of Park House; in 1784, to his executors, Richard Cleaver, Keene Stables and Philip Deare; in 1791, to his heir, Arthur Annesley Powell, and, in 1823, to John Powell Powell.

When the original house was built, or by whom, is uncertain. According to local tradition, the first owner of the little inn was a man named Keene. In course of time the host of the "Wheatsheaf" was gathered to his fathers, but his spirit was restless and returned to earth. In the narrow alley which we have just mentioned, Keene's ghost would be seen at night mounted on the back of a donkey riding up and down the defile. After awhile the ghost of the host of the "Wheatsheaf" ceased from troubling and the name of "Keene's Alley," which the village folk had applied to the scene of old Keene's escapades, was beginning to be forgotten. But the worthy landlord did not intend that posterity should for all time efface his remembrance, for, when he was in the flesh, and was apparently building the "Wheatsheaf," he caused to be inserted in the front wall, at a height of two or three feet from the ground, a couple of bricks engraved with his name. On the demolition of the old house the bricks were found covered with cement. On this being removed, it was found that one bore the word "KEENE," and the other, the name and date, thus, "KEEN 1616." A more singular find has seldom been made, for, whatever be the truth about old Keene's apparition, it proves that local tradition had at least accurately preserved, for over two centuries and a half, the name of the old innkeeper.

Wheatsheaf Alley, looking south.
From a photograph by Mr. T. S. Smith, 1896

The new "Wheatsheaf Hotel" was built in 1889, and was opened in March of the following year. The two old bricks were inserted in the wall at the side of the house facing Wheatsheaf Alley. The ponderous old copper signboard, said to be nearly two hundred years old, was, in 1891, rehung outside the new "Wheatsheaf." A stone, in front of the "Wheatsheaf Hotel" is inscribed, beneath the representation of a sheaf of wheat,

>Erected 1616
>Rebuilt 1889.

The foundation stone bears the following inscription:

>This Stone was laid by
>Robert Bartholomew
>1889.

The old "Wheatsheaf."
From a water-colour drawing by Miss Jane Humphreys

Near the top of Wheatsheaf Alley stood a tall house called Spratt Castle, pulled down some 70 years ago. It was long in the occupation of Christopher and Thomas Grinsteed. In the Highway Rate books it is first mentioned in 1771.

Between the "Wheatsheaf" and the western boundary of the grounds of Walham Lodge, was Bolingbroke House, Lodge or

Hall, in its later days divided into two tenements known as Dungannon House and Albany Lodge. Mr. Crofton Croker writes:

> "Tradition stoutly asserts that this united cottage and villa were, previous to their division, known by the name of *Bolingbroke Lodge* and that here Pope did more than once
> 'Awake my St. John'
> by an early morning visit."

Fortunately the Rate books set the matter at rest. It was not the great statesman and political writer of the days of Queen Anne, but his nephew, Frederick, 6th bart. and 3rd Viscount St. John, who resided here from 1785 to 1787, the year of his death. In 1788 the entry in the Rate book stands:

"Major Gall late Lord Bolingbroke."

The house was probably divided into two about the close of the last or the commencement of the present century.

The western portion was known as Dungannon House, or Acacia Cottage, from a tree of that kind which grew in the garden. For some years it was the residence of Joseph Johnson, a distinguished member of the Society of Booksellers in London. He has not inaptly been described as "the father of the trade." He was born at Liverpool, in November 1738. At the age of fourteen he was sent to London, and was apprenticed to Mr. George Keith of Gracechurch Street. He began business for himself as a medical bookseller in a shop in Fish Street Hill, whence he moved to Paternoster Row. In 1770, his house and stock being destroyed by fire, he removed to St. Paul's Churchyard, where he conducted a most successful business. The precarious nature of Mr. Johnson's health caused him to spend much of the later period of his life in quiet seclusion at Fulham. He died 20 December 1809, and was buried at Fulham (see vol. I, "Fulham Churchyard" chapter). In St. Paul's Churchyard there is a large monument to his memory.

Charles Joseph Hullmandel, the eminent lithographer, was another noteworthy resident at Dungannon House. Hullmandel, who was the son of a distinguished German musician, was born 15 June 1789. He commenced his experiments in the then new art of lithography in 1818. His success attracted so much attention that he determined to devote his time entirely to lithography. According to Croker, Hullmandel resided at Dungannon House in 1839-40. From 1841 to 1847 we find him assessed for Laurel Bank House in the New King's Road (see "New King's Road: Burlington Road to Parson's Green" chapter). He died in 1850.

The house was, from 1857 to 1868, known as Dungannon Nursery, kept by Mr. George Glenny, an eminent authority on gardening.

Albany Lodge, the eastern half of Bolingbroke Hall, was for some years the residence of Mr. Henry Milton, brother of the famous authoress, Mrs. Frances Trollope. During his residence here the house bore the name of Heckfield Lodge, from Heckfield in Hampshire, a parish of which his father, the Rev. William Milton, was vicar. From 1865 to 1874 Albany Lodge was in the occupation of Mr. William Fielder. From 1875 to 1879 it was the home of the Vokes family, the well-known comedians, by whom it was re-christened Lilian Lodge.

Dungannon House and Albany Lodge were taken down in 1891.

Walham Avenue and Lodge Avenue are two names which, taken together, remind us of Walham Lodge, formerly Park Cottage, built about 1780. The house stood in some two and a half acres of grounds surrounded by a brick Park wall. The frontage to the Fulham Road was about 230 feet. The grounds were adorned with finely grown timber and magnificent shrubs.

From 1829 to 1834 Walham Lodge was the residence of William Thomas Brande, D.C.L., F.R.S., the eminent chemist and editor of the "Dictionary of Science, Literature and Art." Brande, who was the son of an apothecary, was, in 1802, apprenticed to his brother, a licentiate of the Society of Apothecaries. Subsequently he became a pupil at the Anatomical School in Windmill Street, and studied chemistry at St. George's Hospital. In 1809 he was elected a Fellow of the Royal Society, and in 1813 he accepted the appointment of professor of chemistry in the Royal Institution. He particularly distinguished himself by a course of lectures on geology, which he delivered at the Royal Institution in 1816. The honorary degree of D.C.L. was conferred on him by the University of Oxford. He died in 1866.

In 1835 Walham Lodge was taken by Capt. Balmain. Its next occupant was Mr. Timothy Richardson. Mr. John Radermacher resided here from 1844 to 1858. During his occupancy the house was known as Park Cottage or Park Lodge. From 1859 to 1871 Walham Lodge was the residence of Mr. William Freeman, founder of the famous horse mart now known as Aldridge's.

In 1880 the estate was sold for building purposes. On the demolition of the house, the workmen, in excavating under a chestnut tree, discovered a potful of old gold coins, which they secretly disposed of.

Between Walham Lodge and Melmoth Place were the market gardens of George Bagley. The Police Station, which stands upon a portion of the site, was built in 1863.

The "George," at the corner of the Fulham Road and Melmoth Place, is a hotel of modern erection, but it marks the site of an interesting little roadside inn, with a heavy pitched roof and bay windows. The extensive stabling extended back as far as the Police Station.

The earliest known reference to the "George" occurs in the will of Sir William Powell, dated 2 December 1680. Sir William, as we have seen (see "Fulham Road: Munster Road to Percy Cross" chapter), devised the "George" to Thomas and Dorothy Bishop, who, at the date of the execution of the will, were then in the occupation of the house. In the Court Rolls the inn is first mentioned in 1682. In the Overseers' Accounts for 1716 is the following entry:

"Paid for the Examination of the Souldiers wife at the George 2s. 0d."

The old Fulham Bridge Commissioners sometimes held their meetings at the "George." The Church Registers record:

1764. Samuel Latham, a poor man from the George at Walham Green bu. 17 Apl.

The house, which was rebuilt in 1867, was for some years in the occupation of Richard Hartley, who ran a half-hourly service of omnibuses between his house and the City. Hartley, who was also a clerk in the Bank of England, was one day called into the Bank parlour by the Governors and informed that he would have either to give up his omnibuses or retire from the Bank. He preferred the latter, saying the omnibuses paid him better!

On the Fulham Road, somewhere near the "George," was a field called Pinzar. We also hear of Pinzar Stile and Pinzar Gate. In 1577 William Collingwood and Humphrey Adames were ordered to make a bridge called a shot bridge "between Payre Cause and Pinzer." In 1581 George Payne had to make a bridge "out of Pynzare to the highway."

In 1615 Robert Rose was required to scour his ditch sufficiently "along the highway from Pinsur Bridge to New Ditch." In 1641 allusion is made to "Great Pinsor," and, in 1682, to the ditch "from the sign of the George to Pinzar fields and Pinzar style." The Jurors, at a View in 1682, presented Thomas George for not laying a footway which formerly led "from the signe of the George within the hedge unto Pinzar feilds." The last we hear of the spot is in 1693, when Thomas Earsby surrendered land "near Pinser Gate."

SOUTH SIDE

Opposite the "Wheatsheaf" is the new London County Council Fire Brigade Station. The old station was built about 1869. The new premises were erected in 1895-6, the foundation stone being laid by the Earl of Carrington, then Chairman of the Fire Brigade Committee. It is a handsome structure of redbrick, relieved by Portland stone dressings. On the ground floor are the engine room, stables and usual offices. In the upper portion are quarters for the engineer in charge, for twelve married men, six single men and a coachman. In the centre of the structure, rising to a height of ninety feet, is a watch tower. The architect was Mr. C. Blashill. Messrs. Holloway Bros, were the contractors.

On the site of the "Swan" Brewery was Ravensworth House. The original house was built by John Ord, Master in Chancery, who resided here from 1756 till 1814.

John Ord, who was born in 1729, was the only son of Robert Ord, Chief Baron of the Court of Exchequer in Scotland. He was educated at Hackney and Trinity College, Cambridge, which he entered in 1746. In 1750 he graduated B.A., and afterwards obtained a lay fellowship. In 1762 he vacated the lay fellowship through his marriage with Eleanor, second daughter of John Simpson, of Bradley, co. Durham. After being called to the bar at Lincoln's Inn, Ord practised in the Court of Chancery. In 1774 he entered Parliament as member for Midhurst. Four years later he was appointed Master in Chancery. Subsequently he sat as member for Hastings and Wendover. He retired from political life in 1790, and in 1809 he resigned the office of Master in Chancery. He was a Fellow of the Royal Society.

John Ord was a skilful horticulturist and delighted in his garden at Fulham, which, for the beauty and rarity of its trees, became second only to that of Fulham Palace. Lysons describes it in his "Environs of London" (1796). Priscilla Wakefield, in her "Perambulations of London," writes:

> "Mr. Ord's garden, at Walham Green, also afforded us a fine show of trees and plants from foreign climates; but nothing was so striking as a bed of moss-roses, measuring nearly one hundred and fifty feet in circumference, spread, from a single stem in the centre, over the ground, like a carpet of most exquisite beauty."

Ord is said to have been the first to introduce the moss rose into this country, a distinction which is also claimed for the Renches of Southfield Farm (see "Parson's Green: South Side" chapter).

John Ord, who possessed a valuable library, chiefly of legal works, died at his house at Walham Green, 6 June 1814, aged 85, and was buried in Fulham Churchyard. Mrs. Ord, who died in 1818, was also buried at Fulham. Mrs. Anne Simpson, sister of Mrs. Ord, died at the house in 1824, aged 81. She is buried in the family vault (see vol. I, "Fulham Churchyard" chapter).

On the night of 9 September 1807 a great fire occurred at the "garden house" of John Ord, which raged so furiously as to burn the principal gardener, an old and valued servant, almost to ashes, before any help could be afforded him. The conflagration was made the subject of a sermon by Mr. Ord's great friend, the Rev. John Owen, M.A., curate. This sermon was printed in 1807. A second edition was published in the same year and a third in 1808. The third edition bears the following title page:

"The Uncertainty of the Morrow. The Substance of a Sermon preached at Fulham Church in the afternoon of Sunday the 13th of September 1807, on the occasion of the late awful fire in the premises of John Ord, Esq., by which his principal gardener was burnt to Death. By the Rev. John Owen, M.A., Curate of Fulham, Middlesex."

In Mr. J. Roe's "Diary" is the following comment on the sermon:

1807 13 Sept. Sunday. A Sermon this evening on the Merits of White a servant of Mr. Ord's who was burnt to death and buried last night together with a Horse of Mr. Ords."

At Ravensworth Castle there is a portrait of Robert Ord, the father of John Ord.

In 1825 the house became the residence of Lord Ravensworth, who much enlarged and improved it. Lord Ravensworth was the brother-in-law of John Ord.

Ravensworth House.
From a photograph by the late Mr. William Appleton

The Right Hon. Thomas Henry Liddell, Baron Ravensworth and the 6th baronet, was the eldest son of Sir Henry George

Liddell, 5th baronet, who died in 1791. At the coronation of George IV, in July 1821, he was raised to the peerage as Baron Ravensworth, a title which had been extinct since the death of Sir Henry Liddell, the 4th baronet, who died without issue in 1784. Lord Ravensworth married, in 1796, Maria Susannah, daughter of John Simpson, of Bradley, co. Durham. She died at Ravensworth Castle, 22 November 1845. Lord Ravensworth had eight sons and eight daughters.

Lord and Lady Ravensworth made Ravensworth House famous for its "breakfasts," or garden parties, as we should now call this species of entertainment. William IV and Queen Adelaide were on one occasion his guests. On 26 June 1840 Queen Victoria, accompanied by the Prince Consort and the Lady Georgina Liddell, one of Her Majesty's ladies-in-waiting, and herself the daughter of Lord Ravensworth, attended one of these breakfasts. Great preparations for this event were made at Fulham. A triumphal arch, covered entirely with evergreens, was erected in the Fulham Road opposite what is now known as "Vincent's Corner." From a

"List of Subscribers with the amount of their Subscriptions towards defraying the Expenses of the ornamental arch erected in honour of Her Majesty's and Prince Albert's visit to Lord Ravensworth at Percy Cross on Friday June 26 1840,"

we learn that the structure was designed and arranged by Mr. P. Phillips.

Lord Ravensworth died in 1855. He was succeeded by his son, Henry Thomas, 2nd baron and 7th baronet, who was born in 1797. He sat as M.P. for Northumberland from 1826 to 1830, for North Durham from 1837 to 1847, and for Liverpool from 1853 to 1855. He was created Baron Eslington, of Eslington Park, co. Northumberland, and Earl of Ravensworth in 1874. He married Isabella Horatia, daughter of the Marquis of Hertford, and died at Ravensworth Castle, 19 March 1878. His lordship was a distinguished scholar.

Ravensworth House was sold at Tokenhouse Yard, 2 July 1878, by Messrs. D. Smith, Son and Oakley.

The mansion was, in January 1879, opened by Dr. Æneas

Munroe as a hospital for women, but the scheme failed.

Ravensworth House was an old-fashioned residence, enclosed by a brick wall. It had a frontage to the Fulham Road of 187 feet. The house contained several large reception rooms and about 18 bed and dressing rooms. It overlooked beautifully timbered grounds, given, in Maclure's "Survey" of 1853, as 4a. 1r. 7p. Feathered songsters, including the nightingale, made the grounds a favourite haunt.

In 1880, Messrs. Stansfeld and Co., of the "Swan" Brewery, Walham Green, purchased the property, their old premises at the Broadway being required for improvements. The new brewery, which was built on the site of Ravensworth House, was erected from the designs of Mr. William Bradford, the contractors being Messrs. G. H. and A. Bywaters. The plant of the brewery was supplied by Messrs. H. Pontifex and Sons. We are indebted to "Noted Breweries of Great Britain and Ireland" for the following description of these extensive premises:

> "All the buildings are of red brick, with Corsehill stone dressings, and covered with Broseley tiles, and the construction throughout is of a most substantial description. Cast-iron columns, stairs and roofs; wrought-iron girders, concrete arches, and asphalt flooring have been used throughout, wherever applicable, while some portions of the plant, usually constructed of wood, such as malt hoppers and grist cases, are made of iron.
> The arrangement of the brewery is distinguished by extreme simplicity, free from any twists or odd corners, and wholly within reach of the master's eye. The plant is a sixty-quarter one, with ample space for extension in every department, when the exigencies of trade require it. Opposite the entrance gates, occupying the margin of the site, is the brewhouse, boiler and copper-house, and chimney shaft. At right angles, at one end of the block, extends the fermenting house, beer store, and loading-out stage; at the other end, divided by a roadway, a range of stables for over fifty horses, forage stores, chaff-cutting rooms, and foreman's dwelling house.
> On the frontage, adjacent to Fulham Road, there has been erected a commodious and imposing block of buildings, containing the commercial offices, wine and spirit cellars, and manager's residence. The central portion of the courtyard is enclosed and covered with a light zinc and iron roof, carried on cast-iron columns, for the accommodation of the cooperage and cask-washing apparatus, which are of an exceptionally extensive character, there being eight small

casks to wash as against every ordinary barrel of the wholesale breweries. Ample space in each department is essential for the efficient conduct of the business at this brewery, on account of the very mixed nature of its operations, which comprise, in addition to the ordinary public house trade, large deliveries of ale to private consumers, as well as a supply of wines, spirits, bottled beers, and mineral waters."

Trafalgar House, No. 637, Fulham Road, possesses little interest. The front portion, which is the oldest, was probably erected about the beginning of this century, the name, doubtless, suggesting the period of its erection. It was long a well-known laundry.

Fairlawn, now the home of the Fulham and South Kensington Branch of the Young Men's Christian Association, is a handsome, square, brick house. It was built about 1858-60, by John Dawson, from the designs of Mr. Andrew Moseley, for Dr. Henry Pawle Ree, who resided here down to 1872. Dr. W. E. Lee and Dr. Carver subsequently carried on practice here.

In 1891 the house, which had been purchased by the late Mr. G. W. Thornton, was acquired by the Young Men's Christian Association.

Fairlawn, back view.
From a photograph by Mr. H. Ambridge, 1874

The Fulham branch of this society was formed in 1879. For the first three years it had a lingering existence, holding its meetings at the "Three Cups" Coffee Tavern, Walham Green. When it was on the verge of falling to pieces, it was resuscitated, chiefly by the efforts of one or two earnest members who sought to bring it more in line with the original intention of the work. The room at the "Three Cups" ceasing to be available, the little society was removed to No. 1, Moore Park Road. Its next move was to No. 27, Barclay Road, where it remained till 1891. In January of that year the annual meeting was held at the Town Hall, but no one, at that moment, had the remotest idea of the vital epoch which was at hand in the affairs of the little struggling association. Very shortly after the annual meeting the members learned that the Barclay Road house had been sold over their heads, and that therefore they must go. It was at this juncture, when the society knew not where to look, that Fairlawn opened out. A meeting was hastily called at which it was decided to purchase the property, if the terms could be arranged, and not long after the whole thing was carried through to a satisfactory termination. The new premises were opened on 8 June 1891.

Since that date the association (which, in 1888, enlarged its sphere of operations and became the Fulham and South Kensington branch), has made rapid progress. The branch, in its present quarters, has added to its other useful features that of a boarding home for young men.

The picturesque Peartree Cottage with its fine old pear tree nailed to the wall, adjoined Fairlawn on the east side, forming, really, a portion of the Fairlawn estate. It is chiefly noticeable as having been, for many years, the home of Miss or "Mrs." Mary Ansted or Anstead, who moved here from Elysium Row. She came to Peartree Cottage in 1832, and lived here till her death, which occurred 2 March 1863, at the extraordinary age of 101. It was a tradition in Fulham that, when a baby in long clothes, she had black ribbons attached thereto as a sign of mourning on the occasion of the demise of George II. As, however, the King died 25 October 1760, while baby Ansted was not born till 28 February 1762, it is difficult to see how the story can be true. Except that she was slightly deaf, the old lady retained all her faculties to the last, and took a keen interest in literary and scientific matters. She was wonderfully cheerful and bright, with a hearty, resonant laugh, such as one seldom hears nowadays. She was aunt to the late Prof.

David Thomas Ansted, the eminent geologist. She lies buried at All Saints (see vol. I, "Fulham Churchyard" chapter).

The house, in later days known as Lawn Cottage, was turned into a laundry. In 1895 it was pulled down. Here are now the Walham Green Post Office and a Postal Sorting Office, formerly in the Broadway, Walham Green.

Peartree Cottage. From a photograph by Mr. T. S. Smith, 1894

SECTION IV: WALHAM GREEN TO STAMFORD BRIDGE

NORTH SIDE

This last section of the Fulham Road covers from Walham Green to Stamford Bridge. Midway between the south end of Melmoth Place and Jerdan Place stands the "Red Lion" (Nos. 490 and 492, Fulham Road), an old inn about which extremely little can be gathered. The first mention of it by name is in the Highway Rate books for 1770. The accounts of the Overseers for 1771 record the following payments:

> Martha Hibert being brt to Bed at the Red Lyon 2s. 0d.
> Paid the Midwife 5s. 0d.
> Relieved her at times 3s. 0d.

Since 1850, the "Red Lion" has been the home of the Peterborough Benevolent Society.

The "Red Lion." From an old photograph

Passing Broadway Buildings, we reach the "King's Head" (No. 476, Fulham Road). It is unquestionably one of the oldest inns in Fulham. An inscription in front of the house reads: "King's Head 1680." An inn, known as the "Hare and Hounds," is said to have stood on the spot three centuries ago. At a Court Baron, in 1695, license was granted to one Thomas Carlisle, "to let a certain cottage called the Kinges Head at Wansdons Greene."

Among the Sloane Manuscripts in the British Museum (No. 228 pt. II. fol. 286), is a poem, late 17th century, addressed "To Sr Ch . . . B . . . and Sir Will . . . B . . . from Epsom Wells," in which is the following reference to this house:

"We having at ye King's head din'd
Where veale and mutton, oxen chin'd
Hang on ye shambles, next we pace
To Putney's Ferry."
     (lines 5-8)

The allusion to "ye shambles" possibly points to the character of Butchers' Row, at the south end of which the "King's Head" stood. The old house was a very small inn, with a bar to the right and a taproom to the left of the entrance. It had a covered-in skittle ground.

The "King's Head" at Walham Green was one of the inns at which the Scots Greys were quartered when William IV was crowned.

The original water-colour drawing, from which the accompanying illustration is taken, bears on the back the following words:

"Butcher row
Lingham's row
Exeter place
Wandom otherwise Walham Green,
        Fulham,
                Middlesex.
1810 The Beggar's Rest now the White hart."

The old "King's Head." From an original water-colour drawing, now in the possession of John Wiltshire, Esq., made by a child in 1810

The drawing was perhaps executed from a window of the "White Hart," from which, of course, the "King's Head," Butchers' Row, etc., could easily be seen.

Walham Green Station, on the Metropolitan District Railway, was opened when the new line was extended to Putney, 1 March 1880.

The angle in the Fulham Road, where the Walham Green Station now stands, marks the commencement of old Salem Place, so called from Salem Chapel, now represented by the Wesleyan Chapel to which we shall shortly come.

Wansdown House, which lies back from the main road, was built by Oliver Stocken, the founder of the "Swan" Brewery, for his son William. It was erected about the end of the last century and called in perpetuation of the memory of the old Manor House of Wendon, which, in its later days, became incorporated in the premises of the "Swan" Brewery. William Stocken, who, in partnership with his brother, eventually succeeded to the "Swan" Brewery, was a brandy merchant, and, it is related, used to do a profitable business with smugglers whose wares he purchased. In 1879, the Wansdown House property, being required by the Metropolitan District Railway for the extension of their new line to Putney and the erection of a Station at Walham Green, was purchased of Mr. Frederick Stocken. In 1881 the house, with a portion of the site, was sold to the Wesleyan Methodists and now forms a part of their trust property.

A little further on is a handsome chapel, erected in 1891-92, belonging to the Wesleyan Methodists. It was near here that, about 1811, the first dissenting place of worship in Fulham was built.

The Wesleyan Methodist movement in Fulham originated in connection with Sloane Terrace Chapel, some of the supporters of which determined to journey to Fulham on Sundays for the purpose of holding prayer meetings, etc. A small building, which became known as Salem Chapel, was leased by the Trustees. In this primitive little chapel the Wesleyan Methodists carried on their work down to 1881, when, the lease having expired, it was decided to erect an iron church, capable of accommodating 450 persons, on the site where the permanent chapel now stands. This piece of freehold land, which had then recently been purchased by the Trustees from the Metropolitan District Railway Company, was secured for the small sum of £1,400. To the Fulham Road it has a frontage of 75 feet, and it extends back to the District Railway, a depth of 270 feet.

Old Salem Chapel was turned to secular uses, being fitted up for a shop. Its walls still remain, incorporated in the premises of Mr. Henry Jannaway (No. 452, Fulham Road).

The iron chapel was taken down in 1891, when the present structure, which seats some 700 worshippers, was built. The foundation stone, just beneath the south window, is inscribed:

> This Stone was
> laid by
> W. W. POCOCK, Esqre, B.A.
> of Wandsworth.
>
> Architect   Builders
> FRED BOREHAM.   Messrs. J. ALLEN & SONS.

The new chapel was opened 7 April 1892.

Before the building of St. John's, Walham Green, old Salem Chapel was often used by church people residing in the district, for Fulham Church was too far away, and the Fulham Road a lonely thoroughfare, which, after dark, was not altogether free from the presence of the knight of the road.

By the side of the chapel is Garden Row, a small cul de sac, at the end of which is Wansdown House.

We next come to Stamford Villas, a terrace of twenty-three houses, now incorporated with the Fulham Road. They were built between 1838 and 1840.

The first, Stamford Villa, now No. 446 Fulham Road, is of little note. Belbrook (No. 444) is associated with the memories of that versatile actor, the late John S. Clarke. Mr. W. H. Swanborough, another member of the same profession, resided here.

The next house, the Rosery (No. 442), is said by Frith in his

"Autobiography" to have been for awhile the residence of Samuel Carter Hall, of whom we shall speak in connection with Wentworth Cottage. The house was for a time the home of Napoleon III during the unhappy days of exile. Ita Villa (No. 440), long the home of the Mundays, is now occupied by Mr. W. Weeks, the florist.

No. 438 Fulham Road was formerly the property of the Earl of Stradbroke. In 1839 it was leased to Mr. Charles Beville Dryden. Subsequently it was purchased by the London and North Western Railway Company, who, in 1863, sold it to Mr. R. E. Chester Waters, the genealogist. In the same year it passed into the possession of Miss A. A. Fryer, whose executors, in 1892, sold it to Mr. David Shopland, Registrar of Births, Deaths and Marriages for Fulham sub-district and Clerk to the Fulham Burial Board.

Hermitage Lodge (No. 436) recalls the names of Dr. Mellor and Dr. Tom Godrich. At No. 432, known as Percy Villa, resided Mr. John L. Shine, another popular actor. No. 426 is the home of Mr. Ernest Rinzi, the miniaturist. No. 424 is now the Fulham Grammar School, established as the Moore Park Grammar School, in 1880, by Mr. R. E. Cranfield. At No. 416 resided, until recently, Mr. George Thorne, whose name has obtained an imperishable renown in connection with "Our Boys." Appropriately enough, he christened the house "Thorne Leigh." No. 412 has, for 22 years, been the residence of Dr. William Edward Lee, the oldest medical practitioner in Fulham.

No. 410 is associated with memories of the late Thomas Johnson, correspondent of the Paris Figaro. During his occupancy of the house, numberless distinguished persons resorted to it. For the past four years it has been the home of that brilliant figure painter, Mr. J. W. Godward. At No. 406 died 21 August 1846, Mr. A. J. Kempe, author of "A History of the Royal Free Chapel and Sanctuary of St. Martin-Le-Grand." In 1828 he was elected a Fellow of the Society of Antiquaries. He was for some time on the staff of the Gentleman's Magazine. He lies buried in Fulham Churchyard (see vol. I, "Fulham Churchyard" chapter). It was at No. 404 that Hablot Knight Browne, the immortal "Phiz," of the "Pickwick Papers," resided from 1844 to about the middle of 1846.

Between Stamford Villas and Stamford Bridge are the grounds of the London Athletic Club, which extend northwards along the

West London Extension Railway as far as the Western Fever Hospital.

No. 404 Fulham Road (the White House), the residence of "Phiz."
From a photograph by Mr. T. S. Smith, 1895

SOUTH SIDE

Facing Melmoth Place is Berwick House, the residence of Dr. R. Rouse, who committed suicide here in 1850. About 1866 it was taken by the Fulham Overseers. It was also used for Vestry purposes until the building of the present Town Hall in 1890.

From the Pound, now the site of No. 589 Fulham Road, to Bonney's Lane, now Argon Mews, was King's Row, some old cottages built about 1790.

From here to the "Swan" (No. 571 Fulham Road) were the premises of the old "Swan" Brewery, founded by Oliver Stocken in the year 1769. In connection with the brewery was a "tap," known as the "Swan," or "White Swan," one of those old-fashioned wayside inns which Dickens so admirably describes. It had pleasant recreation grounds and gardens.

There is evidence that a brewhouse and extensive hop gardens existed on the site many years before Oliver Stocken came to Walham Green, but the particulars concerning them are very scanty. In the London Evening Post, for Tuesday, 26 August to Thursday, 28 August 1740, is the following advertisement:

> "To be Lett, and enter'd on immediately For the Remainder of a Term of about eight years to come.
> A very convenient and well accustom'd Brew House at Walham Green, in the Parish of Fulham, with the Malt-house, Dwelling-house, and all Manner of useful Offices thereto belonging, and also four Acres of Hop-Ground lying behind the same.
> For further Particulars enquire of Mr. Thomas Haywood, Attorney, in Thavie's Inn, Holborn."

In 1746 Henry Temple, of St. George's, Hanover Square, was admitted to "two pieces of customary land at Wansdon's Green," on one of which was erected a messuage "known by the name or sign of the 'White Swan.' " He shortly afterwards surrendered the property to John Carwell. For these two parcels of land a yearly rent of two pence was payable to the Lord of the Manor.

Oliver Stocken, founder of the "Swan" Brewery.
From an oil painting in the possession of A. W. Stocken, Esq.

Oliver Stocken, the founder of this important brewery, came of the ancient family of Stockinge, Stockyng, or Stokyng, which seems to have been settled in East and West Anglia as early as the thirteenth century. For many years that branch of the family, from which the founder of the brewery was descended, resided at Linton, Cambridgeshire. Richard Stocken, or Stockin, grandfather of Oliver Stocken, the brewer, was buried at Linton on 19 March 1714-15, and here his son, Oliver, was buried on 15 October 1741.

The son of this Oliver Stockin, a second Oliver, was baptized at Linton on 6 June 1736. Little is known of his early life beyond the fact of his marriage with a lady named Ann Hale, a native of Sussex. Young Oliver Stocken was the first of the family to seek his fortunes in London. At Walham Green he established himself in business as the proprietor of a small ale house. The story runs that, when he brought his newly-wedded wife to Fulham - the journey being effected in a covered-in van - the good lady sat down on the doorstep of her future home and wept at the sight of its humble character.

Under the management of Oliver Stocken the business developed into a brewery of considerable note. He conducted it down to his death, which occurred at Fulham, 21 November 1808. He was buried in Fulham Churchyard. His wife predeceased him, dying 7 November 1797. They had a family of six children, Oliver Frederick (b. 1769), Thomas (b. 1770), Frances (b. 1771), Henry Charles (b. 1774), William (b. 1776) and John (b. 1777). Oliver Frederick married Ann, daughter of Dr. Layton, of Putney. <u>The marriage took place at Fulham Church, 15 May 1794</u>. Oliver Frederick Stocken died at Lambeth, where he was buried 22 December 1823. Thomas Stocken died 12 December 1784, aged 14. Frances Stocken married James Stockdale, the founder of the business of Messrs. Stagg, Mantle and Co., of Leicester Square. Henry Charles Stocken died 31 December 1793. William Stocken married, first, Sally King of Fulham, who died 9 March 1802, and, second, Mary Ann Bettesworth, daughter of John Bettesworth, of Chelsea. She died 13 September 1812. John, the youngest son, married Jane Maria Turtle, who died 15 September 1819.

On the death of Oliver Stocken the "Swan" Brewery was continued by his sons, William and John. John Stocken died 31 May 1820, the business being continued by his surviving brother William. The latter died 23 February 1824, when the concern passed to his son, Oliver Thomas Joseph Stocken, who was then only 24. The second Oliver greatly increased the popularity of the brewery, which he managed down to the time of his unfortunate failure. On 1 June 1841, the "Swan" Brewery was sold at the Mart, in one lot, by Mr. W. W. Simpson. It now passed into the hands of Mr. William Chambers, the son-in-law of Mr. O. T. J. Stocken. About 1852 Mr. Sidney Milnes Hawkes acquired the brewery. Two years later this gentleman sold it to the late Rt. Hon. Sir James Stansfeld. As stated earlier in this chapter, the old brewery was, in 1880, taken down and removed to its present headquarters on the site of Ravensworth House.

Facsimile of frontispiece of an old price list of the "Swan" Brewery

In the days of the Stockens, the "Swan" Brewery acquired a wide and justly earned celebrity. It had a very aristocratic connection, including the patronage of George IV, the Duke of York and the Prince of Saxe-Coburg. Their small beer was reputed to be better than any fourpenny ale to be obtained in Fulham. Some of the local farmers used to fetch away the waste grain from the brewery and tread it into the tubs for their pigs, which are said to have fattened upon it wonderfully!

The old "Swan" tap, in connection with the brewery, eventually developed into a well-known tavern. It remained in the hands of the Stockens down to 1840, in which year it was sold by order of the assignees of Mr. Oliver Thomas Joseph Stocken.

The Parish Books contain several entries relating to the "Swan." The Overseers' Accounts for 1787 include:

> "Expences at Walham Green with the Magistrates at Petty Sessions at the Swan at Walham Green searching the public houses for disorderly persons £2 10s. 4d."

Old "Swan" Brewery, back view. From a water-colour drawing

PEDIGREE OF STOCKEN FAMILY
(see next page)

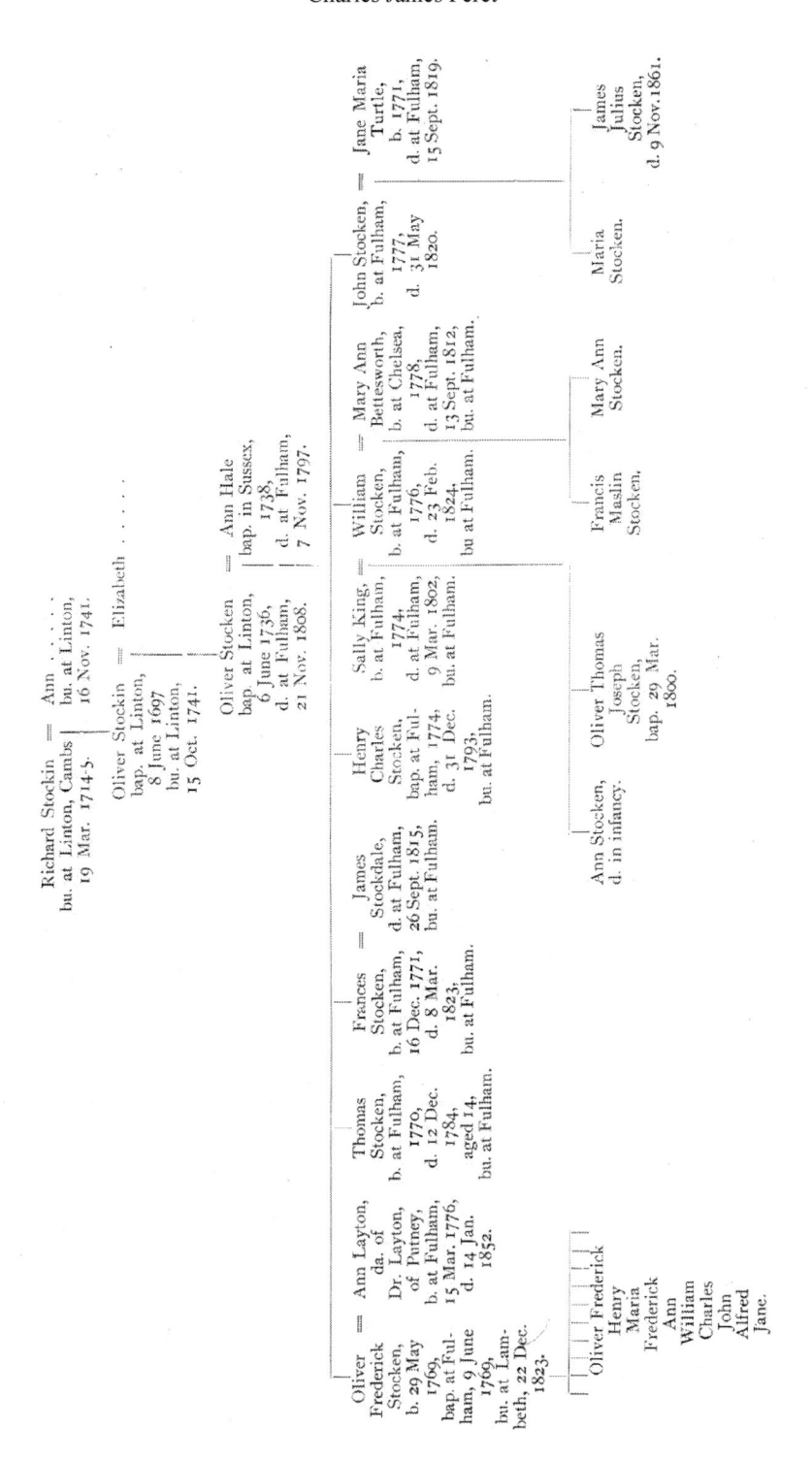

Richard Stockin = Ann ......
bu. at Linton, Cambs | bu. at Linton,
19 Mar. 1714-5. | 16 Nov. 1741.

Oliver Stockin = Elizabeth ......
bap. at Linton,
8 June 1697
bu. at Linton,
15 Oct. 1741.

Oliver Stocken = Ann Hale
bap. at Linton, | bap. in Sussex,
6 June 1736, | 1738,
d. at Fulham, | d. at Fulham,
21 Nov. 1808. | 7 Nov. 1797.

Oliver = Ann Layton, Thomas Frances = James Henry Sally King, = William = Mary Ann John Stocken, = Jane Maria
Frederick da. of Stocken, Stocken, Stockdale, Charles b. at Fulham, Stocken, Bettesworth, b. at Fulham, Turtle,
Stocken, Dr. Layton, b. at Fulham, b. at Fulham, d. at Fulham, Stocken, 1774, b. at Fulham, b. at Chelsea, 1777, b. 1771,
b. 29 May of Putney, 1770, 16 Dec. 1771, 26 Sept. 1815, bap. at Ful- d. at Fulham, 1776, 1778, d. 31 May d. at Fulham,
1769, b. at Fulham, d. 12 Dec. d. 8 Mar. bu. at Fulham. ham, 1774, 9 Mar. 1802, d. 23 Feb. d. at Fulham, 1820. 15 Sept. 1819.
bap. at Ful- 15 Mar. 1776, 1784, 1823, d. 31 Dec. bu. at Fulham. 1824, 13 Sept. 1812,
ham, 9 June d. 14 Jan. aged 14, bu. at Fulham. 1793, bu. at Fulham. bu. at Fulham.
1769, 1852. bu. at Fulham. bu. at Fulham.
bu. at Lam-
beth, 22 Dec.
1823.

Oliver Frederick   Ann Stocken,   Oliver Thomas   Francis   Mary Ann   Maria   James
Henry Maria   d. in infancy.   Joseph Stocken,   Maslin   Stocken.   Stocken. Julius
Frederick Ann   bap. 29 Mar.   Stocken.   Stocken,
William Charles   1800.   d. 9 Nov.1861.
John Alfred
Jane.

The "Swan" Brewery property included a fine old house which faced the Green. Anciently it had been known as Wendon or Wandon House, otherwise Dowbeler's tenement. Of this we shall speak when we deal with Walham Green.

It was for some time the property of the Whites of Fulham Pottery. In 1774 it was leased by William White to Frederick Nussen or Nussan, the musician, a great friend of Oliver Stocken. Here, in 1845-49, the Rev. William Garratt, minister at St. John's, resided prior to the building of the Vicarage House in Dawes Road. In Mr. Garratt's time it was much resorted to by literary men.

Mrs. Chambers, now, by second marriage, Mrs. Smith, daughter of Mr. O. T. J. Stocken, still owns the land on which the "Swan" Brewery stood. It is let on building leases.

Turning into Effie Road we come upon a yard, on one side of which is the Welsh Presbyterian Church, established here by Mr. Timothy Davies in 1897. A Welsh Sunday School was commenced at Walham Green on 1 March 1891 by the Welsh Church at Hammersmith. In October 1894 services were begun on Sundays in addition to the Sunday School. The London Welsh Presbytery decided, on 21 March 1897, that a church should be formed, and on that date 44 members were enrolled.

The present "White Hart" (No. 563 Fulham Road) marks the site of another old inn, a little quaintly-fashioned house, with a thatched roof. A house, bearing the name of the "White Hart," stood here as early as the time of Charles I. In 1632 the Churchwardens

"Pd. to one Mr. Chamberlyne a pooer mynyster lyinge sicke at ye Whytt hart att the nayboures request 1s."

In the Highway Rate books the house is first mentioned by name under the year 1771.

For nearly 45 years the old "White Hart" was conducted by the late Mr. Charles Morrison. "Charlie" Morrison was perhaps the best known man in the Fulham of his day. He was the son of a farmer. When a lad nothing would do for him but a roving life on the sea. He went, but he soon had more than he cared for. His ship got caught in a calm and provisions ran extremely short. A biscuit and a glass of water hardly constituted a diet substantial enough for "Charlie" Morrison. It chanced, however, that he had the job of attending to a number of dogs on board. These were fed on what are known as greaves, the insoluble parts of tallow gathered from melting-pots and made up into cakes. "I used to go shares with the dogs," said Morrison, recounting the story in after days,

> "though it was hardly the fare one would care for. The chaps on board used to say they were bothered if they knew how I kept my strength up, and I took care not to tell them I had a feed on the greaves."

On 28 July 1885 a curious accident occurred at the "White Hart," one of the side walls falling in, doing great damage. The house, having been rebuilt, was re-opened on 5 November 1885. It was once known as the "Beggar's Rest."

On the site of the Fulham Town Hall stood a house known as Elton Villa. Not much is known regarding its history. From 1869 to 1874 Mr. W. H. Liston, the lessee of the Queen's Theatre, lived here.

The old "White Hart."

In the grounds was a venerable mulberry tree, which tradition alleged had been planted either by Nell Gwynne or her royal lover. It was destroyed in 1888 when the Town Hall was built. Its branches were converted into walking sticks.

This handsome block of municipal buildings, erected in 1888-90, has a frontage to the Fulham Road of 91 feet, and extends back to a distance of 175 feet. The whole ground floor is devoted to official purposes, comprising the rooms of the Clerk to the Vestry, the Surveyor, the Medical Officer of Health, the Accountant, the Vestry Clerk, the Rate Collectors, etc. The Council Chamber, where the Vestry meets, is at the rear, on the ground floor. It is 40 feet long by 38 feet wide, and has at one end a public gallery. Adjoining are Committee and Sub-Committee rooms.

Fulham Town Hall.
From a photograph by the late Mr. William Appleton

The principal staircase has a double flight leading to an arcaded corridor, which extends the full length of the hall. Two other staircases lead from side entrances.

The first floor is entirely devoted to public rooms. The large hall, a very handsome apartment, occupies the whole of the central portion. It is provided with two retiring rooms, a platform and a gallery, in an arcaded recess, facing the platform. It is, inclusive of the gallery, 103 ft. 6 ins. long, 45 ft. wide and 44 ft. high. Leading from the corridor is a smaller hall or supper room, 50 feet by 40 feet, with an ante or serving room attached.

The basement floor contains kitchen offices, store rooms, cellarage, muniment room, etc.

Interior of the Large Hall, Fulham Town Hall.
From a photograph by Mr. T. S. Smith, 1895

The front facade presents an imposing appearance to the Fulham Road, rising to a height of 67 feet. It is built of Portland stone. The design is classic and of a substantial character. The architect was Mr. George Edwards, F.R.I.B.A., and the builder was Mr. Charles Wall. The contract amount was £20,438. Including the freehold site, the furnishing, etc., the total cost was £31,535.

The first meeting of the Vestry in the new Town Hall was held

29 September 1890. In 1894 the interior of the Hall was decorated by Messrs. Nepperschmidt and Herrmann. The foundation stone bears the following inscription:

This Stone
Was Laid by Frederic Horatio Fisher, Vicar,
Chairman of the Vestry
10th December 1888.

The district on the south side of the Fulham Road, between Eelbrook and Stamford Bridge, is known as Moore Park, a region of comparatively modern growth. In the Parish Books Moore Park is first mentioned in 1857, though it was planned a few years earlier. It was named after the seat of the freeholder, J. Perceval Maxwell, Esq., Moore Park, in the county of Waterford. It is intersected, east and west, by the Moore Park Road, which runs from the north end of Stamford Road to Musgrave Crescent. This road was built about 1859.

At No. 6, Moore Park Road lives Mr. Edmund L. Von Weber, the well-known sculptor. By birth Mr. von Weber is a Hungarian. After studying at Vienna, Munich, Dresden and Rome, he came to England, settling at Fulham, where he has lived for a quarter of a century.

Harwood Road, which now extends from Walham Green Broadway to the King's Road, was named in memory of William Harwood, a market-gardener who long resided in the vicinity during the earlier years of the century. The south end was built in 1868. Ann's Terrace, its oldest part, dates from 1848 and recalls the name of Mrs. Ann Harwood, the widow of William Harwood. Cedar Road, the next turning, appeared as Cedar Terrace about 1857. Waterford Road was begun in 1850. The Britannia Road, built about 1852, perpetuates, of course, the name of the "Britannia," a somewhat noteworthy house which occupied the site of the present tavern. The old house dated from about 1770. Maxwell Road, formerly Maxwell Terrace, erected about 1860, recalls the name of the freeholder, Mr. J. P. Maxwell. Cornwall Street was built in 1852.

At the junction of Moore Park Road with the Fulham Road is a granite drinking fountain, about 14 feet in height, erected by Mr.

J. Veitch, the eminent florist. It is inscribed:

> In Memory of Arthur Veitch 1880.
> "With joy shall ye
> Draw Water out of
> The wells of Salvation."
>   Isaiah xii. 3.

At the back of the column are the words "Dedicated by his brother."

The houses along the Fulham Road facing Stamford Villas were known as Moore Park Villas. Cambridge and Albert Villas were another terrace of houses, near Waterford Road.

Opposite Moore Park Villas, between Nos. 391 and 495 Fulham Road formerly stood one of the old Turnpike Gates, with a curiously fashioned octagonal toll house.

St. James's Church, which stands at the south-west corner of Maxwell Road and Moore Park Road, was erected on a piece of ground given by Mr. J. Perceval Maxwell.

The building of this church was due to one of the many religious efforts of the Baroness Burdett Coutts. The movement started in 1865, in an Iron Room, the gift of the Baroness, which stood on the site of the present vicarage house.

St. James's Church was erected by Messrs. Cubitt and Co. in 1867, at a cost of £4,118, from the plans of Mr. H. A. Darbishire. It has accommodation for about 700 worshippers. The church was consecrated by the Bishop of London (Dr. Tait) on 13 December of the same year. The Order in Council for the formation of the consolidated chapelry of St. James's is dated 14 May 1868. The new district assigned to it was taken out of the southern portion of the parish of St. John's, south of the Fulham Road.

The style of St. James's is Early English. The interior, which is considered very beautiful, has a fine wooden roof, stencil plated all over. There are twenty-nine stained glass windows, the united gifts of the vicar, Rev. W. H. Denny, Mr. George Dodd Harris, the late Mrs. Noble, Messrs. William and John Bray, Mrs. Pepper, and the late Mr. Henry Stone. There are two large oriel windows, the one on the north side representing Moses, Abraham, and the Prophets Jeremiah and Ezekiel, and the one on the south side, the Four Evangelists. The organ was built by Messrs. J. W. Walker and Sons. The pulpit is of stone, supported on marble columns. It was the gift of Mr. W. Clutton. The chancel, recently redecorated, the organ chamber and choir stalls were added in 1870, at a cost of £ 1,700.

St. James's Church. From a photograph by Mr. T. S. Smith, 1895

St. James's Church, east end.
From a photograph by Mr. T. S. Smith, 1895

There were originally two galleries, on the north and south sides, the one on the north being used for the organ and choir. These were removed when the chancel and organ chamber were added. A handsome reredos, the gift of Mr. Frederick Noble, was, in 1897, placed in the chancel.

The church plate consists of a silver flagon, paten and cup, given by the late Mrs. Baker, wife of the Rev. R. G. Baker, four additional cups, the gift of the Rev. H. Dening, and a brass plate for collections.

The Vicarage house was erected in 1871, from the designs of Mr. Ewan Christian. Adjoining St. James's, at the south-east corner, is a Parochial Room.

The present Vicar, the Rev. William Henry Denny M.A., has had charge of the church throughout.

Near Stamford Bridge was a very old footpath, which led from Fulham Road to the King's Road, called Bull Alley, from the inn of that name which stood near its southern end (see "King's Road: Waterford Road to Stanley Bridge" chapter).

At a meeting of the Vestry, held on 4 Aug. 1853, a resolution was carried assenting to a proposal, made by Mr. William Moore, to stop up

> "the Publicway or passage called Bull Alley, leading from Fulham Road to the King's Road, and to open in lieu thereof a new road of the width of 40 feet, contiguous thereto and in lieu thereof, provided that in consideration of such assent Mr. Moore do give the sum of £200 to the endowment of the new almshouses in Fulham Fields."

The roadway thus formed by Mr. Moore was named from the adjacent Bridge, Stanford Road. The name has since been changed to Stamford Road.

Stamford Bridge, which now crosses the West London Extension Railway, continuing the Fulham Road eastwards into Kensington and Chelsea, marks a point of some interest. Before we proceed to explain the curious confusion which has brought about the name "Stamford," we will quote some references to the original bridge, which, in ancient times, spanned the Creek which separated Fulham from the parishes to the east of it.

The first mention of a bridge at this point occurs in the Court

Rolls for 1410, when the Lord of the Manor was presented for his unrepaired bridge called "Samfordbregge." At a View, in 1424, it was presented that

> "The Lord should amend the bridge called the Samfordbregge where it is broken."

Again, in 1442,

> "The Lord ought to repair Samfordebregge lying between the village of Chelchehethe and ffulham."

In 1443 the name is spelled "Samfordbregge" and "Samfordesbregge." In 1450 a presentment was made for the repair of "Sampfordbregge." In 1479 the Lord of the Manor was again called upon to amend "Samfordbregge." For the first time, in 1509, we find the name spelled "Stamfordbrigge." The Court Rolls for 1569 contain the following reference to the section of the Fulham Road lying between Stamford Bridge and Walham Green, the name of the former, for the first time, appearing as "Standford":

> "Widow Tamworth and Thomas Bonde are to cut and lop their trees overhanging the Queen's Highway between Standford Bridge and Wendongrene before St. John Baptist next or (forfeit) xiid per perch."

At a Court General, in 1582, it was reported that:

> "A Bridge called Samford Bridge should be repaired by the Bishop of London and the Lord of Chelsey equally."

At a Court Baron in 1627 it was ordered:

> "No person hereafter to lay any manner of soyle or dung at Stanford Bridge unless he remove same within one month after on pain of 10s. for every month after."

In 1680 we find certain landowners presented for their ditches at "Stanforde Bridge," and elsewhere.

When the village of Little Chelsea, now West Brompton, grew to importance, the bridge was commonly called Little Chelsea

Bridge. The name is so printed on Rocque's "Map," 1741-45.

The quotations which we have given from the Court Rolls show that the oldest form of the name was Samford or Sandford Bridge, or, in other words, the bridge at the sand ford. In Sandford Manor House, hard by, the original name has, curiously enough, come down to us unaltered. The form Stamford, which, it will be observed, does not occur till 1569, is due to what grammarians term "contamination," i.e. a confusion of forms. Two bridges crossed the Creek between Fulham and Chelsea. The one on the London or Fulham Road was the bridge at the sand ford, correctly called Sandford, Sanford or Samford Bridge; the other, on the King's Road, was, as we have already observed, the Stanbrigge or Stone Bridge, doubtless from the material of which it was composed. It was simply the "contamination" of the two forms, Samford Bridge and Stanbridge which produced the spurious growth, Stamford, Stanford or Standford Bridge.

CHAPTER VII: WALHAM GREEN

The quondam village of Walham Green lies at the bend in the Fulham Road, midway between the northern and the southern limits of the parish.

Originally it was a very insignificant place, comprising some half a dozen old homesteads, mostly freelands. About the centre was the Green, a piece of Waste of the Manor. Facing it, on the site of what is now the busy Broadway, stood the ancient Manor House of Wendon or Wansdown, otherwise Dowbeler's tenement, while, dotted around in the vicinity, were other manor farms. Northward of the Green was the village pond, at which commenced a narrow lane leading to the hamlet of North End. Such, in primitive times, was the spot known as Wendenesgrene or Wendon Green.

Our first concern is to explain the name, and account for the mutation from Wendenesgrene to a form so different as Walham Green. The name has never yet been satisfactorily explained. Lysons, in his "Environs of London," says:

> "Walham Green takes its name from this manor (Wandowne); it was formerly Wendon Green, and was afterwards varied to Wandon, Wansdon, Wandham, and at last Walham Green."

A theory, which has, at least, the merit of ingenuity, has been advanced to the effect that the name Wendon has come from some such primitive form as Wodnes-dun or Woden's-down, the down or "hill" dedicated to Woden, the chief god of northern mythology. It is to Woden and to his wife Friga that we are indebted for the style of two days of our week, while the name of the former is probably enshrined in such place-names as Wednesbury, Wednesfield in Staffordshire, Wodensbury in Kent, Wedensbury in Suffolk, Wansdyke in Wiltshire, etc. It has also been urged that we should remember that, though the worship of Woden spread over all the Scandinavian lands, it found its most zealous followers in Denmark, where the god still rides abroad as the wild huntsman, rushing over land and water in the storm-beaten skies of winter.

The Danes, as we have historic evidence to show, did sojourn at Fulham during the winter of 880-81, so it is not impossible that a party of their followers may have taken the opportunity of journeying a short distance inland, along what we now call the Fulham Road, there to erect to their "All Wise" god, Woden, a rude altar before which they might worship and beg for the success of their expedition.

Let us examine the name. With regard to the first syllable, it will be observed that the variations Wendon, Wandon, etc., imply a varying vowel. The suggested solution Wōdnes-dūn or Woden's-down, would be a perfectly legitimate form as it occurs in Wēdnes-dūn. The change of the ō in Wōden to an "ē" we also find in Wednesbury and Wednesday, which likewise show the complete loss of the "d" to the ear. In Wansdyke we have the vowel change to "a," just as we have in Wansdon, etc. The ancient spellings of the name, which we are about to quote, make, however, the "Woden" theory impossible.

We will now turn to the actual history of the name. To clear the ground we have collected from a variety of sources the following list of representative spellings of the name ranging over a period of three centuries and a half, namely, from 1383 to 1732, when the present form Walham had become the recognized spelling:

1383 Wandangrene
1387 Wendanegrene
1391 Wendenesgrene
1396 Wendenesgrene
1397 Wondenysgrene
1402 Wendensgrene
1414 Wandensgrene
1422 Wendengrene
1422 Wendenesgrene
1425 Wendenesgrene
1437 Whendengrene
1442 Wendenesgrene
1442 Wendengrene
1443 Wendengrene
1445 Wendenesgrene

1458 Wendengrene
1460 Wandongrene
1465 Wendongrene
1471 Wendengrene
1474 Wandongrene
1477 Wendongrene
1480 Wendengrene
1485 Wendengrene
1486 Wendengrene
1488 Wendongrene
1491 Wendengrene
1496 Wendongrene
1507 Wandongrene
1508 Wadengrene
1509 Wendongrene
1514 Wendongrene
1526 Wandonsgrene
1540 Wendongrene
1546 Wendongrene
1550 Wendongrene
1552 Wendengrene
1554 Wandongrene
1555 Wendongrene
1560 Wendongrene
1565 Wandownsgrene
1566 Wanamgrene
1569 Wendongrene
1573 Wandongreen
1576 Wendongreen
1577 Walhamgrene
1577 Wachinggrene
1577 Wanhamgrene
1578 Wanhamgrene
1583 Wendonsgreene
1584 Wendonsgreene
1604 Wansdonsgrene
1606 Wandonsgreene
1610 Wandonsgreene
1611 Wanhamgreene

1613 Wanhamgreene
1627 Wandownegreene
1628 Walhamgreen
1646 Wandonsgrene
1647 Wandownsgreene
1657 Wandonsgreene
1658 Wanhamgreene
1665 Wandonsgreene
1666 Walhamgreene
1668 Wansdongreen
1669 Walhamgreene
1673 Wansdongreene
1675 Wadsdongreene
1675 Wandensgreene
1675 Wansdongreene
1680 Wandonsgreene
1682 Wandonsgreene
1683 Wandhamgreene
1683 Wondongreene
1690 Wansdongreene
1693 Wandownegreene
1693 Wondsdongreene
1694 Wansdonsgreene
1695 Wansdonsgreene
1697 Wansdonegreene
1700 Wansdonsgreene
1701 Walham Green, alias Wandons Green
1701 Wansdons Green
1701 Walham Greene
1705 Wansdon Green
1706 Wansdon Green
1709 Walham Green
1709 Wandowne Greene
1710 Walham Green
1710 Wansdons Greene
1710 Wodsdon Green
1713 Wansdons Green
1714 Wansdons Green
1716 Wallom Green

1717 Wansdons Green
1718 Wansdons Green
1722 Wansdown Greene
1724 Wallum Green
1724 Wansdown Green
1726 Walham Green
1727 Wansdons Green
1730 Wansdowne Green
1732 Wallom Green

 The quotation of 1383 is the earliest known use of the name in reference to the place itself, though, as a personal designation, the form (de) Wendon occurs as early as 1274.
 A careful perusal of the foregoing list will show the reader that the oldest known forms of the name are Wenden and Wendenesgreen. As a rule, the safest way to arrive at the meaning of a place-name is to consider the geographical character of the place denoted. The hill, the valley, the ford, the river, all contribute very largely to the elements which go to make up the names of the habitations of men. The neighbourhood of Walham Green is still, generally speaking, a somewhat low, flat district, but there was once a far greater difference of level. Contiguous to it, on the south, lies Eelbrook, a name which, as we have seen, means the "brook at the hill." In the Court Rolls we frequently hear of this "hill" or elevated piece of land. The village, which was formed immediately to the north of this common, would by contrast naturally appear to lie in a slight hollow. Hence the forms Wenden and Wendenes suggest that we should search for an origin which should give this sense, and, at the same time, afford us some explanation of the variations between these two forms, in the earlier spellings of the name. The Anglo-Saxon *děnŭ*, a valley, dale, was feminine and made the genitive case *děně*, which would easily be shortened to *den* in the middle of a word. But there was also a masculine form *děně*, with the same sense, which made the genitive *děněs*. Thus the variation of forms which we actually find (Wendengrene: Wendenesgrene) point strongly in the direction of these two words forming the root of the second syllable in Wenden and Wendenes. Moreover, *děnŭ* or *děně* is extremely common in many place-names, such as Tenterden, Marsden, Ealing Dene, etc.

Accepting this as the source of the latter part of the name Wenden or Wendenes, we have now to account for the former. Here the ground is not nearly so certain. Most likely the Anglo-Saxon forms, could they be traced, would be found to be Went-dene (*fem.*) and Went-denes (*masc.*). The word went occurs in the Laws of the Northumbrian priests. It is said to mean "stranger," and to occur in the Welsh *gwent*, an open region. It is also used as an old name for a part of Monmouthshire. The only form like it is the unexplained *Wen-* in Wen-lock, Wen-ham, Wen-haston and Wenn-ington. Wem-brook was formerly Wen-brook and Windrush was Wen-risc. Wen-ham would suggest that Wen was once a personal name. There are several roots to which it might belong, but, in the absence of an Anglo-Saxon spelling of the name, it is impossible to explain it with certainty.

It has been suggested that the name may possibly imply a reference to the Danes, and that therefore the Green was that of the Wen-Danes. Such a reference is, however, grammatically impossible. The Anglo-Saxon for *Danes* is *Dene*, a plural substantive, of which the genitive case is *Dena*, which, in later English, would be *Dene*; and could not, without great force, produce the genitive plural *denes* so early as 1391, when the genitive plural in -e was still in occasional use. The probability is, therefore, that the name signifies a wide, open depression.

We have now to explain the remarkable transition from Wenden or Wendenes-green to Walham Green. The change from den to ham, as shown in the foregoing list, is apparently so wanton as almost to suggest that there may have been, from the very first, both a Went-ham and a Went-dene or Went-denes, convertible names for the same place. Far more likely, however, the change arose in the following way. The foregoing list shows that, down to 1566, the latter part of the word was regularly written -den, -denes, -don. In 1566 comes the intermediate form Wanam, followed in the next few years by the -don form again. In 1577 we have the first occurrence of the present spelling Walham, to be succeeded only by an obstinate fight among the forms Wandon, Wanham, Walham and their allies, ending in a final victory for the last named.

The successive changes which have been rung upon this name were due, doubtless, to ignorance and a slovenly pronunciation.

Originally the ancient name Wendene or Wendenes was trisyllabic, as is shown by the 1397 spelling Wondenys, which, becoming dissyllabic, was clipped to Wenden or Wendens, Wendon and Wendons, Wandon or Wandons, and, by confusion as to the place of the "s," changed to Wansdon and even to Wansdons.

The intermediate form Wanam or Wanham Green arose, in all probability, from mistaken etymology with Ful-ham and cognate forms in -ham. Had it really existed from the first we should surely find some evidence of it ante 1566.

Such spellings as Waldon, Walden, Wallom, Wallon, are manifest examples of slovenliness in speech. Waldon, which was due to confusion, stands for Wandon, by change of the liquids n and l, just as flannen is now spelt flannel. The Waldon was altered to Wallon, which gave birth to Wallom, precisely as randon produced random. Lastly, the vulgar Wallom shaped itself into the more chaste Walham which the learned had devised as far back as the time of Elizabeth.

Old houses on the site of Walham Green Broadway.
After a sketch by the late Mr. Philip Vincent

Walham Green, though an interesting portion of the parish, was never the residence of the better-to-do section of the community. Bowack describes it as "a village in which lives a very considerable number of people, most gardeners, whose kitchen greens, plants, herbs, roots and flowers dayly supply Westminster and Covent Garden; here are no houses of any considerable note."

The Court Rolls contain many entries relative to Walham Green, which afford us a very fair idea of the character of the village in the olden time. In 1383 Robert Harding, a baker, was fined "xijd" for cutting down "a certain elm upon his lands at Wandangrene without license." In the minutes of a Court Baron, in 1387, it is entered:

"To this Court came John Kelle and pledged to the Lord xs for trespasses done to the Lord by cutting 16 great Elmes in the same lordship near his tenement at Wendanegrene."

The first recorded encroachment on the "common" or green occurs in the minutes of a Court General in 1422:

"John Coraunt has made a certain encroachment at Wendenesgrene accroaching to himself from the king's highway there and from a certain common and has thereon erected a new barn unjustly, to amend the same before next court or (be amerced) vjs viijd."

In 1437 John Sudbury, chaplain, and Richard Naps were presented for having boughs "overhanging at Whendengrene." John Heth was, in 1460, fined "viijd" for digging "a pit at Wandongrene for clay (luteo) without license." At a View, in 1476, the Jurors were informed by the beadle that Margaret Grenleff of "Wandongrene" was a common breaker of the hedges of her neighbours. John Grove was, at a Court General in 1507, presented because he had the "boughs of his trees overhanging the king's highway in London lane towards his lands at Wandongrene." The removal of sand, etc., from the highways of the parish was once an offence of no infrequent occurrence. At a Court General in 1561:

"It is ordered by the whole Homage that no person after this monition dig soil, clay or sand within the hamlet of Wendongrene to the nuisance of the king's lieges or in the ways, footways or way leading to the church or to the Common fields."

At a View, in 1568, William Turvyn was ordered to remove his "dunghill at Wendon Grene" before March or forfeit 3s. 4d. The following curious minute occurs in the Rolls for 1573:

> "It is ordained and agreed that Joan wife of Nicholas Hill keeps a tavern at Wandon Green obtaining a pledge of the Lord of the Manor according to the Statute and find two sufficient places (l'cos) to entertain a traveller."

In the following year Roger Bentley of "Wandon Green" was fined at a View 13s. 4d. for keeping a tavern contrary to the orders of the previous Court. In 1583 William Canon died possessed of a messuage including

> "one smith's forge (*un' fabricam ferream*), one barn, one garden, one orchard, two parcels of land called Beane haughs and one croft adjacent containing three acres situate at Wendons Grene."

Robert Okeham, "barber chirurgion," in 1605, purchased of Robert Jarvis "half a cottage at Wandons Greene." Evidently Dr. Okeham did not expect a large practice. He must certainly have been gone by 1626, for in that year, Widow Colles, chancing to break her "leege," the parish authorities had to pay 6d. to one John Gate for fetching "Mr Pou the surgun from Branford." The "seting" of the "leege" cost £1. 10. 0. In 1610 the Jurors at a View decided that "Davies the Taylor of Wandons Greene shall turn the beard of his hedge towards his owne ground." In 1611 it was ordered that

> "Allan Burton or his tenante John Weston shall make his fence sufficientlie between them and Edmunde Houlden at Wanham Green before Christmas next uppon paine to forfeit and lose to the Lord for not so doinge the same eyther of them xxs."

Down to the death of Queen Elizabeth, the population of Walham Green must have been very small. In 1625 there were only 24 ratepayers assessed, representing, say, a population of about 120. The rated inhabitants in 1633 numbered 23, and in 1649, 31.

One of the presentments at a Court General, in 1658, was in respect to a Widow Gates:

> "for that shee diuers hoggs unyoked doth keep in a hogg sty neere the Comon high way ouer Wanham Greene to the annoyance of the people of this Comonwealth therefore she is amerced vs."

Walham Green Broadway. From a photograph by Mr. T. S. Smith, 1895

In 1721 there was paid "for posts and rails" around the Green and for "ditching" at the pond, 17s. As late as 1739 only 57 persons were rated for houses at Walham Green.

The Lord's Common or Green was a triangularly shaped piece of sward along the London Road, occupying, as nearly as possible, the site of St. John's Schools, now the Broadway Buildings, reaching backwards towards the houses on the east side. A row of elms extended along this edge of the Green. In former times games were often indulged in on the Green. May-day sports were religiously observed. Sack races and climbing a greased pole for a joint of meat were the favourite pastimes of the male portion of the community, while the fair sex of Walham Green displayed their athletic prowess in running for smocks and gown pieces.

In early times the pigs of the Lord's tenants often got on the Green, damaging the turf. At a Court General, in 1476, it was presented that "Rose Baily has one pig not ringed upon the Lords

Common at Wandongrene." In 1520 it was ordered at a Court General:

> "No Tenant resident or inhabitant to permit his pigs to go and wander (ire et vagare) in the Common of the Lord at Wandongrene to scatter and root up the said common or for every pig so going iiijd. "

Bonfires on the Green on 5 November were a custom of which the boys were very fond. Cartloads of fagots would be brought here, piled in a heap and set alight, the fire sometimes burning for three days. Once it was the custom for the parish to defray the cost of bonfires. The Parish Books for 1689 contain the following:

> "It is order'd in Vestrey ye 23 of Aprill 1689 yt for ye futur no churchwarden shall hereafter bring in any charg for bonfires to this pish."

In its later years the southern end of the Green was enclosed and planted by the Stockens of the "Swan" Brewery. Occasionally the Green was called Fulham Green. In 1447 John Romsey, of Dawes Lane, was amerced "ijd" because he had placed a dunghill in the king's highway at "ffulham grene."

Walham Green had its stocks and whipping post for the punishment of petty offenders. These primitive implements of chastisement stood at the north-west corner of the Green, in the full gaze of passers-by along the London Road. The first reference to them occurs in the minutes of a Court General in 1657, when the Jurors ordered:

> "Henry Norwood to fill upp the gutter neere the Stockes in Wandons Greene which carrieth the water from before the barne into the horse ponnd before 10 April next or forfeit 10s."

Though they survived down to the erection of St. John's Schools, they had long previously fallen into disuse. The two youths last whipped here were Jack Riley, in 1826, and Thomas Henshaw, some two years later, fruit stealing being the offence in each case.

The Parish Pound immediately faced the Stocks, standing in King's Row, on the high road, its site being now marked by No.

589 Fulham Road.

The Pound was a time-honoured institution for the temporary incarceration of stray animals. Sometimes a cow or a horse, a donkey, or perhaps a pig, would betake itself to a neighbour's pasturage in preference to its owner's. If so, the trespasser was pretty sure to be escorted to the Parish Pound, with withy sticks twisted round its neck, to await its ransom.

The Pound at Fulham, anciently the poundfald, pondfald, or pinfold, existed from very remote times. Throughout the Court Rolls are scattered references to "estrays," that is valuable animals found straying in the Manor and of unknown ownership. Such animals were held until redeemed by the payment of a fine, and, if not redeemed, were appraised by the tenants of the Manor and sold. In 1442 the Jurors at a View presented:

> "That a horse colour red sorellyd which by chance came as a stray about the feast of All Saints last past is in the custody of Henry Brook the firmar."

> "That 2 sheep which chanced to come about the same time are in the custody of the said Henry."

At a Court in 1446 it was presented that a black ox had come as a stray. In the minutes of a Court General, in 1478, we find it recited that John Payne had made restitution to Robert Lovell, the bailiff,

> "for taking and leading a horse towards the Poundfald of the Lord which was upon the demesne lands in the tenure of the said Robert."

Another entry of the same date reads:

> "A heifer which came astray and remained in custody ij years, being appraised at vs was nevertheless afterwards sold by the Bailiff of this Liberty for vjs."

At a Court General, in 1543, it was reported:

> "One pig appraised 16d has come as a stray, and has been kept till since St. Luke the Evangelist last past, wherefore precept to the Bailiff to

make proclamation and the same to remain in the custody of William Holden."

At a View in 1571, it was reported that:

"One boar colour sanded with black spots has been within the Manor these 2 years as a stray and now remains in the custody of George Burton."

"Another boar as a stray has been since the feast of All Saints last and now remains in the custody of Richard Coggs."

The bailiff of the liberty or lordship of Fulham, regarding estrays as a kind of perquisite, sometimes disposed of them in other of the Bishop's Manors, over which his liberty extended, much to the grievance of the Fulham tenants whose customary right it was to appraise them and sell them as they saw fit. At a Court General in 1630, the following stringent regulation was passed:

"The Baylief of the liberty belonging to the Bishop of London for the Mannor of ffulham shall not at any tyme hereafter carry or take away any horse cowe or sheepe or any other Beast proving a stray of what kinde soe ever from out of the pishe of ffulham but there to be praysed and kept in the Custody of the Tenaunts according to the custom wch hath bin formerly used or els to forfeite to the Lord for eu'y such Beast xxxiijs iiijd."

The position of the Pound in Fulham, before 1649, is not precisely known, though, from certain entries in the Court Rolls, it is clear that it was in the immediate vicinity of Parson's Green. Why it was removed we do not know, but it is not unlikely that, when Parson's Green became the aristocratic quarter of Fulham, objection was made to the continuance there of such an humble institution. At any rate, at a Court General in 1649, the following presentment was made:

"Wee present that the fittest place (as we conceiue) ffor a pound ffor ffulham side is to bee att Wandons Greene betweene the highway and Douses Channell or between the Morris ditch and the horse pond."

The removal of the Pound to Walham Green was followed by the passing, at a View in 1649, of the following Order:

"Every tennant and Inhabitant wthin ye Mannor shall pay for every drift of Cattell yt shalbe impounded wthin ye said Mannor two pence and all other Tennts not residinge wthin the said Mannor for every such drift and impoundinge iiijd."

The first allusion to the Pound, as being actually located at Walham Green, occurs in the minutes of a Court Baron in 1695, when the will of William Dodd, gent., deceased, dated 7 February 1692-93, was read. The testator devised to his wife for life "divers lands in Wansdon Green," "lying and being in Wansdon Green aforesaid neare ye Pound."

The Pound at Walham Green was shifted about the time of George I, for, in 1727, the Bishop granted to one John Morris, junior, "one parcel of the waste at Wansdons Green upon which a pound (parcus) formerly stood." It is most probable that the Pound had previously stood on a portion of the Common, whence it was removed to the site we have mentioned on the London Road. It was evidently near the high road in 1727, for the Highway Rate book for this year records an expenditure of 9s. "To Mending the Brick Drain by the Pound."

The old Pound was a square enclosure with a gate from the road. The house next to the Pound, going southwards, was long a basketmaker's shop, kept, during the earlier part of this century, by Samuel Sexton, whence arose the stock joke that at Walham Green baskets of every description were sold "by the Pound."

The parish Pound was finally removed to the entrance to Eelbrook, down "Swan" Lane, by the side of the "Swan" Brewery.

A pond was generally an adjunct of the village green. At Walham Green it was, in its later days, separated from the Green by a block of old houses, its site now being marked by St. John's Church. At one time it was doubtless clean and undefiled, but, towards the close of its existence, it was a great nuisance to the neighbourhood. In old records it is often termed a horse-pond. In the Court Rolls the first allusion to a pond at Walham Green is in 1607. Faulkner, in 1812, remarks:

"There is a large pond adjoining the road in the centre of this village, which it has lately been in agitation to fill up, and to erect upon the site a Chapel of Ease for the use of the inhabitants, they being at so great a distance from the mother church."

A severe frost in the winter of 1814 having thrown many men out of employ, the parish authorities decided to give some of them the work of filling up the old pond. The sand for this purpose was brought from the Queen's Elm. For some years the site became a second village green, for the "chapel of ease," to which Faulkner refers, was not actually commenced till 1827.

In connection with the pond an amusing story is told of old Salter, a well-known market gardener. He was driving home from town one day, when he was importuned by some young wenches for a "lift." Salter complied, but, on reaching the pond at Walham Green, he quietly drove his cart into it, and, letting down the "tail," gave the girls a good ducking.

St. John's Church, circa 1828.
From a coloured print at the Hammersmith Public Library

In 1826 preparations were made for the erection of a church on the site of the old pond. The need had, by that time, become very urgent. The only churches which then existed in Fulham were the Parish Church, by the river side, and St. Mary's, in the extreme north of Fulham. The London Road, especially after dark, was by no means safe for pedestrians, and North End Lane was little, if any, better. Moreover, the distance from either church was very considerable.

The Rev. William Wood, at this time Vicar of Fulham, issued the following typical circular regarding the proposed new church. It is dated from the Vicarage, October 25, 1826:

> "New Church at Walham Green.
> Mr. Wood is happy in being able to inform the subscribers and the parishioners at large that, after so much painful delay, there is still reasonable hope of commencing this year to Build A Church, for which they are all so justly anxious.
> By a <u>letter from the Commissioners</u>, it appears that the plans are at length approved of in all their details; and the Architect announces, that the Builders are ready to contract for the performance of the works. The moment therefore is now arrived when the subscriptions should be realized, without which, even if the Commissioners might consent, it would not be prudent to lay the first stone.
> An account has been opened with Messrs. Child's under the name of 'Fulham Church Fund,' to which account there has been already paid the large sum of £3,324; and it is now desirable that the remaining promises should be made good without delay.
> Mr. Wood has to apologize to many respectable parishioners for not having yet given them the opportunity of sharing in this pious and noble undertaking; but he trusts that whether he calls upon them or not, they will show the same zeal as others have done for the welfare of their parish and the glory of God."

In 1826 Dr. Howley, Bishop of London, made His Majesty's Commissioners a grant of the site of the old pond, measuring 2 roods 35 poles. The conveyance describes it as a parcel of land, "part of the waste lands lying within the Manor of Fulham." As compensation for the right of common upon this piece of land, the Commissioners paid to the Churchwardens of Fulham the sum of £5 "to be applied according to the directions contained in the Act passed in the 58th year of the reign of his late Majesty King George III."

On 1 Jan. 1827 the foundation stone was laid by the Bishop of

London. The church, which was built upon arches, was completed in about eighteen months. On 14 August 1828 Dr. Howley, attended by the Rev. Herbert Oakley, his chaplain, and the principal inhabitants, and by the Rev. John Nelson, M.A., minister-designate of the new chapel, the Rev. William Wood, etc., performed the consecration.

St. John's, which was designed by Mr. J. H. Taylor and cost over £12,000, is built in the style known as Pointed Perpendicular. In plan it displays the usual arrangement of nave, aisles and chancel. The tower, which is situated at the west end, is considered by some to be too narrow, being of less breadth than the nave of the church. The west front is, in consequence, vertically divided into five portions. The central is occupied by the tower, which advances about half its plan beyond the nave. It is divided into three principal stories, the exterior angles being supported by buttresses. The whole is surmounted by an embattled parapet, having crocketed pinnacles at the four corners, displaying a curious medley of styles.

St. John's Church. From an original water-colour drawing by R. B. Schnebbelie, 1828, in the possession of the Author

On either side of the west door is a smaller door of corresponding design. The aisles have arched windows bounded by neat cornices. Each aisle is made by the buttresses into six divisions, having windows similar to those in the west end. In the clerestory the windows are similar to those in the aisles, though, of course, smaller in size. At the east end, the chancel is lit by a handsome three-light lancet window, similar in design to those in the tower. It was originally filled with painted glass, representing the Transfiguration (after Raphael). This window, which was renowned for the beauty of its colouring, was blown in during a great snowstorm which occurred on 17 January 1881. The present window, which cost £200, represents our Blessed Lord as Prophet, Priest and King. The central light was the gift of the Rev. W. E. Batty and his brother, the Rev. G. Stanton Batty, in memory of their mother, Mrs. Agnes Batty. The clergy vestry, with windows in the square-headed Tudor style, occupies the angle between the end of the south aisle and the chancel.

St. John's Church. From an engraving by E. Rouse, circa 1828

The interior is plain and neat. The lower story of the tower forms a porch at the west end, and a part of the nave is appropriated for a vestibule communicating with the aisles, a portion being occupied by the staircases which lead to the galleries. The latter run east and west nearly the whole length of the church and across the west end. The aisles are separated from the nave by five pointed arches, supported by piers octagonal in plan.

The roof consists of an open frame of timber, perhaps the finest feature of the interior.

In 1893 extensive alterations were carried out at St. John's. The old high pews were removed and the church was completely reseated. The windows, except that at the east end, were taken out and replaced by others more in accordance with modern ideas. The north and south galleries, which had extended the whole length of the aisles, were shortened by the removal of the portion in the easternmost bays, which were filled in with oak screens. The choir, which had formerly been located in the organ gallery, was accommodated with stalls in front of the screens. The galleries, which are of oak, were much improved in appearance by the removal of the coats of varnish which had obscured the wood. The alterations, which were carried out from the designs of Mr. E. P. Warren, cost about £1,600.

St. John's Church, east end.
From a photograph by the late Mr. William Appleton

The original pulpit and reading-desk were a curious feature. They stood in front of the altar, the pulpit to the north and the desk to the south. They were high wooden structures, irregular octagons in plan. The desk was removed about 1861, being replaced by a smaller one. The old pulpit survived till the restorations of 1893, when the present small oak pulpit was erected.

St. John's Church, after the 1893 restoration

The original reredos, beneath the east window, consisted of three arches covered with angular pedimental canopies, crocketed and divided by buttresses groined with pinnacles, executed in composition in imitation of stone. This reredos was removed in 1893. The present handsome sanctuary hangings were the gift of Mrs. Hailstone, of Elm Park Gardens, Chelsea. The altar, which is of plain oak, is approached by two stone steps. The brass candlesticks upon the altar were also the gift of Mrs. Hailstone.

The font consists of an octagonal basin supported on a pillar, and has a cross purée in a quatrefoil in each face. It formerly stood in a pew near the western entrance. In 1893 it was removed to the south-west corner. On the occasion of the alterations, a choir vestry was added. This was placed at the south end of the spacious vestibule, facing the font. The organ, which is in an oak case, stands in the centre of the west gallery. It was built by Mr. Bates.

The clock in the tower has three faces. Its cost, including that of a dial for the inside of the church, was 114 guineas.

The church, as originally seated, accommodated 826 persons in pews and 544 in free seats, making a total of 1,370. The accommodation is now for 797 persons. In 1893 pew rents were abolished.

St. John's Church. From a photograph by Mr. T. S, Smith, 1896

St. John's remained a chapel-of-ease to Fulham until December 1835, when, by an Order in Council, it became a separate ecclesiastical district under the name of " St. John's, Walham Green," in accordance with 59 Geo. III, cap. 134. Under

19 and 20 Vic., cap. 104 (Lord Blandford's Act), it became a distinct ecclesiastical parish.

The present church plate, purchased in 1879, consists of the following articles: 2 silver chalices, 1 silver flagon, 2 silver patens, 1 brass ewer for font and 1 brass alms dish. The brass ewer for the font was the gift of Mrs. Edmund Batty.

In the churchyard no less than 532 persons lie buried. The first interment took place on 10 March 1836 and the last on 24 October 1853, on which latter date the churchyard was closed by an Order in Council. The existing headstones number under a dozen.

The successive incumbents of St. John's have been:

MINISTERS
Nelson, Rev. John, M.A. 1828 to 1838.
Caddell, Rev. Henry, M.A. 1838 to 1845.
Garratt, Rev. William, M.A. 1845 to 1862.

VICARS
Batty, Rev. W. Edmund, M.A. 1862 to 1892.
Vincent, Rev. George Herbert, M.A. 1892 to -

The St John's national Schools were commenced in 1836, the site on which they were built being the ancient village green. The erection of the schools was gratuitously superintended by the architect, Mr. Browne, to whom the Building Committee were indebted for the original plans. The contract was carried out by Mr. James King. The boys' and infants' schools were opened on 18 July and the girls' school on 12 September 1836. The cost of the schools, exclusive of furnishing, was £797 4s. 5d., while the gross amount of grants, subscriptions, etc., was £880 5s. 2d. During the first year of the existence of the schools, the children numbered: boys, 111; girls, 73; and infants, 76.

In 1846 the schools were enlarged. By deed, dated 11 Novenber 1846, made under the Schools Sites Acts and enrolled in Chancery, 5 December 1846, the Bishop of London formally conveyed to the minister and churchwardens of St. John's, as Trustees, "the triangular piece of land, formerly waste of the Manor, situated at Walham Green."

In 1867 a drinking fountain, erected at the public expense, was placed at the south end of the schools. It was built of stone from old Blackfriars Bridge.

As the site had become no longer suitable the Trustees, in 1894-95, pulled down the schools and rebuilt them on a site at the rear of Mitford Buildings, Dawes Road. Broadway Buildings occupy the site of the old schools.

St. John's National Schools, Walham Green.
From a coloured print at the Hammersmith Public Library

Melmoth Place extends from Shorrold's Road to the "George Hotel." The west side of this Place, along the high pavement, was formerly known as The Terrace, Walham Green Terrace, or St. John's Terrace. The row of houses along it, pulled down in 1897, was built about 1785. At No. 8 lived, from 1852 to 1866, a noted Waterloo veteran, Major William Maclean.

No. 10, Melmoth Place was the site of the original "Cock," one of the old inns of Fulham. It is believed to date from 1713. In 1813 the "Cock," together with four other lots of freehold and copyhold property in Fulham, was sold at Garraway's. In the auctioneer's particulars of sale it is thus described:

> "The Cock: The particulars of a valuable estate part freehold and part copyhold consisting of a well established public house called the Cock situate at Walham Green together with four pieces or parcels of land situate in Fulham field in the parish of Fulham, in the county of Middlesex, which (by order of the trustees of Mr. William Maton, deceased), will be sold by auction at Garraway's Coffee-house in 'Change-Alley, Cornhill, London, on Friday, the 17th of December 1813 at twelve o'clock, in five lots."

The first lot, which consisted of the tavern, is thus described:

"Lot 1 Copyhold. A substantial brick dwelling house, commonly called or known by the name of the Cock Public House, very desirably situate at the north west Corner of Walham Green, by the Road leading from the said Green to North End, in the parish of Fulham, and County of Middlesex, and now in the Tenure or occupation of R. Goodwin, as Under-tenant to Messrs. Meux, Benson and Young, who hold the Premises on lease, of which seventeen years will be unexpired at Christmas, 1813, at the low yearly Rent of £25 payable Quarterly, clear of all taxes (except the Land and Property Tax)."

The other lots were in Fulham Common Fields.

Old houses which stood on the site of St. John's Terrace, a pencil sketch in the possession of the Author.

In the early part of the present century, its best known landlords have been John Price, Ed. Sadler, and Cox. In 1845 Mr. Cox sold it to Mr. Charles Agar, from whom it passed to his son, Mr. F. W. Agar, and, in turn, to the latter's son, the present Mr. Charles Agar.

Until 1894 there swung in front of the house an interesting sign, painted on mahogany. Mr. Agar, who had it sawn through the centre, has placed the two halves, on each of which a cock is depicted, in his bar. In 1894-95 the old house was pulled down, when the present "Cock Hotel" was erected, the site being increased by the inclusion of No. 8, Melmoth Place. The new hotel is a fine building. The Arcadian annexe, which adjoins the saloon bar, decorated with palms and other plants, makes a delightful lounge.

The old "Cock." From a photograph by Mr. T. S. Smith, 1894

No. 24 Melmoth Place was a baker's shop, taken by Mr. Charles Griffin, senior, on his removal, about 1810, from the ancient tenement at the south-east corner of Dawes Road. Here he died in 1840, and here his son, the last parish constable, continued the shop for ten years longer.

At the rear of No. 26 Melmoth Place, rebuilt by Mr. W. J. Furber in 1897, a curious discovery was made. Beneath what had been a kitchen was found a kind of chamber, the walls of which, on the north and south sides, were 14 feet, and on the east and west, 10 feet long. When found, it was filled with fine earth. When this was removed, a red brick floor was revealed, about 12 feet from the top of the chamber. Near each of the four corners of the floor was a well, about 10 feet deep. On the north side of the room were two semicircular arches, from one of which a flight of steps led to the bottom of the apartment.

A little further along Melmoth Place, then South Parade,

between Dawes Road and the "George," was a small turning, known, from Joseph Lewis, a farrier, as Lewis's Yard. It was at the corner of this Yard that the first regular Police Station was established.

In ancient times the police force in the entire Manor of Fulham numbered six men: a constable and two capital pledges or headboroughs for Fulham, and a similar service for Hammersmith.

In 1583 one John Pulton was constable for Fulham. Lysons gives the following extract from the now lost Churchwardens' Accounts:

> "*Anno* 1583. Note of the armore for the parish of Fulham, *viz*. Fulham side only. First a corslet with a pyke, sworde and daiger; furnished in all points, a gyrdle only excepted. Item, two hargobushes with flaskes and towch boxes to the same; two morryons; two swords, which are all for Fulham side only; all which armore are and do remayne in the possession and appointment of John Pulton of Northend, being constable of Fulham-syde the yere aboue wrytten.
> N.B. All sett (qy. sent) owte into Flanders anno 1585, by Rowland Fysher, except one hargobusse with flaske and towch boxe, one murryon with sword and dagger remayning in his hands."

The office of constable appears to have been an annual one, and exemption from service could be secured only by the payment of a fine. William Williams, a baker of Fulham, was, in 1689, fined £5 for declining to serve.

In 1802 Messrs. T. C. Porter and John Druce, two local justices of the peace, "acting in and for the County of Middlesex and residing in the parish of Fulham," laid down a "ratio to be observed in the charges of the constables and headboroughs of the said parish" for certain special services. One of these ran:

> "To each officer on the 5th of November, when directed by the parochial magistrates to go round the parish to prevent squibs and crackers being thrown and it appears they do attend and do their duty accordingly 2s. 6d."

As late as the beginning of this century only three constables were employed to maintain order. It is, therefore, not surprising that robberies and outrages began to grow numerous. After nightfall the high roads leading to Fulham were exceedingly dangerous. So serious did matters become that, in 1810, the Vestry appointed a Committee to prepare a plan for "An association against robberies and other depredations committed within this parish." At a meeting held on 21 November 1810 a series of resolutions were adopted. The first of these ran:

> "It is the opinion of this meeting that the most effectual method of discovering and punishing offenders in the case of robberies committed within this parish would be by the respectable housekeepers themselves patrolling the parish at proper periods, suitably armed and under the directions of persons to be hereafter named, and by offering rewards and holding out protection and indemnity to all who may be able to give intelligence respecting the offenders and by prosecuting such offenders at the general expense."

In order to carry out this scheme, a society was formed, called the Fulham Association against Robberies, consisting of such householders in the parish as were willing to become subscribers to the fund. The Association seems to have been short-lived, for we hear little more of it. Robberies from farms and private houses, highway outrages, etc., continued apace. In 1818 the Fulham Vestry again set itself to adopt

> "such measures as may seem expedient for the protection of their property against the depredations of robbers and for putting a stop to the shameful practices of loose and disorderly persons on the Sabbath day."

At a meeting of the Vestry on 11 June 1818, it was resolved:

> "That in consequence of the frequent robberies lately committed in this parish, an association be now formed for the mutual protection of the persons and property of those who shall become members by subscribing to a general fund for the support of it.
> That the subscriptions shall be in any proportion which may seem fit to the subscribers themselves, nevertheless that they shall not be less than 10s. each."

This second Association did not long survive. Even as late as 1825 there were only five constables in Fulham.

In 1830 a proposal was made to establish a system of Parochial Police, under the control of the Vestry, to be paid out of the parish rates. This scheme, we learn, was "with the view of averting the more expensive measure which it is in the power of the Government to introduce into the parish" - an ingenious piece of opposition to the reorganisation of the police force which Sir Robert Peel, as Home Secretary, was then carrying out. At a further meeting it was found that the Vestry had no power to make a rate for paying a parochial police, so it was, for the third time, resolved:

> "That an Association be formed, as heretofore, for the mutual protection of the persons and property of those who shall become members of it by subscribing to the fund for the support of it."

This scheme proved as abortive as its predecessors. The Vestry, as a last effort, sought permission for a deputation of the inhabitants to wait on Peel, to urge the objections of the inhabitants to the proposed new police. On 28 January 1830, the Rev. William Wood reported to the Vestry

> "that he had been honoured by Mr. Peel with a very friendly conference on the subject of extending the new police to Fulham and that he had been dismissed with the following answer: 'I cannot give you an assurance that the new police will not be extended to Fulham; Government may see fit to do it for great reasons of their own, but so far I will say that you are not in danger of it at present.'"

Eventually Fulham had to fall in with the rest of London in the matter of "peelers." As already stated, a police station was, in 1830, established in Lewis's Yard, where about a dozen men were stationed.

No. 62 Melmoth Place, now occupied by Mr. T. H. Belcher, was long the residence of Mr. John Knight, "the King of Walham Green." He was by far the largest butcher in Fulham, often having, at a time, a score of bullocks and fifty sheep on his premises for slaughtering.

The east side of Melmoth Place consists of a terrace of old houses formerly known as Carpenter's Row. About the centre of the row still exists a weather-beaten stone inscribed:

R. E.
Carpenters Row
1768

In 1877 subsidiary names were abolished, the thoroughfare being re-christened Melmoth Place.

Jerdan Place runs from Melmoth Place to Fulham Road, and thence to Vanston Place. It was formerly known as Market Place, a name which was abolished in 1877, together with the subsidiary names of Frederick Place and Prospect Place. On the west side of Jerdan Place were formerly some old tenements known as Wells Cottages.

Jerdan Place. From a photograph by Mr. T. S. Smith, 1895

The three ancient houses on the east side of Jerdan Place (Nos. 1, 2 and 3, shown in the above view are probably two centuries old.

The quaint tenements from Farm Lane to the north end of Jerdan Place were named Pond Place. The name, now abolished, of course recalls the pond which once faced it. Some of the houses here are very old.

Vanston Place, which runs from the North End Road to Fulham Road, is another new name, devised in 1877, to supersede two or three subsidiary names. From Walham Grove to Farm Lane the houses were known as Robert's Row. From Farm Lane to the site of the Butchers' Charitable Institution was Farm Place, previously King's Place. From here to the Fulham Road was Exeter Place or Lingham Row, named after Thomas Lingham, who resided here down to 1817. An earlier name for this line of old houses was Butchers' Row, an appellation which is suggestive of the trade of its inhabitants. The parish records contain numerous references to the butchers of Walham Green. Here are two from the Churchwardens' Accounts:

1639 "pd to Kich a butcher to relieve him in his sickness at Wandon greene at seuerall times 12s. 0d."

1639 "pd. more to the butcher 3s. 0d."

1640 "Itm to Thomas ___ a butcher at Wandon Greene in tyme of sickness 4s. 6½d."

Pond Place. From a photograph by Mr. T. S. Smith, 1895

No. 17 Vanston Place, at the north-west corner of Farm Lane, is an old inn, known as the "Maltsters." In Rocque's "Map," 1741-45, a house is marked here, but nothing whatever can be gathered as to its history. It is highly probable that, facing Walham Green Pond as it did, it was identical with a house called in the Court Rolls for 1606-7 "the Pond head on Wandons greene." The present house appears to be some 200 years old. Many years ago a quantity of coins, some as early as the second Charles, were found during some alterations to the room over the bar. Between the floor of this room and the bar ceiling the space was filled with sand, which had percolated through the crevices. It was in this sand that the coins had lodged. At the same time a mummified cat was discovered. The house has, in recent times, been much enlarged.

"The Maltsters." From a photograph by Mr. J. Dugdale, 1896

On the east side of Vanston Place is the Butchers' Charitable Institution, founded 16 October 1828. The object for which it was established was to afford Charitable relief to decayed and distressed master butchers, master pork butchers, cattle and meat commission salesmen, hide and skin salesmen, their widows and orphans. For some years the relief thus given took the form of "out-pensions" only. In 1839, James Julius Stocken, son of John Stocken, the brewer, sold to the institution a piece of land, about three acres, known as "Knight's Field," on which a row of almshouses was commenced. On 1 July 1840 Lord Ravensworth laid the first stone.

Year by year the two little rows of picturesque Gothic houses have lengthened out as friends have come to help the institution on. There are now about 150 pensioners on the society's books, about half of whom reside at the almshouses, the rest receiving out-pensions. The annual expenditure of the institution averages about

£5,000.

The houses are built in two rows, running east and west. Those which were erected in 1840-42 consist of the first five or six in the north row, including the lodge adjacent to Vanston Place. On the west side of No. 1, near the ground, is the foundation stone. It is inscribed:

Anno Domini
1840.

Near the middle of the north row is a building containing a fair-sized room, used for Committee meetings, prayers, etc. Beyond this is a newer part.

The Butchers' Almshouses (north side).
From a photograph by the late Mr. William Appleton

On the south side there is a lodge, corresponding to the one on the north side. Next to this are some houses erected in memory of the late Prince Consort. The first one is inscribed, on the west side,

Albert Memorial.
These houses were erected
By the friends of the
Butchers' Charitable Institution
To perpetuate the memory of their late Patron
His Royal Highness the Prince Consort
A. D. 1863.
"Blessed is he that considereth the poor."

A memorial stone is inscribed:

> The foundation stone of the
> Albert Memorial
> Was laid 25 March 1863 by
> Francis Healey, Esqre
> J.P. President.

In continuation of the Albert Memorial, other houses have since been erected.

It is a fact possessing a melancholy interest that Mr. John Knight, who rented from the Stockens the site of this institution, a man at one time worth £20,000, died a pensioner in these almshouses.

The Butchers' Almshouses (south side).
From a photograph by the late Mr. William Appleton

Passing Jesmond Cottage, we come to Hope Bower, formerly Jesmond Villa. From Vanston Place we enter by a little gate. Before us lies a piece of pleasant sward and a neatly-kept garden. Beyond this, at a considerable distance from the road, is Hope Bower, the home, for over forty years, of Mr. S. J. Walden.

Between Farm Lane and Exeter Place nearly all the land, on the east side of Walham Green, was, in the last century, in the possession of the Whitbreads of Bedfordshire, the famous brewers. In 1802 Samuel Whitbread sold certain portions of the family estates. That at Walham Green, consisting of 5a. 0r. 22p., was purchased by John Stocken, son of Oliver Stocken, of the "Swan" Brewery. At the time of the sale the land was in the occupation of William Layton of Mullincer House, Putney, a "horse doctor" (whose daughter Ann married Oliver Frederick, eldest son of Oliver Stocken), and of William and James Maton, market gardeners. These 5a. 0r. 22p. included "Knight's Field," sold by J. J. Stocken in 1839, and the sites of Jesmond Villa and Claremont Villa.

Jesmond Villa or "Bower," as it was occasionally called, was built by John Stocken shortly after his purchase of the land. Here he resided till his death which took place in 1820. Shortly afterwards the Jesmond Villa property was purchased by the Waldens.

Mr. Samuel Walden, a successful London tradesman, came to settle at Fulham in 1823. In this year he purchased a small estate at Eelbrook on which he built Pomona House. Thence he moved to No. 8 Exeter Place.

Mr. Walden is best remembered as the prime mover in the foundation of the Peterborough Benevolent Society, of which he became the first president. It is a strange fact that this institution owes its existence, at least indirectly, to the great Reform Bill. On 6 June 1832 Lord John Russell's famous measure became law. The men of light and leading in and around Walham Green determined to celebrate this great event in a manner still dear to the present generation of Englishmen, namely, by means of a big dinner, to which they invited the poor of the parish. In the month of July of that year, the dinner came off at Claremont Villa, Walham Green, Mr. S. Walden himself occupying the chair. The rejoicing was great and the feeling round the festive board on that memorable evening was that the passing of the Reform Bill ought to be marked in Fulham by the accomplishment of something tangible. Walden thought over the matter very seriously. In his capacity as Overseer of Fulham, he had to collect the poor rate and go to the old Workhouse to pay the poor, as was then the custom. This brought him into contact with numerous sad cases and he saw many there who, he thought, might be kept off the parish if only a little aid were rendered to them in their distress.

In the bar parlour of the "Peterborough Arms" several of the leading men of Fulham were accustomed to assemble. Driving home from London one night, Mr. Walden, as usual, paid a visit to the "Peterborough." Here he chanced to meet a small party of friends, comprising Mr. Knight, Mr. John Butt, Mr. W. H. Richmond, Mr. Blackey, Mr. G. Strutton and Mr. James Young. The scheme these seven gentlemen discussed was that which had been mooted at the dinner at Claremont Villa a few months before, *vizt.*, the establishment of some charity which should commemorate the passing of the Reform Bill. "What shall we call ourselves?" one and the other asked. Mr. Butt said, "Let us form a society, to give poor creatures in distress a little money or a few coals." "So we will, Butt," said Mr. Walden. Thereupon Mr. Butt proposed and Mr. Walden seconded a proposition to establish a benevolent society for Fulham. The proposal was agreed to and thus the society started. Mr. Butt was elected its first secretary. This memorable meeting at the "Peterborough," was held on 12 June 1833.

For some years the institution was called simply the Benevolent Society, but, in 1867, when other charitable agencies had sprung into existence, it became necessary to give it a distinctive name, and so it was called the Peterborough. The Peterborough Benevolent Society was inaugurated on a Wednesday, and on that day its members have ever since met. Down to 1850 the members used to assemble at the "Peterborough Arms," but in the following year they migrated to the "Red Lion" at Walham Green.

From No. 8 Exeter Place, Mr. S. Walden retired to Merton Villa, Slough, where he died, 14 July 1863. His son, Mr. S. J. Walden, moved to Jesmond Cottage, which his father had partly built, and finally to Jesmond Villa, which he renamed Hope Bower.

Adjacent to Hope Bower, on the south, is Claremont Villa, which was also built by the Stockens. Here resided Frederick Stocken, son of Oliver Frederick Stocken, and the step-sons, Messrs. Cullum and Sharpus, whose business is now of world-wide reputation. It was in the grounds, which measure 1a. 0r. 10p., behind this house that the Reform Dinner, to which we have just alluded, was held.

Just at the back of St. John's Church is Farm Lane, a bit of old

Fulham, which has fallen on evil days. In Rocque's "Map," 1741-45, there are no houses shown on either side of it. Long subsequent to this date splendid orchards lined both sides of the lane.

Farm Lane. From a photograph by Mr. H. Ainbridge.

Down to 1825 there were but three houses in Farm Lane, namely the High House, at the top, Wynyaw House, and a noted laundry known as "Pat Power's" at the bottom.

Wynyaw House was long the residence of Samuel Webb, a wealthy and eccentric man. The grounds, which included an extensive farmyard and meadow, measured 4a. 2r. 30p.

Farm Lane. From a photograph by Mr. T. S. Smith, 1896

The name Farm Lane does not occur in the Parish Books till 1806. The appellation is doubtless due to the ancient farm called Chayhames or Cheames, of which we shall presently speak.

An old house in Farm Lane. From a photograph by Mr. T. S. Smith, 1896

The **Manor of Wendon,** otherwise Dowbeler's Tenement, lay between Eelbrook and the Fulham Road, the ancient Manor House facing the Green, on a portion of the site now known as the Broadway.

In the Court Rolls these freelands are never spoken of as the Manor of Wendon, but as Dowbeler's tenement, after one John Dowbeler.

About 1440 this messuage was, together with other property, sold by Nicholas Philpot and William Huntley to Sir Thomas Hasele, of whom we have spoken in connection with the Manor of Rosamond's (see "Parson's Green: Parson's Green Lane" chapter). In 1442 we find Sir Thomas presented for having "encroached on the Common at Wendensgrene."

On his death, about 1448, his widow, Dame Agnes Hasele, continued to hold the property, but, on her remarriage with Gilbert Debenham, she alienated the messuage to Sir Henry Waver, kt., a kinsman. On his death, in 1469-70, his widow, Christian, inherited all his lands in Fulham, etc. She died in 1479, but she probably disposed of Dowbeler's in her lifetime.

In 1492, Dowbeler's was in the occupation of Thomas Broun or Browne. In the following year we find the Essex family here. This powerful family held lands in different parts of the Manor of Fulham. William Essex, in 1460, was fined 4d. as a tenant in default. In fact he was generally absent from the Lord's Courts. He died in 1481. Between 1485 and 1512 we hear of Thomas Essex, doubtless the heir of William. At a Court in 1508 the following presentment was made:

"The lands of Thomas Essex have branches overhanging the way leading from Fulham to Wandon- grene." (i.e. the Fulham Road).

His son, Sir William Essex, knight, succeeded to the estates. In 1512 Sir William was required to scour his ditch "between Dowys-canell and Helbroke." (See first reference note for "Walham Green.") This was doubtless as the tenant of Dowbeler's. Sir William died in 1548. At a Court General, held in this year, his son, Thomas Essex, was admitted.

The Manor House of Wendon, latterly incorporated in the premises of the old "Swan" Brewery

The will of Sir William, dated 27 January 1547-8, was proved 18 Aug. 1548 (P.C.C. 12 Popuwell). The testator, who seems to have possessed lands in a dozen English counties, left all his "Manors, Lands, hereditaments, Rentes, Annuities, reversions, and services in Westowne, Wandons, Butterwyks, Kensington, ffulham, Westmynstr and Yeling" to his son Thomas Essex the younger.

At a Court in 1550 it was ordered that:

"Thomas Essex Esq. be distrained for Relief on the lands whereof his father Sr William Essex died seized *viz.* a tenement at Wendengrene formerly John Dowbeler and after of John Hasele and late of Henry Whafer,"

and other lands.

The Essex family held Dowbeler's till the reign of Elizabeth. It was next alienated to John Tamworth of Parson's Green. In 1565 he settled the "Manor of Wandowne" upon his wife, Christian. He died in 1569. Next it passed into the possession of Thomas Sidney. This gentleman sold the estate to Sir Thomas Knowles, who, as we have seen, in connection with Parson's Green, inherited Tamworth's lands at Fulham. Knowles sold Dowbeler's about 1603. The purchasers were Nehodiajh Rawlin, Rawlins or Rawlings and William Danson.

A room in the old Manor House of Wendon

The name of Nehodiajh Rawlin appears in the Rate books down to 1641. The portion of Dowbeler's estate held by the

Dansons seems to have lain westwards of Rawlin's estate, near Cowlese, a portion of the Manor of Rosamond's.

On the death of William Danson the land was held by his widow, "Mistress Danson," and her son John. John Danson's name occurs in the parish records down to 1625.

Dowbeler's messuage or Manor of Wendon or Wandown was subsequently cut up. A large part of it came into the possession of the Stockens of the old "Swan" Brewery. The ancient tenement, attached to the brewery and overlooking Walham Green, may be regarded as the surviving representative of the Manor House of Wendon. With the later history of this house we have dealt in our account of the "Swan" Brewery (see "Fulham Road: Walham Green to Stamford Bridge" chapter).

Other ancient tenements of note at Walham Green were Green's, *alias* Bird's, Goldhawk's, Chayhame's, Symonds', Lane's, Towes' and Edgehill.

Of Green's we hear as early as 1447. From 1573 to 1580 it was the property of John Powell, of whom we have spoken in connection with Munster House. Its precise position is unknown. Goldhawk's was so called after John Goldhawk atte Sonde, of whom we shall speak under Sands End. It is first mentioned in the Court Rolls under the year 1395. This old farmstead, which lay between Dawes Lane and Fulham Road, passed through numerous hands. At a Court, in 1510, the Lord's bailiff was ordered to seize "a tenement called Goldhawkes at Sond at Wendon Grene," of which one Thomas Stoddert, had made waste. We last hear of it about the middle of the eighteenth century. The houses on the west side of the south end of Melmoth Place probably mark the eastern limits of Goldhawk's messuage.

Chayhame's, Cheame's or Sheame's was an extensive farm which was situated south of Beaufort House grounds, reaching as far as Farm Lane. It owed its name to one Robert de Chayham, who owned it in the time of Edward II. In a re-grant, in 1392, to John Sampford, the messuage is described as "one tenement and eleven acres of wareland." The Rev. Matthew Kerby, S.T.P., who died in 1722, left "Sheames" to his only daughter, Mary, who had married Sir James Edwards, bart., of Walton on Thames. The old farm house, which stood at the east end of Farm Lane, survived till about 1816. Symonds' tenement, which is referred to in the Rolls as early as 1461, stood at the "south end" of Walham Green. The last we hear of it is in 1704, when Sir Michael Wharton was chosen reeve for it. Lane's tenement was situated on the west side of North End Road, near Walham Green. It was named after the Lanes. John Lane, the last of the family, owned it circa 1410. It next passed to the Leventhorps through the marriage of Joan, daughter of John Lane, with John de Leventhorp. In 1438 John Hasele, "clerk to the Crown of our Lord the King," purchased the estate of John de Leventhorp. The subsequent history of Lane's is mainly identical with that of Rosamond's at Parson's Green. It eventually came into the hands of the Whartons.

Lane's Tenement: Deed of feoffment dated 24 April 9 Eliz. (1567), in the possession of the Author

Of Towes' tenement we hear as far back as 1386. Its precise position at Walham Green is doubtful. Edgehill was, in the reigns of Elizabeth and James I, the residence of John Powell, who died in 1606, leaving an only child, Elizabeth, wife of Sir William Stonehouse, bart. Sir William and Lady Elizabeth Stonehouse appear to have let the house. In the Poor Rate Assessment book for 1640 appears the following entry:

"The Lady Eliza Stonehouse 5s.
Nil sol. quia nemo habitat in domo," [no money (collected) because no one lives in the house.]

and in 1641:

"Itm for the Lady Stonehouse the tenn^{te} beinge dead and gone, and ye new tenn^{te} not to be charged 7s. 6d."

In 1647 Dame Elizabeth Stonehouse was elected reeve or bailiff in right of this tenement. By her will, dated 20 January 1652-53, she devised all her customary lands to her grandson, John Stonehouse, second son of Sir George Stonehouse, bart., who was admitted in 1663.

OTHER NOTEWORTHY RESIDENTS OF WALHAM GREEN

John Marten, in his will, dated 19 September 1500 (P.C.C. 7 Blamyr) describes himself as "of the Chapell of our sou'aigne lord the king." To his wife, Alice, he left all his lands and tenements, "at Wandongrene in the Parishe of ffulham." The will was proved 7 February 1501-2.

John Norden, the topographer and surveyor of the King's lands in the reign of James I, resided in a cottage at Walham Green. At a Court General in 1604 he was, "uppon paine to forfeit to the Lord xiij^s iiij^d," ordered to remove a nuisance at his house at " Wandons Greene."

Norden, who was born about 1548, was admitted to Hart Hall, Oxford, in 1564. He was the first Englishman who attempted so vast a design as a complete series of county histories. In 1596 he published a "Preparative" to his " Speculum Britanniæ," which he described as "a reconciliation of sundrie propositions by divers persons (critics, wise and otherwise) tendered," concerning his great undertaking. The book was dedicated to his patron, Lord Burghley, "at my poore house neere Fulham."

Norden wrote some strange books on divinity with whimsical titles, such as "Antithesis, or Contrariety between the Wicked and Godly set forth in a Pair of Gloves fit for every man to wear," etc. Among his other writings are a "Pocket Companion, or Guide for

English Travellers" (1621), and "A Surveyor's Guide." The work by which he is best remembered was that which he commenced "neere Fulham," but which he did not live to complete. The " Speculum Britanniæ" was intended to have been a historical and chorographical description of all England. The only portions published were Part I, containing a description of Middlesex (1593), and Part II, containing Hertfordshire (1598). The work was reprinted in 1637.

John Norden. From an old engraving

Norden got little from the great Lord Burghley beyond his patronage. In his old age he obtained, jointly with his son, the post of Surveyor to the Prince of Wales. From Walham Green he moved to Hendon. He is believed to have died about 1625.

From 1630 to 1634 there lived at a house near Dawes Road, Walham Green, the Rev. John Weston, only son of John Weston, D.C.L., prebend and treasurer of Christ Church, Oxford.

John Weston was born about 1599. He was educated at Christ Church, Oxford, where he matriculated, 12 October 1621. He proceeded B.A., 27 November 1621 and M.A., 17 June 1624. His first living was the vicarage of Cholsey, near Wallingford, Berks, to which he was instituted 26 July 1622.

About 1627 he married, at Fulham Church, Martha, fourth daughter of Stephen Pearse, keeper of the Wardrobe to Queen Elizabeth, James I, and Charles I. On 29 January 1630-31, Weston was installed as prebendary of Peterborough. On 6 January 1633-34 he was presented to the rectory of All Hallows, Lombard Street.

In the course of a few brief years Weston fell on evil days. On 10 November 1638, writing "from my Lodging," in a letter addressed to Sir John Lambe, Dean of the Arches, he remarks:

> "My low and dangerous condition has not only hindered my waiting on you but also prevented my attendance on my church and parish, but I have now obtained some liberty and shall perform all double diligence in my place only my request is that you would pass by these scapes occasioned through my deep extremities. There is one Jones has got a sequestration on my tithes for £160. I am most unjustly dealt with by him. I owe him not half the moneys he claims. I beseech you to stay payment till it appear before the Lord Privy Seal what I owe him, in whose Court he is to give account. Mr. Willett I owe not a penny for serving of my cure; he was employed by Mr. Walker my curate who says he has fully satisfied him. I am indebted to St. Paul's Church three years pay which is £6; I beseech you let that be paid in the first place." (Cal. S.P. Dom. vol. cccci.)

In the following year Weston presented a petition, couched in piteous terms, to Dr. Laud, Archbishop of Canterbury, praying his Grace to rescue him and his family from poverty. It is dated 12 February 1639-40 (Cal. S. P. Dom.).

Weston's subsequent career is difficult to trace. Walker, in his "Sufferings of the Clergy" (1714), tells us that he "was sequestered by the House about 1643," while Newcourt, in his "Repertorium" (1708), states that he "was for his loyalty sequestered by the Rebels about 1642." On 16 December 1647 he was ejected from the vicarage of Cholsey. Nothing is known of his closing years, which must have been spent in poverty and suffering. He is said to have died in 1660.

By his wife Martha, the Rev. John Weston had five sons and five daughters. John, the eldest, was baptized at Cholsey, 17 September 1628. The Fulham Church Registers record:

> 1676. John Weston gen. sepult. 16 Maij.

It is, however, doubtful whether this person was identical with the eldest son of the Rev. John Weston. Ann Weston, his eldest daughter, was baptized at Richmond, 24 August 1630 Henry Weston, the second son, married Mary daughter of John Buckler of

Radipole, co. Dorset. The fourth child was Mary. It is traditionally believed that Henry and Mary Weston were born at Fulham between 1630 and 1634, the period, it will be observed, for which John Weston is assessed for his house at Walham Green. The other children were: Elizabeth, baptized at All Hallows, Lombard Street, 26 Jan. 1634-35, Theobald baptized at Cholsey, 25 April 1638, Robert baptized at Cholsey, 14 May 1641, Martha baptized at Cholsey, 28 March 1643, William baptized at Cholsey, 1 June 1644 and Maria baptized at Cholsey, 17 October 1647.

MISCELLANEOUS NOTES

The following miscellaneous notes relating to Walham Green follow in a chronological order.

1555. The Acts of the Privy Council for 1555 furnish the following quaint details concerning a "seditious bill" which had been cast into the house of one John Smythe, of Walham Green. The matter was heard at a meeting of the Council held at " Grenewiche the xix of Septembre 1555."

> "A lettre to Sir Henry Tirrell and Anthony Browne with a copie enclosed of a seditious bill latelie cast into the house of oone John Smythe of Odam Grene in the parrishe of Fulham, who brought the same himself for his oune declaracion and knoweth not who cast it into his house; and for that the same bill mentioneth the reasorte of some lewde feallowes in Essex unto the said Smith if he would come among them. The said Mr. Tirrell and Mr. Browne are required to have eye to any suche reasorte and to use thier discretions in meting betymes with all assemblies about them and to punnishe the offendours as they thinke convenient and to certifie allso their doinges."

1574. From "Middlesex County Records" (vol. i. p. 92):

> "25 March, 17 Elizabeth. —True Bill against Hugh Meredith of Wannam Grene in the parish of Fulham co. Midd. for keeping there a big, noxious, biting dog, given to worry and bite the Queen's subjects, which dog had on the day aforesaid at Wannam Grene bitten and injured Katherine Yonge, a girl of eleven years of age. G. S. P. R., Easter, 17 Eliz."

The following are from the Churchwardens' Accounts:

1637. It. pd. for a woman that laye in at Wandon greene at severall times 7s. 6d.

1640. Itm. to a poore woman of Wandon greene that came sicke of ye water 3d.

1640. Itm. to Ales Clarke an Auncient wooman at Wandon greene for her weekely mayntenance at 12d. ye weeke for 20 weekes £1. 0s. 0d.

1640. Itm. to Mary Ashwell an Auncient widow att Wandon greene for her weekely maintynance she beinge sick and lame 13s. 4d.

1641. Itm. for the reliefe of Elizabeth Joanes searcher being shutt vp in a visited house att Wandons Greene from the 15 of Aprill 1641 to the 24 of May 16s. 0d.

1641. Itm. for a trusse of strawe for her to lie on 3d.

1669. To a poore woman sicke in a barne at Wandons Green 2s. 6d.

1713. Gave a woman that Lay in a ffitt in Walham Green and victuals and drink and getting her out of the Parish 5s. 0d.

1727. From the Court Rolls:

"We present Thomas Best, Richard Ackers and John Morris for laying timber and large lops of trees over Walham Green where the same must be a nuisance to the neighhours and more to strangers. Therefore if the said trees is not removed in due time the persons named above shall be Amerced at the next Court day."

1730. The following from the *London Evening Post*, No. 367, for Tuesday, April 14 to Thursday, April 16 1730:

"Last Monday Evening two Men and a Woman were robb'd in Fulham Stage Coach, near Walham Green, by two Foot-Pads, who took from them about £3, and the woman's Velvet Hood, and made their escape."

1756. From the Church Registers:

A man that Dropt down Dead at Walham G^n, unknown bu. 27 Feb.

CHAPTER VIII: NORTH END

North End, the greater part of which is now dignified by the name of West Kensington, was a hamlet of Fulham which lay on either side of a long and narrow lane, now the North End Road. Bowack speaks of it as "a small but pleasant airy village, inhabited mostly by gardeners." Faulkner tells us that, in his day, it contained some "very good houses on both sides of the road, occupied by several eminent and remarkable characters." In the Court Rolls, North End is first mentioned under the year 1523, when it is reported that:

"William Broune, Joshua Yonge, John Esyate, John Adam and Thomas Adam have unscoured ditches at Northende."

Before dealing with North End, we will pay a visit to Butts Close and No Man's Land.

Westwards of Gibbs Green, on the North End Road, lay a field, consisting of some six acres, known as Butts Close. At its east end was a smaller close known as Noman's Land. The site was bounded on the east by what is now the North End Road. Southwards the boundary lay along Payne's Lane, now the Lillie Road. Westwards it extended about as far as Church Path.

Butts Close was originally a portion of the glebe lands belonging to the rectory of Fulham. Not improbably it was devoted by some early Rector to serve as a common ground for the use of the tenants of the Manor to practise archery.

It was once incumbent upon the male population of the Manor to practice archery and to keep their bows and arrows in serviceable condition. In accordance with a statute passed in the reign of Mary, we find, from time to time, the tenants of the Manor amerced by the Homage for failing to have bows and arrows. Thus, in 1566, Roger Whythed, was fined 12d., William Denby, 4d., 6, Richard Tyner, 8d., Thomas Bonde, 12d., William Browne, 6d., Roger Sharpe, 12d., and Nicholas Clyfton, 8d., because they "have neither bows nor are there any to instruct in the art of making of arrows according to the statute."

When archery fell out of vogue, Butts Close was turned to other purposes, chiefly for the cultivation of market produce and the rearing of hops. It is impossible to say exactly when Butts Close ceased to exist for its original purpose, but at a Court General, in 1611, the Homage presented:

> "That they have no Butts nor any fitt place or piece of grounde to sett them uppon whereuppon theire artilerye hath not been putt in use according to the Statute."

The earliest allusion to the close, or rather to the entrance to it at Gibbs Green, is in 1439, when one William Bench, or Ben'ssh, was presented at a View because he had "enclosed before a gate called Butts Gate (*una porta voc' Buttes Gate*) at Gybbes grene." As early as 1522 "four acres in the Buttes" were sold to Michael Dormer, of North End.

In 1567 the "constable of ffulham" was ordered to see the butts made before Pentecost or forfeit ten shillings. Again, in 1568, we find the Jurors, at a View, ordering:

> "All the Inhabitants to make the butts of Fulham and Ham'smythe sufficient before Penticost next or x^s."

An order at a Court General in 1612 reads:

> "Widow Prowe shall make her fence sufficient between her Hopp garden in Butts and Mr. James Knowles his land there before candlemas."

We learn from a codicil, dated 12 December 1614, to the will, dated 23 January 1613-14, of James Knowles, of Walham Green, that between the dates named he had purchased of Allan Burton certain customary lands in the Manor, including "a close of six acres called Buts Close and a parcel of land adjoining to the east called Noemans Land."

On the death of James Knowles in 1614, Butts Close and the parcel of land called Noman's Land became the property of William Paulden, of Wakefield, who, in 1618, sold it to Richard Powell, of Cambridge.

It is clear from the above statements that the ancient Butts Close at Gibbs Green must then have ceased to have been used for its original purpose. In 1616 the Homage again presented:

> "That wee have no Butts neither doe wee knowe any place convenient to sett them on."

After the time of Charles I we hear little more of Butts Close under its old appellation. The field became generally known as Noman's Land, Butts Close being called Great Noman's Land and the smaller piece at its eastern end Little Noman's Land. Butts Close, in 1631, passed into the hands of John Gresham. In 1641 James Walsham surrendered "lands in the Butts and ffulham field" to Ralph Hartley. The subsequent history of Butts Close merges in that of Noman's Land.

From what we have said regarding Butts Close and the smaller field to the east, the reader will have gathered the earlier history and position of that tract of land eventually known as Noeman's or Noman's Land.

It is by no means easy to account for the origin of the name. Seebohm, in his "Early English Village Community," thus explains the term:

> "Corners of fields, which from their shape could not be cut up into the usual acre or half acre strips, were sometimes, divided into tapering strips pointed at one end and called 'gores' or 'gored acres.' In other cases little odds and ends of unused land remained, which from time immemorial were called 'No Man's Land' or 'Any Man's Land' or 'Jack's Land,' as the case might be."

The first occurrence of the name in the Court Rolls is in 1492, when it was presented that

> "Thomas Coxston has not amended a common way prejudicial to those who go near Noemansland in ffulhamfeld. to which he was commanded at last Court, wherefore he forfeits xij^d."

This way through Noman's Land was probably the path from Old Greyhound Lane to Payne's Lane or Lillie Road, an ancient thoroughfare which has borne a name of somewhat unsettled orthography. Originally it was Noman's or Noeman's Lane, then Norman or Norman's Lane (or Road), now Normand Road.

Down to quite recent years Norman's Lane had hardly any houses. At the date of Maclure's "Survey" (1853) only six tenements stood here, including Normand House, on the west side, and Normand Farm and Normand Villa on the east. At the point facing Bramber Road was a very ugly bend caused by the line of the old wall of Normand House. In 1894 the Vestry widened the roadway, the wall of Normand House being set back to its present position.

Normand House, south front.
From an engraving published in Faulkner's "Fulham," 1813

Normand House dates from the time of Charles II. In 1649 Thomas Wyld, of the Inner Temple, purchased of Ralph Hartley the six acres of land known as Butts Close together with the piece called Noman's Land. He was, in 1652, chosen one of the "Overseers and Collectors for the Poor of Fulham." In 1659 he increased his estate at North End by purchasing of William Powell, alias Hinson, two acres in Fulham Field "against Somerhouse Close to east." These two acres must have adjoined Butts Close and abutted on what is now North End Road, on the east side of which lay Somerhouse Close.

It was doubtless during the years 1649-61 that Normand House arose. Down to this date we hear only of Noman's Land, but soon afterwards mention is made of a customary messuage called "Noeman's." Thomas Wyld, in 1662, was elected the Lord's reeve or bailiff in right of this tenement. The date of his death is unknown, but it occurred before 1676. He left a son, Thomas, and three daughters, Dorothy, who married Richard Eustace, Sara, who married Gilbert Travis, and Margaret. His widow Susannah Wyld married, as her second husband, Richard Davys or Davies.

Thomas Wyld, junior, in 1687, obtained license to "let to farm one messuage called Nomans land and three acres at North End" to Sir James Chamberlayne.

Bowack, in 1705, speaks of the house as called "Noman's End House."

In 1708 Thomas Wyld, junior, was licensed "To let to farm one customary messuage called Great Nomans Land and Little Nomans Land in Fulham." He died in 1715. His son, William Wyld, was the next owner of "the messuage called Noemansland." In 1731 it became the property of Mrs. Sara Travis, widow, only surviving child of Thomas Wyld. From the Wylds the messuage passed to the Dodds. The first of these, William Dodd, in his will dated 1755, is described as of the Horn Tavern, Westminster, vintner. Descendants of the daughters of this William Dodd, in 1878, sold the property to Mr. James Farmer.

The old Entrance Gates, Normand House.
From a photograph by Mr. T. S. Smith, 1896

In 1812 Normand House was in the occupation of Mr. Jonas Hall and Miss Pope, who kept here an asylum for insane ladies.

During Mr. Hall's proprietorship a young lady escaped from the asylum under circumstances which, at the time, created much excitement in Fulham. Lady Jane ___ , the inmate in question, who had been put into a strait jacket, managed one day to get on to the wall overlooking Normand Road. Here she attracted the attention of a man. "Do write me a letter," she exclaimed, "I am no more out of my mind than you are; I was put here for trying to marry a gentleman." The wayfarer, who had been appealed to, not possessing the needful ability to write, promised the lady that he would get a "mate" of his. This he did, and a letter was in this fashion despatched to a certain address. In a day or two, a gentleman drove down in a coach and four to Normand House. Ringing the bell, he asked to see Mr. Hall. Upon the appearance of that gentleman, the stranger sought permission to take his "sister" out for a short drive. Mr. Hall explained that it was against the rules, but, after a good deal of persuasion, the young lady was allowed out for the suggested airing. The carriage drove three or four times up and down in front of the house, then, at a pre-arranged signal, the coachman whipped the horses, and the equipage was speedily lost to view. The young lady was not recovered, and the writer of the letter, though a well-known Fulham man, was never traced. The incident we relate upon information furnished to us by the son of one of the two men concerned.

In 1816 Normand House was taken by Mr. Edward Talfourd, who continued it as an asylum. On his death, in 1836, it was conducted by Mrs. Talfourd, who died here in 1861. Mrs. Talfourd was the mother of Judge Talfourd, the poet and miscellaneous writer. On the death of Mrs. Talfourd, the asylum was continued by her daughter, Miss Ann Talfourd, down to 1880, when the institution was broken up.

Over the coachhouse in Normand Road was the padded room, from which at times agonizing shrieks were heard.

For a brief period Normand House was used by the pupils of Princess Helena's School before its removal to Ealing. In 1884 it was temporarily taken by Cardinal Manning as a pauper school for boys.

In the following year it was purchased of Mr. Farmer by the Mother Superior of St. Katharine's Sisterhood and made the Mother House of the community, the employment of the Sisters being prison rescue work among young women convicted of a first theft. The girls are trained by the Sisters in laundry, house and kitchen work.

The Mother Superior's Room, Normand House.
From a photograph by Mr. T. S. Smith, 1896

The grounds formerly extended westwards as far as Church Path, the southern boundary being Crown Road, now Lillie Road. The venerable brick gateway, which faced this road, was taken down about 1866. It bore the date 1661. Behind it was an elegant pair of iron gates attached to two square pillars of hand-made red bricks; these are still *in situ*, just behind the gardens of the houses on the north side of Lintaine Grove. The gateway, in olden times, had evidently formed the main approach to the house.

During the present century the ancient messuage has been very much reduced in size. In 1812 it was about eight acres, but when Maclure surveyed the parish in 1853 the grounds were only 1a. 2r. 11p. The Mother Superior, by the purchase of two plots of ground, including Normand Cottage, on the north side, has increased the site to about two acres. The original house has, from time to time, been considerably enlarged and altered. Quite recently another story has been added.

The Grand Staircase, Normand House.
From a photograph by Mr, T. S. Smith, 1896

The Ancient Staircase, Normand House.
From a photograph by Mr. T. S. Smith, 1896

The only entrance now existing is from Normand Road. From east to west a corridor runs through the house. The most ancient part of the building is that on either side of the first portion of this passage. To our left, as we enter, are two of the most interesting apartments in Normand House. These are small but finely panelled rooms, with somewhat low ceilings, overlooking the lawn which faces the south front. The first of these is now appropriated as the Sisters' Room and the second is the Mother Superior's. In the south wall of the latter room is an ancient door, now blocked up. This disused door faces the ornamental iron gates of which we have spoken, and was doubtless the original entrance on this side of the house. On the north side of the corridor are two adjoining staircases. The first, which is shut off from the corridor by a door, is by far the more ancient. The present grand staircase, which lies just west of its older neighbour, bears the Tudor rose decoration. The architraves and hand-made mouldings of the doors in the oldest part of the house are very fine. On the left side of the main corridor are also the library and guests' room. On the north side is the old dining-room.

On the north side of the house the Mother Superior has recently had erected an extensive range of buildings, containing cubicles for the inmates, laundry, drying rooms, etc. connected with Normand House by means of covered-in passages. A permanent chapel has just (1899) been erected in the garden adjoining Normand Road. It is from the designs of the late Sir Arthur Blomfield.

In 1836, during some repairs to the walls of Normand House, the workmen dug up, from under the foundations, three ancient jugs, known as greybeards, from the circumstance of their being ornamented with the faces of old men. A few years ago, in pulling down an old boundary wall, a farthing, dated 1627, was found.

Faulkner mentions a tradition to the effect that the house was, in 1665, used as a hospital for persons recovering from the plague. It is, of course, quite impossible to say what amount of truth there may be in this story, but there is no doubt that, at the western end of the grounds, a burial pit did exist. The West Brompton Railway Mission now marks the precise site.

Lintaine Grove, Silvio Street, Mooltan Street, and Tilton Street all stand on what was once a portion of this ancient estate.

Normand House, south front.
From a photograph by Mr. T. S. Smith, 1896

About the centre of Normand Road, on the east side, stood, until 1888, Normand Villa, a low, two storied house, along the front of which ran a verandah. It was shut in from the road by a high wall, in front of which were some old elms. Its grounds, which measured 1a. 2r. 5p., were laid out with great taste. Close to the gardener's lodge was a gigantic walnut tree, estimated to be three centuries old. It bore fruit down to the last.

Between Lillie Road and Star Road, running behind Normand Villa, was Normand Farm. These market garden grounds, which covered 4a. 1r. 29p., formed a portion of the Earsby's rent charge (see "North End Road: Gibbs Green to Hammersmith Road" chapter).

On the west side of Normand Road are Queen's Club Gardens, surrounding a fine central square of about 2½ acres. On the north side, they abut on Old Greyhound Road. They were commenced by Messrs. W. H. Gibbs and Co. in 1891.

The mansions, which are built of red brick, are of handsome elevation, in the favourite Queen Anne style. They comprise thirty-one blocks, containing about 600 suites of rooms. The site covers some twelve acres.

CHAPTER IX: NORTH END ROAD

SECTION I: WALHAM GREEN TO LILLIE ROAD

Anciently North End Road was variously designated. William Adam, in 1477, was presented at a Court because the boughs of his trees overhung "the way called Gybbesgrene lane." In 1488 the lane is spoken of as "the North-strete." The Court Rolls for 1567 describe it as "a certain street or road of ffulham called the Northeande." In 1646 it is "the King's highway leading from Wandons Greene towards Northend." The term "North End Lane" occurs for the first time in 1649. "The North Lane" is the expression used in 1657. In 1658 we again find "North End Lane." "The Lane of North End" is a description which occurs in the Rolls for 1662.

The northern portion of North End Road was sometimes called Furbushe, Fursbushe or Furzebushe Lane from a close known as Furbushe, Fursbushe or Furzebushe, which lay to the east of the lane. Fursbushe Lane is last mentioned in the Rolls for 1682. The furze covered common which once trended away from North End Road westwards towards the Black Bull Ditch explains the name.

WEST SIDE

North End Road commences at the junction with it of the Shorrold's Road. The name Shorrold's Road recalls that of an ancient messuage, once the property of the Sherewolds, and, on the eastern fringe of which stood, until recent years, three houses, known as North End Lodge, St. John's Lodge and Shorrold's.

On the north side of Shorrold's Road stands the Fulham Conservative Club, erected in 1884, with the object of providing suitable headquarters for the Conservative party in the parish, Fulham, at that time, forming part of the parliamentary borough of Chelsea. The older (western) portion of the club was built by Dr. Murdoch (Mr. P. A. Pasley-Dirom), on a piece of ground which he had purchased for the purpose. The Club was opened on 10

December 1884. With a view to extending the accommodation, Dr. Murdoch purchased a plot of ground on the east side. On this, in 1894, an additional wing was erected. The Club numbers over 700 members.

The Conservative Club. From a photograph by Mr. T. S. Smith, 1896

Proceeding up the North End Road we will take the three houses we have named in the order in which they stood. The first, North End Lodge, almost faced Walham Grove. It and its neighbour, St. John's Lodge, were built about the beginning of the century.

Its first owner was Mr. John Leach Panter, Commissioner of Roads, who resided here from 1808 to 1855. The chief interest attaching to the Lodge was the residence here, for a brief period (1858-60) of Mr. Albert Smith, the famous drawing-room entertainer.

Albert Richard Smith was born at Chertsey, 24 May 1816. He was brought up for his father's profession, that of a doctor, but he early took to literature and lecturing. Perhaps no monologue entertainer ever proved more successful in amusing an audience than this genial and versatile humorist. The arena of his greatest successes was the Egyptian Hall. Here, on 15 March 1852, he opened his "Mont Blanc."

It was Mr. Smith's custom to be driven home from the Egyptian Hall to North End. In those days "cabby" did not always know his fare and sundry disputes would occur between the entertainer and his driver. To obviate these, Mr. Smith had inserted in the brick wall close to the gate of North End Lodge, <u>a stone bearing the words "From Hyde Park Corner, 3 miles 17 yards.</u>"

It was while his Chinese entertainment was being given at the Egyptian Hall that this bright lecturer broke down with bronchitis. He died at North End Lodge, 23 May 1860. About a year before his death he married the eldest daughter of Mr. and Mrs. Keeley, herself a charming actress.

In the garden, at the side of North End Lodge, Mr. Albert Smith built a large concert or reception-room. Some of the "principals," which supported the roof of this apartment, are now incorporated in Estcourt Hall and in a shed nearly opposite this building. In the centre of the carved work is the monogram "A. S."

On Albert Smith's death, the house became the residence of the late Mrs. Keeley, the veteran actress, and her husband. In 1867 the property was purchased by Mr. Boleyne Reeves, the harpist. It was pulled down in 1879. Its grounds measured 1a. 2r. 34p.

St. John's Lodge, which joined North End Lodge, was, from 1811 to 1818, the residence of the Misses Sotheby. The next owner was Mr. John McAdam, who died here in 1824. From 1830 to 1838 it was the home of the Rev. John Nelson, the first incumbent of St. John's. It was during Mr. Nelson's tenancy that the name St. John's Lodge arose, its previous designation having been Grafton House.

In 1840 St. John's Lodge was taken by Mr. James Nicholas Mahon, a well-known barrister. On his death, in 1871, the Lodge was purchased by Mrs. Drew who resided here till 1895, when the house was pulled down.

A few yards further up the road stood Shorrold's, a picturesque looking house, in beautiful grounds which measured 2a. 2r. 0p.

The name Shorrold's is identical in origin with that of the ancient messuage called "Sheroldes" at Sands End, which, as elsewhere explained, means Sherewold's tenement, after one John Sherewold, who owned it in the time of Henry V and VI.

In the early years of the present century, there stood a small cottage on the site of Shorrold's, the property of a dentist, named James Thompson, who greatly enlarged it. About 1820 Thompson sold Shorrold's to Mr. Benjamin Coates, the coachbuilder, who, in 1844, disposed of it to Mr. James Lammin, the father of the late Mr. W. H. Lammin, its last owner.

Shorrold's. From a photograph by Mr H. Ambridge

Shorrold's was a plain brick house. It is said that, in its lovely garden, there might be found every tree and shrub which could be grown in the open air. A splendid magnolia, which covered two sides of the house, was one of the sights of Fulham. The pine pits at Shorrold's were also famous. The house was demolished in 1881.

Epirus Road marks the site of the beautiful avenue of trees which formed the approach to the house.

Immediately beyond Shorrold's there was little of interest. St.

John's Place, as it was called, included a few little houses, known as Chestnut, St. John's, Beech Albion, Ansford, and Raven Cottages.

Some tenements on a portion of the site of these dwellings belonged to the Withers family, of whom we have spoken in connection with Holcroft's. It was upon these that William Withers left a yearly rent charge of £5 for the maintenance of his father's tomb in Fulham Churchyard (see "Fulham Road: High Street to Munster Road" chapter). Against an extract from his will, in the ancient "Register Book," is the following:

"Novr 27th 1772.
A Publick House the Sign of the three Tuns and several other Tenements with two Acres of Land behind the three Tuns."

This property is now represented by Nos. 314 to 334 North End Road and Nos. 1 to 62 Tournay Road. In the Parish Books the "Three Tuns" is many times mentioned. The Overseers' Accounts for 1775 contain the following entry:

"Paid for carrying Elizabeth Holmes from the three Tunns to the Workhouse being very ill 2s. 0d."

Haldane Road, originally Wellington Road, was built in 1852, the year of the death of the Iron Duke.

The "Jolly Brewer" (No. 310 North End Road) was originally a very small house. Mr. Charles Mallous, in whose family the house has been for twenty-three years, rebuilt it in 1891.

From the "Jolly Brewer" to Buckle's Alley the houses were known as North Row. A weather-worn tablet, between Nos. 300 and 302, is inscribed "North Row 1795." Thence we passed Orchard Place, Holt House and Woodbine Cottage to St. John's Villas.

St. John's Villas were two small houses, the southernmost one of which is celebrated as the home of Delattre, the engraver.

Jean Marie Delattre was born at Abbeville in 1745. In 1770 he came to England, in company with another Fulham engraver, William Wynne Ryland. Here he soon became one of Bartolozzi's numerous pupils, and, in 1782, followed his master to North End.

Much of the work which is supposed to be by Bartolozzi, and which bears his name, is really the work of Delattre.

Delattre died at St. John's Villas, 21 June 1843. His daughter, Miss Delattre, died here in 1851. The Church Registers record:

> 1783. Juliet Ann daughter of John and Mary Ann De Lattre bap. 6 Feb.
> 1834. Ann De Latte Northend aged 84 bu. 17 July.
> 1843. John Marie De lattre Northend, 98 years bu. 30 June.
> 1851. Charlotte Mary De lattre Northend, aged 71 bu. 6 Sept.

The "Norfolk Arms" (No. 272, North End Road), is a comparatively modern house. It was extensively enlarged in 1894, when its front was brought out.

A little further down, on the site of Stanhope Nursery, is the North End Road Board School, built in 1880. This school was opened 28 February 1881. It accommodates 360 boys, 360 girls and 480 infants; total, 1,200.

Just beyond is a somewhat old inn, known as "The Crown" (No. 248 North End Road), which gave its name to old Crown Lane. In the Parish Books it is first mentioned under the year 1771. In 1791 the Overseers

> "Paid Jurymen's Groats and other expences at the Crown at North End sitting on the Body of Harwood's Child."

The house, which has been rebuilt at least three times, was, fifty years ago, kept by Host Marshall, a tall man whose boast it was that, while he stood at his door, he could reach with his own hand the nearest row of tiles on the roof of his house! The present house was erected in 1879.

In some of the earlier Court Rolls mention is several times made of one Philip or Philpot Mathews, whose holding lay on the west side of North End Road, near its junction with Crown Road.

The first we hear of it is in 1417, when John Coc surrendered 4 acres "parcel of Philip Mathews ten[t]." Among other families who successively owned it were the Lyndes, Burtons and Cutlers. The last we hear of it is in the time of Elizabeth.

EAST SIDE

We will now take the east side, starting at Walham Grove. This road, which runs from North End Road to Farm Lane, was commenced about 1862. It marks the site of some noted fruit grounds, celebrated for their Windsor pears.

On the south side is the United Methodist Free Church. It was about 1858 that the nucleus of this church was first brought together, old Salem Chapel being the meeting place. The present church in Walham Grove was opened in 1866. The cost was about £2,500. It contains two memorial tablets to the brothers Charles and Joseph New, who were both educated at the school in connection with this church. They volunteered for missionary work in Africa, where both lost their lives.

At the corner of Walham Grove, where Nos. 291 and 293 North End Road now stand, was Walham House, an old-fashioned residence. Faulkner states that, in his day, it was the property of Mr. J. Gregory, and that it was then called York House. For many years it was occupied as a school for young girls, kept successively by Mrs. Yates, Mrs. Skegg and Miss Clara Burbidge. The house was taken down in 1877.

The Mr. John Gregory alluded to by Faulkner was the father of another John Gregory. The property on the site of Walham House still belongs to this family, Mr. J. D. Crace, the present owner, being the grandson of the daughter of the second John Gregory.

On the site of Dungannon Terrace was an ancient messuage which survived till 1877. The house, in early times, was known as Copt Hall, and was probably built about the time of Charles I. The first we hear of it is in 1645, when William Dodd, of Fulham, yeoman, surrendered his

> "tenement of new erection called Copthall situate at Wansdons Grene to Mary his wife in recompense of dower."

William Dodd, whose will is dated 7 February 1692-93, died in 1695. The property next came into the hands of William Nourse, and, in 1717, into those of Matthew Child. On the death of the latter, in 1720, Elizabeth Cutler, widow, his only daughter, was admitted. This lady sold the property to Prudentia Trevor, of Knightsbridge. Until recently the estate belonged to the late Baron Trevor, of Brynkinalt, to whom it came from his aunt, the Countess of Dungannon, a descendant of Prudentia Trevor.

Little is ascertainable about the occupants of the old house, known in its later days as The Grange. About 1834 Mr. Anthony Gattenby established here the York and Lancaster Tea Gardens, a kind of miniature Cremorne, but the venture did not prove a success. For some considerable time The Grange was the residence of the late Mr. Charles Batty, one of the first pioneers in carrying on building operations of any magnitude in the northern and central portions of the parish.

The Grange. After a photograph in the possession of Mr. F. Batty

The Grange, which stood at the south-west corner of what is now Eustace Road, had grounds of about 6½ acres. The exterior brickwork of the house was "rough cast." To the left of the entrance was the dining-room, the walls of which were lined with panelled wainscotting throughout. To the right was the drawing-room. Behind the dining-room was the kitchen, underneath which was a very ancient cellar. Each room on the ground floor was fitted with double casement doors, all of which were of oak. The chimney-pieces were narrow and of quaint appearance. The low ceilings of the ground floor rooms were supported by enormous beams.

The grounds bore indications of a former greatness. In the centre of the lawn, behind the house, was a very fine drooping ash, while nearer the Creek was a lovely mulberry tree. Just to the left of The Grange was a tiny building known as Rose Cottage, and beyond came a range of old farm buildings.

In Halford Road is the Halford Road Board School, opened 18 August 1890. It was enlarged (200 places) in 1889 and (400 places) in 1891. It accommodates 480 boys, 480 girls and 629 infants; total 1,589.

There has just been erected, at the bottom of Anselm Road, the permanent church of St. Oswald's, the foundation stone of which was laid by Lady Edward Spencer Churchill, 25 April 1898.

A few yards southwards of Beaufort House were Clarence and York Cottages. The latter, from 1840 to 1854, was the home of James Baker Pyne, the distinguished landscape painter.

Mr. Pyne was born at Bristol on 5 December 1800. He was originally intended for the law, but he soon determined to relinquish that profession in order to devote himself to art. In 1821 he travelled on foot to Cumberland with his knapsack on his shoulder and the proverbial half-crown in his pocket.

In 1835 he quitted his native city to seek his fortunes in London. In spite of great difficulties, he soon came to the front, a self-taught man. In 1836 he first exhibited at the Royal Academy. Mr. Pyne became a member of the Society of British Artists in 1842 and was Vice-President from 1845 to 1855. It was while he resided at York Cottage that he completed the series of beautiful water-colour drawings of English Lakes, a commission from Mr. Agnew, the founder of the present firm of Messrs. Agnew and Sons. In 1855 he removed from York Cottage to Camden Road, where he died, 29 July 1870.

York Cottage, in 1878, was pulled down. By the side of Clarence Cottage, which stood just southwards of York Cottage, was the ancient pathway which led to the bridge over to Earl's Court fields.

Between the site of Beaufort House and the boundary Creek

was a piece of swampy ground, the size of which is variously given as from seven to twelve acres. At each high tide the water in the Creek would rise and overflow this low-lying tract. From the character of the place it was, appropriately enough, called Marshmansfield, Marshmanscroft or Marshcroft, a name which, in later times, was corrupted to Mashcroft or Mayescroft.

In the Court Rolls the place is mentioned as early as 1392, when we find the "croft called Mersshmanfeld," which had formerly been in the possession of John Goldhawk, was let by the Lord to John Hamond till Margery, the daughter of John Goldhawk, came of lawful age.

Subsequently we find Marshcroft in the possession of the Plumbes, Dormers, Greshams, Earsbys, Plucknetts, Marshes, Dancers and other well-known families residing at North End.

In 1650 John Plucknett was ordered "to lay out ye footway leading from Northend lane through his land in Mascrofte." This was the footway which led to the bridge over the Creek.

Marshcroft is, in the minutes of a View in 1691, mentioned as herbage or lammas land:

> "We p^{r}sent ye certaine Lands called Readings and Marshcroft lying and being in the parish of ffulham wthin the Man^r aforesaid have been time out of mind and now are herbage ground after the crops are carried off."

Samuel Foote, the dramatist, of whom we shall speak when we reach The Hermitage, rented Marshcroft from 1769 to 1776 and, apparently, built stabling on a portion of the site. About 1803 Marshcroft or Marsh Close, as it was sometimes called, became the property of Mr. James Gunter, who bought the 12 acres of a Mr. Snowden. In 1835 his son, Mr Robert Gunter, paid £50 to the New Almshouses in Dawes Road for the Vestry's permission to close the right of way in Marshcroft.

In 1822 a little child was found in Marshcroft, abandoned by its friends. The Church Registers record:

> 1822. Felix Marshcroft bap. 23 Jan. The Christian and surname unknown, abode, etc. unknown. Found in Marshcroft the 19 of Oct. last in the dead of night: ascertained to be about 4 months old when found.

The little foundling was baptized by the Rev. William Wood, who took a great interest in it, and generously paid for its maintenance. It lived, however, only a few years. The Church Registers record:

1826. Felix Marshcroft, Parson's Green, 5 years bu. 6 Dec.

In Maclure's "Survey," 1853, the measurements of Marshcroft are as under:

Meadow and Ditch 8a. 1r. 12p.
Oziers 1a. 1r. 34p.
Bank of Canal 0a. 1r. 9p.
(Total) 10a. 0r. 15p.

Mascottes Bridge, from Marshcroft to Earl's Court, was very ancient. It is mentioned in the Court Rolls as far back as 1442. The Highway Rate books record, under the year 1800:

"Paid a moiety of the expence of mending the Bridge over the Creek by Earls Court fields, £5. 5s. 0d."

It disappeared about the time that Mr. Gunter closed the lane across Marshcroft.

A pasture to the north of Marshcroft bore the name of Somerhouse or Summerhouse Close. In 1649 it was called Somerhouse Field, and in 1650 "ye Somershott in Marscrofte." Reading or Readings was another pasture on the south of Marshcroft.

Among the various forms of the name of Marshcroft, the following occur in the Court Rolls: Mersshmanfeld (1392), Marshmansfield (1442), M'ssh'mansfield (1442), Mershmannes croft (1479), Marshemans Croft (1567), Marshmansfeild (1604), Mercemans fielde (1613), Marshcroft (1649), Masemansfeild (1657) and Marsh close (1720).

Beaufort House, which stands on a portion of Marshcroft, is believed to have been built about the middle of the last century. It was purchased by the late Robert Gunter, and is still the property of his son, Col. Robert Gunter.

Beaufort House. From an old drawing at Beaufort House

As early as 1753 an asylum, called the St. John's Asylum for the Insane, was established here. A few years ago, an old card, which had evidently been used for professional purposes by some former proprietor, was found at Beaufort House, bearing the above description and date. In 1826 Dr. Robert Salmon conducted Beaufort House as an asylum. In 1847 it was in the occupation of Dr. Charles Wing.

Beaufort House. From a photograph by Mr. T. S. Smith, 1896

Beaufort House, in 1859, became the headquarters of the South Middlesex Rifle Volunteers. The first Commandant of this Corps was the late Lord Ranelagh. Since its occupation by the

South Middlesex, the house has, on the north side, been considerably extended. The old Rifle Butts at the back of the house were taken down in 1871.

Pursuing our walk, there is nothing further to detain us till we reach Lillie Road. At the corner, where Nos. 171 to 179 now stand, was an old house known as Hermitage Lodge. Foote, who lived at the Hermitage just opposite, is said to have built stables here. From 1845 to 1862 Hermitage Lodge was occupied by the Misses Stephens, schoolmistresses. About 1864 it was purchased by Miss Joanna Taylor, and, in 1866, by Mr. J. T. Peacock, of the firm of Nurdin and Peacock.

In 1868 Hermitage Lodge became a Carmelite Convent. It was taken down in 1879. On a portion of the grounds, which were rather over an acre in extent, the present Convent in Lillie Road was built.

SECTION II: LILLIE ROAD TO GIBBS GREEN

WEST SIDE

At the junction of the Lillie Road with the North End Road was an old-fashioned straggling brick residence, which stood in somewhat extensive grounds. The house, known as Cambridge Lodge, lay a little way back from the road.

Here it was that Francesco Bartolozzi, the distinguished Florentine engraver, came to reside in 1780, some six years after his arrival in England. He was then in his 53rd year, and at the height of his fame. Mr. A. W. Tuer writes in "Bartolozzi and his Works":

> "Mr. Carey says that when he passed the engraver's house - which he frequently did - late at night or in the small hours of the morning, the lamp in his work room was generally burning; and in regard to the time at which he began his labours in the morning, Mrs. McQueen (the mother of the present members of the firm of J. H. and F. C. McQueen, the fine art copper-plate printers) remembers her father having frequently to go to Mr. Bartolozzi's house at Fulham (where he had a copper-plate press) at six o'clock in the morning, to prove his plates under the artist's personal superintendence."

Bartolozzi made money easily and spent it freely. "His benevolent disposition," says Faulkner, "was shown in many instances, and the poor of the neighbourhood frequently experienced his liberality."

He was a great snuff-taker. In his studio at Cambridge Lodge he used to keep a large box at his side, from which he took frequent pinches, throwing the remains on the floor, so that by the end of the day quite a heap had accumulated !

Lucia Elizabeth, the elder of Bartolozzi's two granddaughters, the children of his son Gaetano, is known to have gone to school at Manor Hall, Fulham Road, so that it is quite possible that this little girl, who was destined to become the famous Madame Vestris, lived with her grandfather at Cambridge Lodge. Amongst the few letters of Francesco Bartolozzi which have been preserved, is one (in Mr. Tuer's possession) dated North End, Fulham, 6th July 1800, written in Italian, to his friend, Signor Colnaghi, commending to the care of his friend, Signor Gasperini and his wife "my little girl," who seems to have been setting out for a journey. In the course of sundry instructions, he observes:

> "I beg you also to tell them they had better give her no meat for supper, and as little butter as possible, and that they should keep their eyes upon her, for she is so lively that she might escape them and run some danger, particularly in carriages and (sedan) chairs; she must not go near the door, a thing which children are very fond of doing. Let them be careful not to allow her to sleep in damp beds."

Who the "dear little girl" was, we do not certainly know. Bartolozzi says in the letter that

> "though she is not my own, I am as much interested in her as though she were, having taken a particular affection for her."

Mr. Tuer suggests that most probably she was one of Bartolozzi's granddaughters. It is possible that it might have been the elder child, the future Madame Vestris, who was born in January 1797, and would, therefore, have been in her fourth year at the date of this letter.

After a sojourn of thirty-eight years in England, Bartolozzi accepted from the Prince Regent of Portugal an invitation, coupled with the promise of a pension and a knighthood, to take charge of the National Academy at Lisbon. He accordingly left Fulham, and on 2 November 1802 sailed for Portugal. He died at Lisbon 7 March 1815, aged 88.

During his residence at North End, many of Bartolozzi's old friends and pupils made the neighbourhood their home. Among these were Giovanni Battista Cipriani, James Anthony Minasi, Jean Marie Delattre, J. J. Van der Berghe, Mr. Scheneker, Pietro William Tomkins, A.R.A., Pietro Bettelini and Thomas Cheeseman.

Bartolozzi's successor at Cambridge Lodge was John Vendramini. This artist, who was born at Basano in 1769, came to London and completed his studies under Bartolozzi. In 1802 Vendramini was married at Fulham Church to Miss Lucy De Faria. He resided at Cambridge Lodge till 1809. He died at his apartments in Regent Street, 8 February 1839.

Francesco Bartolozzi. From an engraving by J. Vendramini

The subsequent history of the house is of little interest. About 1840 Cambridge Lodge was taken by Mr. George Feuillade, who used it as a farm and laundry in connection with St. James's

Hotel. He left in 1857. For a few years the Lodge, which had been struck by lightning and injured, stood empty and dilapidated. It was taken down in 1873. The estate was purchased by Mr. James Farmer.

The old messuage Churchgate's Tenement, which not improbably occupied the site of Cambridge Lodge, recalls the name of the Churchgates, a family who resided at Fulham as far back as 1400. In the Court Rolls it is first mentioned under the year 1483. Among the more noteworthy occupiers of Churchgate's were the Bedells, Canns, Dormers, Greshams, and Wylds. Its history is traceable down to 1731, when Mrs. Sara Travis, the only surviving child of Thomas Wyld of Noman's messuage, was admitted.

At the south-east corner of Chesson Road stands Bethel Chapel, otherwise the West Kensington Methodist New Connexion Church, built in 1887.

About the middle of this century the Connexion had a small chapel at Radnor Street, Chelsea. From this chapel, about 1860, a move was made to Fulham. In 1873 an impetus was given to the movement by the erection of a little iron building, which stood on a portion of the site now occupied by the present chapel.

Bethel Chapel is built in the style known as Geometrical Decorated. The architect was Mr. A. H. Goodall. The cost of the building, including the purchase of the freehold, was about £3,900. Beneath the chapel, which seats about 600 persons, are a large school-room and three vestries.

At the south corner of Archel Road, adjoining North End Road, stood Elm House or Cottage. Croker thus describes it:

> "Immediately beyond Bartolozzi's house is an old wall, apparently of the time of Charles II., enclosing a tall, peculiar looking house, now called Elm House, once the residence of Cheeseman (or Cheesman), the engraver, of whom little is known except that he was a pupil of Bartolozzi."

Thomas Cheesman, who was born in 1760, was one of Bartolozzi's best pupils. He is believed to have died about 1835. The old wall, to which Croker refers, ran from Cambridge Lodge to Elm House.

Elm House, some twenty years ago, was altered into a beershop, known as the "Elm." This house was rebuilt in 1899.

A short distance further is Fane Street, formerly Sun Street. This poor thoroughfare was mainly built about 1825, though a few of its tenements are from a century to a century and a half old. On the north side, near the west end of Fane Street, is the Fane Street Mission Hall, erected in 1888 on the site of an old iron room.

The name of Star Road (formerly Star Lane), the next turning, was devised in allusion to the "Seven Stars," on the opposite side of the North End Road. The first cottages here were built on the south side by Mr. David Shuter in 1824-25. Facing Shuter's Terrace were the market gardens of Thomas Fuller, subsequently converted into a brickfield.

The "Old Oak" beershop, at the corner of Star Road, was once a curious looking little place, with a quaint bay window.

May Street, which was formed about 1870, runs from the North End Road to St. Andrew's Church.

A very ancient messuage at North End, abutting east upon the North End Road, near Noman's Land, bore the name of Huntley's, after William Huntley, who, in 1449, alienated his lands in Fulham to Sir T. Hasele. It was owned by several noteworthy families, among these being the Burtons, Barengers, Arnolds, Potters, Norwoods, Smiths and Lawrences. It survived down to about the middle of the last century.

EAST SIDE

At the north corner, where Lillie Road joins North End Road, stands The Hermitage, or Hermitage House.

Anciently the estate comprised between 14 and 16 acres, extending along the North End Road, north and south, of what is now the Lillie Road. In the old brick wall, which still separates the property from the adjoining coal wharves, is a bricked-up arch which once doubtless led to a close or garden on its north side. On the south side of this wall was a narrow strip of copyhold land. In the grounds was a large lake, on the site of which the "Cannon" Brewery now stands.

In the early part of the last century the property belonged to Richard Prat. From 1739 to 1741 the house was tenanted by the

Rev. Dr. George Lavington, a man whose memory is chiefly noteworthy on account of the violent attacks which he made upon what he called the "enthusiasm" of the Methodists. Dr. Lavington, in 1747, was raised to the see of Exeter. He died in 1762.

From 1742 to 1750 it was the residence of Dr. Willmott, and from 1761 to 1766 of Sir Edward Willmott. In 1767 the estate was purchased by Samuel Foote, who rebuilt the house.

The Hermitage, east front, about 1800.
From a drawing in the possession of Mrs. Lovibond

Samuel Foote, who has been dubbed the "English Aristophanes," was born at Truro about 1721. He was educated at Worcester College, Oxford. In 1747 he opened the Haymarket Theatre with some humorous imitations of well-known characters. Having thus discovered where his strength lay, he proceeded to write a series of farces. He continued to perform at one of the winter theatres every season, often bringing out some of his own pieces. In 1766, while on a visit to Lord Mexborough, he was thrown from his horse. His leg, which was fractured in two places, had to be amputated. "As a compensation for this loss," says the writer of his life in the Dictionary of National Biography, "the Duke of York obtained for Foote a patent to erect a theatre in the City and Liberties of Westminster with the privilege of exhibiting dramatic pieces there from 14 May to 14 September during his natural life. This was a fortune. Foote purchased his old premises in the Haymarket and erected a new theatre on the site, which he opened in May 1767 with the "Prelude," in which he referred to the loss of limb and to the generosity of his patron."

Samuel Foote. From an engraving by W. Greathatch, after a picture by Sir Joshua Reynolds

In consequence of the state of his health, Foote resolved to go for a trip to France. He put up at the "Ship Inn," Dover, where he was seized with a succession of shivering fits. He expired there, 21 October 1777- His body was brought to London and buried in the west cloister of Westminster Abbey. No monument is there erected to his memory, but, in the Church of St. Mary the Virgin, Dover, there is a tablet inscribed:

> Sacred to the Memory of Samuel Foote Esq[r] | Who had a Tear for a Friend, | and a Hand and Heart ever ready, | to Relieve the Distressed. | He departed this life Oct[r] 21st 1777 (on his Journey | to France) at the Ship Inn, Dover. | Aged 55 Years. | This inscription was placed here by his | Affectionate Friend — Mr. William Jewell.

Davies, in his "Life of Garrick," thus sums up the character of Foote:

"Foote was certainly a great and versatile genius, superior to that of any writer of the age; his dramatic pieces, most of them, it is true, unfinished, and several of them little more than sketches; but they are sketches of a master, of one who, if he had laboured more assiduously, could have brought them nearer to perfection. Foote saw the follies and vices of mankind with a quick and discerning eye; his discrimination of character was quick and exact; his humour pleasant, his ridicule keen, his satire pungent, and his wit brilliant and exuberant."

Foote was a man of great conversational power and rich humour. Dr. Johnson says of him that he subdued arrogance and roused stupidity. With perfect frankness the great lexicographer relates the following anecdote of what occurred, on one occasion, to himself:

"Having no good opinion of the fellow, I was resolved not to be pleased; and it is very difficult to please a man against his will. I went on eating my dinner pretty sullenly, affecting not to mind him; but the dog was so very comical, that I was obliged to lay down my knife and fork, throw myself back upon my chair, and fairly laugh it out. No, sir, he was irresistible."
(Boswell's "Life of Samuel Johnson.")

In the "Festival of Wit," 1789 (p. 108), the following amusing anecdote is related by Garrick:

"Foote, who could never keep any very valuable article long out of a pawnbroker's hands, was made a present of a very handsome service of plate, which he exhibited a few days after to a splendid company who dined with him at North End. One of the noblemen was particularly smitten with the fashion of it, and begged to know what it cost. 'Upon my word,' replied the wit, 'I cannot answer that question; but if your Lordship will favour me with a visit in a few days, I can tell you pretty near what it is worth.' "

On Foote's death the house was taken by Charles William, first Earl of Sefton, who resided here till 1779. In 1780 it was rented by Dr. Turton. For some years the history of the house is of little interest.

In *The Times* for 22 June 1815 appears the following

advertisement of the property:

> "Delightful Freehold Villa with Offices and rich Meadow Land, within three miles of Hyde Park Corner. By Mr. Herman at the Auction Mart, on Wednesday June 28, at 12.
> A Singularly Desirable Freehold Residence, called the Hermitage, pleasantly situated at North End, near to Fulham and Hammersmith, in the County of Middlesex, within three miles of Hyde Park Corner, with standing for two or three carriages, stabling for six horses, and appropriate offices, extensive gardens partly walled and clothed with the choicest fruit trees, pleasure grounds beautifully laid out, sheet of water stocked with fish, and three enclosures of very productive Meadow land, the whole containing about 16 acres. To be viewed till the Sale, and printed particulars had on the premises, and of Mr. Herman, Conduit Street, Hanover Square."

The house was purchased by Major John Brown, who lived here till 1822, when Major-General Sir John Scott Lillie, C.B., purchased the property.

Sir John, who was born in 1790, was the son of Mr. Philip Lillie of Drimdoe, Roscommon. He played an important part in the campaign in the Peninsula, being present at almost every action from Roliça to Toulouse. He was, in 1831, selected by the Regent of Portugal to command an expedition to that country to support the claims of Queen Donna Maria.

Sir John was a clever inventor, producing, among other things, the Lillie Rifle battery, an early form of machine musketry, and also a pavement composed of wood and gravel, somewhat resembling in appearance our modern wood pavement.

It was during Sir John Scott Lillie's residence at Fulham that the road from North End Road to Lillie Bridge was made. The building of the Hammersmith Suspension Bridge in 1826-27 necessitated the opening up of a new and more direct route through Fulham. This want he accordingly met by constructing through his grounds the thoroughfare now the Lillie Road. He left North End in 1837.

Sir John Scott Lillie, who died 29 June 1868, is buried at Brompton Cemetery.

From 1838 to 1842 The Hermitage was the residence of the Hon. Sidney Campbell Roper-Curzon, and, from 1846 to 1850, of

General Anthony Bacon. In 1854 the estate was purchased by Mr. James Park. In 1866 Mr. Henry Lovibond, the well-known brewer, came to reside at The Hermitage, the freehold of which, in 1867, he bought of Mr. Park for £4,000. At the rear of The Hermitage, Mr. Lovibond, in 1867, erected the "Cannon" Brewery.

The Hermitage.
From a photograph by the late Mr. William Appleton

This well-known brewery he originally established at Langport, Somersetshire, in 1831. Subsequently he removed it, first to Vauxhall and next to Chelsea, finally bringing it to Fulham. In January 1871, Mr. Lovibond took into partnership his son, Mr. Valentine Locke Lovibond, the business being continued under the style of Messrs. H. Lovibond and Son. Mr. Henry Lovibond died in 1873. Mr. V. L. Lovibond, who married Miss O. A. F. Fleay, died 22 December 1895. By this union there were five daughters and two sons, of whom four daughters survive. In 1897 the brewery was turned into a limited company, Mrs. V. L. Lovibond acting as managing director.

Mrs. Lovibond is herself a practical brewer. It was in 1873 that she commenced to assist her husband in the management of the brewery, studying chemistry and taking a full brewer's certificate. In 1898 Mrs. Lovibond gave evidence before the

Parliamentary Committee on Beer Materials.

On the sale, in 1897, of The Hermitage to Messrs. Jones Bros, for building purposes, a new boundary wall, separating the brewery from the recently disposed-of site, was built.

The Hermitage, which now (1899) stands empty, is a curiously contrived building. Every room has two doors and some possess even three. The dining-room, to the left of the hall, is an apartment which had once been two smaller rooms. To the right of the entrance is the drawing-room. A door at the end of the dining-room led to the billiard-room, added by Mr. Lovibond in 1887. A door, on the north side of the billiard-room, led to a large swimming bath, erected in 1878. In the basement was very extensive cellarage. When Mr. Lovibond purchased the property, it had evidently been much patched about, and parts, apparently, rebuilt with some of the old materials. Some beautiful weeping willows, which overhung the picturesque old pond, were destroyed when the land was drained.

Just beyond The Hermitage there stood, on the site now occupied by coal wharves, a house known as Walnut Tree Cottage, once the home of John Singleton Copley, R. A., the eminent American painter, whose "Death of Lord Chatham," now in the National Gallery, established his fame in this country. Copley, who was the father of John Singleton Copley, created, in 1827, Baron Lyndhurst, Lord Chancellor of England, died 9 September 1815.

Edmund Kean, the great English tragedian, is erroneously said to have lived here.

Walnut Tree Cottage, which took its name from a fine old walnut-tree in the forecourt, was pulled down about 1857. In Maclure's "Survey" (1853) it is described as dilapidated and in Chancery. Its grounds measured 2a. 0r. 38p.

The site of Walnut Tree Cottage became a brickfield. Afterwards it was used as a paddock in connection with Cambridge Lodge opposite. About 1870 the land was taken by a person named Fox, who established here the Star Running Grounds. On Mr. Fox's death, his nephew, Mr. Daniel Edwards, conducted the grounds in partnership with Mr. David Broad. About 1879 the land was acquired by the Midland Railway Company as coal wharves.

Calton Cottage (No. 169 North End Road) also belongs to the Midland Railway Company.

Next to No. 165 North End Road, going northwards, is a winding turning which leads to an old and dilapidated building called Randel House, formerly known as the Old Malt House.

Gloucester Lodge (No. 153 North End Road) has not the happiest of memories. About the middle of the century, in an upstairs back room at this house, was discovered one day the body of Mr. Edward Goslin, the brewer.

He had committed suicide in order to elude capture by the Excise Officers, who were after him for making contraband malt. Under the back sitting-room of the adjacent house (No. 155 North End Road), then a portion of the maltings belonging to the Goslins, there still exists a dark cellar, 23 feet in length, where the malt was stored. The cellar has three secret openings in the top, and at its far end was once a tank. The cement around the wall still adheres, showing precisely what was the position of this receptacle. Above it, just beneath the staircase, is one of the secret openings. Down this opening the barley was shot into the tank. The other two apertures leading to this cellar are situated beneath the back sitting-room. It was through these that the malt was taken up.

Dr. Hornton, who committed suicide in consequence of a reprimand which he once received from a Coroner at an inquest, was another resident of Gloucester Lodge.

The "Seven Stars" is a quiet roadside inn, first mentioned in the Parish Books under the year 1771. In olden times the "Seven Stars" is said to have been much frequented by the knights of the road. The house was in the heyday of its glory in the time of James Stratton. An old brown jug was a curiosity of the bar of the "Seven Stars." It bore the date 1730.

The Garden Entrance to the Earl's Court Exhibition covers the site of Acacia Cottage and Garden Cottage, picturesque bits of old Fulham. Facing May Street were some market grounds long in the occupation of Mr. Adam. Here, it is said, were grown the finest tomatoes to be found in England.

On the east side of Gibbs Green are a couple of tenements, some two centuries old. The first was long occupied by Lee and Coxhead, the music publishers.

Subsequently, it was turned into a dairy, occupied successively by Hey, Denew and Pearson. Warwick Dairy, formerly Edith Dairy, was purchased by Messrs. Pearson and Sons, some twelve years ago. This old firm was established at Kensington in 1817 by the great-grandfather of Mr. J. C. Pearson, the present proprietor of the business. About 1876, Messrs. Pearson and Sons moved to Walham Green, and, in 1878, to West Kensington. Messrs. Pearson and Sons have farms at Thame and Swindon and a home farm at Heston near Hounslow. For many years Messrs. Pearson's .milk came from the Earl of Macclesfield's farm at Shirburn Castle, Oxfordshire.

The Seven Stars. From a photograph by Mr. T. S. Smith, 1896

Passing Seymour Place (No. 125 North End Road), we reach the "Round House," now occupied by the London County Council as a Fire Station.

The spot, which is still known as Gibbs Green, is one of considerable antiquity. In the Court Rolls it is mentioned as early as 1428, when the name is spelled Gybbesgreene. The rector of Chelsea (Thomas Boleyn, LL.B), in 1442, improperly dug for loam at Gibbs Green. The offence is thus recorded in the Court Rolls:

"The Rector of the Church of Chelchehitche has dug six cartloads of loam at Gybbesgrene and carried away the same without license (and is) amerced xl^d."

In 1491 Robert Walsshe was presented because he had made "a dunghill" at "Gybbesgrene."

The Commissioners engaged on the "Surveys of Church Livings," 1647-58, speak of the place as "a little Greene called Gibbs greene." Till within living memory there was a small green in the centre of the roadway.

Old Tenements at Gibbs Green.
From a photograph by Mr. T. S. Smith, 1895

From a very early period a bridge existed in the neighbourhood of Gibbs Green. It spanned the ancient Creek between Gibbs Green on the west and Earl's Court on the east. In 1423 the Jurors presented: "The Lord to amend a bridge at Gybbesbregge." His Lordship apparently paid little heed to the request of his Jurors, for, at a View in 1428, it was again presented "That the Bishops of London Lords of this Manor have time out of mind repaired the Bridge called Gybbesbregge." A similar presentment was made in 1435. Again, in 1438, "The Lord should amend Gybbesbregge." In 1477 it was reported at a Court General "The Lord has a bridge called Gybbysgrene bregge ruinous and broken down, wherefore they will counsel the said Lord."

Two years later the Jurors again reported on the state of the bridge and advised that the Lord of the Manor should be spoken to. In 1488 the Jurors presented that "The Lord has not repaired a bridge called Gybbesbregge in Northstrete near Wendongrene."

From year to year come with monotonous regularity presentments by the Jurors respecting the failure of the Lord to mend his bridges. In 1571 they reported, "The Bridge at Gybbes Grene is ruinous and the Lord ought to keep it in repair." And, again, in the succeeding year, "The Jurors present that the Lord ought to lay a whelm at Gybbes Green and make a bridge for carts there."

SECTION III: GIBBS GREEN TO HAMMERSMITH ROAD

WEST SIDE

At the north-east corner of May Street stands the Clarence Hotel, built in 1864 and enlarged in 1894.

Just beyond is a little *cul de sac* known as Lanfrey Place, formerly Little Ebenezer Place. Ebenezer Place, a row of mean cottages along North End Road, was built by Mr. James Wild in 1848. This gentleman also built, in 1853, Little Ebenezer, now a shop, No. 112 North End Road, originally used as Sunday and Day schools. It once bore a tablet on which was some verse, composed by Mr. Wild. Two lines ran:

> "The writer spent his youthful days
> In teaching children Wisdom's Ways."

Opposite what is now Beaumont Terrace were Myrtle Villas. At No. 2 lived, from 1878 to 1882, Mr. C. Napier Hemy, R.W.S., the artist.

Passing Victoria Cottages, we come to Baron's Court Road, old Potter's Lane, as it was formerly known. (See later in this chapter).

Just north of Baron's Court Road, where the District Railway now crosses to Hammersmith, was North End Grove, for some years the residence of Capt. Dawson and afterwards of Mr. George Keane. The shops along Baron's Court Road are still known as

Keane's Terrace. North End Grove was also the residence of the late Mr. Charles Augustus Howell, the well-known dealer in works of art. From North End Grove, Mr. Howell, as we have previously mentioned moved to Chaldon House (see "New King's Road: High Street to Burlington Road" chapter).

Between Nos. 7 and 9 West Kensington Terrace, was the entrance to a lonely lane which trended away westerly from North End Road to the cottage of a market gardener named Warner, where it crossed a small bridge, which spanned the Black Bull Ditch, at the point where the latter turned north towards Hammersmith Road. Thence Deadman's Lane, as this way was called, ran north-westwards till it reached the south end of Red Cow Lane, now Colet Gardens, at its junction with Great Church Lane. In a cottage about the centre of the eastern side of Red Cow Lane lived the Deadmans, a family of market gardeners, after whom, of course, this second North End Lane, as it was anciently styled, was called.

An old House in Deadman's Lane, removed in 1880-81 in laying out St. Paul's School. From an original drawing in the possession of the Author

Until Edith Road was formed, about 1880, Deadman's Lane was the only thoroughfare which led from this part of North End through to Hammersmith. In 1882 the necessary steps were taken under the Highways Act for stopping up and diverting Deadman's Lane from the end of Great Church Lane to North End Road, in lieu of which Talgarth Road had been constructed.

The land in the neighbourhood of the Cedars and Baron's Court estates was known in ancient times as Broadfield or

Broadmead. In the Court Rolls "Bradmede" is mentioned as early as 1392. Subsequently we hear of Great Broadfield and Little Broadfield.

Much of the land in this part of Fulham, including Edith Villas, is the freehold property of General James Gunter, brother of Colonel Robert Gunter, whom we have mentioned in connection with Beaufort House. (See earlier in this chapter).

James Gunter, the grandfather of these two distinguished officers and the founder of the family and its fortunes, was of old Welsh extraction. With great judgment he invested his money in the purchase of market gardens about Earl's Court and Fulham. As we have already seen, Marshcroft was among the number. On his death, about 1819, the property went to his son, Mr. Robert Gunter, whose two sons, James and Robert, now possess the valuable inheritance. Col. Robert Gunter, to whom Beaufort House belongs, possesses most of the Kensington estate, and a good deal of land in Fulham and Chelsea. Throughout the Crimean War he served with the 4th Dragoons. General Gunter, who is the freeholder of most of the Fulham property, served in the Crimean, Indian and Chinese wars, where he commanded the 1st (King's) Dragoon Guards. A good story is told of Gunter in connection with the Guards. When, in 1851, he joined as a cornet, he was a good deal chaffed. "Your father was a confectioner, Gunter, wasn't he?" suggested a friend. The young cornet assented. "I wonder," continued the wit, "he didn't make you a confectioner, also." "Your father was a gentleman, was he not?" queried Gunter. "Yes," said the friend, "he was." "Then," rejoined Gunter, "I wonder he didn't make you one, too."

The Cedars estate was built by Messrs. Gibbs and Flew, who began their extensive building operations in this district in 1876. This estate, which took its name from The Cedars, mentioned in our account of the Hammersmith Road, is bounded on the south by the District Railway, and on the north by the grounds of North End House (on which Fitzgeorge Avenue is being built) and the high road. Running east and west is are Edith Road, named after Edith Gunter, Gunterstone Road, recalling the name of the freeholder, and Gwendwr and Talgarth Roads, names taken from an old estate in Breconshire belonging to the Gunter family. Trending north and south are Trevanion Road (late Tretower Road), Glazbury Road and Gliddon Road. Auriol Road, which runs from Edith Road to Hammersmith Road, is built on land the property of the parish of St. Dunstan's in the West, and is named after the Rev. Edward Auriol, a former rector of that church.

Among the more noticeable residents of the Cedars estate are (or have been) the late Madame Patey, the distinguished contralto, of 22 Edith Road, Herr Isaac Barrett Poznanski, the violinist, of 37 Auriol Road, Signor Giovanni Focardi, the sculptor, author of "The Dirty Boy," of 10 Auriol Road, Mr. Francis Henry Macklin, the actor, of 13 Gunterstone Road, Mrs. Mary Ann Swanborough, manageress of the Strand Theatre, who died at 16 Talgarth Road, 7 January 1889, Mr. Edward Onslow Ford, R.A., the sculptor, of 3 Matheson Road, and Lt.-General Sir Lothian Nicholson, of 4 Gliddon Road, who died at Gibraltar, of which he was governor, 27 June 1893.

At No. 29 Edith Road died, on 2 December 1884, that distinguished Crimean medical hero, Dr. Daniel John Duigan, C.B. He came of an old Kilkenny family. Entering the naval service in 1844, he served for seven years in the Mediterranean. It was during the Russian war that he earned his chief distinction to fame. Through the terrible winter of 1854-55, he served in the camp of the Royal Naval Brigade as surgeon in the charge of its second division hospital. Subsequently he served in the batteries and trenches before Sebastopol, where he exhibited unflinching devotion to duty.

On the south side of the Talgarth Road, facing the grounds of St. Paul's School, stands the Froebel Educational Institute, established for the purpose of demonstrating the excellence of Froebel's principles of education. The first portion of the scheme consisted of the erection of a Training College for Teachers. In September 1894 Madame Michaelis' College was transferred here. In January 1895 classes were opened both for the students of the Training College and for a few children in the Kindergarten. To afford further accommodation, a new wing, for a model Kindergarten and School, was, in 1896, erected on the east side of the College. A final addition was made in 1899. At the present time there is accommodation for 160 pupils. The Empress Frederick of Germany is the patroness of the Institute.

Gliddon Road Bridge, which connects the Cedars with the

Baron's Court estate, was built by Messrs. Gibbs and Flew in 1885-86.

The Baron's Court estate was planned by the late Sir William Palliser. The title was devised in allusion to the Court Baron held by the Lord of the Manor, and was, perhaps, suggested to Sir William by the name of the neighbouring district, Earl's Court.

Site of St. Paul's School. From an etching by Robert Harris, Esq.

The estate extends from Perham Road on the south to the District Railway on the north. The roads on the Baron's Court estate form a series of parallelograms. Running east and west are Baron's Court Road, Comeragh Road, Castletown Road, Charleville Road, Fairholme Road and Perham Road, intersected, from north to south, by Challoner Street, Vereker Road, Gledstane Road and Palliser Road. The last-named thoroughfare is named after Captain Wray Gledstane Palliser, R.N., brother of the late Sir William Palliser. Comeragh Road was named after Comeragh, co. Waterford, the Captain's home.

Major-General Sir William Palliser, C.B., M.P., who died 4 February 1882, was the youngest son of Lieut.-Colonel Wray Palliser. It is chiefly through the projectiles, which bear his name, for piercing armour-plated ships, and for many practical advances, both in offensive and defensive armament, that Sir William's name will be best remembered.

The Froebel Educational Institute

Baron's Court Estate.
From a photograph by Messrs. A. C. and C. G. Wright, 1898

In 1883 Messrs. Gibbs and Flew purchased that part of the Baron's Court estate which embraces the present Queen's Club and the adjacent houses, from the executors of Sir William Palliser and erected the houses which overlook the grounds of that institution, as well as those on the west side of Vereker Road. They laid out the land as a cricket ground, but for some considerable time no steps were taken towards the actual establishment of a club.

It was, indirectly, the closing, in 1887, of Prince's Rackets and Tennis Club which brought about the establishment of the Queen's Club at West Kensington. The scheme of the promoters was the acquisition of a site which should serve the purposes of an athletic club, and, at the same time, become the home, as far as possible, of the inter-University contests.

The Queen's Club, which was opened for lawn tennis on 19 May 1887, comprises an area of about eleven acres. On this are several extensive club buildings, consisting of a central pavilion, facing east, with a large club-room in front; tennis courts to the north of the pavilion and racket courts and the secretary's and clerks' offices to the south. Further southwards is an asphalt rink which, when flooded in frosty weather, forms a beautiful skating surface. On the west side of the pavilion stand the covered lawn tennis courts, opened, upon the enlargement of the grounds, in April 1889. On the lawns inside the running track and on the side banks, some thirty grass lawn tennis courts can be marked out. There is a good cricket pitch. A part of the ground is reserved in winter for first-class football matches, one of the most prominent features of the Queen's Club. The Oxford and Cambridge Sports were first held at the Club in March 1888. The Club is managed by a representative committee. The members, who number about 1,100, are elected by ballot.

King's House, Baron's Court.
From a drawing in the possession of Mr. F. Winfield.

The main entrance to the Queen's Club is at the south end of Palliser Road, just under the Grand Stand. Over the entrance to these offices is the inscription, "The Queen's Club, 1895."

West Kensington Congregational Church, which stands at the junction of Challoner Street with Castletown Road, was built in 1882-85, at a cost, including the site, of nearly £18,000, mainly raised by the members of the Congregational Church in Allen Street, Kensington. It is built in the Early Gothic style, and is generally considered to be one of the handsomest churches in London.

It was erected by Messrs. Howell and Son, from the designs of Mr. James Cubitt. It is capable of seating from 900 to 1,000 people. The foundation stone was laid 2 November 1882 by the late Earl of Shaftesbury. The church was opened on 4 June 1885.

The West Kensington Lecture Hall, adjacent to the church, was built at a cost of about £2,500, from designs by Mr. C. W. Stephens.

Among the more noteworthy residents of the Baron's Court estate may be mentioned Admiral Sir George Elliot, K.C.B., of 6 Castletown Road; Commissary-General Downes, C.B., of 28 Charleville Road; the late Sir Arthur Colin Curtis, of 2 Perham Crescent; and Charles Dickens, junior, son of the great novelist, who died at 43 Fairholme Road, 20 July 1896.

We will now continue our journey along North End Road.

At Edith Road the North End Road makes a great bend, going first north-eastwards and then north-westwards. In ancient times there stood at this bend, on the west side of the road, a tenement known as the " Dog and Duck," possibly an inn. As early as 1641 we find a "John Milles att the dogg," rated to the poor at a shilling. The Church Registers record:

1713. Jobe Shaw from the Dog and Duck bu. 1 July.

The pond in the grounds of Grove House, built near the site, went by the name of the "Dog and Duck" Pond down to within living memory.

Little can be gathered about the early history of Grove House or Grove Cottage, which stood at this bend in the road. It seems to have been identical with an ancient messuage, consisting of an acre and a rod, called Scroves, Sroves, or Groves, alias Shores. In 1648 Thomas Walter, of Fulham, sold the house to George Kelsey, cutler.

Grove House was once tenanted by William Wynne Ryland, the celebrated engraver. Ryland, who was born in 1732, attained great excellence in his art. In order to extricate himself from some financial embarrassments, he committed forgery on the East India Company. He was brought to trial, found guilty and executed in 1783.

Ryland's house at North End became, about 1817, the home of Dr. William Crotch, the musical composer. Born in 1775, baby Crotch, at the age of two years and three weeks, taught himself "God Save the King." In 1779 he came with his mother, the wife of a Norwich carpenter, to London to astonish the town with a display of his marvellous ability. In the public journals for 18 October 1779 appeared an announcement that

> "Mrs. Crotch is arrived in town with her son, the Musical Child, who will perform on the organ every day as usual from one o'clock to 3 at Mrs. Hart's, Milliner, Piccadilly."

He was at this time a delicate though lively boy, and "next to music, was most fond of chalking on the floor." Young as he was, he could play the violin, the pianoforte and the organ. In 1786 the lad went to Cambridge, where he studied under Dr. Randall. In 1788 he went to Oxford, and in 1794 he took the degree of Mus. Bac., proceeding in 1797 to that of Mus. Doc. In this year he was appointed Professor of Music in the University of Oxford. Dr. Crotch left North End in 1821. In 1822, on the establishment of the Royal Academy of Music, he was appointed first Principal, a post which he held till 1832. He died 20 December 1847.

On the demolition of Grove House, the estate was built over. On the southern portion of it was built a small inn, called "We Anchor in Hope." On the site of this house the "Cedars Hotel" was built by Messrs. Gibbs and Flew in 1883. The other tenements erected round this bend still survive. Lawn and Ashton Terraces, to which we next come, were built between 1850 and 1856, and Grove Terrace, the northern end of the Grove House estate, about the same time.

Passing Grove Terrace, we come to North End House, formerly North End Villa, a commodious residence, which formerly stood in well-timbered grounds, measuring 5a. 1r. 20p.

North End House. From a photograph by Mr. T. S. Smith, 1897

About the middle of the last century, the estate, then comprising 6½ acres, was owned by Gilbert Joddrell, who resided at The Grange, on the opposite side of the North End Road. In 1750 Joddrell sold it to Joseph Pratt. By his will, dated 28 April 1763, Pratt devised it to his wife and others. Joseph Stephen Pratt, in 1792, sold the land to Richard Feild who, in the same year, granted a lease of five acres of it to William Cunnington.

By an agreement previously made (22 November 1791) between the parties, it was arranged that Feild should retain to himself and heirs "one clear acre not taking more than one hundred feet in front of the road," that Cunnington, in consideration of the lease granted to him, should build on the land, within nine months, two substantial messuages on the front next the road, and, within five years, erect ten more substantial brick houses. How far this agreement was carried out we do not know. At any rate, Cunnington built North End Villa and the five houses, pulled down in 1899, known as North End Terrace.

In 1796 Captain John Corner took North End Villa, and, two years later, purchased the estate. By his will, dated 15 August

1817, John Corner left North End Villa to his brother, Robert Sedgley Corner, who died in 1824. His brother, Charles Corner, a major-general of the forces of the United Company of Merchants Trading in the East Indies, let the estate. From 1825 to 1830 it was in the occupation of Mr. Isaac Barker.

In the following year (1831) North End Villa was let to Mr. James Wild, who, in 1833, purchased the property. He spent a considerable sum of money in laying out the grounds. About 1840 he added to the house by building on the present frontage.

Mr. Wild was a man of keen business habits. He was frequently to be seen at sales, where he purchased largely. In the course of years there accumulated at North End Villa a curious collection of furniture, books, and miscellaneous items, including even stone and leaden coffins. The old Hammersmith Turnpike, when it was taken down in 1863, was one of Mr. Wild's purchases. He died 1 May 1866, in his 86th year.

In 1873 North End Villa was taken by Mr. Daniel Pearce, of the firm of Messrs. Phillips and Pearce, glass-ware manufacturers. On his retirement in 1884, the house was taken by Mr. James Stenhouse Scott, who conducted here, for some ten years, a boarding school for boys. It was Mr. Scott who changed the name to North End House.

In 1896 the property was sold to Mr. Charles Julius Knowles. The ground is now (1899) being built over, and a handsome road, named Fitzgeorge Avenue, opened out through the estate. In the grounds, north-westwards of the house, was formerly a large lake.

Between Deadman's Lane and Hammersmith Road was an ancient farm known as Washes, from the family of Walsshe, or Whasshe, who held lands at North End and in other parts of Fulham. John Whasshe, who died 11 March 1551-52 was the last of the family to own this farm. On his death his widow, Agnes, sold it to Thomas Buckmaster. It is described as "One messuage at Northende and 30 acres of land and woodland appurtinent." Subsequently Washes Farm was owned by the Greshams. For a lengthened period it was the property of the Earsbys, a well-to-do family of market gardeners, who settled at Fulham in the reign of Queen Elizabeth.

In the reign of Charles I we find two brothers, William and Thomas Earsby, sons of John Earsby, of Parson's Green, living at two separate farms at North End, the former residing at Washes. William Earsby died 18 October 1664, and was buried in Fulham Church (see vol. I, "Fulham Church: Its Monuments" chapter). By his will, dated 9 October 1664, William Earsby gave his son, John Earsby,

> "Three pieces of lande in Fulham Fields abutting upon Aylands to the north and to the Worple near Hanger Parrebridge containing by estimation 4½ acres and ½ acre more near Parrebridge, in all 5 acres, on condition that he and his assigns should, with the rents and profits of the said 5 acres, buy thirty yards of Hampshire Kersey, worth 4s. the yard, the said cloth to be by him or his assigns made in six petticoats and waistcoats with good bindings and clasps; and the six suits so made up to be delivered by his said son or his assigns on the first day of November after his decease to six poor widows on Fulham side, of good repute and quiet conversation, and so be continued, six one year and six the next year twelvemonth, as they were in the time of his life until the world's end."

The above is quoted from the old "Register Book." The charity was, some years ago, allowed to lapse. By his wife Mary, William Earsby left three sons, Thomas, John, and Joseph. His widow died 30 December 1679, and was buried at Fulham. Thomas Earsby, the eldest son, appears to have lived at a farm on the lands which his father surrendered to him in 1657, south of Beaumont Road, between North End Road and the Creek. John Earsby, the second son, succeeded to Washes Farm. He died 9 September 1687, and was buried at Fulham. Joseph, the youngest son, lived in the parish of St. Margaret's, Westminster. Mrs. Martha Earsby, widow of John Earsby, died in January 1690-91, and was buried at Fulham (see vol. I, "Fulham Church: Its Monuments" chapter).

The children of John and Martha Earsby were William, who was buried at Fulham 4 November 1697; John, who settled at Pinner; Thomas, who succeeded to the estate at North End; Mary, who was baptized at Fulham, 26 April 1675; a second Mary, who was baptized 24 August and was buried at Fulham, 30 August 1678; Elizabeth, who was baptized at Fulham, 9 May 1683, and Martha, who married Edward Billingsley, of St. James's, Westminster (see vol. I, "Fulham Church: Its Monuments" chapter).

In 1702 Thomas Earsby, who resided on his property at Hammersmith, mortgaged Washes Farm to his brother-in-law, Edward Billingsley. He died in 1718, and was buried at Fulham.

PEDIGREE OF EARSBY FAMILY

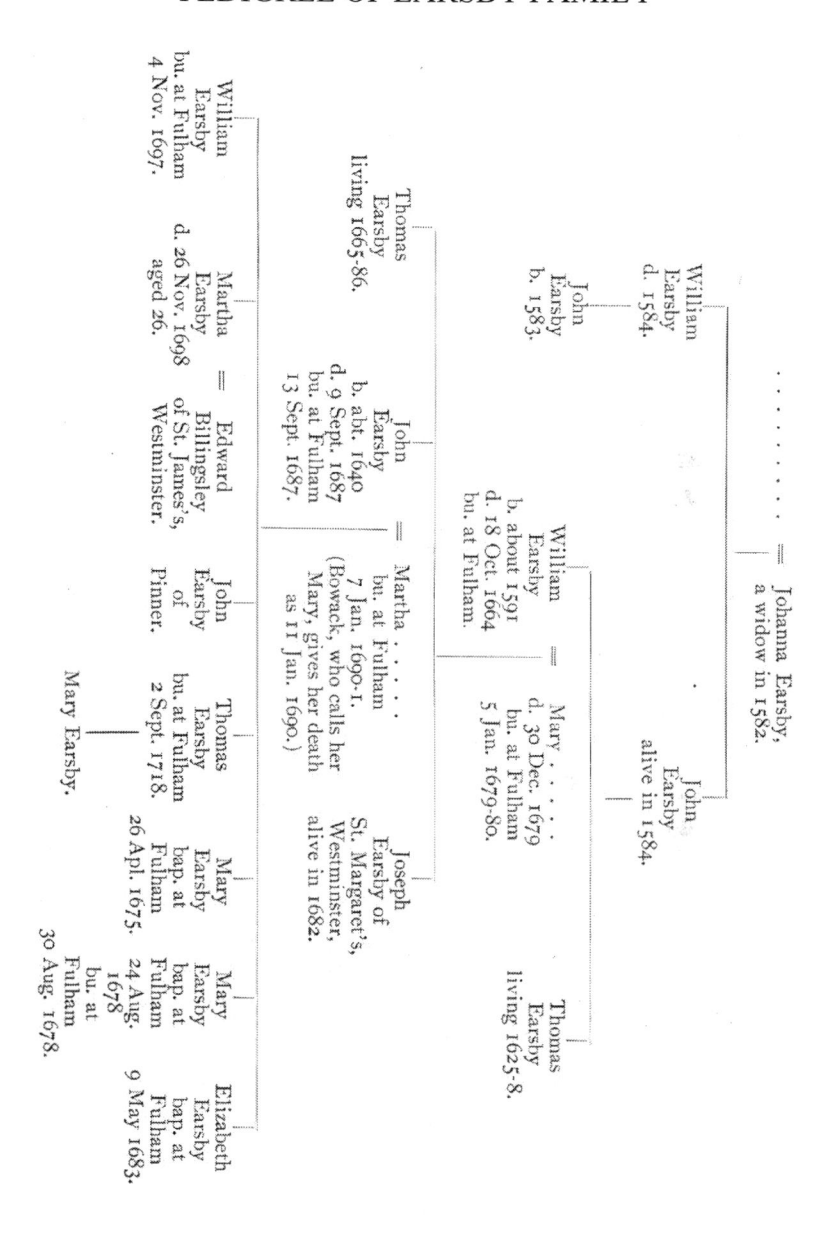

```
                                    Johanna Earsby,
                                    a widow in 1582.
                                          |
                         ┌────────────────┼────────────────┐
                         |                                 |
                    William Earsby                    John Earsby
                    d. 1584.                          alive in 1584.
                         |
          ┌──────────────┼──────────────┬──────────────┐
          |              |              |              |
       John          Thomas         William         Mary .....       Joseph         Thomas
       Earsby        Earsby         Earsby          d. 30 Dec. 1679  Earsby of      Earsby
       b. 1583.      living         b. about 1591   bu. at Fulham    St. Margaret's, living
                     1665-86.       d. 18 Oct. 1664 5 Jan. 1679-80.  Westminster,   1625-8.
                                    bu. at Fulham.                   alive in 1682.
                         |
          ┌──────────────┼──────────────┐
          |              |              |
       John          Martha .....   William
       Earsby        bu. at Fulham  Earsby
       b. abt. 1640  7 Jan. 1690-1. bu. at Fulham
       d. 9 Sept. 1687 (Bowack, who calls her
       bu. at Fulham  Mary, gives her death
       13 Sept. 1687. as 11 Jan. 1690.)

    William         Martha       =   Edward          John          Thomas        Mary         Mary         Elizabeth
    Earsby          Earsby           Billingsley     Earsby        Earsby        Earsby       Earsby       Earsby
    bu. at Fulham   d. 26 Nov. 1698  of St. James's, of Pinner.    bu. at Fulham bap. at      bap. at      bap. at
    4 Nov. 1697.    aged 26.         Westminster.                  2 Sept. 1718. Fulham       Fulham       Fulham
                                                                                 26 Apl. 1675. 24 Aug.      9 May 1683.
                                                                                              1678
                                          |                                                   bu. at
                                     Mary Earsby.                                             Fulham
                                                                                              30 Aug. 1678.
```

455

Robert Foot, who purchased Washes Farm in 1706, died in 1714. By his will, dated 6 April of that year, he devised the farm in moieties to his wife, Ann Foot, and to Samuel Lambert, a London merchant, son of his niece, Sarah.

Samuel Lambert died in 1728. By his will, dated 22 January 1727-28, he left his moiety of Washes Farm to his grandson, William Bagnall. Subsequently the property passed into the possession of Godfrey Clarke, of Chilcote, co. Derby, who, in 1743, sold the messuage to Elizabeth Ashhurst, of Crutched Friars. This lady, in 1751, disposed of Washes Farm and the lands attached to it, in all, 35 acres, to John Whittle, junior, of St. John's, Hackney. The farm must have been broken up soon afterwards.

Westwards of Washes Farm was, in ancient times, a piece of woodland, known as Stylegrove, Scillegrove, Stillgrove, or Stillgroves, 16 acres in extent. The earliest mention of it occurs in the minutes of a Court in 1422. It existed down to about the middle of the last century.

Crabstocks was an ancient heriotable messuage at North End, surrounded on three sides by Washes Farm. The fourth side, the east, abutted on the North End Road. To Crabstocks, we are told, were attached orchards, yards, gardens, and dovehouses.

In the Court Rolls the name Crabstocks first occurs under the year 1545. It was successively owned by the Adam, Gresham, Lidgould, Reading, Burkett, Matthewes and Westbrook families. It survived down to about 1740.

EAST SIDE

The first point of interest was a sombre building, erected by Mr. Tom Slater, the well-known Kensington butcher, in 1834.

For a long time Kensington Hall stood tenantless, and, on this account, doubtless, arose the sobriquet of "Slater's Folly," by which it became known. It was, in 1839, taken by Mr. James Dale of Streatham, whose wife brought hither a young ladies' school. In 1843 the school was transferred to Mr. Robert Johnson and his wife.

In 1860 the Rev. A. S. Lendrum took Kensington Hall, which he renamed St. Margaret's College. He conducted it as a school for young gentlemen down to 1865. In 1875 it was taken by the benevolent Society of St. John of Jerusalem and turned into a Convalescent Hospital, but the scheme had to be abandoned, and Kensington Hall once more stood tenantless. About 1880 the mansion was taken by a Roman Catholic Sisterhood and called St. Joseph's Orphanage. In 1891 this institution was removed to new premises at Brook Green. It was sold in 1896, and in the spring of the following year the "Folly" was demolished to make way for the Kensington Hall Gardens Estate.

This heavy looking, brick building had an ornamental cement elevation, relieved by fluted columns with balcony above. From the upper windows, and from the lead flat to roof, an excellent view over Fulham could be obtained.

On entering we found ourselves in a large outer hall, 26½ feet in length, stone paved and having double doors opening into an inner hall. On the right of this was the dining-room, 41 feet by 17 feet, a plain apartment with an oak floor, opening, in the rear, upon a conservatory, which ran the whole length of the back of the house. The drawing-room, 27¾ feet by 17 feet, also opened on to the conservatory. The library was 20 feet by 17 feet. Two stone staircases extended to the upper floors, on the first of which was the reception-room, 40 feet by 17 feet. On the second and third floors were numerous bedrooms.

In the drying-room attached to the laundry, in the basement of the premises, was a stone inscribed

T. S.
1834,

the initials of the builder and the year of the erection of the house. In the centre of the garden, at the back, was a disused fountain, and, between it and the house, a semicircular stone alcove. To the right was an additional piece of ground used as a playground. The grounds measured 2a. 2r. 28p.

Next to Kensington Hall, going northwards, was North End House, also the property of Mr. Slater. In 1852-53 it was the residence of Dr. Smith, in whose time it had a large medical museum. From 1872 to 1876 Mr. Alfred Thrupp, the carriage builder, lived here. It was taken down about 1877, when Beaumont Road was formed. It is said that it was once the residence of the notorious Madame Rachel. Its grounds measured 2a. 0r. 28p.

Kensington Ball. From a photograph by Mr. T. S. Smith, 1896

At the end of Beaumont Road, overlooking the railway, is the studio of Mr. Albert Bruce Joy, the sculptor, one of Foley's most brilliant pupils.

Near to North End House was a residence known as Tyfrey, and, later, as King's Cottage. The house was pulled down in 1873-74. The Metropolitan District Railway was extended to Hammersmith in 1874, when North End Station was built on the site of King's Cottage. The new line was opened on 19 September 1874. In 1877 the name was changed to West Kensington Station.

An ancient house at North End was named Pheasants. We first hear of it in 1581, when "John Cryspe" was elected the Lord's bailiff for "Vesaunces" tenement. "John Cripps," in 1612, was chosen bailiff for "ffeysaunts." On 13 May 1625, Peter, son of John Cripps, surrendered to Thomas Dolwin, citizen and bricklayer of London, "a messuage called in English the tenement of Pheasants with appurtenances and six acres at North End." This messuage, we learn, lay between the lands of Thomas Earsby on the south, Earl's Court on the east and the King's highway on the west. Its precise position was between the North End Road and the old Creek. Northwards its site terminated about Edith Villas, and southwards in the neighbourhood of Beaumont Road.

The Camells next held Pheasants. Richard Camell in 1630 died seized of it, when his son, Richard, was admitted.

The next we hear of Pheasants is in the time of Charles II, when it was owned by Robert Hicks of Parson's Green. His widow, Mrs. Aurelia Hicks, was, in 1695, elected the Lord's reeve for Pheasants. At a Court Baron in 1713 we find proclamation made for the heirs of the trustees of Robert Hicks, his widow and both trustees appointed under his will being dead. The heir proved to be Hicks Burroughs, who, in 1714-15, sold Pheasants to John Millett, senior, a well-known market gardener of North End. Richard Bradley, in his "Philosophical Account of the Works of Nature" (1739), mentioning some of the more noted kitchen gardens, speaks of "Mr. Millet's at North End," which "affords us Cherries, Apricocks, and curiosities of those kinds, some months before the Natural Season." Millett, who had other grounds at North End, in 1717, sold the estate to Edward Keepe.

Pheasants next came into the possession of the Scotts, a family of brickmakers. In 1749 Thomas Scott died seized of "one customary messuage and 6 acres of land called Pheasants at North End." At his death his sons, John and Thomas, were admitted. They probably pulled down Pheasants.

The "Three Kings" was built by the Scotts about the middle of the last century. The Church Registers record:

1763. Daniel Elsley (a Stranger Died with the Small Pox at the 3 Kings) bu. 22 Aug.

1791. A man found dead near the three Kings North End name unknown W. H. bu. 8 Apl.

For many years the "Three Kings" was kept by Mr. John Shephard and by the Ropers. Mr. John Roper, who took the house in 1845, died 8 July 1848. His widow, Mrs. Lilly Roper, conducted it down to her death in 1866.

We next come to Edith Villas, commenced, about 1843, by Mr. Robert Gunter, on the site of the brickfields of "Squire" Scott.

At No. 1 lived for 45 years Mr. John Blachford, chairman of the Board of Guardians. No. 3 was once the residence of the Rev. Beaumont Byers, M.A., vicar of St. Mary's, West Kensington. At No. 6 resided his father, the Rev. John Sparks Byers. No. 14 is the home of Mr. John Melhuish Strudwick, the Pre-Raphaelite painter. Mrs. Scanes, known in the world of art as Miss Maude Goodman, resided until 1894 at No. 15. At No. 19 died, on 1 March 1897, Mr. J. Wilton Jones, the well-known writer of pantomimes.

The Villas were named after Edith, daughter of Mr. Robert Gunter, who died 10 February 1849, aged 7. She lies buried at Brompton Cemetery.

In 1895 Nos. 24 to 26 were pulled down to make way for the present block of flats, known as Wellsley Mansions, and the shops called Bank Parade, North End Road.

On the site now covered by the Mornington estate was once a noteworthy residence known as Browne's House, probably so-called from a family named Brown or Broun, prominent people at North End as early as the time of Henry VII and VIII.

Browne's House was long in the occupation of the Arnolds. In 1548 Richard Arnold was elected bailiff for Browne's. At a Court, in 1604, it was ordered that "Thomas Stynt shall avoyde his Tenn^{te} at Browne's house." Afterwards it formed part of the estate of Sir Nicholas Crispe. In the time of the Commonwealth, Browne's House was in the occupation of Elizabeth Porter, who died about 1658.

John Hicks, who held the reversion of Elizabeth Porter's lands, including Browne's House, surrendered it to his son, Robert Hicks, who was admitted in 1658. Hicks let the estate to one Wells. Subsequently it was in the occupation of Lord Griffin.

Robert Hicks, who died in 1669, surrendered the whole of his estate at Fulham, which included three separate messuages, to his wife, Mrs. Aurelia Hicks, for life, with reversion to his daughter, Elizabeth, who had married one Boroughs or Burroughs.

Mrs. Aurelia Hicks survived till 1713, when Hicks Burroughs, described as of Burrough, co. Leicester, grandson of Robert and Aurelia Hicks, came into possession of Browne's House and the other property. In 1717-18 Hicks Burroughs sold Browne's House to Sir John Stanley, bart., who had come to reside at North End some three years previously. Lysons writes:

"Mrs. Pendarves (afterwards Mrs. Delany), well known for her beautiful imitation of flowers in mosaic, writing to Dr. Swift in 1736, says that her employment that summer had been making a grotto at Northend for her grandfather Sir John Stanley."

Sir John, who was one of the Commissioners of Customs, continued to reside at his villa at North End, which he called Paradise, till his death in December 1744. His nephew, William Monk, of the Middle Temple, succeeded to the estate. In 1748 Browne's House was purchased by Francis Greville, Earl Brooke, recorder of Warwick and Lord Lieutenant of Warwickshire created, in 1759, Earl of Warwick.

In 1751 Earl Brooke devised his estate at North End to Wills Hill, Earl of Hillsborough, the second and only surviving son of Trevor Hill, first Viscount Hillsborough. In 1753 the Earl obtained the Lord's license to pull down seven tenements on his estate at North End, the site of which he took into the great yard of his mansion house. He occupied numerous posts. He was Comptroller of the Household of George II, Joint Postmaster General, Secretary of State for the Colonies (1768-72 and 1779-82), and Registrar of the High Court of Chancery, Ireland. He resided at North End ten years. He died 7 October 1793.

In 1761 Browne's House was purchased by Sir Gilbert Heathcote, bart., who greatly improved the property.

Sir Gilbert married first, in 1749, Margaret, youngest daughter of Philip, Earl of Hardwicke, and, secondly, in 1770, Elizabeth, only daughter of Robert Hudson, an East India captain and director. He died in November 1785, and was buried at Normanton, in Rutland. A manuscript note, by an unknown hand, in a copy of Faulkner, at the Hammersmith Public Library, reads:

"His funeral was very grand. The parish beadle attended. I can just remember getting up to the house in time to see it on its journey and went with the cavalcade as far as Hammersmith Turnpike. It took place early in the morning and my brother James was with me."

The estate, in the days of Sir Gilbert Heathcote, consisted of 11a. 0r. 14p.

The Dowager Lady Heathcote continued to occupy Browne's

House down to her death in 1798. The succeeding baronet, another Sir Gilbert, sold the estate for £11,000. Faulkner adds: "The house has been since pulled down, and the gardens converted into brickfields." The demolition took place in 1800. Messrs. John and James Scott, who owned a large amount of property in the parish, were the purchasers of the estate.

Mornington Lodge, which stands in the North End Road, just north of Mornington Avenue, was built about 1834 by Squire Jones, of Mornington House. From 1837 till 1846 it was the residence of Mrs. Lamb. From 1847 to 1852 it was the home of Mr. William Schan Lindsay, the great ship owner, who moved here from St. Peter's Villa, Percy Cross (see "Fulham Road: Munster Road to Percy Cross" chapter).

Mornington Lodge. From a photograph by Mr. T. S. Smith, 1897

Mr. William Samuel Burton (1853-66) and Mr. Edwin Burton (1867-74), of the firm of Burton and Ripon, ironmongers, and Mr. R. Herbert (1876-77) were succeeding tenants. Mr. William Henry Gibbs, C.E., who came to reside at Mornington Lodge in 1878, built, in partnership with Mr. J. P. Flew, the Cedars, Salisbury, and other estates at Fulham. In 1889 he greatly enlarged and improved Mornington Lodge, to which he added a new wing. The grounds, which originally measured 2a. 3r. 34p., were considerably reduced by the construction of Mornington Avenue. After standing empty for awhile, the house was bought by the late Mr. Howard Nalder, of the firm of Nalder and Colyer, the Croydon brewers. It is now in the occupation of Col. John Mount Batten, who married the widow of Mr. Nalder.

Mornington House was erected early in the present century on a portion of the site of Browne's House. It is said to have been built as a shooting box for the Right Honourable William Wellesley-Pole, third Earl of Mornington, elder brother to the famous Duke of Wellington. Nothing, however, is known about his residence here. The house, which faced the North End Road, just north of Mornington Lodge, was, in 1824, taken by Mr. William Jones. Squire Jones, as he was better known, resided here till 1836. In 1843 Mornington House was purchased by Mr. John Thornton Down, gentleman-at-arms in Her Majesty's Service, who resided here till 1874. Mr. Down also purchased Mornington Lodge. He died at Putney, 25 February 1878.

Mornington House was pulled down by Messrs. Gibbs and Flew in 1878-9, when the site was covered by the Mornington estate.

The grounds contained some fine trees. In one corner, near what is now the end of Matheson Road, was a celebrated grotto, which, according to an old tradition, was Pope's grotto, brought from Twickenham. The grotto, which is said to have cost £1,000, held some forty people. From its roof depended numberless beautiful stalactites. The area of the grounds, in Maclure's "Survey," is given as 6a. 3r. 13p.

Between what is now Stanwick Road and the West London Extension Railway was Versailles Nursery, surrounded by a high wall. For many years, about the middle of this century, it was conducted by John Salter, a noted chrysanthemum grower, who lived in an old-fashioned house, which abutted upon the railway. The nursery ceased about 1872. Its extent was 2a. 0r. 21p.

Resuming our walk along the North End Road, we next reach The Grange, the history of which dates back to the time of Charles II. The estate then comprised three acres of land, on which stood two cottages. The first we hear of them is in 1669, when Mrs. Elizabeth Hill died seized of them. Mrs. Hill was the widow of Mr. Emery Hill, of Westminster, father of Mr. Emery Hill, who, in

1708, founded the charity in Rochester Row, known as the Emery Hill's Almshouses.

On the death of Mrs. Hill, the two cottages and three acres at North End came into the possession of her daughter, Jane, wife of Humphrey Grinsell, of St. Margaret's, Westminster. By her will, dated 28 September 1670, Jane Grinsell devised the property to her husband and heirs for life, with remainder to certain persons in trust "To putt forth children yearlly to apprentice for ever." This charity has been lost.

The Trustees sold the estate to Hopton Shuter, of the Inner Temple. Charles Frothingham was the next owner. In 1682 the property was in the occupation of Sir Edward Dering, and, in 1687, of Alexander Davenant. In 1687-88 it was purchased by Sir William Cranmer, who, in 1691, sold the estate, still in the occupation of Davenant, to John Kendrick, of Godstone, Surrey.

The next owner was John Smith, or Justice Smith, as he is sometimes called in the Rate books. He held the two cottages and three acres by a copy of Court Roll dated "Wednesday in Whitsun week 1713."

There is little doubt that Justice Smith, on his admission, pulled down the cottages and erected the twin houses which, about 1836, came to be styled "The Grange." On one of the stackpipes, at the back of the south house, is the date 1714, a date which was confirmed by an interesting discovery made a few years ago. On the removal of the ancient wainscotting, which formerly surrounded the walls of the dining-room of the south house, there was found, rudely written in white chalk, on the back of a panel which had been fixed over the mantel-piece, the following inscription:

> "This room was wincoted In ye year 1714 August ye 20 On ye first year of his Majesty George the 2."

The date, "1723," which appears on the sundial on the top of the south house, has been taken to indicate the date of the erection of the house, but more probably it merely records the year in which the dial was added. There was formerly a similar dial on the north house.

The Court Rolls for 1714 record:

"Wee present Mr. Smith at North End for lopping and cutting downe my Lord's Trees upon the Waste before his doore without leave for which wee amerse him one pound."

The Grange. From an engraving by T. Rickards, circa 1800

Justice Smith lived in the north house. The south house was, in 1717, let by him to the Countess of Ranelagh, widow of Richard, third Viscount and first Earl of Ranelagh.

John Smith, in his will, dated 10 March 1721-22, devised

"All that messuage in which I now dwell and one messuage adjoining in the occupation of the Countess of Ranelagh, Samuel Vanderplank and their assigns to John Smith, son of Henry Smith, ironmonger, and his heirs."

A codicil, attached, dated 5 December 1724, provides as follows:

"All my household goods in my Dwelling House at North End in the Parish of Fulham are to remain in the said House, as also whatsoever is on the p^{r}misses, Stable, Coachhouse or Gardens and the House in which the Countess of Ranelagh now lives is not to be separated but to be and remain joyntly together with my dwelling House, as also all the Goods in the kitchen or any other part of the House, which belongs to me All which I give and bequeath to my executor Samuel Vanderplank before named in my will and the same to have and enjoy during his natural Life and after his Decease to his issue Male and in failure of Male Issue then to my other executor Henry Smith and his Issue Male."

Justice Smith died about 1724-25. It is clear from the foregoing will that the south house, in the time of the testator, was in the joint occupation of Lady Ranelagh and Mr. Samuel Vanderplank. In the Rate books the name of the former appears for some years alone, but in 1726 and 1727, the names are conjoined.

Under the will of John Smith, junior, dated 17 November 1740, Samuel Vanderplank inherited the whole estate, to which he was formally admitted, upon a recovery thereof, 18 November 1747.

By his will, dated 11 January 1748-49, Samuel Vanderplank devised his estate to his daughter, Ann, who had married Gilbert Joddrell, of Lincoln's Inn. He died in 1749, leaving a son, James. At a Court in 1750 the Homage found that Samuel Vanderplank had lately died seized of divers copyholds, including:

> "All that customary messuage or tenement with the garden land and appurtenances adjoining in which John Smith formerly dwelt near adjoining to a messuage heretofore in the tenure of the Countess of Ranelagh and was then lately separated therefrom and also the said messuage or tenement with the garden land and appurtenances thereto belonging, formerly in the tenure of the said Countess and held by the yearly rent of 1s. 2d.," etc.

This allusion to "lately divided" shows that The Grange, which is still two houses, must have been subject to the partition in the time of Samuel Vanderplank. Not unlikely it was Justice Smith who divided it when the Countess of Ranelagh became his tenant. Gilbert Joddrell and Ann, his wife, who were admitted in 1750, resided in the south house.

In 1739 Samuel Richardson, the originator of the English novel, came to North End, taking a lease of the north house, in which he resided for fifteen years.

Mr. Reich ("Richardson Corr.," by Barbauld i., clvi.) refers to Richardson's villa by the name of Selby House, but this appears to have been a fanciful, rather than an actual, appellation. A discussion in "Notes and Queries," as to the origin of this name, was solved by Col. W. F. Prideaux, who, after consulting "Sir Charles Grandison," wrote to that journal (8th S. X., 14 Nov. 1896):

"The first few pages of that work sufficed to solve the mystery. 'Selby House' was the residence of the uncle and aunt under whose roof the beautiful Miss Byron spent her orphan girlhood. 'Sir Charles Grandison' was published in 1754, and it seems clear that the circle of friends who, as we learn from Miss Highmore's sketch, were in the habit of listening to the novelist whilst he read to them the manuscript of 'Grandison,' were wont to playfully bestow upon their host's abode the name of the residence which had sheltered his heroine's youthful years."

Samuel Richardson.
From an engraving by E. Scriven, after a picture by M. Chamberlyn, 1811

Richardson was born in Derbyshire in 1689. He was, at the age of seventeen, apprenticed to John Wilde, a London printer. After serving his time, he worked as a compositor and corrector of the press. At length he took up his freedom and set up in business for himself, in Salisbury Court, Fleet Street. Through the influence of Mr. Onslow, Speaker of the House of Commons, he obtained the contract for printing the "Journals." Nearly the whole of his literary work was done at North End. Here he wrote "Pamela" (1740), "The History of Clarissa Harlowe " (1748), and "Sir Charles Grandison " (1754). The second won for him a European reputation.

Norris Brewer, in "London and Middlesex," written in 1816, describing the North End Road, observes:

> "On the eastern side of the road, in the close contiguity of Hammersmith, is still remaining the house in which Richardson first sought a resemblance of rural retirement. The exact period at which he became a resident does not appear; but it is unquestionable that much of 'Clarissa Harlowe,' and the greater part of 'Sir Charles Grandison' were written at North End. The house in which he lived forms part of a large building said to have been erected by Lady Ranelagh early in the last century. The original structure is now divided into two tenements and probably was subject to such a partition when Richardson was an inhabitant. The rooms are spacious and several are ornamented by carving in an agreeable style. The gardens are large and in one of these is still remaining a grotto of extensive proportions, and embellished with shells, spars and some curious fossils. We may suppose that this was the spot, to which Richardson repaired, with the first light of morning, to form those fanciful pages which afterwards afforded so much pleasure to the public; and that here those friends assembled who were first favoured with a perusal of the result of his labours."

The position and identity of this famous grotto are points which have been much discussed. Mr. Austin Dobson, in his "Eighteenth Century Vignettes," tells us that it is described by Mr. Reich, of Leipzig, as being "in the middle of the garden, over against the house," and contained a seat in which the novelist was accustomed to work. Mrs. Barbauld, in her "Life of Richardson," prefixed to his "Correspondence," writes:

> "He used to write in a little summer house or grotto, within his garden, at North End, before the family were up, and, when they met at breakfast, he communicated the progress of his story, when every turn, and every incident, was eagerly canvassed."

In the novelist's "Correspondence," published by Sir Richard Phillips, are, in vol. iv, a view of the house, and in vol. ii, a coloured engraving, made by Miss Highmore, of the interior of the grotto, with Richardson reading the manuscript of "Sir Charles Grandison" to a party of admirers. Brewer, who visited the house about 1816, could find but little similitude between the grotto or summer house, as then existing, and this drawing.

The explanation is that there were two summer houses, one pulled down about 1801, and one which perished in a great storm in 1836. The summer house which Brewer saw must have been the latter one, and, as this bore but little likeness to the coloured engraving by Miss Highmore, we are forced to the conclusion that Richardson's grotto was that which disappeared about 1801. In a deed in the possession of the owners of the north house, dated 13 December 1791, mention is made of the "tool house at the east end of the said garden under the summer house." In a paper of 1801, it is noted:

> "Since Mr. Jackson's purchase the tool house and summer house have been pulled down which stood in the North East corner of the Gardens and the end wall there has been taken down and a new one built further eastward on the other part of the land purchased by Mr. Jackson of Mr. Vallotton by which the garden is lengthened."

The new wall which was then built, "further eastward," was doubtless the present boundary wall, against which the garden studio of the late Sir E. Burne-Jones now stands. The position of the summer house taken down about 1801 must therefore have been somewhat westward of this wall. When the second summer house was built we do not know. It is, however, quite possible that some of the old material was used in its erection. Of its destruction in 1836 we shall speak later.

The following anecdote concerning Richardson is told by Sir Richard Phillips:

> "A widow kept a public house near the corner of North End Lane, where she had lived about fifty years; and I wanted to determine the house which Samuel Richardson the novelist had resided in in North End Lane. She remembered his person, and described him as a round, short gentleman, who, most days, passed her door, and she said she used to serve his family with beer. 'He used to live and carry on his business,' said I, 'in Salisbury Square.' 'As to that,' said she, `I know nothing, for I never was in London.' 'Never in London!' said I; `and in health, and the free use of your limbs?' 'No,' replied the woman; `I had no business there, and had enough to do at home.' 'Well, then,' I observed, `you know your own neighbourhood the better. Which was the house of Mr. Richardson, in the lane?' 'I don't know,' she replied, `I

am, as I told you, no traveller. I never was up the lane; I only know he did live somewhere up the lane.' 'Well,' said I, 'do you go to church?' 'No,' said she, 'I never have time. On Sundays our house is always full. I never was at Fulham Church but once, and that was when I was married, and many people say that was once too often, though my husband was as good a man as ever broke bread. God rest his soul.' "

Boswell, in his "Life of Johnson," tells the following good story of Richardson's inordinate vanity:

"A literary lady has favoured me with a characteristic anecdote of Richardson. One day at his country house at North-end, where a large company was assembled at dinner, a gentleman who was just returned from Paris, willing to please Mr. Richardson, mentioned to him a very flattering circumstance, that he had seen his 'Clarissa' lying on the king's brother's table. Richardson, observing that part of the company were engaged in talking to each other, affected then not to attend to it. But by and by, when there was a general silence, and he thought that the flattery might be fully heard he addressed himself to the gentleman, 'I think, Sir, you were saying something about - ,' pausing in a high flutter of expectation. The gentleman, provoked at his inordinate vanity, resolved not to indulge it, and with an exquisitely sly air of indifference answered, 'A mere trifle, Sir, not worth repeating.' The mortification of Richardson was visible, and he did not speak ten words more the whole day. Dr. Johnson was present, and appeared to enjoy it much."

In 1754 Richardson moved to Parson's Green. Mrs. Delany notes under date 30 October 1754:

"Richardson is very busy, removing this very day to Parson's Green." ("Delany Corr.," iii. 296.)

John James Vallotton, of whom we shall speak when we reach Otto House, next door, was admitted to the north half of The Grange in 1795. In November 1801 he sold it to John Jackson, of whom we have spoken in connection with the summer house. Two years later (1803) this portion of The Grange was bought of Jackson by Mr. William Ludlam, a merchant, of Earl's Court.

About 1816 the south house was taken by Mr. Archibald Sinclair, whose widow lived here till 1824.

It was during the residence of Mrs. Ludlam, the widow of Mr.

William Ludlam, that the second summer house was destroyed by a storm. The following interesting account of the occurrence we quote from a letter, dated "Northend, Fulham, Dec. 11th 1836," from Mrs. William Ludlam to Mrs. James Ludlam of Netherbury, Dorset. This letter is now in the possession of the latter's granddaughter, Miss Edith Harrison, by whose courtesy we are enabled to quote from it:

> "It was this day week that I fully intended writing to you, my dear Elizabeth, but the unexpected arrival of Col. D'Arcy in Town and his proposal of dining with me on that Day prevented me from putting my good intention respecting you in practice and all this week I have been so busy and so interrupted that I have found it impossible. . . . but first let me congratulate you upon not having been blown off the Island and set down in Ireland, or Spain or perched upon one of the Andes or having your pretty cottage fall down and bury you beneath its ruins. . . . alas, alas, though we may now talk of such things with a light heart and a smile upon the lips a week or ten days ago the thought of them made us tremble, at least I did for I slept immediately under a Stack of Chimneys which I knew to be loose. Sleep I could not but laid watching the rising gales and determining to rise at the first rattle of tiles or bricks and make my escape in time and at all events to sleep below the next night, but upon investigation I found there was another stack of chimneys close to that apartment more likely to fall than the other, so I remained till bricklayers could venture up with safety and I could be put into safety, but it was no easy task to procure either tiles or chimney pots, slates or bricklayers, the last were engaged everywhere the former used up in the course of the first four and twenty hours and their value increased to three times their usual cost, all this week I have had men chipping and knocking over my head and the Kitchen Chimney was obliged to be nearly taken down and re-built for safety, so I suppose I shall have or shall suffer a loss of some pounds, in the gardens I have been more favourably treated, lost only one Tree and the old Summer house which was torn up root and branch. . . . it was in a dilapidated state and I did not have it repaired on account of the threatened Rail road which I now begin to think will really take place and is not only to cross my Meadows but will go through Mr. Stanley's house and he has received a notice to quit which is very pleasant, particularly as he has just renewed his Lease and been painting and repairing said house at a great expense, he comforts himself by making them pay well for it, and I must endeavour to do the same, but nothing will recompense me for the pleasure which I have had in the shrubbery and the delight I have found in its walks and solitude, and Mrs. Pratt is

a fellow mourner with me, but to return to the tale of the Tempest again, you have no doubt read of all the miseries-it has occasioned and the loss both of lives and limbs and I consider that it is a fresh call upon my gratitude to the Almighty that not only myself but all that are dear to me of my Friends have been spared from all evils but those which it is in the power of Money to alleviate and to cure."

The Grange. From a photograph by Mr. T. S. Smith, 1896

On the death of Mrs. William Ludlam, the north half of The Grange was, in 1843, let for three years to Mrs. Macnamara, who resided here with her accomplished daughter, Louisa Cranstoun Macnamara (Mrs. Nisbett), perhaps the most delightful actress of her day.

Louisa Cranstoun Macnamara was the daughter of Mr. Frederick Hayes Macnamara. Her birth took place at Ball's Pond, Islington, on 1 April 1812. Her earlier appearances on the stage were under the name of Miss Mordaunt. She first appeared at Drury Lane on 26 October 1829. In 1831 she married John Alexander Nisbett of Brettenham Hall, Suffolk, a captain in the First Life Guards. Seven months after her marriage, she was left a widow, her husband having been killed by a fall from his horse. Returning to the stage, Mrs. Nisbett achieved an enormous success.

On 13 October 1844 she married, at the Chapel at Fulham Palace, Sir William Boothby, bart., of Ashbourne Hall, Derbyshire, Receiver-General of Customs. Sir William, who was 62 years of age at the time of his marriage, <u>died at his country seat</u>, 21 April 1846. On 12 April 1847 Lady Boothby reappeared at the Haymarket. Her final engagement was under Mr. James Anderson's lesseeship of Drury Lane in 1851, when failing health led her to limit her performances. She died at St. Leonard's, 16 January 1858.

Mr. John H. Pollock lived at the north house from 1850 to 1855. In November 1867 it was taken by its late occupant, Mr. (afterwards Sir) Edward Coley Burne-Jones, bart.

This distinguished Pre-Raphaelite painter was born at Birmingham, 28 August 1833, and received his education at King Edward's School in that town. In 1852 he gained an exhibition at Exeter College, Oxford. It was at Mr. Comlie's, of the Clarendon Press, that he first saw the works of the Pre-Raphaelites, including Holman Hunt's "Light of the World." While at college he met William Morris, who became his life-long friend. In the Christmas vacation of 1855 Burne-Jones came to London, where he met Rossetti, and in the following year took lodgings with him in Sloane Terrace. He married in 1860 Miss Georgiana Macdonald. In 1881 he was made an honorary D.C.L. of Oxford, and in 1890 was decorated by the French Government with the Legion of Honour. He died at The Grange, 17 June 1898.

Since the time of Mr. A. Sinclair, the successive occupants of the south house have been Mrs. Henry Green (1825-1834), Mr. Richard Sparkes (1835-1839), Mr. Solomon I. Paine (1845- 1851), and Mr. John Paine (1852-1862). Mr. John Paine died very suddenly as he was one day entering the house.

From 1863 to 1866 The Grange was the residence of Frederick William, fourth Marquis of Londonderry, who <u>threw the two houses into one</u>, and made several structural alterations.

In 1867, when Mr. Burne-Jones took the north part of The Grange, the houses were again divided. In 1868 Mr. Charles Johnson, who died 23 September 1894, purchased the south house, which is still the residence of his widow.

The portion of The Grange in which the late Sir E. Burne-Jones resided has now a stuccoed front, with large single windows in lieu of the small windows which it once possessed. This change was probably made to save the window tax. There is, outwardly, now little identity in appearance between the two portions of The Grange, though they were once precisely alike. It is impossible to say at what period the act of vandalism, which still hides the old red bricks of the north house, was carried out, but it was doubtless in the early years of the century. While the south half of The Grange has suffered comparatively little at the hands of the "improver," the northern portion has undergone numerous changes. The entrance to the house was, like the other half, originally at the side but now it is in the front. Entering the north house we find ourselves in a spacious vestibule, once a room. Facing us, a staircase, of spotless whiteness, leads to the upper floors. To the left of the vestibule is the dining-room. Adjacent to this room is the kitchen. Beyond this, built upon what was once a portion of the garden, is an extensive addition to the house, made, probably, some sixty years ago. The bottom portion was, till recently, the great artist's drawing-room. Over it, on the first floor, is a large studio, originally a drawing-room.

The grounds of the north part of The Grange are 3r. 6p. in extent. On the north side they are bounded by the old wall of Otto House. On the south side is the wall which divides the two gardens of The Grange. At the far end stands Sir E. Burne-Jones's garden studio. Facing the drawing-room is a pleasant lawn with here and there a notable tree. One is an old mulberry, which bears just as good fruit as it did when North End was a rural hamlet. Another familiar friend in this part of the grounds of The Grange is a wonderful apple-tree, which, however, now year by year loses a limb. Nearer the house is a fine old thorn, on which Samuel Richardson must often have looked.

The south house is a very pleasant one. Inside its gate, one might almost imagine oneself in the heart of the country, so restful the environment. The drawing-room, overlooking the lawn at the back, is an elegant apartment. On one of the French windows at the end of this room is scratched the name "Johnson 1762," supposed to be the signature of Dr. Samuel Johnson, a great admirer of Richardson, whom he described as "an author who has enlarged the knowledge of human nature and taught the passions to move at the command of virtue." The dining-room, in the front, had, until

Mr. C. Johnson's time, its walls wainscotted. The panels are said to have been painted by Lord Londonderry's sister. It was, as we have already said, on the back of one of these that the inscription, referring to the wainscotting of the room in 1714, was found. This fine old red-brick house has fortunately escaped the stucco embellishments bestowed upon its neighbour.

The grounds, which now measure about one acre, contain some noteworthy trees, especially a mulberry, reputed to be three centuries old, a walnut-tree of extraordinary proportions, and, until 1895, when it was cut down, a lovely briar rose, which Sir E. Burne-Jones has immortalized in his picture of the "Sleeping Beauty."

In the roadway before The Grange were once two or three fine chestnut trees, one of which attained a great size. The north and south houses are now numbered respectively 49 and 51 North End Road.

Next to The Grange is a large white residence known as Otto House (No. 47 North End Road.) It was built, towards the close of the last century, by Colonel Otto, whence, of course, its name. The original house, which served the purpose of a shooting box, was only a small building. The present verandah shows the width of the frontage at the time of erection. Its next owner was Mr. John James Vallotton, who resided here from about 1795 to 1804.

The house is still surrounded on all four sides, by a high brick wall built by Mr. Vallotton. In Lisgar Terrace, at either end of the wall which faces north-east, are tablets inscribed:

"This wall is the | Property of | Mr Jno Ja^s Vallotton and two feet of ground NE."

The building of walls within two feet of one's ground was due to an old custom, the two feet being reserved as a space on which ladders, etc., could be placed in case of the walls requiring repair. Two similar tablets are affixed to the north-west and south-east walls.

After a brief residence here by Mr. Willoughby Rooke, Otto House was purchased by Colonel Benjamin Ansley, who lived here from 1809 to 1835. In 1836 it became the property of Dr. Alexander Robert Sutherland. On his death it came into the hands of his son, Dr. Alexander John Sutherland, and, on the latter's death, into those of the present owners, Dr. Henry Sutherland and Mr. Arthur Henry Sutherland, sons of Dr. A. J. Sutherland. Thus, Otto House has been in the possession of this family for three generations. It is a licensed house for the reception of ladies of unsound mind.

From time to time the house has been considerably added to. The north-west wing was built by Dr. A. R. Sutherland and the south-east wing by Dr. A. J. Sutherland. The extension on the north side of the house was added by the present owners.

The spacious hall runs through the house from front to back. The view of the well-kept grounds, from this point, is very picturesque. At the back of the house are some fine trees, certainly over a century old. In the days of Colonel Ansley and of the first Dr. Sutherland, when North End was still in its pristine beauty, the grounds of Otto House produced an abundance of fruit, including peaches and nectarines. Five old elms used to stand in front of the wall of Otto House.

Otto House. From a photograph by Mr. T. S. Smith, 1896

Just before we reach Portland Street is Ebenezer United Methodist Free Church, formerly known as the Wesleyan Chapel or Ebenezer Chapel, built by Mr. James Wild, a Wesleyan

Methodist, in 1842. This was the second Wesleyan Chapel in Fulham.

The foundation stone of Ebenezer Chapel was laid by Mr. Wild's son, James Anstey Wild. The stone, which is at the south-west corner of the building, is inscribed on one face

J. W.
Ebenezer

and on the other

Laid by
James Anstey Wild
30th June 1842.

The Chapel cost about £1,000.

Portland Street once bore the more picturesque sobriquet of "The Willows" from the willow hedge on either side. A stone let into the wall at the south-west corner of the street is inscribed

"Portland Street, 1792."

An old beer shop at the opposite corner has the curious sign of the "Live and Let Live."

At one of a row of seven small houses, called Portland Place in the North End Road, just north of Portland Street, was the old village post office.

On the site of the "Cumberland Arms" and Cumberland Crescent was a pretty country house known as Cumberland Lodge. In Maclure's "Survey" of 1853, it is described as "dilapidated." It must have been soon afterwards pulled down, as Cumberland Crescent was built in 1857.

Just beyond Cumberland Lodge, in the North End Road, was Willow Place, popularly called "The Bay," chiefly occupied by brickmakers.

At the north-west corner of Bishop King's Road is St. Mary's Protestant Mission Hall, in connection with St. Mary's Church. On the front is a stone inscribed:

> "This
> Memorial Stone
> was laid to the honour
> and glory of God
> by Miss Annie Louisa Davis
> of Sheepstead House
> Abingdon
> on June 20th 1895."
>
> C. Bradshaw Foy, M.A., Vicar
> B. Pollard } Churchwardens.
> A. Williams }

The building cost £2,600.

SECTION IV: MISCELLANEOUS

A tenement called Ottersale's at North End abutted upon "Earlesfield," i. e. the fields at Earl's Court. It obtained its name from John Ottersale, who lived at Fulham in the time of Henry VI. He surrendered his holdings about 1459. The Court Rolls, down to 1567, contain many references to "Otersales," " Ot'sales," etc.

From the time of Richard II down to that of Edward VI there stood at North End a tenement known as Richard's. In 1394 William Hunt died possessed of "a messuage and 10 acres in Benerssh called Richardes" when his son Robert was admitted. Through marriage the tenement descended to Gerard Hokelem, William Conyngton, and John Adams. In 1485 Idonea, widow of John Adams, died possessed of several holdings, including "Ricardes in Benerssh," when her son, William Adams, was admitted. Richard's tenement is not mentioned after 1551.

A messuage called Bearcroft lay in Great Broadfield. It is first mentioned in the minutes of a Court General in 1688, when it was the property of the Earsby family, in whose possession it long remained. In the last century it came into the hands of the Scotts. It was latterly divided into two tenements.

A messuage at North End was known as New Close. It abutted on the north on "a lane leading from North End Lane (i.e. Deadman's Lane) to ffulham Field." In 1724 it was sold by Sarah and James Sanders to Jacob Tonson, the bookseller. In 1737 it became the property of Samuel Tonson, his great nephew.

A messuage called Oade Close, Woade Close or Wood Close lay just south of Fursebush Close. It is not mentioned in the Court Rolls till 1613. It belonged to the Crispes from whom it passed to the Glovers. In 1714 Benjamin Glover surrendered "One messuage and 4 acres called Woade Close at North End to the use of his will." He died in 1715. By his will, dated 14 September 1714, he devised Woade Close to

> "my loving sisters Mary Garroway and Bridget ffriend equally, which estate at North End my father, Mr William Glover purchased of Henry Crispe."

OTHER NOTEWORTHY RESIDENTS OF NORTH END

In the early years of the last century, Mr. Tanegue Azier, a manufacturer of gunpowder, resided at Noman's Land. The Church Registers contain the following entries:

> 1701. Mary Juman servant maid from Mr. Aziers Nomans land bu. 30 Oct.

> 1705. John the son of Taneguy Azire Gunpowder maker bapt. 11 April.

> 1706. Ann the Dau. of Tanegue and Hester Azier Gunpowder maker bapt. 23 June.

> 1711. Tanegue the son of Tanegue and Hester Azier bapt. 2 Mar.

The Dormers were a great family in North End in the 16th century. Godfrey Dormer of Thame, Oxfordshire, had five sons, William, Geoffrey, Michael, who became Lord Mayor of London, Peter and Edward. The first we hear of the Dormers is in 1515, when Thomas Cann surrendered Churchgate's (See earlier in this chapter), and other copyholds in Fulham to the use of Sir Michael Dormer of London, mercer. This was the third and most distinguished son of Godfrey. In 1522 Michael Dormer sold to his youngest brother Edward the tenement called Churchgate's at North End. At a View, in 1522, the following presentment was made:

"Michael Dormer has broken the halve (*le halve*) at North End so that the water is not able to run on its course. To replace same before next Court or (forfeit) vj^s viij^d."

At a View, in 1525, Michael Dormer was ordered

"To lop his boughs overhanging a way from Gybbes grene to Benyssurs (i.e. Ben'ssh's near Marshcroft).

Edward Dormer died in 1539. His will, dated 21 Jan. 1538-39, was proved 12 Jan. 1539-40 by Katherine Dormer, his widow. (P.C.C. 1 Alenger.) To Fulham Church he left two torches.

Katherine Dormer became the wife of Sir John Gresham. Sir Michael Dormer died in 1545. At a Court Baron, in 1547, his youngest son, Ambrose Dormer, was admitted to the estate, belonging to the Dormers, in "ffulham strete."

The connection of this family with North End was due to the marriage of the widow of Edward Dormer with Sir John Gresham.

Sir John Gresham was the third son of John Gresham of Holt, in Norfolk, where he was born. He was a member of the Fishmongers' Company, and was admitted a mercer in 1517. In 1537 he was Sheriff of London and was knighted the same year. In 1546 he founded the Grammar School at Holt. He was Lord Mayor of London in 1547, when he revived the pageant of the "Marching Watch" on Midsummer eve. He died of fever at his house in Bassinghawe, London, 23 October 1556, and was buried in the church of St. Michael Bassishaw on 25 October. His will, dated 12 February 1552-53 and 18 September 1554, was proved 26 November 1556. (P.C.C. 28 Kitchen.) The first wife of Sir John Gresham was Mary, daughter and heiress of Thomas (or William) Ipwell or Ipswell of London, mercer. She died 21 September 1538, and was buried at St. Mary, Aldermanbury. His second wife was Katherine Sampson, the widow, as we have already observed, of Edward Dormer. By the first marriage, Sir John had five sons and six daughters.

Sir John Gresham's lands at North End descended to his widow, the Lady Katherine Gresham and to John Gresham of Mayfield, co. Sussex, his third son. In 1567 John Gresham sold a considerable part to William Smythe. Lady Katherine Gresham died in January 1576-77 and was buried at St. Michael's Bassishaw, 9 January 1576-77. At a View in 1577, it was reported that

> "Lady Katherine Gresham died since last Court seized of free and customary lands and Elizabeth, now wife of John Gresham, Esq., is daughter and next heir and of full age."

John Gresham died in November 1578, and was buried in the vault of his cousin, Sir Thomas Gresham, in St. Helen's, Bishopsgate, 3 December 1578.

Elizabeth Gresham, the wife of John Gresham, was the daughter of Edward Dormer of North End by Katherine, subsequently the wife of Sir John Gresham. She was therefore step sister to her husband. The marriage took place at St. Michael's Bassishaw, 17 July 1553. She survived her husband and subsequently married William Plumbe of North End.

The issue of John and Elizabeth Gresham were three sons, Thomas, William and Edmund (or Edward). Of Thomas, to whom the Fulham property descended, we shall presently speak. William married the widow of James Baynton. The date of his death is not known. Edmund (or Edward) died 7 May 1593, aged 16, and was buried at Fulham Church (see vol. I, "Fulham Church: Its Monuments" chapter).

Thomas Gresham married, first, Isabel, relict of ___ Gibbons, and, second, Judith, daughter of Sir William Garrard of Dorney, Buckinghamshires. He <u>died at Fulham on Tuesday, 11 July 1620</u> and was buried in the Parish Church. His eldest son, John Gresham of Fulham and Albury, was not quite ten at his father's death. His other children were James and Penelope Gresham. His will, dated 8 July 1619, was proved by Judith Gresham, his widow, 17 July 1620 (P.C.C. 74 Soame). To the poor of Fulham he left £4. <u>He left all his lands</u> in the parish to his wife, Judith. The following note is appended to the will:

> "Memorandum that upon Twesdaye the eleaventh of Julye of one thowsand six hundred and twentie between seaven and nyne of the clocke in the foore noone or thereaboutes this will of Thomas Gresham Esquier was founde in the pockett of his hose ymediatelie after his decease by Master ffrancis Plumbe his brother in the presence of

Anthony Mountague and others."

John Gresham continued rated for his messuages at North End down to 1641. His son James probably disposed of the property, as we hear nothing further of the Greshams in connection with North End.

PEDIGREE OF GRESHAM FAMILY
(next page)

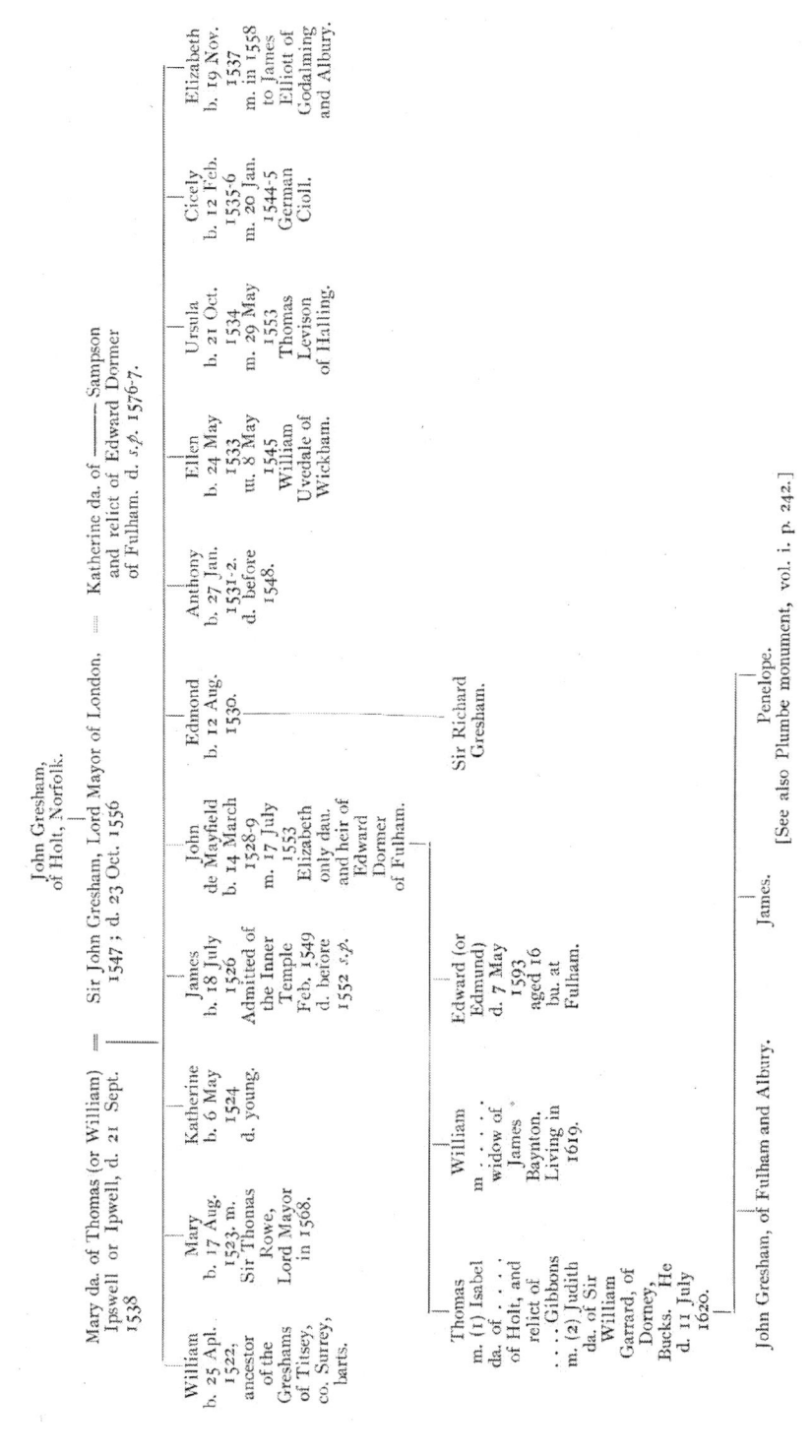

John Gresham,
of Holt, Norfolk.

Mary da. of Thomas (or William) Ipswell or Ipwell, d. 21 Sept. 1538 == Sir John Gresham, Lord Mayor of London. 1547; d. 23 Oct. 1556 == Katherine da. of ——— Sampson and relict of Edward Dormer of Fulham. d. s.p. 1576-7.

Issue of Mary:

- **William** b. 25 Apl. 1522, ancestor of the Greshams of Titsey, co. Surrey, barts.
- **Mary** b. 17 Aug. 1523, m. Sir Thomas Rowe, Lord Mayor in 1568.
- **Katherine** b. 6 May 1524 d. young.
- **James** b. 18 July 1526 Admitted of the Inner Temple Feb, 1549 d. before 1552 s.p.
- **John de Mayfield** b. 14 March 1528-9 m. 17 July 1553 Elizabeth only dau. and heir of Edward Dormer of Fulham.
- **Edmond** b. 12 Aug. 1530.

Issue of Katherine:

- **Anthony** b. 27 Jan. 1531-2. d. before 1548.
- **Ellen** b. 24 May 1533 m. 8 May 1545 William Uvedale of Wickham.
- **Ursula** b. 21 Oct. 1534 m. 29 May 1553 Thomas Levison of Halling.
- **Cicely** b. 12 Feb. 1535-6 m. 20 Jan. 1544-5 German Cioll.
- **Elizabeth** b. 19 Nov. 1537 m. in 1558 to James Eliott of Godalming and Albury.

Issue of John de Mayfield:

- **Thomas** m. (1) Isabel da. of .... of Holt, and relict of .... Gibbons m. (2) Judith da. of Sir William Garrard, of Dorney, Bucks. He d. 11 July 1620.
- **William** m .... widow of James Baynton. Living in 1619.
- **Edward (or Edmund)** d. 7 May 1593 aged 16 bu. at Fulham.

Sir Richard Gresham.

John Gresham, of Fulham and Albury.   James.   Penelope.

[See also Plumbe monument, vol. i. p. 242.]

In an ancient house at Noman's Land resided the Plumbes. The first of the family to settle at North End was William Plumbe of Eltham, of whom we have spoken in our account of his monument in Fulham Church (see vol. I, "Fulham Church: Its Monuments" chapter). In the Court Rolls his name first appears in 1581. At a Court Baron in this year it was presented that

> "Wm Plumbe gent, in violation of an order of a former Court has permitted his cattle to feed in the Common Fields after the Feast of All Saints to the waste of the hedges in that neighbourhood, vizt. a horse colour grey, which is always upon the neighbouring hedges, wherefore (he forfeits) vj^s viij^d."

In 1583 it was presented that

> "Wm Plume, Esq., keeps three animals in the Common called Wormehall (i.e. Wormholt Wood, now Wormwood Scrubs) beyond the hedge (*ultra semita*) and contrary to the order made, wherefore he is in mercy iij^s iiij^d."

Joshua Sylvester, the "Silver-tongued Sylvester," poet and translator, author of "Lachrymæ Lachrymarum," a lament on the death of Prince Henry, son of James I, was a nephew of William Plumbe, whom he used to visit at North End. In one of his poems entitled "The Wood-man's Bear," he thus puns on his uncle's name:

> I was wont (for my disport),
> Often in the Summer season,
> To a Village to resort,
> Famous for the rathe ripe Peason,
> Where, beneath a *Plumm*-tree shade,
> Many pleasant walks I made.
> (Stanza 30).

William Plumbe died at his house at North End, 9 February 1593-94. By his first wife, Margaret, daughter of Thomas Nevil, he left no issue. By his second wife, Elizabeth Dormer, widow of John Gresham, he left one son Francis, whose descendants for many years dwelt in the parish. One of these, Nicholas Plumbe, was elected Overseer in 1672 and Surveyor of the highways in

1676.

At the Bodleian Library, Oxford, is preserved an interesting deed, dated 3 November 39 Elizabeth, bearing the signature of Elizabeth Plumbe, and her seal "erm. on a bend vaire," relating to an exchange of lands, lying "near the common called Gibbes Greene" at North End (Middlesex Charters, No. 177).

MISCELLANEOUS NOTES

The following miscellaneous notes relating to North End follow in chronological order:

1522. From Court Rolls:

> "John Burton has grubbed up a way mere from Shortland towards Northende. To make said way mere as it was from ancient time or forfeit xl^s."

1640. The Parish Books show that this year North End had twenty-four rated inhabitants.

1646. At a meeting of the Vestry, on 19 May of this year, information was brought by the parish constable, Thomas Walter

> "Of Mr. Smith at Northend that he doth keepe an Inmate one Mrs. Collins, with three small children hauing no husband, Wherevpon it was Agreed that the said Thomas Walter should prosecute according to the statute in that case made and prouided."

1650. The Parish Books this year show only eleven persons assessed under North End.

1666. The assessments this year, under " North ende," number thirty-six.

1670. From the Churchwardens' Accounts:

> "To a poore woman att Northend in her sickness and want 4s. 0d."

1675. From the Church Registers:

"A man childe left in the outhouse of John Bowchiers at North End and was Baptized by the name of Fulham to wch name of Fulham is added Northend as his surname bap. 23 Mar."

1680. From the Church Registers:

" Hannah, a poor woman y^t dyed vpon ye highway at Northend bu. 26 Oct."

1718. From the Churchwardens' Accounts:

"16 Feb. To John Paul (the parish undertaker) for a coffen and shroud for ye man
that died at North End and buring 9s. 6d."

"To money paid for bringing the man to church 2s. 6d."

1755. From the Church Registers:

"A man that Died on a Dunghill at Northend bu. 19 Feb."

1764. From the Overseers' Accounts:

"Relieved a man and woman and two children all being ill with a fever at North End 1s. 6d."

1788. From the Overseers' Accounts:
"Relieved a poor woman at North End with a lame leg 1s. 0d."

CHAPTER X: HAMMERSMITH ROAD

The only portion of the Hammersmith Road which lies within the parish of Fulham is the south side, from Counter's Bridge, now the site of Russell Road Bridge, to No. 155.

Counter's Bridge, from time immemorial, spanned, at this point of the old Roman road, the Creek or ditch which divided Fulham from the parishes of Kensington and Chelsea. Its maintenance, in common with that of the other bridges within the Manor, was in the hands of the Bishop. The first we hear of it is in 1421, when, at a Court General, the Homage presented that the Lord should repair "Contessesbregge." In 1422 the name appears as "Contassebregge," and in 1445 as "Cuntassebregge." In 1475 it was reported at a Court General that the "bridge called Countesbregge is ruinous and the Lord ought to repair it." At a Court General in 1517 the following presentment was made:

> "The Lord to repair a bridge called Countes lying in the highway leading from London towards Hounselowheth."

In 1617 the name is, for the first time, spelled "Countersbridge." In Rocque's "Map of London," 1741-45, the name is given as Counter Bridge, and in Pigot's "Atlas of Counties," 1831, as Counter's Bridge. Caunter or Caunter's Bridge is a less frequent spelling. The origin of the name is doubtful.

The Creek some way south of Counter's Creek bore the name of Billingwell. In 1410 John Lane was presented at a View for his unscoured ditch "at Byllingwelle." In 1437 the name is written "Billingwell Dyche." At another View, in 1484, the tenants were required to cleanse the ditch from "Countasbregge to Billyng Wellditch."

Adjoining Counter's Bridge, and abutting upon the Hammersmith Road, are three acres of land which, with two acres at Parr Bridge, constitute the trust known as Dr. Edwardes' and Bishop King's Charity.

This valuable benefaction owes its origin to Dr. Thomas

Edwardes, Chancellor to Dr. John King, Bishop of London. Dr. Edwardes, by a codicil, dated 13 January 1618-19, to his will, dated 9 January 1618-19, left a sum of "one hundred poundes to the poore of ffulham to buy them land." Dr. King, by his will, dated 4 March 1620-21, gave £20 to be bestowed upon the poor of Fulham parish in bread, beef and money, at the discretion of his executrix. This £20 was, however, with the consent of Mrs. King, added to the gift of Dr. Edwardes, making £120, which sum was invested in the purchase of five acres of land, namely, the two at Parr Bridge, of which we shall speak later, and the three up in this far-off corner of North End.

From the ancient "Register Book" we learn that Sir William Bird, kt., Dean of the Arches, Dr. Edwardes' executor, duly paid the £100, which was "imployed for Purchasing of Landes to the use of the Poore of the sayd Parishe," and that the £20 was employed with the consent of Mrs. Joan King, the executrix of her husband, Dr. King,

> "towards the purchasing of Lands for the use of the Poore of the sayd parishe, that thereby the rather there might be a continuall and a yearlie remembrance of the sayd Legacye, that which could not have been if it had been bestowed all in one yeare at once."

Accordingly,

> "The sayd Summe of Twenty Pounds was added to the Hundred Pounds given by Dr Edwards: and made up the Summe of Six score Pounds with which Six score Pounds there was purchased Six Poundes a yeare for ever to the use of the Poore of the sayd Parishe."

The meaning of this last remark is that the copyhold land which the Trustees purchased with the combined legacies produced a rental of £6 *per annum,* which was distributed every year in beef and bread to the poor on Fulham side and Hammersmith side.

At a Court Baron, held on 13 May 1623, Sir Edward Powell, kt., and others were admitted to hold the lands at North End

> "on trust, to permit the wardens of the church of Fulham, and the overseers of the poor of the same town, from time to time, for ever, to dispose of the rents and profits thereof, to the use of the poor

inhabitants of the said parish for ever according to the intent of the two wills of Dr. Edwards and Bishop King respectively."

In 1682 Joseph Earsby, youngest son and heir of William Earsby, of North End, then deceased, and last surviving Trustee of the "poores land," surrendered the trust. The North End portion is described as

"Two Closes near Counters Bridge, between the lands of Thomas Earsby Esq. on the south and the King's highway upon the north, and upon the Common sewer (*i.e.* the Creek) east and a lane called ffurbush lane leading from the King's highway to North End, west."

The new Trustees appointed were Joseph Earsby, Edward Saunders, *jurus consulti,* John Perry, Esq., Thomas Earsby, Esq., Richard Stevenson, clerk, Vicar of Fulham, William Cleeve, William Dodd, John Earsby, Anthony Nourse, Jonas Morley, Nicholas Goodwin, John Plucknett, William Holden, Edward Dodd, William Pannett, Philip Morley, Edward Nourse and John Leasy.

At a Vestry, held on 24 October 1721, Reginald Marriott, Esq., William Withers, Esq., Mr. Alexander Wells, senior, and Mr. Christopher Gray were chosen Trustees for the poor land at North End.

A detailed description of the estate administered under Dr. Edwardes' and Bishop King's Trust is given in Court Roll of 16 April 1836. The trust is dealt with at pp. 13-17 of the Rev. R. G. Baker's "Benefactions" and pp. 20-22 of the Rev. F. H. Fisher's "Endowed Charities of Fulham."

By an indenture, dated 24 June 1786, the greater part of the site was let on "building lease, for a term of 99 years, to Mr. William Vale. About 1788 Mr. Vale built Vale Place, a row of twenty-six houses, facing Hammersmith Road. At the east end of Vale Place was a small inn, described in the lease as the "Rose and Crown." Under this name the house is mentioned in the Highway Rate books as early as 1771. Its stables and gardens covered 2a. 3r. 13 poles. The inn is believed to have been rebuilt by Mr. Vale, who re-named it the "Hand and Flower." It is so called in the minutes of a Court Baron, held in April 1838.

Along the Creek, starting from the "Hand and Flower," Mr. Vale erected a row of genteel but somewhat dismal houses, still called Portland Place. These were completed about 1816. Here, at No. 7, lived William Belsham, the celebrated Whig historian. He was the author of a "History of Great Britain." Mr. Belsham died at Portland Place, 17 November 1827, aged 75.

At No. 4 Portland Place, lived, from 1845 to 1847, Mr. Gilbert A'Beckett, author of "A Comic History of England, *etc.*" and one of the chief contributors to *Punch* magazine.

To the south of Vale Place there were built on this estate, Portland Place, in the North End Road, Willow Place, Little Vale Place, nicknamed "Vinegar Yard," and John's Place. William Street, which commenced about the centre of Vale Place, running southwards to the north-east corner of the grounds of Otto House, was built about the same time. It recalls the Christian name of Mr. Vale. About halfway down it, on the west side, were the St. Mary's Girls' and Infants' Schools, built in 1840 by the Rev. Sparks Byers. William Street Board School, erected in 1874, now covers the site of these Schools. It was opened 5 April 1875. It was enlarged in 1885 (476 places) and in 1889 (420 places). It accommodates 448 boys, 444 girls, and 476 infants; total 1,368. In 1899 a Higher Grade School was added.

Mr. Vale's lease fell in on 24 June 1885. Since then the character of this part of Fulham has been completely changed. Vale Place has made way for a line of handsome shops and of residential flats. Behind these a new road has been formed, called Bishop King's Road, running from William Street to North End Road.

Wending our way westwards and crossing the northern end of North End Road, we reach the site of the old turnpike, which crossed the road opposite Blind Lane (now Blythe Road). Under the Act of 1863, turnpikes were abolished. That across the Hammersmith Road was taken down on 1 July 1864.

Just westwards of the top of the North End Road, on the high road, is Dorcas Terrace, Nos. 89 to 119 Hammersmith Road, so called after the Christian name of the wife of Mr. Payne, who built the houses in 1824.

Devonshire Street, Munden Street and Vernon Street, which were built rather over half a century ago, call for little mention.

Most of the property about here belongs to the Vernon Investment Association. This company was formed in 1846 by some tradesmen at the Bloomsbury end of the Hampstead Road. They held their first meetings at the "Vernon Arms," No. 418 Southampton Street, Pentonville, whence, of course, the name of the Association arose. The property at North End was bought in 1848, for the purpose of creating leasehold ground rents, but the scheme was not successful. The company ultimately built Devonshire Street and Sun Street. The latter was re-named Vernon Street.

In 1856 a piece of land lying in Vernon Street was surrendered by the Association to the Commissioners of Police for the purpose of building a Police Court to meet the increasing needs of this district. It was at first known as the Vernon Street Police Court. Subsequently it was called the Hammersmith Police Court. Finally, in 1889, its name was changed to that of the West London Police Court.

Monday morning at the Police Court.
From a photograph by Mr. T. S. Smith, 1895

Between Munden Street and Auriol Road was an old fashioned brick house known as The Cedars or Cedar House. In its forecourt grew two fine old cedars, which conferred their name upon the house. They were trees of immense girth. The grounds measured 2a. 3r. 5p. A portion of them was known as the Wilderness.

In 1779 the house was taken by James Branscombe. This person had, in early life, been a servant in the employ of the Earl of Gainsborough. According to Faulkner's "Hammersmith," he carried on, for upwards of forty years, a lottery office in Holborn. He was a Common Councilman of the Ward of Farringdon Without. In 1806 he served, with Sir Jonathan Miles, in the office of Sheriff and received the honour of knighthood. His name disappears from the Fulham Rate books after 1787. The Hunts were the next occupants of The Cedars. James Hunt died here in 1799. Mr. Richard Hunt, who built St. Mary's Chapel, now Church, died here in 1818. From 1821 to 1868 The Cedars was a girls' boarding school conducted, from 1821 to 1842 by Miss A. C. Fryer, and, from 1843 to 1867 by Miss Anne Rawlinson, who died in the last named year.

The Cedars. From a drawing by H. W. Burgess, lithographed by C. J. Hullmandel, *circa* 1840

The house, which was popularly said to be haunted, long stood tenantless. In 1882 it was pulled down, when the site was built over. (Nos. 129 to 135 Hammersmith Road.)

Chapel Garden, a gardener's cottage, and Chapel Place, a row of four houses, which stood where the Edith Road now joins the Hammersmith Road, reminds us of the proximity of St. Mary's Chapel, now Church. Just beyond the top of Edith Road is St. Mary's Church House, originally built as a school, in connection with St. Mary's, for the education of thirty boys and thirty girls. The school house was erected on a part of the churchyard. With a view to the enlargement of the premises, a deed, bearing date 5 May 1848, was executed, by which the Rev. J. S. Byers conveyed, under the School Sites Acts, "to the Minister and Chapel Wardens of the District of St. Mary," a small piece of land, the buildings erected upon which were to be used for a school "for the education of children and adults, or children only, out of the labouring, manufacturing and other poor classes in the said district." The school was to be in union with the National Society. Upon the piece of ground thus conveyed additional buildings were erected, and the enlarged school was devoted entirely to boys, the girls and infants being, as we have seen, otherwise provided for.

St. Mary's Church, which faces the Hammersmith Road, was erected as a proprietary chapel in 1813-14 by Mr. Richard Hunt of The Cedars.

At Fulham Church on Sunday, 7 February 1813, the Rev. William Wood, the Rector, gave out the following notice:

> "Whereas it is intended to build a Chapel at North End, it will be necessary first to set apart some land for a Burying Ground and in order to the Consecration thereof, a grant of the said land must be made to the Parish under an agreement, that it shall be given back to the proprietors by Lease; the Parishioners are desired to meet in Vestry on Thursday next at 12 o'clock, to signify their assent in Form to the Contract which is proposed."

On the motion of the Rector the following resolution was carried at a meeting of the Vestry held on 11 February:

> "That the Inhabitants now present do give their consent that Richard Hunt, Esqre. of North End, be permitted to Erect a Chapel on his own

Estate there situated, and that the said Inhabitants agree to accept (as a Gift to the Parish) a certain portion of Land to be appropriated as a Burying Ground to the said Chapel."

St. Mary's was the second church built in Fulham, and was intended by its proprietor to meet the spiritual needs of the growing population of the northern portion of the parish and the adjacent district.

The original building was a plain rectangular edifice, composed almost entirely of brick, with ordinary glass windows, possessing not the least pretension to beauty of form or design. A deep gallery ran round three sides of the church, which, singularly enough, was so arranged that the chancel came at the south end. By way of fiction this south end is called the east, while the other parts of the church are correspondingly miscalled.

St. Mary's was consecrated by Dr. Howley, Bishop of London, on 6 May 1814. It continued to be a chapel of ease to Fulham down to 1836, when, under 59 George III, cap. 134, a district was assigned to it. In 1856, under Lord Blandford's Act (19 and 20 Vic., cap. 104), it became a separate and distinct ecclesiastical parish.

Mr. Hunt died four years after the building of the chapel. Against the south wall is the following tablet to his memory:

"In a Vault beneath are deposited | the mortal remains of | Richard Hunt, Esquire, | born the 6th November, 1748, | and died the 28th May, 1818. | This whole sacred edifice | which he built at his sole expence | and in which he now lies entombed | is his noblest and most lasting monument | and will record whilst it endures | his zeal for God's glory and the national religion. | Also Elizabeth his wife, | who died Nov[r] 13th 1821, aged 78 years, | and also Mary-Anne | their daughter, | who died June 24th 1822, | aged 34 years."

In 1883 St. Mary's Church was considerably enlarged and improved, the accommodation being increased from 1150 to 1700 seats. The improvements, which included the present facade facing the Hammersmith Road, a new chancel and transepts and a wooden roof, cost about £4,000, towards which the Rev. John Macnaught, the Vicar, contributed £1,500. The church was re-opened on Sunday, 27 January 1884.

St. Mary's contains many stained glass windows, the chief of which were placed in the church by the Rev. John Macnaught. In the apse or bay, in which the communion table stands, are three two-light windows, of beautiful design, inscribed:

> "Erected by John Macnaught, M.A., vicar, 1884, in loving memory of John Macnaught, M.D. died 1883; Harriet Macnaught, died 1884; Charlotte Macnaught, died 1876."

At the end of the west transept is a fine stained glass window of four lights inscribed:

> "Erected by John Macnaught, M.A., vicar, 1884, in loving memory of Dorothy, his wife, Dora Redwar, Elisabeth Say, Ellen Agnes, their daughters."

At the end of the east transept is a square window of stained glass. In the side walls of the original building some of the plain glass windows have made way for others of stained glass, placed there to the memory of the Prince Consort, Mr. C. J. Parker, Mr. Francis Robert Jago, R.N., Mr. John Beaumont Byers and his wife Marian.

To the left of the chancel is the organ, an instrument of fine tone. It was placed in its present position when the church was enlarged in 1883. Previously it had stood in the centre of the north gallery, where the choir was also located. It was erected by subscription in 1819, and was built by Kendall and Co., of Kensington. It was enlarged in 1899. A door to the right of the chancel leads to the vestry, formerly two rooms, now thrown into one.

Beneath the window at the end of the west transept is a marble tablet inscribed:

> "M.S. | Anne Rawlinson | of 'The Cedars,' Northend; and of Retford, Nottinghamshire | Born May 10th 1786, died February 11th 1867 | 'Faithful unto death' | This tablet is erected by numerous affectionate pupils | who, through a period of 50 years, | were taught, by her bright example, to look to | Jesus, as 'The way, the truth, and the life.'"

Against the south wall is a brass inscribed:

"In affectionate memory of the Rev[d] John Flowers Serjeant | who died April 19th 1881 after labouring for six years | as the faithful and well beloved vicar of St. Mary's, Fulham | . This inscription and a granite monument in the churchyard | were set up by those to whom he was dear | and the sum of £75 was entrusted to the Charity Commissioners | for the benefit of sick children to be selected | by the vicar and wardens of this church."

One remarkable feature of St. Mary's is the number of mural tablets fixed against its walls. The font, which is square in shape, is situated just to the right of the north door.

In 1890 the walls of the apse and transepts were beautifully decorated, the cost of the improvements reaching over £500. In 1896 the side galleries were removed. The removal of the galleries reduced the seating accommodation by only 150 sittings, as a large new gallery was built at the north end. In 1899 new oak choir stalls and a wrought iron screen were added.

St. Mary's Church. From a photograph by Mr. T. S. Smith, 1896

The vaults, now disused, are a peculiar feature of St. Mary's. They are entered by means of a small door at the south end of the church, underneath the whole length of which they run. At one time these vaults, which are absolutely dark, contained 130 bodies, the decay of which caused a fœtid odour to constantly pervade the church. During alterations in 1883, the Vicar obtained an Order in Council for the removal of the corpses from the vaults to the churchyard, where they were re-interred in a huge grave on the west side.

The first Register of Burials at St. Mary's, containing the years 1814-28, is incorporated, year by year, with the Registers of Fulham Parish Church. The original Registers for 1829-36 are missing. Fortunately there is still preserved a list of the burials, from the commencement to 1836, made by Mr. Lancelot Bathurst.

The churchyard, which was closed by Order in 1881, is completely honeycombed with graves, though the stones are neither numerous nor important. From the Church Registers it appears that no less than 2,601 persons have been buried at St. Mary's. Perhaps the most noteworthy interment was that of Mr. Joshua Jonathan Smith, Lord Mayor of London, by trade a sugar baker, of Bennet's Hill, Doctors' Commons. In 1803 he was elected Alderman of Castle Baynard ward, and in 1808 Sheriff of London and Middlesex. He was Lord Mayor of London in 1810. He was, conjointly with Lady Hamilton, executor of the will of Lord Nelson. He died 15 July 1834, aged 69, at his residence in St. Mary Abbott's Terrace, Kensington. On 21 July his remains were interred in one of the vaults beneath the church.

One of the oldest stones in the churchyard is that to the memory of a Mr. John Southcombe, of Bratton-Fleming, Devonshire, who was, the epitaph records,

> "unfortunately killed on the High Road near this place by the Bath Mail Coach on the 21 of Oct. 1814 in the 50th year of his age."

The Overseers' Accounts for this year contain the following entry:

> "Paid Adkins of the Hand and Flower for the expences of the Jury which sat several times on John Southcomb who was killed by the Mail Coach £1. 8s. 6d."

Beneath the Iron Room in the Edith Road, built by the Rev. J. F. Serjeant, are also several graves. The churchyard extends on both sides of the church and also at the rear of St. Mary's Place.

The successive incumbents of St. Mary's have been:

MINISTERS
Elms, Rev. Edward, M.A. 1814 to 1822
Lateward, Rev. Frederick 1822
Wesley, Rev. Charles, M.A. 1823 to 1837
Byers, Rev. John Sparks, B.A. 1837 to 1856

VICARS
Byers, Rev. Beaumont, M.A. 1856 to 1874
Serjeant, Rev. John Flowers, M.A. 1874 to 1881
Macnaught, Rev. John, M.A. 1881 to 1886
Alcock, Rev. Henry Jones, M.A. 1886 to 1888
Foy, Rev. Charles Bradshaw, M.A. 1888

The Rev. John S. Byers purchased the advowson of the Bathurst family, to whom it had descended through the marriage of one of Mr. Hunt's daughters with Mr. Lancelot Bathurst, J.P. The advowson has now passed into the possession of a prominent Nonconformist.

Beyond St. Mary's Church are four houses, formerly known as St. Mary's Place. Here the Black Bull Ditch, coming from Shepherd's Bush, reached the Hammersmith Road, which it crossed under a brick arch. The "Black Bull" inn, just outside the Fulham boundary, occupied the site of the residence of the High Master of St. Paul's School.

The bridge over the ditch was anciently called the Brook Bridge. The Court Rolls contain numerous presentments respecting the failure of the Lord of the Manor to keep it in good condition. The earliest is in 1422.

END OF VOL. II

NOTES

Chapter I: Fulham Church and Churchyard (Miscellaneous)
As Shakespeare reminds us:
"*May*. Sirrah, go fetch the beadle hither straight,
[Enter a Beadle with whips."
2 Hen. VI., ii., I.
1547-48: There is no date above the Fulham return, but at the commencement of the Roll are the words "Primo Die Januarij Anno primo Rex Edwardi VI."

Chapter II: Rectors And Vicars Of Fulham
Sir William Vigorous: "Sir" was a title formerly given to clergymen.
He died 20 Feb. 1495-96: Newcourt says 14 Feb. 1495-96.
Reports, Hist. Manuscripts Com., vol. vi. House of Lords' Cal.: In the Institutions at the Record Office, Adoniram Byfield is stated to have been "admitted and instituted to the Rectory of ffulham, 12 Nov. 1646, on Presentation of the King." This is, of course, merely a legal fiction, the King being credited with all presentations to the benefices sequestered by Parliament between 1645 and 1649.
The name of Adoniram Byfield appears among the minutes of the Fulham Vestry from 8 May 1644, down to 19 April 1652: Unlike other incumbents, he never appended any designation, not even that of minister, to his name.
Presented to the former in 1645 by Edmund Harvy and to the latter in 1657 by Cromwell: 1645 is probably a slip for 1654, the date of Knight's formal admission to the rectory of Fulham. 1657 is the date of his formal admission to the vicarage.
Katherine Byfield, on 12 Feb. 1660-1, took out letters of administration: The writer of Byfield's life in the D. N. B., who does not mention the will above quoted, assumes that the Letters of Administration refer to Adoniram Byfield, rector of Collingbourne-Ducis. Far more probably they refer to his son, whose wife was also called Katherine.
In the Parliamentary Survey, made in 1649-50 "for Examinyng and finding out the number and yearly values of all parsonages and

ecclesiasticall and spirittuall lyvings and benefices," etc.: Augmentation of Livings, v. 12, p. 210, Lambeth Palace Library. The original document, with seals affixed, is at the Record Office.

Became minister at the chapel of St. Paul's, Hammersmith: In the Survey of Church Livings, made by order of Parliament, Isaac Knight, who is described as "Mr of Arts," is stated to be "a very zealous and painfull Preacher of the gospell of Jesus Christ."

Received from Col. Harvey presentation to the livings which were in his gift: From an entry in the Admissions at Lambeth Palace Library, there is reason to believe that Col. Harvey presented him to the rectory of Fulham on 4 Nov. 1652.

Dated at Whitehall the 24th day of November 1654: Admissions, Lambeth Palace Library, No. 585.

The Commissioners on 21 Feb. 1655-56: Augmentations of Livings, Lambeth Palace Library.

Appointed chaplain to Bishop Sheldon, who, on 11 Jan. 1660-61, presented him to the rectory of Fulham: In the State Papers (Dom. Charles II, vol. xxv. 9), is a petition from Geo. Stradling to the King, soliciting presentation to the rectory of Fulham.

His brother, Dr. Francis Turner, Bishop of Ely: Bentham, in his "History of the Church of Ely," states that the advowson of the rectory of Fulham had, for that turn, been granted to the Bishop of Ely.

Cock of Debden in Essex: This Debden rector who visited Fulham was the Rev. John Cock, D.D. The Rev. W. C. Muriel, who was formerly rector of Debden, unlike his predecessor, John Cock, *did* exchange his rectory for Fulham!

Admitted and instituted by the King: The Bishops' Registers at the P.R.O. (Henchman, 10) state that Keene was presented to the vicarage by the Bishop of London by lapse.

Chapter III: Tithes

In the Lambeth Register: We have been unable to verify this statement, since the Library at Lambeth Palace now contains no Register of Archbishop Langton. The earliest is that of Archbishop Peckham (1279).

Col. Arthur Eyre: In the State Papers the name is sometimes given as Arch. (Archibald?) Eyre, and sometimes as Ant. (Anthony?) Eyre.

The vicarial tithes are commuted at £900 a year: At the present value of tithes, this would represent about £650 per annum, but a large amount has been redeemed, while investments made by Queen Anne's Bounty in "Goschens" and Ground Rents probably reduce the actual endowments of Fulham Vicarage to under £600 a year. In 1836 the Tithe Commutation Act was passed, by which all tithes were commuted for money payments.

Chapter IV: New King's Road

Fulham National Schools: The official designation of the schools at the Education Office is the "All Saints, Fulham, School (National)."

ANNO DOM°: It is somewhat curious that the error "Anno Dom°" for "Anno Dom^i" has so long escaped observation.

The boys wore jackets and waistcoats of brown frieze with cord trousers. The girls had blue serge dresses and white straw bonnets: According to an ancient tradition, the practice of clothing the charity children arose out of an alleged bequest by Bishop Vaughan, who, chancing to fall into the Moat, was luckily rescued by some of the boys. Nothing, however, can be discovered respecting the gift by the "good Welsh bishop." The practice of clothing the children at the expense of the schools was discontinued about 1846, on account of the funds being insufficient to cover the additional expense caused by the stringent requirements of the Education Department.

Tree in the school-yard: Mr. Popple planted the two trees which still exist in the girls' playground.

The Schools from 1830 to 1862 comprised three buildings, one each for boys, girls and infants: Between these years the boys' school was behind the teachers' residence, No. 212, New King's Road, the girls' to the east of this house, and the infants' to the west.

He proceeded B.C.L. of Christ Church, Oxford, 17 Dec. 1661: It is by no means unlikely that Dwight obtained this degree through the influence of Bishop Walton. From Foster's "Alumni Oxoniensis" it does not appear that he ever matriculated.

Nor can the exact date of his advent be ascertained: An inscription outside the Fulham Pottery now reads "Estabd. 1671," the date of Dwight's first patent. This is certainly wrong. It formerly read,

"Established 1675."
<u>ffell</u>: The baptism of this child cannot be traced. There is no doubt that the boy was so christened after John Fell (Bishop of Oxford, 1675-86), either as godfather or else as friend of his father. Samuel Dwight, another son of the potter, was christened after Samuel Fell (Dean of Christchurch, Oxford, 1638-47), father of Bishop Fell.
<u>White Gorges</u>: A kind of pitcher.
<u>Formerly M.A.</u>: This is a mistake. John Dwight never took an M.A. degree.
<u>His wife Millicent</u>: Mrs. Millicent Dwight died about 1742, Administration of the goods, *etc.,* of Millicent Dwight, "late of the Parish of St. Clement Danes," was granted to John Dwight, her husband, 23 Aug. 1742. (P.C.C. Act Book).
<u>William White, or Wight, as the name is occasionally spelt</u>: George, "son of Willm and Lidya White," was buried at Fulham, 2 Apl. 1755.
<u>Hawkins's Alley</u>: Abraham Hawkins, gardener, *temp.* Geo. II.
<u>Mr. William Hyde, the magistrate</u>: In the British Museum is a copy of a letter from Mr. William Hyde to Sir John Danvers, bart., justice of the peace for Leicestershire and Middlesex, regarding the licensing of the "Duke's Head Alehouse." [8vo Lond. 1791].
<u>Mr. Hodgson's carter</u>: Dr. Hodgson lived at North End.
<u>The wall of Lot 1</u>: This old wall is still standing behind the houses in Pomona Place.

Chapter V: Parson's Green
<u>Great brick house</u>: Probably Brightwell's, *q. v.*
<u>High white house</u>: Albion House.
<u>Mary</u>: "Mary" is an error for "Martha."
<u>Tyrringham Backwell, son of Alderman Edward Backwell</u>: In a letter from John Verney to Sir R. Verney, dated London 8 Oct. 1677, the following passage occurs:

> " . . . In Whitefriars were burnt 4 or 5 houses also to the ground, and as many more defaced. Mr. Carpenter, in whose chamber the fire began, was burnt in his bed; Alderman Backwell's son's chamber was burnt, and he thought to be in it, but by good luck he went that evening to Fulham."
> - Hist. Manuscripts Com. Reports, vol. vii. p. 470.

Robert Hicks or Hickes, the son of John Hicks, a woollen draper, lies buried in Fulham Church: This Robert Hicks, for a few months in 1662, was an Alderman of Bridge Ward, but, paying his fine, he was discharged service. By his will, dated 1 June 1669, he devised his property to his wife Aurelia Hicks, who died in 1713. He left a daughter, Elizabeth, who became Elizabeth Burroughs. Her son, Hicks Burroughs, inherited the estate.

William Rumbold: William Rumbold was apparently residing at Fulham before the date of this admission. A letter in the Record Office, from his brother Henry, is dated "Follam 13th July 1664."

In an information, sworn 23 Oct. 1690: Starkey *v.* Rumbold, Chancery Proceedings.

Francis Villiers: This was the Frank Villiers or "Villain Frank" of the State Papers. He died 1 Feb. 1693-94, and was buried in Westminster Abbey.

Charles Chambrelain, an alderman of London: He and his wife, Rachel, are buried at St. Helen's, Bishopsgate, where an elaborate monument to their memory was erected by Lemyng and Abigail Rebow.

Albion House School was continued down to about 1828: It was at this school that Robert Banks Jenkinson, 2nd Earl of Liverpool, K.G. (b. 1770, d. 1828), Prime Minister, received his early education.

Henry Waver: Esch. 19, Ed. IV, No. 65. The name is spelled Waver, Wavers, Waffer, Wafers, *etc.*

Sir Michael Wharton, or Warton, knight, in possession: The Whartons were connected with the Careys of Brightwells, hence, possibly, the association of the former family with this district. Lady Philadelphia Wharton, the mother of Sir Thomas Wharton, was the daughter of Robert Carey, Earl of Monmouth and, consequently, sister to the Hon. Thomas Carey, who married Margaret, daughter of Sir Thomas .Smith.

He died 8 Oct. 1655: Some authorities say 12 Oct. 1655.

This was High Elms House, familiar to a later generation as Park House: It may be noted that it is specially mentioned in the leases of this half acre strip that the south wing of the mansion built by Mr. Powell stood on the adjacent freeland. The exact position of the house will be seen from the sketch plan taken from one of the leases.

Sr Nicholas Smyth: He became Vicar of Fulham in 1550. Dr. Simon Heynes, Rector of Fulham, 1536-52.

Survey of Church Livings: Public Record Office: Survey of Church Livings, vol. iii., co. Middlesex, 1656.

This Living being worth some Ages since £800 per annum, which building is now let in tenements: This is an obvious error. The sinecure was never, at any time, worth anything approaching £800 a year.

Three acres of wet marsh common ground: This piece of wet marsh ground lay on the east side of Peterborough Lane, almost facing Bell's Alley.

Thomas Ranch: The name is variously spelled Ranch, Wranch, Wrenche, Wrench, Rench, etc.

Messrs. James Veitch and Sons, whose connection with this property dates from 1870: The earliest reference to Southfield occurs in the Court Rolls for 1486, when mention is made of "Litill Southfeld."

He died at Parson's Green, 19 April 1569: We make this statement on the authority of the Funeral certificate which states that he "departed at his parisshe at ffulham on Tuesday, the xixth of Apryll in A° Dn^i 1569."

My cousin Wythe: This was the wife of John Wytte or Whitte subsequently of Hore's tenement, Parson's Green (see "Parson's Green: East Side" chapter).

Marye Smithe of the Savoy London, spinster, daughter of Smithe: Mary Smith married Thomas Andrewes of St. Sepulchre. The license issued by the Bishop of London is dated 23 Feb. 1595-96.

The house was usually known as Villa Carey, or Carey House: In Seller's "Map of Middlesex," published in 1730, it is shown as "Villa Carey."

Lady Mordaunt (nee Elizabeth Carey) enters in her "Diary": "The Priuate Diarie of Elizabeth Viscountess Mordaunt" covers the years 1656-78, and contains, *inter alia*, references to the Great Fire, the Plague, the Restoration, etc. The handwriting is difficult of decipherment and the spelling highly curious. It is in the possession of Lord Roden. See Appendix E.

Gardening was one of his favourite recreations: In Evelyn's "Philosophical Discourse on Earth" (1678) occurs the following passage: "But there you have a neat and useful hotbed, as I have been taught to make it by the Right Honourable the late Lord Viscount Mordaunt at Parson's Green whose industry and knowledge in all hortulan elegancies requires honourable mention."

Through his mother, owner of the estate at Parson's Green: The 44 acres of copyhold land, which the Bishop of London granted to Lord Mordaunt in 1666, descended to the uncle of Charles Mordaunt, Harry, second Earl of Peterborough.

During the residence of Mrs. Robinson at Parson's Green, she had a kind of musical academy there: Sir John Hawkins, in his "History of Music," vol. v., p. 305, states that Anastasia Robinson came to live at Peterborough House in 1723 and established a musical society there. According to tradition it was at Vine Cottage in the Fulham Road that Mrs. Robinson and her daughter lived. The Rate books show that a Mrs. Robinson lived at or near Parson's Green during 1724-9. Judging from the assessment, the house was a large one, but its exact position is not ascertainable. The Earl seems to have gone to reside permanently at Peterborough House in 1724, his name appearing thenceforward in the assessments down to the time of his death.

1743. Sr Mordaunt Lawson Bart. bu. 13 Aug: On the death of Sir Mordaunt Lawson, the title passed to a cousin and at last expired in 1806 when Sir Wilfrid Lawson, the tenth baronet, died without issue. He devised his estates to Thomas Wybergh, of Clifton Hall, Westmorland, a nephew of his wife. This Thomas Wybergh assumed the surname of Lawson and died in 1812. He was succeeded by his brother, Wilfrid Wybergh, who also assumed the surname of Lawson and was created a baronet in 1831. He married a sister of Sir James Gresham. The present Sir Wilfrid Lawson, bart., the well-known advocate of teetotalism, is his son.

Lord Mohun, who was killed in a duel with the Duke of Hamilton: A Colonel John Mohun was buried at Fulham 5 April 1731.

Conveyed Peterborough House and the greater portion of the grounds to Major John Scott Waring, who resided here till 1813: The Fulham Church Registers record:

> 1812. John Scott Waring Esq. of Peterb. House in this par. a widower and Harriet Pye Esten of the par. of St. Geo. Han. Sq. in the County of

Middlesex, a widow were married in this Church by license 15 Oct.

Chapter VI: Fulham Road

<u>Countless ruts, and, in wet weather, seas of mud</u>: Sir Arthur Blomfield in his lecture on "The Olden Times of Fulham," delivered in 1856, gives a graphic description of the condition of the Fulham Road in by-gone days.

<u>Augusta Lacrimans</u>: i.e. "London Weeping."

<u>Midd. Liberi Tenentes</u> . . . : Harleian Manuscripts 1711, n.1.

<u>Held the messuage down to about 1626</u>: At a Court Baron, held 18 October 1626, it was presented that "Thomas Claybrooke" had made default, and, in consequence, was "in mercy iiij^d."

<u>Mrs. Carey's name disappears from the Rate books after 1827</u>: In *The News* of 5 July 1812, is the following: "The Marquis of Sligo is said to be the purchaser of Mrs. Clarke's cottage, at Fulham, which is now occupied by Madame Chery, the dancer, of the King's Theatre." The report turned out to be inaccurate. Mrs. Clarke was another of the Duke's favourites.

<u>Belonging to Sir Joseph Williams or his son, Joseph Williams</u>: These names are incorrect. They should be Sir John Williams and his son William Williams.

<u>Ehrengarde Mélusine von Schulenberg</u>: She was the mistress of George I, not George II, as wrongly stated by Croker.

<u>Captain Richard Powell</u>: He was one of the Captains of the Trained Band, co. Middlesex.

<u>Barbara, daughter of Henry Cary, of Clovelly</u>: This lady was buried in the chancel of St. James' Church, Clerkenwell, 23 October 1656.

<u>On one side is a view of Munster House</u>: It may be interesting to note that the original drawing was made by M. T. Hosmer Shepherd. It is now in the possession of T. H. Ellis, Esq., of Normanhurst, Addison gardens, Kensington, whose father engraved the plate for Mr. Elliott. Our illustration, by the courtesy of Mr. T. H. Ellis, is taken from the original drawing.

<u>Thomas Holmes was presented "for his ditch"</u>: This was doubtless in respect to his ownership of the Manor of Rosamond's (see "Parson's Green: Parson's Green Lane" chapter).

<u>Keene's ghost</u>: An old resident of Fulham and a firm believer in the apparition, informed us that, some fifty years ago, he was one

day returning along the Fulham Road, when, on nearing Keene's Alley, as Wheatsheaf Alley was then called, he saw the ghost of a man with a dog and a donkey, the latter of which he was driving. He informed a policeman of what he had seen, but the officer was incredulous. "You know, sir," he remarked to us, after narrating the above, "it is given to some people to see these things."

The marriage took place at Fulham Church, 15 May 1794: A. W. Stocken, Esq., of Halkin Street, Belgravia, the grandson of this Oliver Frederick Stocken, has in his possession a curious little prayer-book, on the fly-leaf of which is written "This book was given to Ann Layton in Fulham Church by Oliver Frederick Stocken, 1793."

Chapter VII: Walham Green

Douses Channell: This was a ditch or gutter, which ran, probably, from Walham Green Pond to Eelbrook. It is mentioned in the parish records as far back as 1491, when the name is spelled "Dowes canell." In 1540 it is "Dowys Canell," and in 1680 "Dowse kennel." Cf. O. Fr. chanel, canel. Lat. canalis, a water-pipe; whence also canal and kennel, a gutter.

Letter from the Commissioners: The Royal Commissioners for Building New Churches.

Chapter VIII: North End

James Knowles, of Walham Green: The will of James Knowles, which was proved in the Prerogative Court of Canterbury, 27 April 1615, is preserved at the Bodleian Library, Oxford. It contains some curious passages. He left "to the poore of ffulham streete, Wandons Greene, Parsons Greene and Northende to every householder that will take it twelve pence; I doe not meane to every Rogue or Inmate but to him or her that is reputed the owner of the house."

Norman or Norman's Lane: About the latter half of the last century, the name Noeman was mistakenly written Norman, the confusion, at a somewhat later date, being increased by the addition of a "d" at the end of the word.

Chapter IX: North End Road

A stone bearing the words "From Hyde Park Corner, 3 miles 17

Printed in Great Britain
by Amazon

HOLD TIGHT

Bennett Security Book 4

HANNAH SHIELD

Prologue

Faith Townsend woke to the sound of men's voices.

One was Jon's. Whiny and pleading. "I told you, I don't have it here."

The other voice was hoarse. Angry. "'Cause you snorted it all up already? That what you're telling me?"

"*No.* I'm clean now. I stored it somewhere else. It's safe."

"Bullshit. You think I'm trusting you? Where'd you stash it, man?"

Her bedroom was dark. Light bled around the door, coming from the living room. She pushed the covers away, and cold air met her bare legs. Jon always liked to keep the house so cold at night.

But she hadn't even known he was home. He'd been gone a lot lately, rarely bothering to make an excuse.

She went to work, visited their families, smiled during church on Sundays. But in her heart, she prayed for a way out of the mess her marriage had become.

She'd told her mother and her pastor the truth, and they'd scolded her to be patient. Be strong. Somehow, their idea of "strength" meant staying silent. And she'd had *enough*.

But the solution to her problems was far less clear.

She crept to the crack in the door and looked through. Anger rushed through her at what she saw.

Her husband stood in the entryway. The front door was open behind him. The other man was pawing around their couch, searching beneath the cushions. He was skinny, even skinnier than Jon. He wore a hoodie and dirt-stained cargo pants.

"Kyle, please. You have to trust me. I'll get the stuff to you, but not all at once."

"I'm the one with the buyers. I call the shots."

"But we're partners on this, right? We have to work together. You know what those guys will do to us if they find out."

What is going on? she thought. *What's Jon done now?*

"You mean, what they'll do to *you*. They're your friends, not mine."

"You're involved too, though. It's both of us now."

Kyle whirled on him, his eyes sharp as flint. "You threatening me?" He pushed Jon up against the wall, a sunburned hand tightening on Jon's throat.

Faith gasped.

Kyle went still. He turned, and his cold gaze locked onto her.

Faith backed away from the doorway. But she already knew it was too late. Kyle came bursting into the bedroom.

Jon was running after him. "Leave her alone," he whined.

Kyle grabbed her by the arms. "So this is Faith. I heard you had a pretty wife, but that was an understatement. Sexy little thing, isn't she?"

She tried to wriggle away. "Let me go!"

Jon tried to yank on his arm, but Kyle knocked him aside with an elbow. He pulled Faith close enough that she could smell the man's rancid breath.

"You know what your husband's into, Faith? Or are you as dumb as he is?"

She'd suspected. But knowing the truth didn't mean she had a clue how to fix it.

Faith stared into his cruel eyes. "I want you out of my house."

"Not until you get the message." He turned her around, holding her tight against his ribcage. She couldn't see Jon, couldn't even hear him. She wondered if he'd left. Simply abandoned her here. Faith tried to wriggle away, but her arms couldn't move.

Kyle put his chapped lips to her ear. "You listening, Faith?"

She forced down the urge to vomit. "Go away. This is my home and you can't just—"

Kyle pushed Faith down onto the mattress. She felt his hand on the back of her head, tight in her hair. His knees straddled her thighs.

His bony fingers squeezed the inside of her leg. Shoved beneath the edge of her shorts. She tried to scream, but she couldn't breathe. He wouldn't let her.

Faith's lungs started to spasm with panic. She kicked, but he easily avoided her.

Kyle's lips brushed her ear. "If your husband doesn't hold up his end of our deal, you're the one who's going to pay for it."

Then, suddenly, the pressure lifted.

He was gone. So was her husband. Faith was all alone.

Finally, she knew what she had to do. It would mean leaving everything behind. But she still had to find the courage to go through with it.

Chapter One

Faith grabbed her phone. Her thumbs flew across the tiny keyboard on the screen. *SOS*, she typed. *Emergency. Help.*

Within ten seconds, Sylvie's name appeared with an incoming call.

"Faith? What's going on?" She sounded breathless.

"This is a disaster."

"What is? What's happening?"

Faith looked at the piles of clothing strewn over the floor. "I just pulled every item from your closet, and I still have no idea what I'm going to wear."

Sylvie blew air into the phone. "Jeez, you nearly gave me a heart attack."

"My brain is stalled. I'm freaking out."

Faith switched the call to video. Sylvie's face appeared, fingertips pushing her chunky pink glasses up her nose. She was in the Bennett Security workroom, a huge open space filled with desks and computer terminals, like Mission Control for NASA. Faith could hear other people talking in the background. *Houston, we have a problem.*

"This has to be quick," Sylvie said. "I'm swamped."

"I know, I'm sorry. I wouldn't usually bother you." But, to be fair, Sylvie had worked late every night for the past three days. Faith hadn't seen her since Tuesday, even though they shared the bottom floor of a townhouse and Faith's "bedroom" was really the living room couch.

"Crap, Max is calling my work phone. Hold on. Here—talk to Tanner."

Sylvie shoved her cell into the hands of Tanner Reed, who looked back at Faith mildly, like this wasn't an unusual occurrence at five o'clock on a Friday. But Tanner was always completely calm. The man was a bodyguard and ex-Navy SEAL. Nothing flustered him.

"Hey, Faith. Did a suitcase explode?"

She sighed. "No, but it's still a fashion-related emergency."

Tonight would be her first time going out with a guy since she'd moved to California. But even more significant? It would be her first date since leaving her husband. And considering that she and Jon had been together since they were teenagers, and he'd never actually taken her on a real date to begin with?

This was kind of her first date…*ever*. At thirty years old.

No pressure or anything.

"I need to figure out what to wear on my date tonight," Faith said.

"Just wear whatever makes you feel like yourself." He ran a hand through his unruly curls.

"That is *so* not helpful."

Faith wanted to be herself, but at the same time, she hardly knew what that meant at the moment. After eleven years in a loveless marriage, she wanted to find out what she'd been missing—in other words, *everything*.

But she had to be careful, too. This was her brand new start. She couldn't mess up again. She knew how quickly one bad decision could drag you irreparably down the wrong path.

Maybe it was silly to pin so much importance on an outfit choice, but every single thing about this night felt significant.

"All right," Tanner said. "Give me some options."

"Here's number one." Faith picked up the first contender, a long black sundress. It went past her knees, and she didn't mind the ruffles at the neck. A nice balance of flirty and conservative. Though it looked like something Sylvie might've worn to a funeral.

"And here's another." Faith lifted a tiered lace babydoll dress. This was more her best friend's typical style, a mix of cute, funky, and sexy.

"Wait, are these Sylvie's clothes? Is that why they're all black?"

"Yes. Keep up, Tanner. Time is of the essence here."

Faith had already ruled out every item of her own. The clothes she'd brought with her when she left Jon didn't scream "going out." They were either scrubs for wearing to work or baggy pants and blouses she could only describe as "church-appropriate." Not the look she was going for.

Hence, the raid on Sylvie's closet.

Men in West Oaks weren't like the ones she'd grown up with in the Texas Hill Country. They wore fancy clothes and wrote screenplays. Okay—not Tanner. But Luke, the guy she was going out with tonight, fit those descriptors. He also seemed funny and smart, from their brief conversations so far. She needed to look just right.

She showed Tanner two more dresses.

He screwed up his lips, rubbing his beard like he was considering this decision carefully. "Definitely the one on the right. With the strappy things."

"You don't think it's too short for a first date?" She was several inches taller than Sylvie.

"Only wear it if you feel comfortable. But if you were my date and wore that, I'd think you looked pretty amazing."

Tanner had spoken matter-of-factly, which was the tone he used for everything. But Faith still felt her skin flush in a pleasant way.

Sylvie grabbed the phone. Her face reappeared. "Okay, I'm back, but Max needs me upstairs. Can't this wait until I get home? I promise, I'll help you tear apart my closet then."

Faith huffed, dropping the dresses in a heap on Sylvie's bed. "You said you'd meet me at the restaurant, not at home. That's only a few hours from now."

"But your date's tomorrow."

In the background, Tanner said, "Uh, no, it's tonight. Keep up, Sylvie."

Panic crossed Sylvie's face. "Whoa, wait. That's not possible."

Faith sank onto the bed on top of the clothes pile. "Are you about to bail on me?" How could Sylvie have forgotten? Faith had only mentioned it about three million times.

"I am so, so sorry. I won't be out of here until late."

Sylvie and her boyfriend Nic were supposed to double date with her. Faith had wanted her friends to check Luke out and give their approval.

But maybe Faith should've expected this. Not because Sylvie was unreliable, but because her job was extremely demanding. The employees of Bennett Security were busy solving life-or-death problems and helping people in danger, which Faith totally got. That had to take precedence.

"It's okay," Faith rushed to say. "We could reschedule."

Sylvie groaned. "No. Let me just see, if, um… Well, Nic could still go with you."

"That's not a double date. That's a creepy three-way."

In the background, Tanner was snickering.

"You could ask Ethan, too," Sylvie suggested. He was Sylvie's cousin and their upstairs roommate.

"Ethan has plans."

Tanner's head popped in again. "You don't want to go by yourself?"

"No, she doesn't," Sylvie snapped. "I'm supposed to be her wingwoman. Nothing wrong with that."

But her friend's tone implied the opposite. Faith knew it was borderline pathetic to be thirty years old and this nervous about a simple night out.

It was one thing to chat with Luke from the next table at the coffee shop where they'd met. But the idea of going to dinner alone with him made her feel like the room was spinning. She'd only split from Jon a few months ago, left her family and her home, taken the biggest risk of her life... It was like she'd needed eleven years to save up enough bravery to leave, and now she had nothing in reserve.

Maybe you can't do this, she thought. *Maybe you should just cancel.*

She really, really hated that voice.

"I'm available," Tanner said.

Sylvie looked over at him. "You and Nic are going to double date with Faith?"

"Nic's your boyfriend, not mine." Tanner shrugged a massive shoulder. "I'm a good wingman. I'll hang out nearby to make sure the dude's not a creep. I mean, if you want, Faith." His large brown eyes met hers through the screen. "Up to you."

"Um. Sure."

She felt a little sheepish about bringing a bodyguard on her date, but maybe it would actually help with her anxiety knowing Tanner was nearby.

"You sure it's okay?" Sylvie asked.

Faith managed to smile. "Yeah. I'll owe you one, Tanner. Thanks."

"No worries," he said breezily.

If only, she thought.

She texted him the info on where and when to meet. Then

she got dressed, taking extra care with her makeup. Most days, she didn't wear any at all, but she'd looked up some tutorials on YouTube.

By 6:30, Faith was pacing the apartment.

And her laptop kept taunting her from its place on the bookcase.

You have to check it at some point, she told herself. *Better to do it now when you have something else to look forward to.*

Grumbling, she opened the computer and logged on to her email.

She'd blocked Jon's number on her phone. But she still needed a way to get in touch with him. She didn't have the money for fancy divorce lawyers who'd handle communications, and he certainly didn't. Plus, she figured if he didn't have *some* way to vent, he'd do something more drastic. Jon tended to be impulsive.

Sure enough, there was an unread email from Jon Townsend, right at the top. Subject: *Please read this Faith. SOS.*

Holding her breath, she clicked on it.

It's an emergency. I need your help. Please call me so we can talk?

The echoes of her text to Sylvie weren't lost on her. She remembered other texts she'd sent to her husband over the years. *SOS.* Sometimes tongue in cheek. Other times, deadly serious. Who had started using that reference first, her or Jon? When would their lives cease to overlap?

The cursor hovered over the reply button.

They'd married as teenagers, for reasons that still tore at her heart. She'd tried for years to fit the image of the "good wife" that her mother and community had pressed upon her.

Giving up is weak, they'd said.

But not once had Jon considered what was best for her, and she hated how long it had taken her to realize it.

Finally, Faith had chosen *her* version of strength, even though her family would never forgive her for it. She'd chosen her own happiness.

And how's that going? she asked herself. *Happy yet?*

Faith deleted Jon's message. Her eyes felt damp. She rubbed at them, and her fingers came away black with mascara. Closing the laptop, she hurried to the bathroom to redo it.

Chapter Two

As soon as the call with Faith ended, Sylvie whirled on Tanner. "You need to look out for her tonight."

"Obviously. That's what a wingman does."

As Sylvie should know, since they'd been friends for years now, and Tanner had been a solid wingman to her, too.

"No, seriously. Faith is… She's trying to move on from her shitty ex-husband. From what she's hinted, her marriage was nowhere near healthy. She won't even tell me all the details, which is a clue in itself, don't you think?"

"Yeah. Sounds rough." The idea of some asshole hurting Faith made his stomach twist.

Tanner knew that Sylvie and Faith hailed from the same tiny town in central Texas. But while Sylvie had left over a decade ago, Faith had only moved away recently. The few times he'd hung out with her, she'd seemed sweet and open. She had a bubbly laugh that could work its way under your skin.

"It's a big deal for her to be going out at all," Sylvie said. "I'm trying really hard to be supportive."

Tanner hooked an arm around Sylvie's shoulders. "Aww, you're like a protective mama bear."

"Who's bailing on her friend. I suck."

"No, you're busy. Speaking of—Max is looking impatient." He pointed up at their boss's glass-walled office, where the man himself was pacing. "You'd better head up there. Don't worry, I'll take care of Faith."

She gave him a quick hug. "Thank you. I know you will." Sylvie raced upstairs. Tanner watched her go, hands in his pockets, then headed for the elevators.

Faith had given him the address of a restaurant on Ocean Lane, the main beachfront strip in West Oaks. He had a couple hours till he had to be there, which meant plenty of time for a workout.

Since it was Friday afternoon, the Bennett Security gym was deserted. The rest of the bodyguards had already bounced, which was just the way he liked it. He loved his co-workers, but the guys could get rowdy at times. Tanner needed the peace and quiet.

He changed into workout clothes in the locker room, then set his phone and towel on a bench.

As he loaded the squat bar with his warm-up weight, Leon Kozinski walked in.

His least favorite teammate. Just great.

Kozinski strolled over to the dumbbells. "Jeez, Tanner, don't you ever leave this place?"

"Nope. This is my natural habitat."

Kozinski's brow wrinkled, like he was working hard to puzzle out what that meant. Then he caught sight of himself in the mirror and got distracted.

The guy had done a stint in the army and had a black belt in something-or-other. But he was annoying as hell, and Tanner still couldn't believe their boss Max had hired him.

They'd been short-staffed lately. Maybe decent bodyguards were hard to come by at the moment.

"What I don't understand is why *you're* still here." Tanner lined up his shoulders beneath the barbell and stood to unrack it.

Kozinski grabbed a couple of twenty-five-pound weights. "Just getting a pump before going out."

"Of course you are."

For Tanner, it had been a while since he'd had plans for a Friday night. Lately, most things beyond his basic routine were just…too much. He'd been trying to keep his stress levels down. But he also didn't like to think he'd been hiding out or choosing the easy path. Avoiding discomfort had never been his style.

Faith was getting herself back out there, not letting her past keep her down. Tanner admired her for it.

If she could do it, why not him?

Besides, helping out Faith wouldn't be a tall order. All he'd have to do was sit at a bar by himself, right? Not so bad. It would probably be noisy and crowded, which made his chest tighten up. But worst case, if the bar scene got to be too intense, he could sit outside on the curb.

No worries.

His mantra these days.

Six punishing sets of squats later, he unloaded the plates and put away the equipment he'd been using. Then he picked up Kozinski's dumbbells, too, which the guy had left strewn across the floor.

Some assholes didn't know how to clean up after themselves.

As he got ready in the locker room, he couldn't stop picturing Faith in that strappy short dress. He could already imagine her long, tanned legs…

Which he really shouldn't do. He was supposed to be her wingman for a date with some other dude.

Still, the thought of her in that dress made him want to look decent, too. His usual shorts and graphic tee combo seemed insufficient.

Hair still damp from the shower, Tanner dug into his locker until he found a pair of jeans. He had a black T-shirt in here, too, folded up and clean. He pulled it on.

The locker room door opened, and footsteps echoed on the tile. "Damn, actual pants?" Noah Vandermeer clapped a hand on his shoulder. "That's like formal wear for you. You got a date tonight?"

"Just with your mom." Tanner slid his flip-flops on. He could only compromise on his wardrobe so much.

Noah flipped him off. Practically a gesture of love.

Like Tanner, Noah was a retired SEAL. They went way back to when they were tadpoles. He and Noah had been swim buddies during BUD/S and tight ever since. Much more than friends. Brothers.

"Haven't seen you all week," Noah said. "You okay?"

"Yeah. Why wouldn't I be?"

"Just that we missed you last weekend. The kids were all asking for you. You gonna be there next time?"

He and Noah volunteered with teens who were interested in the military on the weekends. "Planning on it. Wasn't feeling well before."

"Since when do you get sick?"

Since that shitstorm a few months back, Tanner thought. The concussion that had knocked him on his ass in so many ways.

But he'd beaten this kind of crap after he'd first left the SEALs. He would beat it again. The last thing he wanted was his friends wasting their energy worrying about him.

"Just a stomach thing."

Noah studied him like he could tell that wasn't the whole story. "If you ever want to talk, you know where to find me."

"You want more of my sparkling personality?"

"Always." Noah leaned against the next locker. "So, Max wanted me to ask you about that other captain spot that opened up. You given it any thought?"

"You know that's not my thing."

Noah was a Bennett Security bodyguard too, but he'd been promoted not long ago. Being a captain meant Noah had supervisory responsibilities, plus all the administrative nonsense that went along with the higher pay. He was welcome to it. Tanner had no interest.

"But you're one of the most senior guys here. Don't you want to stand up there next to me? Boss the idiots around?"

"Like Kozinski? No, thanks. I get enough of him as it is."

Tanner just wanted to train, do his job, then wake up and do it again. That was all he asked out of life—to be useful, serve a cause greater than himself, and wear a smile as he did it.

"Don't let a tool like him affect your decision," Noah said. "Besides, aren't you the guy who's all about welcoming challenges?"

"I'm just not feeling it. Okay?" He struggled to keep the testiness out of his voice. Tanner's armpits were starting to sweat, and his lungs were clenching, refusing to fill all the way. Why did this room feel smaller than it had before?

"Whatever," Noah said. "Fine. We'll see what Max has to say about it. Pretty sure he's got his mind set on you."

Then Max will be disappointed, Tanner thought.

Noah's head tilted. "You didn't say if you had a date or not."

"It's a favor to Sylvie, that's all. Faith is meeting up with some guy. I'm going to hang around nearby in case she needs an out."

"Oh, it's Faith?" Noah's eyebrows hitched in a way that Tanner didn't love. "I remember when she came by the office. Huh. She's something."

"Yep," Tanner ground out.

"I didn't know she was dating again after the whole divorce situation."

"Apparently so."

"If this thing tonight doesn't go anywhere, you think Sylvie would mind if I ask her out?"

Tanner threw his stuff into his locker a little harder than he'd intended. "How the hell should I know?" he growled.

Noah's head turned sharply toward him. "Somebody's in a mood."

He didn't even know why he was annoyed. Not like he had any right to care who Faith went out with. He barely knew the woman. And as far as guys went, Noah was one of his best friends and as stand-up as they came.

Maybe he was just getting sick of all the questions. Noah didn't know when to let up sometimes.

"I must be getting hangry. I'd better grab some food before wingman duty. See you later."

He grabbed his wallet, slammed the locker shut, and turned tail. He wasn't proud of it. But sometimes there was no way out but to retreat.

∼

TANNER'S FLIP-FLOPS slapped against his soles. He'd walked several miles along Ocean Lane to get to the restaurant. He had a car but preferred to drive it as little as possible. Walking cleared his head, helped him focus on the present moment. Just taking in his surroundings, keeping up a steady rhythm. It soothed him.

The sun hovered low over the horizon. Lights, music, and voices spilled from restaurants as he passed.

Tanner double-checked the message Faith had sent. She was meeting her date at a sushi place. It had an Irish-themed pub next door, and he'd planned to take up space at the bar and sip a Guinness. Faith was supposed to text him if she needed anything.

But when he reached the pub, he found himself frozen on the sidewalk, looking through the windows.

The place was packed. People were practically on top of each other, shouting and laughing as they watched a soccer game on the televisions. Shoulders pressed against shoulders, noise deafening even from outside.

Too much input. His mind was already buzzing from it. Sweat prickled all over his skin. Tanner's vision started to blacken at the edges.

Somebody bumped into him as they pushed past. "Excuse me," the guy said irritably, then looked up at him, eyes widening. "Uh, sorry."

"No worries." He knew he was in the way. He also knew nobody would call him on it unless they were slightly closer to his size. It was a privilege of usually being the largest person in the vicinity.

He waited a moment, hoping the panic would subside, but apparently his brain wasn't going to cooperate. In fact, his breathing grew shallower, his throat seeming to swell.

Shit. This wasn't a convenient time to start with that nonsense. But he didn't want to be sitting on the curb like some lost kid when Faith walked by. He had to at least *try* sitting inside.

Tanner took a few steps down the sidewalk, checking out the view inside the sushi restaurant. Way less crowded, and it had a bar with an open seat on one end. Far more doable.

Faith wouldn't mind, right? Not like he was going to introduce himself to her date. He'd just sit and wait like he would've next door.

He opened the door for a couple exiting, then went in. At the bar, he ordered a Sapporo and squeezed onto the stool.

He could feel the exits around him like pulsing warning signs. Front door, plus the swinging kitchen door at the back, which would lead to an alley. A hallway with the bathrooms. None directly behind him, though. He angled his body to improve his peripheral vision.

Everything's fine, he repeated to himself. *No worries*.

"Need a food menu?" the bartender asked while making a cocktail in a shaker. Her eyes flicked over him, and she smiled.

"Nah. I'm good. Just the beer." His stomach was too knotted up to eat, though he probably should.

Tanner drummed his fingers on the stone counter as he waited, taking deep breaths and counting. *In, two, three, four. Out, two, three, four.*

The bartender returned with the Sapporo bottle and popped the cap. "Nice ink." She nodded at his arms. "You here alone?"

"Sort of."

"That's mysterious." Someone down the bar tried to get her attention, but she remained focused on Tanner as he sipped his beer. "If you think of anything you need, let me know."

He smiled back. She was friendly. Or was she flirting?

Sylvie liked to tease him for being clueless about women. He didn't think that was true, but his exes had said similar things. *You don't know how to flirt*, they claimed. *You talk to women the same way you talk to guys.*

He didn't see how that was a problem. Somehow, he'd ended up with plenty of girlfriends, so he couldn't be doing *everything* wrong.

Tanner was still friends with almost all his exes. They had a weird tendency to get engaged to the very next guy after him. Or girl, for the ex who'd fallen in love with a woman. He got a lot of invites to weddings.

At an engagement party a couple months back, he'd overheard his ex talking about him to her maid of honor. *You know that sorbet some fancy restaurants serve between courses? That's Tanner. He's the perfect palate cleanser before the main course—when you're ready to cut the shit with all the juvenile guys, but you haven't found 'the one' yet.*

He wasn't sure if it was good or bad. Was he cool and refreshing? Or...did he have no flavor at all?

Either way, he wasn't the type anyone wanted to settle down with. Which was okay with him. He wasn't avoiding commitment, necessarily. More like commitment was avoiding him.

He was glad to be single at the moment. For the last six months, he'd been too focused on keeping his head together to have extra energy for dating.

The front door to the restaurant swung open, and Faith appeared.

She was wearing the strappy dress, and damn—she looked even better in it than he'd imagined, even with the little cardigan she'd thrown over it. Faith's legs were slender and toned. Her long, cornsilk-blond hair hung over her shoulders. His dick perked up, showing interest, but Tanner told his body to behave itself.

Perving on Faith was against the wingman code.

Her date walked in behind her, resting a hand on the small of her back. What had she said his name was? Luke?

Luke was a lucky guy.

Tanner turned to face the bar so she wouldn't notice him staring.

The bartender smiled over at him again, and he returned it. His lungs were breathing easier, relaxing. Almost felt like his old self.

A small win, but he would take it.

Chapter Three

Luke flared out his jacket so he wouldn't sit on it. "Sorry again about being late."

Faith hung her purse on the chair. "It's okay. We're here now, right?"

At least she'd only been standing outside for ten minutes. She was glad Tanner hadn't seen her through the window from his seat at the bar.

She'd been surprised to see Tanner here, since they'd planned on him waiting at the pub next door. She'd watched him from the corner of her eye as he smiled at the bartender and sipped his beer.

Tanner reminded her of professional athletes she'd seen on television. The wild hair, the big muscles. The man had a certain appeal.

They'd become friends through Sylvie, and they'd hung out countless times since Faith had moved to West Oaks. But always in groups, never one on one.

Her seat was facing away from the bar, which was a good thing. She was supposed to be thinking about her date, not the friend doing her a favor.

"Busy day?" she asked.

"It's been crazy, actually. Practice ran over. Then I had to shower, and—yeah. Time got away from me." He'd worn jeans and a blazer. He looked cute, but also jittery. His fingers kept swiping through his hair.

Faith opened her menu. "What were you practicing?"

"Football." His eyes drifted downward toward her chest, then snapped back up.

"Oh." Some kind of adult rec league? "Great way to stay active."

"I try." He flashed his handsome smile, and she felt relieved. There was the Luke she remembered from the coffee shop.

They were getting past the awkward part. And he'd never seen her in a low-cut top before, so that explained why he was suddenly struggling to maintain eye contact.

Luke usually took the table next to hers on Tuesdays at her favorite coffee shop. She liked to spend her afternoon off from work there. They'd started chatting about a month ago, which had turned into sharing an oversized peanut butter chocolate chip cookie whenever they saw one another.

There'd been something youthful and energetic about him. Mischievous, even. When he'd asked her to have dinner with him, she hadn't hesitated.

And he'd let her pick the restaurant, too. *I'm up for anything*, he'd said. *Tell me where you want to go.*

"What kind of sushi do you like?" Luke asked.

She scanned the menu, but she had no idea what she was looking at. "I don't know, actually. I've never had it before. That's why I picked this place. To try something new."

"Never tried sushi?"

She shrugged. "Didn't have much variety where I grew up in Texas. Sometimes we drove into Austin, but we always got barbecue."

Luke's grin grew even broader. "I'll order for you, then."

When their waiter returned, Luke listed a bunch of items from the menu. He got a beer, so Faith did as well.

Their drinks arrived, and they clinked the glass bottles together.

Luke took a sip. "So, Texas. I've never been. What's it like?"

She didn't know how to answer. "Big? Um, but the town I come from is tiny. Lots of cows. The bowling center-slash-arcade was the popular hangout."

"Did you have any high scores?"

"*House of the Dead 2* was totally my game. I splattered those zombies all over the place." She and Sylvie had spent countless afternoons there over summer breaks in high school. Their parents wouldn't have approved, but the girls usually snuck over from the roller rink.

Luke tipped his head back, laughing. "I love it. I can just see you with that light gun. What a badass."

Faith sipped her beer. "I'm glad we're doing this. I was a little nervous, to be honest. I haven't been out in a while."

"Yeah, me too, actually. Not since—"

His phone rang. He fished it from his blazer pocket and looked at it. "Shit, it's my mom. Hold on. I'll be right back."

He was up and crossing the room before she could say anything. Luke stepped out of the restaurant. Faith could see him talking animatedly through the front window.

His mom? Was she sick or something? Faith hoped not. She couldn't imagine answering a call from her mother during a date. Not unless it was an emergency.

Faith's phone buzzed with a message. She checked it.

Tanner: Everything okay?

She turned around. Tanner waved at her from the bar.

Faith: I think so. He's talking to his mom.

Tanner: Is she sick?

Faith: That's what I was wondering!

Tanner: So what do you think? Do you like him? Is he a keeper?

Faith: Still deciding. Started out slightly weird but improving.

Tanner: Roger that. Your wingman is standing by.

She smiled over her shoulder at him, but Luke stepped into her line of sight instead.

"Sorry about that." He slid back into his seat.

She set down her phone. "Is anything wrong with your mom?"

"Oh, no. She just wanted to remind me of something." He rolled his eyes. "So, anyways. You were saying you hadn't been out in a while?"

"Yeah." It was probably time to tell him. "I'm going through a divorce."

Luke had just lifted his beer to his lips. Now he covered his mouth, coughing, and set the glass roughly on the table. "*Divorce?*" he choked out.

"Are you all right?"

It took another minute for him to be able to speak. Faith resisted the urge to clap him on the back. Other patrons were staring.

Luke dabbed his mouth with his napkin. "You must've gotten married really, like…*young*."

She nodded. "In hindsight, it was a mistake."

His mischievous grin reappeared. "But you also must be pretty experienced."

"I…guess." What were they talking about right now?

"With relationships, you mean?" She thought the opposite was true. Faith knew almost nothing about a normal, healthy relationship. She and Jon had never had one.

"Yeah." He leaned his elbows on the table, and his leg brushed hers. "Divorce sounds rough."

"You have no idea."

He was shaking his head. "It's just so hard to imagine. But I guess it's the small-town thing? That's why you got married young?"

"Probably. Yeah." She didn't want to get into the real reasons.

"And your parents were okay with it?"

"Definitely okay with the marriage. Not so much with it ending."

"Wow. So, is that why you moved here? Because of the divorce?"

Faith picked at the label on the beer bottle. "I needed a fresh start."

"But it must've been hard, settling into a new school and everything."

She sat up straighter. "I'm sorry. Did you say…school?"

"Yeah. Unless you've already graduated?"

Faith blinked at him. "Wait. Do you think I'm in college?" She'd been told she looked young, but *that* young? It was a little creepy, actually. Luke thought he was out with a college girl?

"I wasn't sure. I just figured, since you don't go to West Oaks Prep, like me…"

"West Oaks *Prep.*"

She didn't realize she'd shouted until the couple at the next table looked over. A panicky feeling was crawling across her skin, setting off goosebumps.

No. This cannot be happening.

A bunch of different clues suddenly clicked together in Faith's mind into a horrifying image. It was worse than the splattered zombies in *House of Dead 2.*

"Luke, are you in *high school?*" Her voice had gone all high and shrieky.

"Not so loud. It's cool. I'm a senior."

Faith's teeth ground together. "I assure you, this is very much *not cool.*"

"Why? How old are you?"

Instead of answering his question, Faith got up, spun around, and marched over to the bar.

Tanner saw her coming. "What's up?"

"I have a situation."

Fury darkened Tanner's features. "Did he do something?"

"No, it's what he *is*. Luke is…" She could only whisper the next part. "He's a senior in high school."

She expected shock. Horror. Instead, Tanner started snickering. "You cannot be serious."

"You think I'd make this up?"

"If you had a twisted sense of humor, maybe." He leaned out to look past her.

"This isn't a joke, Tanner."

"For real? The dude is *eighteen?* Must be an early bloomer."

She shushed him. "It's not funny. He ordered a beer! I'm contributing to the delinquency of a minor." How on earth had she not realized he was so young? The football comment, the call from his mom… Ugh. She wanted to curl up and disappear.

Tanner closed his mouth, though mirth still danced in his eyes. "We'll fix this."

"*How?*"

He slid off his stool, towering over her, his big hand resting on her arm. "Come with me. We'd better let him down easy."

Together they walked back to her table. Luke watched their approach with wide eyes.

Tanner put his hands on the back of her empty chair. "Hey, Luke. I'm Tanner. Afraid I'm going to have to confiscate that." He reached out and snagged the beer from Luke's hands.

"But—"

"Nope, no arguments. Now, it seems there's been a misunderstanding. We can either cause a scene in here—which your mom won't like when she gets called—or we can go outside and request you an Uber."

Tanner had spoken quietly, but Faith still felt half the restaurant staring at them.

"Okay. Sir." Luke's face had turned beet red. Hanging his head, he got up and shuffled toward the door with Tanner behind him.

The waiter appeared with their sushi order on a serving platter. "Ma'am? Is something wrong?"

"There's been an emergency. I'm really sorry." Faith got her purse and took out her wallet. "Could I get that to-go?"

A few minutes later, she met Tanner outside the restaurant with a shopping bag full of takeout containers. "Is Luke gone?"

Tanner pointed at a pair of brake lights. "He's headed back home. He's going to be more careful next time he picks up an older woman."

"Did you tell him how old I really am?"

"Same age as Sylvie, right? Thirty? Yeah. I don't think he believed me, but he was too busy trying not to piss his pants to argue. I told him I'm an undercover alcohol enforcement officer." He chuckled.

Faith sank onto a bench beneath a bus stop sign. She was humiliated. "The day I got married, he was seven. *Seven.*"

"To be fair, he looked at least twenty-two."

Faith made an exasperated sound. "I thought he was twenty-eight." She covered her face with her hands. "My first real date since…*ever*, and I pick a child."

Tanner moved the bag of takeout to sit beside her. He took up almost the whole bench.

"I thought Luke was writing a screenplay. He must've been doing his *homework*." She groaned, looking up at the sky. "What the heck is wrong with me?"

He nudged her shoulder. "Nothing's wrong with you. You were nervous about dating again, so you picked a dude who wasn't intimidating. He didn't seem like a bad guy."

She'd been through so much awfulness with Jon. Seen the dark things people were capable of doing to themselves, to each other. Was Tanner right, and she'd picked a guy who didn't scare her?

A kid. Because apparently, she was too scared of *men* to want to date one. If that was true, then she was more messed up than she'd realized.

It was one thing to leave her husband, another to get over the scars of what happened during her marriage. Scars that even her best friends didn't know about.

"Please don't tell Sylvie about this? Or anyone? Ever?"

"I won't. Wingman's code of secrecy."

She managed a small smile.

"The night's young." Tanner smoothed a hand over his bushy beard. "You could still have your first-date-since-ever. If you want."

"How?"

"Well, for one, you've got a lot of sushi to eat. And two, unlike some people, you and I don't have a curfew."

Faith snorted.

"What do you say?" he asked.

She looked up at him. Tanner's warm brown eyes gazed down at her. "Okay. What should we do?"

He held out his hand. "Leave it to me. Your first date is going to be epic."

Chapter Four

Tanner hadn't expected to take over as Faith's date tonight. But she'd looked so disappointed and dejected. Like all kinds of self-defeating thoughts were running roughshod through her brain, tearing up her confidence.

He knew exactly how it felt to think you were making progress, to get your hopes up, and then, *wham*—end up back on your ass again. It sucked.

She deserved something special, and no way was he going to let her down.

He picked up the takeout bag with one hand and led her across the street with the other.

"Where are we going?" she asked.

"To a spot I know." He paused. "If that's okay. You trust me?"

She didn't answer right away. "I do." She sounded certain, like she'd really considered it.

He glanced at her sandals. "Are your shoes comfortable? The spot I'm thinking of isn't too far, but it's all relative."

"Didn't you drive here? I would've, but I don't have a car."

"I walked from the office."

"In flip-flops?"

"I like the wind between my toes."

She laughed, and the sound made him smile. "My shoes are fine. Let's go."

It was that time of twilight when the sun had disappeared below the horizon, yet the sky still blazed with fading color.

As they strolled along the paved beachside path, Faith's hand remained in his. "Being near the ocean is my favorite part of living in West Oaks," she said. "Aside from Sylvie, of course. Back home, the beach was so far away we only went a few times. And it wasn't this pretty."

"I'm totally an ocean guy. Give me water and sand and fish tacos, and that's pretty much all I need."

He glanced at her sidelong. The breeze was ruffling her hair across her face. He wished he had a third hand so he could tuck it behind her ear.

"Did you grow up on a cattle ranch, like Sylvie?" he asked.

"Actually, my dad's a dentist. My mom stayed home with me and my four brothers and sisters."

"Are you the oldest?"

"I am. How'd you know?"

"Lucky guess." He paid attention to people. Being observant had served him well, both in the military and as a bodyguard. But it wasn't exactly hard work paying attention to Faith.

"Did you grow up near water?" she asked.

"No, I wish. I grew up near Bakersfield."

"Where's that?"

"It's north of here, in the Central Valley. Hot as hell in the summer, foggy in the winter. Couple hours to the beach, but I didn't even know that until I was in high school." Most of his family had stuck close to home. He was the weirdo who'd joined the Navy and traveled the world.

They walked in silence for a while. The path led to a set of stairs onto a raised walkway along the sea wall. At the top, Tanner pointed to a bench.

"We missed the main part of the sunset, but it's still a great view."

"Wow," she breathed, settling in. "It's incredible."

"It is." He forced his eyes to examine the view instead of her.

The coastline curved into the distance, and lights winked from ships out near the horizon. People milled on the beach below. Tanner liked sitting up here, being a part of things yet separate, too.

"Also a great spot for a picnic." The plastic takeout bag crinkled as he set it in his lap. They took out the boxes. "You ordered a lot of food."

"It was Luke. I've never had sushi before, so he made all the choices."

"Poor kid, didn't even get to eat his dinner."

"I know. But it's not like he paid. Then I *really* would've felt bad."

"Good thing. This would've taken his whole allowance." Tanner was glad when Faith giggled. He was always willing to laugh at himself and expected his friends to do the same. Laughter had a way of taking the sting out of shitty situations.

"So, never had sushi before?"

"I haven't had the chance," she said defensively. "I want to try new things."

"I admire that. It's not where we come from, it's where we're going."

"I'm not trying to say I'm ashamed of where I'm from. There's good in it, too. But I want...more. I'm tired of missing out."

"Why have you been missing out?" he asked gently.

Faith turned away, her focus on the far-off distance. "I thought I could save someone who didn't want to be saved. Then I realized if I didn't protect myself, nobody would."

Tanner couldn't tell if she meant that literally. But either way, it worried him. "You needed to protect yourself from your ex?"

"From his mistakes."

"Are you safe from that now?"

"As long as Jon stays out of West Oaks? Sure." She huffed a laugh. "Sorry. All that sounded way more serious than I meant it to. Can we eat? I'm starving."

He knew a deliberate change of subject when he heard one. Tanner had pulled that maneuver enough himself. But if she didn't want to tell him, he wouldn't push.

He popped open the first lid. "Let's see what we've got here. Tuna, that's yellowtail, eel…"

"*Eel?*"

Tanner narrowed his eyes. "Now we know where you should start. Embrace the fear."

"I'm not scared." Gingerly, she picked up the rectangle of rice and fish and nibbled the edge of it.

"You have to put the whole thing in your mouth."

"Oh, do I?" She started snickering.

"Faith, get your mind out of the gutter. Haven't you corrupted enough innocents for one night?"

She shoved the piece of sushi into her mouth and chewed. Her face went from hesitant to surprised. "It tastes like…barbecue."

"I know, right?"

"Is there more?"

He tilted the box. "You can have the other piece."

Watching her eat was more entertainment than he'd had in a while. Her face was so expressive. She kept closing her eyes, making humming sounds. Making no secret of her enjoyment.

Okay, it was kinda turning him on.

Finally, she protested that she couldn't fit another bite, and he helped finish up the rest. His appetite had returned with a vengeance. Now, she was the one watching him eat. Tanner made the same kinds of faces and noises she'd been making, only even more over the top.

"Damn, that's good."

She poked his side. "Don't make fun of me."

"Imitation is the highest form of flattery."

"Is that right?" She dug her fingers into her hair to tousle it, then pulled some of the long strands to cover the lower half of her face. "Wingman for hire." Her voice was gruff. "Pay me in fish tacos or sushi."

He turned toward her, arm stretching over the back of the bench. "It's like looking in a mirror." He smoothed his beard.

"I'm also available for practice first dates," she said in the same ridiculous growl.

"How am I doing with that so far?"

She dropped her hair. "Not bad."

"Not *bad?*" He grabbed the trash and threw it into the nearest garbage can. "Let's see if I can improve my rating at the next stop."

"There's more?"

"I promised you this would be epic." He held out his hand again, and she took it. Her skin was cool and smooth. "I can't have you telling future customers my dates are just 'not bad.'"

Her face lit up when she saw where they were going.

As they neared the boardwalk, the path grew denser with people. But the open air above his head kept the buzz of unwelcome thoughts to a whisper. Or maybe it was Faith's hand in his.

Upbeat music and happy shouts drifted over from the game booths.

"What should we play first?" he asked.

"This one. It's my favorite." Faith dragged him toward the milk bottle game.

He dug a few ones out of his pocket. "Okay, but the winner gets to pick the next game, and the loser has to pay."

"You're on."

Tanner handed the bills to the game operator.

He picked up the first beanbag, tossing it in his hand. He missed. Same with the next one, though it was closer.

"Ouch," Faith said. "The big strong bodyguard can't even hit a stationary milk bottle?"

"That was a warm-up." The next beanbag grazed one, but they didn't tip. "Oh, come on."

"My turn." Faith grabbed a beanbag. She eyed her target for a moment, shifting her feet back and forth. Finally, she wound up her arm and threw.

The beanbag hit the lowest tier at the perfect angle. The bottles toppled over. She threw her arms up and jumped up and down, shouting.

The operator gave her a fuzzy blue teddy bear, which she tucked into her purse so its head stuck out.

Tanner clapped his hands. "We've got a ringer here."

"Surprised?"

"Not really." With Faith, he was quickly learning that he should be prepared for anything. "Where to?"

Faith got a devious look in her eyes. "I know the perfect thing."

She grabbed his hand, pulling him along behind her.

"Step right up, test your strength on the high striker," a barker shouted. "Who's mighty enough to ring the bell?"

Tanner laughed, just shaking his head. "I'm happy to show off for you, if that's what you want."

Faith shrugged. "We'll see. I'm giving you the chance to redeem yourself after that devastating milk bottle loss. Hopefully, you'll make use of it and not choke."

That sounded distinctly like a challenge.

The operator's eyebrow's shot up as he approached. "I'll take a swing," Tanner said.

The man accepted his money. "Gather round, folks.

Contender for the world's strongest man right here. Let's see what he's got."

Faith smirked. "No pressure."

"What you don't know is, I'm at my best under pressure." Tanner took the mallet, weighing it in his hand. He swung it in the air, getting a feel for it.

A ring of people had gathered to watch.

Tanner lifted the mallet above his head a couple of times, enjoying the grumbles around him as he kept frowning and readjusting like a ballplayer stepping up to bat. But finally, he swung the mallet upward and brought it down on the target. The bell rang, and the crowd cheered.

He turned to Faith, and her grin was the biggest of all. That was worth every prize in this place put together. "Did I redeem myself?" he asked.

"That was…"

"Don't say 'not bad.'"

She pursed her lips together, which only made him focus on her mouth.

This isn't a real date, he reminded himself. She'd just said it a few minutes ago—this was only a practice. Fun between friends.

After a few more games, they got ice cream cones and walked back down along the beach.

They each took off their shoes, their feet pressing into the soft wet sand. The lights of the boardwalk reflected off the waves as they strolled along the shore.

"It's surreal, being here right now," Faith said. "Walking on the beach, eating sushi. I never would've thought a year ago I'd be doing all this."

"Why not?"

Faith blew out a heavy breath. "I've been miserable for a long time. Practically since before I got married."

"What happened?"

She stopped and stared out into the waves. "Sylvie and I

were best friends in high school. We had this grand plan where we'd both go to school in Austin and have all the freedom we'd been lacking. But I got waitlisted. I chose a school closer to home and was still hoping to transfer." Faith shrugged. "But then, Sylvie decided to follow her cousin to California. Just like that, she was gone."

"Did she ask you to go?"

"Yep. I almost did. But I let my parents talk me into staying. They didn't have to work that hard, though. I was so scared of failing and having to come back home, so I… I made some reckless, stupid choices that *guaranteed* I couldn't leave. And I got stuck with Jon as a result."

Tanner could tell there was a lot more to that story. But he didn't want to pry if she wasn't ready to talk about it. Talking about the past could be overrated.

"I'm just so sick of missing out. On love and affection and…" A smile broke through her world-weary expression. "And sushi."

It made his heart sick to think of Faith living a life without love. She deserved all of that and so much more.

"You've done a lot of the work getting yourself here, opening up to new experiences," he said. "You'll find what you're looking for."

"What if I've already missed it? I just feel like I've wasted so much time." She shook her head as if to clear it, then took another bite of her melting ice cream. "I'm scared of making the same mistakes. Getting stuck and settling for an easy life, even if I'm not happy."

Tanner finished his ice cream cone. "You have to get comfortable being uncomfortable."

She made a skeptical face. "That sounds like a bumper sticker."

"I'm serious. The more you can exist with physical discomfort, the less any type of stress will affect you. Then you'll never be tempted to choose what's easy instead of what fulfills you."

"What am I supposed to do? Wear flip-flops for miles-long walks?"

"That's an option. Or what about taking a nighttime swim in a freezing cold ocean?"

She looked over at him, eyes wide. "Do not tell me that's act three of this date."

"It wasn't until now. But if you need to practice getting uncomfortable…"

"If you want me to get in that water, you'll have to pick me up and throw me in."

"That could be arranged."

Chapter Five

Tanner's eyes flashed in the low light, taunting her.
"You wouldn't dare," she said.
He took a few steps closer to her, flip-flops dangling from his hand. The waves continued to crash, water spilling around their feet before pulling back again.
"I wouldn't do anything you didn't want me to do." His voice was husky, and a thrill of arousal ran from her stomach down between her legs.
Oh. Okay then.
It was possible she had the tiniest of crushes on Tanner Reed.
This night with him had not been what she'd expected. Not even close. They'd gone from the friend zone to…something else. But she wasn't even sure it was intentional on his part. Maybe he was just this kind to everyone. She'd believe it.
Tanner was one of the most giving people she'd ever met. Funny, sweet. And silly in a way she was starting to really like. Even his overgrown beard was getting sexier, though she imagined he would be cuter if she could see more of his face.
She had no complaints about the rest of him. When he'd rung the bell on the boardwalk, his muscles all tense

and flexing? Desire had flooded through every part of her, taking her completely by surprise. The dirtier parts of her mind had instantly wondered what he'd feel like up against her.

But she didn't know what to do with that feeling.

Well, she knew what she *wanted* to do.

But this date wasn't real. He'd seen her ridiculous attempt with Luke, and he'd taken pity on her. That thought quashed any naughty images lingering in her brain.

Faith tossed her sandals onto the sand. She took off her cardigan and set it atop her purse to hide it.

"Okay. Throw me in." She turned away from him, facing into the waves.

"Really?"

She closed her eyes. "Yes. I want to do something crazy and uncomfortable I've never done."

Nothing like my old life. I'm never going back to that. Ever.

Strong arms looped around her hips from behind. She yelped as Tanner tossed her upward, catching her against him as if she weighed nothing. She grabbed hold of his arms, desperate for anything to hold onto.

"You sure about this?" His voice rumbled against her ear. Her back pressed into his chest. My god, the man was solid.

Faith nodded, and he waded into the surf, jeans and all. Goosebumps rose on her bare legs.

"Four, three, two—" His arms lifted, and she braced herself for the cold. Then he laughed. "You were seriously going to let me do it?"

"You jerk—" Faith wiggled until he let go her. Frigid waves reached to her knees, shocking a scream out of her. Cold. So cold.

She scooped up the icy water and splashed him.

"Oh, now it's on." Tanner grabbed hold of her again, but this time her chest was mashed against his wet shirt. "Hold your breath." He sat down in the water and tipped them both sideways. A wave crashed into them. Faith held her breath as she went below the surface for a split second.

When he pulled her back up, she was sputtering and screaming and laughing. Both of them were soaked from head to toe.

His fingers brushed her hair from her eyes. Tanner's was plastered against his head. "That crazy enough for you?"

Not even close.

He stood all the way up again, still holding her. She looped her arms around his neck. His large hands were on her bare thighs. Her dress seemed to be somewhere up around her waist.

They were both panting, and she knew she should be cold, but Tanner's warmth burned through their wet clothes.

And his eyes. The light from the boardwalk and the night sky reflected in them, like two deep pools. She wanted to dive in and stay under for as long as she dared. Faith licked her lips, tasting salt.

He was so close she felt his exhales against her skin. "Should I set you down?"

Not yet, she wanted to say. But she didn't get the chance.

"You two all right?" someone shouted.

"We're good, thanks." Tanner set her gently back on her feet.

That moment, whatever it had been, was gone.

They waded back to the sand, Faith pushing her dress down the best she could. She really hoped the fabric wasn't dry-clean only, otherwise she was going to owe Sylvie a new one.

"Is my mascara everywhere?"

"Nah, only a little. Here, use my shirt. It's already black."

Faith used his sleeve to wipe below her eyes, cracking up at how ridiculous she must look.

Her teeth chattered as she wrapped her dry cardigan

around her shoulders. Tanner didn't seem bothered by his soaked clothing.

"Since we're both a mess now, I guess I should walk you home?" he asked.

"Probably."

"But that's how every good date should end, right? Both participants too disheveled for polite society."

"Is there an innuendo in there somewhere?" she asked.

"Hey, you're the one with the dirty mind, not me."

They walked along the sand for a while, until their feet were dry enough to put on shoes and go back onto the paved path. Their hands kept brushing.

"You're not too cold, are you?"

She felt him looking down at her. She'd been focused on the street, the waves, the other passersby. Anything to keep herself from staring at him, though her gaze kept wandering in that direction.

"No," she said through chattering teeth. "I'm fine."

She hoped he might put his arm around her to warm her up, but she wasn't going to ask for it. And he didn't volunteer.

"If Sylvie is mad about her dress," Tanner said, "tell her it's my fault."

"Pretty sure it was my fault, too. But if she asks, I'll tell her the dress's sacrifice was worth it."

"Yeah?"

This time, she couldn't resist looking at him. He was grinning in that easygoing way of his.

If only daily life could be as smooth for her as it seemed to be for Tanner. He walked back and forth across their town, dispensing advice and swooping to a sad girl's rescue like it was effortless.

There was no way he could possibly understand how much this evening meant to her. She didn't think any man had ever been so thoughtful and wanted so little in return, just her laughter and her company.

But if she kept thinking along those lines, she was going to embarrass herself by crying. And she'd already had enough humiliation today. She didn't want to spoil the time they'd had by making it into anything more than it was: a really good time between two friends.

In fact, she should've been thrilled to have a friend like Tanner.

By the time they got back to her townhouse, Faith had resolved to forget about her crush and just be grateful for his friendship. That was what he seemed to want from her.

Maybe he already had feelings for someone else. Or maybe he had no interest in her that way at all. It wasn't her business.

But as they stood there on the porch in their salt-crusted clothes and their messy hair, she felt far more awkwardness than she should've if he were just a friend.

Tanner hooked his thumbs in the pockets of his jeans. "So, what's the final verdict on tonight? Not bad?"

She tilted her head, as if she had to think. "It got better. I would say you were adequate."

He clutched his heart. "How can a guy handle this many compliments and stay grounded?"

"It's a feat. But somehow, you do it." Faith looked down at her sandals. "Actually, it was pretty much perfect. Thank you. For everything."

"It was my pleasure, believe me. I can't remember the last time I had this much fun."

"Me, neither." She looked up into those deep brown eyes again.

If he kisses me, she thought, *I'll kiss him back.*

She really wanted that. And it had nothing to do with capping off the perfect first date, or building up her confidence, or with anything else at all except *him*.

Maybe she would even invite him inside.

But neither one of them closed the distance. So finally, she reached into her purse and pulled out the blue stuffed bear she'd won at the boardwalk. "Here, this is for you."

"But you won it."

"For my date. Isn't that how it goes?"

"I'll cherish it always." He grinned and accepted the gift.

Faith said, "Goodnight. See you later?"

He nodded, backing away. "Any time."

Chapter Six

Tanner paused outside the rec center, bracing a hand against the stucco wall. He took several breaths to steady himself, repeating his mantras.

Embrace the uncomfortable. No growth without fear.

Then he pasted on a smile and walked inside.

Noah was already here, chatting with some of the kids who were regulars.

Damien, who was around fifteen, raced over as soon as he saw Tanner. "Hey, where were you last time?"

"I was feeling under the weather. Really missed seeing you guys. I would've been here if I could."

Damien's eyes had grown as big as monster truck tires. "I didn't know you could get sick. I thought Navy SEALs were like, superhuman."

A girl named Julie walked up. She was a freshman in high school, wore her hair buzzed on one side, and had a sardonic sense of humor. "You don't think Tanner's superhuman? Look at him."

He laughed off their comments. He'd heard it all before, and he knew they didn't mean to be hurtful. The exact opposite. But this was the very reason he volunteered to spend time with these kids. To make sure they understood that everyday people, from all walks of life, could be heroes. Invincibility wasn't a requirement, nor was it realistic.

"We get sick just like anybody. And injured. We even cry."

Damien looked skeptical.

Tanner felt the kids tense up as a newcomer walked into the room. But the new guy was someone Tanner knew well.

"Hey, man!" Sean Holt pulled him into a hug.

"Good to see you. Been too long."

"No kidding. I don't get over here from L.A. often enough." Sean smirked. "Though it does help to get an invite. Makes me think Noah's the only one who still loves me."

"Maybe I'm just shy."

"Or maybe you're full of it." Sean looked over at Damian and Julie. "This guy seem shy and retiring to you two?" They beamed at being pulled into the conversation.

"If Tanner's shy," Julie deadpanned, "then the rest of us are, like, comatose."

Sean had been a Marine at the same time Tanner and Noah were SEALs. They'd carried out some missions together overseas. Since leaving the service, Sean had joined the LAPD. Now, he was a detective with the Gang and Narcotics Division.

Noah strode over. "Sean, you made it." They hugged, pounding each other on the back. "Thank you so much for being here."

"Happy to help."

"Hey everyone, listen up," Noah said. "Detective Holt is going to tell us a little about himself and his work with the LAPD. I brought him in today because he's got some amazing stories, both from his days in the Marines and on the streets of L.A. But I want all of you on your best behavior so we can represent West Oaks right."

After everyone had settled down and Sean had launched

into his war stories, Tanner leaned against a table on one side of the room.

He loved giving back by volunteering with these kids. Many of them had trauma in their backgrounds, and they were here for mentors they could trust. The military might not be a great fit for all of them, but at least they could explore the option in a safe space with open communication. And Tanner knew that, sometimes, the best kind of healing was devoting one's life to others.

He just wished someone had told him back at the start of his military career that healing wasn't a straight line. That the choice not to give up had to be made every single day when things got hard. When he'd been a SEAL, he'd had no idea some of his toughest days would be ahead of him as a civilian.

But maybe he wouldn't have listened, any more than Damien wanted to hear that stuff now.

Hell, Tanner wasn't all that good at following his own advice. He'd told Faith she had to get comfortable being uncomfortable. But when was the last time he'd really pushed himself?

Case in point: he'd been a coward about asking her out again.

It had been two weeks since his "date" with Faith. The date she'd called "practice." But by the end of it, he'd wanted it to be real.

On her front porch that night, he'd looked for any sign she might be feeling the things he was feeling. It had taken all of his willpower not to just say, *Fuck it*, and kiss her.

But he'd known she was in a vulnerable place. She'd told him more than enough to convey that her marriage had a dark side, one that she was still struggling over. It wouldn't have been right for him to get all handsy with her, not unless he'd known for sure she wanted it.

In the days that had followed, he'd only gotten less sure of himself. He'd texted with Faith a couple of times, testing the waters. But now, it seemed Faith had put him squarely back in the friend zone.

He could've taken the risk of just asking her to go out with him. But that would've required a bit more nerve and backbone than he seemed capable of at the moment.

Superhuman, my ass.

Sean had taken off his LAPD windbreaker, and he walked casually across the front of the room as he spoke, holding the kids' attention. "One of the worst things I have to see in my job is people your age, people who haven't even graduated high school, dying because of drugs."

Sean went over to his bag. "There's something I carry with me at all times. Anybody know what this is?" He unzipped the leather duffle and pulled out a small white package.

"That's Narcan," Damien said.

Tanner hated that the kid knew it by sight. Damien's mother had almost died of an overdose just a few months before. Both parents had been in and out of jail. Tanner had met the boy's grandmother, who was his caretaker. Thank goodness she was looking out for him.

"That's right. Tanner knows about this stuff too." Sean gestured at him. "When he was a SEAL, Tanner had to have all sorts of equipment ready to treat the wounded in a war zone. But all of you know there are dangers here at home, too. You'll find Narcan in any squad car, in local libraries, your schools—because these days, an overdose can happen anywhere. A classmate might buy pills on social media, thinking it's one thing, and find out only too late that it's lethal. Now, I'm going to show you exactly how to use Narcan nasal spray just in case you're called upon to save a life. Who wants to help me out with a demonstration?"

A dozen hands shot up.

But Sean pointed at someone who hadn't volunteered. "What about you? Damien, right?"

The kid shook his head, obviously uncomfortable. Shit.

Sean hadn't known about Damien's history, which had been an oversight on their part. Tanner was mentally kicking himself for not mentioning it.

"I'll do it." Tanner stepped forward. "And Julie will help out. She's going to save me."

Julie jumped up, mugging for the others.

Tanner went over and lay down on the floor at the front. He put his hands behind his head, smiling.

Sean poked him with his foot. "You're supposed to be suffering an overdose, not laying out to get a tan. Somebody needs to give this guy some acting lessons."

The kids hollered and laughed, which was of course the idea. Lightening the mood.

Tanner sprawled like he was unconscious and closed his eyes.

"First," Sean said, "you need to check for signs of an opioid overdose. His breathing will be very slow, irregular, or might have stopped. His pupils will have shrunk to pinpricks. Try to wake him by shouting and shaking him by the shoulders."

Julie did as Sean instructed. She peeled back one of Tanner's eyelids, her face appearing in front of him.

"Next, and this is very important, have someone call 911. Then grab your Narcan, like so."

Sean took her through the rest of the steps, ending up with Tanner in the recovery position on his side. He opened his eyes to watch the kids, noting that even Damien was smiling shyly.

Another pang of guilt and regret shot through Tanner for missing the last session. He knew in theory that being here, among these incredible kids, was just as cathartic for him. So why had it become such a struggle to show up? Why couldn't he do the things he knew he needed?

His body was capable. He was grateful for that. Yet his mind kept getting in the way.

AFTER LEAVING THE REC CENTER, Tanner and Sean went to a cafe down the street. Noah had to get back to work for a weekend shift. Everyone had them sometimes, but Noah did almost every week. The curse of being a captain, as far as Tanner was concerned. Too many planning meetings, too much time spent checking up on other guys.

Inside the cafe, a singer-songwriter type strummed an acoustic guitar and cooed lyrics into a microphone. They ordered iced coffees and grabbed a table on the patio, where shade trees cut the afternoon sun. The air smelled of jasmine and fresh cut grass.

"Thanks for being there today," Tanner said. "The kids loved it."

"Maybe. They definitely love *you*. That was great to see. You're making a big difference in their lives."

"Trying to."

Sean crossed his legs. "When's the last time I saw you? Six months ago?"

"Something like that."

"You know what I've been up to. Working my informants, the occasional bust, and spinning my damn wheels, same as always. We make progress taking down a bad guy, and three more pop up. Like the Silverlake Syndicate. They bit the dust, but even worse people have taken over their territory."

Tanner knew the Syndicate's history well. They'd been a small but powerful presence in the L.A. underworld for decades. But recently, after a deadly battle with another group of mobsters, the Syndicate had fallen apart.

"We've got cartels moving black tar and fentanyl in and out of our city," Sean said, "and it's like a whack-a-mole game."

"That sounds almost like whining. Not that I'm surprised. You jarheads were always a little soft."

Sean took a gulp of coffee, shaking his head. "There's that ornery S.O.B. I know and love. How have you been keeping busy? Still got a different girl on your arm every month? I swear, it was like flipping a calendar."

"Can't help it if the ladies love me."

"And you never had to lift a finger. That pissed me off. I happen to still be single. Dating in L.A. sucks."

Tanner cracked up, thinking of Faith's mishap with the high school kid. "It's not so easy here in West Oaks, either. But I'm single, too. Have been for a little while."

"Needed a breather?"

Tanner drew his finger through the condensation on his iced coffee. He wasn't sure what he'd say until he opened his mouth. "Actually, I got injured. Not long after I last saw you."

"I think Noah mentioned something about that. What happened?"

"Got knocked on the head pretty bad. Concussion."

He'd been on bodyguard duty, working an assignment involving Sylvie's boyfriend, Nic, and the Silverlake Syndicate. Tanner and Sylvie had been ambushed. That had been bad enough, getting caught by surprise. Embarrassing as hell. Tanner had fought back against the assailant, thinking he could keep the situation from spinning fully out of control.

Then another bad guy had appeared out of nowhere. He'd clocked Tanner over the head with a blackjack, knocking him instantly unconscious.

When Tanner woke, he'd found his friends gone. He hadn't remembered where he was. And all he could think of was Afghanistan, like that shit had happened the minute before, and not years back.

The panic had been enough to send him into unconsciousness again.

The next time he'd woken, Tanner had been in a hospital. He'd careened out of bed, knocking over equipment and sprawling onto the floor with his ass hanging out.

Good times.

"How's the recovery been?"

"Uh, not so great actually." His throat had gone dry. He sipped his drink.

Tanner wasn't even sure why he was telling Sean this. Maybe it was because Sean didn't see him every day, didn't work with him. This confession didn't feel like such a risk.

The words started tumbling out of him. "Physically, I'm better. That's what everyone says. But there's this buzz of thoughts in my brain, always in the background. Like I can't fully calm down. Like I know something else is about to happen, any second, and when it doesn't come that just makes it worse."

Sean folded his arms on the table, leaning in. "Have you talked to any professionals about this?"

"Not recently. I went through something similar a few years ago. I know…what it is." He'd been diagnosed. Why couldn't he just say the words? "But I thought I was over it."

"You had PTSD?"

Tanner couldn't even nod. He just sat there.

Sean knew about how Tanner had been wounded overseas. Tanner had left the SEAL Teams not long after.

"There's no shame in that, man. You're far from alone."

"I know that, believe me. I was the damned poster boy for self-acceptance and mindfulness and all that shit."

Sean snickered. "Of course you were."

"That's what makes me so…" *Mad*, he thought. *So fucking mad*. All that work he did, and none of it mattered. He was sitting on a coffee shop patio with strains of indie rock drifting from inside, and he had to swallow down the urge to scream.

Sean shifted his weight in his seat. "Okay, I think I'm getting it. You had symptoms like this not long after you discharged. But you thought you'd dealt with it. And now, after the concussion, it's back."

It sounded so straightforward coming out of Sean's mouth. "That's the story. Basically."

A few steps forward, a dozen back.

"Does Noah know?"

"A little. But he'd probably overreact. I don't want to get stuck behind a desk at work."

Being a bodyguard could get tense on occasion. But most of the time, Tanner stood around looking intimidating while rich people went about their business. He provided peace of mind. It was a far cry from the action he'd seen in the teams, and sometimes, he missed that constant pressure. When they hadn't been fighting, they'd been training hard to fight. Every. Single. Day.

The quieter everything else got, the lighter that pressure, the more the shit in his mind could start to swirl.

But being a civilian had given him the opportunity to make his community better in other ways. And he loved the camaraderie he'd built with the other Bennett Security bodyguards. Most of them, at least. He couldn't stomach the idea of giving that up. Not even temporarily.

If he was saddled with desk duty, that buzz in his head would only get worse.

"I can do my job," he said, "but I can't stand people second-guessing me."

"That's part of being a team, though. Knowing your brothers are looking out for you."

"Yeah, and I'm looking out for them. I'm not going to let them down. Period. I just needed to say this to *someone*."

Sean touched his shoulder, squeezing it. "I'm glad you did. How can I help?"

"I don't know. I'll figure it out. It just sucks."

But when he conquered it this time—because he would—how long until he found himself back here again?

That thought probably scared him most of all.

Chapter Seven

Faith went out to the waiting room to call the next patient. "Gabriella? You can come on back."

An eight-year-old with ribbons on her pigtails bounced off the couch, running toward Faith. Gabriella hugged her around the knees.

She had to smother a laugh. If only all her cleanings were so enthusiastic.

"Honey, give Faith some space." Gabriella's mom hurried after her daughter. "Sorry about that."

"It's okay. I'm glad to see her too."

Faith had only been working for Dr. Petrie a few months. The dentist didn't seem to be a huge fan of kids, so Faith had quickly become the resident child wrangler. She loved it. Kids were by far her favorite patients.

Gabriella had been in several times recently for hyperdontia. She'd needed oral surgery to remove the excess and impacted teeth and had experienced various other complications. Each time she'd come in, Faith had spent extra time reassuring her.

Thankfully, today was just a cleaning. Gabriella's mom helped her up into the chair.

"I have a little something for you." Faith dug into her pocket and held out a folded piece of paper. "Have you seen one of these before? It's a cootie catcher."

The girl giggled. Faith stuck her fingers into the slots to make it pop into shape. "I'll show you how it works. It tells your future." And of course, all the predictions were specially tailored to the little girl, who wanted to be a veterinarian someday.

Gabriella's mom leaned over. "I used to love those when I was a kid. Did you do the drawings? They're beautiful."

Faith nodded. She'd just drawn small decorations on the paper, but the compliment made her smile. After she showed Gabriella the game, she handed the paper toy to the girl.

A loud hammering sound interrupted them. Faith resisted the urge to grimace. "Just the construction over at the hospital. Sorry about that. Now, how about you show me all those pretty teeth?"

She stayed focused on Gabriella and her mother throughout the cleaning. But after they left and Faith's next patient didn't show, she had time for her mind to wander.

Which, lately, was not necessarily a good thing.

She finished prepping the room for the next appointment, then went into the break area. Myra, the other hygienist, was eating her lunch and flipping through the latest issue of *Cosmo*.

Myra turned her magazine around and pointed. "Look, there's a whole article about worst dates ever. You should totally write in, because yours beats every single one of these, hands-down. Even the one where the guy showed up in assless pants." She clapped a hand over mouth. "Dang, I shouldn't say assless in the office. Petrie might hear."

Myra had no problem discussing explicit sexual topics, yet she avoided four-letter words. Usually this dichotomy made Faith laugh, but she wasn't feeling so cheery today.

Faith sank into a chair, groaning. "Why did I tell you about Luke again?"

"Because you love to entertain me?"

"Pretty sure it was because I thought I'd get some sympathy."

Myra squinted at her. "Have you met me?"

Myra was a few years younger, fresh from getting her certificate, and Dr. Petrie was the first dentist she'd worked for. Faith often heard laughter coming from the other rooms where Myra was working. If Faith was the calming presence in the office, Myra was the jovial one.

"But what about that other guy who was with you that night? The one who bailed you out of there."

"Tanner?"

"Yeah. What's the story with him?"

"We're friends." Whenever she had a few moments to herself, her mind kept going back to their walk along the beach, the freezing cold swim, and the heat that had built in her stomach when he'd held her.

That same heat was spreading through her veins right now.

But Faith had shared the details with her best friend Sylvie, who'd acted like that night hadn't been anything unusual. *He's the best, isn't he?* Sylvie had said. As if Tanner might've done the same for anyone.

"Uh oh, somebody's blushing."

Faith pressed a hand to her cheek. The curse of being a pale blond. "Am not."

"Have you seen this Tanner guy again? A bodyguard, right? That sounds hot."

"He's just a friend. That's it, end of story."

Myra shrugged, flipping through her magazine. "Okay, if you say so. I was just hoping for some more dating stories because it's not like I've got any."

Myra was always complaining about the awfulness of dating apps. That was why Faith had steered clear of them. And after almost hooking up with an eighteen-year-old, she wasn't exactly eager to line up the next potential guy. She was way too nervous now.

It didn't help that the only man she seemed to think about lately was Tanner. Because obviously, that wasn't going anywhere. They'd barely even texted in the last couple weeks, and he hadn't shown any interest in getting together again.

It wasn't so bad, though. Tanner was her first crush, unrequited or otherwise, since high school. A milestone in itself. Baby steps were still steps.

The front desk receptionist strolled into the break room. "Faith? There's someone here to see you."

She walked to the waiting area and nearly choked.

Jon.

Jon was here.

Her husband. *Ex*-husband, as soon as those divorce papers were signed and processed.

Jon hadn't looked well the last time she'd seen him, but he'd lost at least ten pounds since then. Back in high school he'd been a handsome football player. Blond, cleft chin. Cocky smile. But you'd never know it from his gaunt cheeks and sallow skin.

"What are you doing here?" she sputtered. "You're supposed to be in Texas."

"We need to talk."

"You can't be here. This is… It's not…" Faith was going to hyperventilate. She wasn't prepared for this.

"Is everything all right?"

Faith turned around. The dentist stood behind her. Dr. Petrie was in her fifties, with a streak of white in her otherwise dark hair. "Is this a patient?"

"No, I'm her husband, and I need to speak to her." He'd spoken softly, but there was that familiar edge underneath. Like he was barely holding himself together.

She had to get him out of here.

The dentist pursed her mouth with disdain. "Your

husband, who was making all those calls and disrupting my office?"

She'd made the mistake of giving her work number to her mother, and her mom had a soft spot when it came to Jon.

He wants to be a good man, her mom would always say. *You just have to give him a chance.*

As if she hadn't given him a thousand chances.

The calls had been embarrassing enough. The receptionist had to block his number. Either he'd somehow traced this address from the phone number, or Faith's mother had shared that with him, too.

"I'm sorry, Dr. Petrie. I had no idea he'd do this. Could I step outside for a minute?" Faith grabbed Jon's arm and pulled him out the door.

In the parking lot, she rounded the side of the building. The fenced-in construction site lay beyond, heavy machinery digging into the dirt. Dr. Petrie's office was located in a medical building next to the hospital, which was constructing a brand-new wing.

The noise had been bugging everyone in the dental office for weeks. But today, the sounds put Faith even more on edge. Her skin tingled with frustration and fury.

"Jon, what are you doing here?"

"I need your help."

She wanted to scream. "Why didn't you say you were coming to California?"

"Because I knew you'd tell me not to. I have good reasons for being here. I had to drive two whole days."

He scratched at his arm. Faith watched the motion, studied the twitch at the corner of his mouth. You couldn't spend eleven years with someone without getting to know them, inside and out.

"You're using again. Aren't you?"

He turned away, face crumpling. "I can't take you being down on me, too. But I'm a month clean, I swear."

"You can do what you want, Jon. I realize now that I can't stop you. But you can't interfere in my life, either. Our marriage is over. It has been for a long time."

His eyes were rimmed with red, and dried skin dotted his nose. "I want a new beginning, too. I just need a little bit of help first."

She looked at the construction site. A huge truck was backing up, beeping a warning. "What do you want, exactly?"

He shuffled his feet. "I've got a business opportunity. I need some startup funding."

"You have got to be kidding me. I'm not giving you money so you can get high."

"I'm *not*. I'm selling antiques and things. I've got business partners back in Texas, finding stuff cheap. I'm going to sell it here for top dollar to rich people. They love all that rustic crap."

"What happened to *your* money?" She'd left his share in the bank account, plus the deed to the house that his parents had helped them buy.

He just shrugged. That answered her question. They both knew where the money had gone.

"I can't give you money, Jon. We can both predict where it'll go."

"So, you still think the worst of me. That feels great." Jon wiped at his nose. "I'm living out of my truck right now, you know."

She spotted it across the parking lot—a beat-up Ford F150 with a tarp over the bed. "I'm sorry to hear that. I have to get back to work. You need to go."

He started toward the truck, then turned back around. "Maybe I could store some things at your place? Just for a little while, till I can figure some stuff out? That would really help."

"*No*, Jon. You can't. I hope this new business works out for you, but you'll have to do it yourself."

He stormed off, shaking his head.

～

FOR A WEEK, Faith saw no sign of her husband. She started to hope he'd given up and gone back to Texas.

Then the package arrived.

She was in the break room at work, exhausted after a long morning. No cute kid patients, just grumpy ones. Oh, and a middle-aged man who'd stared openly at her chest area the whole time, even though her clothes were so baggy even the outline of her breasts was indistinct. She suspected he'd enjoyed having his gums prodded. *You could do that a little harder*, he'd urged. So gross.

The receptionist poked her head in. "Faith? Package just came for you."

"A package?"

Faith got up from the table and followed the receptionist to the front. She stepped behind the desk, where a huge cardboard box took up half the counter. It was battered and dirty, with tape crisscrossing the top.

"This must be a mistake." *Please, let it be a mistake.*

The receptionist took her seat. "All I know is the guy said it was for you."

Dread uncoiled like a snake in her belly. "What guy?"

"That blond guy who came here for you before. Your ex-husband? You should probably get that out of here before Dr. Petrie sees."

"Before I see what?" Dr. Petrie strolled over, eying the cardboard box with distaste. "What on earth is that?"

"Faith's package," the receptionist supplied. Which was not particularly helpful.

"You know I don't like personal packages arriving here."

The door to the waiting room opened, and a patient walked in. He glanced at the box as he approached the desk.

"Get it out of sight," Dr. Petrie hissed.

Faith grabbed the box and carried it toward the back. The dentist stayed on her heels. "I already warned you after your ex-husband came here. I expect a certain level of professionalism."

"I know. It won't happen again."

"See that it doesn't." Dr. Petrie turned and went toward her office.

Faith set the box on the floor in the break room.

Myra was heating up a Lean Cuisine in the microwave. "What's going on?"

She clasped her hands behind her back to hide the way they were shaking. "My husband left this for me, after I told him not to. And Dr. Petrie saw it. She's pissed."

Myra peered at the box. "You going to open it?"

"Not if I can help it."

For the rest of the afternoon, she kept herself busy. But that cardboard box kept nagging at her. She felt it sitting in the back room like an abscessed tooth. She could ignore it all she wanted, but eventually, she'd have to deal with it.

Faith went to the break room and glared at the box on the floor. There was no way she could leave it here. But she couldn't take it back to Sylvie's townhouse, either.

Not without knowing what was inside.

Myra walked in. "I thought you'd left. Everyone else has."

"Without my box? I don't think Dr. Petrie would be very happy about that."

Myra grimaced. "Just open it, already. I'm dying of curiosity now."

"It could be something illegal."

The other hygienist laughed. "What, like it's a bomb or something?" She took a step back when Faith didn't say anything. "Wait, for real, it's not a bomb. Right?"

"No." Jon was a lot of things, but he wasn't homicidal.

He'd never once raised a hand to her. But was he capable of all kinds of other shit? Without a doubt.

"Then what?"

"Maybe…drugs."

It was just the type of twisted thing Jon would do if he thought the police—or worse, his druggie friends—were after him. *Here, hold this for me so I won't get caught with it.* Fury burned in her stomach.

Myra's over-plucked eyebrows arched. "Oh, heck. Really? There are a *lot* of things I don't know about you, Faith."

"You have no idea."

What was she supposed to do?

She couldn't open a box of illegal narcotics in the dentist's office. That was a guaranteed way to get fired, if not arrested.

Calling the police wasn't a good option. For one, she didn't know for *sure* this contained drugs. But even worse, police would mean drawing attention to her problems for the whole world to see and judge. What if they accused her of being involved? *She* was the one in possession. Jon was in the wind.

Should she open the box outside in the parking lot?

So a construction worker can see? Great idea.

Throw it in a dumpster?

She didn't want to leave this stuff where someone could find it and get hurt.

Which left Sylvie's townhouse, and Faith had already ruled that out. No way was she bringing this mess home.

There was only one other place she could think of. But it would mean telling Sylvie about Jon's issues. It was hard to admit the entire truth—that Faith had spent years with a junkie who'd probably never loved her. Who'd made her feel worthless and unsafe in her own home.

But at least Sylvie and her coworkers at Bennett Security would know what to do. They'd know how to dispose of the contents safely, maybe even turn it over anonymously to the police.

"Any chance you could you give me a ride somewhere, and then take me home after?" she asked Myra. There was no way she could carry that bulky thing on her bike. It was hard enough to manage her regular bag with her lunch and extra scrubs.

"Is it going to be fun?"

"Well…maybe?"

Myra arched a skeptical eyebrow. "Is there at least a possibility of attractive men being there?"

"That likelihood is high."

"Then I'm definitely in."

∼

MYRA OPENED THE GLASS DOOR, and Faith carried the cardboard box into the front entrance of Bennett Security. It was in a three-story brick building right on the water. The brick looked aged from the outside, like a converted warehouse on an old wharf.

But inside, the company's headquarters were sleek and modern. Black leather chairs were arranged in the waiting area. A potted palm tree sat by a floor-to-ceiling window.

The receptionist wore a little microphone on her head. She smiled politely as they came in, though she cast a curious glance at the box.

"May I help you?"

"Could I speak to Sylvie Trousseau?" Faith asked. She'd tried calling on the way, but her friend hadn't answered.

"Let me check."

The box was heavy, yet Faith didn't want to set it down. It was her burden, and she had to see this through. She just hoped Sylvie could help her figure out what to do with it.

If not for Sylvie, Faith would never have had the courage to move to West Oaks at all. They'd lost touch for over a decade, and when Faith had finally given up on Jon, she'd reached out. She couldn't believe how forgiving Sylvie had been, even though their rift had been entirely Faith's doing.

And here she was, bringing her problems to Sylvie's workplace. If she'd had any other option, she would've taken it.

Maybe she was overreacting. But sadly, Faith knew her husband too well.

Her throat was tight as she waited for her best friend to appear.

"This place is swanky." Myra craned her neck. "And there are definitely some sexy men in here. Like those two. Dang." Myra grabbed Faith's elbow, jostling the box. "Look, they're coming this way."

Faith looked. Tanner and a preppy-looking guy had just stepped out of the elevator.

She glanced around for some means of escape. She didn't want to bring Tanner into this, too.

But it was too late.

Tanner did a double take when he passed reception. A grin split his handsome face.

"Faith?"

Chapter Eight

"Tanner. Hey." She was holding a huge cardboard box, looking bewildered. A curvy woman with bright red lipstick stood beside her. Both women wore medical scrubs, and Faith's long hair was in a messy bun. Her face, which was usually so vibrant, seemed pale and withdrawn.

He and Noah had just finished a training session, sparring with some of the other guys. Tanner wished he'd cleaned up, but then he might've missed her.

"Need some help?" He took the box out of Faith's hands.

"I was hoping to find Sylvie. I tried calling, but..."

Her anxiety was palpable. He wished he could put his arms around her and say something ridiculous to make her laugh.

Noah was leaning against the wall, arms crossed over his tight T-shirt. "Sylvie's on an assignment. Some crisis with a security system, and the client was important enough to get Max *and* Sylvie to make a house call." He stepped forward, sticking out his hand. "I'm Noah, by the way. Faith, right?"

"We met when I was here before, with Sylvie."

"How could I forget?" Noah flashed one of his oh-so-charming smiles, and Tanner fought the urge to roll his eyes.

"And I'm Myra," the other woman said with a wave. "I work with Faith, obviously. With clothes like these, we're either in the medical field, or a cult."

"What can we do for you both?" Tanner asked.

"I got that package this afternoon." Faith nodded at the box he was holding. "I hoped Sylvie could check it out. But I don't want to bother you."

Instantly, he went into threat assessment mode. He glanced down at the item in his hands. "You think it could pose a danger?"

"It's *not* a bomb. It's from my husband. *Ex*-husband."

Tanner did not feel reassured. And he felt a lot confused.

"What's the reason for your concern?" Noah was using his "in charge" voice. Normally, Tanner was perfectly happy for his friend to take command of a situation. But at the moment, the move grated on him.

There was a pause. When Faith responded, she was so quiet he could hardly hear her. "It could be drugs."

Tanner took a step forward, leaning in to hear her better. "Could be? What's your level of certainty?"

"Fifty-fifty." She cleared her throat. "Jon moved to the area not long ago."

"Your ex is in West Oaks?" He remembered what Faith had told him the night of their "date." That she'd be safe so long as Jon didn't show up here.

But apparently, he had.

"Jon asked me to hold onto some of his stuff. He claims it's for some resale business. But he's...um, he's a heroin addict. And he's been a dealer in the past." Faith's cheeks flushed red. A strand of hair escaped from her ponytail and onto her forehead, but she didn't brush it away.

There was silence in their group. Tanner's chest tightened with fury at her ex. And with empathy for her. She hadn't wanted to confess this.

"Then let's take a look," Tanner said.

He and Noah led the way to a conference room. Tanner grabbed some supplies. He and Noah slipped on latex gloves.

The kit in his bag also included Narcan, the overdose treatment his buddy Sean had mentioned when they were volunteering at the rec center. Sean hadn't exaggerated. Pretty much any medic out in the field carried the stuff with them. Every employee of Bennett Security did, too, in their standard-issue first aid kits.

Tanner used a knife to carefully cut the tape holding the cardboard box closed.

Noah stood beside him and pulled back the flaps, while Tanner moved forward to inspect the inside.

He felt a twinge of guilt at being annoyed at Noah before. He trusted this guy with his life. So what if Noah liked female attention? Even if the female in question was Faith.

Tanner did a visual scan of the contents. The box was filled with items wrapped in paper or bubble wrap. They brought out each item in turn, checking carefully for any signs of powder or pills.

But it was just a bunch of old-looking dishes and knick-knacks. No matter how closely they examined everything, nothing suspicious appeared. The stuff didn't even look expensive enough to be worth stealing.

"Guess it was a false alarm," Noah said. "I have no doubt your ex has done shady things in the past, Faith, but at the moment he seems to be legit."

Tanner removed his gloves.

Faith wiped a hand over her face. "I'm sorry. I just assumed."

"No need to be sorry." Noah gestured at the box. "Where did Jon say this stuff came from?"

"From Texas. He's going to resell it here." She walked over and looked at the various dishes, only half of which they'd repacked into the cardboard. "And he was telling the truth, for once."

Tanner was about to reassure her, but Noah spoke first. "Given your ex's history, I would've been worried, too."

Faith's eyes were on the tile floor. "Thank you again."

Myra rested a hand on the table, cocking her hip. "So, you guys are bodyguards?"

"That we are." Noah puffed out his chest. Tanner held back another eye roll.

"How in shape do you have to be? Scale from one to ten, with ten being the dudes who're on the cover of romance novels?"

Tanner wasn't going to touch that one.

While Noah did his best to answer with a straight face, Faith slipped through the doorway.

Tanner went to follow.

He found her leaning against the wall outside the bathrooms, wiping tears from her eyes.

"Oh, hey." She sniffled. "Sorry. I'm not sure why I'm crying."

He propped against the wall beside her. "Crying is a natural physiological response to stress. In other words, you gotta let that shit out."

"More of Tanner's words of wisdom?"

"That one's a little long for a bumper sticker."

Tears streaked down her cheeks. "It's so humiliating. Having to tell you and Myra and Noah about my drug dealing husband. I haven't even told Sylvie, but I need to."

"Nobody could blame you for that. None of this is your fault."

"Isn't it?" She took a shaky breath. "I tried to leave Jon once before. Three years ago. I went to my parents' house, and my mother told me I was being cruel. She called in our pastor, too, and they lectured me about how weak I was. Even when I told them Jon was an addict. And...I started to believe them. I took Jon back because that was what my family wanted." She squeezed her eyes closed. "*Now* you want to tell me this isn't partly my fault?"

"Faith, they gaslighted you. Or maybe they believed what they were saying? I don't know. But you're living your life differently now. That's what matters."

"Maybe Jon's trying to change, too, and I'm being unfair to him. But I can't trust that he won't put me in danger again."

"Has he threatened you at all?"

"No, it wasn't like that."

"You know you can call me if you ever feel unsafe, right?"

She nodded slowly. "To hire you as my bodyguard?"

Tanner shrugged. "Pay me in fish tacos." A smile snuck onto her face. "I also have hugs available. If anyone needs one."

"I do," she whispered.

He opened his arms, and Faith walked into his embrace. She laid her cheek against his chest.

Tanner didn't want to admit how much he'd been longing to touch her. How he'd craved feeling her skin against his after that night on the beach.

She smelled like seagrass and coconut and the ocean breeze on a summer day. Or maybe those were just the memories she brought to mind. Small, perfect moments that felt like home to him. Moments he wanted to bottle up, so he'd have them on rainy days.

He felt a pang in his chest, knowing how soon he'd have to let her go.

"Why haven't you told Sylvie this stuff? She wouldn't judge you."

"I know, but…" She shifted her head against his pec. "It's usually hard to talk about all this. Except with you."

Her hand moved to his abs and lightly gripped his shirt. Tanner held his breath. Suddenly he was acutely, painfully aware of every nerve ending in his body, especially the ones in contact with her. The rest of him really wanted to join in. The more contact, the better.

Which, sadly, wasn't going to happen.

"You seem to be around for all my humiliating moments in West Oaks," she said.

He laughed, and he felt her moving in response, snuggling into him. "I could ask my mom to send some middle school pictures of me if you want to even the score. My hair was even crazier."

"Is that possible?"

"And my beard was longer then, too."

She swatted his chest with the back of her hand. "I *do* wonder what you'd look like without the beard."

"You want this ugly mug on full display?"

"Ugly? Yeah, right. Is that why you have that bushy beard? You're hiding behind it?"

"Me? I don't hide. I let it all hang out."

She glanced up at him, tilting her head and smirking. God, he loved it when she gave him that look. Like they were fully in this moment together, sharing a private joke that didn't need words.

"Hey Faith, where'd you go?" Myra called out.

She pushed back from him. Tanner missed her already.

Faith's eyes were bloodshot. "Thank you for being such a good friend."

He should've been happy to hear it, but damn. That word still stung.

"Happy to help." Tanner returned her smile, though it felt like rubbing lemon juice into a cut.

She went back into the bathroom for a few minutes. When she emerged, her eyes were clear, and her smile had returned.

He and Noah walked the two of them to the exit and watched them go.

Noah spun around, dimple sinking into his cheek. "So. What's up with you and Faith?"

Tanner jammed his fists into his pockets. "We're just friends." Faith had made that clear just in case he'd gotten confused.

And he wasn't in the right headspace to try for anything more. It wouldn't be fair for him to weigh her down with the shit he was going through. Not when she already had problems of her own.

"You really wouldn't mind if I ask her out?"

Tanner's response was stuck in his throat.

Noah was a good guy. The best. The kind of man Tanner would fix up with his own sister if she were single. It would be an asshole move of colossal proportions if he stood in Noah's way out of petty jealousy.

"Yeah, no. I don't mind."

Noah clapped his hands together. "Perfect. Think you can put in a word for me? As her friend?"

Tanner forced out a laugh. "Please tell me your game is better than that."

"Whatever happened to brotherhood? We're supposed to be a team."

"But it's so fun to see you flail around."

"Fine. Next time you need help getting laid, don't come to me."

Tanner knew that Noah was only kidding. Noah was more a serial monogamist than a man whore. Nor did the guy need help scoring a date.

But protectiveness still roared through Tanner's veins. "You'd better treat her right. She's been through a lot."

"Easy, big guy. You know I will."

Shit. He did know. Noah would be great with her, and Tanner hated it. Which made him the worst wingman—and friend—in existence.

Chapter Nine

After work the next day, Jon finally called.

"Where have you been?" Faith asked.

She'd unblocked his number to demand an explanation after the box had arrived. Yet there hadn't been a single peep from him until right now. She'd actually started to worry something bad had happened to him.

"I'm sorry. I've been working to raise the startup money I need."

Which she'd refused to provide. Faith ignored the subtle guilt trip. "I told you I wouldn't store your stuff."

"I know, but I didn't have any other options. I'm saving for a storage unit. You know my credit is shit."

And so is mine, thanks to you, she thought. But she wasn't going to get onto that subject. It would only lead to an argument.

"Have you found a safe place to stay?" she heard herself asking. Gah, she didn't want to care what he was doing. Why did she?

"Still in the truck. But thank you for asking. That means a lot, you know."

"It doesn't mean anything."

"But you could've trashed my stuff. Sounds like you didn't."

Tears pressed at her eyes. "I came to California to start over on my own. *Please.* Just let me do that. Let me go."

There was silence on the line. She heard him sniffle.

"I'll come pick up the box. I can do it right now."

This was what she'd wanted. For him to take it back. But she was *not* giving him her address.

"I'll leave it at the bus shelter on Ocean and Third."

"The *bus shelter*? Why?"

"Take it or leave it. I'll text you where to go."

"Jeez…fine. I won't bother you again." He hung up on her.

She felt good about this small victory. But she knew better than to believe anything he said. *Especially* when it was what she wanted to hear.

~

JON HAD BEEN a one-night stand when she was nineteen. It had happened after Sylvie left for California. Faith had been too afraid to leave with her best friend, so she'd punished herself instead—hooking up with Jon Townsend, a boy she and Sylvie had both despised. A bully from their high school football team, notorious for his antics at parties and for screwing anything that breathed.

Faith had been drunk. She barely remembered that night except for flashes here and there. The loud music, the sourness of the cheap beer. Jon's fumbling hands. It had all been over in a matter of minutes. The encounter left her completely disgusted with herself. Exactly the point.

But less than a month later, Faith's period failed to arrive.

She panicked and told her sister, which led to her parents finding out. Suddenly, she and Jon were sitting side by side, receiving tongue lashings. There wasn't a question of *whether* they would get married, just a question of *when*.

Both sets of parents decided on a quick visit to the Justice of the Peace, before either of their children could think better of it and refuse. In a daze, Faith moved into Jon's house with his family. At the urging of the pastor at their church, Jon promised to stay sober and get a steady job.

The strange thing? She and Jon turned to one another out of sheer loneliness. They'd been cut off from all their other friends. Over those months, as her stomach grew, Jon went to all her doctor appointments and spent time with her. She thought maybe she'd been wrong about him, that he'd just needed a purpose to force him to grow up.

One night, he promised he would be a good dad and a loyal husband. *I know you don't love me*, he said. *But someday you will.*

She'd wanted to believe it. And maybe it would've happened if their baby had lived.

After that terrible loss, their families closed ranks around them, offering support but also making clear that their marriage was a permanent arrangement. They both lay awake every night, crying for everything they'd lost. That anguish bound them together.

Jon did try to keep his promise to be a good husband, at least on the surface. For years, they coasted along. Faith resigned herself to never finding real love, but at least she had stability. A home. She focused on getting her Associate Degree in dental hygiene, starting her career.

But all that time, Jon hadn't been okay. Not at all.

She remembered the first time she'd walked into the bathroom and found him shooting up between his toes. She'd turned right back around, walked into the yard, and thrown up.

Faith had insisted he get help. Once she'd understood how bad things really were, she'd done everything she could think of. Offering support. Yelling. Kicking him out. Trying, and failing, to leave. But he had a disease, and no matter what she said or did, it only seemed to get worse.

Looking back, Faith couldn't believe she'd let it go on for so long. When she'd suspected he was dealing, she knew something had to change. Then that horrible man had appeared one night. *Kyle*. Hinting that Jon had gotten himself mixed up in something even worse.

Kyle had terrified her. Threatened her. While he'd been in her bedroom, she'd been convinced he was going to hurt her in the worst possible way.

Faith had almost called the police. But half the sheriff's deputies were Jon's old high school buddies.

So she'd made the decision to leave for good instead. Leave her job, her family, her life, and go so far away that nobody could force her back. All in the hopes of starting fresh.

Thank goodness she was in West Oaks now, surrounded by friends who cared about her. She refused to let Jon hijack her life again. Jon could come knocking all he wanted, but she wasn't going to let him in.

Chapter Ten

Tanner pushed the barbell up to unrack it. He lowered the weight until it brushed his pecs, enjoying the burn in his muscles and the momentary quiet in his head. On the next exhale, he repeated the set, keeping his movements smooth.

Then Kozinski's voice broke through his focus. "Bro, she was all over me. Seriously."

Tanner grunted as he pushed the barbell up again. It clattered onto the rack.

"I thought you were doing sets of six?" Devon Whitestone was spotting. The former Army Ranger had joined their bodyguard team in the last year. Now, he was one of Tanner's closest friends at Bennett Security, second only to Noah. "That was just three. You okay?"

"I'm a little off today."

"Don't think I've ever heard you say that. Is it a joint issue?"

Tanner rubbed his shoulder. "Who knows. Maybe."

"Better get that looked at. Especially if you're going for captain. You'll have to keep up with the rest of us idiots."

"You too about that captain shit?" Tanner sat up on the

bench, grabbing his towel to wipe his neck. "Why don't you apply if it's so great?"

"Because I don't have anywhere near enough experience. Besides, my girlfriend is the boss's sister. Max would never want to seem like he's doing me special favors, nor would I ask for any."

"I don't want favors, either." Tanner wished their more senior bodyguards hadn't retired. He wasn't a fan of being the "elder." It was one thing to play the mentor to the kids at the rec center, another when it came to his teammates at work.

Even if he'd wanted the promotion, trying for captain would mean more scrutiny. More time under Max's watchful eye. All things Tanner didn't need. He handled himself well under pressure, yet he also worried one of these days his composure would finally slip, and they'd all see beneath his mask.

They'd all figure out what he was trying to keep locked down inside.

"And then I was like, 'That's what she said,'" Kozinski shouted from the other side of the room. Like every guy here wanted to hear his dumb exploits. Some people were laughing, though. Dude was a bad influence.

Tanner cast a glare toward their loudmouthed teammate. "I can't concentrate in here."

Devon followed his stare. "Yeah, he needs a volume control."

"Or better yet, an off button." Tanner wiped his face with his sweat towel.

Kozinski peacocked over to the bench press, where Tanner was still sitting. "Bro, you done with that yet?"

He felt anger prickling along his skin and fought to keep it down. "I've got one more set."

"Then speed it up, old man. The rest of us got places to be."

Old man? Really? He was still in his thirties. "Are you

kidding me? After you've been wasting time running your mouth for the last hour?"

"I was *kidding*. Relax."

"Don't tell me to relax." His breathes were shallow. Blood rushed in his ears. *No worries. You're fine. No worries.*

"What happened to all your 'Zen' bullshit, Reed?"

Tanner jumped to standing, fists clenched.

"Whoa, stand down." Devon stepped in between them. "We all have a team meeting in ten. Maybe everyone should focus on that instead of bickering?"

Kozinski walked back toward his little fan club, shaking his head. Like *Tanner* was the one with a problem.

Tanner's fingers opened, then tightened into fists again.

Devon was watching him. Everyone was watching him.

"I need to take care of something," Tanner said. "I'll be back later."

Devon followed him toward the locker room. "What about the team meeting?"

"Tell Noah it was an emergency." He had to get out of there before he put his fist through something—like Kozinski's face. The air was too stale. He needed to be outside with the pavement pounding against his feet.

~

TANNER WALKED down the sidewalk along Ocean Lane, dodging people on their lunch breaks.

Lately, too many things rubbed him the wrong way. The way the metal plates clanked when he loaded the bar in the gym, the way his clothes were arranged in his closet. The scratch of his T-shirt label. Everything set him on edge like nails dragging down a chalkboard.

Tanner caught sight of his reflection in a window and was surprised by the scowl that met him.

He thought of what Faith had said—that she wondered what he'd look like without the beard. That he was *hiding*.

Was that true?

It was the same beard he'd had for years. Same unruly hair. But he wasn't the same on the inside, was he? His brain was a shifting mess, and the things that had felt right before didn't fit him anymore.

He worked hard to project a certain image. The laidback bodyguard, approachable yet strong. Ready with his bumper sticker wisdom, as Faith called it. His "Zen bullshit" to use Kozinski's obnoxious and offensive phrase.

But he didn't like thinking his mask was literal. And he *really* didn't like that Faith had picked up on it.

He walked into the first hair salon that didn't seem busy.

A bored-looking stylist glanced up from her magazine. "Need a trim?" She had the scratchy voice of a smoker.

"More than a trim."

"That'll take a while," she muttered.

He ran his fingers through his curls. "I was thinking a buzz cut. Make it easy for you."

Now, she studied him. "Nope. That won't work."

"Isn't the customer always right?"

She snorted, tossing her magazine aside. "Just leave it to me. I'll make you look good. What about the beard? That thing needs a weedwacker."

"I'm getting the impression you'll do whatever you want, no matter what I say."

She cracked her knuckles. "I'm Gladys, by the way. You should know who you're trusting."

"Tanner. I'm in your hands, Gladys. Don't let me down."

He swallowed down his nervousness and fought the sudden urge to run. It was just hair. It would grow back. He needed to face the discomfort, conquer the fear.

She washed his hair with cool water, which felt nice. To his surprise, each snip of her scissors made him feel lighter. Like he was cutting away the old, worn-out parts of himself. Starting fresh.

He found himself wondering what Faith would think of his new look. He'd been worrying about her husband's presence in West Oaks, but so far, she kept insisting all was fine whenever he texted.

"I'm curious, Tanner. What inspired this makeover?"

"Just…seemed like it was time for a change."

"Uh huh, sure. More like, trying to impress someone you like."

That was partly true. If Faith hadn't said anything about his hair, would he be here right now? "If you already knew, why'd you ask?"

Gladys seemed to contemplate this question. "I suppose I like to leave room for surprises. But most people are predictable."

If he was trying to impress Faith, it didn't make much sense. As far as he knew, Noah hadn't asked her out yet. But he'd laid a claim. Even if Tanner had thought it was a good idea to make a move on Faith—which it probably wasn't—he couldn't now.

Gladys buzzed the sides short but left it longer on the top. He didn't know if it looked good, necessarily, but it was different. She smoothed some product through, taming the curl.

Then, she took her clippers to his beard. Tanner couldn't breathe as she got closer and closer to his skin.

"Don't pass out on me." The barest smile ghosted over her face. "I thought you wanted a change?"

"I do. But maybe not *too* much change."

"All right, don't get your undies in a twist. We're keeping the beard, but it'll be short."

He let out his breath.

When she was done, the whiskers followed the contours of his face. Tanner ran his palm over the short bristles.

And…yep. He could see himself more clearly. Interesting. He'd almost forgotten this face.

Gladys ambled over to the register. "That'll be sixty bucks."

"Ouch. Prices have gone up since my last cut." He handed over his credit card.

"You know how much they charge for rent on Ocean Lane?"

"Nah, I'm kidding. It was worth it. Thanks, Gladys."

She winked. "Good luck with whoever you're trying to impress."

I'll need a lot more than luck, he thought. Maybe a time machine. Because when it came to Faith, he'd missed his chance.

Chapter Eleven

Faith dumped her bags of groceries on the kitchen counter. "Who else is hungry?"

A silent house greeted her.

Right. She'd forgotten Sylvie and Ethan both had plans tonight in Los Angeles with their significant others. That meant she was on her own till the morning, which seemed to happen a lot lately.

Of course, she would never complain. Sylvie and Ethan had been incredibly kind about letting her stay here. She'd basically shown up on their doorstep, a homeless charity case after she left Jon. Her friends had helped her get back on her feet.

She owed Sylvie and Ethan everything.

Faith was paying her share of the rent. Her friends hadn't asked her once about finding her own place. They were giving her time. Still, she knew her next step toward independence was overdue.

Tanner would probably tell her to do something uncomfortable if it would mean growing as a person. He'd be right. But it was so much easier to *know* the right thing than to actually do it.

And now that she was thinking of Tanner, she couldn't stop. She could invite him over for a friendly dinner. It made more sense to cook for two than for one.

Before she could grab her phone, the doorbell rang.

Faith went over to the security panel. Sylvie and Ethan's townhouse had a Bennett Security system. On the camera, a man stood on the porch. He was facing partly away from her, looking back and forth over the street. He was lanky, his arms roped with sinewy muscles.

He had his hoodie up, keeping his face in shadow.

A sudden rush of fear spiked through her.

But this was her home, however temporary. She wasn't going to cower and hide.

Faith opened the door by a few inches. "Yes?"

The man scratched at his nose. "You got a package for me?" he mumbled.

"A package?"

"Yeah. From Jon."

"If Jon sent you, there's been a mistake." She hadn't heard from her ex in the last few days, and she'd taken that as a good sign. "You need to leave."

She went to close the door. But the guy slapped a hand on the wood, pushing it back open.

His eyes lifted, and his face came into view. Panic spiked in her chest.

It was him. *Kyle.* The man who'd threatened her. Pushed her down in her bedroom in Texas.

Faith put her weight behind the door, trying to close it. But he pushed even harder. He was trying to get inside.

No, *no*. This couldn't be happening.

"I'm calling the police," she yelled.

The door slammed against her. Faith fell backward onto the floor. Kyle stood over her. He grabbed her by the hair, hauling her up so she had to face him. "Did you think we were finished? Just because you left town? That's not how this works."

"I don't have any package. Jon took it."

"Are you lying to me?" He raised his hand and brought it down. The smack caught her on the cheekbone near her eye. Sharp pain and disbelief overwhelmed everything else.

"*No.* I don't have anything you want."

"You don't think so?" Kyle pulled her even closer, jamming his bony nose into her hair. "Maybe we should find out."

He took her hand and put it on his thigh. Faith yanked it away. She sucked in a breath and screamed as loud as she could.

Terror blanketed her, stealing every thought except, *Fight.*

She kicked at his knee. He let go of her and stumbled, cursing.

Faith sprinted for the front door, bumping her shoulder on the frame. Her breaths were ragged and loud in her ears, mixed with sobs.

"Help me! Someone, please!"

She banged on the next-door neighbor's place, but the windows were dark. Nobody answered.

Faith ran. She had no clue where she was going, just that she needed to get out of sight. The row of townhomes ended, and she saw a gate leading into someone's backyard. Her fingers slid over the latch. Finally, she managed to open it, and the hinges creaked. She hurried around the side of their house and crouched in the shadows behind a bush.

Her body was shaking. This was surreal. A nightmare. The past had come for her, and she was running. *Again.* When would it ever stop?

She felt a weight in her pocket. Her phone.

She rapidly pressed the side button to activate emergency calling. Back when she'd been with Jon, she'd learned the method just in case her husband overdosed.

Now, she waited for a voice to pick up. "911. What is your emergency?"

"A man named Kyle broke into my house. I need help."

The operator offered to stay on the line with her while she waited for the officers. Time seemed to be frozen.

How had Kyle found her? Jon didn't even know her address.

She was so angry, she thought she'd choke on the feeling. First Jon was in West Oaks, and now Kyle? Why? Why was this happening? Why couldn't they just *leave her alone*? She felt nauseating rage at Jon for bringing that shit to her door. It wasn't *right*.

A few minutes later, sirens climbed in pitch, turning onto her street.

Faith emerged from her hiding place. Her chest was so tight she was lightheaded from lack of oxygen.

The neighboring houses up and down the street were all the same, yet they'd changed in some indefinable way. Like she'd stepped into a dark, twisted mirror.

Two squad cars pulled up in to the curb in front of her, and multiple West Oaks P.D. officers got out.

She explained what had happened, how Kyle had forced his way into the house. She'd stopped crying and now spoke in a listless monotone. The despair was almost too much. She just wanted to sit down somewhere quiet. Hide away from what had happened.

She'd thought she was safe.

The police were here now. But what would happen after they'd left? How was she supposed to fix this?

Three of the officers went inside the house to see if the intruder was still there. The fourth stayed with her. He wore glasses and couldn't have been more than twenty years old. "Ma'am, is there anyone you'd like us to call?"

Immediately, she thought of Tanner.

Chapter Twelve

Tanner stood in the doorway of Sylvie and Ethan's townhouse. "Faith?"

She was sitting on the couch, hugging herself around the middle. She looked up, and Tanner didn't even think. He opened his arms.

She dashed toward him. He wrapped her up and held her tight. She'd sounded so terrified on the phone, telling him some guy had broken into her house. Tanner had hardly breathed on his drive over here. He'd run a couple of red lights, too, which hadn't been the wisest decision. But he was here now. He'd make sure she was safe.

There were police officers milling around and filling out paperwork, but he didn't pay them much attention.

"Did they catch the fucker?" Tanner asked, a dark edge to his voice.

"No. He was gone by the time they arrived."

"Jesus, you're hurt." She had the beginnings of a bruise on her cheek. "Did anything else happen? Do you need to go to the hospital?"

"No. Just... I was so scared." Faith buried her face against his chest. Her tears wet the fabric of his shirt. He wished he knew what to do to make her feel better, but he figured this would work for the moment. Just holding her, comforting her as best he could.

She explained that the officers had searched the house, but there'd been no sign of the intruder. She'd pulled up the video of him on the security system and was supposed to send the clips to the police via email.

"Did he take anything?" Tanner asked.

"I don't think so. He went through the house like he was looking for something." Faith blinked rapidly. "His name's Kyle. He's one of Jon's…not friends. But someone Jon knows."

Her ex. Tanner's pulse raced again.

"Kyle was asking for a 'delivery.' But it made no sense. Jon had already taken that box. And I don't even see why Kyle would want those old dishes."

Unless he hadn't been talking about the same delivery.

"Ms. Townsend?" an officer said. "We just have a few more things to go over for your statement."

"Oh. Sure."

Tanner went into the living room with her, and he didn't leave her side while she finished reciting every detail she could recall.

"Do you know where your husband is living?" the officer asked.

"No. But I can give you his license plate. He said he's been sleeping in his truck."

Somehow, her ex was tied up in this. But if Jon and this Kyle guy were working together, then why had Kyle expected to find a package at Faith's house? Why wouldn't the two men have just talked to one other?

What were they up to?

The officers finished up and promised a detective would contact her. She and Tanner walked to the front. The police left, and Faith shut and locked the door.

She turned around, fully looking at Tanner for the first time since he'd arrived.

Her eyes shot wide, and she covered her mouth with her hand.

"It's just a haircut." He scratched at his beard, what little of it there was left.

"I can't believe I didn't notice before."

"You were distracted."

"It's, um..."

"Not bad?" he supplied. "I hope?"

She snickered. "Not bad."

He hoped it was slightly better than that. He didn't even know what he'd been expecting. She viewed him as a friend, right? Why would she care if he changed his look?

Faith ducked her head. "Thanks for coming tonight. I just didn't know who else to call."

"I offered to be your bodyguard if you ever needed me, and I meant it. I'm happy to be here. Always."

"Right." But she seemed resigned instead of reassured. Probably because she never should've needed a bodyguard at all. He wished he could box up Jon and Kyle and ship them to the North Pole. *Here's your delivery, assholes.*

"I need to clean up the mess that's left," she said.

"I can help."

Tanner went around the house with her, putting things back into closets and wiping up dirty shoe prints.

Faith kept sneaking looks at him as they worked.

"You're making me self-conscious," he said.

"Why? You...look good. I promise."

"You're laughing at me."

"I'm *not*. I was thinking maybe I should get a haircut, too."

He frowned at her. "Don't do that."

"Why?" Faith gathered her hair into her fist. "I've always worn it long, and I think I'm tired of it. This stuff is always getting in the way."

Because your hair is beautiful. Because I want to run it through my fingers. Feel it brush my bare skin while we...

Okay, those images were not appropriate. He was supposed to be comforting her right now. Not picturing her naked.

"Please don't cut it?" Tanner said, softer this time.

She glanced away. "Maybe I won't."

They finished cleaning and went back to the downstairs living room.

"Are Ethan or Sylvie coming back here tonight?" he asked.

"No. They're staying in Los Angeles. Theater tickets or something with Nic and Luis." Her eyes shone with tears again. "I'm sure one of them would come back if I asked, but I don't want to ruin their night."

He couldn't just leave her here. "Then why don't you stay at my place? With me?"

"What?"

"I'd stay here with you, but I was thinking you might prefer a change of scenery. Or, I could drive you to a hotel. You make the call." Maybe he'd been indulging in some naughty fantasies about her naked, but his intentions were entirely honorable. He just wanted her to be able to sleep and feel secure.

"Your place sounds good. If you don't mind."

Without his permission, his heart did an eager dance in his chest.

"Grab your stuff, lock up here, and we'll head over."

Chapter Thirteen

Faith sat in the passenger seat of Tanner's Jeep. She realized she'd never seen him drive before. He usually walked places. But thank goodness he'd driven because he wouldn't have fit too comfortably on her bicycle handlebars. Nor did she have the energy to go by foot.

Faith was still unsettled after what had happened, but Tanner's presence relaxed her. The inside of the Jeep smelled like him, a mixture of laundry detergent and something she could only describe as masculine. She inhaled deeply, wanting more of it.

Tanner was constantly thinking of other people. She already owed him for all the kindness he'd shown her. She didn't see how she'd ever pay him back.

He'd do anything for a friend, Sylvie had once remarked.

She'd been a little shocked to see Tanner's haircut earlier, but it was a lot better than "not bad." She'd wanted to see more of his face, and that instinct had proved correct.

The man was gorgeous.

His jaw was strong and angular. The cords of his neck followed graceful curves, equal parts beauty and strength. Somehow, his eyes had become even more striking, lighting up all her nerve endings as he gazed back at her. Combined with the tattoos snaking up his arms, the way his T-shirt hugged every contour of his chest...

Her senses were already heightened from all the adrenaline in her body. But now, more pleasurable chemicals were speeding through her bloodstream.

"Here we are." He put the truck in park. The night sky was clear, the moon half full. Streetlights gave the surroundings a yellow glow.

Faith grabbed her bag and followed behind him. Before they'd left her house, she'd changed out of her scrubs and into leggings and a T-shirt.

Tanner lived in a clapboard bungalow with white railings along the porch. Shaker-style shingles covered the roof, framing a dormer window.

"Your house is adorable."

"Are you sure? I thought it was ruggedly manly."

A giggle snuck out of her. "You should complain to your real estate agent."

"Too late now. I'll have to stick with adorable." He unlocked the door and showed her inside. Faith set her bag on the floor.

The interior was sparser than she'd imagined it would be from the outside. Picture frames leaned against a wall in the living room, waiting to be hung. In the kitchen, some of the cabinets were missing their doors, and the walls had patches of different paint colors.

"I have a lot of unfinished projects," he said. "I had to save for a long time to afford this place, but it's still needed work."

"It has great bones. I'm jealous. In my old house in Texas, I *always* had something unfinished, and it wasn't nearly this nice." She admired the exposed rafters in the ceiling, walking through the open first floor.

Tanner sat on the arm of the sofa. "What was your house like?"

She pictured it. Narrow, one-story, shotgun style. Her in-laws had helped her and Jon with the down payment. Her mom hadn't liked it. *You'll be able to trade up to something bigger once you have kids.* To her mother's chagrin, that hadn't happened. Faith had an I.U.D., and her mom would've been livid had she known.

Her mind stuck on the memories of Jon, like a scratched record. But Tanner was still waiting for a reply.

"I don't think that place had a single straight line in it. Everything was wonky. But it was mine. Well, partly mine."

Back in Texas, she'd spent years making a home she didn't feel safe in. She'd tried to find the freedom to start over. Yet here she was, running from her disastrous marriage once again.

The urge to cry burned in her nose.

"Have you had any dinner?" Tanner asked.

"I..." She couldn't remember. But her stomach was rumbling. "I don't think so. Have you?"

"Nope. Let's see what I've got, though I can't promise it'll be gourmet." He opened the fridge, and Faith came into the kitchen behind him. Tanner pulled out a loaf of bread and a block of cheddar cheese. "Do you like grilled cheese and tomato soup?"

She almost cried, but this time with relief. Comfort food was exactly what she needed. "That would be *perfect*. You're my favorite person ever."

He grinned, and wow—she could see his mouth more clearly now with his shorter beard. His lips were full and soft-looking. "Have a seat, and I'll have this ready in a bit."

"Can't I help?"

"If you want. Sure."

Faith grated the cheese, while Tanner started on the soup. "I hope you don't mind canned."

"Are you kidding? My mom made Campbell's tomato all the time when I was growing up. There were five of us, and she usually spent so much time cooking. She was a fan of easy lunches. Made-from-scratch tomato soup is fantastic, but canned tastes like home."

"Same here. But my mom likes to add some extra ingredients."

"Really? Like what?"

He winked. "Can't give away the Reed family secrets."

She finished grating enough cheese for two sandwiches. They almost ran into one another as they jockeyed for position around the stovetop.

"Sorry," she said.

"No, go ahead."

He stood next to her, stirring the pot as the soup heated. Her pulse thrummed in her neck at having him so close.

Friends, she reminded herself. *We're just friends, and that's fine.* Anybody would do well to have a friend like Tanner.

"Has Noah gotten in touch with you?" he asked.

"Noah? No. Why?"

Tanner shrugged. "Just something he said. He…wanted to ask you out."

"*Oh.*" She felt flustered. She didn't know what to say. Did Tanner approve of this idea? "Really?"

"Can't be that surprising. You must have guys hitting on you all the time."

"Not so much." She cringed. "Just high schoolers." They both laughed.

"Noah's an upstanding guy. You wouldn't have anything to worry about with him."

It seemed like Tanner *really* wanted her to date his friend. But the idea of more time with Noah didn't excite her.

"Since Myra and I went to Bennett Security, she keeps talking about you. She might have a little crush." Faith melted butter in a skillet, added a slice of bread, then layered cheese and a second slice on top of it.

"Oh, yeah?" Tanner watched, gripping the back of his neck. "Are you trying to set me up?"

"What? I—no." Setting up Tanner and Myra would've been the last thing on her mind.

Tanner rested his hip against the counter, facing her. "Myra seems great. I'm just…not sure she's my type. I hope that doesn't make me sound like an asshole."

Faith tried to hide how much she liked hearing that. "You're just being honest. What *is* your type?" When she glanced over, he was looking at her.

"Someone who's funny. Sweet. Willing to put up with my nonsense." He'd taken a step toward her, his voice lowering. "Beautiful doesn't hurt."

"And you don't think that's Myra?"

Hesitation passed across his features. "You're right, she could be. I should give her a chance."

Now Faith was cursing herself for saying anything.

They finished cooking and sat down to eat, but their conversation didn't flow as easily as it had before. She couldn't tell if Tanner felt it, or if it was just her.

Despite the shift in the mood between them, Faith felt her nerves calming even further. The food warmed her from the inside out. "The soup is really good. It's so creamy. And I don't know what that flavor is, but it's good."

He shrugged. "I added half-and-half instead of milk, and dried thyme."

"I thought you weren't giving away the family secrets."

Tanner stirred his soup around in the bowl. "I decided to make an exception for you."

Her phone rang. Faith got up and found the device in her bag. Ice flooded her veins.

"Who is it?" Tanner asked.

"It's him." She answered, turning to face away from Tanner. "Hello?"

"Faith." Jon sounded breathless. "Someone might come by later."

"He already did. It was Kyle. You found out my address, didn't you? You gave it to him."

"*No*. I don't know how he figured it out. I tried to explain to him that—"

"He pushed his way into the house." She lowered her voice to a whisper. "He hit me, Jon."

"Oh, shit. Shit. I'm so sorry."

"I called the police."

He moaned. "This is so bad. It wasn't supposed to…"

"What the hell is Kyle doing in West Oaks?"

She felt Tanner watching her. Faith couldn't stop her body from trembling.

"It's a long story."

"What have you gotten yourself into?"

"You always think it's my fault. I tried to tell them you couldn't be involved anymore, and I was going to make another plan. I *tried*."

"Tell me the truth. Is there any 'antiques' business, or are you dealing again? Is that what this is really about?"

"Why can't you just trust me?"

She put her hand over her eyes. "Go back home to Texas. *Leave me alone*."

The call cut off.

Faith sat on the couch in the living room. Tanner came over and sat on the next cushion, leaving a couple feet between them. "Do you want to talk about it?" he asked softly.

"You heard me giving my statement to the police. And you heard…" She lifted her phone.

"I don't mean for me. You've been through something traumatic and discussing it can help."

She felt tied up in knots inside. "You were in the military, right? And you're a bodyguard. I know how much you did for Sylvie and Nic in the past. How do you stand it? Being in danger. Facing people who want to hurt you."

The bruise on her cheek ached. Kyle had hit her, and he'd threatened to do far worse. The uncertainty and confusion were tearing at her heart.

She put her hand over the mark on her face, feeling the shame as her skin heated.

"It's not easy," Tanner said. "The fear can be worse after the action is over. I try to focus on helping other people."

That didn't surprise her at all. Faith liked to think she was a kind person, too. But she was nowhere near as giving as Tanner. She'd spent so much of her life absorbed in her own problems.

"You knew this guy Kyle in Texas?"

Faith wrung her hands in her lap. "I'd suspected Jon was dealing. He never told me anything, but I could see the clues. Then, he disappeared. After he came back, I could tell something worse than usual had happened. Jon was really freaked out. Then, that guy Kyle came to our house one night. They were talking about how they were partners in something, but neither trusted the other. I was in the bedroom, and Kyle heard me, and…" She couldn't keep going.

"Faith, what did he do?"

Her thumb swiped a tear from her cheek. "Scared me, mostly. Pushed me. Said he'd make me pay if Jon didn't do what he wanted."

She felt the fury radiating from him, though Tanner hadn't moved a single muscle.

"Did you get any sense of what Kyle intends to do next?" he asked.

"No. This feels different than what happened in Texas, though. Because it's *here*. In West Oaks. I don't understand why Kyle is here, but it has to be something big. Right? Otherwise, why come all this way?" Except for the fact that *she* was in West Oaks. But Faith couldn't see why Kyle would chase her here, when he'd left her alone for the last eight months.

"Could it be related to whatever he and Jon were up to in Texas?"

"Maybe. Just now, on the phone, Jon said he didn't want to involve me, but other people were making him." She slowly shook her head. "I don't want him to suffer. I wish he could be happy. But… I think I deserve happiness, too." Her voice broke as she said this. Tanner reached over to place his hand over hers.

"You deserve that and a whole lot more."

"Thanks. So do you." Then she felt silly. Tanner wasn't sitting here asking for her advice or her approval.

He shifted his hand and laced their fingers together. Faith looked up at him, and she saw something different in his eyes. Something deeper and more tender. An ache started in her chest.

After the night she'd had, she wanted to sink back into his arms and take comfort in him. *Not* just as a friend. But that would've been crossing a line. Tanner was already giving so much to her, and she was being selfish to want even more.

Reluctantly, she pulled her hand away from his. "I'm really tired."

He got up, collected their dishes from the table, and brought them to the sink. "I was thinking you should take my room upstairs, since I don't have a guest room."

"I'll just sleep on the couch. I'm used to it, believe me."

"But you'll be more comfortable upstairs, knowing I'm here by the doors. Right?"

This man. Why did he have to be so perfect all the time?

There was no way in hell she could sleep in his bed, smelling him. Thinking of him. She'd be up all night imagining him next to her.

"I'll be more comfortable on the couch."

"Fair enough. I'll get you a pillow and some blankets."

He helped her set up a makeshift bed. Faith used the bathroom, where she followed her nighttime routine as best she could. She was already wearing comfy clothes, but she slipped off her bra.

When she came back out, Tanner was sitting on the end of the couch opposite her pillow. He stood.

"Thank you for everything," she said.

Tanner gently brushed his fingertip across her cheek, just below the bruise. "I'm really sorry about what happened. But I'm not sorry you're here."

"Neither am I."

"Goodnight, Faith."

Her gaze followed him as he climbed the stairs.

∽

FAITH OPENED HER EYES. She'd heard a crash.

She sat up on Tanner's couch, gasping for breath. Instantly, her body filled with panicked energy. She couldn't remember going to sleep.

Her eyes scanned the living room and kitchen. Both outer doors seemed secure.

There was a light on upstairs, shining down from the second floor. And now that her mind was fully awake, she realized the noise had come from up there, too.

Tanner's bedroom.

She didn't know if there was any reason to be worried, but fear clawed at her all the same. Was Tanner still awake?

Was he okay?

Pushing away the blankets, Faith got up. She padded over to the base of the stairs. Her foot pressed onto the first step. The wood made a popping sound. She paused.

"Tanner?" she whispered.

Somewhere upstairs, he moaned.

Chapter Fourteen

*G*unfire roared in Tanner's ears. Scotty went down in front of him. Night vision goggles painted the scene in a surreal, green haze.

The enemy had come out of nowhere, mouth a snarl of hatred and fear. Hands pointing a rifle. The black circle of the barrel stared like an inhuman eye.

The muzzle on Tanner's M4 flashed.

The guy's body convulsed as the bullets hit him. Skinny arms and legs flailed, then stilled, limp and lifeless.

In Tanner's ear piece, his chief was yelling orders to their right flank team. An explosion rocked a nearby building.

Scotty was on the ground. Tanner turned his teammate over and saw blood gushing from a ragged hole in his neck. He tugged the NVGs off Scotty's head, and his teammate's eyes rolled back.

Tanner grabbed for the gauze in his kit. He had to stop the bleeding. "Stay with me, okay? Stay—"

He woke up curled in a fetal position, covers twisted around his feet. His limbs trembled, still half trapped inside his nightmarish memories.

Fuck. He couldn't get any air. Panic was overwhelming him. He forced his lungs to relax enough to take a breath.

Then a tiny pop came from below. He knew that sound. Someone was on the stairs.

Tanner jumped to his feet.

His bedroom was the only space up here, more of a loft than anything, and he had no door. No protection. His instincts screamed, *Danger. They're coming. Get ready.*

Then he heard his name.

"Tanner?"

It was Faith. He leaped down the steps, grabbed her around the waist, and hauled her back up. He pressed her up against the wall, covering her body with his. His lips whispered against her ear. "Stay quiet. We can't let them hear us."

It had to be her ex-husband. And the other one, Kyle, who'd hurt her last night. They'd followed her here.

Faith tensed, hands gripping his arms. He wore only a pair of sleep shorts, and his bare chest was slick with sweat. Her breasts rose and fell as she breathed.

Everything else was silent except his pulse pounding in his ears.

He needed a weapon. He had to protect her.

"I need my gun."

He tried to move toward the stairs, but Faith wouldn't let go of him. "Wait, are you sure anyone's outside? I heard a noise, but I thought it came from up here. Did something fall?" She pointed. "Was it that?"

His alarm clock lay on the floor. Tanner blinked. He remembered hearing Faith on the stairs, her voice. But then...

He grabbed his phone and opened his Bennett Security app. The cameras on his front and back door didn't show a thing. Same with the sides of the house.

Nobody's there, the rational part of his brain said. *You've been feinting at shadows.*

Fuck. This was bad. He shook his head, trying to clear away the last remnants of his nightmare.

That night in Afghanistan. The worst night.

The images remained vivid in his memory. Shooting the hostile who hadn't been older than fifteen. Then watching Scotty bleeding out, unable to do a thing to stop it. The things that happened after…

He bent to pick up the clock and set it on his nightstand. Three in the morning.

"I think you're right. I'm sorry."

Thank god his weapon was locked in the safe downstairs, where he always left it. And *this* was why, so he couldn't wake up confused and grab it without thinking. He tasted bile at the back of his throat.

How was he supposed to explain this to Faith?

His bedside lamp was on, just as he'd left it. He rarely slept more than an hour at a time, but even that would've been impossible in pure darkness.

Tanner sat on the edge of his bed, pulling himself together. When he looked up at her, she had her arms crossed, shoulders tight. Her nipples poked at her thin T-shirt.

He huffed a laugh. As if there was anything funny about this. "I was having a nightmare, and I guess I knocked over the clock. I think my brain didn't wake up with the rest of me."

"When I saw your light on, I thought you were still up. I didn't mean to scare you."

"I must've fallen asleep with the lamp on." Like it was some mistake. But no way was he telling her he needed a nightlight.

"It's okay. Maybe we're both stressed about what happened earlier?"

"That must be it."

"I'm glad it's not just me." She walked over and sat beside him on the mattress.

His awareness perked up again, but this time it was in attention to her. Faith's hair was loose, hiding part of her face.

Without thinking, he swept it back over her shoulder, fingertips brushing her neck. She exhaled with a small sigh.

That sound went straight to his dick.

He recalled how he'd been pressed up against her body just minutes ago, their chests separated by only the fabric of her shirt...

Nope. Bad brain. Think of the ice-cold Pacific. Pretend you're swimming five miles in January.

Noah had made it clear that he liked her. His friend. Noah, his brother, whom he cared about and would never betray.

He could *not* get hard right now in front of her. In these shorts, there wouldn't be any hiding it.

"I don't think I can sleep any more tonight," she said.

"I doubt I will, either. I don't sleep much in general."

"Why?"

"Don't know. Just how I am." He was so full of shit.

"We might as well be awake together."

"It would be silly not to." He grinned, and he only had to fake it part way. "Want to go for a morning swim?" That would take care of his rebellious nether regions. His balls would be trying to disappear into his abdomen.

She shivered. "Absolutely *not*. I've had enough discomfort for one twenty-four-hour period."

"That's true. You have."

She glanced at the mattress. "Could we lie down? Would that be weird?"

Shit. Lying next to her in his bed wasn't going to help his body behave. But Faith needed comfort. He would never deny her that.

"If it makes you feel better, who cares if it's weird?" They were two friends, seeking solace in closeness. *Platonic* closeness. And he could use some comfort, too. Having her in his room made him feel more awake by the minute. The nightmare was fading away like foam on an ocean wave.

Faith crawled across the mattress and settled onto one of his pillows. Then she reached down and pulled the covers up to her waist.

Tanner got in beside her, careful not to touch any part of her. He lay on his back, staring at the ceiling.

"I sent a text to Sylvie and Ethan before bed." Faith adjusted the pillow under her head. "But I don't know if they've read it. I feel so awful. Kyle went into *their* house because of me. What if they get back and find something's missing that I didn't realize?"

"We'll get it figured out. I promise, they'll be a lot more concerned about you."

"But…" She breathed like she was trying not to cry. "I feel like I brought this to their door."

"It's not your fault. You know that, right?"

"Yeah. But knowing and feeling are different."

True words. "If you remotely think that guy could come back, maybe we should arrange a bodyguard detail for you. Or a car to keep surveillance on the house."

"I'll think about it. I just want Jon to leave town. I was finally doing better before this happened."

That sentence spoke directly to his soul. It was exactly how he felt. Tanner put his hand on top of the blanket, palm up. He didn't want to reach for her and force the contact. But he was hoping.

She brought her hand out, too, resting it against his.

"If Jon doesn't go back to Texas," she said in a whisper, "maybe I should."

"Do you want to go back?"

She hesitated. He turned his head to look at her. Faith was biting her lip, which only drew his attention to her mouth.

"Sometimes. There are things I miss."

"Like what?"

"My family. Open spaces. Rolling hills, and the sound of

wind rustling the leaves. Line dancing on ladies' night with my friends."

"Line dancing, huh?"

"It was really popular when I was in school. Don't laugh."

"I wouldn't. I'm a country boy. I can boot scoot."

A smile broke across her face, like the first rays of the sun coming up. "I thought you grew up here in California."

"California's got plenty of farm country. Where do you think all that produce comes from? Or all those happy cows?"

"When you say it like that, it's obvious. What're *your* favorite things from home?"

"Mom's tomato soup. Her cranberry French toast at Christmas. Playing chess with my dad and drinking beers with my siblings." His fingers shifted against hers. "Foggy mornings when it feels like the rest of the world doesn't exist, and everything's quiet."

"That sounds nice. I wish I could see it."

I wish I could show you, he thought. He wished a lot of things.

Faith's eyes closed. Tanner looked at the ceiling and listened to her regular breathing until he drifted off too.

∼

"TANNER, could you be a dear and hold my shopping bags?"

Mrs. Zhang had a home in West Oaks, and whenever she visited from Hong Kong—every month or so—she arranged for a team of local bodyguards. Usually, she preferred Tanner to escort her around. She seemed to think it was hilarious to make her six-five bodyguard carry around pink shopping bags or look after her pampered Lhasa Apso.

"Of course, ma'am."

Today, they'd made the trek into L.A. to shop in Beverly Hills. Mrs. Zhang had stopped at every boutique on

Robertson Boulevard, inching her way toward The Ivy, where she'd be stopping for lunch.

There was constant activity around them, but it didn't rile Tanner's nerves. He was in bodyguard mode, scanning for threats. His suit, earpiece, and matching scowl gave off the kind of *don't-fuck-with-me* vibes that made people steer clear.

Periodically, he passed her purchases over to the other bodyguard working with him—who, today, was unfortunately Leon Kozinski.

"Seriously, more?" the guy muttered. "Why should I carry all this shit?"

"Because this stuff looks better on you. Watch out for the glitter."

He'd resolved not to let Kozinski bug him anymore. Tanner wasn't going out for captain, but he could at least set a good example for the more recent hires.

He still felt unnerved by the episode a few nights ago when Faith had stayed over. His nightmares didn't usually trigger such vivid flashbacks, and he was pissed at himself for making Faith witness it. He'd been redoubling his meditation and mindfulness efforts. A couple of times, he'd almost called the therapist he'd used to see. But that would've been an admission that he'd fully regressed to the same shitty place he'd been years ago. This time around, he could handle it on his own.

Finally, it was time for Mrs. Zhang's lunch reservation. Once she was seated, Tanner turned to Kozinski. "I'll be back in fifteen." He was going to take a quick break to meet his friend Sean, the detective with the LAPD Gang and Narcotics Division. "But I'll be on the comm if anything comes up."

"Yeah, go. I got this."

Tanner walked half a block down to a coffee shop. It had white subway tile on the walls and way too many indoor plants draped over every surface.

Sean was in line. He gave Tanner a quick hug. "This place

isn't my usual speed. Are those prices in dollars? American dollars?"

"It's my treat. I appreciate this."

"If you're paying, then I'll get a ten-dollar cookie, too. Gotta say, I'm curious what they're putting in that thing. Gold leaf? Magic mushrooms?"

"You could ask, but that's not the fun way to find out."

They took their drinks outside and stood by the curb to talk. "I got some info on the guy in that photo you sent me," Sean said.

Tanner's blood rose at the thought of the man who'd attacked Faith. Tanner had told Sean all about the assault and shared the video footage.

"I spoke to a friend at West Oaks P.D.," Sean explained. "They ran his prints and found his record easy enough. Piece of shit named Kyle Spaulding. He's been inside for assault in Texas. Suspected of a lot more, but the witnesses have a tendency to clam up."

"What about drugs?"

"Possession of marijuana with intent. But according to everyone I asked here in L.A., he's not known to work for any of the cartels who currently run things in this region."

"Is he just a street dealer?"

"Possible, but if he's low-level, why the stuff with these deliveries? It would suggest he's got more of a role."

"Huh." Faith had been convinced Jon was back into dealing. "If not drugs, then what's it about?"

"Could be some sort of financial scam. You wouldn't believe the sleazy schemes people come up with to make a few bucks."

No matter what, Jon had no good reason to be connected to someone like Spaulding, and no justification for bringing Faith into it.

"But here's the thing," Sean went on. "Even if someone gets lucky and picks Spaulding up, he's only looking at a misdemeanor assault charge in West Oaks. He'd be out on bail in no time."

"Are you serious? What about burglary? He invaded her home."

"Burglary would require intent to commit a felony when he entered the house. From what you've told me, there's only weak evidence of that. He'll probably claim he was looking for his property inside, since he was there for his alleged package."

"After what he did to Faith? That's bullshit."

"That's reality." Sean took a bite of the cookie. "A mandatory restraining order will have issued, but that'll just be one more misdemeanor if Kyle goes near her again. As for her ex, there's basically nothing to suggest Jon Townsend has committed a crime."

So the police were doing nothing. Not what Tanner wanted to hear.

"Has her ex bothered her again?" Sean asked. "If he's harassing her, Faith could make a complaint with West Oaks P.D."

"Faith hasn't mentioned anything. I've texted with her. I'm closer to Faith's roommate Sylvie, my coworker, and she hasn't seen him around either."

Sylvie had called him up the day after the incident. Most of the time, Sylvie was a badass who kept her cool under the direst of situations. Except maybe when she'd first met her boyfriend, Nic.

But when it came to Faith, she'd once again been in mama-bear mode. *Could Faith really be in danger?* Sylvie had asked. *Should I talk to Max about arranging a safe house?*

Tanner had already thought about that. But Faith's life had been disrupted enough. He'd joked about being her bodyguard, but she didn't actually seem to want protection. If she preferred to stay put, they needed to respect her choice.

But had he been worrying about her? Of course. It was nagging at him like so much else.

Tanner hoped Jon took Faith's advice and went back to Texas.

"This cookie's actually pretty good." Sean broke off a piece. "Want some?"

"No, thanks." Tanner's stomach was too unsettled.

"How've you been feeling?"

He didn't want to talk about that. Probably should never have brought it up last time.

Tanner glanced down the block, where Kozinski was looking bored outside The Ivy's luxe dining patio. "I'd better go, man. Break's over. Thanks again."

Chapter Fifteen

Faith was finishing up a patient's chart when Myra nudged her. "I think someone's here to see you."

She looked up, dread plunging through her veins. Was it Jon?

She could see into the waiting room past the reception desk. Tanner's friend Noah had his elbows resting casually against the counter. She breathed a sigh. Just Noah. Thank goodness.

Then she realized why he might be here. Tanner had said Noah wanted to ask her out.

Oh, god. No.

He flashed a dazzling grin at their receptionist. "I was hoping to make an appointment."

"Why do you think he's here for me?" Faith muttered to Myra.

"Because when we were at Bennett Security that time, the guy only asked me about you." Myra pumped her eyebrows up and down.

Faith elbowed her coworker. "Quit. He's going to see you."

Noah's eyes flicked over to meet hers.

"Usually people call for appointments," their receptionist

said. She was a no-nonsense gatekeeper, an old battle axe in a twenty-five-year-old's body.

But Noah's smile didn't falter. "Phones are so impersonal. Plus, I didn't have the number."

Faith could only see the back of the receptionist's head, but she could imagine the glare Noah was receiving right now. "It's on our website. But I'm happy to schedule something for you." She woke up the computer.

Myra leaned over to whisper, "I think now is when we save him."

Faith shrugged. "Unless he really wants a cleaning." She was trying to be optimistic.

"I guarantee you, a guy with teeth that nice already has his dental care well established." Myra walked over to the reception area. "You're overdue for a break, right? I can take it from here. Noah's a friend."

The receptionist eyed her warily. "You'll answer the phones?"

"Faith and I don't have any more appointments. We've got it."

Shrugging, the receptionist got up and walked toward the back. Faith glanced after her. It was almost the end of the day, and Dr. Petrie had already left. Still, she was nervous about the receptionist mentioning this visit later. Faith couldn't afford to anger her boss after what had happened with Jon's visit and the "delivery."

Faith walked over to the desk. "Are you really here to schedule an appointment?"

"That was my clever ruse to get in the door. Do you think your receptionist will forgive me?"

"That probably depends on why you're really here." She tried to keep her tone neutral. She suspected he was flirting with her, and she didn't want to give him the wrong idea.

His clean-cut, boyish looks probably let him get away with

plenty. With enough time, Faith thought even their battle-axe receptionist wouldn't be immune.

"It was true when I said I didn't have the phone number I needed. But I was hoping I could get yours."

Definitely flirting. Because Tanner—the guy she was actually crushing on—had probably encouraged it. Ugh. This was awkward.

Myra grabbed a sheet of note paper, leaning over the desk. "She'd be happy to. Why don't I write it down? Or, even quicker, you could just tell her now whatever you were going to say on the phone."

Noah's eyebrows drew down thoughtfully. "That would be more efficient. I was going to ask if you're doing all right. Tanner told me what happened. The break in?"

"Oh. Yeah, I've been good."

Neither Kyle nor Jon had bothered her further. She was really hoping the whole mess was behind her. Any other possibility made her feel like throwing up. Myra and Sylvie had both been great about it, checking in almost every day on how she was feeling. Sylvie had made sure Faith didn't have to spend the night alone, and Myra had been driving her to and from work, so Faith didn't have to bike.

Tanner had texted several times, too. Faith was determined to be grateful for *all* her friendships.

"That's a relief," Noah said.

Myra huffed. "Really? You came all the way here to ask that? Bor-ing," she said in a singsong voice.

Noah laughed. "C'mon Myra, give a guy a chance. I wasn't finished. I *also* planned to ask if she'd have dinner with me."

And there it was. Faith had known this was coming, but she still felt her cheeks blushing.

"If you're going to get shot down, sooner is probably better," Myra pointed out.

"So true." Noah and Myra both looked to her, waiting for her to say something.

In theory, Noah was exactly the kind of guy she should want to go out with. In objective terms, he was cute. Classic good looks, expressive green eyes. Defined muscle showed beneath his polo shirt. Noah seemed friendly, kind.

He just wasn't Tanner. And Tanner wasn't interested in her.

She kept thinking his name. *Tanner.*

And then, she realized she'd said it aloud.

Noah looked confused. "What *about* Tanner?"

Faith's jaw snapped shut. Crap. Why had she said that?

Sorry Noah, but I can't stop thinking about your friend. Because, when it comes to men, I'm only attracted to the ones I can't have. First Luke, now Tanner. It was like her subconscious didn't want her to have sex ever again.

Noah was still waiting for an explanation. But Myra saved the day.

"Oh, that's a *great* idea." Myra waved her hands excitedly. "What about all of us going out together? You and Faith, me and Tanner."

Noah hesitated, then shrugged. "No objections here. Is that what you meant, Faith?"

"Well…"

If the four of them went out, they'd probably have a good time together. It meant another evening spent in Tanner's company. Because he was her *friend*.

And maybe, if she gave Noah a chance, she'd feel something for him. He was the guy she should be interested in—handsome, a full-grown adult. Available and interested.

"Sure."

"How about tomorrow?" Noah asked.

Faith couldn't think of any reason to say no. "Tomorrow works."

"Then it's a double date."

Chapter Sixteen

Tanner saw the lights of the restaurant ahead. The sun had set, and waves were crashing into the rocks far below the path. He was on the south side of West Oaks, a five mile walk from Bennett Security's headquarters.

His pace slowed, but not because he was tired. If anything, he wanted to just keep on walking, all the way down along the coast with no destination. He'd been dreading tonight since Noah had ambushed him yesterday with this stupid idea, and now that it was here, he didn't know how he'd get through it.

Embrace the fear, he repeated in his head.

But fuck that. He was tired of his heart racing, of not sleeping. The buzz in his head had only been getting worse. Days at work were okay, but nights at home were near unbearable.

Almost a week had passed since Faith had slept over. He'd boomeranged between wanting her so much his entire being ached for her and torturing himself over the guilt. Not healthy, yet he couldn't stop doing it.

Tanner kept putting one foot in front of the other, right up to the parking lot of the seafood place. Through the bank of windows, he could tell it was rowdy. Large groups of people were already crowded around the communal tables, laughing and shouting.

Damn it. He'd known this place would be busy but hearing the noise and seeing all those people stoked his panic even more than he'd been expecting. His heart drummed in his rib cage.

It was bad enough he'd have to see Faith with Noah, but to have all this chaos around him?

No. He couldn't do it. He had to bail.

"Tanner!" Myra jogged toward him across the parking lot.

And now he was stuck.

Then he felt ashamed of himself for even thinking about ghosting this poor girl. She was supposed to be his date, and he owed her his best effort.

He forced a smile onto his face. "Hey, how's it going?"

"Better now. Thank jeez I'm out of the office. Dr. Petrie was flipping out today because somebody—I'm not naming names—forgot to restock the nitrile gloves." She shrugged. "Okay, it was me. But whatever. It's not a war crime." Then she glanced at him again and gasped.

"Holy crud, your hair. What happened to it?"

He rubbed a hand through his shorn locks. "Felt like trying something new."

"Dang, boy. New is good. You've upped your hotness quotient by like, a thousand."

He probably looked like some animal caught in headlights before it was turned into roadkill. Myra burst out laughing. "Okay, I need to say this. Nobody technically asked you if you wanted to be my date before we planned it, which my therapist tells me was rude. Apparently, I have boundary issues."

"You have a therapist? Are they any good?" In case he wanted to see one again. Maybe.

"Yeah, she's a buzzkill, but she's also right a lot of the time. So, you're off the hook tonight."

"I am?"

"Yep. Let's just consider this a friends thing."

Tanner exhaled, and his shoulder muscles unwound a few notches. His adrenaline was still up, but at least this was one fewer thing to worry about.

Myra rolled her eyes. "You don't have to look *that* relieved."

"Sorry. The truth is, I'm hung up on someone else, and that's not your fault. I wouldn't want to give you the wrong idea."

"That sounds juicy. Do tell."

Thankfully, Noah's Maserati SUV rolled into the parking lot right at that moment. While Tanner and Myra had agreed via text to meet at the restaurant, Noah had said he was picking up Faith from her house.

"Whoa, sweet ride," Myra said.

"Noah comes from money. Grew up in the fancy part of West Oaks." Tanner realized how dismissive and judgmental that had sounded. "He doesn't act like it, though. When we served together, I had no idea until he invited me to spend a few days' leave on his family's private island."

"For real?"

"Don't mention I told you that. He gets self-conscious."

"Yet he's driving that car around?"

"I didn't say it made sense."

She mimed locking up her mouth.

The passenger door opened, and one long, tanned leg appeared, then the other. Faith's blond hair was braided down her back. She'd worn a pale blue dress ending just above her knees.

He thought about her lying in his bed, that hair splayed on the pillow, nipples jutting through her shirt…

Stop. That's your friend's girl. Or at least, she probably will be.

Myra nudged his side with her elbow. "Hung up on someone, huh?"

"Boundaries," he muttered.

He still didn't want to be here. But that didn't matter, did it? The operation was underway. It was full speed ahead until he was out the other side.

In the restaurant, the hostess was busy with another party, so they waited. Faith and Myra stood a few feet behind, chatting.

Noah clapped a hand on Tanner's shoulder. "You know, I haven't had a chance to ask about your extreme makeover."

"My haircut? I thought that was old news. I did it days ago."

"But I haven't given you any shit for it yet. Some kind of TikTok challenge?"

"Nope. Just felt like it. Don't know why."

"It's one of those mysteries of the universe?"

"Like how you manage to get any action wearing the same clothes as my dad."

Noah popped his collar. "Faith hasn't complained yet about my polo shirts."

"Matter of time." Tanner smiled, gnashing his teeth together.

The hostess reappeared and led them to a table right in the middle of the interior. Tanner was already starting to sweat. There was a sea of people around him, noise, distractions. His chest was seizing up.

He pulled on his T-shirt to get some air. "Are there any tables outside on the patio?"

"Not for another hour."

Shit.

Skin crawling, he slid into a chair beside Myra and across from Noah. The hostess handed out menus. The server arrived, and they ordered a round of beers, along with some fried appetizer things. They chatted until the drinks arrived.

Noah held up his beer. "A toast to old friends and new beginnings," he shouted over the noise. They clinked bottlenecks together.

The table behind them exploded into raucous laughter, and Tanner flinched.

Noah leaned toward him. "Something wrong?"

He sipped his beer, shaking his head.

I'm calm, he told himself. *I can manage this. No worries.*

Myra set her beer bottle on the table with a *thunk*. "Okay, I just realized something. Is Noah the only person at the table who doesn't know Faith corrupted an eighteen-year-old?"

Faith groaned, covering her face with her hands. "Please, don't."

"Boundaries, Myra," Tanner warned. "Didn't we talk about this?"

But Noah was looking at them expectantly. "You can't say something like that and not explain."

Tanner held up a hand. "Either Faith tells it, or we change the subject."

She blew a strand of hair from her forehead. "Fine, I'll tell Noah. But he'll probably lose all respect for me."

She started the story reluctantly, then grew more animated as she went on. Myra and Noah were both rapt. Tanner loved seeing Faith like this, confident enough in herself to let both her humor and sweetness shine through.

And when he focused only on her, the rest of the noise fell away for a little while.

"The kid actually ordered a beer?" Noah asked.

"And commented on how 'experienced' I must be, since I'd been married."

"Wait, he what?" Tanner hadn't heard that part before.

"And then Tanner fixed everything by taking me to the boardwalk and for a walk on the beach." Faith tipped her beer back. "We even went on a nighttime swim, and I nearly froze my butt off."

Noah eyed him. "Why haven't I heard about this?"

His discomfort reared back to life. "I was just doing what any good wingman would've done."

"I don't think so," Myra said, poking his arm. "Sounds to me like you went above and beyond."

Noah grinned. "But that's Tanner. Like when we got paired up as swim buddies when we were qualifying as SEALs. He and I were miles off Coronado Island doing a timed swim, and I was about ready to succumb to hypothermia…"

Noah told a well-worn story about Tanner supposedly dragging him back to shore, though Tanner remembered the whole thing differently. The anecdote felt patronizing. Like Noah was patting him on the head. *Good boy, Tanner. Good for you. Saved your buddy's precious life so Noah could someday make captain and get the girl and the happily ever after.*

And there went the rest of his decent mood.

After that, Faith and Myra launched into stories about their months working for Dr. Petrie.

But somewhere along the way, the noise in the room turned into a constant roar in Tanner's ears. Every time someone passed too close to their table, he felt the tension in his body winding tighter.

He tried not to notice Noah's arm draped over Faith's chair. The brightness of her smile and the shine of her hair. Faith seemed to pull at his vision, like all the light in the room began and ended with her.

Then a guy in a baseball cap stood up from the table next to them, holding an ice-filled drink aloft. His friend pushed him. Baseball cap stumbled back.

Tanner saw it all unfolding like it was slow motion.

Baseball cap knocked against Faith's chair, an elbow slamming into her head. His icy drink spilled into her lap.

Tanner was out of his chair before he'd even realized it. He shoved the baseball cap guy away from her. The guy fell against his own table, disrupting half the drinks and sending people scattering.

Tanner grabbed the guy's shirt and yanked him back up. Baseball cap's friends shouted in protest.

"Apologize," Tanner growled.

Noah appeared at his shoulder. "That's enough, man. Stop."

Baseball cap scowled at them both. But people couldn't just go around being reckless, with no regard for the harm they caused. Didn't they know how dangerous it was? How any second the world could tip on its side and go straight to hell?

"You hurt her. Don't you *care?*"

"Jeez, okay. I'm sorry."

Tanner let him go.

The guy readjusted his cap. "Fucking psychopath."

Loud music still played, but many of the voices in the restaurant had gone silent. Tanner felt like he was coming out of a fog.

He looked over at Faith and Myra. They were wiping off Faith's dress with a napkin.

Noah smiled at the other group. "It was just an accident, right? Everyone's sorry. Another round of drinks on us. Okay?" He pulled Tanner back to their table, while the baseball cap guy and his friends returned to theirs, muttering to each other. But it seemed like Noah's peace offering had smoothed things over.

Tanner sat roughly in his chair. His heart was racing so fast he thought it would explode.

"Are you all right?" he asked Faith hoarsely.

She stared back at him with shock in her eyes. "I'm fine. What about you?"

No. No, I'm not.

Myra tugged at Tanner's shirt. "Dude, you need to chill. That was exciting, but you have to pace yourself. I don't want to get thrown out before we finish dinner."

Noah made some joke, and the rest of them tried to get on with their evening like nothing had happened. Yet Tanner still felt like he was inside a haze of relentless input. His heart rate wouldn't calm down.

He felt Faith watching him, her shoulders tense, like she was waiting for him to blow up again.

Tanner knew he should get out of here before he did something else he would regret, but he couldn't bring himself to get out of his chair and leave the table. All his energy went to staying still. Acting normal.

Finally, the night was winding down, and the crowd inside the restaurant ebbed. He and Noah split the check, while Faith and Myra went to the bathroom.

"You want to get some air?" Noah asked.

"Yeah. That would be good."

Tanner let his buddy guide him out into the parking lot. He gulped down the fresh air as the noise and lights of the restaurant receded. Ocean waves crashed in the background.

They walked halfway across the lot toward Noah's Maserati. Then Noah turned around. "What is up with you tonight?"

"What do you mean?"

Noah sighed. "Scaring the shit out of that kid who spilled his drink? That's not like you."

"I just thought Faith deserved an apology."

"Faith is my date, remember? If she couldn't handle it herself, then I could have."

"I'm sure you could." He kept thinking of Noah's arm on her chair.

"And you still seem pissed off. Right now. Why?"

Tanner paced across the gravel, balling his fists. "I saw that guy hit her in the head, and I reacted. You're right, I shouldn't have. But after what happened at her house a few days ago, when she got hurt, I guess I'm sensitive."

"That would make sense if we were in a dangerous situation. But we weren't. It was just some drunk losing his balance."

Fucking psychopath, the guy had said.

"I was looking out for her. Faith is my friend."

"Like the way you took her out after her bad first date? A little nighttime swim?"

"Pretty much."

Noah's expression tightened with the dawning realization. "You sure that's the truth? She's just a friend?"

Chapter Seventeen

In the bathroom mirror, Faith brushed her hair away from her face. Myra had gone into a stall.

She couldn't believe Tanner—*Tanner*, of all people—had nearly gotten into a fight with some random guy.

When Noah had picked her up, she'd resolved to be optimistic about tonight. Even if she wasn't interested in Noah romantically, she needed new faces in her life, new experiences. That was the whole reason she'd moved to West Oaks.

And she especially needed to get her mind off Jon. She hadn't heard anything else from her husband. But the police hadn't tracked down Kyle either, according to the detective she'd been communicating with.

Faith smoothed a flake of mascara from beneath her eye. Nope, she was taking tonight off from all that stress. Unfortunately, worry over Tanner had taken its place.

In the car on the way here, Noah had been a perfect gentleman. She'd wished for some kind of chemistry with him. But despite the pleasant smell of his aftershave and his usual dazzling smile, she hadn't felt a thing. She'd almost told him, right there in the car, that nothing would ever happen between them. But it would've embarrassed him, and the rest of the night would've been excruciating.

During dinner, she'd had to force herself not to stare at Tanner. As far as she'd been concerned, no other man had existed in that room but him. And then, seeing the casual way Myra would nudge Tanner's arm or joke with him... It had fired up her blood with jealousy in a way she'd never experienced before.

Having a glass of icy alcohol splashed into her lap had probably done her some good. At least it had cooled off the heat pooling in her lower body. Seriously, dampening her panties over another guy while her date sat right next to her? Her body's reactions weren't totally voluntary, but she'd still felt shitty.

She was going to tell him they couldn't go out again. The minute they got into Noah's car, she'd thank him for dinner but make her feelings clear.

A toilet flushed. Myra came out of the stall and washed her hands. "This has been a weird night."

"No kidding."

"For a moment there, I thought we had a bar fight on our hands." Myra grabbed a paper towel. "But those other guys took one look at Tanner and backed down. Smart move."

"He wouldn't have actually fought them. That's not how Tanner is."

Myra checked her makeup in the mirror. "I dunno, he was pretty pissed off. But I can't tell if he was really challenging the guy who knocked into you, or if he was challenging *Noah*."

"Why would he challenge Noah?"

Myra side-eyed her. "Maybe because of the hardcore possessive vibes flying across the table?"

"*What?*"

Had Myra noticed how she'd been staring at Tanner? Had *Noah* noticed it?

Her coworker huffed. "Faith, you in no way fit the 'dumb blond' stereotype. But sometimes, I swear…"

"If I'm so dumb, then you'd better spell it out for me," she snapped.

"Well, chill. Tanner is not the only one with a short fuse tonight. Look, you're into him, and he's way into you. It's not that complicated."

Faith sputtered. "No, he's not. He sees me as a friend." She glanced at her reflection in the mirror. Her face looked as red as Tanner's tomato soup. Stupid pale skin.

Myra was snickering. "Sure, a friend he'd like to fuck." She clamped a hand over her mouth. "Dang. That's five bucks I owe the swear jar."

Faith didn't bother to look in the mirror again, because she could feel her blush deepening to an even brighter shade of crimson. She didn't think Myra was right about Tanner's feelings, but the rest of Myra's assessment had been spot on.

You're into him.

"Are you mad?" Faith asked.

"Why would I be? Yeah, I had a crush on Tanner for like, five minutes. But I have a short attention span. Besides, he and I agreed to be platonic before you and Noah even arrived."

"You did?"

Myra leaned in conspiratorially. "He said he was hung up on someone else. Which must be *you*."

"Are you sure?"

"He was making it pretty obvious."

Faith's stomach was flipping around like a roller coaster on the boardwalk. But she still couldn't quite believe it.

"Now do you see why Tanner got all territorial when that guy bumped you?"

"Maybe. It still doesn't seem like him."

"Lust makes men do strange things." Myra shrugged one shoulder. "And women, too. Basically, we're all a bunch of animals."

Could Myra be right? Tanner had feelings for her?

She didn't want to hurt Noah by going after his friend. And she definitely didn't want to come between the two men.

Why on earth would they think she was worth it?

She and Myra went to the restaurant's front entrance. Tanner and Noah were visible through the window, talking with serious expressions.

When they stepped outside, Noah's voice carried toward them across the parking lot.

"You told me you were okay with me asking her out."

Faith stopped walking. Were they talking about her?

"I...tried to be."

"So you *weren't* okay with it." Noah's shoes scraped in the gravel. "Do you have feelings for her? Is that what this is about?"

Myra nudged her. Faith's guts had jumped up into her ribcage.

Tanner glanced over right then, and his eyes landed on hers. He bowed his head. Looked away. Didn't answer.

What was going on?

Myra strolled over. "Well, this is awkward."

Tanner looked in the other direction. "Myra, do you mind giving me a ride home?"

"Oh, we're doing the avoidance thing? Sure. My chariot awaits."

The two got into Myra's car and drove away. Faith watched him go, confusion making her head swim.

That left Noah and Faith standing there sheepishly.

"I guess you heard some of that?" Noah asked.

"Some. I'm not really sure what it was about."

"Neither am I." He scratched at his scalp. Noah looked different without his usual smile. Younger. "I should get you home."

They got into Noah's SUV. The car pulled smoothly out onto the road. Music played quietly from the speakers. Faith wished he would turn up the radio to drown out the things they weren't saying.

But she had to bring it up. "Noah? We should probably talk about, you know, what happened?"

"Yeah." Noah's fingers tapped against the steering wheel. He cleared his throat. "Tanner's been my friend a long time."

"I know."

"If I had realized he had a problem, I wouldn't have asked you out. No matter how much I wanted to."

"Right. I feel the same way."

But Tanner had suggested the opposite. He'd encouraged her to go out with Noah. Why would he have done that if he felt something for her?

Faith had never really dated, not even before Jon. She kept feeling like she must've done something wrong, missed some signal. Was this why dating was so difficult? Because nobody said what they really meant or felt?

She would've thought Tanner would be an exception.

"And then you came up with the whole double date thing," he said.

"*Me*? It was Myra."

"Myra, then. Anyways. It was supposed to be fun, and I ended up hurting my friend." Noah pressed his lips together. "What I'm trying to say is, this can't happen again. You and me. I hope you understand."

"Oh. Yeah." She finally connected the dots. "That's what I was about to say to you. Even before Tanner got upset. I *wanted* to like you. Because you're great. And I thought Tanner just saw me as a friend."

Noah chuckled, eyes fixed on the road. "It's cool. You don't have to make me feel better. I just wish I could've set you two up instead of getting in the middle of this."

She couldn't believe she was having this conversation with Noah, when at the start of the evening he'd been her date.

This had to be uncomfortable for him. "We don't have to talk about Tanner. This is kind of weird, honestly."

This time, Noah laughed out loud. "Weird for sure. Not how my dates usually turn out."

He seemed like someone who would be easy to fall for. The right woman was going to be extremely lucky to end up with Noah. And hopefully, they'd get together without so much drama.

With Tanner, Faith struggled to know where she stood. Yet, she also had that swoopy, dizzying, roller-coaster feeling whenever she thought about him, like the world was falling out from beneath her and nothing had ever felt so good.

As they drove, the Friday night crowds emerged on the popular parts of Ocean Lane. Faith had lived here for months, but she still marveled at how busy it was on nights like this. When everyone seemed to be going somewhere, dressed in trendy clothes and heels. Out to impress.

Her chest filled with longing. She wanted to be with Tanner right now, with his flip-flops and ratty shorts and graphic tee. She loved that he didn't care what anyone thought.

Was he hurting right now? Because of *her*?

She glanced at her purse, which held her phone. Should she text him? But what could she say? Even if Tanner felt something for her, that wasn't the same as wanting to *be* with her.

Noah rubbed his chin. "You know, Tanner's seemed a little off for a few months now, and I've wondered about it. But that's around the time you moved to West Oaks, right?"

"Maybe." Was he suggesting Tanner had been interested in her all this time? That couldn't be right.

"Tanner's as good as my brother. He's been one of my best friends for over a decade. I'd do anything for him. I just want him to be happy, and if that's with you, I'm all for it. Even if I might wish I got there first."

He gave her a charming, lopsided smile. She was glad to see his sunny expression back.

But Noah was talking like he had some idea of where this was headed. Tanner hadn't said anything to *her* about how he felt. He'd chosen to avoid her.

"I have no idea if he wants to be with me." From the way he'd acted so far, she guessed the opposite.

"You'd need to ask him. But how do *you* feel?"

"I care about him. A lot." The flutter in her chest told her everything she needed to know.

Suddenly, Noah tapped the brakes. "Fuck it. You know what? Let's go talk to him."

"Right now?" Her voice squeaked. "The both of us?"

"Better to get it all out in the open."

She admired the impulse. But Faith had never lived her life that way. Growing up, there were so many things that simply were not discussed. Even when she'd gotten pregnant, her father hadn't been able to say the word aloud until after she was married. Neither of her parents had *ever* discussed how her pregnancy had ended.

Faith considered herself an honest person. But that wasn't the same as just putting it all out there, the way Noah was suggesting.

She *wanted* to be that kind of person, though. Bold and unafraid. Ready to go after what she wanted. To speak up about what she was keeping inside.

"Alright. Let's go."

At the next intersection, Noah made a U-turn, then sped down the road.

Chapter Eighteen

Tanner stalked down the sidewalk. He figured he looked pissed off because people kept crossing the street to get away from him.

It was near midnight, and he scowled at every bar and dance club that he passed, thinking of all the happy people inside. It wasn't that he was jealous they had what he didn't. He was angry at himself for not being like them. For not being the person he'd been six months ago.

He couldn't believe he'd been such an ass tonight in front of Faith. And he'd been a jerk to Noah, who didn't remotely deserve it.

The guy had asked for his permission to go out with Faith, and Tanner had given it. The stupid double date hadn't been his idea, but he could've put a stop to it. Instead, he'd ruined everyone's night.

He'd acted like some twenty-year-old, testosterone-addled bully.

He'd already apologized to Myra as she drove him away from the restaurant. She had assured him it was no big deal, though he didn't see how that could be true. She didn't even know his excuse. Not that he intended to excuse his behavior by shifting the blame.

Tanner was well aware that mental illness was no weakness. If anyone had dared suggest that about one of his fellow veterans, he'd have vigorously listed all the arguments to the contrary. But somehow, when it came to his own problems, he couldn't speak up.

All he knew was, he'd needed to get out of Myra's car before they'd gone a mile. He'd asked her to pull over, and then he'd walked down to the beachside path to pound the pavement.

Questions had peppered him with every step.

What was he supposed to say to Noah and Faith?

What was he supposed to do if they actually liked each other? If he had to see his best friend with the girl he kept fantasizing about?

The walking had helped, as it usually did.

By the time he turned down his street, he was breathing easier. He didn't feel a deep scowl furrowing his face anymore. He just felt sad.

But his relative calm lasted only until he saw Noah and Faith sitting on the steps of his porch.

What were they doing here?

Did they want his permission? His blessing?

Fuck me.

He almost turned around right then to keep on walking.

But Noah jumped up and jogged toward him. "Tanner, Jesus. Where have you been?"

His eyes strayed over to Faith, who still remained sitting.

"Decided I felt like taking the long way home. What are you doing here?"

Noah dug his hands into his jeans pockets. "We need to talk, and I didn't think it could wait. Not with how we left things."

So Tanner's instinct had been right. Noah wanted to start

something up with Faith, and he needed to be honest about it or some other honorable shit like that. Maybe he intended to take Faith home right now.

The thought of her in Noah's arms, in Noah's *bed*, made Tanner's guts twist. He couldn't fucking stand it.

Only Noah would think talking about something like this was necessary.

"You could tell earlier I'm pissy tonight," he growled, "and I promise you, things haven't improved."

Noah came over and wrapped an arm around his shoulders, though he had to reach up to do it. He steered Tanner a few yards away, probably so they'd be out of Faith's earshot.

"You'll want to hear this."

"I guarantee, I don't. You don't have to worry. I'll get over it. Just… You don't have to rub it in my face."

Noah tipped his head back and burst out laughing. "Really? You like this girl, and you're giving her up that easily?"

Tanner squinted at his friend. "What, am I supposed to fight you?"

Don't tempt me, he thought. *Don't fucking tempt me.*

"No, you're supposed to shut your big yap and listen."

But he didn't want to do that. In fact, he was feeling more unreasonable every second. "I jerked off thinking about her. More than once. Sure you don't want to punch me?"

Noah's eyes closed. "Jesus Christ, dude. This would've been a lot simpler if you'd come out and told me how you felt before. Instead of pulling all this drama shit. And now that I know, I'll get out of your way. All right? That's what I've been trying to say."

He didn't understand. "Out of my way? What do you mean?"

"Why are you making this so difficult? Do you have feelings for Faith or not? *Real* feelings, not just…" Noah rolled his eyes. "Jerking off," he muttered.

He turned to look over his shoulder. She was still there on his porch. A few locks had fallen out of her braid around her face.

"I do. I want the chance to make her happy. So bad." He wanted to see her hair fanning over his pillow again, but it was a lot more than that. He wanted to make her smile, hear her laugh, and be able to kiss her right after. "But she doesn't feel that way about me. And even if she did, I thought she'd be better off with someone like you."

Noah scoffed. "That makes no sense. More importantly, she doesn't agree—on either of those counts."

Tanner's head swiveled back to his friend.

"The rest is for her to say, not me. But can you promise me one thing? Try not to screw this up?"

Noah spoke briefly to Faith, then got in his car and drove away. He'd left her behind.

Crickets were chirping, but otherwise, the street was quiet.

Tanner didn't know exactly what was going on here, and he still felt like a mess on the inside. But he was starting to hope. It felt like a glimmer of sunshine after a string of gloomy days.

He went up to his porch. "Hey."

"Hey."

"I'm surprised you wanted to see me. Wasn't at my best tonight. Really sorry about that."

"I wasn't either." She stood, brushing off her dress. His eyes traced over her.

"But you didn't almost start a brawl."

The corner of her mouth twitched. "Maybe I did. You weren't with me every minute."

"I wanted to be." He held her gaze. He really needed to know if what Noah said was true.

Then she said something he hadn't expected. "Should we take a walk?"

He checked her shoes. Sandals, but not the impractical heeled kind some women wore. "Where to?"

"Anywhere."

For the first time in hours, he felt himself almost smile. "Okay."

His house was only a few blocks away from the beach, so he turned back in the direction of the shore. She fell into step beside him. She had a small purse on a long strap, and she put it over her head so it crossed her body, which made him think of his hands following the same path along her shoulder, over her breasts, to her waist…

Did she want that?

God, this was torture. But he wouldn't be anywhere else for the world.

For a while, they didn't say anything. When they reached the shore, they took the paved beachside path.

He was thinking of their first "date" together. Even though it hadn't been a real date, that night had meant something to him, and its significance had only grown as the weeks passed. He'd had his reasons for not pursuing her before, even aside from thinking he was in the friend zone. Those realities still existed.

He needed to be honest with her. Noah had told him, *Don't screw this up*. He really didn't want to.

"There's something I need to tell you."

Faith stopped and turned to him.

"It would be easier if we kept walking."

"Oh. Okay." She hesitated, but they resumed their course.

"The other night, when you were at my house, and I freaked out when you came upstairs… I knew exactly why it happened, but I didn't want to tell you the truth." He took a breath. "I have PTSD. Post-traumatic stress disorder."

"Because you were in the military?"

"It's related to that, yeah."

"What's it like?"

The question surprised him. He thought about how to describe it. "Like there are so many signals coming into my brain I can't make sense of it. I feel overwhelmed, convinced something bad is going to happen. I'm always bracing myself for it. Certain days are worse than others. Certain nights."

"You have nightmares? Like the other night?"

He nodded. "I told you I don't sleep much, but this is the real reason why. Sometimes it gets intense." Like he was running from something, and if he stopped moving, it would lunge out of the shadows to consume him.

"Is it intense now?"

"Lately? Yeah."

"That sounds awful. I'm sorry."

Ocean Lane was practically deserted now. The occasional car drove past, and a few people remained on the beach. When Tanner was out late like this, he sometimes saw homeless people in sleeping bags or bundled with blankets. In a few more hours, nearly everyone would be alone, their expressions glazed. Sometimes, Tanner wondered if he looked the same to others he passed in those early hours of the morning.

"I don't want to make excuses for what happened tonight. I shouldn't have lost my temper."

"It wasn't so bad. You didn't hit the guy."

"But I wanted to."

When he was at work, he could focus. The world shifted back into clarity. But outside his job at Bennett Security, Tanner felt unmoored. Adrift in a chaotic world he could no longer navigate. Yet the world hadn't changed. Just him.

Faith tugged at the purse strap crossing her torso. "When I'm around you... Do I make it worse?"

He rested a hand on her upper arm, stopping her. "No. Not at all." He never wanted her to think that. "It's complicated. But it feels good to be around you."

"I like being around you, too. A lot."

They were far from the nearest streetlight. Her face was

half bright, half shadow. He reached up to run his thumb along her cheek. She turned into his touch.

"I suck as your wingman, though. Because I'd rather not see you with anybody else."

"I don't want anybody else. Just you."

Tanner was struggling to get enough air in his lungs, but for once, it wasn't anything like panic.

Faith reached for his hand. Their fingers wound together. "Should we keep walking?"

"That works for me." He didn't want to fuck up this moment. But at least she hadn't run in the other direction. She was still walking with him. Holding his hand.

"Have you told Noah about having PTSD?"

"He knows I went through something a few years ago. But not about how it's been recently. I got a concussion. It happened before I met you."

"Sylvie told me. It was when you were protecting her?"

"Yeah. It's like getting knocked in the head rewound the clock in my brain. When I woke up, I thought…" He didn't want to rehash those memories with her. That was a place he'd prefer not to go. "Anyway, Noah wouldn't judge me, but I'm worried he'll make me take time off. When I'm protecting people, that's the only time I feel calm. Or most of the time when I'm with you." He huffed a laugh. "As long as I'm not thinking about Noah making moves on you."

"I really thought you didn't see me that way. I thought I had a hopeless crush."

"So did I." He marveled to think Faith had been feeling the same.

But Sylvie had always said he was clueless about women liking him. Of course, there was more to it. The fear of dragging her down under the weight of his issues. But now he wondered if he'd had it wrong. If denying his feelings for her had only made the stress worse.

"I got my hair cut because of you."

"Me?"

He brushed his palm over the shortened strands at the side. "You said you wanted to see more of me. And once that idea was in my head, I couldn't get rid of it. You said I was hiding, and you were right."

She squeezed his hand. "I don't want you to hide. But you don't have to change anything for me, either."

He needed her closer. Tanner let go of her hand so he could wind his arm around her waist, drawing her against his side as they walked. Being able to touch her this way was the best thing he could imagine. Well, second best. No clothes between them would be slightly better.

"But I do like the haircut," she added.

"Myra told me I upped my hotness quotient."

Faith stopped to study him. Her eyes moved around his face, settling on his mouth. "She's not wrong. It wasn't easy to keep my hands off you that night at your house."

He hummed. "It wasn't easy lying next to you in my bed, trying to be good."

"I didn't want to be good, either. Still don't."

His cock jumped, responding to the heat in her gaze. He pulled her into a walk again.

"Where are we going?" she asked.

"Same place I took you on our first date. The bench with a spectacular view of the shoreline."

"Our practice date. Are we still practicing? Or is it opening night?" She giggled.

He swallowed a groan of longing. "There's that dirty mind of yours."

His fingers massaged her waist through her dress. The thought of her skin with no barriers—just Faith, blond hair spread beneath her, panting under his touch—sent jolts of arousal down his spine.

The path sloped upward. Unlike the last time they'd walked this way, when he'd been on good behavior, his dick was getting harder by the second. Her teasing sounded less like a joke and more like a naughty promise of things to come.

He wouldn't move too fast with her. But damn, now that he knew she felt the same way, it was not easy to focus on being patient.

But there was more he needed to say.

They settled onto the bench. This midnight view was more subdued than their last visit here. Lonely lights dotted the coastline. Tanner pulled her close and rested his cheek on her head.

"I've been crushing hard on you since the night we came here," he said. "I thought about asking you out for real. But I knew if you were around me enough, you'd eventually see what I was hiding. I was afraid I'd scare you away."

Faith sat back enough that she could lock eyes with him. "People think I'm innocent or naive. I'm not."

"I know." She'd told him enough about her past to make him realize that. "But haven't you been through enough?"

"You don't think I'm strong enough to handle it?"

"I know you are. But I only want happiness for you."

"This makes me happy—you and me, being honest with each other." She cupped his face in her hands. "Nothing about you could ever scare me away."

He wanted so badly to believe that.

Faith caressed the whiskers on his chin. He felt her breaths on his skin. Their mouths were just inches apart. She craned her neck, eyelids heavy.

Tanner touched his lips to hers. They both pulled back, eyes meeting.

She dove forward to kiss him again. Faith's lips were so soft. He wanted to suck on them, to taste all of her, but he forced himself to be calm.

Then she draped one of her long legs across his lap, and he couldn't stop himself. His tongue licked at the seam of her lips. Faith opened her mouth to deepen their connection. Her tongue slid against his. The slick motion, the heat—it combined to make his insides feel like they were combusting.

She made a little moan, and it was the sexiest thing he'd ever heard.

This thing between them, however she wanted to define it, was so new and surprising that he hardly believed it was happening. But she felt so right in his arms. He was going to hold onto this girl if he could help it.

Chapter Nineteen

Faith hadn't made out with someone like this since...ever.

Tanner had started out gentle, clearly testing the waters with her. But she was so ready for more. She laced her fingers behind his neck, kissing him back unabashedly. Her tongue stroked his, and it felt so damned good. Being held. Being *wanted*. Her body was on fire.

Distantly, she thought of what he'd confessed. Some things made more sense. His nightmare, the incident in his bedroom, his temper at the restaurant. The way he sometimes seemed different from his easygoing self. But she hadn't seen anything that frightened her.

Faith had been married to someone trapped by addiction and despair for over a decade. Someone who'd refused to open up to her, no matter how much she'd tried. In all those years, Jon hadn't shown her as much kindness as Tanner had in a matter of weeks.

The unfairness of the world infuriated her. She ached to think of *anyone* struggling with trauma, but Tanner especially. Was it arrogant or misguided to imagine she could give him some happiness? She wanted to believe it was possible. She'd just be returning the favor.

And wherever this was leading... They didn't need to define it yet. They cared about each other, wanted each other. For now, that was enough.

Her palm flattened against his chest, which only made her think of how big he was, how much skin and taut muscle he had for her to touch. She'd seen some of it the other night in his bedroom when he'd had his shirt off.

She wanted all of him under her hands, up against her. Inside her.

Their mouths had fused together, tongues licking into each other's mouths, but she couldn't slow down.

Tanner put a large hand on her calf and slid it up along the side of her leg, and her clit throbbed in response. She thought she might come from that contact alone, as if every inch of her skin was directly connected to her core.

And the thought of his fingers between her legs, his tongue, his... *Ughn.*

A car raced by on the road, its engine rumbling and loud music blaring from its speakers.

Faith jumped, shocked back into awareness of the rest of the world. Both of them were gasping for breath.

It was the middle of the night, but they were still sitting on a bench in a public place within full view of the street.

She didn't care who saw them. But she wanted to get a lot naughtier than this. He seemed to have the same thing in mind.

"Can we go back to your place?" she asked.

Lust darkened his expression. "I won't argue with that."

He stood, grabbing her hands to pull her up. Tanner tugged her along the path, practically making her run to keep up with him.

"My sandals are great for walking, slightly less practical for jogging."

He stopped, cupped his hands around her ass, and lifted her against his hip. She yelped, wrapping her legs around his waist and her arms on his neck. He kept one hand propped beneath her. "There. Will that work?"

"It'll work." She could hardly get the words out, she was so turned on.

She bounced slightly against him, and his hip bone rubbed right at her clit. Her arousal was climbing to a fevered pitch. Faith kissed his neck, sucking gently at his skin. The vein in his neck pulsed rapidly beneath her tongue.

"You don't know what you're doing to me," he murmured.

"I think I have *some* idea. Same thing you're doing to me."

"And what's that?"

"Making me want you."

He walked even faster.

They'd taken at least half an hour to get to the bench overlooking the coastline, but it didn't take nearly that long for Tanner to make it to his house.

They mounted the steps onto the porch. Tanner set her down to unlock the door. Faith stood behind him, wrapping her arms around his middle. She was taller than average, about 5'8", and on her tiptoes her head rested perfectly at the base of his neck. His round ass pressed into her stomach. She felt giddy. When was the last time she'd touched anyone this much? Wanted anyone this much?

The door opened. She swept past him and went inside. The living room was dark. Tanner switched the light on, shutting the door.

Faith spun around to face him. Tanner's eyes were hooded.

"You want me to take you upstairs? Undress you?" His voice had dipped.

She walked back over to him and laced their fingers together. Her heartbeat accelerated again. "Yes. That. So much."

"My room is messier than the last time you were here. I really wasn't planning on company."

"I don't mind messy."

He studied her like he was deciding if that could be true.

She pulled his hand, nodding toward the stairs. "Trust me, I'm messy, too." *So much more than you know.*

The wooden steps creaked on their way up. "Watch your head," he said as they neared a low rafter, and Faith had to laugh as she passed beneath it.

"I didn't even have to duck."

"Guess it's just me."

The last time she'd been here, it had been night, and she'd been focused on other things than the room. Now, she studied it more closely.

The ceilings were sloped, and his king-sized bed took up most of the space. Against one wall, a row of paperbacks were lined up on the floor. A laptop and various chargers lay on a nightstand.

The sheets and blanket were rumpled, the pillows half crushed. Clothes were strewn over the floor. A few forgotten water glasses. She couldn't have cared less. These were all pieces of him, and she didn't want perfect. She wanted *real*.

Tanner closed in on her, eyes molten. His tongue swiped across his lower lip. "We can take this slow. You just tell me."

"I can't. I need you too badly."

His hands went to the back of her head. He crashed his mouth onto hers. This kiss was searing. The scruff of his beard scraped her chin, and she wondered how it would feel against her thighs.

His tongue thrust deep inside her mouth, pulling a needy groan from her chest. She grabbed hold of his T-shirt to keep herself upright. His skin was hot underneath. The anticipation was almost painful. She couldn't remember ever being this swept up in a moment.

"Off," she said against his mouth, reaching for the bottom

of the shirt. He broke the kiss long enough to tug the thin fabric over his head.

Her breath caught as she stared at him—a golden expanse of smooth skin broken by intricate black tattoos, an impossibly broad chest, a wide V of muscle leading down to his waistband. He'd looked like this the other night, too, but now she was allowed to stare all she liked.

His erection was prominent beneath the fabric of his shorts. She heard a whimper, and realized she'd made the sound.

He was big. *Really* big.

Faith hadn't had sex in a long time. She liked to think she would remember what to do. It had to be easier than riding a bicycle. Just a different kind of ride.

But that monster in Tanner's pants would be a lot to handle for her first time back.

She imagined how it would be to take him in her mouth, and tingles broke out over her entire body. Her nipples poked at the cups of her bra.

Slowly, he backed her up until her legs met the bed. She fell onto the mattress, catching herself with her hands, then scooted until she'd reached the middle. Her legs were bent, her dress bunching up around her hips.

He crawled toward her, stopping between her knees to stroke his palms along her outer thighs. Faith lay back. He moved his hands to either side of her head, caging her in. Their bodies weren't touching as he hovered just above her.

She didn't know how to interpret the look he gave her. His expression was full of longing, as if she were an impossible distance away instead of inches.

Faith lifted up onto her elbows until their lips met. Then it was like a switch flipped inside him. He growled into her mouth and the rest of his body lowered, pressing her into the mattress. His hips thrust against her. She opened her legs wider, making room for him. The crotch of her panties was soaking wet against her skin. She felt the hard length of Tanner's cock in his shorts, lining up with her swollen clit through the layers of fabric.

His kiss was unrelenting. Her nails lightly scraped over the curves of his back—the angular lines around his shoulder blades, the bumps along his spine. His scent and taste and the solid weight of him were overwhelming.

It was already almost too much sensation to take in at once. How would it be once all their clothes were on the floor, and all of his skin was sliding against hers?

She wanted to find out.

Chapter Twenty

Faith was, by far, the sexiest woman he'd ever had in his bed. He felt the heat between her legs through their clothes. The scent of her arousal was heady in his nostrils, driving him wild.

Tanner was struggling to pace himself and keep his control. All he really wanted to do was tear away those panties, free his dick, and sink himself into her. The thought was so encompassing that it drowned out everything else. The noise in his brain, the knowledge that they were moving too fast.

He wasn't sure what she wanted out of this, and he really didn't like to think it was a one-time deal.

He'd told her about his PTSD. That wasn't something he'd talked about with many women. A girlfriend had known about it when he'd first been dealing with the symptoms. She hadn't been able to handle it, the way his moods could shift, the nightmares. She'd rolled her eyes at his mantras and his need to walk in order to clear his head.

He could already tell Faith wouldn't be so dismissive. She'd claimed she wouldn't get scared away. He was sure she believed it.

But she didn't know yet what it would be like. How tough it could get.

If she got close to him and couldn't stand it, or didn't think he was worth all the hassle, it could send him into an even darker spiral.

Yet the intensity of their chemistry together, right in this single moment—it wasn't something he could pull away from. He hadn't even realized he was so desperate for her touch, for this connection, until Faith had offered it. He couldn't deny his need for her anymore.

Even if he might end up getting hurt.

Tanner rutted himself against her. His heart was stuttering in his chest, but he only wanted more. More bare skin, more heat, more of her body. The problem? He had to stop kissing her if they were going to undress.

Suddenly, she cried out around his tongue, back arching. Her hips bucked upward, grinding against his cock through their layers of clothes. He felt her shuddering, heard the strain of pleasure in her moans.

When she stopped shivering, he braced a hand on the mattress to look down at her. Faith's eyes were wide.

"You came?" A smile tugged at his mouth.

She nodded.

Tanner hummed appreciatively. He didn't mind working hard to get someone off, but the responsiveness of her body sent jolts of desire to his balls. His cock was so thick it was aching, but somehow, her orgasm had gotten him even harder. Precum dampened his boxer briefs.

"It's, um…been awhile. Since I've done anything like this." She glanced away. "Or since anyone's touched me? Not counting myself, I mean." Her voice wavered. "I guess I was slightly starved for contact."

"I am, too." He'd been so turned on, he was a little surprised he hadn't come in his shorts. "A little dry spell is nothing to be ashamed of." It helped explain why they were both so frantic.

Her eyelids kept blinking. "Three years?"

"Wait. Three *years?*" But she'd been married. How could a woman this beautiful and sweet be denied pleasure for that long?

Faith's eyes squeezed closed. "I wish I hadn't said that out loud. It's pathetic."

"It's not pathetic." Tanner shifted to one side of her, so he wasn't holding her down. And so his dick wasn't poking her and making its demands.

He was aware of the significance of tonight for his own battered heart. How risky it was to let her close enough that she'd see the darker spaces in his head.

But now he was thinking of what this intimacy meant for *her*.

She'd obviously been through something terrible with her ex. There was probably a lot more to it she hadn't shared.

Faith had gotten married as a teenager, and the guy had turned out to be a drug dealer. Right now, Jon Townsend was *still* trying to keep his hooks in her. Just a few days ago, that lowlife Kyle Spaulding had terrorized her for no other reason than her connection to her ex.

Fuck, Tanner thought. *I can't do this.*

Faith sat up. "I spoiled the mood, didn't I?"

He ran his hand down her leg. "Not even close. But I think reality might."

"Reality?"

He traced his thumb across her cheek. "I like you, Faith. A lot. You make me want… So many things. I can't let myself mess this up."

That was the terrible thing about hope. It gave you something else to lose.

"I don't want to mess it up, either."

Tanner propped himself against the pillows beside her.

"Maybe we should slow this down, even though neither of us wants to."

"You'd better not be saying we should date other people. We both saw how that went."

He bit down as a surge of possessiveness went through him. "That's *not* what I want. I plan to keep my cool and seeing another guy's hands on you isn't going to help with that." He wrapped his arm around her, drawing her against him. "But I want us to figure out…what this means."

She'd started out this night with someone else. When he and Faith got completely naked together, when he was finally inside of her—close as they could get—Tanner wanted to be able to say she was *his*. And he wanted her to feel the same about him.

"You're probably right." She bit her lower lip, and he saw vulnerability in her expression. "I really like you, and I can't imagine regretting anything we do. But slower is probably smarter."

"I can tell you're worth the wait."

She dragged her fingers between his pecs and down his stomach. "So are you. Even though waiting sounds like torture at the moment."

"Hey, at least you got an orgasm."

"I could help you with that."

"Nope, my dick can be patient." Though his body was protesting the opposite.

He kissed a line from her ear down her neck. That led to their mouths meeting again, but it was less urgency and more anticipation. "Stay here tonight?"

"You trust me not to jump you?"

He fit his hand against her neck, loving the way her pulse throbbed under his palm. "I'll take my chances."

"I'd better text Sylvie where I am. Considering the fact that Noah picked me up at the start of tonight, she's going to give me such a hard time tomorrow."

"That'll be nothing compared to the shit she'll give me for moving in on you."

"But you and Noah are good, right?"

"Yeah. We're good." Better than that. Tanner owed him.

He gave Faith one of his shirts to sleep in. He found a new toothbrush for her to use, and while she got ready for bed, he cleaned up his room.

In his nightstand, he found the blue stuffed bear Faith had won on the boardwalk. He left it on the pillow he was already thinking of as "hers."

She came back upstairs. His shirt nearly reached her knees. "Is that the bear I gave you? You kept it?"

"Of course I did. A pretty girl won it for me."

They slid under the covers together. Tanner pulled her toward him. Her body fit perfectly against his. He couldn't believe he could touch her like this. Exploring her curves over the fabric of her sleep shirt, kissing her neck while she sighed with pleasure. It made him realize how lonely he'd been in this room, struggling alone with his demons.

Which you haven't even told her about yet, he thought. *Not really.*

But before tonight, he hadn't said "PTSD" out loud in years. That had to mean progress.

He'd changed into a pair of form-fitting sweats, hoping they'd rein him in. But after about ten seconds of touching and kissing, his excitement was undeniable.

Faith pressed her thigh against his hard-on. "I'm really trying to be good here, and you're making it difficult."

"Worth the wait," he reminded her. And himself.

"Then we have to put some space between us."

He grumbled, but she had a point. They shifted apart by a couple of inches, but he kept his hand on her stomach, needing to feel her there.

"Do you have plans this weekend?" He wasn't volunteering at the rec center tomorrow, so his schedule was free.

"Not yet."

"Want to spend it with me?"

"That could be fun." He could tell she was trying not to smile, and somehow, that just made her happiness all the more obvious.

He decided, right then. He'd do anything to keep her looking at him that way. Faith seemed to believe he was something special, and it had been so long since he'd felt that. He couldn't let her down.

It didn't take long for her breathing to grow smooth and regular.

She hadn't asked him to turn off the light. He reached for it. But his fingers froze on the switch. The thought of the darkness made his throat start to close.

He left it on.

Tanner rolled back to face her. He closed his eyes and tried to sleep, hoping he wouldn't dream of anything but Faith.

Chapter Twenty-One

Faith woke up to bright morning sunshine and a cold bed.

Tanner wasn't here. She could hear him walking around downstairs. She sat up, smoothing down her bedhead.

Giddiness filled her chest. She'd woken up in Tanner's bed before, but this was nothing like the first time she'd slept over. Her chin was the slightest bit chafed from his beard. She was wearing his shirt. And she still felt the heat of his hands.

Her bare legs rubbed together, but that minimal friction just teased her. If anything, she was even more turned on than she'd been last night.

The stairs creaked under his feet, and Tanner appeared. "Hey. Good morning."

Ugh. He wore the same low-slung sweatpants from the night before, no shirt. He braced one arm against the wall, making his muscles flex. Her breath quickened.

"Could you put some more clothes on?" she asked. "Because that's just cruel."

He looked down at himself, then smirked. Tanner crossed the room to grab a shirt from his closet.

She'd been frustrated at first that Tanner wanted to wait,

but it was for the best. They could start fresh and just enjoy being together. No more pointless jealousy or misunderstandings. And when they did finally take things to the next level—which she hoped was soon—they wouldn't be focused on anything else but each other.

Please let it be soon. Otherwise she'd be thinking of sex every minute they were together. It was going to get distracting.

She'd never felt this kind of physical need for a man before. She hadn't even thought it was possible to get this insanely, overwhelmingly horny. Like if she didn't have him, her body would stop functioning.

It was really annoying.

Faith tore her eyes away from him and stood up. "What time is it?"

"Seven."

"How long have you been up?"

He shrugged. "A while. I needed to make some calls. I had an idea for this weekend if you're game."

"Yeah?"

Tanner had his hands on his hips, gaze on the wood floor. Like he was nervous. He was *so* cute when he was uncertain. "You mentioned you like to go dancing, and there's this bar. I think you'd like it. But it's in my hometown. Couple hours away."

"Yeah? Sounds like an adventure."

"But I haven't been home for a while, and my mom's been asking me to visit… I'd need to see my family, too. I'd be a dick not to. And I do miss them."

She stepped in to put her hands on his chest. Tanner's arms latched around her waist. "You want to take me with you to see your family?"

"Yeah. My mom wants us to stay there, not a hotel. Is that too much, too soon?"

"I'd love to." It might've seemed soon with some other

hypothetical guy. But everything with Tanner felt natural. Right.

"Good," he murmured. That softness in his eyes, the heat radiating from his skin beneath the shirt—this was quickly becoming a moment. But if he started kissing her again right now, she might explode from all the need building inside her.

"Of course, my mom's already rounding up my siblings and planning enough food for a SEAL platoon. So, I hope you like pot roast. And noisy nephews. And dogs. My family's a lot."

"Mine is, too. I'm one of five, remember?"

Faith missed her rowdy siblings, that energy of a big family she remembered from childhood. She'd grown apart from them since she'd gotten married, probably because they'd seemed to love Jon so much. To them, he was still the football star, the popular golden boy. Her siblings never would've believed the truth if she'd tried to tell them. Her mom certainly hadn't.

"You sure it's okay?" Tanner touched her chin to lift it.

Her smile had slipped. She pushed her thoughts of her family away. "A trip to the California countryside sounds lovely." She wanted to see where Tanner had grown up. She wanted to see every part of him he was willing to share. And she'd feel less tempted to jump him with his family around. "I just need to pack. I don't have anything with me."

"Then let's swing by your place before we hit the road."

This felt like more than just an impulsive trip. She was trying not to read too much into it.

But whether he realized it or not, he was very close to making her fall for him. And, like everything else when it came to Tanner, it felt so good she didn't want to stop.

FAITH STUCK her key in the lock, but the townhouse door flew open of its own accord.

Sylvie stood there, one hand perched on her hip. "So you're both here. That's good. I don't have to track you down."

"I texted you. I told you where I was."

"Yeah, and what you were *doing*."

"Hey," Tanner said, "there was no 'doing.'"

Faith smothered a laugh.

Sylvie glared at him. "All I know is, she starts out on a date with Noah, and she ends up at your place, texting me that you two hooked up. Care to explain?"

"I'll do my best." He held out a bag of croissants and a tray of lattes, which he'd picked up on the way. "But doesn't this buy me a few brownie points?" He'd insisted on bringing it as a peace offering. Which had clearly been a wise move.

Sylvie grabbed the bag and looked inside. "A few points. First, you can go upstairs and say hi to Nic. Ethan and Luis are up there, too. I need to talk to my friend."

She took Faith's arm, and they went into her bedroom.

Once she'd closed the door, Sylvie's scowl broke, replaced by a mischievous grin. "What happened? I'm dying here."

"You're not actually mad at us, are you?"

She rolled her eyes. "Miffed, perhaps. Mildly irritated—that I had no hint of these developments until now. But mostly, I like giving Tanner a hard time. As long as you're feeling good. You are, right?" Sylvie flopped onto the bed.

"Yes."

"That's all you're giving me? My entire career is built on information, Faith. I hate being out of the loop. I have a *need* to *know*."

Faith sat down, crossing her legs. "We like each other, and we both figured that out last night. Noah's okay with it. And Tanner is..." She slowly exhaled, trying to calm the rapid beating of her heart. "Amazing."

"He is. Tanner's been a great friend to me, and he clearly has been to you. I just worry."

"We didn't have sex. I wanted to, but he thought we should wait. We're going to take it slow."

Sylvie nodded. "He just earned a few more points from me."

"He's taking me to meet his family this weekend."

"And this is moving *slowly*?"

Faith threw up her hands. "He asked me, I said yes. It feels right." They'd been friends first, so they already knew a lot about each other. Meeting his family and seeing his hometown seemed like a natural next step.

"I've never heard of him taking a girl home before. He must be serious about you."

"He misses his family, and he thought I'd enjoy coming along. There's a bar. We're going dancing."

Her friend gave her a wry look. "If you're going to a different town to meet his mother, it's a big deal."

Faith wondered if Sylvie knew Tanner had PTSD. He'd only mentioned that Noah was unaware. She figured she shouldn't say anything on the subject, since it was his business.

"I'm excited for you, really," Sylvie said. "But rebounds can lead to heartbreak."

"Tanner's not a rebound." She didn't think he was. "I'm kind of crazy about him."

Sylvie pulled her into a hug. "Just be careful. I don't want two of my favorite people to end up hurting each other."

"Neither do I."

∼

AN HOUR LATER, they were on the highway, speeding away from the coast in Tanner's Jeep.

"Did Sylvie give you a lecture, too?" she asked.

"A small one. If I break your heart, I'm on her shit list for life."

"She implied I'm on the rebound."

He glanced at her sidelong. "Are you?"

"*No.*" Emotionally, her marriage had ended years ago. And didn't you have to be in love with someone else first to have a rebound? Faith had *never* been in love. She didn't know how it felt.

Tanner reached across the gearshift, palm out, and she took it. Her hand fit into his.

"Neither of us wants to piss off Sylvie," he said. "Let's agree right now. Nobody gets their heart broken."

"That's a lot to promise."

"You planning to be rough on me?"

"I didn't mean…" She shook her head. "We can't help it if one of us feels something the other doesn't."

He studied the view through the windshield. "Sylvie asked me if I'm serious about you. I am. I want to be with you, exclusively, if you'll have me." Tanner glanced over again, like he was checking her reaction. "You don't have to say anything. I'm not pressuring. I just need you to know where I stand, and that I'm a patient guy. When I have to be."

She wanted to be with him, too. She wanted his heart, and hers was nearly gone already.

But those words stayed stuck in her chest.

Faith hadn't thought before about the risk of hurting *him*. When it came to love, she had no track record. She had no clue what she was doing.

If this didn't work out, she'd be losing one of her closest friends in West Oaks.

A minute had passed before she realized she hadn't answered him. But she still wasn't sure how to capture in words what she was feeling.

Tanner tuned the radio to a country station. A Luke Bryan

song came on, and Faith sang quietly under her breath. Tanner smiled with his eyes on the highway.

It felt so good to be out on the road under the open blue sky. She hadn't even realized how much tension she was holding until it fell away. Her head rested against the seat, and she looked up at the clouds through the window. But Tanner's hand around hers kept her grounded right here, in this moment.

They were risking a lot. But she couldn't imagine wanting to be anywhere else.

An hour into the drive, Tanner pulled off the freeway and into a gas station. "Tank's getting low. Need anything?"

"I'll stop by the restroom." While he punched buttons at the pump, Faith went inside.

After a quick pitstop, she walked back out, stretching in the sun. Tanner was standing by the Jeep, hands in his shorts pockets. He looked over and smiled.

Flutters spread through her insides. Part of her still thought she must be dreaming. She and Tanner were on a trip together. And they were…if not *truly* together, they were at least heading that way.

He wants me. She smiled at the simple pleasure of that knowledge.

Then her phone rang, and she came crashing back to the real world.

It was Jon.

Shit. After days of silence, he had to pick now?

She thought about not answering. But maybe he'd tell her he was on his way out of California. If she could be so lucky.

"Jon, I only have a minute."

"Hey. I'm sorry."

Apologizing already. That wasn't a good sign.

"Are you sick?" she asked. His nose sounded stuffy.

"Can you switch to video?"

Faith rounded the side of the gas station building, then

leaned back against the stucco wall. She pushed the button for video. Jon's face appeared.

She covered her mouth to hide a gasp.

He had two black eyes. A bandage covered his nose, and scabs dotted his eyebrows and cheeks.

"Oh my god. What *happened?*"

His voice wavered. "I tried to tell them I'd set up a different arrangement. But they wouldn't listen."

"Who? Was it Kyle?"

"It's better not to ask."

With an eerie chill, she remembered the way Kyle had pushed his way into the townhouse. "It was. Why is he in West Oaks, Jon? What is going on?"

"This has gotten really messed up. It wasn't supposed to go down like this, I swear to you." Snot ran down to his lip. "I have to ask for your help again. With another package."

"Jon, *no.*" She rested her forehead in her hand.

"I have no choice. They won't let me change the plan. It was Kyle's idea to use your place, and I should never have agreed. I know I wasn't thinking it through, but it's too late now."

He kept saying "they." Who else was involved in this? More people like Kyle? "How could you do this? These people know where I live now. Where my *friends* live."

"You just have to hold onto a few more deliveries, starting next week. That's it. That's all they want."

"I won't be a part of anything illegal."

"It's not." Lying through his teeth. Unbelievable. But at least he wasn't going on about "antiques" anymore. She didn't understand why that first box had been full of dishes and knickknacks, and really? She didn't want to know.

"Just do what I'm asking Faith, please. If you do, I swear I'll sign the divorce papers with any terms you want. I'll go back to Texas. I'm begging here."

She looked around, relieved to see Tanner hadn't followed

her. But soon, he probably would. He'd wonder where she'd gone.

"I know I've let you down so many times," Jon said. "It's my fault I lost you. But after this, I'll never ask you for anything again."

"You expect me to believe that?"

They'd had almost identical conversations countless times in the past. The repetition had worn grooves into her heart. She felt the stress piling on her like a physical burden. No matter how much she fought it, she always seemed to end up in the same place with Jon.

"I don't want those people near my house," she said. "Especially not Kyle. I told the police about him, and I sent them the video from the doorbell camera."

"It won't be Kyle. I already made sure. I swear on our daughter's grave."

She felt like he'd ripped out her lungs and shown them to her. Tears welled up. She wiped them quickly away.

"I'm done with this conversation. I need to go."

"Wait. The next package will be ready late next week. I'll call you to arrange the drop-off."

"Jon, I *said no*. You're not listening."

He kept talking. "But there's one more thing. They said if you call the police again…" Jon's throat worked as he swallowed. "They'll do a lot worse to us both. Okay? So don't."

Faith ended the call, feeling like she'd be sick.

She went back inside to the bathroom. The cold water splashed into her eyes, washing away the tears. She forced herself to take deep breaths, overcoming the urge to hyperventilate.

"You need anything, sweetie?" an older woman asked.

Faith smiled. "I'm fine, thanks."

When she came out, she ran into Tanner near the register. He was buying bottles of water. "Grab something if you want it."

"I'm all right. I'll meet you outside."

She waited by the car, shifting her feet on the asphalt as the sun beat down. Tanner returned, and they both got in.

He set the waters in the cup holders. "Is everything okay? You disappeared there."

"I just had a phone call. From…my mom." Inwardly, she cringed at the lie. But she didn't want to explain it to Tanner and ruin their day.

Jon had created this mess. She should just let him deal with the consequences.

But seeing him beaten up, hardly able to breathe, had pulled at something deep inside her—the part of her that felt guilty for leaving him. For not being able to help him during their marriage, even though she'd tried.

She hadn't been able to escape that guilt yet, and she never would unless Jon left her in peace.

But how could she make him stop when nothing she said made a difference?

Chapter Twenty-Two

The moment Tanner walked in the door, Isabella Reed ran toward him. "My baby's home!" She grabbed his cheeks, examining him. "You look so handsome. Finally listened to your mama after all these years and got a haircut?"

Then she caught sight of Faith, who'd just walked in the door behind him, her backpack slung over her shoulder.

His mother arched an eyebrow at him. "Or did someone else convince you?"

On the phone that morning, Tanner had mentioned he was bringing a friend. His mom had asked all sorts of questions, but he hadn't known how to answer them.

Faith wasn't his girlfriend yet. So, he'd just said she was someone special. Someone he cared about. But Faith was different from any other woman he'd been with. That much, he knew. He'd never felt like this. So elated to have her in his life that anything seemed possible.

Tanner set his duffel on the kitchen floor. The dogs were jumping at him, nearly as excited as his mother. Their tails whipped side to side. Isabella snapped her fingers at them, and the two Labradors calmed.

"You must be Faith. Aren't you a beauty? It's such a pleasure to meet you."

"Thank you for having me." Faith dug into her backpack and produced a metal tin. "This is for you. I hope you like chamomile."

"If anyone doesn't, they're wrong. You're such a sweetheart. You didn't have to bring a gift." Tanner's mother beamed.

"My mom would be scandalized if I didn't bring *something*. But it was short notice."

"Short notice is right. I had to run to the grocery first thing this morning. My son could've given us a little more warning, couldn't he?"

He wasn't going to mention that they'd only started… whatever this was last night.

"Any other faults I should be aware of? I swear I'm listening." Tanner knelt down to rub Scout behind the ears. She was the older of the two dogs, and her muzzle looked grayer than he'd remembered. He'd let more time go between visits than he'd meant to, something he was probably going to hear about endlessly on this trip. He spoke to his parents at least once a week by phone, but his mom usually saved up her pestering to do in person.

"Tanner, I've got Faith in your sister's room. I set it up with fresh linens but let me know if there's anything else either of you needs."

"Kaylee's room, huh?"

His mother gave him a knowing smile. "I thought Faith would enjoy the view from there. Prettiest side of the property."

And also the smallest bed. No way Tanner could fit in there with her.

"What about me?" he asked.

"You can share with Brayden."

His little brother. It was a good thing he and Faith were

taking things slow, because he clearly wasn't getting any action in this house. Not that he'd expected to. Isabella Reed ran a tight ship. Tanner's former bedroom had long ago been converted into her sewing room.

He took Faith upstairs. The walls were painted a cheery pale yellow, with white wooden trim. Yellow and white gingham curtains hung over the windows.

"It's so cute. You grew up here?"

"Yep. Farm chores every morning and afternoon, especially during planting and harvest. My parents have lived here since they got married. My sister Kaylee and her husband live in the other house you saw as we drove in. They built it a few years ago. They took over the day-to-day business of the farm so my parents could retire. Brayden works the farm, too, but he still lives here."

"You never thought of coming back and running it yourself? As the oldest?"

"I wanted to see the world. Then, I fell in love with the ocean."

They walked down the narrow hallway, which was lined with family photos dating all the way back to when he and his siblings were babies. Faith walked slowly, examining each one.

In the car, he'd put how he felt on the table, and it was a relief to have done it. Saved any more agonizing about when he should tell her. He didn't want his feelings to be any secret, not after he'd almost lost his chance with her. But she hadn't responded at all.

Was that a sign she was considering his words carefully? Or that he'd freaked her out?

He'd been worried back at the gas station that she was upset. She'd had that mysterious phone call, which she'd said was from her mom. It had seemed odd that she'd taken it around the side of the building.

His mind had naturally gone to her ex-husband. Would

she lie about talking to Jon? But Tanner also didn't want to spoil the trip by accusing her of something.

She pointed to a photo of Tanner when he was eight, flanked by his two younger siblings. Their mom had stuck all three in matching outfits, which should've been barred by the Geneva Convention.

"You were cute back then. You still have the same smile."

"Yeah, it's too bad about the rest of me. Don't know what happened there."

She jabbed a playful elbow at his side. "Fishing for compliments, are we?"

He leaned into her from behind, bringing his mouth to her ear. "I do like fishing. Anything biting?"

She gave him a scorching look over her shoulder. "We'll have to wait and see."

Tanner showed her Kaylee's old room. It still had a twin bed with a pink, ruffly canopy over the top. At least Kaylee had gotten rid of the unicorn sheets and comforter back in high school.

"I'll be way at the other end of the hall. We've officially been separated. No hanky-panky allowed."

"Will you get in trouble for being in here with me?"

"Only one way to find out." He closed the door to the hall.

Faith set her backpack on the bed. "I want your mom to like me."

He grinned at that. "She does. For one—you're you, and anyone would like you. Second, she credits you with cleaning up my appearance." Tanner dropped his duffel at his feet.

"You know, you haven't kissed me all day," Faith said.

"I was waiting for you to make the first move."

"Hasn't that been our problem this whole time?"

He took a step toward her, lowering his head to brush his lips against hers. Her mouth pressed back, still closed. Her hand fisted the back of his shirt like she had to hold on, and she made a small whimper.

His pulse rocketed upward. He didn't know how such a chaste kiss could set his blood on fire. But she did that to him.

She had everything he needed. All he had to do was win *her*. This trip was part of the effort. But his mind whirred, dreaming up more ways to make her happy. If he could make the highs high enough, then the lows—when they came— might not be as bad. Right?

"Does it feel good to be home?" she asked.

"It's good to be here with you." But he guessed she probably meant the unwelcome buzz in his brain. The shadow that followed him. Amazingly, he seemed to have left it behind in West Oaks. "I'm feeling like myself."

He hadn't slept great last night, but at least he'd skipped the nightmares. And since he'd woken up beside her, a positive mood had come easily to him today. Maybe opening up to her had helped.

Whatever it was, he wanted to get everything he could out of their time here together.

Tanner rested his hands on her hips. "We have dinner with my family, but after that, I want to take you out on a real date, just us."

"The bar you mentioned?"

"Yep. Going dancing, and we're doing it right. I'll even borrow my brother's cowboy hat and boots."

She tilted her head. "But will your jeans be tight enough?"

"Painted on. Wait till you see my ass in them." He kissed her again. "Any other requests?"

She ruffled his hair. "You have to dance every song with me. Even the cheesy ones."

"Planning on it. And afterward, we're going stargazing. I'm betting you miss the stars?"

She gasped. "*So* much. How'd you know?"

"Lucky guess." He'd seen her looking at the night sky when they'd been out together. But anywhere near L.A. was hopelessly light-polluted. Here, they were still close enough to civilization that it wasn't ideal, but he knew a place she would like. Nice and quiet and romantic.

Faith had said she missed home. The Central Valley wasn't Texas, but it was as close as he could get within easy distance. And he already knew all the good spots.

He intended to prove he was worth the effort. If this was his shot with Faith, he had to make every moment count.

∽

UNFORTUNATELY, he had to run the gauntlet of dinner with his siblings first.

That afternoon, Brayden came in, half covered in mud. He did a double-take when he saw Faith sitting at the kitchen table. Tanner was getting beers out of the fridge. "Hey, bro, this is Faith. Faith, Brayden."

"Hi. Are you Tanner's girlfriend?"

She opened her mouth, then closed it.

"I'm still working on that." Tanner grabbed an extra beer and handed it to his brother. "But thanks for pointing it out."

Brayden snorted. "Was this trip your idea, Faith?"

She shook her head. "Nope, it was his."

Brayden looked skeptical. "But clearly, it's more about you than us. Because I don't see what Tanner's doing here otherwise."

Tanner didn't appreciate what his brother was implying, especially because it was true. "I can't come visit my family?"

"Obviously, you can. But you don't. Not anymore."

Tanner gestured around them. "Then what is this?"

Brayden popped the tab on his beer. "Whatever," he grumbled. "Tell your girl what you like. Welcome back."

"You'd better clean up. Chow's almost on." The pot roast was finishing up in the oven, and their mother had gone upstairs to change.

Tanner's brother stomped up the stairs.

Brayden was six years younger. Before Tanner had left home for the Navy, they'd been close. But now, his brother resented the fact that Tanner hadn't returned to the farm. He got annoyed when Tanner visited and annoyed when he didn't.

But he'd been rude in front of Faith, which was totally uncalled for.

Tanner was going to apologize to her, but then his parents came down, and Kaylee and her brood arrived—three boys under five. The dogs ran around as the kids screamed. Faith went to help his mom get the food on the table.

The circus had officially started.

Brayden reappeared just before they ate, dark hair damp from his shower. The whole crew gathered around the dining table, elbow to elbow.

Tanner put his hand on Faith's leg. "Noisy enough for you?" he said into her ear.

"Throw in my niece and her tambourine, and it would be just about right."

Sometimes lately, a cacophony like this could set off Tanner's inner alarm bells, overloading his senses. But tonight he was handling it. Even his brother's bad mood had slid off him easily enough.

It helped that he had a mission. He was taking Faith out later tonight, and nothing could get him down.

After dinner, he and Kaylee took dish duty while the others settled into the living room.

His sister rinsed off a plate, then handed it to him to load in the dishwasher. "What's the story with Faith?"

"I like her."

"That's obvious. Where's she from? How long have you been dating?"

"Um, Texas. And…a day?"

"*What?*"

"We were friends first. Got to know each other."

Kaylee handed him another plate. "She must be special for you to bring her home."

"She's from a small rural town, and I thought she'd like it here."

"Ah. So, you're not here to see *us*. Why am I not surprised?"

"You sound like Brayden, complaining about me having my own life someplace else. I've just been busy. "

"That didn't used to stop you from driving up. And Mom and I have come down to West Oaks. Like when you were injured with the concussion?"

"Yeah. I really appreciated that." Those first couple weeks after the injury, he wouldn't have been able to take care of himself otherwise.

"What's been so different lately? When I heard you were bringing a girl home, I thought that might explain it. If you've been head-over-heels in love and haven't thought about anyone or anything else. But if she's so new, that doesn't explain months of absence."

He grabbed the dish towel to wipe his hands. Now that he'd told Faith, it was easier to imagine telling his sister the truth. But this wasn't the moment for that conversation. "I'll try to do better."

"I hope so. You know I love you. We all do, even Brayden." She pulled him into a hug.

After another hour, the kids were crashing out, and it was fully dark outside.

Tanner found his brother sitting on the back porch. Frogs were making a racket down by the creek, and moths fluttered around the porch light.

"Any chance I could borrow your truck?" Tanner asked.

Brayden barely looked up. "Why?"

"I'm taking Faith out tonight, and I need it. We're going to look at stars."

His brother propped his elbows onto his knees and glared. "You are not having sex on my truck bed."

"Jeez, I won't." Tanner grabbed a chair and sat. "I'm sorry I haven't come up in so long. I've been dealing with some stuff."

"Like what?"

"Like..." He cleared his throat. He didn't let himself think too much, just said it. "Since that concussion I got. I haven't been feeling so well."

Tanner thought his brother needed a little bit of truth. And unlike Kaylee, he wouldn't get too worked up over it.

"That sucks. Do you need anything?"

"Aside from your truck?"

Brayden snickered. "Okay, fine. Take it. Have fun."

"Thanks." Tanner squeezed his brother's shoulder.

"This thing since the concussion. Is it physical? Or..."

"More mental. I guess."

"Like the issues you had before? When you came back from overseas?"

"Probably." This was a little deeper than Tanner had intended to go.

"Mom and Kaylee have been afraid of something like that."

Tanner's guts swooped. He didn't like that his problems were so transparent. His family saw through him too easily. Which was likely the reason he'd stayed away.

"I don't want any of you to worry."

"That's what family does though. The more you shut us out, the worse the worry gets."

"I'll keep that in mind." Brayden didn't understand that their worry made Tanner *feel* even worse, too. He was the big brother. The eldest son. He'd already chosen a life that took him away from them. He couldn't turn around and expect them to hold him up.

"Everything will work out," Tanner said. "Love you, bro."

"Yeah. Me, too."

Chapter Twenty-Three

Faith jumped down from the cab of the truck, boots crunching in the gravel. Strains of banjo and steel guitar streamed from the building ahead of them.

Tanner slammed the driver's side door. He fit the white hat onto his head and offered her an arm.

She'd always thought Tanner had a bit of a surfer vibe. But he looked damn sexy in those jeans—skintight, hugging his ass. His black T-shirt was snug, showing off his biceps. She was finding it difficult to keep her hands off him.

"This way, ma'am," he said in a drawl.

"I didn't know you were hiding a cowboy under those tattoos."

"You bring out this side of me."

Faith had borrowed a pair of calfskin boots from Kaylee. Her white sundress was a recent purchase, bought the same time as the blue one she'd worn last night. Her hair draped in a long braid over one shoulder.

She took Tanner's arm, and they walked toward the roadhouse.

People were visible through the open door, shouting and

dancing. Faith saw Tanner's mouth tighten into a thin line as they neared.

"It looks crowded," she said. "We could always go somewhere else if you'd rather."

"No way. I'm good." He moved his arm to her waist, fingers shifting as he gripped her side.

They showed their IDs, then walked inside. A wall of heat and noise hit them, and Faith drank it in. This was so familiar, a scene she'd been missing. Nights spent out with her girlfriends, letting off steam and chasing freedom even for a few hours before she had to return home. Jon had never taken her out like this. He drank plenty but didn't like dancing.

Don't think of him, she told herself. She wanted to stay in this moment, right here, not in the past.

"Something to drink?" he asked.

"Bourbon and soda?"

They stopped at the bar, and he ordered one for each of them. Tanner hugged her closer against his side as they made their way toward the edge of the room, where there was free space at a bar-height table. He seemed to relax as he leaned against the wall, sipping his drink.

Faith stood with her back to his stomach, watching the crowd. The colors, the music. All of it sang through her veins. Being here with Tanner made all of it better.

She'd already been so comfortable with him as a friend, and that hadn't changed. But her excitement and anticipation had skyrocketed. She'd heard other people describe the heady rush of falling for a friend you already knew and trusted, but to actually experience it? Faith had never imagined being this lucky.

He fit his arms around her and kissed her neck. "You're the prettiest girl here. I want to make sure everybody knows you're with me."

Warm tingles spread through her, and it wasn't just the whisky.

From the minute she'd stepped into the Reed family home, she'd felt welcomed. She loved that his family was big and messy, just like hers. His younger brother's grumpiness had actually made her feel more at home. The Reeds weren't perfect. They fought and disagreed. But it was obvious how much they loved each other. Loved *Tanner*.

His nephews had climbed all over him, overjoyed to see him, and Tanner had hugged them and spun them around till they squealed.

His family had made it clear how much they'd been missing him. She guessed Tanner had been staying away because of his struggles lately. But she was glad to see him back here reconnecting with them. He'd chosen to share this side of himself, and she felt honored.

Faith relaxed against him as they both swayed gently to the beat of the music. His thumbs drew circles over her hipbones, and Tanner's nose tucked behind her ear, breathing her in, leaving a kiss behind.

She'd been torn all day about keeping her conversation with Jon to herself. But she wanted tonight to be only about the two of them.

The opening strains of *Ain't Goin' Down Till the Sun Comes Up* started, which had a fast-paced line dance she'd loved since her school days. She looked back at Tanner. "Should we dance?"

"You go first. Show me how it's done."

Faith worried he didn't like being here. But his soft smile and heated gaze encouraged her.

She joined the line, sinking into the muscle memory as she danced. The energy of the song and the fast movements made her euphoric. As she swayed her hips, she locked eyes with Tanner through the crowd. He tilted his head, watching her, and she could feel his attention from across the room like a physical touch.

Arousal sped to her nerve endings.

All she could think of was his mouth, his hands. Every part of him that she wanted on her.

When the dance was over, she crossed back toward him, chest heaving. But that look in his eyes wasn't helping her catch her breath.

He took off his hat and set it on the table. "I couldn't take my eyes off you."

"I didn't want you to."

Faith laced her fingers into Tanner's. He surprised her by pulling her back toward the dance floor.

He danced the next one beside her, hitting every step and looking damn good doing it. No question he'd done this before.

Faith noticed other women looking at him, and she hooked a finger in the back pocket of his jeans as the music shifted into a slower song. Tanner's arms formed a circle, cinching her right up against him, and his forehead dipped to rest against hers. They were both sweating and smiling.

"This is our first real date. How'm I doing so far?"

She pretended to think. "Not bad."

"You're a woman of tough standards. Notes for improvement?"

Faith tipped her head back. "More kissing."

Tanner slanted his mouth onto hers. His lips teased hers open. He tasted like whiskey and heat and adrenaline, like every sexy country song that ever turned her on. She loved the brush of his beard against her skin.

Then his fingers slid into her hair, changing the angle of her head as he fit his tongue into her mouth. His kiss was rough and intimate, so hot she felt a thrill at being in public, among these other women who'd cast him interested glances. He was claiming her in front of all these people. Some might've been staring at them, disapproving, but she hardly noticed or cared.

The universe seemed to shrink down to just the two of

them. Her breath was skipping in her chest, her whole body aching to have him even closer.

Tanner had wanted to take this slow. But then he went and kissed her like that. There was just no way she could resist this man. There wasn't a single thing about him that wasn't sexy. He made her feel safe and seen and beautiful.

A long time ago, she'd set her life on the wrong path by doing something risky and impulsive with the wrong person. But Tanner wasn't Jon. He practically wasn't even the same species.

As they kissed and swayed to the music, Faith realized she'd been falling for Tanner since that first night they'd spent walking on the beach weeks ago. Laughing on the boardwalk and keeping each other warm in the cold Pacific waves.

She was getting light-headed when he pulled back, licking his lips and gazing down at her.

"What are you thinking about?" he asked.

"How much I want to get you alone."

"But what about dancing?"

"We could still dance. Just without so many other people." She stood on her toes, whispering in his ear. "Right now, I only want to be with you."

"I can make that happen."

Tanner went back to the table for his hat. Then he took her hand, leading her through the crowd toward the exit.

Chapter Twenty-Four

Tanner drove off the highway onto a dirt road. The truck's high beams cut through the darkness, lighting up trees and open expanses of farmland. There wasn't another set of headlights for miles.

He parked and shut off the engine. It was a perfectly clear night, a riot of stars visible through the windshield.

When he turned to Faith, she was already smiling at him. His stomach did a backflip.

Watching her dance at the bar, he'd felt like he must be dreaming. He'd been to that same roadhouse plenty of times in his younger days, but never with anyone like her. There'd never been anyone like Faith in his life before.

He was still working on being completely open with her, but he could see himself getting there. Telling her about the nightmares. About what had really happened in Afghanistan. And it didn't scare him nearly as much as he'd thought.

With his focus on her while she'd danced, the overwhelming noise and chaos of the bar had faded away. The world had felt right. He didn't want that feeling to stop. He wanted to take care of her, and he suspected she was more than ready to care for him. He wanted to believe she could.

"What now?" she asked.

"We get outside. The stars are waiting."

Tanner grabbed the blankets and throw pillows he'd stored in the backseat. He'd raided his mom's linen closet before they left. Mom would probably be annoyed if she went looking for an extra layer tonight.

He removed the cover from Brayden's truck bed and spread out the blankets. Then he helped Faith climb up onto the tailgate. They both slipped off their boots and socks.

It was a perfect night, not too chilly, with a breeze rustling the leaves in the trees. Crickets chirped in the dark. All the truck's lights had switched off, and Tanner's eyes were adjusting. Faith was bathed in starlight and moonlight as she knelt on the blankets, and he'd never seen anything so beautiful.

Tanner crawled over to lie down. Faith snuggled against him, both of them facing the star-strewn sky.

Now that they were alone, the heat between them had lowered to a simmer. But he knew this feeling. This was the same anticipation he'd felt just before their first kiss. How was it possible that had been just twenty-four hours ago?

Last night, he'd put on the brakes. But if she wanted this as badly as he did, there was no way he'd turn her down again.

If she wanted this.

Their shoulders were pressed together. He rested his hands on his stomach. "I hope it hasn't been awkward, meeting my family."

"No, it's been the opposite. It's been great."

"Except for Brayden. I meant to apologize about that. He gets testy with me, and I wish he'd waited until we were alone instead of hashing it out in front of you."

"It's all right. He told me he was sorry. Though he did make it clear he was still mad at you."

"When was this?"

"When you were doing the dishes after dinner."

"What else did he say?"

"Just that he misses you. He wanted to know how your job's going. Stuff like that. I wasn't very helpful. But I did talk about how amazing you are, and he nodded like he already knew. He said you were the best big brother when he was a kid."

Tanner didn't understand why Brayden could say those things to Faith, a woman he'd just met, but not to his own older brother.

"Your family just wants to know what's going on with you," Faith said. "Are you going to tell them?"

"Eventually. I don't want them to be disappointed in me for going backward, when I'd made so much progress."

"They wouldn't be. You can't think that."

He wanted to move on from this subject. "What's your family like?"

"Like yours, in a lot of ways. They get mad at each other, bicker at the dinner table, hug and make up. But they tip-toe around me. I'm the one they whisper about. 'Poor Faith, with her sad marriage and no kids.' That's how it used to be, anyway. Now they probably talk out loud about 'poor Faith, with her sad divorce.' Whenever I talk to my mom, she tells me she prayed at church for me and Jon to reconcile."

Something twisted painfully in Tanner's chest. "They don't realize how unhappy you were?"

"It's not the kind of thing they'd think about. Not because they're heartless. But that's how we were raised. Wives are selfless. Literally. They exist for their husbands and families, and that's all they need."

Tanner rolled onto his side to face her. "What do *you* need?"

"Freedom. Laughter. Pleasure." She said these words staring up at the sky, like she was speaking to the stars. Then she turned to him. "You."

Tanner inched closer to her, letting his eyes run over her

face. Long eyelashes, which looked even more lush in the low light. Her pale, glowing skin.

He waited until he couldn't stand it another second. He needed his lips on hers.

Faith opened up to his kiss, taking the moment from zero to sixty in an instant. Her hand slid up the back of his T-shirt, her leg draping over his hip.

Tanner was regretting his wardrobe choices. Fuck, these jeans were tight.

Faith broke off the kiss, though her lips were still close enough to brush his. "You told me earlier you want to be with me, and that's what I want, too. But I can't wait. I need all of you."

"I'm yours. For as long as you want me. Tell me you're mine."

She'd said she needed freedom, and he could respect that. Just as long as they belonged to each other tonight, right now. Even though he already knew this single moment could never be enough.

"I'm yours," she whispered.

Tanner cupped the back of her neck and claimed her mouth.

He rolled them so he was on top of her, his weight supported by his forearms. He knew she'd feel his hard length straining the seams of his jeans. Faith's legs wrapped around him, holding him tight.

For a while, he just kissed her, appreciating this gorgeous girl underneath him. He didn't really know why she'd chosen him, but he was going to pay back her trust. He'd make this good for her because she deserved to have everything she'd been missing, pleasure being first on his list.

He knew just where to start. There was something he'd been craving.

Tanner pushed back onto his knees. Her dress was already up near her waist. Her panties were pale pink, lacy. So feminine and sexy. He hooked them with his fingers. Faith lifted her hips, and he slid the scrap of fabric over her thighs and off.

She propped onto her elbows to look at him, legs bent, knees knocked together. Her lips were parted, eyes darkened with lust.

Tanner kissed each of her knees, running his hands along her outer thighs. "Open up for me?"

She parted her legs. His eyes had adjusted to the starlight, and the sight of her bared before him made his chest seize. His breathing grew ragged as he imagined how she would taste.

His dick was caged in his pants, desperate to get free. But that wasn't happening until he gave Faith what she needed.

Tanner brushed his lips down her inner thigh, teasing her skin.

"That feels so incredible."

"I haven't even gotten started." He grabbed a throw pillow. "Put this under your hips?"

Now he could see her better, reach her better. Tanner dipped his head between her legs and dragged his tongue over her soft folds.

She cried out, fingers digging into his hair.

There you go, he thought. *Now we're getting somewhere.*

He tongued lower, moving deeper into her core, and meeting her opening. She was already slick with wetness. It coated his tastebuds. Sweetness and summer—that was how she tasted.

Tanner pushed his tongue inside of her. She made a desperate sound. He could feel how tight she was. He needed to get her nice and ready for the rest of him.

If she wanted that. Fuck, he hoped she did.

Faith's back arched. He glanced up at her. She was still braced against her elbows, but her eyes had closed, her mouth open and gasping. Tendrils of blond hair framed her face.

"You're killing me," he murmured.

Her eyes popped open. "What?"

"You're just so beautiful." He was riding a wave of euphoria and didn't ever want it to end.

He nudged her thighs wider as he fucked her with his tongue. Her panting grew faster, the pitch of her moans increasing. The moment he switched his attention to her clit, she cried out, shuddering and thrusting her hips against his face.

"Tanner. Oh. *Yes*."

He loved how responsive she was to his touch. He needed to hear her say his name like that, over and over.

His lips closed around her clit, sucking to coax every last shudder of pleasure from her body. When he was sure she was done, he sat back against his heels, wiping his beard with his T-shirt sleeve.

Tanner crawled up to kiss her. "Did you like that?"

She smiled and made an incoherent sound, which he figured was a good sign.

"Can I get you naked?"

Faith sat up and wiggled out of her dress, pulling it over her head. She wasn't wearing a bra. He sucked one of her dark pink nipples into his mouth. All he wanted in the world was to worship her body for a while, kissing and caressing, not leaving one square inch of skin unaccounted for.

But Faith was looking at him with a wicked smile. "Your turn. Get naked for me."

He fisted the back of his collar and tugged his shirt off. His jeans were less cooperative. But finally, he kicked them off. Damn, it felt good to have those out of the way. He lay back and reached for the waistband of his boxer briefs, but Faith got there first, yanking them down.

His dick caught on his underwear and sprang back up, hitting his stomach with a slap.

Her eyes flared. "I knew you'd be big, but…wow."

"Too big?"

"I'm up for a challenge." She knelt between his legs. One of her hands rested on his stomach. The other gripped the base of his shaft, stroking him hesitantly.

"You don't have to do anything you don't want to."

"I know. But I've been wanting you in my mouth all day."

His dick must've liked the sound of that. A bead of precum glistened at his tip. Her tongue played at the corner of her mouth. She started to bend forward.

"Wait." He reached for her braid, sliding off the hair tie. His fingers worked through the strands to free them. "That's better."

When she bent over him this time, her hair fell in a wavy curtain onto the bare skin of his hip. Faith's tongue darted across his slit, sending lightning bolts of desire up and down his spine. He clenched his jaw and moaned. His glutes tightened as he forced his hips to stay still.

Her lips closed around him. She couldn't take much more than the head, but he had no complaints. Faith's tongue slowly moved up and down his length while her hand did the same. The feeling of her hot, wet mouth was overloading his pleasure receptors.

This was every fantasy he'd had in the last month, coming to life—Faith naked and on her knees while her sweet mouth worked over his cock. No way was he going to last long. It was a little embarrassing, actually.

He slid his fingertips along her chin. "Baby, I'm close."

Faith took him deeper and suctioned her lips around him, shocking a guttural groan out of his chest.

Tanner couldn't hold himself back. His cock jerked and he spurted into her mouth, the orgasm crashing over him in waves.

Chapter Twenty-Five

Tanner's cum hit her tongue and the back of her throat. Faith tried to swallow it down, but there was so much. She felt it dribbling from the side of her mouth. The vein on the underside of his shaft kept pulsing.

She wanted everything this man had to give.

His dick was still hard, but the rest of him went limp. Giving him one last suck, she sat up, gathering her hair to one side. Her nipples tightened as a breeze caressed her skin.

Faith's gaze traced over the panting, naked man splayed before her. His chest was smooth to show off his intricate tattoos, but he'd left his happy trail untouched. She dragged her fingers down the line of hair, past his belly button down to where it met his crotch. His cock twitched.

She crawled up his body, pressed herself flat against him, and looked into his eyes. They were shining with reflected starlight. His square jaw, his prominent nose—all the lines of him were softened by the dimness.

Tanner's palms rested on her lower back. "You've got something here." He lifted one hand to touch her chin with his fingertip.

"Do I?" She couldn't hide her naughty grin.

He licked the trail of cum off her chin and then kissed her. The move was so shameless, so intimate. Faith moaned into his mouth. She'd been the good girl for too long, and Tanner brought out the bad side she'd been dying to set free.

His arms cinched around her. She rested her head where his neck met his shoulder. They lay there for a while, listening to the trees. Something howled in the distance. The night air was chilly on her back, but the man beneath her was like a furnace, keeping her warm.

Tanner's hand squeezed her bare ass cheek. "That was the best blow job of my life."

She scoffed. "I could barely fit you in my mouth."

"And that was hot. All I know is, I saw stars when I came, and not just the ones in the sky."

She didn't think Tanner would patronize her, but she still felt self-conscious. "You must've been with a lot of people, and I've just been with…you know." With her and Jon, there'd never been anything like a honeymoon phase. Satisfying sex had seemed like the realm of books and movies, not reality. Not until Tanner.

"Why should that matter?"

"It *shouldn't*." But she was thinking of those women eying him at the bar. How easily he could've taken one of them home. He'd probably had endless opportunities in the past. Partners who would've known exactly what they were doing.

"You made me come so hard, it wiped anyone else from my memory." Tanner brushed her hair back.

"Right. So plausible."

"*Like a virgin…*" he crooned in a falsetto.

She giggled, lifting up to look at him. "Stop. That's awful. And it feels like you're making fun of me."

A wrinkle appeared between his eyes as he frowned. "I'll admit I'm a terrible singer. But I'd never make fun of my girl."

My girl.

Her insides were getting melty.

Tanner kissed her forehead. "My dirty, dirty girl."

His calloused hands roved over her skin. His hips moved, gently thrusting against her. She felt him getting hard again against her thigh. Desire threaded through her bloodstream, setting off an ache between her legs.

"What do you say?" he asked between kisses. "You want to take my virginity? I know you're into younger, innocent guys. Who may still be in high school…"

Faith growled, pushing back on his chest. "You are the *worst*."

"Maybe, but I think you like it when I tease you." He grabbed her and flipped them over. Tanner's body covered hers, all that skin hot against her.

She wasn't in the mood to joke anymore. "I like everything you do to me."

His hips rolled, grinding his dick into her hip. He was thick and rock hard again. "I have a condom in my wallet. Should I get it?"

She nodded.

His jeans were lying a few feet away. He grabbed a cuff to pull them over and fished into his pocket.

Tanner knelt over her and rolled the latex onto his impressive hard-on. Faith watched, awestruck at how sexy he was. She'd never felt this kind of brazen lust for a man before. But it was more than just his body. She was falling for him so fast, everything else was a blur.

She was nervous, though. "Um, it's been a while."

"I know." Tanner stretched out over her and kissed her. "I want this to be good for you. Tell me what you need."

"Just you." Faith couldn't imagine how sex with Tanner could be anything but good. But she wanted him to enjoy it, too. What if she was terrible?

"I'll go slow."

He teased her breasts with his mouth. His fingers traced down her body until they were between her legs. He pressed the flat of his hand against her sex, then slowly started to massage her.

Faith made a grunt of frustration. "Too slow."

Tanner's mouth moved to her neck. "Gotta be patient."

His fingers stroked her, parting her folds until finally, *finally*, his fingertip brushed her clit. "There," she panted. She could feel how slippery she was. Wet and eager.

"I know." It was infuriating how calm he was being about this. Tanner's fingertip massaged circles over her clit. It felt impossibly, agonizingly good. Even better, somehow, than his tongue. Probably because of what they were building up to. She dug her fingers into his hair, pushing her feet against the blankets.

Faith gasped when he pushed a digit inside her. "*Yes.*"

He added a second finger, and she felt the stretch. But it wasn't enough. His fingers had only awakened a deeper sense of need. The idea of waiting another moment for his cock was making her crazy.

"I'm ready. I want you. So bad."

"Then you'll have me. I've got you, baby."

She loved when he called her that.

The pressure of his fingers disappeared. Tanner readjusted his weight, his forearms braced to either side of her. His tip met her entrance. He just barely pushed inside. Pain hit her and immediately she tensed, gritting her teeth.

Tanner went still.

"I'm okay." Her voice was strained. "Keep going."

He pulled her into a deep kiss, his tongue stroking hers. Her breathing evened out. His cock edged forward, stretching her further. The burn increased. Her fingers dug into his biceps.

Three years was a long time to go without any kind of sex, and Faith worried for a moment this wouldn't work. What if her body had decided to close itself off? Maybe self-denial had become too ingrained for her to fully open up. Was that possible?

But Tanner was gentle, taking his time. He started to pump lightly into her, even though he couldn't have much more than the head inside. His kisses increased in intensity. He kept making sexy humming sounds and whispering things almost too low to hear. "Fuck, that's good, Faith. I almost can't take it."

With each thrust, he slid further into her channel.

She sucked in a breath as his cock suddenly filled a new part of her, and his hips rested flush against her body.

Tanner paused, his eyes fixed on her. "How're you doing?"

"Is that all of you?"

He smirked. "That's not enough?"

Faith breathed a small laugh. The burn had stopped, and now the stretch felt indulgent. Like a luxury she'd forgotten she could enjoy.

She rocked against him. "It feels good," she said. "Really good."

Slowly, Tanner pulled out of her, then slid forward again to fill her. Faith tipped her head back.

"Yes. Oh god, yes. Do that again."

The smooth slide of his thick cock was like nothing she'd ever experienced. He'd joked about the "like a virgin" thing, but that was just how she felt. Like whatever she'd done before, it hadn't been in the same category as this—Tanner on top of her, filling her, taking such care.

This man was going to ruin her for anybody else.

Chapter Twenty-Six

Tanner lifted himself on one hand, looking down at her. His eyes devoured her. Blond hair in a messy halo, luscious curves, legs wide open. All that sweetness just for him.

He bent his knees and gripped her thigh with his free hand, pushing even deeper. Her body was all tightness and heat. The pleasure made his head swim.

He moved in and out of her, still gentle, until she bucked upward to meet each thrust.

"Harder," she said. "Make me feel you."

Tanner's eyes fluttered closed. She didn't know how hot it made him when she talked that way. How he was barely holding onto his control.

He'd been trying to pace himself to make sure she was right there with him. It had been a long time for her, and he was afraid of rushing or pushing her too far. But Faith made him feel savage.

A feral part of him—totally uncivilized—wanted to mark her irrevocably as his own.

"I don't want to hurt you."

"You won't. I want everything you've got. Don't hold back."

His legs were trembling with keeping himself motionless. Tanner pulled back his hips, then pistoned them forward.

Faith cried out. "Not enough. More."

The lust in her expression unlocked that primal need in his chest. Tanner yanked her even closer and drove his cock into her.

He started giving in to the heat and the rhythm. Now that he'd stretched her, their bodies fit like they were meant for each other. She was still tight, her pussy so perfectly snug around his cock. Faith held onto his shoulders, her breasts jiggling in time with his thrusts. He glanced down to see his shaft pushing into her, the pleasure almost more than he could bear.

She was stripping away all his barriers. He felt raw, like a broken thing with sharp edges.

But he wanted to trust what she'd said. That he shouldn't hold back. That she could take it.

Everything he had.

His eyes met hers, asking the same silent question, and she nodded.

Tanner slammed their bodies together. She lifted her hips eagerly to meet him. He fucked her with abandon, letting go of every other thought in his head. His grunts were rough. This wasn't graceful or polite. Fuck, it wasn't even romantic. But right now, romance wasn't what either of them needed.

This was a connection Tanner had never experienced. It went beyond words or anything he could begin to explain. They were both exposed and vulnerable. Holding nothing back. But he watched Faith, locked into her gaze, knowing she was sharing this moment with him. Nothing mattered but her moans of pleasure, his own ferocious need, the wide-open sky above them. He felt uninhibited. Free.

Faith's body squeezed around him as she started to shake.

She threw her head back, breasts bared as she arched her spine. Tanner's glutes flexed. He drilled hard into her, chasing his own climax. Then he was over the edge. The release took him over, wiping his mind clean, stealing his breath. More than just pleasure. This was like free-falling into a sky dive. His balls emptied until he had nothing left.

When they'd both finished, he stared down at her, forcing himself not to look away. Faith reached up to touch his cheek.

Her smile was dreamy. "That was perfect."

"If there's any perfect around here, it's all you."

He lay down next to her, and they held one another. He couldn't remember the last time he'd felt this mellow, or when his brain was this quiet. Probably not even before the concussion, when he'd thought he felt like normal. But "normal" had still been a heightened state. He'd sensed something was slightly off, and the something had been *him*.

With Faith in his world, Tanner felt like he fit.

He was drifting in and out of sleep. The moon had changed places in the sky. He had no clue what time it was, nor did he care. It was somewhere between light and dark, but the shadows tonight held nothing that he feared.

"You still with me?" he whispered.

Somehow, she'd known he wasn't just asking if she was awake. "I'm right here. I'm not going anywhere."

∽

"TANNER. *TANNER.* WAKE UP."

"Mmmm?" He squinted as sunlight flooded his vision. Tanner rubbed his eyes, sitting upright.

"It's morning, and we're still naked. We have to get back."

"Oh, shit. What time is it?"

Faith checked her phone. "Almost seven."

"That's fine. You scared me for a minute. Thought we'd be late for church."

He couldn't believe he'd slept so long and so peacefully. Hadn't stirred except a couple of times, when he'd checked that Faith was still curled up beside him. She had a tiny snore, ridiculously adorable.

She yanked her dress on over her head. "*Church?*"

Tanner reached for his underwear and jeans. "My mom will be pissed if I'm in town and don't show."

Faith groaned, trying to work the tangles out of her hair, though Tanner liked it messy. "We've been out sinning all night, and now we have to face your family at church? Do you think your mom's awake yet?"

He laughed. "Oh, she's awake by now. They all are. They're farmers. Nobody's going to miss our walk of shame."

"What's your mom going to think of me?"

He pulled Faith into his lap. The fly of his jeans was undone, and he hadn't found his shirt. But he was starting to think about getting undressed again. "Probably that you're my girlfriend. I was vague on that before. Unless you'd rather I say something different?"

Faith circled her arms around his neck and shrugged. "Girlfriend seems...slightly less scandalous."

He pressed his lips to hers. "Certainly wouldn't want to scandalize the locals." Their kisses started to get heated, and Faith pulled away.

"We have to head back before it gets any later. I cannot go to church looking like this."

Tanner dressed, wrapped up the blankets and pillows, and stuffed them into the backseat. He'd drop them off at a dry cleaner later.

He and Faith got into the truck, and he started back toward the farm.

"You can wear whatever you want to this church. It's really informal. You can go looking like you do now."

"I'm not attending Sunday services with sex hair," she muttered. "What denomination is it?"

"Unitarian Universalist. You know it?"

"No."

"It's a little bit of everything. They use prayers from Buddhism and the Bible and Torah, quotes from humanist philosophers. They sing Beatles and folk music. Members can believe whatever they want. It's inclusive."

"You say 'they' like it's not your church."

"It's not, really. My family started going while I was in the Navy. My mom wanted comfort, I guess. Somewhere to go to pray I'd come home. I get it. But it feels more like her thing, not mine."

He had nothing whatsoever against religion or spirituality. Plenty of his teammates were believers. But it hadn't been a part of Tanner's life when he was growing up, and he hadn't felt compelled to join as an adult.

"I should've asked before if you were okay with it," he said. "We don't have to go." He'd gathered that Faith had mixed feelings about her church back home.

"I want to. It sounds different. And you know I like to try new things."

"I *do* know that." His tone dripped with innuendo. He reached over to squeeze her thigh.

"Stop. I need to calm down before I see your parents or I'll be thinking of what we did last night, and my face will turn bright red."

"*I'll* be thinking about what we did. All the way through church."

She smiled, shaking her head.

They pulled up in front of the farmhouse and got out. Tanner went in through the back door, and Faith trailed in behind him. Conversation stopped. His mom, dad, and brother looked up at them from the kitchen table.

Isabella popped up from her seat. "Morning. Would you like some coffee? You missed breakfast, but we saved some eggs. Faith, how about you?"

"I'm all right, thanks. Just coffee."

Isabella poured a couple of mugs. Faith took hers and dashed upstairs.

Tanner's father was pretending to study the Sunday paper, while his brother sat back in his seat, staring with one eyebrow raised.

"So where've you been?" Brayden asked. "We were worried."

"Who's this 'we?'" Isabella asked. She stuck a mug of coffee into Tanner's hands. "Your *mother* was worried."

"I took Faith dancing. I was showing her a good time."

His brother grunted. "I'll *bet* you did."

"None of that, boys, thank you." Isabella hit Brayden's chest with an oven mitt. "It's good to see you alive and well, Tanner. The caravan leaves for church in forty-five minutes, so everyone be ready, please."

Tanner started toward the stairs, but his mom pulled him into the office. "Can we have a word?"

"Am I in trouble for staying out all night?" Tanner took a gulp of coffee. "I'm not seventeen."

She closed the door. "No, you're a grown-ass man, and you can do what you like. But a text might've been nice, instead of leaving us wondering what happened."

A fair point. "Sorry."

"I don't intend to pry, but I would like to know what's going on with my son. Are you and Faith together?"

"Yes."

"Are you in love?"

He choked on a mouthful of coffee. "I'm...not sure." But maybe he was. At least, he thought Faith was the kind of woman he could fall in love with.

"But she makes you happy?"

He felt warm as he recalled holding her as they'd danced. How easily she made him laugh. "Very happy."

"That's all I want for you." She pulled him down into a

hug, then let him go with a pat on his shoulder. "I just hope you'll bring Faith around again soon. And if you do... I'll consider getting a double bed for Kaylee's old room." This last sentence came out in a rush. She cut her hands through the air. "So you can both stay there, instead of running around town and coming home embarrassed. That's all I'll say about it."

"Thanks, Mom."

"Now, go get yourself presentable. You smell like something unmentionable."

∼

TANNER WAITED OUTSIDE THE BATHROOM. Faith came into the hall, combing her damp hair. She wore a simple skirt and blouse, no makeup, and if anything she looked even more beautiful than last night.

She glanced up and down the hall. "What did they say?" she whispered.

"It wasn't a big deal. I told my mom how happy you make me, and now she loves you."

"It's still embarrassing. They have to know we..."

"Oh, they know." He circled an arm around her waist, needing some kind of contact. Now that his mom had brought up the "L" word, he couldn't get it out of his head.

Maybe it was too soon. But he'd been pining for Faith for weeks. The more he got to know her, the deeper he got. And after the explosive chemistry they'd shared last night? He'd never felt this way about anyone. He hadn't even known he *could*.

He rubbed a drop of water from her collarbone. "This weekend has meant a lot to me. I want you to know how crazy I am about you."

She gave him a quick kiss. "I'm pretty crazy about you, too. I'm glad I make you happy. I'm just returning the favor."

He gave her a squeeze, and then she went back to Kaylee's room to finish getting ready. He jumped into the shower.

Tanner was happier than he'd been in as long as he could remember. But discomfort still nagged at him underneath, despite the bright sunlight today. That inner sense that something bad was waiting just out of sight, ready to tear him back down.

He and Faith were happy right now. But what would happen once things got harder? She'd said nothing he did could scare her away. But that would only be true until it wasn't.

The more he cared about her—the closer he got to the big "L"—the more it would crush him if he lost her.

So, he wouldn't let it happen. He wouldn't let his mind go back to those dark places anymore. He'd managed at the bar last night, so he'd keep doing it. Staying focused on her, knowing she wanted him back. That was exactly what he'd needed.

Tanner showered and got out, toweling off. He stopped to stare into his reflection in the bathroom mirror.

"You're going to do it for Faith. You won't let her down."

There was no other option.

Chapter Twenty-Seven

Faith and Tanner rode along in Kaylee's Suburban. The boys bounced around in the third row while Tanner told them knock-knock jokes. She loved watching him with his family.

She still had trouble believing Tanner's mother had taken their walk of shame so well. If it had been her family, they'd have greeted Tanner at the door with a shotgun and a preacher.

Granted, he was a son instead of a daughter. But Faith bet her parents would react that way if one of her brothers did the same. Premarital sex was never acceptable in their eyes. They'd had a point, she had to admit, since she'd ended up pregnant at nineteen.

"Why are you holding hands with her?" the oldest nephew asked.

Tanner winked at Faith. "Because she's my girlfriend."

"Do you kiss her?"

"I'm thinking about it."

Kaylee turned around in the front passenger seat. "I hear you might've kissed her last night."

Faith felt her cheeks flushing. All morning, Tanner had kept sneaking kisses, touching her like he couldn't bear to have her too far away. Public affection around family wasn't the norm for her, but she liked it. Not having to hide. Not being ashamed. Shame about sex was clearly not a trait of the Reed clan.

"Not you, too," Tanner said. "You're embarrassing her."

Kaylee snickered. "Sorry, Faith. You're one of us now, and that means taking s-h-i-t from us."

"I'm starting to get used to it."

The elated feeling in her chest was almost painful. Kaylee's words meant more than the other woman could know. Faith missed her own family, imperfect as their relationship was, but to have a group of people like the Reeds accept her—she was beyond grateful.

Tanner had given her so much this weekend. She never could've expected someone like him to come into her life.

This might not be love yet. She only knew the whirlwind inside her mind and body the last couple of nights was entirely new. Nausea and euphoria and utter terror, which all somehow combined into the best sensation she could imagine. It was a pure adrenaline rush. Faith had never taken recreational drugs—despised them, in fact—but she wondered if this was how a high felt to Jon, except life-affirming instead of detrimental. She never wanted to come down.

If things didn't work out with Tanner, how could any other man ever compare?

Maybe this was just the result of mind-blowing sex. But it felt like something real. Something precious she was afraid to lose.

If anyone could spoil this for her, it would be Jon. His stupid schemes and his packages and phone calls.

She hated that he kept haunting her mind, even now.

They parked and piled out of the Suburban. People streamed up the stone steps of the church and through a huge set of wooden doors. Parishioners greeted them on the way in, stopping to hug Tanner's mom and chat with Kaylee and her husband.

Slowly, everyone worked their way toward the seats. Strains of Leonard Cohen's *Hallelujah* drifted from a piano.

Tanner waited to be at the very end of the row, and she wondered if he didn't like being surrounded by so many people. Faith squeezed his hand.

Tanner's sister handed her a songbook. A parishioner walked up to the front. "Our theme for this month is Love." He launched into a reading from the Dalai Lama. "The more you are motivated by love, the more fearless and free your action will be." After he'd finished the reading, the man lit a chalice on a pedestal.

Fearlessness, she thought. *That's what I need more of.*

Everyone stood as the pianist started to play. Tanner clasped his arm loosely around Faith's hips and shared her songbook, pausing to kiss her cheek every so often.

She couldn't help thinking of Sunday mornings spent in Texas during her marriage. Standing next to Jon, pretending all was well. Singing had always been her favorite part of the service. Those were the times she could close her eyes and escape for a few minutes, longing for something better.

After those services, her mom would usually whisper something like, *I prayed for you and Jon to get through this rough patch.* Or, *I prayed you'd get pregnant again. Isn't it time?*

Her mom had no idea how much those statements carved her empty inside.

Faith had sent up her own prayers on Sundays while she sang, though she'd never repeated those to her mother. Or to anyone.

She'd prayed to be made whole again, for her broken pieces to be healed, for some way out of the purgatory she'd been stuck in.

For someone who'd love *all* of her back. She'd been

waiting a long time to love someone, and be loved, with her entire heart.

She looked over at Tanner. It was hard not to imagine *he* was the person she'd been waiting for. But it had taken her leaving home, giving up everything she'd known, to find him.

A drop of water fell onto her hand. She was confused until she touched her face.

She was crying.

Tanner looked over at her. "Hey," he whispered. "What's wrong?"

"I'm sorry. I'm…" The tears kept falling. She rushed out of the room.

A sign for the restrooms pointed down a hallway. Before she could reach the bathroom door, she felt a hand on her arm. "Faith? What's going on?" Tanner had followed her.

What little composure she had dissolved. She put a hand over her mouth and sobbed.

Tanner's thumb wiped tears from her cheek. "Tell me."

"I don't know."

But she did know. She'd almost told him last night. Tanner had shared his struggles, even though he'd worried about scaring her away.

But Faith had sorrow and ugliness in her past, too, and she'd been keeping the worst of hers inside.

"I lied to you."

He pushed his tongue inside of his cheek. "What about?"

"Not here."

They went out the front doors and sat on a patch of grass in the shade of a tree. Singing still came from inside, though it was muffled.

"I can't believe I ran out of there."

"I've run out of nicer places. And worse ones."

"Being here, it just reminded me of things back home. I wasn't ready for it."

Tanner ran his fingers down her arm.

"Have you ever had a moment where a bunch of things suddenly make sense for the first time?" she asked.

"Maybe. Kissing you was a little like that. So was last night."

His statement made her smile, though tears still dotted her eyelashes. "Yeah. But this one, just now, wasn't nearly as fun." She tugged up a few blades of grass, gathering her courage. "Yesterday, on the way here, I said my mom called. But I lied. It was Jon."

His expression was hard to read. "I thought that might be the case. I saw how upset you were afterward."

"Why didn't you say anything?"

"I figured you had your reasons. Or you'd tell me later. I trust you."

"I'm sorry." She rested her head against his shoulder. Tanner kissed her forehead. "I need you to understand how things are between me and Jon."

She felt him tense. "Okay."

He was probably thinking the worst. "We've never loved each other. Not the way a husband and wife should. I've told you that, and it's all true. But there's other stuff I left out. Because it's…" She swallowed down a fresh wave of tears. "Really hard to think about, much less say."

He was silent, waiting for her to keep going. A car drove past on the road.

"I lost my virginity with Jon at a party. I'd been drinking. And I got pregnant. Within a couple of months, I had a husband. A baby on the way. I wasn't thrilled, but I started to think it could turn out happy for all of us."

Tanner massaged the back of her neck. He could probably tell how this story was going to go.

"Jon was willing to try to be a family. But then…" She sniffed, wiping a stray tear. She knew this part was nothing to be ashamed of. It hadn't been her fault. Or Jon's. But the pain was still fresh, even a decade later.

"I had some complications at six and a half months. We found out the baby had a genetic defect, which hadn't been detected because we didn't do any testing until then. She wasn't going to live past her birth. There wasn't anything we could do. I carried her to term, but…"

Faith couldn't keep going. Each word was taking something from her. Like she was cutting them out of her skin.

Tanner pulled her into his lap, rocking her as her tears soaked into his shirt.

In a rush, she told him about the nights she and Jon had cried together, both before and after the funeral. The headstone bearing the name *Lorelei Townsend*. The unbearable guilt she'd felt, knowing she hadn't wanted the child in the first place.

"Oh, Faith. I'm sorry."

"I've felt broken for so long."

"That's okay. We can be broken together."

Her arms cinched around his torso, holding onto him as tightly as she could. Her arms shook from the effort, but she didn't let go. Faith breathed through the pain in her chest.

Sometimes, it felt like the anguish would just keep coming. It would never stop. She'd never get free.

But Tanner was here, solid and steady. Holding her up when she wanted to fall apart.

Finally, she could speak again. There was a lot more she needed to say.

"Jon was the only person who understood what I was going through. I saw the good in him. The kindness. For years, I kept looking for it, hoping I'd find it again." Her husband had been a selfish person his whole life, but he'd loved their child. That wasn't something she could easily forget.

"Eventually, I gave up hoping he'd be the husband I needed. But that's why I can't pretend he means nothing."

"Do you want him in your life?"

"What would you say if I did?" She looked up at Tanner's face and saw no judgment there.

"It's not my place to have a problem with it."

Faith stiffened in his arms, not knowing what he meant by that.

"I'd never tell you not to see someone you care about. Even if it's him." He traced her cheekbone with his thumb, right where the bruise had faded. "Even though I don't like that he's hurt you."

Did she care about Jon?

A part of her always would. But in all the years she was married, what she felt for Jon had never come close to what she already felt for Tanner.

"He never wanted my help. I've given him enough chances to know he's not going to change. And I've realized I played my own part. Maybe if I hadn't forgiven him so many times, it would've forced him to take a different path."

"Sounds like you're blaming yourself for his choices."

"I'm trying not to. But I have to take responsibility for my actions. Leaving him was the scariest thing I've ever done, but it's no wonder he didn't take me seriously. Now that he's followed me here, I can't fall into the same old cycle."

Accepting his excuses. Letting him get away with more and more.

On the phone, Jon had sworn on their daughter's life. He'd known what that would mean to her. But it didn't mean the same to him. His addiction and his desperation always won out.

Standing and singing in that church pew, she'd felt it in her soul—enough was finally enough. She didn't know yet what she'd do about Jon's new request. But speaking up for herself wasn't sufficient. She needed a plan. *Actions*, not words.

Faith ran her fingers through Tanner's hair. It had a slight curl on top, just a hint unruly after the cut. "I want to be braver," she said. "As brave as you."

The skin around his eyes crinkled. "You're already braver than me."

She didn't see how that could be true.

"Why? Did I scare you away?" she asked.

A smile broke through the sadness in his eyes. "Nah. Gonna have to do better than that. I'm not going anywhere."

Tanner gave her a soft kiss. Singing came from inside the church again. Faith rested her forehead against his, and the sun shining down on them through the leaves of the tree felt a little like grace.

Chapter Twenty-Eight

By the time Tanner and Faith went back inside, the service was ending. His family sent questioning glances Faith's way. Kaylee pulled her into a quick hug. That was his family, giving love when someone needed it without demanding much in return. Tanner had to keep reminding himself of that so he wouldn't let so much time pass before his next visit.

They gave him a hard time, but it was all out of love. He was grateful to see they were showing Faith the same.

After a big Sunday lunch—his mom's famous pulled pork sliders and cole slaw—Faith went upstairs to pack her things. Tanner wanted to follow to continue their conversation from earlier, but his dad put a hand between his shoulder blades.

"How about a drive around the property? Been a while since we've done that. I can show you what's new."

It was a small tradition of theirs whenever Tanner came to town. His dad liked chatting about everything going on around the farm. He wasn't managing its day-to-day affairs anymore, but this land had been the man's life. Tanner understood how much it meant to him.

They climbed into the old truck along with Scout, who wagged her tail from the backseat.

Tanner's father was a man of few words. He'd always been affectionate and kind. He'd never made Tanner feel guilty about the choice not to return here after his discharge. But Dad also kept his feelings close to the vest. Tanner couldn't help wondering if his dad felt the same as Brayden did.

"Kaylee and Brayden have been doing a good job with the place," Tanner said.

"That they have. All my kids keep making me proud."

"Even me?"

"You kidding? Especially you. I couldn't be prouder to call you my son."

It felt good to hear his dad say it.

"How's the job at the security company going?"

"It's good. I still like it."

Tanner had never considered doing anything else. Unlike Noah, he'd never had any interest in pursuing grander ambitions. He kept waiting for the day that Noah would announce he was moving on to some bigger opportunity. Tanner had never felt the urge.

Despite his recent struggles, he still felt Bennett Security was the right place for him. But he found himself opening his mouth to say more. "There's a captain position. One of the senior guys retired. You remember my buddy, Noah? He's been encouraging me to apply."

"That sounds right up your alley. People have always looked up to you. Like the other SEALs. They always used to ask for your advice, didn't they?"

That was true, even though he hadn't been the most experienced of the operators there. For some reason, a lot of the guys had seemed comfortable sharing things with him. "But I don't know how much my advice is really worth. And I don't like dealing with all the headaches of being in charge."

"Aren't you the guy who always says to embrace what's uncomfortable?"

He'd walked right into that one. He'd brought this up, after all. Maybe he was giving the captain spot more serious consideration than he'd realized. "I wasn't going to apply. But I don't know. I might reconsider."

"Perhaps Faith is the reason behind that?"

"Why would she be?"

His dad gave him a knowing glance. "A man wants to put his best forward when the woman he cares about is watching. Like how I bought the neighbor's land just before I asked your mother to marry me? Wanted her to think I was going places, so to speak."

Tanner huffed a laugh. "It's possible."

"Was Faith okay this morning?" his dad asked. "She seemed upset during the service."

"She's all right. She felt bad about leaving, though. I told her nobody minded."

"Not in the least. I assumed she was moved by whatever spirit she believes in. But I can tell she's got a kind heart. And it's the kind-hearted people who sometimes end up hurting the most." His dad patted Tanner's shoulder. "I love you, son. No matter what. Always will."

"I love you, too."

Back at the house, Faith had her backpack ready by the door. They said goodbye to Tanner's family, spreading around the hugs. His nephews jumped around, getting in a few last piggyback rides.

"I hope you'll come see us again soon, Faith," his mom said. "I would say the same to my son, but he'll accuse me of being a broken record."

"Nobody understands that reference anymore," Brayden complained.

Their mother shrugged. "Maybe Faith's one of those trendy people with a vinyl collection. You don't know."

Dad carried Faith's bag to the car.

On the back porch, Tanner's brother came in for a hug, smacking him on the back. "So Faith's your girlfriend now?"

"Seems that way."

"You're an asshole."

"What? Why?"

"You totally had sex in my truck," Brayden muttered.

"Duh."

Brayden flipped him the bird, hiding the gesture so their mom wouldn't see it.

"I'll buy you a gift card for a detail," Tanner said.

"You'd better. Take care of yourself, jerk."

"Love you too, dumbass."

Tanner felt peaceful as they headed out on the highway. It was hard to wrap his head around how much had changed in his heart in just a few days.

Now, they were heading back into their everyday lives. Reality.

He wanted to believe he could keep his fresh mindset going. That he could keep his promise to himself not to let Faith down.

Yet he also couldn't deny the fact that Faith had been more open with him than he'd been with her. He hadn't been exaggerating when he'd said she was the braver of the two of them. She'd pretty much bared her soul. Tanner was still holding the toughest memories back.

He'd told the kids at the rec center that so-called "heroes" were just humans. Real heroes got sick. They cried. But when was the last time Tanner had let anyone see him like that on purpose?

With Faith, he wanted to get there eventually. But right now, she needed him to be strong. She had enough to deal with. He couldn't lay more burdens at her feet, no matter how much she claimed she could handle it.

Maybe she could, but that didn't mean it was right for him to do it.

"Thank you for taking me with you this weekend," she said. "It meant a lot."

"Thanks for coming with me."

"In more ways than one?"

He snickered. He couldn't get enough of this girl and her dirty mind. How she could find a way to laugh no matter how much she was hurting.

As they made their way back toward the coast, Tanner asked, "Did you want me to take you to the townhouse? Or... back to my place?" He wouldn't blame her at all for wanting to go home. They'd spent almost forty-eight hours together, minus sleeping apart last night.

But he was relieved when Faith gave him a wicked smile. "Your place." She reached over to massage his leg. Tanner shifted in his seat as his dick responded, pressing into the seam of his shorts.

"You could spend the night again. If you want."

She didn't even hesitate. "Could you swing by my house on the way so I can get what I need for work tomorrow?"

"You got it." He drove a little faster.

˷

THE MOMENT they got inside his house, Faith pounced on him. "Upstairs," she said between kisses.

"You don't want to talk more about earlier? What you told me during church..." He'd waited to bring up the subject again, worried about pressing her too much. He couldn't hold her while he was driving. But now that they were home, he wanted her to know he was more than willing to listen.

She made an adorable grumbling noise. "Talking can wait. I want you in your bed."

He wasn't going to argue with that.

Tanner grabbed her around the waist and picked her up. Faith squeaked, holding onto his shoulders. Her legs wrapped around him, and his fingers gripped her thighs. The climb up the narrow staircase was slightly awkward. They both laughed when he knocked his head on the low rafter.

Tanner dumped her onto the mattress and sprawled on top of her, kissing her fiercely. Letting himself take what he wanted from her mouth. Faith had told him not to hold back, and he didn't intend to.

Last night had been just about perfect, but that experience had only whetted his appetite. Now they were back home in his bedroom. Twice before, she'd slept here beside him, but neither time had he gotten what he'd wanted.

Tanner wasn't anywhere near done claiming her.

Faith scratched her nails along his back beneath his shirt. His cock felt ready to burst through his zipper. With a growl, Tanner pushed onto his hands and knees.

"We both should be naked."

Faith nodded her head against the mattress. "Yes. That."

He backed up until he reached the edge of the bed, then stood. He fisted his T-shirt and yanked it over his head. His shorts and boxers were next, shucked off to the floor and kicked into a corner.

His cock pointed forward at her. Tanner gave himself a long, slow stroke.

Faith hadn't removed a single item of clothing. Instead, she crawled toward him on the mattress, a naughty gleam in her eye.

When she got close enough, she licked his slit. Groaning, Tanner rested one knee on mattress. Faith took the head of his cock into her mouth, closing her eyes and moaning like it was the best thing she'd ever tasted.

He felt conflicted. He *really* loved what she was doing—on her hands and knees, sucking and tonguing his dick like a lollipop—but he also needed her naked right now. It was a conundrum.

Then he remembered what an intensely emotional day she'd had. Revealing so much about her past, opening up about her heartache.

Tanner planned to take good care of her, so she knew just how incredible she was.

He gently touched her hair, hips pulling back. His tip popped out of her mouth. "You're not naked yet. Let's fix that."

Tanner took her by the hands. She got up from the bed and stood in front of him. Her clothes stripped away easy enough, and he circled his arms around her, drawing her against him. His cock folded up against his body, pressed into her stomach. His forehead touched hers, and it was just like last night at the bar when they'd been dancing. Except now, there was absolutely nothing between them, and they didn't need any music except their heartbeats. He swayed her back and forth.

"Never seen anything so beautiful as you," he murmured.

She touched his cheek, and then they were kissing again. This was calmer, sweeter, not so urgent as before. Yet his need for her felt even deeper, going to a place inside him he hardly recognized. It was scary, but he didn't want it to stop.

He wanted to give everything to her. He wanted to be brave enough for that.

Reluctantly, Tanner broke their kiss. He grabbed a condom and a bottle of lube from his nightstand, then lay flat on his back on the bed, one knee casually bent.

He beckoned his fingers. "Come here."

Faith seemed to know what he wanted, climbing over to straddle his thighs. She leaned forward at the same time that he lifted onto one elbow, their mouths meeting in the middle.

She moaned when his fingers dipped between her legs.

While they kissed, he used his hand to make sure she was wet and ready.

Tanner lay back to roll the condom on and lube himself up. He knew she might need the extra moisture in this position, especially with how tight she'd been last night.

Faith watched all this with her lips slightly open, a haze of desire in her expression. "You want me on top of you?"

Other men—he wasn't going to think their names, not right now—had made her feel weak and helpless. He wanted to give her complete control over how this went. She'd set the pace. Tanner wanted her to chase her own pleasure and use his body to do it.

"Yes. You want that, too?" He was still holding his cock upright.

She answered by moving until she was right over him, her opening at his tip. She took a sharp inhale as she lowered herself. The progress was slow at first, as it had been last night. But Tanner relished every moment of this. Seeing the look of wonder on her face as he slid ever deeper inside her.

Finally, she was seated all the way onto him. Her lips pressed together. She breathed through her nose.

"You okay?" he asked.

"Just admiring you. I can see you better than last night." Her eyes raked over him.

"Yeah?" He couldn't explain the sudden twinge of shyness he felt. "Do I meet with your approval?"

"Expectations were high," she said in a businesslike tone. "But you keep exceeding them."

Faith rocked her hips, and Tanner groaned involuntarily. Her movements were slow, even hesitant, forcing him to use that patience he'd promised her before.

But this view was pretty damn amazing. Her legs spread over him, her round breasts swaying.

She worked up to a steadier rhythm. Her breathy pants and moans increased in speed. Faster. Rougher. Her eyes fluttered closed. Tanner's hands ran all over her. Up her thighs and stomach and tits. Down her arms and shoulders.

He lifted up again onto his elbow. Her palms landed on his chest, and Faith's hair fell like a curtain around them. Tanner nipped at her lower lip, rolling it between his teeth.

She thrust herself against him. Fucking herself on his cock.

He saw the very moment she came undone. Felt it. He already felt so attuned to her. Like they'd both landed on the same frequency. Faith dug her fingers into his hair as she rode that wave. Tanner grabbed her hip with one hand and pumped into her. Didn't take much before he was right there with her, coming apart and pulsing and groaning.

She collapsed onto him, head on his chest. Tanner drew circles onto her back.

A few minutes later, they were curled up together beneath the covers. They hadn't had dinner, and it was nowhere near bedtime. But neither made a move to get dressed.

Faith exhaled, and he felt her mood shift.

"Jon wants me to accept another of his 'deliveries.'"

Tanner clenched his ab muscles, keeping back the tirade he wanted to unleash at her ex.

"I'm *not* going to do it," she said. "But I don't know how to handle it."

"You can't just tell him no?"

"I tried. He wouldn't listen, probably because he's so desperate. When he called yesterday, he made sure I saw him on video. Somebody beat him up. Black eyes, broken nose, cuts all over his face."

"Shit. For real?" Tanner almost felt bad for the guy. But it sounded like Jon had used the beating to manipulate her.

"I think it was Kyle."

Kyle Spaulding. The man who'd threatened her. Attacked her. If only Tanner could track the asshole down and make him experience the fear he'd put into Faith. "My friend Sean is a detective in the LAPD Gang and Narcotics unit. I asked Sean to look into Kyle. I'm sorry I didn't tell you before." He hadn't wanted to upset her further by bringing up the subject unless it seemed necessary. Now, it was.

"What did Sean find out?"

"Kyle hasn't been in the L.A. area for long. He's got a record back in Texas, including possession with intent to sell. But nothing specifically ties him to drug trafficking in California."

"Jon said it was Kyle's idea to use my place for storing these 'packages.' I can't believe this is a legitimate business."

"No, that's unlikely, given Kyle's record. And your ex's history."

She nodded. "I got the impression Jon's not in control of what's going on. He said, 'They won't let me change the plan.' And he said if I go to the police, they'll come after me."

"So it's more than just Kyle?"

"Maybe." She rubbed the skin between her eyes. "Jon swore Kyle wouldn't come near me again, which means other people are involved in this, too. It scares me."

"I'm not going to let anybody touch you." He felt the surety in his bones, even though he wasn't sure of many things these days.

Her eyes raised, but she didn't look reassured. "But I don't know what these people will do if I won't cooperate."

If it were up to him, Tanner would've turned this whole mess over to Sean and the other authorities. But he worried Faith wouldn't be willing to go there.

How could Tanner protect the woman he cared about if she still had these ties to her ex?

"You know Jon's just taking advantage of your kindness, right?" he said softly. "He wants you to feel sorry for him."

"I do feel sorry for him, but I'm *not* going to do what he wants." She spoke adamantly. "I need to figure out what I *can* do. How I can finally get free of him without also getting Jon killed or anyone else hurt."

Tanner didn't care much what happened to Jon. But these people had threatened her, too.

"Would it be easier if I talk to him?" Tanner asked. "So you don't have to?"

Her head fell back against his shoulder. "I don't want him to know about you if I can help it."

That smarted. "Why?"

"Because he'll turn it into another guilt trip. 'You already have a boyfriend, and we're not even divorced.' Jon has a way of turning things…ugly."

Tanner tried to project a laidback persona. But fading into the background when someone was in danger? Especially someone he cared for? Not his style. Not even close.

"I'm confused," he said. "Do you want my help with this?"

"I do. But I don't want you to take over for me. I need to fix this myself somehow. Jon and Kyle have both made me feel powerless. I'm stepping up and taking responsibility."

He understood. Faith had told him again and again she needed freedom. She didn't want anyone making her decisions for her.

"Tell me what you want me to do," he said.

"Stay next to me as I try to figure this out? I need to talk to Sylvie and Ethan, too, since it could affect them."

"Sounds like wingman duty." He flashed a grin. "I can handle that. I'll be right by your side, and we'll sort it out together."

Even though his natural instinct was to bear the brunt of it himself.

Chapter Twenty-Nine

*I*t took a few days to get everyone's schedules aligned, but on Thursday afternoon, they met in Sylvie's living room. First to arrive was Ethan, Faith's upstairs roommate and Sylvie's cousin. Then Nic, Sylvie's boyfriend. Faith hugged them both.

"Have the police found anything more about the guy who broke in?" Nic asked.

"That's what I need to tell you all about."

Sylvie and Ethan both knew this was about Jon. But Faith had only seen Sylvie for a few minutes here and there since her weekend with Tanner. They had a lot to catch up on.

Faith had spent every night with him since they'd returned to West Oaks.

When they were in each other's arms, laughing, making love, she could pretend nothing else mattered outside the walls of his house. But afterward, the worries kept coming back.

Jon hadn't called again yet, but it was only a matter of time. She had to be ready.

Sylvie and Tanner walked in the front door. Faith's roommate dumped her bag and keys on the ground, rushing over to wrap Faith in her arms. "I'm sorry we're late. It was hard to get away today. You'd think that place couldn't function without me."

"I guarantee it can't." Tanner gave Faith a heart-melting smile. "Hi."

"Hi." She couldn't resist giving him a quick kiss. Her body instantly responded to having him near, and she wished she could focus on him instead of the mess involving her ex-husband.

"Ugh, you two are so disgustingly adorable," Sylvie said. "Are we talking business or what?"

Faith forced her attention away from Tanner. "What do you mean? I'm all business." Despite her happiness at seeing her boyfriend—she loved saying that—the trouble with Jon had been weighing heavily on her mind.

They all took seats in the living room.

"Sylvie, Ethan, this affects both of you. I wanted you to be involved in this decision. Same with Nic and Tanner because you both have experience dealing with…things like this."

"Criminal conspiracies?" Nic asked wryly.

Ethan's eyebrows shot up behind his wire rimmed glasses. "That sounds ominous."

Faith wished she could joke about it. But this situation felt too serious. "I'll tell you everything I can, and let you decide for yourselves."

She went through the chain of events so far. How Jon had reappeared at her workplace, asking her to store things for him, and an innocent package had soon followed. How Jon's old associate Kyle had shown up at the house, demanding another delivery.

"At first, Jon seemed apologetic. He promised he'd leave me out of whatever scheme he's mixed up in. But he never keeps his promises." She told them about his latest call over the weekend, asking her to receive another delivery here.

"That asshole," Sylvie said. "He's really unbelievable."

Faith had no interest in defending him. Nor did she want

to rehash the full, tragic story. "The people Jon's involved with are threatening us. They beat him up. He's in way over his head, and I feel stuck. If I keep refusing, I have no idea what they'll do to Jon or me. And if I go along—which I won't do—he'll just keep asking for more."

Nic brushed his dark curls away from his forehead. "It's typical for the cartels to have storage places for their product when it arrives from overseas before it gets moved for sale. Makes sense an innocent person like you would be attractive as a stopping point in their distribution chain. You wouldn't be on the radar of the DEA or local authorities."

Nic was one of the most physically beautiful men Faith had ever met, though of course he had nothing on Tanner. Yet Nic was also soft-spoken and unassuming. Sylvie had mentioned he had a checkered past, including personal experience with organized crime—on the wrong side of the law—which was hard for Faith to believe. These days he worked for an art gallery and consulted with law enforcement to help catch bad guys. But when it came to subjects like drug cartels, she had to assume he knew what he was talking about.

"But Jon hasn't asked her to store a whole stream of product," Sylvie argued. "Just a box here and there."

Nic looked skeptical. "Still sounds drug related to me. The kinds of people we're talking about? Who dole out beatings as punishments? They don't make elaborate plans unless there's money in it. And not many kinds of contraband would be as valuable as cocaine or high-purity heroin or fentanyl pills coming in from overseas."

Faith was inclined to agree. "Because of Jon's past, how he was a dealer before in Texas, I've thought from the beginning this was about drugs. But if Jon was involved in the drug trade here, why didn't Tanner's friend in the LAPD find any evidence of it?"

Tanner rested his elbows on his knees, looking down at the carpet. "I'm not sure."

Nic propped his foot on the coffee table. "If Jon's moving drugs, but he's doing it outside the cartels who have ownership of this region, it would be insanely dangerous. Both for Jon and anyone else who touches this."

Faith didn't want to mention that Jon had passed on a threat against her if she reported his associates. It probably went without saying. Tanner already knew.

Sylvie jumped up from the couch, pacing on the rug in her combat boots. "But we've faced down murderous thugs before. I'm not going to let anyone intimidate my friends."

Nic looked up at her fondly from his seated position. "I'm right there with you. But we have to be smart about this."

"Exactly," Ethan said. "We let the police handle it. Not us."

Which she'd also considered, despite Jon's threats.

Tanner lifted his head. "We should let Faith decide." His brown eyes were soft as he regarded her. "Do you have a plan in mind?"

She shifted on the cushion. "I might. I mentioned two options so far. Refuse Jon altogether or go along. I don't like either one. So, here's number three. When Jon contacts me about the next drop-off, I'll act like I'm on board. But when the delivery comes, we'll see if the package has drugs inside, hidden somewhere. Tanner, maybe your friend at the LAPD would be willing to check it out?"

"Sean will help us unofficially. But the police will want concrete evidence before devoting their resources."

"So, we're running a sting operation?" Sylvie had stopped pacing. Her arms were crossed over her petite frame.

Faith nodded. "Basically. And if it's really something illegal, as it probably is, we'll have the evidence the police need to get involved. They can catch the person who comes here to pick up the delivery."

Tanner's knee brushed Faith's. "But what about Jon? If it's drugs, he'll be implicated, too."

"I know. I've spent too long covering for him. I'm done."

Nic pushed out a breath. "This sounds dangerous."

"I guess there's a fourth option," Faith said. "I leave town. I can't imagine Jon or Kyle, or anyone would still bother you if I'm not here." Though nothing would stop them from coming after her.

The others made sounds of disapproval. Tanner frowned, reaching for her hand.

"This is only happening because of my presence. Sylvie and Ethan, you invited me into your home, and I brought this mess along with me."

Sylvie crossed her arms over her black tank top. "Out of the question. We'll follow your other plan, option three. And no matter what, we're in this together."

Faith let out a breath, sagging into the couch with relief. None of this was going to be easy. But having her friends beside her made her believe she could do it.

～

AFTER THEIR MEETING, the five of them ordered takeout for a quick dinner. But the whole time, Faith couldn't wait to get Tanner alone.

He seemed to be thinking the same. The moment she stepped out of Sylvie's dining room and into the hall, he followed. "I've missed you all day." Tanner lifted her up, pressing her into the wall and kissing her.

Faith put her hands on his cheeks, enjoying the scratch of his whiskers on her palms. All she wanted was to curl up with him and wish everything else away. "I missed you, too."

Myra had commented at work on how she wouldn't stop smiling. Faith's coworker had also demanded details about what happened after their infamous double date. But despite much cajoling, she'd only given up that she and Tanner were official now.

What they did when they were alone belonged only to them. She cherished each new memory they'd been making.

This thing with Tanner was only a few days old, still brand new. Faith didn't know any more if they were going fast, slow, somewhere in between. She only knew how right she felt whenever they were together. Why should she question this feeling when it was so good?

And the sex... Faith hated the word addiction. Yet it was the only term that fit the overwhelming craving she felt for this man. Whenever they weren't tangled up together, she was distracted by her longing for it.

But no matter how happy she was, her problems with Jon still hung over their heads. She wanted the bad parts to be over.

He set her down. "My place again tonight? I drove here from work."

"You don't want to walk? I don't mind."

"Nah, I'm good. I haven't felt like walking as much lately. Cuts into our alone time."

Faith had already changed out of her scrubs into comfier clothes. In the living room, she grabbed a few things from one her suitcases to take with her.

Sylvie, Nic, and Ethan were still sitting at the table, nibbling on Thai food. "Sleeping at Tanner's again tonight?" Sylvie asked.

Faith's cheeks warmed. "You don't mind, do you?"

Nic grinned. "I certainly don't. I've been staying here the past couple nights, and without you sleeping in the living room, Sylvie and I can be as loud as we want."

Ethan rolled his eyes. "You think I can't hear you upstairs?"

Sylvie covered her face, laughing. Faith figured that was a good time to slip away. She grabbed Tanner's hand before he could add to this oversharing session.

The sun was down, and headlights streamed past them as they drove.

"Have you spoken to Noah?" Faith asked. She knew Tanner had wanted to check in with his friend in person, given all that had happened over the weekend.

"Not yet. He's still on assignment, and every minute I've been at work this week, I've been busy. Hardly any time to slow down and think, which is probably for the best. Every time I do, I end up worrying about things."

"About Noah?"

"No, not him. I'm sure Noah's fine with us being together. I worry about you."

"I don't want you to."

He chewed his lip. "I should be there when the drop-off happens. I can stay out of sight if you want. Just as long as I'm nearby."

"I agree. I want you there."

"So you'll tell me as soon as you hear from Jon about the drop-off date and time?"

"*Yes*. I promise I will. But for the rest of tonight, let's pretend none of that's happening. I want it to be just us."

He stopped at a red light and leaned over to kiss her.

The minute they stepped inside his house and locked the door, they were pulling off clothes. Tanner got rid of his shirt and shoved his shorts and briefs down, his thick erection bobbing as he stepped out of them. She couldn't get enough of his body. The contrasting pieces of him, soft and hard, rough and smooth.

Faith pushed him toward the couch. "I can't wait. I need you now."

"You're not even naked yet."

"I will be."

He sat down and lay back against the cushions, lazily gripping his shaft as he watched her. Faith had already discarded her T-shirt. She slid her knit pants off her hips, kicking away the loose fabric. She crawled onto his lap, knees straddling him, and rubbed the crotch of her panties against his cock. The contact made her shiver.

These moments were almost better than the climax itself. The anticipation of having him, imagining how he would feel and taste, the noises he'd make. How she'd drive him wild, and he'd do the same to her.

Faith had never expected sex with anyone could be this good. But with Tanner, each time kept getting better. Somehow, knowing just what would set him off made the act that much more satisfying.

Tanner flicked her bra straps past her shoulders, then tugged down the cups to expose her breasts. He palmed her ass, lifting her higher, mouth landing on her nipple. His tongue swirled over the bud just before he nipped it with his teeth.

Her panties were soaking. Mouth still on her breast, Tanner slid the fabric over her crotch to one side and penetrated her with his middle finger. She dug into his hair, holding his head in place.

"You have a condom down here?" she asked.

He pulled off of her to speak. "My wallet. In my shorts."

"Do you always have one in there?"

"Around you, I do."

Faith got up and grabbed his pants. She tossed him the condom, shucked off her underwear, and unhooked her bra.

Once his cock was sheathed, she knelt over him. Fucking him the past few days had made this part easier. The first few times he'd left her sore, but now she slid herself easily onto his length. The stretch still made her gasp.

Tanner's moan was primal. "You on my cock is the sexiest thing I've ever seen." His big hands squeezed her ass, forcing her to move slower.

"I think my view's better." Faith had never thought of

herself as such a visual person. But she could've stared at Tanner naked all day.

Waking up with him in the morning light in his bed, she'd noticed scars all over his body. Different shapes and sizes. Some circular ones on his arms, partly hidden by tattoos, which looked like gunshot wounds. Faith had asked, but Tanner had mumbled something vague about training maneuvers. She didn't need explanations if it was too hard to talk about. She'd just kissed every spot. All of him was beautiful.

Tanner's grip on her ass lessened, allowing her to move. Faith rolled her hips, whimpering at how indulgent this felt. The friction against her clit combined with the pressure of him inside her.

He sat forward to kiss her, beard scratching deliciously against her skin.

She let go of every worry, lost her sense of time. Everything else faded away as she rode him. Their eyes were locked, both of their gazes soft, breathing one another's air. Her hands pressed into his chest, enjoying the rumbling vibrations as he panted and groaned.

Faith was so wrapped up in him that her orgasm caught her by surprise. She held onto his shoulders and thrust herself against his dick, crying out so loud she bet the neighbors could hear.

Her hips stilled. Faith struggled to catch her breath.

Tanner held her by the waist, lifting them both up so he was on his knees on the couch. He tipped her back onto the cushions. His weight landed on her, driving his cock forward and shocking another gasp out of her. They were only half on the cushions, but Tanner didn't seem to care. He braced one foot on the floor, his hand on the frame of the couch.

Her orgasm had left her even wetter. His cock pistoned in and out of her, the heat between them building to a frenzied pace. She loved when he was like this. Rough and uninhibited.

He wasn't usually the typical alpha-male type, but when he fucked her like that? She loved how dominant he was.

"Wait." She could barely get the word out. "I want you to come on me."

His head bent down to kiss the dip between her collar bones. "That naughty mind never ceases to amaze me."

Tanner pulled out of her. He knelt to either side of her, stripped off the condom, and beat his cock. The tip was red and leaking inside his fist. The sight was downright indecent.

Tanner's free hand cupped his balls. The grunts he was making went straight to her clit, reigniting her arousal even though she still pulsed with the aftershocks of her release.

A guttural roar erupted from him. Ropes of cum shot from his tip onto her breasts and stomach. His fist kept milking his shaft until he was spent.

Chapter Thirty

Faith looked down at the mess he'd left. "I need to get that on video so I can watch it whenever I want."

Tanner leaned forward to rest his hands on either side of her face. He was panting, his chest tight as he gulped in air. "What are we going to do with that mouth of yours?"

"Make it dirtier?"

He dragged a finger through the cum on her chest. When he brought the fingertip to her mouth, she sucked it in, eyes never leaving his.

This woman was going to be the end of him.

"Now I'm going to clean you up." Tanner scooped her off the couch and into his arms. He carried her to the bathroom, setting her on the counter while he turned on the water and waited for it to warm. But he didn't want to lose contact for too long. He trailed gentle kisses down her neck and shoulders until the water was hot enough.

They stepped into the shower. Tanner made sure she was under the spray so she wouldn't get cold. Shower gel lathered between his hands, and he massaged the suds over her breasts and stomach and back, alternating with deep pulls from her lips with his mouth.

At work, he was used to forcing everything but the present moment from his mind. But all that week, whenever he'd had a spare minute alone, his thoughts had immediately returned to her. To her slender, toned body and the long sweep of her hair. The way she gave herself to him completely, never hesitating to voice her desires. Her laugh, her bravery, and the aura of innocence she still somehow embodied. Like she was choosing to see only the good in him.

For the past several days, since they'd returned to West Oaks, Tanner had woken up next to her every single morning. No nightmares. Only the slightest hint of unease during his sleepless periods. He'd been able to switch off his lamp at night for the first time since the concussion. A huge accomplishment, though he hadn't explained that to Faith.

He'd promised himself he would conquer his issues for her, and miraculously, it seemed to be working. He was managing. Even tonight, when they'd been at Sylvie's and the stress had started to build, he'd handled it.

Well, the voices of his friends had gotten a bit too shrill, the lights a little too bright. He'd felt panic rising up. But he hadn't let it take him over.

Tanner couldn't stand the thought of a lowlife like Kyle Spaulding targeting Faith. He hated this "sting operation" of hers. But she'd insisted on handling this problem herself, and in truth, he couldn't think of a better solution.

Until Jon and Kyle did something more blatant, the police couldn't nail them. Sean had made that clear.

Even if Faith refused to play along in their scheme—whatever it truly was—they wouldn't leave her alone. Worse, Kyle or somebody else might punish her for defying them anyway. When Faith double-crossed them, the danger was probably even higher, but at least the police would be willing to get involved. These assholes would finally see some kind of consequences.

And no matter what, Tanner was going to be there to protect her.

Once they were both cleaned up, they went upstairs to his bedroom. She put on one of his T-shirts and slid beneath his covers, her damp hair leaving droplets on the pillowcase.

Faith was already fitting effortlessly into his life. She was under his skin. In his bones. He felt the knowledge that she was *his* in every part of him. Not his to control, because Tanner had never wanted a relationship like that. But his to care for.

His to love.

His mom had asked him just a few days ago if he loved Faith. This still felt too new to say it, but whatever this feeling was in his chest—this overwhelming longing, even when she was right in front of him—he couldn't deny it. He couldn't hold it back, either.

Tanner stretched out beside her, propping his head against the pillow to face her. "I have a question for you."

"Oh?" She sounded sleepy and relaxed, the way she usually did after love making. He relished knowing these small, intimate things about her. Like the freckles on her inner thighs. The dimples on her lower back.

"How would you feel about moving in with me?"

Her eyes widened. "Really?"

"I know it's fast. Some people will say too fast. And they'd have a point."

"They would."

"Also, fair warning, my friends and family all agree I'm annoying."

"Are you trying to talk me out of it?"

He pulled her into his arms and kissed her head. "No. I want you here with me. Every day. You make me a better man." Better in so many ways. He didn't want that to be a burden on her, some kind of responsibility to add to the pressures already on her shoulders. But it was true.

He *needed* her here. Maybe more than he was willing to admit.

"Then I would be honored to move in with you. I want to be with you every day, too. Just like we've been doing."

His grin was so wide it made his cheeks ache. That was what he wanted. For every day forward to be just like this.

∼

BLOOD POURED from Scotty's neck. Tanner packed gauze into the wound, the hot liquid burning his hands, but it kept coming. A bubbling waterfall of red.

Stay with me, *he thought.* I've got you.

Something thumped Tanner hard in the body armor on his back. At first, he thought it was the teammate at his rear, hammering him to get his attention. Which didn't make much sense.

He looked over his shoulder. Saw the flash. Heard the pop. Another hard thump, jarring him. Movement, eyes, shouts, coming toward him.

In a split second his M4 was in his blood-soaked hands, but it was too late. They were already on him, shoving cold metal against the back of his neck.

He knew what came next. The darkness. Pain.

It was already here. He kicked his legs, as if that could force away the panic.

No air. They were suffocating him. He couldn't breathe.

Sickening images seared his vision. Scotty on the ground in a pool of blood. The trail stretching behind as they dragged his lifeless form. Made Tanner watch what they did.

No. No.

He fell onto the ground and scrambled back till he met a wall. The wall of his prison. Scotty's mangled body was lying somewhere nearby. Tanner's hands were sticky with his friend's blood. He wheezed, gasping for air.

A light switched on. "Tanner?"

Why was Faith here? He didn't want her in this place. They were going to hurt her.

"Get away from here. Run."

She climbed down onto the floor beside him. Her hand touched his knee, and he flinched.

"*Don't.*"

"I'm sorry." She sat across from him with her back against the bed. "Was it a nightmare? What can I do?"

"Just go. Please."

He was terrified they'd hurt her. But as clarity started to cut through the panic, his fear shifted.

Tanner was afraid *he* would hurt her.

Faith wrapped her arms around her knees. Her eyes watched. He saw the shine of tears.

Slow down and breathe. The voice of his rational mind was kicking in. *You can get through this.* Even though he wanted to scream and fight. Even though this feeling—trapped, overwhelmed—was intolerable.

Faith was here, and she was seeing everything.

He wanted her to look away.

It felt like a year passed before his lungs worked. The terror started to recede, like floodwater slowly draining. But it left its mark behind. He felt dirty. Ruined.

He'd sworn he wouldn't do this shit anymore. He thought he'd been managing. Sleeping with the lights off, like that was worthy of a fucking medal. He'd wanted to believe things would be different—because he had Faith now. He wasn't supposed to let her down.

But it hadn't mattered, had it?

He'd known, deep down, the darkness would come back for him eventually. Like internal bleeding. You might not see it on the outside, but at some point, it would break you down. He wanted to cry, but at least he'd regained enough self-control to keep that in. Faith had seen enough for one night.

"It's been a while since I've had one that bad." He sounded hoarse. As if he'd been screaming, though he was pretty sure that had only been in his head.

"I can go if you really want me to."

"No. Please don't go." He opened his arms. "I'm so sorry, baby."

Faith hugged him. "Don't be sorry. It's okay."

How could she say that? It wasn't okay. The truth was, it would never be okay. If she kept on seeing how ruined he was, eventually she'd see that truth, too.

Chapter Thirty-One

"We'll see you in another six months." Faith led the patient to the front desk. After he was gone, she went to the exam room down the hall, ignoring the incessant hum of construction noise coming from outside.

The door to the exam room was cracked open. Faith popped her head in. Gabriella sat in the chair, while her mother and Myra hovered around her.

"How are things going?"

"Just finished up x-rays," Myra said, "and now we're waiting for Dr. Petrie."

Gabriella had been suffering pain after a recent procedure. The girl's demeanor was radically different from the last time Faith had seen her. Gone was her bubbly vivaciousness. The little girl barely glanced up.

Faith stepped inside, pulling a folded piece of paper from her pocket. "Hey Gabriella, I was hoping you might be able to help me with something."

The little girl made a sound of assent, perking up slightly.

"I've been having some trouble with this drawing. Any suggestions?" Faith unfolded the piece of paper.

Gabriella sat forward. "A horse. She's so pretty. What's her name?"

"She doesn't have one yet. That's exactly what I hoped you could help with." Faith shared a smile with Gabriella's mom, who was watching all of this quietly.

"Is she a real horse?"

Faith knew what the girl meant—whether a real horse had been the inspiration. "As a matter of fact, she is. She wasn't mine, but she lived not far from me when I was your age. I used to go visit her sometimes and give her carrots. She had a little diamond shape right on her nose, like I drew here."

Gabriella studied the image. "I think her name is Starlight." She nodded like this was a very serious discussion. "Yes. That's definitely it."

Faith handed her the paper, and Gabriella's eyes brightened even further. "Think you could hold onto her for me? She might seem like she's just a drawing, but she gets lonely. Now that I'm a grown-up, I don't have nearly enough time to visit. Starlight needs someone who can really take care of her."

"I promise I will."

Dr. Petrie arrived, eying Faith. "Did you need something?"

"No, just saying hi." Faith retreated, and Gabriella's mom joined her in the hall.

"Thank you. She's really been struggling. That tooth keeps bothering her, keeping her awake at night from the pain. I wish I knew what to do."

Faith understood better than the woman could know. "I hope she gets some relief soon."

"Me, too. But thanks to you, her spirits are back up."

Faith wished there was more she could do. It wore a person down, feeling so powerless. Seeing someone you cared for suffering in front of you yet being unable to stop it.

Two days had passed since Tanner's vivid nightmare. Every time she'd woken on the nights since, he hadn't been there in bed. She wasn't sure if the nightmares had recurred, or if he simply couldn't sleep. He'd been leaving the light on and asked if it bothered her. Of course, she'd said no. But when she'd tried to discuss his nightmare further, he'd told her not to worry about it and changed the subject. She couldn't force him to open up to her more than he already had.

And maybe there wasn't anything else for him to tell. Maybe this was just what he'd talked about before. How it was going to be hard. She had no intention of getting scared away. If she was scared at all, it was only for him.

It was one thing to hear in general terms what PTSD was like for him. But it had been another to see Tanner huddled against the wall, unable to bear her touch.

Just go. Thank goodness she hadn't listened.

Somehow, they'd get through it. She believed in him. And she was willing to wait and support him as long as it took. She just wished she knew how to reassure him without that pained look crossing his face—like she was only making him feel worse.

Faith carried on with her day until she received a text message. It came from an unfamiliar number.

It's me. I'm outside.

She knew who must've sent it. Only one person would show up at her work, acting all mysterious. A glance through the front window confirmed it. She could just make out Jon's truck parked at the far side of the lot.

She was so tired of this, much too tired to even get angry.

When she was able to take a break, she pushed through the door outside. Shouts and engine noise assailed her from the construction site.

The passenger door to the truck was unlocked. She opened it. But she didn't get in.

"What is it? I thought you were going to call."

"I was afraid you'd get confused because of my new

number. I'm supposed to use this one now." He shrugged sheepishly. "But I wanted to see you, too. I miss you."

Bruises still darkened his eyes, but his face looked better than it had on the video. "What about the delivery? Do you know yet when it's arriving?"

"Can you at least get in, so we can talk like normal people?"

She laughed without humor. "You think this is anywhere near normal?"

But she went ahead and climbed up, closing the passenger door most of the way. This brought back memories, and not all of them terrible. Driving around their town on weekends. Singing along to the radio, even laughing.

Jon rubbed a hand over his mouth. "Sometimes, I think you're the only person who's ever cared about me."

"What about your parents?" Or frankly, hers. So many people had been willing to give Jon the benefit of the doubt.

"But they don't know me. Not the real me. You've seen everything that I've done, and you still stuck around. I hate that I put you through all that. But it felt good, too. Knowing you cared enough to put up with it."

"Do you know how fucked up that sounds?" She stared out the window so she wouldn't have to look at him. "I'm seeing someone," she blurted, unable to keep it in. Maybe so he'd stop talking about their marriage like it wasn't over.

Or, maybe because it would hurt him. A tiny repayment for what he'd done. She wasn't above that.

"Is it serious?" he asked.

"Yes."

Jon's fingers tapped against his knee. "No wonder you changed your mind about helping me. You really want that divorce, don't you?"

She regretted saying anything about Tanner. That had been petty. Pointless. "You don't have to do this, you know.

Whatever you're into with Kyle, you could just forget about it."

Her determination hadn't faltered. But she wanted something better for him. It wasn't too late for him to step up.

"You don't get it, Faith. You never have."

"I guess I don't." She was finished asking for explanations. She said nothing, fingering the handle of the door, ready to bail on this pathetic excuse of a conversation.

But Jon surprised her when he kept talking.

"Back in Texas, I sometimes had trouble with dipping into the supply I was supposed to sell. Kyle helped me balance the books, you could say. Stretch what supply I had left. He found some new buyers and took a cut of the money. But it felt like a deal with the devil." Jon paused. His hands were shaking, which made her wonder again about whether he was using these days. Whether he was getting antsy for another fix. "Kyle kept making demands, wanting to be in control of everything. After he came to our house a while back in Texas, hurt you, I stopped working with him. It was just too risky. In a lot of ways."

Faith stayed completely still, her hand still on the car door handle.

Jon fidgeted in his seat. "Then you left, and I was desperate. I didn't know how I was going to make rent. Or buy food. And I didn't want our parents to figure out, you know, how bad things were. I needed a really big score. The guys I was working for, they agreed to step up my supply. I'd sell more, make more."

"What did you do?" The accusation was clear in her tone.

He screwed up his mouth, looking away, which was all the confirmation she needed.

"I swear, this time it wasn't my fault. Some assholes busted in the house, waving guns, nearly cleaned me out. The product, the money. I was fucked. Completely fucked. I had no idea what to do, how to make it right. The guys I owed, they didn't care about excuses. Either I paid up on time, or I was dead. So I did the only thing I could think of. I called up Kyle."

Of course he had.

"Kyle's got a bad reputation with a lot of people. Doesn't play well with others. But he's the kind of guy with ideas, you know? He's like a snake who can slither through the smallest crack. He came up with a plan for how I could turn things around. He's the one who thought of coming out to Southern California. He knew you were here, and you could be part of our distribution chain. You're totally clean. Practically invisible. Perfect for helping us stay out of sight."

Just as Sylvie's boyfriend Nic had thought. Though Faith couldn't understand what they were selling if Jon had lost his supply. Had they gotten more drugs from somewhere else?

"I hooked up with a few people I met online who live near L.A.," Jon said. "They handled some of the logistical, practical stuff. Then, I had to get you to talk to me again. Get you to cooperate. You already know I realized real quick that was a bad idea, and I tried to change the plan. But I couldn't explain that to Kyle in time. That's why he barged into your house. Which I've already apologized for."

"Why couldn't you contact him?"

"Because…" Jon shook his head. "Forget it. The important thing is, Kyle's in charge now. I have an insurance policy to make sure he doesn't screw me over. But Faith, you're *Kyle's* insurance policy. Do you get that? If I fuck this up, he'll go after you and me both. And if *you* fuck it up? You don't even want to know."

She turned cold. "Is that a threat?"

"I'd never hurt you. But Kyle would. You already know that."

Faith pressed her lips together. Her pulse thumped against her neck. Jon's words had the opposite effect than he'd intended. She'd never help these people. She was more convinced than ever.

Not even to save Jon. Because he would never choose to save her. He'd allowed Kyle to use her as a pawn because Jon only cared about himself.

"Do you know when the delivery will happen? Yes or no."

"It'll be next Tuesday night. I'll send you a text from that new number."

"Are you the one bringing the package?"

"Yeah. It'll be me."

"Fine. I'll be ready." The door handle popped open, and she got out of the truck.

Chapter Thirty-Two

The jeweler placed a yellow diamond and sapphire tennis bracelet on a piece of black velvet. Mrs. Zhang picked it up and held it in the light.

"What do you think, Tanner? Does this suit me?"

"It's as elegant as you are, ma'am," he said evenly. Tanner had his hands clasped behind his back, glancing from the front of the store to the back every few seconds.

She smiled primly, wagging a finger at him. "Very well, I'm not paying you for flattery."

"Don't worry, the flattery's no charge," he said automatically. They'd had this same exchange more than once. A little routine of theirs.

It was Monday, and they were shopping in West Oaks today. Tanner assumed the client frequented jewelry stores all over the world, but Mrs. Zhang seemed particularly fond of this one. Their client typically left this store with tens of thousands of dollars of merchandise.

Tanner didn't see the appeal of the intricate metal designs and massive cut gems. The low light glinted off the facets, tripping along the silver and gold. It was all glare in his eyes.

He glanced through the front windows. Kozinski was

outside. The kid was supposed to be keeping an eye on any pedestrians and cars that approached.

The jeweler brought out a tray of brightly colored rings. "We received a delivery of some brand new designs yesterday. No one else has seen them yet. I think you're going to love these."

The mention of a "delivery" made Tanner think of Faith. He checked his phone, just in case she'd called, even though he wasn't supposed to deal with personal issues while on the clock. She was at work again today, and Tanner didn't like not knowing if she was all right.

She'd told him Jon visited her office last Friday. The delivery was supposed to come sometime tomorrow night, and Tanner was going to be there. He'd already talked to Sean about their plan. Sean had promised to come to West Oaks tomorrow, too, in anticipation of the delivery. He was going to stay away from Sylvie's house to avoid alarming Jon's friends.

But the minute that package had arrived, Tanner and Sean were going to inspect it. They'd find out what Jon was really doing. And if it was drugs, as they all now believed, Sean would call his friends at West Oaks P.D. to bring down the hammer.

There would probably be a few tense days when Sylvie, Faith and Ethan could be in danger. But Bennett Security owned several safe houses. When it came to protecting people, Tanner knew exactly what to do.

And that buzzing in his mind that seemed to be ever-present the last few days? The nightmares that were keeping him up again? He was going to conquer all of it. He just had to work harder. Maintain his focus.

He kept a pleasant smile on his face, even though he was sweating through the armpits of his suit. There was no one else in this jewelry store, yet his nerves were on high alert. He could feel the threats waiting just out of sight.

Besides, in many ways his stress was justified. Danger was everywhere. He wasn't imagining that.

This world was full of too many bad people. Hiding in the shadows, waiting for you to let down your guard.

"*Thoughts*, Tanner?" Mrs. Zhang had her hand up, a ruby and gold ring on her finger. The sharpness in her tone told him she'd had to repeat herself.

"Sorry. It's...very nice."

"You're awfully dour today. Is anything wrong?"

"Not at all, ma'am. Just keeping an eye out."

Kozinski was outside with his hands in his pockets like he was standing by to direct traffic, not protecting a wealthy woman whom any number of people would happily rob.

Suddenly, there was an explosion in the room. "*Get down.*" In half a second, Tanner had Mrs. Zhang on the ground, his body shielding her, his Glock in his hand.

He scanned for the threat in the room and found the store's security guard staring sheepishly at him. The man bent to pick up a metal water bottle from the ground. "Sorry. My fault. Fingers slipped."

Tanner pushed away from Mrs. Zhang as his mind caught up. That loud clang had been the metal hitting the granite floor. No attackers. No threat. But his body was primed to fight, and his pulse raced like a runaway horse.

He tucked the gun away and helped the client up. "Apologies."

"It *was* rather loud, wasn't it?" She brushed off her clothes. "I'm gratified to know your reflexes are in top form."

Tanner felt the jeweler watching him. Mrs. Zhang went back to examining the rings.

Little had changed in the room, but Tanner felt his nerves fraying. Like the stitches at his seams were unraveling. His muscles tightened, trying to keep himself together. Even the gentle instrumental soundtrack coming through the speakers jarred him.

But he was sure of it now. The water bottle had been a false alarm, but something else was happening. Something was coming. He felt it with his entire being. His eyes strained to identify the source.

Then he found it.

Kozinski wasn't out on the sidewalk anymore. He'd disappeared.

Tanner spoke into the comm system that connected him to Kozinski. "Where are you?" There was no answer.

The world pulsed with every beat of his heart. Tanner turned to the security guard, who was leaning his hip against one of the cases and sipping his water.

"I need to check on…" Tanner murmured. "Keep an eye out here." There was no rear exit to the store, thankfully, which was far more secure. Just the front. But if Kozinski was down, that left the entrance vulnerable.

His fingers moved toward the weapon in his shoulder holster again. He didn't draw it yet.

Tanner pushed his way out into the open air. Sun overwhelmed his vision for a split second, grinding his anxiety into an even higher gear. He'd taken off his sunglasses inside, and now he couldn't remember where he'd put them.

Squinting, he scanned the sidewalk and spotted Kozinski over at the next store front. The kid was chatting with a group of college-aged women in front of an ice cream shop.

White hot fury filled Tanner's veins. He stormed down the sidewalk. One of the girls noticed him coming and took a step back, her eyes bulging.

"What the hell do you think you're doing?"

Kozinski glanced over his shoulder, smug grin morphing into a scowl. "What? They asked for directions."

"Why?" Tanner glared at the young women, wondering if this was some set up. Were they here as a distraction? Was the attack already coming? They averted their eyes, shoulders slouching.

"Dude, you're being an asshole," Kozinski hissed.

Tanner grabbed the other man's arm and hauled him back toward the jewelry store. "Get back to your position. We have to be ready."

"Ready for what?" Kozinski shook him off. "For the little old lady to hand us her shopping bags to carry? I stepped away for a single fucking minute. You're the one who's making this a big deal."

"Do you have any idea how many threats are out there? And you're shirking your duty. Fooling around like it's a game." Any moment could mean life or death. Tanner had seen it happen. Someone could lurch out of the shadows and attack. You could be alive one second, then bleed out the next.

No one was safe. *No one.*

His breaths came faster and faster. He couldn't get enough air.

"And you're a damn *head case*."

Tanner rounded on him. "The fuck did you just say to me?"

Kozinski must've seen something in his eyes because he held his hands up and started backing away.

"I've had enough of your antics," Tanner barked. "You don't deserve a place on this team. You're fired."

"You can't fire me. You're not Max, and you're not a captain. So go to hell, Reed."

"*Fuck* you, Kozinski." Sweat rolled down the back of Tanner's neck. He was gasping for oxygen. His vision was clouding at the edges.

He had to get back inside. Protect the client. That was his duty.

Tanner turned around and found Mrs. Zhang and the jeweler outside, watching them. Both wore shocked expressions. Mrs. Zhang's elegant fingers touched the base of her neck.

"What on earth is going on?"

"Nothing. My apologies. It won't…" He forgot what he'd been saying.

"Tanner, you don't look well. Perhaps we should finish early today."

"Not necessary."

"I insist." Her stern tone brooked no opposition. Her mouth was tight with discomfort. "I'm having my driver take me home now." She took out her phone, turning her back on him.

He and Kozinski were both dismissed. Maybe not just for today. Shit.

She'd asked what happened, and he didn't even know. He was only sure of one thing—if he didn't get out of here, the scream building in his throat would escape.

Kozinski was just standing there, gaping.

"Go back to the office," Tanner said. "I'll deal with you later."

"Where are you going?"

He didn't answer. He had to walk. Get away from the panic and the stares and questions.

Tanner took off his jacket and unbuttoned his collar. He crossed the street, and a car's brakes screeched, horn honking. Tanner flinched at the onslaught. Too much input. Too much of everything.

He found his way to the beachside path. At some point his phone rang.

Noah's name appeared on the screen.

Tanner switched off his phone and kept walking, no destination in mind. Just as long as he kept moving, he could breathe.

Chapter Thirty-Three

Faith's cell rang while she was in the middle of a cleaning. She slipped her hand into her pocket to silence it.

But not long after, as she was finishing up the patient's chart, it rang again.

The receptionist glanced over, her annoyance clear.

"I know, you don't have to say it." Dr. Petrie didn't like phones ringing in the office. That woman's list of pet peeves was long and detailed. Good thing this job paid well.

Faith closed the patient's chart and headed for the break room.

Once she was inside, she checked her call log and cursed out loud.

Myra had just walked in. "Yikes, don't let anyone else hear you. What's up?"

"Jon has called twice." The phone started ringing again in her hand. "And now, here he is again."

This couldn't be good. She answered. "Yes?"

"It's me," he said. "The package is ready early. I have it. I need to drop it off today."

"What? That's not what you said before. You said tomorrow night."

"Yeah, I *remember*, Faith. But now it has to be today. Okay? What is it you're not getting?"

"I'm at work."

"How soon can you get home?"

She looked around the break room, thinking about the rest of her day. The phone calls she'd have to make—Tanner, Sylvie, Ethan. Tanner was supposed to be with her when the delivery came. Would he be able to make it to Sylvie's townhouse in time?

"Come on," Jon whined. "This has to be soon. They're expecting it, and these people are not patient. They're pissed enough about the delays as it is."

"All right. I could be home a little after five."

"Fuck, no. Forty-thirty at the latest."

Her anger boiled over. "*No*, Jon. *Listen* to me, damn it." Faith was shocked by the strength she heard in her own voice. But it felt so good to use it. "I'll be home after five."

"Okay, then. After five." Jon ended the call without saying goodbye.

"What's going on?" Myra asked. "You look like you're about to puke."

"I don't have time to puke. I need to go." Faith stuck her phone into the pocket of her scrubs. "Is there any way you could cover my last cleaning? And…"

"Yeah, I'll take care of things here. Because you're sick, right? You look feverish. And probably contagious. Dr. Petrie would not want you around."

She gave Myra a quick hug. "Thank you. I'll owe you."

"Sure you don't want to tell me what this is really about?"

"Maybe after it's over. I really hope that's soon." *I'm going to do what I have to do.*

∾

FAITH CURSED her stupid bicycle as she coasted up to Sylvie's garage. She was sweaty, and her heart wouldn't slow.

At a red light along the route to Sylvie's place, she'd tried contacting Tanner. But the call had gone straight to voicemail, like his phone was off. It was already well after four o'clock.

Faith still had a key to the house. She let herself in. Still catching her breath, Faith called Sylvie.

"Hey, sweetie."

Faith tried to keep the panic out of her voice. "Jon called. He moved up the delivery to today."

"Shit. Okay. Um, we'll handle it. What time?"

Faith was grateful for her friend's cool head under pressure. "He's supposed to be here soon. I just got home. To your place, I mean."

"Right. I'm stuck at work a little longer. But I'll call Ethan and see where he is. What about Tanner? Is he on his way?"

"He's not answering his phone. I hoped you might know where he is. Is he on an assignment or something?" He hadn't mentioned anything out of the ordinary that morning.

"I haven't seen him. But I've been swamped with my own projects all day." She blew out a breath. "This has caught us by surprise, but your plan is the same. Just accept the package, and the rest of us will be there soon."

Faith ended the call, trying to keep herself from panicking.

She'd thought she was ready. But her friends were supposed to be with her. *Tanner* was supposed to be with her.

She sent him a text, followed by another call. Still no answer. She really wished he were here, even just to reassure her with his presence.

But if she had to do it alone, she'd manage it.

Over the weekend, she'd moved her few belongings over to his house. It hadn't taken long. Secretly, Faith had been laughing at herself, thinking it wasn't such a big deal to move in with a guy when your stuff fit into two suitcases and a plastic storage box.

But it *was* a big deal. Tanner wanted her to be a permanent fixture in his life, and she wanted that, too. More than anything.

Sylvie hadn't said much about the move, and Faith knew her friend had been holding back commentary. It was soon, there was no denying it. With so much going on right now, the stress she and Tanner were both under… It was a lot. But being with him still felt better than anything Faith had experienced before. Tanner felt like home to her.

But although she'd moved her things to Tanner's, she and her friends had decided she shouldn't make Jon aware of her new address. It would've just upset her ex for multiple reasons. As far as their plan was concerned, she still lived at Sylvie's place.

Faith kept trying Tanner's number every few minutes. She was starting to get worried about him, but maybe that was ridiculous. They'd only been dating a short while. Maybe his assignments were like this sometimes. Demanding all his attention.

She paced across the living room. *I can do this.*

The change in schedule was nerve-racking. But Sylvie was exactly right. Soon, Tanner and his detective friend would be able to check out the package and decide what to do. Which meant Faith's part in this was already almost over. She had no reason to be so freaked out right now. She was brave. At least, she wanted to believe that.

Faith jumped when there was a knock at the back door.

Through the kitchen window, she could see Jon outside. He stooped to set something down.

She opened the door a crack. He nodded at the taped cardboard box, which sat on the concrete pad.

"There it is. Take it inside. You can't leave it out here." Jon's face was drawn, his bruises faded to a garish green. Bloodshot veins gave his eyes a red cast. He hadn't shaved in days. "You're not going to mess with it, are you? Please tell me you know better than that by now."

Faith hoped he couldn't see the vein pulsing in her neck, a clue to the adrenaline coursing through her. "I won't." She didn't bend to pick up the box yet, just staring at it. Would it be heavy?

"They'll be here to pick it up in half an hour."

Her eyes shot up. "Wait, what?"

Jon frowned. "Half an hour. I thought you'd be happy to be rid of it so fast."

"But... I don't understand." Her chest was clenching. What about the plan? She didn't even know when Tanner and Sean would get here. "You said I was supposed to store it. Why did you bother bringing it here at all?"

"You're a neutral third party."

"What does that *mean*, Jon?"

He muttered something, head bowed as he started to leave. He was going back on everything he'd said—as she'd known he would. But how far off the rails had this already gone?

"Kyle's not coming here. Right? You swore."

"I tried, okay? But..." Jon glanced back over his shoulder. "Just do your part, and everything will be fine. Take it inside and wait. Half an hour."

"Jon. *Get back here.*"

He walked away, leaving her there in the doorway.

Shit. *Shit.*

Faith dragged the box inside and shut the door, locking it behind her. She was all alone here. She couldn't reach Tanner. And Kyle might be on his way.

Tears of frustration pricked at her eyes.

The box waited right in front of her. Taunting her.

What was inside? What was all this really *about*? Why were Jon and Kyle following her, threatening her, torturing her over this?

She had to know the answer. She was so sick of being in the dark.

Faith went to the kitchen and grabbed a knife. If the box held drugs, she'd call 911. No more of this nonsense. The police would be here when Kyle—or whoever—showed up. Kyle and his friends could run if they wanted. They could try to punish her. But if she did nothing, Kyle might hurt her anyway.

She wasn't just going to sit here, all alone, waiting for it to happen.

Faith remembered every excruciating detail of how he'd held her down, pushing her face into the mattress so she couldn't breathe. How his hands grabbed her inner thighs, bony fingers prodding under the edge of her pajama shorts. He'd wanted to terrify her. Make her think he could do anything. Take anything.

He still could.

She wasn't going to let him.

Kneeling beside the box, she tucked the knife beneath the edge of the tape. The blade slid along one edge of the box. Then the other. Then the center, where the flaps connected.

The knife clattered on the tile when she set it down.

The flaps opened at a touch of her fingers.

Bubble-wrapped items lay on the top, just like the last box Jon had left for her. The one that had held only old dishes.

She wondered if he'd known she would open the first package. If she was just that predictable. It must've been a test, a trap. Forcing her to speak to him again, to let him back into her life.

But just now, Jon had looked too worn down to be capable of any more deception. He'd underestimated her. He assumed she was weak and cowed. So many times in the past, she'd proven him right. Maybe this was only the second truly brave thing she'd ever done—aside from leaving him—but she'd make it count.

Faith gingerly lifted the top item and peeked inside the wrapping. Some kind of commemorative plate. *County Fair 1996*. The next few items were similar. Totally innocent. Boring, even.

But then she removed a rounded dish from the box and saw something beige beneath. Off-white powder packaged under clear plastic.

Chills ran along her arms. Faith had almost been starting to doubt herself, but here it was.

Drugs. What kind, she didn't know. Heroin?

They hadn't even made much effort to hide it. The bubble-wrapped dishes on top would only pass the most cursory inspection.

Faith cleared away more of the decoy items. She didn't even know why she was doing it. She had the evidence now. What did it matter how much there was? Yet she kept going until the next layer was fully exposed. Bricks of beige powder, lined up in rows.

The truth was ugly, but she'd needed to see this. Anger burned away her fear. Jon was such a bastard.

Faith's phone rang, breaking her out of her reverie. The minutes were ticking by, and she hadn't called the police yet. Kyle could be here any moment. Jon had claimed she had half an hour, but why should she believe him?

There was no way she could stay here, hoping rescue would come. She had to save *herself*.

Whoever was calling, they'd have to wait. Faith hefted the box into her arms just as a car pulled up in front of the house. The brakes screeched, and the engine cut off.

Panic sped through her. Was that him? Kyle?

Faith rushed into the kitchen and through the door leading to the garage. She closed the inner door and pressed her ear to the wood, listening. Her hands were sweating, and she struggled to keep hold of the bulky cardboard package.

In the main part of the house, the front door opened. "Faith? Are you here?" It was Sylvie.

Faith exhaled with relief. But Kyle could arrive soon. Or some other awful person. She and Sylvie both had to get out of here.

There was a deeper voice talking to Sylvie. Tanner. Thank god. Where had he been?

Faith set the box roughly on the garage floor, losing her grip at the last moment. A small puff of powder erupted into the air, settling onto her arms and shirt. She brushed the stuff away. She could taste it on her tongue, noxious and chemical.

Disgusting.

Faith pulled open the door, stepping back into the kitchen. "I'm here. We have to—"

She caught only a glimpse of Sylvie and Tanner before everything turned to black.

Chapter Thirty-Four

Tanner was walking along Ocean Lane when a car pulled up alongside him. The window buzzed down, and Sylvie looked over.

"Where the heck have you been? Faith and I have been trying to call you."

"What? Why?"

"Get in. We need to hurry."

Anxiety closed around his throat. Tanner jumped inside, and Sylvie sped off, just making the yellow light at the next intersection.

"Jon moved up the drop-off," Sylvie said. "It's happening today."

Tanner put his hand over his eyes. "Is Faith alone?"

"Yes. I left work as quickly as I could."

And Tanner had promised he'd be there. He'd made Faith agree to call him, and he hadn't even left his fucking phone on.

Sylvie turned off Ocean Lane, heading toward her townhouse. "I saw Noah on my way out of the building. He said he couldn't find you, either. Something went down with Kozinski?"

This was such a mess. Tanner was beyond ashamed. Kozinski had called him a head case, and the kid had been right.

All these months, no matter what was going on inside of him, Tanner had been able to do his job. But yelling in front of Mrs. Zhang? Leaving his own post to chase after Kozinski? Unforgivable. What the hell had he been thinking?

Not thinking. He'd been letting his emotions rule him. Why couldn't he just *get control?* Why was this so fucking hard?

He dreaded what Noah would say. The explanations his captain would demand.

While he'd been walking around aimlessly for the last two hours, Faith had needed him. The shame only got worse. This mess in his brain was like the rip tide, pulling at his feet, trying to drag him under.

He had to get himself together before he saw Faith.

"Tanner?" Sylvie kept glancing at him with concern as she drove.

"Sorry. Yeah, some shit went down with Kozinski. Not important right now." He took out his phone and powered it on. Texts and voicemails appeared.

Oh, god. She must've been panicking when she couldn't reach him. If something had happened, he'd never forgive himself.

Tanner tried calling Faith, but she didn't answer.

Sylvie's car roared down the street and turned into her driveway. Faith's bicycle leaned against the fence. She was definitely here.

They both dashed out. Sylvie jammed the keys into the lock. Turned.

The entryway was quiet, though lights were on. "Faith? Are you here?" Sylvie ran into the living room.

"Maybe we should check your cameras. See if Jon's been here." Tanner was thankful some of his old training had surfaced, tamping down his fear. When he'd used to go on missions as a SEAL, an eerie calm had always settled over him. He didn't know where that calm had been earlier at the jewelry store.

The inner garage door opened, and Faith stepped into the kitchen. "I'm here. We have to—"

Her eyes rolled back, and she collapsed onto the tile floor.

Sylvie screamed, running toward her, arms outstretched.

Tanner took two steps forward. Saw the open cardboard box in the garage. The off-white powder inside. In that moment, too many things made sense.

When he spoke, he hardly recognized his own voice. "Don't touch her."

"Why? Oh my god. Faith!"

There was no time to explain. They had minutes at most. "Call 911. She's overdosing. I need your first aid kit from work. Where is it?"

"My car. My car." She held out her keys, hand shaking.

He sprinted outside. Popped the trunk.

Tanner raced back to the kitchen, already unzipping the small case. Sylvie was talking into her phone, but he kept his attention on Faith. As a SEAL, he'd trained as a medic, and those muscle memories came back to him instantly. Tanner gently rolled her onto her back and checked her airways, her pulse.

She wasn't breathing. Her pupils had nearly disappeared.

Tanner pulled the Narcan from its packaging. Cradling Faith's head and tilting it back, he fit the device into her left nostril. Pressed the plunger to activate the spray. He turned her onto her side, still holding her. She was so limp in his arms. Faith's hair was tangled beneath her in a halo.

"Come on," he heard himself say. "Come on. Stay with me." *Please don't leave me. Please.*

The bloody hole in Scotty's neck flashed through Tanner's mind. *No, no, no.* He forced his thoughts to the present.

Sylvie knelt beside him. "The ambulance is coming. Faith, wake up. You have to wake up."

"Go outside, Sylvie. This whole area could be contaminated." He grabbed a second package of Narcan from the first aid kit, keeping it ready. *Come on, Faith. Please.*

Tanner didn't realize he was holding his breath until Faith took one of her own. "She's breathing."

Sylvie started to sob. She hadn't listened to Tanner's warning, but he couldn't blame her.

He set aside the Narcan and performed CPR. Faith seemed too small, too fragile beneath his hands. He couldn't let his conscious mind think too much about what was happening. How he still could lose her. The same words kept running through his mind.

Stay with me. Stay with me.

Time passed in a blur, though it also seemed to be standing still. Suddenly, the paramedics were here. Tanner didn't want to let her go, but he had to.

"What's she taken?" someone asked. The medic wore gloves and a respirator.

"She didn't take it," Tanner choked out. "Accidental. I think it's fentanyl."

He watched them load Faith onto a stretcher and take her through the front door. Tanner was still on his knees on the kitchen floor. Sylvie's hand rested on his shoulder. "Take my car and head to the hospital. I'll stay here to deal with the police."

He was in a daze. "I don't want to leave you alone." *Like I did Faith. I left her alone when she needed me.*

"Ethan and Nic are both on their way."

Tanner got up and they went outside. The wail of the sirens faded into the distance.

"But I would just *love* for Jon and his drug dealer friends to show their faces here." Sylvie's voice was tight with rage. "They're going to pay for this."

All of the shock and panic of the last few minutes crystallized within him, hardening in his chest. "I'm going to make sure of it."

Chapter Thirty-Five

Faith opened her eyes. She was in a hospital room. Something was beeping. It had to be night because there was darkness behind the window blinds.

Tanner sat in a chair, his elbows on his knees, head in his hands.

"Tanner?" Her voice cracked. She tried to sit up and reach for him, but her arm was attached to something. An IV. But even if it hadn't been, she didn't think she could move. Her limbs were heavy and aching, and her head pounded. She felt like she'd been hit by a truck.

Tanner looked up and rushed to the side of the hospital bed. "How are you feeling?"

"Terrible. But it's so good to see you."

He laughed, yet the sadness in the sound made the ache in her chest even worse. "Pretty sure that was my line."

"What happened?" She remembered getting the delivery from Jon. Opening the box. "Oh, no. The package. It had drugs inside."

He sat on the edge of the bed beside her. "We know. You overdosed. You could've—" Tanner cleared his throat.

"I don't understand. How could I have overdosed?" She

remembered something about the powder spilling. A bad taste in her mouth. It was still there, vile and metallic.

"Fentanyl powder. Even in small amounts, it's potent enough to absorb through the skin. It could've been fatal."

She rested her head against the pillows, feeling nauseous. "Can I have a drink of water?"

Tanner reached out for a glass on a nearby table.

Faith sipped the liquid. Her brain was starting to fit the missing pieces together.

How could she have been so stupid?

"I'm so sorry. I did this. It's my fault." The water almost slipped from her hands. Tanner took the glass.

"Don't say that. I was supposed to be there with you. I'm the one who fucked up. If I'd been there, I could've called Sean like I was supposed to, and you never would've been in that position. There was no way you could've realized how dangerous it was to open that box."

"It's not your fault you weren't there. You were at work."

A nurse came into the room. "Look who's up? A lot of people are going to be very happy. I'll need a little room, though, if your boyfriend doesn't mind?"

Tanner sat back to let the nurse check Faith's vitals.

"This guy saved your life. Did you know that?" The nurse tilted her head toward Tanner. "Paramedics hardly had to do anything but get you here."

He looked sheepish. "Sylvie had her first aid kit. Thank god for that. The Narcan did the rest."

"But you thought fast, so good on you," the nurse said. "Take credit when it's offered."

Tanner shrugged. Faith hated that she'd scared him. He'd been under enough stress already.

The nurse held Faith's wrist. "You're recovering nicely. I'll let the doctor know you're awake. But we're going to keep you here a bit longer to monitor you. You had some very nasty stuff in your system."

There was a question in the nurse's tone, not quite an accusation. But Faith felt guilty all the same.

"Thanks."

Tanner returned to her side, and Faith pressed her face into his chest. He wore the button-down shirt and tailored pants he'd dressed in that morning for work. It seemed like a lifetime ago that they'd woken up together, showered, dressed. Like this would be any other day.

"You saved me," Faith said. "I didn't even know."

"Least I could do. Sylvie would've figured it out if I hadn't."

"But you were there when I needed you. You're always there when I need you." Words were inadequate to express the gratitude she felt for him. The tight, achy, overpowering sensations in her heart that had nothing to do with being sick.

"I just…" She struggled with how to explain it. How to make sense of what an idiot she'd been. "I was just so angry. Jon dropped off the box, and he said someone would be there to pick it up right away. He hinted that Kyle might come, even though Jon had promised I'd never have to see him again. I had to do something." Somehow, in the moment, it had seemed heroic to face the truth inside that box. So she could call the police and point her finger and say, *This is what they've done*.

"It's okay," he said. "I understand. Sometimes, a mission goes sideways. Happens to the best of us."

She'd convinced herself she was being brave. But she just kept screwing up. She was tired of feeling like this. Weak and powerless. Yet she kept ending up in the same place, over and over again. Crushed by the weight of her own misjudgments and mistakes. Stupid impulsive decisions. The way she'd gotten trapped with Jon in the first place. She'd tried to convince herself she could break free of all that, but she hadn't. She'd failed.

Tanner was the one bright spot in her life. But he was

sitting in a hospital room right now because of her. If he'd been with her earlier, he might've been the one who'd overdosed.

He'd trusted her enough to go along with her ridiculous plan. She wished he hadn't listened to her. She wished she'd left town when she had the chance so the people she cared about weren't affected.

She felt a fresh surge of panic. "Is Sylvie okay? She was there, too. Wasn't she?" Faith was fighting back the tears.

Tanner cupped her face in his hands. "Hey, look at me. Breathe, okay?"

She nodded, staring into his brown eyes.

"Sylvie is fine. She's meeting with West Oaks police. I've been in touch with my friend Sean at the LAPD, and he's working with the regional drug task force. They're going to take care of everything. You don't have to worry."

Take care of everything I screwed up, you mean, she thought.

Tanner kissed her gently on the lips. She bet she must taste awful, but he didn't complain.

"I'm just so thankful you're here," Faith said.

He grimaced like the words hurt him.

Tanner held her tightly against him. His breathing was ragged, as if he were the one barely holding together. "Faith, I—"

Someone knocked on the door, pushing it open slightly. "Flowers for a Faith Townsend?"

"Yes, that's me."

A woman with a sunburned face carried in an arrangement of daisies. She set it on a table, eyes darting everywhere.

"Need a signature or something?" Tanner asked.

The woman shook her head, slinking toward the door. Tanner frowned, seeming to study her narrow shoulders.

"Who sent the flowers?" Faith said.

Tanner stood up and checked the card. He handed it to

Faith. The card said, *Get well.* No indication of who'd sent it, which seemed odd.

But then Sylvie appeared in the doorway, which the delivery woman had left open. "Hey, can I come in?"

Faith nodded, and Sylvie dashed over, pulling Faith into a hug. "That was awful. Never, ever do that again."

"Play with a box of full of fentanyl? I don't intend to."

"Tanner," Sylvie said, "Noah's out in the waiting room, along with half the people we know. He seemed anxious to talk to you."

Tanner bit his lip. "Shit. I should probably go find him, then." He bent to give Faith a soft kiss. She pressed her palm to his cheek, smoothing it along his whiskers. Faith wondered why he was so tense about seeing his friend.

"See you later?" she asked.

"I'll be back. You can't get rid of me." He winked, then stepped through the door, closing it behind him.

Sylvie was shaking her head. "You two. Just get married and have five kids and a dog, already."

Faith looked down at her blanket, smiling sadly. If only it were that simple. "I'm so sorry, Sylvie. I really messed up."

Sylvie sat beside her. "Come here." They hugged again. Faith wiped her eyes, taking in a shaky breath.

"Any chance you know where my phone is?" Faith asked.

Sylvie picked it up from the nightstand. "This is it, right?"

Faith was relieved it hadn't gotten lost in the chaos. She quickly tried to check her notifications. There were a few, but the display said *No service.*

Sylvie tilted her head, probably noticing Faith's frustration. "I haven't got service in here, either. But most everyone you know in West Oaks is out in the waiting room. Nic, Ethan, Luis. Some other bodyguards from Bennett Security. Myra, from your dental office."

"Myra's here?"

"Tanner had her number, and I called her. Figured you'd

be out for work tomorrow and wanted to make sure your boss got word."

Faith embraced her friend yet again. "Thank you." Dr. Petrie wasn't going to be happy about her missing work, but at least the office had notice. Faith hoped she wouldn't miss more than tomorrow, though. She couldn't afford to.

"Do you want me to ask Myra to come in?" Sylvie said.

"Would you?" That idea brightened her mood even further. Sylvie and Myra were her two closest friends in West Oaks, apart from Tanner. And the two women didn't even know one another.

A few minutes later, Myra raced into the room with all the energy of a hurricane. "What the freaking heck, Faith? Oh-em-jeez."

Faith laughed and accepted yet another hug. She didn't think she'd ever gotten this many hugs from this many different people in a short period. Not even from her family. Myra sat on one side of the bed, Sylvie on the other.

"You know," Myra said, "if I'm being honest? I thought you were paranoid about the drug stuff. Don't get me wrong, I love drama. But I had no idea your ex was actually going all *Breaking Bad*."

"Except it wasn't meth," Sylvie pointed out. "She *wishes* it was meth."

Myra's eyes narrowed. "Which sounds super weird taken out of context."

Faith giggled.

Sylvie looked thoughtful. "Myra, I heard you may have been present at the infamous double date. Is that true? When this girl started out with one guy, then hooked up with another by the end of the night?"

"Um, you mean, hooked up with *my date*?"

"Can we not?" Faith was rolling her eyes.

"Already are," Myra said. "This story is too good to keep to myself."

Sylvie pointed across the bed at her. "Yes. I can tell this lady's a keeper. Leave nothing out."

Myra launched into an over-the-top retelling of that night. Faith's friends snuggled into her, and she let her head fall back against the pillows.

Physically, she still felt like crap. But despite the awfulness of this day, there was a warm sensation building inside of her. A tiny flame that refused to go out.

Chapter Thirty-Six

*I*n the hallway, Tanner found two familiar faces. One was Nic, Sylvie's boyfriend. The other was Max Bennett, Tanner's boss. The two men had been conversing quietly.

Inwardly, Tanner cringed, though he maintained a stoic expression.

Nic and Max were friendly with each other, though they weren't "friends" as far as he could tell. Their backgrounds couldn't have been more different. Tanner hadn't liked Nic much at first, either. But the guy was head-over-heels for Sylvie, and he'd moved on from a pretty dark past. Tanner had to admire that. Maybe Nic could give him a few pointers.

Max patted Tanner's arm. "How's your girlfriend?" He'd never met Faith as far as Tanner knew. He must've heard from Sylvie or Noah about their relationship.

"Getting better. They're going to keep her a little longer."

"You need anything? If you think she's still in danger, you can have your pick of guys to guard her door."

"I could stay, too," Nic offered. "Or grab food. Coffee. You name it."

"Coffee would be great, actually. Black."

"I'll be right back." Nic smiled, obviously happy to have a task. Tanner had mostly needed to get rid of him to have a word with Max. There was no getting around this, and Tanner knew he should be the one to broach the subject.

"I'm, uh, sorry about what happened earlier. With Mrs. Zhang." There was no way Max hadn't heard. Noah would've told him so they could do damage control with the wealthy client. "I meant to call you myself, but…"

"Don't worry about that. Sounds like it was just a misunderstanding. You have much bigger priorities at the moment."

"I take my responsibilities very seriously."

"I know you do. That's why I can count on you."

But would you if you knew all of it?

He owed his boss a candid explanation, but Tanner couldn't bring himself to do it. Not here, outside Faith's hospital room. Not just a few yards away from the waiting area, where a bunch of his teammates were sitting.

"Right now, though," Max said, "you can count on *me*. Sylvie told me how important Faith is to you. Whatever you need, just ask."

"Thank you." The muscles in his shoulders unclenched. "That means a lot."

Max gripped his shoulder again, then let him go.

Tanner wandered over to the waiting area. He spotted Devon Whitestone and nodded in greeting.

And Kozinski was here, too. What the hell?

Noah jumped up from his seat. Sean was next to him.

Noah pulled Tanner into a hug, cursing so loud a nurse looked over and frowned. "I can't believe this mess. It's nuts."

"Tell me about it. What's Kozinski doing here?"

"Showing his support. Like all of us." Noah frowned at him. "Sean said this has something to do with Faith's ex? Like that package she brought to the office before?"

Tanner caught his friends up on the details. Noah and Sean each knew bits and pieces. Yet he tried not to reveal anything Faith had told him in confidence.

"I've been talking to the task force," Sean said. "Jon's delivery was heroin cut with fentanyl. Like you thought, Tanner. Bigger profit margin, and most buyers don't have a clue it's not pure. Just a few months ago, we had a prosecutor collapse in the middle of a courtroom when he was handling the same kind of evidence in front of a jury. Shit goes right through the skin."

"I'd heard that, too." Which was how Tanner had realized what must be happening to Faith. Even in small doses, street fentanyl was incredibly lethal to people who had no tolerance for opiates. Death within minutes unless an antagonist like Narcan was administered.

"Your friend Sylvie will need to have her house decontaminated," Sean went on. "West Oaks is putting together an arrest warrant for Faith's ex-husband, based on the camera evidence of him delivering the package."

"What about the people who were going to pick it up?" Tanner asked. "Faith said it was probably Kyle Spaulding."

Sean shook his head. "There's reasonable suspicion to bring him in for questioning. But unless Kyle confesses, or Jon is willing to point the finger, we might not be able to hold him. Just for the other misdemeanor assault charge."

So, once again, they had little on Spaulding. Faith was terrified of the guy, but that wasn't enough.

"I'm relieved Faith is okay," Sean said. "I need to head back to L.A. Anything else you need, man?"

Tanner appreciated the offer. He'd never had so many people looking out for him. It felt good, but also a bit uncomfortable. He was used to being the one looking out for his friends, not the other way around. "Nah, I'm good. Thanks for all you've done."

"I just wish I could've done more and prevented all this in the first place."

After Sean had left, Tanner turned to Noah. There was so much he needed to say. He thought maybe he could get it out, and if he hesitated even a few minutes, he'd lose his nerve. "Can we go outside and talk?"

"Yeah. Sure."

Tanner double-checked that Faith wasn't alone. Myra and Sylvie were with her. Plus, a handful of Bennett Security bodyguards were still in the waiting room. So he had little to worry about.

He and Noah went through the automatic glass doors into the parking lot. Tanner sat on a concrete bench. The streetlights bathed the lot in pale yellow, and cars drove past on the nearby boulevard.

"I missed your call earlier," Tanner said.

"Yeah. Kozinski got in touch, bitching and moaning about you. I was surprised you didn't pick up."

"I was…walking. Needed to clear my head."

Noah sat next to him. "Not the first time I've heard that from you."

Very true. Even before his concussion, Tanner had relied upon time outdoors to keep himself steady. He'd been convinced he'd defeated PTSD. But he'd had all sorts of crutches. His mantras, his walks. An unfailing positive attitude, masking the uncertainty inside.

Out with it, he thought. *It's time.*

"Remember how I told you a while back I had PTSD? Because of being wounded in Afghanistan after you left the teams?"

"Of course."

"It's not really past tense anymore."

Noah paused, studying him. "Okay. How long have you been having trouble?"

"The concussion. Six months ago."

"Jesus, Tanner. You've been keeping this to yourself that long?"

"At first, I thought it was purely physical. I hoped it would go away on its own as soon as my injuries were healed. But then the nightmares came back. It just seemed to build. I couldn't face the fact that I'd gone backwards. It was so… demoralizing. Knowing I'd failed."

"You didn't fail. You were on a different part of the path."

Tanner snorted. "Bumper sticker."

"What?"

"Never mind." It was what Faith would've said, and Tanner didn't feel like explaining their inside joke. "I didn't tell you because I wasn't letting my problems affect work. When I was working, I felt like myself. Focused. I could tune out all the other noise and just do my job. But today?" Tanner shook his head, sighing. "Today, I was a mess. I couldn't keep it together." He'd been distracted. Even confused. He could've put Mrs. Zhang in real danger—not just by missing something important, but by overreacting.

Tanner had just wanted to keep protecting people. But he couldn't do that anymore. PTSD had robbed him of so much. He wanted to cry, thinking about it.

Fuck. His eyes were stinging.

"I've been wondering for a while if something could be wrong," Noah said. "You seemed off for months. Then after I realized you had feelings for Faith, I thought that explained it. The way you acted that night at the restaurant, flipping out on that guy who ran into her."

"Yeah. It was because of my feelings for her, but also… not. It was more than that."

"And I was more than happy to accept the easy explanation. I should've paid closer attention. I should've asked."

"I wouldn't have told you. With Faith… Is it okay if I talk about her with you? I don't want to be an asshole."

Noah nudged his shoulder. "You are anyway. But I forgive

you. Tell me whatever you want. Not like I was in love with her."

Tanner's heart raced at those words. "With Faith in my life, in my…" His cheeks were burning, which was embarrassing. "In my bed, I feel genuinely happy for the first time in a while. She's the best thing that's happened to me, maybe ever. I thought I could conquer my issues out of sheer willpower to be worthy of her. For a few days, it even seemed to be working. But then the nightmares came roaring back. It was like the highs were higher, but the lows were lower, too. And…"

His voice was breaking up. "Today, when Faith tried to reach me to ask for my help, I wasn't there. I was too wrapped up in my own shit. And she almost died."

He felt Noah watching him. But Tanner couldn't meet his friend's eyes. The words kept flooding out of him.

"I can't ignore this anymore or wish it away or pretend it's not beating me. But I don't know what to do. I don't *know*. I don't…"

A tear streaked down his cheek. A thousand more wanted to follow.

"You've never told me what really happened when you were wounded. I heard you were shot. Captured."

"Five days," Tanner murmured. Yet it had felt like five years. He'd been trained for it, and he'd done everything he was supposed to do, swallowing down the horror and bearing the pain until he was rescued.

The nightmares and the panic only came much later.

"I don't know how to talk about it." Anytime he tried to imagine saying the words, he drew a blank. How could he describe what it had been like? Thinking he'd die in that darkness, knowing what they'd done to Scotty's remains. His thoughts of Scotty's family, his own. Wondering how Mom and Dad and Kaylee and Brayden would feel when they heard he was dead. Mutilated.

"That's okay." Noah put an arm around his shoulders. "I love you. You're my brother, and I love you. No matter what."

He hiccuped. "Even if I stole your girl?"

"She was never my girl, man. She was always yours."

My girl. "I think I'm in love with her."

As he said it, he knew it was true. His heart pulsed, *Faith, Faith.* He loved her.

"Then I'm happy for you. But I want you to have whatever you need to get better. Because I know you *will* get better. At your own pace. Maybe you should take some time off work. Paid, so don't worry about that. But you need to see a professional and get help with this."

He'd known this was coming, and he hated it. "This feels like a punishment. Everything's worse when I have nothing to focus on."

"Shouldn't you ask why that is? Be uncomfortable. Embrace the fear. See what happens."

He flipped Noah off.

Tanner's friend laughed. "Maybe I deserved that. But it's still true. Trust me, if this is a punishment, it's on me, because I'll have to figure out how to do without you. I'll be counting the days till you're back. But let's make sure that, when you do come back, you're ready."

"What will Max say?"

"Same thing I'm saying. You honestly doubt that?"

No. He didn't doubt it.

"What do you think?" Noah asked.

"I think… Yeah. Time off is a good idea. I'll be there for Faith. And aside from that, I'll figure out what to do with myself." He was so tired of fighting. Tanner wanted to figure out how to get back to living.

WHEN HE RETURNED to Faith's hospital room, Tanner found Devon standing sentinel outside. It was ten at night.

"You're still here?"

"Of course. We've got your back. Kozinski's next on the night shift." Devon held out a coffee cup. "Nic brought this over. I think it was for you?"

"That's okay, it's all yours." He reached for the doorknob, then paused. "Tell Kozinski thanks for me?"

Devon gave him a crooked grin. "Maybe you should do that yourself, after your little tiff this afternoon."

"You heard about that?"

"Everybody heard, but trust me, we all knew Kozinski had it coming. You'll make a decent bodyguard of him yet."

"*I* will?"

"Yeah, when you're a captain. Noah can't deal with all these assholes on his own."

Tanner appreciated Devon's vote of confidence. But he was heading into a hiatus from work, not toward more responsibility.

The guys were all going to hear about that soon enough, too.

"I'm going to be taking a little time off," Tanner said.

Devon's eyebrows drew down. "Oh. For Faith?"

"Not really, no. I'll do whatever I can for her. But this is really for me." Tanner scratched his head. He was sweating, and he wondered if Devon saw any redness around his eyes. He'd sat with Noah for a while outside, long after the tears had stopped.

"I have PTSD."

"Damn. That sucks. If you ever need to talk, I'm here."

Second person today Tanner had told, and Devon wasn't looking at him like he was an alien. Tanner had known he wouldn't, of course. But fear wasn't always rational.

Tanner gave Devon a one-armed hug, and his friend

returned it. "Now get in there," Devon said. "Your girl's waiting for you."

Faith looked up when he went in. Tanner's heart lifted to see her. She'd showered and changed into fresh clothes, and her hair was braided over one shoulder. Dark half-moons still bordered her eyes, but her skin had recovered much of its glow.

"How're you feeling?"

"So much better. A West Oaks detective stopped by, and I gave my statement. Sylvie left a little while ago. She and Ethan have to get a hotel until their place is cleaned. I feel really bad about that."

"We're all just thankful you're well. Did the detective say what they're doing to find Jon?"

Faith shrugged. "Not really. He seemed like he didn't want to make any promises. It's frustrating."

"I know." Tanner reached for her hand. "You told the detective about the threats against you, right?"

"I did."

"Even if the police don't catch up to him, Jon lost a bunch of product yesterday. If he was working for a cartel, he's in trouble. And if he *wasn't* working for a cartel? If he was violating some group's territory? He's in even worse trouble. Same with Kyle. They're probably out of the state by now."

"I hope so."

Tanner sat next to her. Faith cupped his cheek, and he leaned down for a gentle kiss that sent tingles of desire down his spine.

"I wish we could go home now," she said.

"You're feeling *that* much better?"

She laughed. "Maybe not. But good enough to enjoy seeing you naked. That's my favorite new hobby."

He flexed a bicep for her, making a goofy face. "They wanted you to stay for observation, right?"

"But I'd rather sleep in your bed."

"Our bed."

"Yes," she whispered. "Our bed."

He loved this woman, and as soon as he worked up the courage, he'd tell her. "Well, as of now, I'm available for all your personal bodyguard needs. You won't be able to get rid of me."

Not until Jon Townsend, Kyle Spaulding, and their drug dealer friends were either in a jail cell, or they'd left town. Or they were down in some other way. If any of them came after her, Tanner would do whatever was necessary.

"What do you mean, you're available?"

He put an around her, settling back against her pillows. "The last few days, my head hasn't been in a great place."

She nodded against him.

"Today, it just got to be too much. I blew up at one of the other guys. I had my phone turned off because I was upset. Which was the worst possible timing." A lump had gathered in his throat at this admission. "That's why I wasn't answering when you called. I can't even tell you how sorry I am."

Faith sat up and ran her fingers through his hair. She didn't need to say anything. The softness of her touch said it all. But he really didn't want her comfort right now. He was supposed to be the one comforting her.

He pressed on. "I told Noah the truth about everything. I told Devon, too. Max will be next. I'm going to take some time off work to get better."

"I'm glad. I want you to have everything you need."

He wanted to tell her he already did, right here in his arms. But that wasn't fair or true. It wasn't Faith's responsibility to heal him. She just gave him all the more reason to seek out healing for himself. Even if that meant opening up and talking about things that terrified him. Talking about the things that happened in Afghanistan. Somehow, he'd figure out how to do it.

But he had to keep his girl out of harm's way. What was the point of saving himself if he didn't save her, too?

"Let's go home," she said. "Tomorrow we can sleep in as late as we want. We don't even have to get out of bed."

That did sound nice. Just the two of them in his upstairs bedroom, secluded from the world. Safe.

Tanner kissed her forehead. "Okay. I'll tell the nurse and see what else we have to do. Then I'm taking you home."

Chapter Thirty-Seven

The nurse removed the IV and told Faith she was cleared to leave. Quickly, she checked her phone, wanting to text Sylvie and Myra about being discharged. They'd asked for updates, no matter how late at night.

But Faith's phone still had no service. Her reception had been spotty since waking at the hospital.

"Ready to head out?" Tanner asked.

She tucked the phone in her pocket. She'd text her friends later. "So ready."

"I'll swing by the nurse's station to let them know, and then I'll go pull the car up front."

The nurse had said she would have to be escorted out in a wheelchair.

Tanner paused in the doorway. "Kozinski's right out here in case you need anything."

The other bodyguard leaned his head in and waved. "Just yell, 'Leon.'"

He was young, probably early twenties, with a heavy layer of stubble on his face. Faith knew Leon wasn't Tanner's favorite person. But he'd won some points with her by helping out. Tanner's fellow bodyguards were obviously the best kind of people—loyal to a fault. Even Leon.

"I'll be fine. I'll see you soon, Tanner."

Her boyfriend winked at her, then took off down the hallway. Faith sat on the bed to wait.

Her mind kept wandering to Jon and Kyle, stressing over where they were. What would happen.

Jon had sounded so desperate when he'd told her about his problems in Texas. The people he owed money. And Kyle... She remembered what Jon had said about him. *He's like a snake who can slither through the smallest crack.* She had a nagging feeling in her gut that there was still more she didn't know.

Yet having Tanner around was doing a lot to keep the fear at bay.

Faith knew taking time off work would be difficult for him. But she was incredibly proud of him, too. Telling Noah had been a very big deal.

Never in her life had she experienced the kind of closeness she and Tanner shared. Despite what they'd both gone through yesterday, they'd come out stronger for it.

She'd nearly died of a drug overdose, and Kyle might still try to come after her. If Jon was prosecuted, she might have to testify or something. But she'd also never felt this excited and optimistic about her future.

An orderly brought the wheelchair into her room. "Ms. Townsend?" she said. "Your ride's here." She had a deeply tanned face and wore scrubs and thick-framed glasses.

"I'm just waiting for my boyfriend to get back," Faith said. "I'll be ready in a sec."

"Oh, there was one more test the doc needed first."

"A test? What for? I thought I was done."

The orderly shrugged, holding out a form. "They just tell me where to go. This is your name, right? Faith Townsend?"

She confirmed the paperwork did indeed have her name

at the top. Had the doctor decided on an extra precaution at the last minute?

"They're expecting us," the orderly said tensely. "Third floor."

"It'll be quick? I'm really ready to go."

"That's what they said."

"All right." Faith sat in the wheelchair. The faster she got this over with, the sooner she could go home.

Kozinski looked into the room. "Should I come with you?"

"That's okay. Wait here for Tanner. Tell him I'll be right back." She didn't want Tanner to return to the room and find her gone with no explanation. If her stupid phone had been working, she could've just texted.

The orderly wheeled her down the hall, going surprisingly fast. They'd turned in the opposite direction from the nurse's station. "Isn't the elevator behind us?" Faith asked.

"There's another down here. Less crowded."

They reached the elevator. The orderly pushed the down button, her hands fidgeting at her sides.

Faith looked over at the woman. "You said the third floor. That's up, not down."

"Whatever. This is the way we're going."

Then the realization hit her. This wasn't some orderly she'd seen around the hospital. This was the flower delivery woman who'd come to her room before.

Faith shot to her feet just as the woman pulled a knife from her pocket.

The elevator dinged, and the doors slid open. "No questions. Get moving." She took a step forward, brandishing the knife.

"*No.*" Faith tried to dart away. The woman grabbed hold of her elbow with a shockingly strong grip. The knife went to Faith's throat. She could feel the blade against the vein throbbing at her neck. Terror made her lightheaded.

"If you scream, you die."

The woman pulled her into the elevator, and the doors slid closed.

Chapter Thirty-Eight

Tanner jogged across the concrete toward his Jeep. It was after midnight now, and the parking lot was quiet. He could see the construction site looming beyond a wire fence, the large vehicles all dark and silent.

The place felt like a wasteland, despite the flowering bougainvillea bushes planted in rows across the parking lot in an attempt to soften the landscape.

He couldn't wait to get Faith to the comfort and familiarity of his house. He was exhausted after the day's events. Yet there'd been good things, too. He'd told Noah and Devon the truth, and that confession had been a relief. Max would have to be next, and Tanner was nervous about that upcoming conversation with his boss. But Max had spent years in Army Special Forces. He would understand.

Tanner just wished he'd made this leap earlier before things had gotten so bad. He shouldn't have needed this terrible situation to force him to finally open up.

Despite everything, Faith hadn't walked away from him yet. If anyone could stick by him through this, he believed it was her.

She'd stuck by Jon for a long time, too, but Tanner knew

this relationship would be different. He couldn't force himself to be well for her, but he could devote himself to the hard work necessary to heal.

And he'd make her feel loved, every single day.

In fact, he was going to tell her as soon as he went back inside the hospital. He felt the words bubbling up.

I love you.

He unlocked his Jeep and opened the driver's side door, glancing around as he always did. Keeping an awareness of his surroundings.

Then he noticed the pickup idling over near the construction site.

It had a tarp over the bed. Just how Faith had described Jon's truck.

Someone was sitting behind the wheel, and exhaust puffed from the tailpipe.

Tanner got into the Jeep and used his keys to unlock the glovebox. He'd stored his Glock inside, since the hospital didn't allow weapons. He had a tactical knife here, too, but he left it in its place. Nor did he bother with his shoulder holster.

This was probably unnecessary. But he felt better with his side arm in his pocket.

He gently closed his driver's side door, then crouched down to move closer to the idling truck.

The license plate was black on white, a star in the middle.

Texas.

It was Jon. The bastard was here, at Faith's hospital.

What the hell did he want?

Tanner looked over at the hospital building, wondering if he should go back inside right now to check on Faith. But Jon was here in the truck, and Kozinski was right outside her door. Leon was an idiot, but he wasn't so stupid that he'd let anyone into Faith's room.

Tanner reared back into the shadows as the truck's door opened.

A man got out. Stringy blond hair, unshaven face. His clothes were rumpled. He looked nothing like Kyle, whose image Tanner had seen on the security video from Faith's house. This had to be Jon Townsend.

Jon started toward the hospital entrance.

Tanner wanted to grab hold of this man and demand answers. Because of Jon, Faith had been miserable for years. She'd almost died. Tanner felt that rage close to the surface, crying to get out. To take revenge on this man who'd nearly killed an innocent woman.

The woman Tanner loved.

But just like earlier, when Faith had been overdosing, his training was kicking in.

Tanner approached quietly until he was within arm's reach. "Excuse me, are you Jon?" He spoke calmly, but with authority. He didn't want Jon to immediately run.

The guy spun around, eyes wide. "Uh, sorry?"

"You're Jon, right?"

He looked Tanner up and down, and that familiar wariness appeared in his eyes. The same thing Tanner had seen in countless others. The privilege of being someone his size.

"Yeah." Jon's voice had squeaked. "What do you want?"

"My name is Tanner. We need to talk."

"About what?"

"Faith." He took a step closer. He could smell the sweat oozing from Jon's pores. The fear.

Jon's gaze darted around, though he didn't speak. Didn't move.

"Do you know what happened to her this afternoon? How she almost died?" Tanner forced himself to keep his voice even, even though he wanted to scream and take Jon by the shoulders and shake him.

Something changed in Jon's eyes. A spark of defiance. "You're him, aren't you? The guy Faith mentioned. You're the one who's *fucking* my *wife*."

"She's not your wife anymore."

"Like hell she isn't. Until I sign those divorce papers, she's still Faith Townsend. That's my name. *Mine.*"

Tanner shoved him up against a parked car with one hand. *Don't be stupid*, his rational mind warned. *Don't do this.* But he didn't want to listen. "Do you have any idea what you did to your *wife* today? You almost killed her."

"That wasn't supposed to happen. If she'd just done what—"

Tanner pulled Jon forward, slamming him again into the side of the car. The guy's whining and excuses made him sick.

He remembered how small and lifeless she'd been. Lying limp on the floor as her lungs stopped working, as her heart slowed.

Tanner pulled back his fist. "Give me one reason that I shouldn't put you in the hospital right now. You're the one who deserves to be there, not her."

Jon flinched and closed his eyes, turning his head away from the coming blow. "You're right. I know."

Tanner's arm trembled. His pulse throbbed in his throat.

Faith wouldn't want him to be doing this.

If she were here right now, he knew exactly what she'd say.

She'd want him to show mercy. To choose to see the possibility of good in Jon, even if the guy didn't deserve it.

Tanner dropped his fist. He let go of Jon's shirt, stepping back. "What are you doing here? Why haven't you left town? Whatever shit you were into, it's over."

"I know I'm pathetic. Okay? If I could go back, if I could change a thousand different things, I would. But I can't." Jon slumped against the car. "I never wanted to work with Kyle again in the first place, but this was my last hope. I have to disappear. But I couldn't leave knowing she could still be in danger."

"So you're here to warn her? Of what? Do you know something specific?"

"Just that Kyle will want blood." Jon blinked back tears. "Please tell me you can protect her."

"I have friends who are with her right now, watching out for her."

He sighed. "That's all I want now. For her to be safe. Tell her I'm leaving town. I swear, I'm not going to hurt her anymore."

Tanner studied the man in front of him. He couldn't tell if Jon really meant what he was saying. Maybe the guy believed it, even though he'd gone back on his word more times than anyone could count.

"I'll pass it along. But she's not yours anymore, Jon. If she ever was."

"I did love her." He lifted his bloodshot eyes. "You'll take care of her, right? The way I never could."

"I will."

Nodding, Jon slunk back toward his truck.

Tanner's anger had faded away. Maybe Jon had finally realized how much he'd lost. That wasn't punishment enough in Tanner's mind for what he'd done, but maybe it was the best any of them would get.

As for the police? He'd call them the minute Jon got in that truck to report the man's location. They could deal with Townsend as they saw fit. But his primary duty wasn't Jon—it was taking care of Faith. He had to get back to her.

Tanner headed toward the hospital. Faith was probably wondering what happened to him.

Behind him, a cell phone rang shrilly.

Jon said, "Kyle?"

Tanner stopped and glanced back.

"I'm…I'm in West Oaks. Yeah." Jon had a look of utter shock on his face.

Tanner felt a change in the air. Jon's sudden terror telegraphed across the concrete.

Tanner started walking back toward him.

"Don't hurt her," Jon choked out. "Kyle, hold on, wait—"

Tanner started running. He was about to yank the phone away when Jon's arm dropped to his side, phone dangling from his fingers.

Tanner waited, holding his breath. But he already saw the truth in the other man's eyes.

"Kyle's got her," Jon whispered. "He's got Faith."

Chapter Thirty-Nine

The sunburned woman pulled Faith out of the elevators and into a dark hallway. Faith felt the tip of the knife poking through the fabric of her shirt into her back.

"What do you want?"

"For you to shut up and do as you're told." The knife moved back to her jugular, almost breaking her skin. "I'm warning you. Stay quiet."

Never. Faith screamed, and the knife cut into her neck with a searing burst of pain. Her scream turned to a choked cry.

"I told you to be quiet."

Hot blood trickled down her neck. Faith held her hand against the cut. Her eyes searched for a way out. She had to get away.

They'd come out on the basement level. The woman pushed Faith in front of her, the knife at her back. The hallway was brightly lit, but it felt deserted. A few doors stood open, revealing offices, all of them empty for the night.

Up ahead, a thick sheet of plastic bisected the hallway. It moved slightly, like the inner membrane of some creature, breathing.

When they reached it, the knife briefly left Faith's back and sliced a long cut through the plastic.

"Hurry up." The woman almost shoved her through the gap. Faith tripped forward, just barely catching herself. Her hand left a bloody print on the plastic.

This part of the hallway looked like the one behind them, with open doors leading into offices. Yet it was like stepping through into a different dimension. The walls were half demolished. Ductwork and pipes lay exposed beneath. Wires hung in tangles. White dust covered everything.

Her skin itched with alarm. Was there some way she could get the knife away from the woman? Could she run into one of the other rooms or hallways and hide?

"Do you work for someone? Is that it?" She tried to keep her voice steady. She had to stay calm. Had to think.

"Stop asking questions."

"Is it Kyle?"

The woman cringed, like the name frightened her.

Panic rose in Faith's throat. She lunged forward, trying to run, but the woman's grip tightened on her arm, and the knife dug into her armpit, cutting her again. "*Stop.*"

"Then do as you're told."

Every moment seemed to stretch endlessly. They kept going, further and further through the broken maze of hallways. Deeper into the construction area.

The air turned cooler, smelling of exhaust and saltwater. Faith thought the woman was taking her outside.

But instead, they turned a corner. There was a light in a room up ahead.

When they reached the open doorway, Faith saw him standing inside.

Kyle. He was here. She whimpered involuntarily.

The woman shoved Faith into the room. She caught herself against a chair. There was almost nothing else here, aside from a built-in countertop and cabinets.

Faith lifted her chin. "My friends already know I'm missing. They'll be looking for me." But she couldn't hide the tremor in her voice. She was afraid.

The last time she'd seen Kyle, he'd hit her. He'd threatened her more than once. And that had been before she'd ruined his and Jon's plans. She didn't even want to think about what he would do to her now.

Kyle glanced at her neck. "She's all cut up."

The other woman shrugged, averting her eyes. "She wouldn't be quiet."

"Yeah, she has a problem with that, doesn't she? I'll teach her." Kyle smirked at Faith, then turned to the woman who'd posed as the orderly. "Did anybody see you, Jenny?"

"There was some guy in the hallway outside her room, but I told him I was taking her for a test. And there was a boyfriend with her earlier when I brought in the flowers."

"Boyfriend already? You move fast." Kyle leered at Faith. "Where's her phone?"

Jenny gave it to him. She must've taken it from Faith's pocket. He switched it off and stowed it in his jacket.

"But nobody saw us come down here. I checked for cameras, like you said." Jenny was fidgeting, moving her feet back and forth. Faith realized it now—Jenny's mannerisms were those of a drug addict who needed a fix.

Kyle held out his hand. "Give me your knife."

"What? Why?"

"Because I fucking *said so*."

Don't, Faith thought. *Tell him no.*

Jenny looked down at it in her hand. "But I need it. I gotta protect myself. You must have your own."

"But I want that one." Kyle grinned. He was enjoying this. Proving his power in the room.

Jenny handed the knife over, and Faith's stomach dropped even further. Kyle palmed it.

"That's more like it." He pulled a small bundle of bills

from his pocket. He held them out, then yanked them from Jenny's reach. "Do I have to remind you what will happen if you tell anyone about this?"

Jenny shook her head vigorously, eyes on the filthy linoleum.

"That's good. Cause I have enough shit to do without having to come after you, too."

Jenny crammed the bills into her coat, then scurried out the door.

Faith heard her footsteps retreating down the hall.

Kyle turned around and faced her. His eyes took her in, glowing with pleasure at what he saw.

"Get away from me." Faith tried to dart past him. She gasped as he lunged at her, pushing her hard into the wall. Faith kicked at his knee, but he easily deflected.

The knife blade went to her ribs, the tip sharp and threatening. The cut at her neck pulsed with pain, sticky and wet with blood.

"You've caused a hell of a lot of trouble for me." His voice was frighteningly soft. Treacherous. "You must've thought I'm as spineless as your husband. Like my word doesn't fucking mean anything. Makes me think you don't know me at all, Faith."

He kept coming, so close that his body pressed up against hers.

Her legs were shaking. Her teeth chattered, even though she clenched her jaw shut. She turned her head to the side, trying to somehow avoid him.

Her eyes caught on something on the ground, down at the base of the wall. A piece of metal.

Kyle grabbed her chin and forced her to look at him. "But don't worry, we're going to get to know each other even better. By the end of this, you'll know just who I am."

"Go. *Away.*"

He pulled back his hand and smacked her across the face. Another starburst of pain made her vision blur.

Kyle backed away, and she sucked in a grateful breath. The knife had left a hole in the front of her shirt, which was already soaked with blood at the collar. Her cheek stung and her eyes watered as she stared at the floor, finding the piece of metal again.

What was it?

Kyle took out his phone and held it to his ear.

"It's me. Try to listen, even though that's hard for you. Where are you right now?"

Faith knew he had to be talking to Jon.

Think, she told herself. *Find a way out.*

But what?

"If you ever want to see your wife again, you'll do exactly what I say. You know what I want. We'll meet in twenty minutes at the West Oaks Hospital. Tell a soul, and she's dead. Have an independent thought in your brain, and she's dead. You just wait for me to call with the exact location for the trade. Got that? Twenty minutes."

Chapter Forty

Tanner's heart had stopped.

"What do you mean, Kyle's got her? That's not possible." She was upstairs in her hospital room. Kozinski was standing guard outside.

Jon's phone made a noise. "Oh, fuck." He held it up.

Faith's picture was on the screen, standing against a white wall, her face a mask of both defiance and terror.

The world fell out from under Tanner's feet. *No. No. This can't be.* Hands shaking, pacing the concrete, he got out his phone and called Kozinski's number.

His voice didn't sound right when he spoke. "It's Tanner. Is Faith in her room?"

Please, he thought. *Please.*

"No," Kozinski said. "An orderly took her for some kind of test. Should be back soon."

Tanner couldn't even speak. He couldn't even think about how stupid he'd been to trust Kozinski for even a second.

Kyle had her. Where was she? What was Kyle going to do to her?

"Tanner?" Kozinski asked. "Is something wrong?"

"Yes," Tanner ground out. "Something's very *wrong*. Faith is—"

Jon's eyes widened. "You can't. I'm not supposed to tell *anyone*. Or he'll kill her."

Kill her. Cold sweat broke out over Tanner's skin.

Tanner punched *End* on his screen, debating what to do. He wasn't about to take orders from Kyle. Or Jon Townsend. But should he call the police? Call Devon and the other bodyguards at Bennett Security?

He needed to think.

Jon bent over at the waist, bracing a hand against the nearest car. "I was afraid of this happening. What are we gonna do? I can't give him... I *can't*."

Tanner grabbed Jon's shoulder and slammed him against the car. "Can't give him *what*?"

Jon's head was darting side to side. Looking for some way out.

Tanner brought his nose an inch from Jon's. "Tell me. What does Kyle want?"

"The drugs. The rest of what I have." Jon's voice was high-pitched. Desperate. "But—"

"You'd better not finish that fucking sentence. There is no 'but.' So this is how you knew Kyle would come after her." This bastard knew he had something Kyle wanted, and Faith was the only bargaining chip. "You have more of that shit you brought to Faith's house?"

"No. Not that. This is..." Jon swallowed. Tanner hadn't loosened his grip on the man's shirt. "It's the rest of the heroin I brought here from Texas. It's pure, worth a lot."

Faith had told Tanner the story Jon shared—about how he'd taken on more product, hoping for a big profit, and then gotten robbed. He'd turned to Kyle for help. "What exactly was the plan?"

"Kyle had the idea to bring the last of my stash to L.A. and cut it with fentanyl so we could stretch it out, make back the money I owed. We'd done it before in Texas, but on a much smaller scale. This time, we needed more people, a bigger market where we'd go unnoticed."

The words kept rushing out of him, as if he could make this better by finally telling the truth. As if it wasn't too late. "I found some guys online who worked in a lab and would handle cutting the drugs, and Kyle was supposed to manage the sales side, keeping under the radar of the L.A. cartels. Faith's house was going to be our transfer site. A place to store the stuff where nobody would pay attention. But Faith was a buffer between me and Kyle, too. Because I didn't trust him, and I know he's never trusted me."

"You fucking coward. You wanted to use her. Used her to protect *yourself*."

Jon squeezed his eyes closed. "I was trying to be careful. I only brought the stuff to the lab guys a little at a time. Then I was supposed to take the final product to Faith's so Kyle could pick it up. Right away, I had second thoughts. I told him Faith couldn't be involved after all, and Kyle was so pissed. He... He tricked me into meeting with him, and then he beat me up. Tried to make me give up the rest of the heroin. But I'd put it in a safe place for that reason. So Kyle couldn't backstab me and cut me out of the deal."

And Jon had lied to her, claiming she'd never have to deal with Kyle again. "So you thought you'd sacrifice Faith instead?"

"I didn't want this to happen. I could've just left town this afternoon when it all blew up, but I didn't. I tried to warn her. I *tried*."

Tanner was getting the impression Jon wished he'd chosen differently. "Where's the rest of the heroin?"

Jon's eyes darted toward his truck.

Dragging the other man along with him, Tanner went back to the Ford pickup. "*Where?*"

"This is all I have left, man. There must be some other

way to get her back."

"You've never been the husband Faith deserved. Have you?"

"I…"

"*Have* you?"

"No." Jon was crying. "I haven't. I'm sorry for it. I am."

Tanner held Jon by the arms, and he was sure if he let go, Faith's ex would fall into a heap on the ground. But Tanner couldn't let him.

The only way this would work was if Tanner took command.

"I know you're sorry," he said softly. "But right now, Jon? Tonight? Faith needs you. And you're going to man up. You're going to finally be the man she needs you to be."

Snot ran from Jon's nose. "How?"

"I'm going to help you. But first, you're going to show me where you're keeping the heroin."

"Okay," Jon whispered. He went over to the truck. He reached up into the wheel well above the rear tire. There was a snapping sound.

Tanner drew his gun and pointed it. "It would not be wise for you to play games with me right now."

"I swear. I'm not." When Jon pulled his hand out—slowly—he held a cellophane-wrapped brick of heroin. "There's eight more of these, hidden all over the truck."

Tanner exhaled, putting his gun in his pocket.

"Where did Kyle say to meet for the hand off?"

"Just somewhere around the hospital. He's supposed to call me in twenty minutes to tell me exactly where. Less than twenty now, I guess."

"Did he know you were here already?"

"No. But I told him in I'm still in West Oaks. He probably thinks I'm driving here now."

"Show me the picture again."

Jon nodded, taking out his phone. "Okay."

Tanner studied the image, ignoring the awful pang in his heart. The wall was white. Stained. He saw the corner of an empty shelf on one edge of the photo. Where had this been taken? *Where?*

"She hasn't been gone long from her hospital room," Tanner said, thinking aloud. "And we'd have seen the car if he'd driven her out of here." Unless he'd gotten her into an ambulance and driven her out that way, but Tanner couldn't imagine Kyle being that resourceful. Besides, he needed to keep her close, which meant he wouldn't have gone far.

There was only one place he'd be able to keep Faith hidden until he was ready for the hand off.

"He's got her in the abandoned part of the hospital. The construction area."

"Then what do we do?" Jon asked. "Just wait for Kyle to call?"

"No. That's not good enough."

Kyle had her *right now*. He could be hurting her. And no way was Tanner trusting Kyle to turn her over as promised.

They had only minutes to find Kyle and catch him by surprise. But to do that, Tanner needed a plan. He needed more people he trusted. More *time*—to talk to witnesses inside the hospital, check cameras. But he had none of that. He couldn't wait for his fellow bodyguards to get here, and he couldn't take the risk of getting the police involved.

Tanner could feel the seconds ticking away. He drew the Glock 22 again, checked the magazine. Jon tensed, cringing away, until he returned the weapon to his pocket.

"You'll need to do exactly as I say," Tanner said.

"You have a plan?"

"The start of a plan." It would have to go just right, no room for error. Which, given the pathetic resources at his disposal, was a fucking nightmare.

Tanner pulled out his phone again and went to his recent calls.

Chapter Forty-One

Kyle ended the call, then held up the phone and snapped a picture of her. She flinched when she heard the camera sound.

His thumbs moved over the screen. "There. Now he's got your photo. He knows I'm serious."

She felt the tiniest bit of hope. Kyle hadn't just taken her for some kind of sick revenge.

She was a hostage. It was a negotiation.

And her gaze kept flicking down to that discarded piece of metal by the wall.

It looked like a scalpel.

Faith cleared her throat, trying to get her voice to work. "You said Jon has something you want? What is it?"

Kyle's eyes hardened as he looked at her. She forced herself to maintain eye contact, though she wanted to stare at the scalpel. Figure out how to get it. The small piece of metal was just a few feet away. But if she went for it, would Kyle stop her? Would he get there first?

"You want to know where I first met Jon? He bought pills from my neighbor in the next trailer over. He was Mr. Star Football Player, the kid everybody loved. That's what you saw in him, right?" He sneered at her. "He thought he owned the world. Used to come to my neighbor's at all hours, making noise like we were just white trash that lived to serve people like him. When pills weren't enough anymore, it was smack. Then he tried to screw over my neighbor, and that guy wouldn't sell to him anymore. Jon came slinking over to me, begging for my help. He's always thought he could ask for help and get whatever he wanted in return with no consequences."

Kyle's cruel grin turned smug. "Now, he knows better. He's not the one in charge. But you know what the truth is? When it comes to Jon, it's not even me who's in charge. It's that need inside of him. He'd trade anything for it. Probably even you."

Kyle leaned against the counter, crossing his ankles casually. "So I guess you better hope he's willing to give me what I'm asking for. This will be the hardest test Jon has ever taken, and I can't wait to see what he does. He either gives me the supply he's been holding back, or he abandons you. And I get to do whatever I want with you."

She didn't want to talk about the second option. Would Jon actually abandon her? Was he capable of it? Just leave her in the hands of someone like Kyle Spaulding?

The sick feeling in her stomach told her the answer.

"What supply? What does that mean?" She shifted her weight, ending up a step closer to the scalpel.

But instead of explaining, Kyle rolled his eyes. "Aren't you Miss 'I'm So Innocent.'" He advanced on her, brandishing the knife. The blade poked another hole into her shirt, this one right between her breasts. "You think you're too good for me. Stuck up little bitch. But here's the secret. Even if Jon trades for you, I didn't promise I'd send you back good as new."

With all her strength, Faith shoved him back and dove to the floor. Her hand closed around the handle of the scalpel.

Kyle was laughing. "You're just making it easier for me." He bent over her, grabbing hold of her hair.

Faith rolled, ignoring the painful yank on her scalp.

She brought up her hand and swiped the scalpel across Kyle's face.

He reared back, screaming. But Faith didn't wait to see how bad he was hurt. She just rocketed upright and ran.

She dashed down the hallway, dodging tools and hanging plastic. Her heartbeat rushed in her ears.

Kyle's scream turned into a bellow of rage. He was coming after her.

Faith kept running down the hallway. She saw a deeper darkness up ahead, beyond the flapping of a loose sheet of plastic.

Outside. She was almost there.

But Kyle's footsteps were closing in.

Faith grabbed a heavy drill and threw it behind her. Kyle grunted. She caught a glimpse of him, hand clutched to his bloody face. Just an arm's reach behind her.

Hurry. Hurry.

She ran through the gap in the plastic and immediately fell, rolling down a dirt slope. She slammed into something huge and solid. The wind was knocked out of her.

It was the tire of some construction vehicle.

She forced herself upright, trying to ignore the ache in her lungs and her head. The stinging at her neck. The hospital towered nearby, windows bright. But the construction site was a dark divot carved into the landscape. Massive vehicles hulked around her.

Faith scrambled forward. She only made it a few steps before Kyle slammed into her. She sprawled in the dirt. He grabbed her arms with wet, sticky hands.

Her shoulder joints protested as he yanked her up.

The blade of his knife pressed into her throat just above the other cut, the pain sharp and cold. She clenched her teeth, whimpering.

"Don't you dare scream." Kyle's voice was slurred. Blood

covered the lower half of his face, and something was wrong with his mouth.

She must've slashed his lip open with the scalpel.

The tip of Kyle's knife traced her windpipe. She was scared to move, scared even to breathe.

"I changed my mind," he said. "When Jon gets you back, it'll be piece by piece." The blade traveled up her neck to her ear, scratching a painful trail along her skin. "Starting with—"

"Kyle, let her go."

Jon. He'd actually come.

Kyle's head craned, looking for the source of the voice. Faith couldn't move her head because of the knife. Then, mercifully, Kyle loosened his grip on her and the blade pulled back.

Faith turned.

Jon held a duffle. He was making his way down the dirt slope of the construction area, shoes sliding.

"What the fuck is this, Jon?" Kyle demanded. "If you think you can get the jump on me—"

Another man appeared at the top of the slope. He was in silhouette, the security lights of the parking lot bright behind him. The metal barrel of a gun glinted, pointing straight at them.

Faith's heart stuttered in her chest. Was it Tanner? It had to be.

Kyle pulled Faith in front of him, her back pressed to his chest. The knife went to her throat. She screamed as the blade bit again into her skin. Another hot drip of blood rolled down her neck.

"I brought what you wanted." Jon threw a duffle into the dirt. The zipper was open, and something white showed on the interior. "All of it. I swear."

Kyle was tense and jittery behind her. Faith could sense his indecision. "Then why is some asshole pointing a *gun* at me, Jon?"

The other man descended the slope at an agonizingly slow pace, one foot in front of the other.

His face came into view. Faith's eyes widened in shock.

Kyle brought his mouth to her ear. "Is that him?" he muttered. "The boyfriend?"

"Y-yes."

Jon grimaced, running his hands through his stringy hair. "Kyle, listen. This is everything you asked for. Everything I have. That was the deal. Just take it. *Please.*"

"No. The deal was, if you told anyone, she was dead. Did you think I was *playing?*"

The knife bit deeper, and she choked back another scream.

"It's not my fault," Jon cried. "He was there when you sent the picture."

Kyle's chest heaved against her back as he breathed. "Here's what's going to happen. Boyfriend is going to set his gun on the ground by the bag. Then he's going to back up, slowly. Either of you tries anything? This knife is going into Faith's jugular."

"Don't—" she began, before Kyle tightened his grip on her, forcing her to cut off her sentence.

Faith's eyes didn't leave the gun as it lowered to the dirt.

Tanner, what are you doing? she thought.

She didn't understand what was happening. How was this possibly going to turn out all right?

Kyle pushed her forward, and she almost fell. "Walk," he said. Together, they went toward the duffle bag full of drugs. The gun lay abandoned on the dirt.

When they got close to the duffle, Kyle pushed Faith onto her knees. "Pull the bag over to you."

She grabbed the straps and dragged it toward her. The knife pressed into the back of her neck. When she tried to stand, Kyle poked the tip of the knife deeper.

"Stay there. Don't you fucking move." He stooped to pick

up the gun. "Thought you'd found yourself someone to protect you?" Kyle murmured to her. "That's where you're stupid. If you can't protect yourself, you're fucked. Nobody can help you. Your boyfriend's about to find that out."

"Don't," she whispered. "Please."

"You still haven't learned yet, have you Faith?" He pointed the gun at the men across from them.

"*No.*"

Faith moved before her thoughts could even process what she was doing. With a sudden surge of rage, she grabbed for the gun. The knife sliced across her skin. But she'd taken Kyle by surprise.

He was forced to drop the knife, and their hands grappled for the gun.

His grip was stronger. The barrel turned toward *her*.

Kyle pulled the trigger.

Chapter Forty-Two

The gun made a hollow-sounding click.

At the same moment, Tanner's arm closed around Kyle's neck. With his other hand, he pointed his tactical knife into Kyle's lower back.

He could feel the shock radiating through the man's body.

Surprise, you fucker.

Across from him, Kozinski smiled. The kid had actually done what he was supposed to do. So had Jon.

The magazine for the gun was back in Tanner's Jeep. The weapon in Kyle's left hand was worthless.

"Let her go." Tanner was giving the guy one last chance.

He didn't take it. Instead, Kyle threw the gun aside and grabbed Faith by the hair. He yanked her head backward, his other hand closing over her throat.

"Get back," Kyle screamed, "or I'm going to snap her n—"

Tanner jammed his tactical knife forward in Kyle's kidney. Instantly, the man's body seized, his grip faltering. Faith broke away from him, falling to her hands and knees and scrambling upright.

Tanner pulled the knife free, ready for the next strike. But

Kyle was already collapsing onto the dirt. Dark wetness soaked the clothes around the wound.

Faith had a hand to her neck. Blood dripped between her fingers. "Tanner."

She had her eyes on the knife in his hand. The metal gleamed red in the low light. His fingers opened, the knife falling to the ground, and Faith ran into his arms.

"You're hurt," he said.

"Kozinski seemed like he was pretending to be you, and I didn't know where you were. I thought Kyle was going to… I couldn't let him…"

"I know. You did great. But it's over now." He kissed her forehead, breathing her in for one blissful second. "I have to let you go for a minute, okay?"

Tanner bent over Kyle. The guy wasn't dead yet, but he'd die soon without medical attention. Tanner didn't need Kyle's death on his conscience, scumbag though he was.

He put pressure on the wound. "Hang in there, asshole. Paramedics won't take long." Tanner looked up at Kozinski, who was standing there watching. "Did you call them?"

"Yeah. Police are on their way. Ambulance, too."

"Where's Jon?" Faith asked.

Good question. Though Tanner wasn't especially concerned. The duffle bag of heroin was still here.

Kozinski shrugged. "Must've just run off. Can't have made it far. Should I go after him, Tanner?"

"Nah, let the police deal with him. At least you didn't let him swipe the drugs."

"I'm not *that* much of a dumbass."

"Coulda fooled me." Tanner let a smile ghost across his face to show Kozinski he was forgiven for the past issues between them. Mostly.

Kyle was unresponsive. His face had turned almost snow-white.

Tanner heard sirens. But if they didn't hurry up, Kyle wasn't going to make it.

"Leon, could you take Faith to the parking lot? She doesn't need to see this."

"I'm not going anywhere," she said, crouching beside him. "Not unless you're with me."

Tanner locked eyes with her. He hadn't prayed in a very long time. Maybe not ever. But right now, he was thanking every god who might be listening that his girl was safe.

∼

TANNER DIDN'T KNOW what time it was when they got home. It was light outside, but that meant nothing. He'd gone beyond exhaustion. Faith looked dazed.

"Come here." He and Faith held one another in the living room. He brushed her hair back, just looking at her. Grateful beyond words that she was standing here with him.

Her neck was bandaged, but thankfully, the cuts hadn't been too deep. The paramedics had cleaned the small wounds. She'd spoken to the police, reassured her friends that she was heading home.

The police had guards on Kyle's hospital room. He was alive, last Tanner heard. There'd been no word yet about Jon, who was running from all the problems he'd helped cause. Tanner had to imagine they'd track him down soon. The police now had more than enough reason.

Tanner also planned to put in a good word for Kozinski with Noah and Max. He still didn't like the kid, but after Leon had helped save Faith, they were square.

Tanner had washed away any visible remnants of Kyle's blood from his skin, but he still felt dirty from the last day's events. He couldn't imagine how Faith must be feeling after what she'd been through.

Now that they were home, all the overwhelming

emotions Tanner had been suppressing started to rise to the surface. Terror at almost losing Faith. Regret that she'd seen him with blood on his hands, even though it had been necessary.

He wanted to take care of her. Make her feel safe. Show her how much he loved her.

"There's so much I need to say. I don't even know where to begin."

"Maybe we should start by getting cleaned up?" she asked.

He smiled. "Yeah. That would be good."

They went to the bathroom. Tanner started the shower to let it heat. They both undressed, tossing their clothes into a pile.

Under the spray, Faith put her face against his chest. He wrapped his arms around her and let the water wash away the sweat from their skin.

He realized she was crying, and his heart nearly broke. Tanner whispered comforting words and held her until she lifted her head, sniffling.

"Okay. I'm done. I really, really want to be done."

"I want that, too." He wished healing worked that way. "What do you need? What can I do?"

"Just take me upstairs. Don't let me go."

He nodded, kissing the wet skin of her shoulder.

They dried off. "I need to fix my bandages," she said. They were peeling away from her neck.

"I'll do it." Tanner grabbed his kit and replaced them with gentle fingers.

They went to the bedroom, hand in hand. Sunlight streamed through the window. Faith got under the covers beside him, using his chest as a pillow.

"Thank you," she whispered. "I appreciate everything you did for me. But I wish I could've done it myself. You know? Stopped Kyle. Kept him from hurting me or anyone else."

"You did a lot. You got him outside, where it was a hell of

a lot easier to find you and get my plan to work. And you tried to save Kozinski's life by going for that gun."

"But if I'd been faster or stronger, I could've gotten away."

"It's okay to need help."

"My new bumper sticker?"

"I have more. Bravery and strength come in all forms. Not just physical. You've made it through a lot, and you're still here."

"So are you." She smiled, another ray of sunshine, but it faded too quickly. "You saved my life twice in the past twenty-four hours. I know you probably would've done that for anyone, given your job, but…"

Tanner put his fingers on her chin, gently lifting her face until she was looking back at him. "You're not just anyone." How could he make her understand how much she meant? How she was saving him in a different way, right now? He could only think of one way. And why the hell was he hesitating?

"I love you. I'm *in* love with you."

A wrinkle appeared between Faith's eyebrows. She frowned, eyes filling again with tears.

Not the reaction he'd been hoping for.

"I…" Faith wiped at her eyes. "I love you, too. I love you so much. I've been waiting a long time to say that to someone and know in my heart I mean it."

"I wish you didn't have to wait so long."

"But it was worth it." Faith kissed him, and Tanner pulled her close. Her skin was smooth. So soft it made his chest ache. Everything about her was precious and beautiful.

They kissed for a while, murmuring I-love-yous in between. Then they lay still, looking at one another.

"Turn over?" she asked.

"Why?"

"I want to admire the rest of you."

Tanner rolled onto his stomach. Faith stretched out over

him, her hair tickling the back of his neck. She dragged her fingertips up and down his spine, following with kisses. He knew she was touching his scars.

"Where did you get these?" Her voice was barely more than a whisper.

"Some of it was training. But the worst ones…" He breathed through the squeezing sensation in his upper body. "Happened in Afghanistan. We were going after a high-value target. But the intel was bad. We got ambushed. My friend Wayne Scott was right in front of me, and I couldn't save him."

Tanner's body armor had stopped the rounds in his back from killing him. There were bullet wound scars on his right upper arm.

Faith laid her head between his shoulder blades, still tracing her fingers along his skin as he spoke.

"I was captured. Tortured." The long scars on his back were knife wounds.

He wanted to tell her all of it if she truly wished to hear it. But it didn't have to be now. They had time, a miracle Tanner felt deep in his bones.

"I'm not okay," he said. "I haven't been for longer than I'd like to admit. But I'm going to do whatever it takes to get better."

"I know. I believe in you."

For several long minutes, they both remained still. Birds glided past the window and clouds moved, making shadows dance through the beams of sunlight on the walls. Tanner felt like he'd let some small part of the past go. Like a few of the spirits that haunted him were flying free.

Then, slowly, Faith kissed each of the scars on his back.

Her kisses and caresses moved to his shoulders, his arms. Then further down. The base of his spine and the backs of his thighs. Pleasure sang in all his nerve endings. His cock swelled, and his hips rocked gently into the mattress, chasing that feeling—urgent and immediate and *alive*.

He turned back over, wanting to see her face. She hummed when she saw his erection.

"We don't have to," he said.

"I want to. I love you." The straightforward way she'd spoken these words—as undeniable truths—made him want to hold her and cherish the incredible gift of simply being alive and in love.

Faith took his cock in her mouth. Tanner tipped his head back and moaned, eyes closed. She licked up and down his shaft, and her hand moved down to cup his balls. "I never thought I'd love doing this so much," she said. "You taste so good on my tongue."

A moan was the only response he could make. He lost himself in the attentions of her mouth and her touch.

But more than even this, he wanted to look into her eyes and sink inside of her. To feel the intensity of their connection.

Tanner sat up, enjoying the view for another moment. "Come here, baby." Faith lifted her head. Her tongue darted over her swollen lips.

He reached toward the nightstand for a condom, then scooped her up with one arm and positioned her beneath him. Tanner sheathed his erection, never taking his eyes off the incredible woman in his bed.

Tanner kissed his way down her body, taking his time getting her ready. His fingers and his tongue worked in and out of her until she was panting, and her opening glistened with wetness. The heady, spicy scent of her was making him lose control. He couldn't contain his need.

Tanner sat up, knees bent, one hand braced against the mattress by her head. He pushed her thighs wider with his own and thrust his cock inside of her. Her body gripped him so tightly he felt weak for a moment.

His free hand gently touched her face. Her blue eyes gazed back at him, hooded with desire.

He bent down so his lips grazed hers. "I love you."

Tanner rolled his hips, fucking her gently but deeply. Faith responded to him like they were completely connected, their minds in sync. Their bodies glided together, finding a steady rhythm. The heat between them slowly increased.

When Faith's breathy panting grew desperate and needy, Tanner turned them over so she was on top of him. Her body reacted almost immediately to the new position. Faith's breath hitched. Her thighs squeezed around him as she shuddered. He would never get tired of seeing her like that—swept away in those moments of pure pleasure. Tanner loved making her feel that. Feel *him*.

He pulled her down and held her close, whispering how beautiful she was. She whispered back I-love-yous. He felt his own climax coming. So close. Almost over the edge. Tanner rolled her back over and pumped into her.

She sighed, her breath hot against his cheek, and he came undone. His cock pulsed inside her.

Mine, he thought. He knew what a gift this was. Loving her, earning her love in return. He wasn't going to waste it.

Chapter Forty-Three

"Faith? Dr. Petrie wants to see you in her office."

As soon as the receptionist left, having borne the bad news, Faith groaned.

"Dude, what did you do?" Myra asked.

A visit to their boss's office was rarely a good sign. Faith ran through the possibilities. Had she forgotten an appointment? Had a patient complained? "Guess I'd better go find out."

The door to the office was open. Dr. Petrie looked up from her tablet computer. "Faith, come on in. Close the door?"

Faith did as the dentist asked and sat down in a chair in front of her desk. The room was perfectly organized, not a paper out of place, not a single picture frame crooked. Even the potted plant had symmetrical leaves.

"Is there something wrong?" Faith asked.

"Why would you say that?"

Faith tried to smile, pretending this meeting wasn't giving her an ulcer. "No reason."

"Well, I just had a call about Gabriella."

"Oh, no." Their eight-year-old patient who'd been having

so much trouble with her teeth lately. "Is she all right?" Faith hadn't seen the girl or her mother in a couple of weeks.

Dr. Petrie flattened her hands on the surface of the desk. "She's doing great. Her mother wanted to let me know they're going on vacation to Costa Rica, and they plan to do some horseback riding. Apparently, Gabriella has talked about nothing else since you gave her a drawing? Of a horse?"

Faith nodded, still unclear what this was about.

"Her mom credits you for keeping Gabriella's spirits up through all her procedures and complications. I'm relieved she's out of pain, but it's thanks to you that she's been handling all of this so well."

Faith hardly knew what to say. "I'm so glad she's doing better. And going on vacation? That's a big step." Gabriella's mom had mentioned before it was hard for them to leave home because the little girl was so often in pain.

"Most kids with her problems would hate seeing me, but her mom is right. You've made this into a relaxing place for Gabriella to visit. Her mom is grateful, and so am I. Well done."

She didn't think Dr. Petrie had ever paid her a compliment before. "Thank you."

"I know you've been going through some tough times lately," the dentist went on. "I had a difficult divorce several years ago myself. I know how it can be. I realize I don't always come across as sympathetic, but I am."

The woman said all this awkwardly, like it wasn't natural for her. But not everyone communicated in the same way. Faith almost laughed, she was so relieved. Dr Petrie actually liked her? Was this happening?

"Doctor, I work hard here. I give our patients my all. You're right, I've been through some tough times, and I haven't always felt supported here. If I give you feedback on office policies, would you be willing to listen?" Faith had been taught to be respectful of her superiors. But that didn't mean sitting quiet.

Dr. Petrie nodded. "I may not agree with you. But I will listen. If there's anything you need, a way I *can* support you, well…you'll let me know?"

"I'm doing much better now, actually. My divorce is final, as of today."

"That's quite a milestone. Are you doing something to celebrate?"

Faith grinned. "I am. I have big plans."

"With your boyfriend?" The dentist must've seen her blushing. "Don't worry. I'm not criticizing. I heard Myra talking about him."

Why wasn't she surprised? "My boyfriend's out of town visiting his family. I'm going out with my girlfriends."

"Sounds like the best way to commemorate the occasion." Dr. Petrie stood and offered her hand. "I'll see you bright and early on Monday, as usual?"

"Yes, Doctor. Looking forward to it."

∽

TANNER'S SISTER Kaylee drove up to the valet stand.

"What do we do now?" Faith asked, craning her neck to watch the activity in front of the restaurant. She'd thought people got dressed up to go out in West Oaks, but that was nothing to the people strolling along Sunset Boulevard.

Myra leaned forward from the backseat. "Faith, have you never parked at a valet before?"

"Are you really that surprised?"

"You are so freaking cute," Kaylee said.

Sylvie piped up. "I'd like the record to show that I did not laugh. However, Kaylee is right. You're *really* freaking cute."

Faith stuck out her tongue at her friends.

She was excited about this night out. Tanner's sister was

staying with her, and the two of them were quickly becoming close friends. Kaylee was ecstatic about having a weekend away from her three kids, and Faith was just happy to be out with her friends.

Except for this whole valet parking thing, which still seemed a little weird. Just turning over the car to some random person? Her dad would never have been okay with it.

The valet finally arrived. They all got out, and Sylvie snatched up the ticket. "I'm holding onto that. I don't want one of you to lose it drinking twenty-dollar cocktails."

"Good," Kaylee said, "because this mama hasn't been out on the town in a year, at least. I plan to get crazy, so look out." She put an arm around Faith's shoulders as they went inside. "There's only one rule tonight—you do not tell my older brother how drunk I get."

Faith scoffed. "I would never."

Inside, loud music, laughter, and chatter filled the air. Servers passed by holding vividly hued cocktails and tiny, Instagram-ready bites of food. This was the fanciest restaurant Faith had ever stepped into. It was like something from a movie, all swanky fabrics and dim lighting and off-duty models as bartenders.

She and her friends had worn sparkly dresses and heels, and Faith felt a little bit like a movie star herself. Going out on Sunset Boulevard in Los Angeles was one of her bucket list items. But it definitely wasn't Tanner's scene. This was the perfect place to experience with her girlfriends, sipping fruity drinks and watching the impeccably dressed people around them.

The prices on the menu made her eyes bulge, but tonight was about celebrating her freedom. She resolved not to worry about it.

A little while later, the four of them raised their glasses in a toast.

Kaylee was sitting next to her in the booth. Sylvie and Myra sat across from them.

"What do you want to bet Tanner is changing a diaper right now?" Kaylee asked.

Tanner was at the farm helping out his brother-in-law with the boys. He'd planned to spend a lot of time with his brother Brayden as well.

Faith cracked up. "I'm sure he'll dive right in. He's all about embracing discomfort."

"Well, he's welcome to it." Kaylee bumped Faith's shoulder with hers. "You miss him, don't you? I see that wistful look in your eyes."

"I can't help it. It's our first weekend apart since we got together. I know it's only been a couple of months, but it feels like longer."

"Doesn't matter how long it is. When you're with the right person, you just know. I miss all my boys like crazy, but it's good to have a little break. I promise, when this weekend is over, you'll enjoy seeing Tanner that much more."

Myra leaned over the table. "And I bet the sex will be that much better, too."

"Don't really need to hear details. But yeah, it's probably true." Kaylee wrinkled her nose. "I just know I've never seen Tanner this happy. I'm glad he has someone like you to look out for him. He's always been so concerned about other people and not as good about watching out for himself."

Tanner had told his family what he was going through. They'd been just as supportive as Faith had expected.

Sylvie raised her lemonade in agreement. She was the designated driver. "That's Tanner exactly. He's one of my best friends, and to see him with another of the people I love? I can't even describe how great it makes me feel."

Faith's nose burned. They were going to make her cry. She'd never felt so loved and supported as she did on a daily basis in West Oaks. It was hard to believe this was really her life. It was more than she'd ever hoped for or imagined.

Faith had spoken with her mother and siblings, sharing the truth about Jon's arrest and the reasons for it. They were coming around to her side. She didn't know how much she wanted her family in Texas to be a part of her life.

But Faith hoped she could have a good relationship with her mother someday, even if her mom never outwardly acknowledged how detrimental Faith's marriage had been.

These women, right here—they were a family to her, too.

The four of them ordered too much food and drank too many cocktails with ridiculous names, except for Sylvie, who rolled her eyes at them. As it got later, a dance floor opened up on one side of the restaurant, and Kaylee pulled Myra over with her.

Sylvie slid into Faith's side of the booth. "So, how does it feel to be officially not-married?"

Faith looked into her near-empty glass. "It's hard to describe. But it's good. So, so good."

She'd had a lot of ups and downs in the last two months since her near overdose. Jon and Kyle were now both in jail, with charges pending related to their drug scheme. Kyle also faced multiple charges for her assault and kidnapping. Both men were expected to plead guilty, which would save Faith from having to testify in court about everything that happened. She would've done it, of course. But she was glad to know with certainty that Kyle would be punished. Both he and Jon faced years in prison.

Jon had written her several emails, but she'd chosen to communicate with his public defender instead. She wished him peace. But a clean break was going to be better for the both of them in the long run.

Both Jon and Kyle were segregated from the main population in the jail after threats on their lives. Apparently, the L.A. cartels had heard about their activities and didn't look kindly on the violation of their territory. She didn't wish for Jon or even Kyle to be hurt. Whatever happened, it was beyond her control, and she simply tried not to think about it.

Everything she'd been through had brought her here to this moment. How could she have any regrets?

"I would never have come to West Oaks if it wasn't for you," she said to Sylvie. "You forgave me and took me in. You're my real family, and I could never pay you back for all you've given me."

"Oh, you can't say stuff like that and not hug me. I'm way too sober for this."

She and Sylvie hugged each other tightly. Once again, Faith was fighting back tears.

Sylvie dabbed at her mascara. "You know, you didn't mention the fact that I introduced you to Tanner. I would've thought that would come first on your list of thank-yous."

"It does rank pretty high."

Somehow, loving Tanner made her feel freer instead of tied down. She couldn't wait to find out what adventures they'd have and what the future held in store for them.

With Tanner, she couldn't believe how fulfilling each day was. For a long time, she'd been missing out on affection and passion, but Tanner was certainly making up for it. Every single morning when she woke up next to him, she was excited about what the day would bring. The jokes they'd share, the new experiences. And of course, the sex.

So much amazing sex.

At some point, she figured the chemistry between them would ebb to a low simmer instead of a full-on forest fire. But there were no signs of that happening yet.

"It seems like he's doing really well," Sylvie said. She'd admitted to being shocked when she found out Tanner had PTSD. She'd felt bad for not realizing how much her friend was suffering. "Whenever I ask, he claims you deserve the credit."

"That is *not* true." He'd done all the work. All Faith had done was be supportive. Loving Tanner wasn't difficult. Nothing felt more natural. She couldn't imagine doing anything else.

"But you were exactly what Tanner needed. And he's what you need. It's the same thing Nic and I have, and I know what a difference that makes—finding that kind of connection with someone. It makes everything else easier. I'm glad you both found where you belong."

"So am I."

Epilogue

"Who would like to get us started?" the group leader asked. "Who's got something they'd like to share?"

Tanner raised his hand. The leader called on him, and he shifted in his hard plastic chair. "I went to visit the wife of my buddy who died."

Everybody here knew who he meant. He'd told them about Scotty's death and what happened after, though he couldn't be too specific on the where and when. He'd told the story enough times now that it no longer felt like his throat was about to close up.

"It was the high school graduation for Scotty's younger son. I'd corresponded with his wife off and on since he died, but it had been a while since I'd visited her in person."

"And how did you feel about seeing her?" The group leader was a former Marine. He'd lost both legs to an IED in Iraq.

This was a support group for veterans. Many of the members suffered from PTSD. Tanner had been attending every week. Sometimes he brought Noah or Sean along with him since they were both veterans themselves. Devon had come a couple of times, and the former Army Ranger had talked about losing his twin brother to violence, though his brother had been a cop, rather than a service member.

Even Tanner's boss Max had attended with him once. The former Green Beret had spoken about some of his own difficult memories from his time overseas, when he'd been racked with guilt over having to leave his younger sister behind in the states.

"It was good to see her," Tanner replied. "But hard, too. It's always been hard thinking about Scotty's family not having him when I'm still here."

Many others in the group were nodding.

"But I was grateful to be there. And proud to see the men his sons have grown up to be."

Tanner and Scotty's widow had stood on the grass, the New Mexico sun beating down on their heads, watching the graduates cross the stage. Faith had come with him on the trip, but she'd stayed at the hotel that day. She would've joined him, of course, but he'd thought it would be better to chat with Scotty's widow alone.

I'm sorry Scotty can't be here, Tanner had said. *He was a hell of an operator. It was a privilege serving with him.*

He loved what he did, his wife had responded. *I know he wouldn't have changed a single thing. Even if it had to mean missing this.*

It was true. If Tanner had been the one who'd died that day, he would've felt the same. He'd never understood why continuing on had posed so many more challenges, but he was starting to.

He'd been seeing a therapist, the same one he'd spoken to a few years ago. They'd talked about his disappointment and frustration with going "backward," as he'd seen it. But she'd assured him there was no right way to recover. That it was something he might be dealing with for the rest of his life in different ways, ways he might not even be able to foresee yet. That idea was frightening.

But his traumas and experiences had also made him into the man he was today. The man Faith had fallen in love with.

He'd also realized he could help others by being honest about his struggles. He'd spoken, in very general terms, about PTSD with the kids at the rec center. He'd also discussed it at a team meeting with the other bodyguards at Bennett Security, too, just before he'd returned to work after his time off.

Max had offered him the position as captain, and Tanner had accepted. Amazingly, he felt his teammates respected him *more* after knowing his story. Even Kozinski was on better behavior, picking up after himself and being more conscientious.

Mrs. Zhang had also forgiven Tanner for his outburst, and he was back on her detail whenever she visited West Oaks.

Each day, one of his teammates came up to Tanner and asked for advice, often in hushed tones. *I'd rather not talk about this with anyone else, but...* It felt good to be able to help in those situations, even if he wasn't always sure of the value of his advice.

The buzz of thoughts in his mind still sometimes got to be too much. But he used his coping mechanisms, and he never hesitated to explain to his friends or to Faith what was happening. He was constantly floored to have so many people who cared about him in his life. Those connections had only gotten stronger and were helping him heal. He liked to think he was paying it forward.

If Scotty were here, his wife had said, *he'd tell us to make the most of every single day.*

That was just what Tanner intended to do.

∼

AFTER THE MEETING, Tanner went outside and found his girlfriend waiting for him. This had become a habit of theirs.

No matter what happened during group, Tanner always had her to look forward to.

She flashed her beautiful smile when she saw him coming, and he wrapped her into his arms.

Faith rose onto her toes and kissed him. "How was it today?"

"Not bad."

He knew that would get a smile out of her. It was another of their inside jokes. After group, it usually meant that things had gone pretty well, but that he didn't want to jinx it.

"I love you," he said, because he hadn't told her for at least an hour.

"I love you, too." She tucked her head under his chin. She could probably hear his heart speeding up at having her so close.

Faith had given him so much. A reason to get better, a source of support and courage, a bridge to reconnect with his family. These days, Faith never hesitated to speak up when she got annoyed with him. Granted, it didn't happen often.

Every day, their connection got stronger, and he felt stronger for it.

"What should we do now?" he asked. "Get fish tacos for dinner?"

She snorted. "You're so predictable. First, I could use a walk on the beach. It's almost sunset. Maybe there's a spot with a good view?"

He pretended to think. "I know a place."

They walked over to the shore and slipped off their shoes, carrying them as they held hands. The damp sand compressed under Tanner's feet. There was a warm breeze tonight. It was the kind of weather that tricked tourists into thinking the water might actually be comfortable. But the waves were frigid when they splashed over his toes. Just the way he liked it.

The water of the Pacific wasn't that ideal turquoise blue of the Mediterranean or Caribbean. It was dark blue and murky.

Sometimes, it was a stormy gray that concealed its hidden depths. But of all the places he'd traveled, the water here was his favorite.

Faith knew where they were headed. He hung back a bit, letting her lead the way. Her hair ruffled around her face, the blond strands glowing in the fading light.

They reached the bench up on the seawall where they'd sat and had sushi on their first date. He didn't think of it as a fake date or a practice anymore. Their friendship had begun before that, but Tanner had realized he'd loved her since that night. He'd fallen in love with the way she opened her heart to new experiences. Faced down her fears.

They sat, heads bowed together, watching the fiery orange and cotton-candy pink of the sunset. At least, that was what Tanner did until he got distracted by the beautiful woman beside him. He trailed kisses along her neck, gently sucking at her skin.

She made that needy sound that never failed to get him hard. "People are watching."

"Don't care. Not my fault I can't resist you."

She glanced at his lap. "I think you need a cold shower."

"How about a cold swim?" He'd only been joking, but when she turned to him, she had a mischievous smile on her lips.

"You're going to have to throw me in."

Tanner stood, lifting her up with him. Her legs wrapped around his waist. She was wearing shorts instead of a dress, so he knew she wouldn't protest that her undies were showing.

He jogged down the stairs to the water and waded in. "You sure about this?"

She shrugged. "I'm not scared. Do your worst."

He tossed her up in the air. She screamed and made a huge splash when she landed. He'd known it was a deep enough spot that she wouldn't hurt herself. But still, she flailed around before surfacing, spitting water. Her hair was plastered to her face. Her clothes were soaked, clinging to her curves.

"I can't believe you actually did it. You *jerk*."

She ran after him as he retreated into the shallows, and he let her catch him.

"You're going to pay for that." She grabbed his hands and yanked him down into the water. Of course, Tanner went willingly.

He kneeled in the surf, pulling her against him and kissing her. She was salty and cold and wet, but her mouth was warm. Their tongues teased and licked each other. The chilly water was doing absolutely nothing to tamp down his desire.

He loved this woman, and he couldn't get enough.

Someday, he was going to marry her, assuming she said yes. But they already belonged to one other. Really, that was all he needed.

A wave crashed into her back, and she screamed, half in shock and half delight. Laughing, Tanner kept a grip on her waist. The waves rolled into them, but he kept them both steady. With Faith in his arms, he could face down anything.

If they were each a little broken, that was okay. Because together, they were perfect.

∼

Don't miss the next book in the Bennett Security series, HUNG UP, Noah and Danica's story!

When Danica Foster-Grant is nearly kidnapped, the billionaire heiress knows she's been betrayed. The only person she can trust? Noah Vandermeer—her former flame, and her brother's worst enemy.

Also by Hannah Shield

THE BENNETT SECURITY SERIES

HANDS OFF (Aurora & Devon)

To keep her safe, he has to keep his hands off…but she has other ideas. A steamy, action-packed romantic suspense.

∼

HEAD FIRST (Lana & Max)

He's protecting his former flame… But can he resist falling for her? A second-chance steamy romance with courtroom drama and heart-pounding danger.

∼

HARD WIRED (Sylvie & Dominic)

Can this bad boy find redemption in the arms of the enemy? A steamy, enemies-to-lovers romance with hacker intrigue and mafia drama.

∼

HUNG UP (Noah & Danica)

Coming August 9, 2022

Her brother's worst enemy is the only man who can protect her. A second-chance romantic suspense between a former Navy SEAL and a billionaire's daughter.

∼

And more books coming soon!

Acknowledgments

I'm so grateful to my beta readers and advance reviewers! Your support means the world to me.

To learn more about the real-life experiences of Navy SEALs who've overcome PTSD, I recommend the memoirs *Perfectly Wounded: A Memoir About What Happens After A Miracle* by Mike Day, and *Battle Ready: Memoir of a Navy SEAL Warrior Medic* by Mark L. Donald.

About the Author

Hannah Shield once worked as an attorney. Now, she loves thrilling readers on the page—in every possible way.

She writes steamy romantic suspense with feisty heroines, brooding heroes, and heart-pounding action. Bennett Security is her debut series. Visit her website at www.hannahshield.com.